All Different
All Equal

The story of my life

Written by

Jim Thakoordin

The author would welcome any comments and feedback from readers who wish to do so and directed through his ,
Email: info@jimthakoordin.com
or
website: www.jimthakoordin.com

For permission requests, write to the publisher, addressed "Attention: Permissions

Coordinator" at the email address below:

Ministry In Art Media Ltd

e-mail: info@miapublishing.com

www.miapublishing.com

ISBN Number: 978-1-907402-68-5

Cover Design: MIADesign.com

Contents

Part 2 (207)

PART 5 (689)

Chapter 22: Jim's legacy and what people say about him   691

Acknowledgements

This book is dedicated to my parents, Dhanraji also known as Mabel, father Ramsahi also known as Jokhan and my eldest sister Betya. I also want to include my wife Doreen, son Michael, daughter Jane and my four lovely grandchildren, Rohanie, Elijah, Aoife and Sarah. They have all given me much love and happiness and the reason to live as well as writing this book. I shall be eternally grateful to all my family who have supported me during the best and worse times in my life. My wife of over fifty years who is also my partner and friend is a remarkable person who has been my greatest supporter as well as my most severe critic on occasions. Love and respect always, Doreen.

I would like to thank all those many people who have helped and inspired me in my long and often controversial life. They are far too many for me to mention.

I also want to thank Sarah Sharp for her practical help and advice in organising and putting this book together.

Preface

Who is Jim Thakoordin? - Professor Fred Walemba PhD

Profile of the author

Jim Thakoordin, born on a sugar plantation in Demerara, Guyana (formerly British Guiana) on 6 August, 1943, has been in the forefront of the struggle for economic, political and social justice; equality of opportunities and access to resources for all ethnic groups within society. Jim has campaigned in support of those who have been oppressed because of their race, gender, disability, social status, religion, age, disability and beliefs, since his arrival in Britain in July, 1961. Jim has been actively involved in major trades union, political and community struggles. He started as a child labourer on the sugar plantation during British colonial rule and continued the struggle on his arrival, age seventeen, in London through the labour movement. For Jim it was a natural continuation of the race and class struggles which has become more intense, with age, experience and knowledge. Despite being seventy years old and in poor health he is still heavily involved in the fight for justice, equality, peace and freedom. He is one of the longest serving Black people alive who have served the labour movement at national levels.

I understand that he was engaged in strikes, sit-ins, sabotage and demonstrations against exploitation and degradation of workers by the plantation owners in Guyana, who were supported by the colonial masters through economic, political and military domination. He was elected as a shop steward at age fourteen, representing child labourers on Plantation Leonora in Demerara. He accompanied his parents during bitter and sometimes violent anti-colonial and workers struggles. He has had very little formal education and arrived in Britain with no family, qualifications or enough money to see him through for a week.

Jim used every opportunity since arriving in Britain to educate himself, promote the interest of his race and class and to secure justice, fairness and respect for everyone, especially the disadvantaged and victims of institutional, ideological and economic discrimination and oppression. He has always been passionate in his commitment to equality and fairness and has used worked tirelessly and consistently and used every opportunity to challenge and influence institutions, political groups, community and trade union organisations, to make them more open, transparent, accountable and responsive to the people they claim to serve. In doing so Jim has given cause to many people to either like or support him or, to dislike, avoid or unite against him. His challenging style, propensity to intervene, interrupt, ask searching questions and holding people and institutions to account distinguishes him from many other activists. He is certainly a no nonsense person who believes in thinking outside the box even if it means creating a measure of chaos, confusion, resentment, or being labelled a militant or maverick.

A colonial boy

His adult life was shaped by his upbringing on the plantation in Guyana where he first worked with his parents and sisters in the cane fields, often from daylight to darkness for poverty wages. He was very attached to his mother, who like his father was illiterate but understood the differences between rights, wrong, justice, exploitation and fairness. They were politically aware of the excesses of colonialism and exploitation of people by the bosses who used every system of oppression and control by the undemocratic state, including destabilisation, persecution, the use of the military, controlled by the British Colonial Office in London to force workers to work for poverty wages, in order to boost profits for the absentee white plantation owners.

Jim was frequently absent from school due to working with his family in the fields and around the home by collecting firewood, helping with the care of the few animals the family had, fetching water and finding various ways of helping his family of eight to put basic food on the table. Life was very difficult as Guyana had no organised social, welfare, healthcare, employment, rights, benefits or community support services. The sugar plantation was the only source of income for the overwhelming majority of the population. Jim can recall when accompanying his mother to the grocery shop once each week for the family shopping there was insufficient money to pay for the basic essentials despite several members of the family working. Families survived through having debts, finding creative ways of surviving and trying to live the simplest possible life. There was no electricity, gas, telephone, radio, television, running water, inside toilet, fridge, cooker or any form of luxury in Jim's home. For many years children slept either on the floor or on bug ridden mattress stuffed with dried grass. The local community rallied to help families in distress in periods of sickness, unemployment and death.

Jim's parents were committed Marxists and strong supporters of Doctor Cheddi Jagan – a Marxist who was imprisoned by the British but eventually successfully led the struggle for an end to colonial rule and became the country's first Prime Minister. Doctor Jagan was much disliked by the British and American establishments.

London calling

At the age of 17 Jim decided to leave Guyana for economic reasons and after a great deal of struggle Jim and his parents saved up enough for his journey to London by foot, rail, steamer, bus, a tiny aircraft, a ship across the Atlantic Ocean and a train from Southampton to Waterloo Station in London, where he was met by a friend who had arrived in England before him and was from his village. It was a steep learning curve for Jim having spent all his time in a small impoverished village with few items of clothing, no shoes or, expensive personal possessions.

However, he was somewhat spoilt at times being the only brother amongst six sisters and in a village where everyone worked hard but was still living below the poverty line.

Jim started off life in London on the dole, but found work as a porter within three weeks, before becoming a London bus conductor. He first met his wife Doreen, a Londoner from Irish and English backgrounds, age seventeen, when she boarded his number 187 bus in Harlesden, North London on her way home from grammar school. It was a relationship which blossomed and it is still going after fifty years of marriage, two grown up children, Michael age fifty and Jane age forty seven and four lovely grandchildren ages eighteen to ten.

Within weeks of arriving in London Jim joined the trade union and the Labour Party as well as other campaigning groups through contacts made at Hyde Park Corner, also known as Speakers Corner where political, social, trades union, anti-colonial, anti-racist, fascist, religious, feminist and other groups and individuals with burning issues gathered on Sundays to explain and passionately argue their case. These were exciting times for Jim as it reminded him of some of the campaigns he took part in on the plantation. At these meetings Jim met and admired many famous speakers including Lord Donald Soper, a well-known Methodist Minister, politicians and those with political aspirations, leaders and potential leaders from home and abroad and extremist groups and campaigners on almost every historical, contemporary and controversial subjects. The speakers were mainly men who were invariably heckled, taunted and verbally attacked by the crowds.

There were also at many political meetings and gatherings at the famous Quaker's Centre, known as Friends Meeting House in Euston Road and the Ambassadors Hotel nearby where he met politicians, campaigners and people involved in the anti-colonial, pro-communist, socialist, feminist, peace and anti-apartheid issues. Amongst the people he met were Kwame Nkrumah, Jomo Kenyatta, Julius Nyerere and many others who led their country after colonial rule. He also met many colourful and well known socialists, philosophers, writers, historians and peace campaigners including Lord Bertrand Russell. Michael Foot, Harold Wilson, Tony Benn, Dennis Healey and many others.

After marrying on 23 August 1963 in a registry Office in Willesden Jim and Doreen moved from London to Luton, in Bedfordshire, some thirty miles from where they had lived. Jim worked on the London Transport Country Buses based in Luton before he moved to the post office. He maintained his trade union and political activities which started in London and was elected a union convenor with the Union of Postal Workers and Secretary of the Luton Trades Union Council in 1968. Jim continued his part-time studies at Luton College of Higher Education, where he started at Harrow Technical College in the evenings, as well as his involvement in postal courses organised by the Trades Union Congress (TUC). He struggled but successfully completed courses in Politics, Economics and Labour Studies, as a mature student with little formal education and a family with two children. In 1974, after many years of activism within the labour movement and community organisations Jim won a TUC Scholarship to Ruskin College, Oxford, where he studied Economics, Social Studies, English Language and Politics. Doreen worked as a teacher and supported Jim throughout his studies.

Jim went on to the University of Essex, after rejecting a place at New College Oxford, as he wanted to move away from the bastion of bourgeois education to a militant "red brick university," where he studied Comparative Government and Sociology between October, 1976 and July, 1978. In October 1978, Jim studied for an M.A. in Industrial Relations at the University of Warwick and at the same time a Post-Graduate Certificate in Education (PGCE) at the University of London. He successfully completed the PGCE, but not the MA course because he secured a full-time post as a London and Eastern Region, Regional Education and Public Relations Officer with the GMB Union, in September, 1979. During the Margaret Thatcher years between 1979 and 1993, Jim was instrumental in the formation of a number of national organisations within the trade union and Labour Party, including the Black Trades Union Solidarity Movement, with his friend and countryman, Bernie Grant who became a Labour Member of

Parliament. Jim was elected as Chair and Bernie the Secretary. Jim was elected the Convenor of the Labour Party Black Section, which took off nationally after the Labour Party Conference in 1983, in Brighton. Bernie Grant, Diane Abbott, Keith Vaz and Paul Boetang were all involved in the Black Section debate and activities and later became Members of Parliament in 1987.

Councillor Jim

In 1981, Jim was elected to Bedfordshire County Council as a Labour Councillor and served on several Committees. He chaired the Education Committee, Special Needs, Employment and other key Committees for many years. He was the Labour Group's Deputy Leader on the Council for a couple of years. In 1983 he stood as Labour's Parliamentary Candidate for Milton Keynes, where he fought a gallant campaign. 1985 Jim Chaired a Committee supported by the Greater London Council and produced a book on *"Race and Trade Unions"*. Jim was one of only three full-time paid black trade union officials in Britain and he was in the forefront of challenging the overt and covert racism and sexism within the trade union and Labour Party. He also challenged the institutional racism within local government, which was responsible for the police, fire service, further and higher education and had reserved seats on the Boards of Universities, Health Authorities and other local, regional and national institutions, public bodies and agencies. Through this process Jim served on the Board of Cranfield University and the University of Bedfordshire as well as the Health Authority, Executive Committees of the Local Government Association for England and Wales and several national Councils and Boards for the Police, Education and Manpower Planning. He was also nominated to the National Employment Tribunals Service and Chaired the governing body of two High Schools and served on the Boards of two Colleges in Bedfordshire.

Jim decided to leave the GMB Union in 1985 and to work for Islington Council as a Neighbourhood officer, in charge of a large decentralised multi-purpose office with over seventy staff. Jim became disillusioned with the trades union movement which lost much of their momentum, direction and credibility, culminating with the historic defeat of the striking miners in 1984, due to the continuous ideological onslaught by Thatcherism. He left Islington Council in 1987 to become the Principal Race Equality Officer in the Planning and Economic Development Department in the London Borough of Ealing. The travelling to West London each day from Luton was too much and he successfully applied for the post of Senior National Advisor to Local Government in England and Wales, with the Local Government Management Board (LGMB) – linking Equality with Quality within the 314 local authorities. Jim developed several specialist projects and courses for Chief Officers, Councillors, Departmental Heads, and other groups of workers from Chief Executives to Community Workers.

He developed and taught on specialist courses for women, Black and disabled employees, to prepare themselves for promotion and career development. One such course for aspiring Chief Executives enabled nine women – eight white and one Black woman to be successfully appointed to Chief Executive Positions over three years. During his work at the LGMB Jim was involved in producing several publications for senior managers and trainers on various aspects of training and development for the strategic and successful implementation of equality, quality and human resources policies, practices, guidelines and good practices. Jim gained national recognition for his work on race equality and training for managers in local government, public services and the private sector, including the design and delivery of courses for trade union officials, negotiators, chief officers and chief executives. Between 1980 and 2010 Jim was a regular contributor to local and national radio, newspapers and professional journals, as well as occasional appearances on regional and national television. He was also the editor of his union newspaper "Candid" which was circulated in London and the Eastern Region. During this work he interviewed lots of important people, including Tony Benn, Neil Kinnock, Roy Hattersley, and Michael Foot, Claire Short and other leading political and trade union leaders. Jim is still a regular contributor to the local radio and media at the time of writing this book.

After leaving the LGMB in 1993 Jim completed a Master's in Business Studies (MBA) in Administration at the University of Hertfordshire and several other qualifications, a course in Counselling, Teaching English as a second Language, and Training Trainers. Jim started his own consultancy business – 'Working for Equality' in 1994 whilst continuing with his involvement as a County, then a Luton Borough and a Parish Councillor. He also maintained his involvement with his trade union at local and national level, serving on several regional and national committees on the TUC and his union.

Equality champion

In 1994 Jim completed an MBA course and set himself up as a Training and Management Consultant. He then secured a long-term consultancy contract with Barnfield College in Luton as the Equality Manager and supported the college, the students and the community until he left in 2005. Between 1995 and 2005 Jim provided consultancy services on various aspects of equal opportunities, race relations and employment law across Britain and in other parts of Europe and North America. Jim also wrote several publications on race, racism, and community issues. His 320 pages book – 'Memories of the 20th Century,' published in 2005 was well received and commented on by many people.

Since 2005 Jim has had to restrict some of his activities due to problems with his health which resulted in several major operations, including a quadruple heart bypass, operation on his kidneys, and fitting of a pacemaker to assist the function of his heart. Despite his age (70 years) and his health Jim continues to serve on several local and national organisations including being a national executive member of his union – the University and College Union and President of the County Associations of Trades Councils in Bedfordshire and Buckinghamshire,

Jim has lived and still lives an amazingly varied and active life and still has time for his delightful family and his other passion, gardening. When I first visited Jim at home over 40 years ago, I found him in his immaculate garden. His latter home where he now lives naturally has a large and well-tended garden full of fruit, vegetable and flowers, and a modest menagerie of animals including friendly ducks!

Jim's autobiography is a fascinating and stimulating read, covering a rich and rewarding life. I can recommend it highly to everyone and especially to those who share Jim's passion for justice and a better world.

Jim Thakoordin, Baroness Doreen Lawrence,
Barrister Michael Mansfield QC and
Sadiq Khan, Member of Parliament

Reflections on the miserable lives of my parents and my sisters especially my eldest sister, Dede convinced me that even though I had tried to support them morally and financially from England, it was not enough as the only son and brother. By the time I was in a position to help my parents and my sisters a lot more financially, my parents had passed away having lived miserable lives. Despite the early humble backgrounds of our lives, all my sisters and their children worked themselves out of poverties and into comfortable lives. They managed this incredible turn around through hard work, taking risks, enduring suffering and hardships and being strong and determined. Education and training has been the key to many of the successes achieved by my immediate and extended family, something my wife and I are committed to ensuring whilst supporting our four grandchildren. I believe that although my family are scattered across three continents and have different cultural, social, economic and political perspectives and careers, we all have a common bond moulded by our past and present experiences.

Writing this book has brought history closer to me and has revealed a lot about my past as well as my vision and plans for the future. I have focussed on a wide range of subjects and issues, which have had a great impact on me and influenced on my life and character. Researching the impact of the slave trade and indenture-ship which brought Africans and Asians together under colonialism and imperialism helped me to select the topics for inclusion in this book. Equally persuasive in my selection of material was the fact that I had matured and sustained a mixed black white relationship for more than fifty years, and both my children are in mixed race relationships. I am proud of my rainbow family and what we all stand for. My wife Doreen has been a tower of strength and support since I met her. My family now have common links with people from African, European, Asian and American descents. There are also family members from various ethnic and religious backgrounds, including Christianity, Hindu, Muslims and atheists. Our ancestral backgrounds span four continents with current roots in Europe, Africa, North and South America. My diverse multi-racial and multi-cultural family has shaped some of my views on race, racism, international relations, equality, justice, freedom and respect for humankind and all creatures on earth, as well as our global environment.

Clarifications on terminology:

I am aware that I have used different terminology to identify and define race and ethnicity in this book. I have interchangeably used Black, Black Minority Ethnic (BME), Black Ethnic Minority (BEM), Asian, African, Caribbean and Ethnic Minorities. (EM) All these categories denote the non-white population in Britain.

I am also aware of that I have duplicated some information in various parts of the book and I feel this is justifiable as each chapter is supposed to be self-contained.

I have assembled the book as far as possible in some sort of logical sequence starting with what the book is about before moving onto Part 1 which is the story of my life in Guyana and arriving in the UK. Part 2 covers my family in the UK and my search for. Part 3 is about my involvement in politics and other public bodies. Part 4 deals with issues I feel strongly about. Part 5 is what people think of me and my legacy.

cars or welfare support except for those senior people who managed the plantation and lived a privileged life in their exclusive and guarded compounds. Our small one-bedroom house was situated some two hundred metres from the main road and beside other similar buildings. There was a large pond some eight metres away in the front of the house and a massive canal one hundred metres to the left. The pond was about five metres wide, two hundred metres long and between one and two metres deep in various places. There were about thirty houses in Gronveldt Pasture surrounded by fields, pastures, a coconut farm and canals in every direction. Our home was just five minutes' walk from the Atlantic coastline. Most homes were also no more than ten minutes' walk from the sugar mill and the associated factories and offices.

People generally used the water from the pond to cook, clean, drink and have showers using buckets and cups, as well as providing drinks for animals. The pond provided local people with a small variety of fish for our meals. A few people constructed small platforms in the pond which was used by women to wash clothes and pots and pans. Children and adults would also use the pond for bathing, swimming and fishing.

There were frequent confrontations and quarrels among the adults about the misuse of the pond by children swimming in it and polluting the water. One elderly neighbour, who lived next door to us and relied totally on the pond's water, occasionally threw broken bottles into the pond to deter children from swimming in it. There was a stand pipe a couple hundred metres from our home, which intermittently provided clean water for cooking and drinking. People in the village were poor, but respectful of each other. They supported each other through difficulties and where possible shared what little they had. It was a traditional environment and almost all of the population were members of the Hindu faith and the rest were Muslims. Everyone respected each other's faith, culture and lifestyles. Some of the properties on the estate, which were built to accommodate the slaves and the indentured labourers from India in the 19th Century, were still habitable and known to us as Logies. These massive uniform terraced buildings were built close to the mill. Sanitation was degrading, unhealthy and poor. There were communal toilets built over trenches which were often stagnant. When there were floods due to heavy rainfall, sewage ran through the village.

In between two rows of logies and separated by trenches on both sides was the main road leading to the factory gate. Workers on foot and white managers in Jeeps, motorbikes or bicycles daily used this dusty road to and from the factory and fields. Trading would take place on both sides of this road every day, but especially on Saturdays as workers had to use this road to go to the factory to collect their wages in cash, and they would shop on their way home. The traders were mainly women and small farmers with anything to sell, including fruits, fish, meat, vegetables, groceries and clothing. Saturday was always a special day for everyone. Children received pocket money and families in employment ate fairly well. Some people went to the local cinema as a special treat.

Family background

My father died when I was only a few months old and my mother was left alone with no close relatives in the village to assist her and her children. She did her best to survive and care for all of us. The welfare state which existed in Britain did not extend to British colonies. There was no support for widows, the unemployed, sick, disabled, or the poor people. My mother was an only child whose mother had died when she was a small child and her elderly father living three miles away was in poor health. Luckily for us, within a couple of years of my father's death a man who lived near to us left his wife and moved in with my mother. His name was Jokhan Ramsahi.

We moved from our house to another small building, a couple of hundred of metres facing the main public road, separated by a canal between the road and our new home. The canal flowed into the Atlantic Ocean each day. It was conveniently used for waste disposal of all types from raw sewage to dead chickens, animals and any other domestic or household waste. The good thing about this was that it was all taken away by the tide and fresh water came in each day.

The large canal that was part of the essential waterways necessary for transporting the sugar cane to the mill ran for many miles into the interior, and was also a resource used for swimming, washing, cleaning and fishing. I can recall as a child of three or four years accompanying my sisters to fetch water, firewood, tend our small garden and take care of our animals. My eldest sister known to all of us as Dede took care of me from a baby and as a result never attended school. All children were expected to do regular chores and treat all adults with utter respect. All adult men and women especially older people were addressed as 'Aunties' or 'Uncles', we would address all elderly people with the same respect we had for own grandparents. Children were frequently called upon to run errands for the elderly, sick and people with disabilities.

I had two elder sisters Betya (whom we called Dede) was the eldest, and my second sister Doreen is three years older than me. I was told that my paternal father and mother had two other children who died soon after birth. Infant mortality was very high on the plantation, due to poverty and lack of medical facilities. My mother, like many women in our village had several miscarriages, often caused by pregnant women working until the start of labour and various accidents around work, or at home. Women were encouraged to marry as young as fourteen and were subjected to a variety of abuse including domestic violence, exploitation at work, working long hours inside and outside the home that involved heavy lifting and fetching of water, firewood, grass for animals and walking for miles in the hot sun barefoot, carrying farm produce. I often worked alongside my mother and sisters doing such chores.

My eldest sister was almost like a mother to me. She took care of Doreen and me whilst our parents were working on the plantation. We loved our parents and also our grandfather who told us that our ancestors were transported on the

SS Hesperus and the SS Whitby from Southern India, which landed in British Guiana on 5th May 1838.

My grandfather, my mother's father, whose name was Ramsakal, told us that his father had told him, that they had received messages from people claiming to be residents from another village where his sister was living, and that his sister was being abused by her husband and would like to return to the family home. My great grandfather then gathered as many men folks he could from his home village and they set out on bullock carts to confront his sister's husband. However, before they entered the next village they saw hundreds of bullock carts and men who were given similar messages being rounded up by armed Indian mercenaries working with the British and were marched to the nearest port, a journey which lasted two days. Upon arrival at the port they were forced to sign documents by the use of their thumb print which indentured them to work on the sugar plantations in Guiana and the Caribbean.

My great grandfather was of the Hindu faith and some members of his family were known as Thakur. My mother's grandparents also originated from India and there were family members known as Din. The name Thakoordin was unknown to me until I was given a birth certificate when I was sixteen years old for the purpose of securing a passport to enable me to travel to England. The clerk at the registry asked my mother who was illiterate lots of questions about her ancestors and took it upon himself to give her the certificate with the name Thakoordin. My name up to the point of securing a passport was James Junniah. No one ever explained to me where the name Junniah came from. It could have been a misspelling or a mix up in the registration of the name of my ancestors upon arrival in Guyana. The first name my parents gave me was Budya and I inherited James when I was christened as a teenager after I decided to join the Anglican Church although my parents were devoted Hindus. My parents were deeply religious and practising Hindus.

My stepfather Jokhan was a tremendous person. He loved us all and treated us all like his own children. Our relationship with him was like any normal relationship between father and children. Jokhan was also extremely tolerant towards our mother whose lifestyle had changed considerably since the birth of my sister Julie. My mother was a very strong person, more so in the mind than body. She was fiercely independent, highly political and was a staunch supporter of the Marxist People's Progressive Party, led by Cheddi Jagan who campaigned for independence against colonial rule. My mother had several miscarriages after she started to live with Jokhan and she also had four more children, all girls. Our father Jokhan was a semi-skilled worker who operated a large water pump, which irrigated the sugar cane fields. When he wasn't required as a water pump operator he worked as a labourer on the plantation. He was involved in community activities and politics and was always willing like my mother to participate in industrial disputes to support worker's rights and anti-colonial struggles. He died in 1967.

During periods of my father's illness my mother had to undertake all sorts of activities to keep the family; which brought even further shame on us as a family. She would often walk from village to village barefoot on the hot road with a basket of fish on her head and the ice used to keep the fish fresh dripping down from her head. Walking for miles in the hot sun every day with little attention to her diet soon made her ill. My grandparents from my father's side were unknown to us and only my mother's father Ramsakal represented our extended family. He was a kind and loving person who lived on his own in a small house near the sea. I used to make regular journeys to see him but I never stayed overnight as he was not in good health and he used to have his meals with a family who lived opposite his house.

However, there was an elderly couple who were related to my stepfather Jokhan and who used to look after me for short periods. They lived in a village named Good Fortune some fourteen miles away. They were a lovely couple who had no children of their own and were always pleased to see me, although I frequently felt lonely and miserable, because I missed my family after a couple of days. I used to cry a lot in bed at night in the dark before falling asleep. I believe my parents sent me to stay with relatives simply for economic reasons, as it was one less mouth to feed and there was an expectation of me returning home with new clothes, some goods and presents for my sisters. They would always send me home after a couple of weeks which seemed like months with a new shirt and trousers and gifts for my sisters, mainly fruits and sweets. Sometimes they would put some money in my pocket and secure the pocket with a safety pin. This was a gift for my parents.

My mother, apart from being fiercely independent, caring and compassionate, was a radical feminist who smoked black tobacco roll ups, enjoyed a glass of local rum and even engaged in relationships with men other than Jokhan. Her values had a profound impact on me during and since my childhood. She was and has been the major source of influence and inspiration in my life and much of my involvement in the trade union and labour movement are due to the beliefs and values I gained from her.

Guyanese women like all women in the Caribbean and the mainland of South America, that were under colonial rule were strong and brave. They had to be strong to stand up against the oppressive employers, but also to challenge sexism, domestic violence and the task of finding food for themselves and their children, in a situation with no welfare support or services. I saw a lot of violence within my village and within my own family, especially against my two eldest sisters by their alcoholic husbands.

My mother died within a few months of my father in 1967. So I lost my father, mother and grandfather within months of each other. I was unable to attend any of the funerals due to lack of money and refusal of extended leave to visit Guyana. As the only son I was protected in many ways by my parents and my eldest sister Dede, whose education was sacrificed in order that she could take care of us younger children. Although I helped Dede and her family a number of ways after I arrived in England I never felt that I had repaid her sufficiently for her love and care. She died in 1994, age around fifty four years. Dede had a difficult life, and some of her children also suffered a great deal, but four of them have grown up to be very successful professional and business people. Her son was a Minister for Local Government in Guyana for many years. All my five remaining sisters are grandparents and have lived successful lives since they broke out of poverty due to hard work after they became adults.

Childhood and childhood memories

My mother was an extremely hardworking person. She always worked from early in the morning until very late at night. My father often had periods of unemployment or absences from work during sickness due to past or recent injuries at work. My mother always undertook the responsibility to ensure her children were fed and clothed. Like most families it was always the women who had to make ends meet within the household. Most families in the village of Leonora were like us who experienced poverty as a normal way of life. All families wanted to educate their children but were forced to frequently withdraw them from primary and secondary schools, either for short periods, or permanently as soon as they became teenagers to assist them at work or in the home, also caring for younger children.

During my parents lifetime they never had the opportunity to turn on electricity. They lived in poor housing and brought us up where there were either oil, bottle or gas lamps but no electricity. We had no running water either in the kitchen or in the yard. We always had to draw water from trenches or from communal stand pipes. Support of any kind came mainly from relatives, friends and neighbours. As my mother's only son, I felt that I had a special role in her life. We were very close and I enjoyed privileges, which were unavailable to my sisters. For example, I was given a small cup of milk either from our own cow or from the milkman who used to travel along the road each day on his bicycle buying and selling milk along his journey. Dede always put our needs before her own and I recall her being extremely protective of me before and after I started school. She used to involve me in her chores, such as fetching water, gathering firewood, cutting and fetching grass for the animals we kept, tending the small garden and spending time fishing in the nearby canals.

My childhood up to the time I started school at age 5, was reasonably good compared to that of my sisters, most likely because I was a boy. I was told that although I was a well behaved child, I used to get up to my share of mischief, such as climbing fruit trees, demanding attention from my sister Dede and I would not let her out of my sight. I was told of an incident when I fell and landed under a machete that was being used to peel coconuts and came down on my left foot. Most of the bone was separated from the flesh and it cost my family all the money they could raise to have a metal plate fitted to repair my foot. This incident ensured that I would never be a runner, or carry heavy objects for long distances.

I learnt a lot during my childhood, especially during the first ten years. I knew wrong from right, the experience of being harassed and bullied, going without food for some days, growing up in poverty under colonialism, having to fight back when cornered, the need to have loving and stable family and the power of people united under common aspirations.

Much of my values to this day have been influenced by my early childhood.

School days

I started school when I was about five years old, in an old community building quite close to the sugar mill on plantation Leonora, some half a mile from our home. My friends and I used to walk without shoes to school in the hot sun along the dusty road with a layer of fine red cinders. We used to sit on long benches without any backrest, and there were up to seventy children in a class, ages from five to eleven years old. Boys and girls were in separate sections. The school was managed by an African-Guyanese middle aged teacher. She was known to us as Teacher Bob, a name she inherited because she charged parents a shilling a week, which was regarded as a 'Bob' for each child she taught. Teacher Bob was probably in her late forties and well built. She would often have a nap during the hot afternoons when the temperature often exceeded eighty degrees Fahrenheit, as heat from the hot sun penetrated the tin roof of a large building without any windows. The children, including myself, would sometimes quietly sneak away and play in the schoolyard or wander around the streets near the school. We even engaged in stealing fruits from surrounding yards or returning home before the end of lessons.

Some of the children had only started school aged seven, eight, or even nine. Teacher Bob taught us basic reading, writing and arithmetic. We used slates to write on with carbon pencils; we never used pens, paper or books except on very special occasions in primary school. I would walk each day to school and walk back at lunchtime to see if there was any lunch at home. Some days there was no lunch, but I was still pleased to see my sister, Dede, who would make me a lime drink and encourage me to return to school. Sometimes she would give me two pennies, which enabled me to purchase a drink and small piece of cake, or a fruit from the elderly female vendors outside the school gate.

We did not have school uniform; the children wore what their parents could afford. I never had any shoes in primary school. I was nearly eleven before I had my first pair of plimsolls, which only lasted a few weeks because of the water and mud on the village roads. I often went for many months without having any footwear and either attended school, or worked with my parents in the field barefoot. My clothes were always clean even though there may have been lots of patches on my short trousers and shirt. We used to play marbles during breaks at school and at home, using buttons as prizes, so it was not uncommon for us boys to have our clothing held together by safety pins, because we had used the buttons at marbles.

I was a very small child in size and very dark in complexion. Pigmentation played a major part in the colonies and to this day in determining social status, acceptability and life chances with whiteness in skin colour being most desirable. Colour was an important element in the stratification of the races, a characteristic that is still prevalent around the world. I was forced to acknowledge my skin colour at an early age. My nickname was pudding and I was often referred to as black pudding. Being black and poor made me an easy and obvious target for the bullies at school. I had very little to share with other children throughout my schooling, as I had very few possessions and hardly any pocket money except on Saturdays when my parents were paid if they had worked the previous week. I was very lonely, frightened and isolated during primary school days.

Teacher Bob regarded me as a fairly bright and attentive pupil for most of the time. I left Teacher Bob's school when I was about seven and went to Anna Catherina Infants and Junior School. This school was a couple hundred yards further away from home. I walked to and from school each day. Some days we came home for our lunch, some days we didn't. My older sister Doreen also attended the same school for a while, so I felt a little protected, because of her presence, from bullying and harassment. I stayed at Anna Catherina Infant and Junior School until I moved to the nearby St. John's Anglican High School when I was about nine years old, and stayed there until I was about thirteen years old.

I never attended school on a regular basis, as I had to do lots of chores helping my parents, especially during harvest time. They had two plots of land about half an acre each on which they cultivated rice and ground provisions some two miles from home. I was often removed from school for long periods to assist my parents when they had difficulty completing their work on the sugar plantation or during planting and harvest time in the fields. I sometimes stayed away from school because I was either ashamed of attending - due to my raggedy clothes, or fear of being bullied. My parents often took us to work to assist them because the work was so difficult or badly priced. It was all piecework and they had to complete the allocated tasks within a certain time to earn a fixed sum before they were given additional work. As a consequence we would lose a fair bit of schooling.

I was fairly bright at high school even though I attended irregularly. Despite the bullying I nevertheless enjoyed most of the lessons. The class sizes were often up to sixty plus children, with one qualified teacher and occasionally a pupil teacher for each class. The teachers were quite strict and they never hesitated to use either the cane or a thick leather strap to punish us if we did anything wrong. This included being late, having dirty fingernails or feet, being inappropriately dressed, not completing homework or having wrong answers, or being disrespectful to other children or staff. Much of the learning was done by rote and by working as a whole class. There were occasions when we did group work such as nature study and going into the field near the school to look at plants, insects and birds.

I had one favourite teacher when I was in my first year at high school. Her name was Miss Melia. She lived about two miles from our home and she had to ride her bike past our house to get to and from school, so I would often see her whilst I was going to fetch water, taking the animals to pasture, or helping my parents. She would often say to me, "James don't be late, see you at school". She was a lovely person in her fifties and she took a particular liking to me, because on a couple of occasions I had made brooms from the branches of coconut trees and given them to her and she used them to sweep her home and yard. My mother would also occasionally give her some fish as a thank you for the help she gave me and she appreciated that very much. I remember one occasion, when the school had organised a play to mark the Queen's Coronation in 1953. Miss Melia asked me if I would like to be involved in the play, I said "Yes", but she said, "You have no proper clothes, your trousers are torn, you have no shoes and you need to dress up in this play like the all the other children". I informed her that I wanted to be in the play but I couldn't take part for the reasons she stated. To my surprise and delight about a week later, she asked me to go into a room, and to try on a really nice new shirt, trousers with a proper belt and a pair of plimsolls, which fitted me perfectly. She said, "Right, James, you can now take part in the school play". I enjoyed the gifts very much, and I was always grateful for her help and encouragement. I saw her before leaving for England and gave her a couple more brooms. She was never married or had any children. She lived with her elderly mother in a nice house in Stewartville about a mile from our home. Her garden had lots of fruit trees and I would frequently visit her to pick the fruits for her and her elderly mother.

I had few friends at school before the age of eight. However, I did have some good friends who lived near to us when I was about ten. One of them was Joseph Ramdial, with whom I still maintain contact, Abdul Sattaur and his brother Abdul Jabbar, and another friend called Buddul. They are all living abroad in America and Canada. We remained friends for many years, even after I had arrived in England. Sattaur and Buddul would often defend me if I was being bullied or harassed by the other boys. My parents knew their parents and we lived very well together in our village. We played a lot after school together and sometimes we would bunk off school and go in search of food or catch fish or crabs, gather firewood, pick coconuts or cut off the coconut branches and use the centre spine to make brooms and then sell them.

I was never very good at sports because I was seldom allowed to participate in it at school. I wasn't allowed to participate most of the time in football or running or anything like that, due to my size and being excluded by the other boys, but I was fairly good at marbles which we played after school with friends, either on our way home or when we got back to our village. I was allowed to join my friends during the evenings after I had completed my chores. My sister Doreen and I would walk the short distance, past the cake shop to play games called choor and rounders with boys and girls in their early teens. Weekends were special for children because our parents were paid and they were at home on Saturday afternoon and most of Sunday. I would also visit the local market either with my mother or just to look at the variety of fruits, vegetables, fish and goods for sale.

We walked to and from school each day, and sometimes returned home for lunch. School started at eight thirty and finished at three thirty. The surface of the road to school was covered with reddish brown cinders, which made it very dusty. Each time a vehicle went by it created so much dust in the atmosphere that our feet, face and arms would often be covered with a thin layer of brownish dust by the time we arrived at school. Sometimes there would be a water cart with sprinklers at the back and that was organised to ensure that white overseers and managers did not have to tolerate the dust when making their way to and from the sugar factory and the offices on the plantation, even though most of them travelled in their jeeps or on the backs of mules. On the days when we managed to catch up with the water cart, we would walk behind it and the water would be pouring at our feet. We enjoyed that very much even though sometimes we got our clothes wet and we got a good thrashing when we arrived at school.

I was reasonably good at arithmetic, grammar, spelling and reciting my tables. I did not do any science subjects such as chemistry or physics as I left school too early to go to work. We did basic reading, writing, spelling, arithmetic, geography, nature study, woodwork, some history, which was very much British or European history and art. Discipline was very rigid at school and the cane or strap was readily available and used by teachers. The boys would bend over a desk and sometimes be held by two other boys and the teacher would administer up to twelve lashes for serious offences. The male teachers were more likely to use the cane and to deliver more stinging and painful punishments. Girls were less likely to have the cane or strap. They would be hit on their outstretched hands, whilst boys were beaten on the backsides for serious wrongdoing and lashed on the hands for minor offence.

I enjoyed all subjects even though I had to struggle a great deal due to regularly missing lessons and having to catch up, using notes that my friends had made. To make up for missing lessons I did a fair bit of homework. My sister Dede, who was illiterate, recognised the value of education and would often sit with me during the evenings with the use of a bottle lamp filled with kerosene oil and a wick made out of rags, to provide light for us. Dede was so encouraging, patient and attentive and told me off when I wanted to go to bed early. As we sat on the veranda we could hear the frogs croaking and the rats scampering over the tinned roof of our house. We had to regularly swat the mosquitoes on our arms and legs. She enjoyed looking at the pictures in the book and me reading an occasional story for her. I loved my sister dearly and hardly a day goes by without me remembering her with great fondness and respect even though she passed away many years ago.

After leaving Miss Malia's class and entering second standard, I had a teacher who gave me a terrible time. He would often flog us boys with a long cane about three feet long, for almost anything, which he considered to be wrong. His name was Tiwari and I remember on one occasion he had me standing in front of the class of around sixty pupils, because I had arrived at school late and my feet were dirty. I had to take my father's breakfast and lunch to his workplace in the field some two miles from the school. I had to run along muddy tracks to carry his food because he had left home very early for work before the food was ready. After standing in front the class for about ten minutes, he decided to give me six lashes on my backside with the cane. Before he completed the six lashes I wet myself and naturally the children laughed at me. I was then teased and bullied even more because of this incident. Sometimes we had to line up without any warning for finger nail inspection, dirty feet, lice in our hair and untidy dressing. I was always likely to be punished for something. How could I have ever been well presented, when I had to complete lots of manual chores before school each day, such as cleaning out the cow shed, feeding the animals, fetching water, and watering the vegetables in the garden?

Even though I had a terrible experience at school on the whole, there were occasions when I enjoyed being at school. On one occasion I fell in love with a pupil teacher, a young African woman who helped me during lessons. I really loved her and I enjoyed it very much when she came close to me to look at my work. I loved her sweet fresh smell, and would often request her attention even when it was not necessary. I would do anything to get her attention, even deliberately getting my sums and spelling wrong so she could come and correct my work. I really used to have fantasies about this woman, being in love with her and even contemplating marrying her when I was older. I was only about eleven years old and an irregular attendant at school. I also took a liking to a young African girl in the class whose name was Jennifer. She was sweet, but in those days, and even to this day in Guyana, children from African and Asian backgrounds seldom mixed.

My crush on Jennifer lasted for a couple of months until I fell in love with another girl. Her name was Jocelyn. Her father had a chemist shop in Anna Catherina. They were people of mixed race, which included Guyanese and European origins. I got on well with Jocelyn but I got the impression that she felt that her status was far too advanced for her to reciprocate my attention. They had wealth and possessions well beyond the average family. In any case she had lots of other friends and took no notice of me. Nevertheless, I continued to like her very much, even to the point of walking the two miles from where we lived to go past her home during school holidays to get a glimpse of her.

I was often taken out of school to work. I was able to raise money using a donkey and cart. I recall a donkey we had called Jack. He was ever so lazy. Sometimes Jack would sit down on the road, fully harnessed and attached to the cart, when he felt he had done enough work. He ignored the lashes and the abusive language. On other occasions if he saw a female donkey on the other side of the road, he would try to make a detour towards her, so we had to keep him under strict and tight control. I remember having a pet dog once. On one occasion I tied this little puppy to a post during the night before going to bed. Unfortunately, the puppy got itself tangled up in the rope and it strangled itself. I never kept a pet dog after that incident. Dogs and cats were seldom allowed into the house; they were very functional creatures. The cats were expected to catch rats that were quite common and the dogs were supposed to provide security. There was no special food for these animals. They generally ate the scraps from the family meal. As a result they were invariably in poor physical condition. There were hardly any scraps from our plates, on the contrary, there was never enough to go around most of the time, we ate every bit of the fish, including the head and the bones from meat when we were lucky to have such a treat.

From a young age I became allergic to dogs and cats. It was very sad to see the state in which these animals were kept; the dogs were often had mange all over, as well as sores and flies. They would often try and make their way towards you when you were eating either on the stairs or under the living area of the house, where a lot of people spent their time. The natural reaction was to chase them away by throwing stones at them. I believe that many people in Guyana and in the Caribbean had a similar approach to dogs and cats. They were seldom treated by working class people as family pets and brought into the house. Instead they were kept outside the house. Sometimes these animals would also be brutalised because they had stolen food or young chickens; they refused to go away from the neighbourhood where they were dumped as strays or because they were sick or disabled.

I kept some turkeys and chickens for food. I was very sad when during special holidays, celebrations, festivals, family visits, weddings or birthdays; my family would have a chicken or turkey for lunch or supper. It used to upset me very much whenever they decided to have chicken or turkey curry, especially when I used to have to catch the poor things and arrange for them to be killed and have the feathers removed. I used to chase the chicken or turkey until they either sought refuge in the poultry pen, or chose to hide in a bush. I would then grab the bird and sadly that was it. It was always a very sad event for me and I would seldom participate in the feast. My favourite turkey called Jack was killed after my sister's wedding. It upset me a great deal.

I spent holidays with my Godmother, Teacher Vann, who was an African woman and knew my mother when she was a child. Teacher Vann lived about four miles from us, in a village called Blankenburg next to La Jalousie where my mother was born. She was a single woman in her late sixties who lived on her own. She was very intelligent and a good cook. She retired from teaching because of ill health and poor sight due to diabetes. Teacher Vann lived alone in small but well-constructed painted wooden house with her cats. I would sometimes spend three or four days at different times during the summer school break with her. I was there because my parents had a small plot of land on which they grew rice and I was a human scarecrow to keep the birds away from eating the seeds of the young rice plants. I would equip myself with a rattler made from old sardine tins and a sling shot made from the old rubber tubes of bicycles.

I would get to the field before the birds were active in the morning and return to my Godmother's home that was about one mile away when the birds had finished feeding in the evening. I enjoyed her company and her cooking. She talked with me a lot, frequently expressed her sympathy for my mother and the problems in bringing up her children with little resources. My godmother would often buy me either a shirt or a pair of short trousers before I returned home after each visit. Even though I loved her, I really used to miss my sisters and parents when I spent time away from home. I visited my godmother in 1974 when I first returned to Guyana, having lived in England for thirteen years. We hugged, cried and welcomed each other. I gave her some gifts and I talked with her; by then she had lost much of her sight. I felt extremely hurt at seeing her in such a condition and I very much regret that I wasn't able to spend more time with her. She was quite ill and passed away soon after my visit.

Discipline at home, school and within the family and community was fairly rigid. Children had to obey teachers, parents, relatives and older people within the village. We were scared of people in authority such as the police, school inspectors, teachers and the village elders. Children caught doing wrong things were often disciplined verbally by older people in the village. They would also report the matter to our parents who would discipline us verbally and physically in the presence of the person who reported the bad behaviour.

I had lots of activities outside school, as I said, including gardening, looking after our animals and poultry, and doing family chores like ensuring there was sufficient firewood and water, selling fruits and ground provisions, using a donkey and cart to transport goods to market for traders, or making brooms from coconut palm trees and selling them at the market. I also helped my parents with farming their small pieces of land to supplement the family income. I can recall lots of pleasant and funny memories of playing with my friends in the village and doing things like catching fish or crabs in the muddy bands of the sea, miles away from home, playing by the beach against the instructions of our parents, gathering fruits, sugar cane and vegetables from various sources and still having some time to get up to some of the tricks and mischief's that young boys indulge in.

I can recall a few incidents that were hilarious to say the least. I was about sixteen years old at the time and my friends and I who used to regularly sit, during the late evenings and nights, beside the main road, on the grass by the large green area outside the Church to engage in all kinds of conversations. The older men would be in the nearby shop that played loud music and sold cheap rum. As boys under eighteen we were not allowed to be seen drinking, so we would sometimes put our pennies together and purchase a quarter bottle of rum to share between us. On one of these nights, someone said they spotted a papaya tree full of ripe and half ripe fruits beside the veranda of a posh house within the overseer's compound. I was nominated to climb the 2.5 metre tree to pick the fruit and pass it on to the boy half way up the tree, who would then pass it on to the boy standing on the ground with large sack. We managed to avoid the security and whilst I was up the tree picking the fruits a white overseer and his girlfriend came out on to the veranda and started making love. I sat on the tree almost frozen to avoid detection. Before they returned indoors he decided to have a pee which drenched the tree and all three of us on and beside the tree. We still managed to return to the road side some 700 yards away to share out the fruits after a good washing. On other occasions we would climb coconut trees, up to fifteen metres or more high that did not belong to us to harvest coconuts. On other occasions we entered the gardens and the cow pens owned by the plantation to provide food for the white overseers, to steal vegetables, milk from the cows and fruits. We never felt any guilt at taking small bits away from those who have far more than they need. We did all sorts of things to fill our hungry tummies and help out our families when they were struggling.

During my time at school I never passed any certificated examinations. I passed the end of term examinations and I moved on from first to second and third standard within eighteen months, before leaving. I left school at thirteen for good and started full-time employment on the plantation pretending to be sixteen years old. I was forced through circumstances to take on duties and responsibilities, which were normally carried out by much older children. The poverty, exploitation and injustices, which were prevalent during my childhood helped to shape my thoughts, feelings and behaviour throughout my adult life.

Working on the plantation

After leaving school with no qualifications I applied for work in the sugar cane factory. I lied about my age claiming to be sixteen instead of nearly fourteen. I was given a job because the father of a friend I knew at school, who was the personnel administrative officer responsible for employing manual workers. Vacancies were never advertised; people had to go to the office and ask if there was work. Employees who were aware of potential vacancies and knew of opportunities would alert family and friends first and even provide some bribes in money, to a person who could assist someone into employment. If your contacts were good you were able to find work in the factory, if not you had to seek employment in the cane fields working in the hot sun in all weather conditions, often doing heavy, dirty, dangerous and seasonal work. I joined a group of some fifteen boys, between fourteen and eighteen who were managed by a man called Hyman and I became part of the notorious Hyman gang within the factory.

We did a range of labouring jobs including cleaning, refuse collection, sweeping the factory floor, carrying messages and running errands, moving materials around the factory with buckets and wheel barrows. We cleaned and tidied the massive factory floor and other areas every day including working overtime on Sundays. The Hyman gang would often use pitchforks to shift the remains of the sugarcane after it had been through the milling machines, onto conveyor belts, which transported the waste to the furnaces that generated the heat to convert water into steam to run the various pieces of equipment in the factory. The waste was constantly recycled; the remains would pile up in massive heaps after being dropped from a conveyor belt. We would have to keep the belt area clear and would have to shift and store this waste, called magasse, up to a hundred yards away, and stack it up in massive heaps several metres high. Sometimes we had to put this waste on a reverse conveyor belt because it was needed as fuel for the massive ovens. The men who worked near the ovens breathed in particles from the magasse which was always in the air. These lead to breathing problems later in life and coughing up blood.

Hyman was a quite a character and well known for his alcohol dependence and his outbursts against any boys caught slacking. Some of the work was very difficult, dirty, and dangerous and the noise was deafening in parts of the mill. We had to crawl in between various pieces of machinery to clean, and to move equipment and material. We used to take unofficial breaks when we could, during the eight hour day. We always had look outs to inform us when Hyman was checking us out. God help anyone who was caught doing anything wrong. It meant that he would be subjected to a tirade of abuse and insults from Hyman, especially if he had, had a few shots of rum. He would scream, shout, make threats, and even sent us home early without pay if he was in a really bad mood. He also expected certain favours from some boys, including bottles of rum, money, and cuddles. I kept clear of him, and would never enter his ramshackle office, which was a storeroom for the equipment we had to use, without the presence of other boys. I was never one of his favourites, especially when he knew that I was attending trade union meetings and reporting some of the things we had to endure under Hyman's supervision. He was seen as an eccentric, but harmless person and no action was ever taken against him when I worked under his supervision.

I also made friends with some older men who were clerks and administrative assistants, apprentices and mature staff who had started an education study group. A number of us from the Hyman gang and other boys working in the laboratory and offices joined this group and attended evening classes. There were no teachers or formal teaching. It was entirely self-help and each one supporting those less qualified. I wanted to escape from this labouring job by gaining skills and qualifications. I managed to escape after about a year from the Hyman gang and secured a job as a laboratory assistant based in a large office and managed by Mr Larson a white chemist from Holland.

Promotion to Laboratory Assistant

My second job on the plantation was as a laboratory assistant. There was only one laboratory that was responsible for quality assurance and monitoring the progress of the sugar production through the various stages. I secured this job through a senior chemist who was one of the organisers of the education group. The main thing that kept the group going was because the plantation Welfare Officer recognised that as most people did not have electricity, or facilities to study at home, they could use his office during the evenings as a quiet place. It had electricity, running water, chairs, tables and equipment to support studying.

I would regularly run around the factory collecting samples at different points and the more senior staff would analyse the quality and inform the production staff to make the necessary adjustments. I assisted the junior staff in some of the work in the laboratory. It was shift work and each of the three shifts lasted eight hours. The pay was reasonable and during the regular factory closure, which enabled the European overseers to return to their country of origin for up to six weeks at a time, we had a relatively easy time. I worked in the laboratory for about a year until I was just over sixteen.

A Strange experience at work

I lost my job soon after I was sixteen because of a strange experience. As part of my work in the laboratory I had to change the cards in the sundial, which was situated outside the massive colonial type house where the Chief Chemist and Head of the Laboratory was living. He lived with his European wife on the overseer's compound, where the majority of white overseers (junior and middle managers) lived. The compound was in an enclosure with a high fence draped by tropical flowers with thorns to keep out unwelcome and unauthorised visitors. The houses on the compound were the best on the entire plantation. They were large properties painted white and other bright colours. Some were concrete buildings and some wood with a number partly concrete and partly wood. The buildings were spacious with lots of modern furniture, equipment, well-cultivated gardens with lots of flowers and well-kept lawns and roads. Recreational facilities such as swimming pools and bars were available only to the European overseers. Each household had their personal servants, maids, gardeners, watchman and people who would run errands for them.

The residents in the compound and the very senior managers who lived in the even bigger individual houses outside the compound for junior and middle managers had permanent security staff. They all had access to meat, vegetables and poultry specially reared for them by specialist local staff. Much of the consumer goods, furniture, equipment, clothing and even household items were imported from Europe. The class system and the system which identified the status of the employee were apparent even amongst the Europeans. For Black and Asian people they were also placed in a hierarchical system determined by skin colour, class and qualifications. Colour was a key factor for anyone seeking work, which involved close contact with the Europeans.

Each morning I would replace the card in the sundial outside the home of the Chief Chemist. I would arrive before sunrise and put a card into the dial, and so when the sun came up it burnt a line on the card indicating the volume and intensity of the sun's heat. Before inserting the new card I would retrieve the used one and return it to the Laboratory. On one particular day I went to change the card, and I was about an hour late because I overslept. The sun was already up, so I was trying very hard to discreetly complete the task and leave. Before I could complete the task I saw the cook, an African female, who asked me what I was doing. I told her what I was doing. She informed me that I was late. I apologised to her. She then asked me if I wanted a drink. I thanked her and said I would like a drink, as I missed my breakfast having woken up late. I followed her towards the kitchen using the stairs reserved for tradesmen. I sat at the top of the stairs and she gave me a cup of coffee and some toast. Whilst I was having the coffee and toast, the wife of the Chief Chemist came through the house and into the kitchen, wearing only a loose dressing gown, which was open and exposed her frontal body. She was naked apart from the dressing gown. She saw me eating and smiled. To my surprise she didn't even attempt to secure her dressing gown. It was such a shock for me because it was the first time I had seen a naked white woman.

For me it was an overwhelming experience, which I felt compelled to share. It was every male teenager's dream to see a naked woman, let alone a European woman. The experience reminded me of white women I had seen in Western European films and the women I adored such as Jane Russell, Diana Dors, Rita Hayworth, Brigitte Bardot, Anita Ekberg, Marilyn Munroe and others. However, I went back to the laboratory feeling very excited and anxious to share the experience with the other laboratory assistants. I told a couple of friends about the incident as we huddled in a corner of the laboratory. I repeatedly described in detail what I had seen. Unfortunately, word got back to the Chief Chemist about the experience I had had at his home. He did not take kindly to this. He later called me into his office and informed me that as I was too old to remain a laboratory assistant and it was time to recruit a younger trainee assistant. He informed me that he would be happy to provide me with a reference which I later returned to collect prior to leaving for England. I am convinced that I was dismissed because of the earlier incident. I then became unemployed.

Distressed and looking to escape

After being unemployed for a few months, I had a discussion with one of my older friends, who used to help me at the adult education centre, about his decision to emigrate to England to further his studies and career. We kept in touch with each other, after he had arrived in London. He encouraged me to move to London, if, and when I could afford to do so. I felt it would be a good idea, even though I would miss my family. The big problem was that I was unemployed; feeling depressed and had no chance of ever saving enough money to pay for my travel to London.

At that point in time my parents were separated and our family was going through a very difficult time. I felt as though I had had enough and life was not worth living. Throughout most of my childhood I had had to cope with insults about my mother's lifestyle, such as her having a mixed race daughter, half African and half Asian, leaving the family home and returning a year or two later with another child, and associating with some women whose reputation was frowned upon by some people. At the same time my eldest sister Dede was having all sorts of problems with her husband who frequently assaulted and abused her and she would come to our house for protection. My other sister Doreen was also in an abusive relationship. Both husbands were alcoholics and violent when they ran out of alcohol and money to purchase more. Somehow these women had to find money for their husbands and their friends to remain drunk for days at a time. I felt so distressed and helpless and vowed to take revenge against these men as soon as I felt I was physically able to do so.

All these problems led me to the decision I think, to drink some poisonous liquid, which was stored for treating diseased and injured poultry and for killing rats after mixing it in food left out at night for rats to feed on. We were told as children, that we should never touch the bottle as it contained a poisonous substance. It was a cry for help and not a determination to die. Fortunately, I was found lying on the floor by a relative who immediately put his fingers down my throat and made me vomit most of the poison before it was fully effective. I survived, but I believe there was some damage to my kidneys and liver which affects me to this day. I survived the experience and my parents then came together and we discussed what I wanted from life. I told them that I would like to join my friend in England, because I wanted to get away from the problems, which had characterised my family and my personal life.

Following this incident my family and I decided that there was no future for me in Guyana. I was unemployed, unhappy and desperately wanted to do something useful. There were hardly any opportunities for me except to follow my parents and work in the sugar cane fields. My parents association with the Marxist People's Progressive Party led by Cheddi Jagan, and the Guyana Agricultural Workers Union was enough to ensure that I would never have a career on the plantation. I was determined to avoid becoming a field labourer for the rest of my life, at any cost. I then became more interested in emigrating from Guyana to England even though I was only seventeen years old with no qualifications or recognised skills. I had a long discussion with my mother who promised to think about it and she explained how difficult it would be to see her only son leaving her for a foreign country, and beyond her personal protection.

When it was decided that I would travel to England, my mother ensured that I had the finance to enable me to make the journey. I remember going with her to the pawnbroker in Georgetown, where she pawned her precious gold jewellery which she had acquired from her grandmother and mother that was brought over from India during the years of indenture-ship. My mother sold what goods she had, accepted small gifts from friends and relatives, and this enabled me to leave Guyana.

My parents were very hard working people and very politically motivated. They were part of the struggle for trade union rights, and the campaign for an independent and democratic Guyana, which remained a British colony until the granting of independence in 1966. Guyana is a country rich in natural resources including gold, bauxite, rice, timber and of course sugar, yet, to this day, most of the inhabitants, (like the majority of people in the ex-colonies around the world populated by Black and Asian people) live in poverty. I knew leaving Guyana was never going to be easy for me as I felt I had a special role within my family as the only son and brother. I felt that my loyalty should be to my parents who were getting old and in poor health. I was torn between staying in Guyana and looking after my parents and sisters who needed support and leaving Guyana to work in England. I comforted myself that I would return from England, with enough money and education to get a good job and to take good care of my family. Guyana was and still is a male chauvinist and violent society. Violence against females was and still is quite extensive. My two eldest sisters, who were already married before I left Guyana, were suffering enormously because of the violent nature of their husbands. It disappointed me greatly and I suffered too.

I left Guyana when I was still seventeen. It wasn't at all easy for me; I felt extremely distressed at leaving my parents, who were getting old and sickly, but still working very hard to make a living. My two sisters Dede and Doreen who were older than me were married and had families of their own. My four younger sisters were all under fifteen years of age and very vulnerable. My brother-in-laws were violent and dependent on alcohol; my father and mother suffered from ill health and they were separated and all this left all my sisters very vulnerable. As the only young and strong male person in our family, I felt it was my duty to stay in Guyana and support them, to stand up to my violent relatives and improve my life. But on reflection, I also felt it was right to leave. Leaving for England was I felt an act of selfishness on my part and I was tormented by the thought of isolation and estrangement from my family. I comforted myself by proceeding with arranging my departure from Guyana with the hope that I would return within three to five years, educated, strong and with money to take care of all my family.

When I was leaving Guyana I said to my mother, "I will come back and look after you, you shouldn't worry". I still see her from time to time in my dreams. I remember her at the airport, a very small, frail lady with no shoes on her feet. She was accustomed to walking barefoot and she refused to wear the sandals, which my sisters had bought for her, but carried them instead. My relatives were ordinary country folks who lived extraordinary lives in order to survive. Before departure on a tiny eight-seater airplane from Atkinson Airport in Georgetown I hugged and kissed my parents and whispered "I love you" to them. I kissed their feet before turning to my two eldest sisters hugged and kissed their feet as a mark of deep respect. I was by then too upset to say anything to the others whose hands I shook before boarding the plane.

Kaieteur Falls – Guyana

First Family picture

Ma and sisters

Jim before leaving for England

Chapter 2:

Ma

My mother and sisters

All mothers are exceptional super-human beings and my mother was no different. No-one knows for certain when my mother was born or how old she was when she died. Neither my mother's birth nor her two marriages were officially ever registered; however, I believe she was born around 1913 in a small village called La Jalousie on the west coast of the Demerara River, Guyana.

La Jalousie, at the time of mother's birth, was a small village consisting of no more than 100 families. The population was almost entirely made up of first, second and third generation descendants of indentured labourers from India.

East Indians first landed in, what was then British Guiana, in 1836, two years after the British Parliament agreed to abolish slavery in the British Colonies. This was during the period of indenture-ship when over two-and-a-half million Indians were transported by the East India Company from India to the Caribbean, various parts of Asia, Africa and South America to work on various European, mainly British owned plantations. This despicable trade in humans across continents was very lucrative for the British nation and owners of the plantations. Queen Victoria, the Parliamentarians, the Christian churches and the capitalists made fortunes from the trafficking of humans who were either kidnapped or lured to be transported under false promises. This trade lasted from 1836 until 1917 when it was finally abolished.

My maternal grandfather, Ramsakal, known as Sakla, was born during the 1880's on one of the ships which sailed from India to the Caribbean and Guyana, with labourers from Bengal, Bihar, Delhi, Madras and Calcutta. My mother knew nothing of her grandparents, or even her mother, since they died when she was just a small child. Her father never re-married nor had he been inclined to have any more children, so my mother grew up as an only child in a house made of mud and straw which was a minute's walk from the coast of the Atlantic Ocean in Demerara.

According to my mother, her childhood was very lonely, isolated and miserable as there were no immediate or extended family to take care of her while her father worked on the sugar plantation. She had no formal training or education and remained illiterate throughout her life. My mother's name was Dhanraji but she was commonly known as Mabel. To us children, she was always referred to as 'Ma'.

Ma did not only have an unusual childhood, but almost all of her life she was characterised by unusual behaviour and circumstances. She was married in her early teens to Junniah. It is possible she was aged between thirteen and fourteen, since she became a mother well before she was 18 years old, after at least two miscarriages. Junniah, who was much older than her, had been married before and had a daughter called Raj. According to word of mouth reports, my mother had several miscarriages before eventually giving birth to a son who was disabled and died shortly afterwards.

Miscarriages and infant mortality rates were very high under the plantation system in which women and children were forced to work for long hours in the hot sun, with grossly inadequate food, and a lack of medical care or support of any kind. My mother had her share of miscarriages due to poor health, heavy manual work and poor diet. Abuse of women and children was also sadly a common feature of the plantation economy. This was mainly due to the plantation owners only being interested in profits and not the people, whose blood, sweat, tears and miserable lives were linked to the profit margins.

At the age of about twenty two, my mother gave birth to my eldest sister, Dede, followed by my second sister, Doreen, before I was born in 1943. My father died when I was less than a year old, so my mother had to struggle without the support of any extended family; since my father was also the only surviving child from his parents. His own parents had passed away when he had been a young man. Life for my mother as a single parent was very harsh due to the fact that there were no welfare services of any kind in place for mothers, children or the elderly.

After losing my father, my mother was again lonely, isolated and severely distressed. She did all she could to bring up her three children on her own, while at the same time working full-time. To add insult to injury, she accumulated another burden to her miserable life; she was abused by a number of men including an African carpenter who carried out repairs to her house. In due course she gave birth to a mixed race African / Indian daughter, which brought even more distress and shame to her and her children. Mixed relationships were extremely rare and frowned upon by fellow Indians whether they were Hindus, Muslims, Christians or Atheists. I believe this pressure and abuse had severe effects on her physical and mental state, as well as her lifestyle and moral values.

Shortly after my mixed-race sister, Julie, was born my mother met and married Ramsahi also known as Jokhan, the person who all my sisters and I regarded as our father, until his death in 1967. From her marriage to Jokhan came three more girls – my sisters Datsie, Joyce and Petsie. They were not all from the same father. My mother continued to work long hours in difficult situations until she became very sick and later died from cervical cancer. I believe that she had had multiple medical problems, including diabetes, which unfortunately had never been diagnosed. I understand diabetes better now; I can see that the states she got into and attitudes she had on occasions which could have been linked to diabetes. Her death followed on a few months after our father had passed away and her own father died soon afterwards. The three tragic deaths in the family seriously shocked me and caused me much pain and distress, which is still felt even to this day. Sadly, at the time, I was unable to attend any of the funerals, something which haunts and torments me even now.

My earliest memories of my mother began when I was about six years old. As the only son, my mother treated me as someone special in her life. From then until I was seventeen and left for England I felt there was a special bond between my mother and I. I loved her dearly and I frequently promised myself to take care of her and to make sure she got all the help and support to enable her to live a comfortable life. Her early death cheated me of this opportunity. I deeply regret that I could not spend as much time with her as I had wanted.

My mother was around four feet nine inches tall and weighed no more than seven or eight stones. She was a typical East Indian Guyanese woman who was the driving force and workhorse of the family. Such women always placed the needs and welfare of their families before their own. Pain and suffering followed them throughout their lives, bearing and rearing children, supplementing their husband's or family income by keeping animals, chickens or cultivating kitchen gardens were part of their daily routine. They were occupied every day of the week from early morning until they went to bed late at night. Many of them were regularly condemned, blamed or brutalised by husbands if things went wrong in the family. Poverty, oppression and pain shaped and defined the lives of working-class women. On many occasions during my childhood I wept at the thought of the constant pain and suffering my mother had to endure to support her children and husband during his frequent illnesses due to undiagnosed and untreated diabetes, or periods of unemployment.

During my childhood it was common for women to get up between 3 a.m. and 5 a.m. to cook breakfast for their husbands who would leave for work from as early as 5 a.m. Often, women would also work on the plantation and both men and women would take other members of their family including children under fourteen and as young as seven or eight years old to work with them. The work was so badly priced that parents felt compelled to involve their children. Even so the wages at the end of the week were insufficient to enable the family to purchase enough food and to pay their bills. Many children from as young as ten or twelve years old were often left behind at home to look after younger sisters and brothers and take care of the family home.

I spent part of my childhood from about eleven to thirteen years staying at home and looking after my younger sisters, when my elder sisters were taken to work by my parents. I kept our family home and looked after the few animals we kept too. I also did my best when I was not looking after my sisters to secure food for my family by rearing chickens, cultivating a small kitchen garden, collecting firewood and fetching water. If I were not doing all these things, I would either be at school for part of the time; working with my mother in the cane fields or rice fields, or selling fruit or vegetables by the roadside in the hot sun.

Workers on the plantation had very little or no choice where they worked or how much they were paid. There were always a large number of people who were unemployed and willing to work at below subsistence wages. The plantation was the only employer for miles around. There were no paid holidays, social or welfare payments, reasonable pension schemes to provide for even the basic necessities of life, nor were there any health and safety facilities, apart from the dispensary provided by the plantation owners. It was not uncommon for supervisors, commonly known as 'drivers' to insult; abuse or cheat their workers. Bribery, corruption and abuse were regular features of plantation life, as were low pay, poverty, powerlessness and a poor diet. Rape, domestic violence, stress and helplessness characterised the lives of most women in our village, yet they continued to put their families before themselves.

My mother had more than her fair share of such degrading experiences. Reporting any kind of violence or abuse to the police was extremely rare due to the fear of further attacks and abuse. It was also known that women and working class people did not have the financial power to secure justice. Women were economically dependent on men and such dependency was re-enforced by social, religious and cultural values.

Despite the hardships my mother had to endure she was fiercely committed to helping others and was physically, emotionally and politically involved in the fight for independence for Guyana from British Colonial rule. She was determined to fight injustice, unfairness and exploitation in every area of life and recognised, despite being completely illiterate, how the misuse of power, colonial occupation, lack of self-determination and oppression determined issues on justice, freedom and fairness. I have inherited all these views from her, plus her boldness in challenging authority and confronting injustice. My mother was an ardent supporter of the People's Progressive Party (PPP) which was led by the great Guyanese anti-Colonial campaigner and Socialist, Doctor Cheddi Jagan. Like many liberation fighters during the anti-colonial struggles Doctor Jagan was imprisoned by the British ruling elite.

I was only ten years old when my mother regularly took me to political meetings to support the struggles ignited by Cheddi Jagan and the PPP. I was taken along to these meetings and demonstrations by my mother as it was not culturally correct for women to be seen at such meetings on their own. Being the only male in the family apart from my father I fulfilled this important role. My father was a great deal less politically aware or involved than my mother, even though he was a staunch trade union member.

One of my mother's favourite habits at election time was to vote early and vote often, and to encourage others to do the same. She was a great agitator and would regularly attend trade union, party political and community meetings. She would passionately encourage other women to attend meetings and to vote at election time, even though such events were almost exclusively the domain of men. I gained a lot of knowledge about political, trades union and community struggles well before I was fourteen years old mainly due to my mother. During my childhood, home was where my mother was. She was frequently away from home for prolonged durations. Yet she gave me the values, vision and determination which influence me to this day, to struggle for a world free from inequality, exploitation, unfairness and injustice. I see my life, my duties towards my family, community, race, class, and the world through the experiences I endured as a child, and the times spent with my mother.

My mother was well-known in our village and surrounding ones. She used to have several jobs apart from working in the plantation, including being part of a gang of women who de-weeded amongst the thousands of rows of sugar cane. Sometimes, this involved getting up early in the morning to listen for the foreman who would announce at several points along the Leonora Road, by shouting messages as to where women workers were needed. This could involve walking barefoot for miles with the necessary equipment and food on mud or gritty roads to get to the actual place of work. The work would not end until either it was completed or too dark and dangerous to continue wielding a machete.

Workers regularly toiled through torrential rain and scorching sunshine with no protection against the weather, or having a change of clothing. It was not uncommon for women to endure labour or even give birth on the way to work, at work or on the way home from work. Women would support each other by stopping work and looking after sick or injured colleagues, using their own clothes for bandages or as wraps for babies born alive or dead. Births and deaths were not always reported and no one appeared bothered about registering such events as far as I was aware. Accidents at work were fairly common as well. Workers would often continue working even after some serious accidents. They would resume work after a brief rest, in order to finish their work. No work, meant no pay, and no pay meant poverty.

Guyana was largely an agricultural economy with the fertile land owned by the absentee plantation owners or the independent farmers. The rich indigenous farmers exploited the large army of poor casual workers who had to work for poverty wages. The small farmers barely earned enough to keep themselves and their families out of debt. The mining and timber extraction industries were firmly in the hands of the capitalists based in London. They extracted large profits, yet were reluctant to invest in local businesses.

Women earned much less than men for work of equal value, even though wages for men were often at or below subsistence level. Despite the fact that my parents worked full-time and were often assisted by us children, there was never enough income to enable us to eat well, have decent clothes or footwear, or enjoy any luxury whatsoever. My parents always seemed to owe money to the shopkeepers for goods we bought on credit during hard economic periods. Workers were often laid off for weeks and even months from the plantation, which was the only employer in Plantation Leonora. During this period, moneylenders and pawnbrokers did good business amongst the poor, which made up about eighty per cent of Leonora's population. On more than one occasion my mother and I were turned away from the shop where we bought our weekly foodstuff, (commonly called 'rations') due to outstanding credit.

The moneylender would sometimes insult my mother in the presence of her children when she was unable to repay his loan at high interest rates. I remember on one occasion saying to the loan shark when he came for payment that my mother was not at home and could he return later, to which he replied, 'I will wait'. After about forty minutes, which seemed like a whole day, my mother appeared from her hiding place in the house to offer him part of the payment which he was entitled to. This shame was obvious to all of us children and I made a promise that I would never owe anyone any money. I am pleased to say that, apart from a couple of occasions, I have kept that promise to this day. On one of the very few occasions I borrowed money; it was to support my family in Guyana after the death of my parents. Even now, I never borrow money from anyone, nor involve myself in any credit purchase. I do not use a credit card and all my purchases are made by cash or cheque where possible.

On many occasions my mother went without meal when we were young children, because there was simply not enough food available, and feeding the children came first. This situation always distressed me and I often thought to myself that, when I grew up, my mother and family would always have plenty of food, clothing and support. It was a treat to see my mother smile and cuddle us children. She spent a lot of her time breastfeeding my younger sisters even though there was often very little or no milk available. Mother's breast milk, when available, was often a substitute for cooked food; at least it calmed the child and put them to sleep for a while.

I remember an incident when my mother was sitting on the floor eating her meal consisting of boiled rice and a few vegetables whilst my baby sister was breast feeding. Suddenly the baby did a wee and some of it went into her enamel plate which was placed on her lap. She enquired whether there was any more food in the pot, and was told that the pot was empty. She then drained the urine away from her plate, sprinkled some salt on the remaining food and ate the rest. This memory has stayed with me since and I always treat food with respect. I seldom, if ever leave food on my plate or waste food, because there was never enough to go around when I was a child. I am totally opposed to food being wasted in rich countries when about a quarter of the world's population do not have sufficient food to eat.

My family was very creative in accessing and cooking food. My parents and eldest sister, Dede, would harvest edible wild crops from fields and trenches, engage in fishing, growing our own and providing food from the cattle and poultry we raised. Ma made the simplest of dishes the tastiest in the world – the only problem was, there was never enough of it, except on special occasions. Sometimes, a small portion of boiled rice with some salt and pepper tasted like a meal fit for a king. We boiled the small amount of rice in a large pot of water. We then used the water, drained from the rice with a sprinkling of salt. For us it was a meal. We never peeled our own vegetables unless we had to, nor did we ever leave any food on our plates. Eating meat was associated with special occasions. A chicken would be a real feast for us. When I got married, this is something we practiced in our own family, even when our economic position became very secure. I am always opposed to wastage of any sort; I hoard things in my loft, garage, sheds and in my house and then pass them on to people in need. I often send books, equipment and other materials to poor countries as gifts.

I valued every moment I spent with my mother when I was between the ages of six to thirteen. I can only express some of my feelings in terms of what my mother meant to me, as I find it difficult to assemble the words that would reflect my inner thoughts. I took comfort in my mother's presence; I watched tears rolling down her face which sometimes triggered off my own tears; listened to her laughter and laughed with her; observed her struggles and shared her vision for what a world could be and what it was in reality. I was often at her side during her many jobs working as a market trader, selling food and vegetables, selling fish from door to door, farming rice and vegetables and doing other tasks. Of the many jobs my mother undertook, I believe that being a fishmonger, walking with a heavy basket of partly-frozen fish and ice-cold water dripping on to her head and body for hours each day, was the most painful.

Walking barefoot door-to-door with a straw basket of wet fish on often hot and muddy roads must have been torture for her. I frequently trotted alongside her as she walked through the villages constantly placing the heavy basket from her head to the ground. She had to make frequent stops to allow customers to see and haggle before they purchased her fish, usually on credit. It was quite difficult for her to lift the basket from her head and place it on the ground. Sometimes I was able to assist her myself. On other occasions customers would help her to place the heavy basket on the ground and then return it to her head until the next stop. To compound matters Ma was illiterate so she was unable to record the names and addresses of the customers and the sale price. When I was with her, I was reasonably competent in making some notes, but it was never fully accurate. Pages would go missing from the book either because the rats had chewed them or someone had torn the page out.

However, my mother would remember most if not all, the details from memory. The problem was when she went round on Sunday mornings to collect her money, quite a number of customers would either deny making the purchase at all, or arguing that they didn't owe as much as she claimed. She had little choice but to accept a lot of lies from people who would turn to other providers should she argue with them. Some of them were so poor and were unable to pay and would even ask her for more credit. After collecting money on Sunday, sometimes having to make two or three return calls during the day, we would often sit and count up the money late in the evening. Ma would then parcel out the various allocations which she had to make to the fishermen or trawler owners from whom she had purchased the fish and then set aside sums for household expenses. Sadly, on occasions there was insufficient money to pay the people from whom she bought the fish, let alone make any profit. These were distressing occasions for both of us because we knew very well what the implications were.

On good occasions, Ma used to save small sums through women's co-operatives. Each woman would put in, for example, two or five Guyanese dollars each week, and one of the group would be paid the total collection, less commission charged by the person who collected the money and underwrote the transaction. We used to have good meals for at least a week when it was Ma's turn to collect. Plus, she was able to clear up any debts. As my two eldest sisters started to earn their own income from the plantation, life became a bit easier for all of us.

Our life changed when my eldest sister, Dede, got married and left our home. We all noticed a real change in Ma. Dede was a tower of strength to our family. Not only was she regarded by me and the younger sisters as a mother figure, but she had worked from her early teenage years until she left our home. Dede's income was an important supplement to the family finances. Dede was always by Ma's side when working in the fields: Ma trusted Dede and depended on her. Dede was very mature for her age and always modest and loyal – never selfish, argumentative, rebellious or extravagant. When she left home, Ma became demotivated and demoralised for many weeks before picking herself up and buying a donkey and small cart. Ma and I made a good team. She bought the provisions and I used the donkey and cart to transport the goods.

On one occasion we stopped halfway home from the market at Parika with a cart full of plantains, eddoes, bananas, yams, oranges and cassava, because we wanted to give the donkey a rest and some food. We pulled up at Ma's friend's house on the main road, which had a large front garden, fed the donkey and let it loose to graze, then had a cold drink and a bun. When we were ready to restart our journey, we couldn't believe our eyes – the donkey had had an adorable, cuddly little foal. So, we spent two days with Ma's friend, and a cart load of provisions which we did our best to sell some from the cart on the side of the road. Eventually, all four of us arrived home safely.

After that, Ma decided that it was too risky having a female donkey and not fair to work her so hard, so we sold the two of them and bought a male donkey, who we called Jack, instead. He was a total nightmare and we soon discovered why he had been so cheap to buy. He would often tear away with the cart in any direction when he saw a female donkey, and would sit down in the middle of the public road whenever he thought he had done enough work. Apart from that, and the fact that he sometimes returned with bites all round his neck when some stronger stallion had remonstrated with him for making a pass at his mare, he wasn't a bad lad. He was strong and powerful with a shining black coat and on the whole a good worker.

Mothers have many talents

Another of Ma's many talents was dressmaking. She made all her own clothes as well as our own and the Singer machine was an important part of the family. Ma would peddle away for hours on end, using a small jar filled with kerosene oil and a lighted wick to enable her to see what she was stitching well into the night. Ma even made clothes for others who were poor in the village. They would buy the material, and Ma would sew it for them on her machine. I used to be a benefactor of this arrangement, because Ma would make shirts for me from the off-cuts. I was often teased by my friends because of my colourful shirts made from bits of dress material.

The sewing, like the donkey and cart, and the fish business had to go, all for the same reason. People wanted goods but they had problems paying. They were either cheats, unemployed or very poor. Ma always felt sorry for poor families and would continue to let many of them have goods on credit, even though they had no means of paying her in the foreseeable future. Many women with several children who were either widowed, sick or had lazy husbands saw Ma as a soft touch and despite her own financial problems she never disappointed them. Ma had a strong social conscience and would often put the needs of other people before her own. She regularly saved a meal for any unexpected visitor or a beggar even when there was insufficient food to feed herself and her family.

After the fish, the sewing and the donkey and cart business, Ma decided she wanted to be involved in growing rice. As there were no rice fields in Leonora she decided to go to an island in the Essequibo River called Hamburg where we had some distant relatives farming. There was no school, shop, cinema or any recreational facilities in Hamburg; the highlight of the lives of these some six hundred people, mainly children, was going over to the mainland by crossing the Essequibo River in small boats sometimes as small as ten feet long, four feet wide and eighteen inches deep. The large steamer which sailed from the capital, Georgetown, stopped each day for a few minutes at the small wharf at Hamburg. People would arrive with purchases they had made and were willing to sell to those people who were unable to, or couldn't afford to travel. It was a small community on this large island owned by a Portuguese family who had a large house that was infrequently occupied by them.

I was twelve years old when Ma decided to take me along with her to Hamburg. It was a dreadfully lonely, isolated and miserable place and I missed the rest of my family and friends. Straight away, I was picked on by a boy about two years older than me, who was seen as leader of the teenage gang. A fight was arranged and we gathered in a field at the rear of some houses; I knew what would happen to me if I lost the fight. Fortunately, I had seen films when men fought each other in a different way to the Hamburg boys. So, I used both my arms, my feet and the rest of my body, unlike the boy who relied on one punch or neck-lock to get me to accept defeat. I won and was seen as the new leader.

Ma worked for a number of rice farmers but was unable to secure some rice land for herself. So, she decided to move from Hamburg to the County of Essequibo about a mile away across the fast-running, deep, rough and dangerous river from Hamburg. We made several trips across the Essequibo River in a small boat about 11 feet long, fourteen inches deep and about 3 feet wide in the widest part, with our few possessions. I got to know the boat and its owner well. The owner was invariably half drunk when he steered the boat known as 'Kill Three' because three people had died while crossing the river in this boat.

So we were now on the mainland of Essequibo which was somewhat more civilised than Hamburg. Ma decided to send me back to Leonora to fetch my sister Doreen, three years older than myself, to help her as she had managed to rent some rice fields. Doreen and I hated the work, having sometimes to work knee-deep in muddy water for long hours, planting rice or preparing the ground for sowing. We rented accommodation and had a hard time feeding ourselves. I was often sent back to Leonora to collect food, clothing and money for our survival in Essequibo. At least I never had to fight there because I never saw or played with other young boys as I was always working.

At one stage, I was so tired and fed up with working so hard and seeing my mother struggle I decided to either run away or injure myself. I decided to use the large machete I was working with to pierce a large vein in my leg and bleed to death. So I closed my eyes and aimed the business end of the machete at my leg. It did cut my flesh but not the vein. I then screamed in pain and my mother rushed to where I was. She bandaged the wound and I was back at work within fifteen minutes. She did curse quite a bit because she suspected that this was no accident.

My father was tremendous; he supported my mother through all her plans. He was always loving, generous and forgiving towards her, regardless of how she treated him. Within a year we had our first harvest and Ma was very pleased.

Doreen and I helped Ma to thresh the rice stalks to remove the rice grains called paddy before the skin was removed and the rice available to be cooked. I became quite strong, manoeuvring the bags of rice which weighed up to one hundred and fifty pounds. Ma and Doreen used to help me lift each bag on to the stack of bags then on to my shoulders and back, and I would carry each bag to the pick-up point. My father never visited Essequibo. He had quite a tough time trying to find regular work and to take care of the rest of the family. I loved him dearly and felt very sorry for him and his often miserable life.

Unfortunately, despite all our hard work, we had to abandon this venture after two years. The rice mill owner cheated Ma by claiming that the quality of the rice was poor. Ma also found a young man who wanted to marry my sister Doreen, an arrangement which my sister totally rejected. Soon after this suggestion both Doreen and I told Ma that we wanted to go home to Leonora, which involved a day's journey by foot, steamer, and rail and again on foot to our house. Ma was then left isolated and alone again in Essequibo. What was an even bigger problem for all our family was that Ma who was a committed and practicing Hindu was on her own and eventually started a relationship with a Muslim man who lived near where she had lodging. Within a few months Ma was pregnant with my youngest sister. Ma stayed in Essequibo and I cried for months because of the separation from her and not knowing what would happen to our family. That feeling about being separated from someone you love most has stayed with me, and regularly re-surfaces whenever I am separated from my wife, children or grandchildren. I also experience the same feeling whenever I visit my family abroad and have to leave them to return home not knowing when I shall see them again. I had the same experience each time I visited my children or they visited me when they were at university and we had to separate.

My mother eventually returned to Leonora with Petsie but decided to rent a house nearby, instead of living with us. She took my sister Datsie to live with her to look after Petsie. By then my sister Doreen was married to a fisherman and was living in Zeeburg some three miles away from our house. My eldest sister, Dede, was having a difficult time economically and within her married life. Both my elder sisters had married fishermen who were addicted to alcohol; prone to violence and not working for long periods. My sisters would normally turn to Ma for support in these situations but she had problems of her own.

This new man in my mother's life started to regularly torment and abuse her. This man was a practicing Muslim and a frequent visitor to the nearby Mosque. He had no shame, principles nor morality and exploited my mother despite her poor health and her confused state. It crossed my mind many times to take revenge against this man and the drunken husbands who abused my sisters. I promised myself that I would sort them out, shame them and teach them all a lesson on respect, but this man died before I returned to Guyana and my sisters managed to sort out their husbands with the support of their children.

Sadly, Ma started to work as a fishmonger again, a year before I let Guyana. I believe she was suffering from severe stress, and had various illnesses, which were never diagnosed or treated. Her behaviour was strange at times and frightening on many occasions. She became excitable, confused and emotional on occasions, but continued to work and live the best she could. I was working in the sugar mill at Plantation Leonora and was unable to spend time with Ma during the day. This man was always tormenting and bullying her as well as threatening her if she visited our family home. Ma left this man and moved nearer to our family home. We used to visit her on a regular basis. I was about fifteen and a half years old at the time. I used to visit her almost every day. I cried each time I left her after a visit. She was still a great cook and always touched my face and stroked my hair before I left. Her home was a tiny room with an earth floor. Most of the time she was alone at night - my youngest sister stayed with the rest of our family most of the time. I was so upset for my mother and my father. He was such a tolerant and loving person and all of us children adored him.

My workmates regularly tormented me about our strange family life, including the fact that I had a mixed race sister. The respect the villagers had had for ma was somewhat diminished. She had had in the village and my poor father must also have had a dreadful time amongst his peer group. He was a practising Hindu and was a member of the local religious group that was prominent in community work. They organised arrangements for celebrating Hindu festivals and community support for Hindu families. Muslims and Christians had their own groups in Leonora. The course took place in the community centre supported by the plantation. A Community Welfare officer was appointed to promote various projects, including a Workers' Educational Association on the estate. A couple of adult friends who used the centre encouraged me to continue my education. My education and status improved through my involvement at the centre. My awareness of the importance of learning increased enormously and so did my desire to make use of any opportunity to improve my knowledge and skills.

I joined the educational group of young and older workers who operated as a self-organised study group. Several of those involved were working either at the local laboratory or in the administration offices. Mixing with this group of committed and self-motivated men gave me a lot of confidence and I shared their aspirations to share knowledge and improve our skills and abilities. We also wanted to build a career within the plantation economy or to seek employment opportunities abroad. My most pressing thoughts were to get away from the problems and misery that my parents and sisters were going through.

London calling

Two members of the study group subsequently left for England and were doing very well. I kept in contact with one of them and he encouraged me to try to come to England.My parents could not afford the passage to England and I became very frustrated. However, I decided to continue to work and to study at the centre during the evenings.

My plan to travel to England had to be brought forward because I knew I would probably lose my job at the laboratory anyway, due to certain incidents at work.

I would have been dismissed in any case when I was eighteen as it was laboratory policy to dismiss assistants when they had reached that age and recruit fourteen-year-olds at lower rates of pay. Having left my job, with a recommendation from Mr Lawson, despite his annoyance with me for seeing his wife in the nude, I decided to have a conversation with my mother about my future. We talked about us returning to the donkey and cart trade, but she told me she could not cope with heavy work anymore. She was uncertain about her own future and decided to continue selling fish, but on a smaller scale. I was terribly upset to see my mother living by herself. We could see her tiny rented home from where we lived.

In addition, I was tormented and frustrated about the dreadful conditions in which my sisters were living and the constant abuse they had to endure from their violent husbands. I decided that I had no way out, I would never get to England, find another job, except as a field worker, and any thoughts of going becoming self-employed was impossible. So I decided to terminate my life which was full of sadness, misery, disappointments and frustration. I realised it was a wrong thing to do, as it was an escape from what was going on. As it happened, I survived and I had a long and painful discussion with my mother about going to England to start a new life. It was a shock for her as none of my relatives have ever travelled abroad. My mother was very supportive and assured me that she would do all she could to assist me. I promised her that I would return after a few years with money to take care of her and the rest of our family.

No one within my family had any idea of what I needed to do to travel to England, except that Britain was our mother country and we were allowed to emigrate as British colonial subjects. My mother happened to have a conversation with a woman who was a fellow fishmonger and she explained that I would need a passport to travel to London. She told my mother that a man called Barsatie knew of the system and he would assist us for a fee. He was one of these people who had failed in almost all his previous adventures to fulfil his dream to make lots of money. Nevertheless, despite his reputation as a bit of a fixer, my mother decided to seek his assistance.

Ma and I then set about with determination to plan and execute all the arrangements including arranging for the travel. The weeks I spent with Ma before leaving for England on 12th June 1961, just eight weeks before my eighteenth birthday, were some of the saddest times in my life. I was torn between going to England and staying in Guyana and looking after my mother, father and sisters. On a couple of occasions I became afraid of leaving my family to make such a long and lonely journey into an unfamiliar culture. Each time, Ma persuaded me that it was the right course of action to take and even promised to come to England and rescue me if I experienced any problems. Ma started to stay for longer periods in our family home and it appeared that we were all under the same roof again as one family.

Our first task was to travel to Georgetown, the capital city of Guyana to secure a birth certificate for me. We travelled together by foot to the train station, then on to a steamer, the Orange which took us across the Demerara River nearly a mile wide. We walked to the Registry Office and we waited in the hot sun for hours. Ma was barefoot, of course and I had well-worn plimsolls, made by BATA on my feet. A woman who noticed us waiting told my mother to go back to the window and show the clerk some money that she was prepared to offer him as a bribe for the certificate which should be issued free of charge. My mother reached into her bra and pulled out some money and the clerk then gave her immediate attention. He told her to be very quick and asked her all sorts of questions, which she could not answer. In the end he gave her a certificate with a single name "Thakoordin".

We returned home and planned the next task. She sorted out all her jewellery which she had accumulated for years and carefully carried with her since she got married. The plan was to pawn the jewellery to pay Mr Barsatie and to deposit it with the travel agent, Jo Chinn and Company, who Mr Barsatie recommended, no doubt for a fee from Mr Chin as well. The pawn shop was familiar to my mother, even though they had a very bad reputation not only for offering a low rate, but also replacing the jewellery with a similar one with much less gold content when they were returned to the owner. One reason for using this pawn shop was that they were the nearest to the port where the Orange was docked and it was safer to reach the shop and return to the steamer without falling victim to the thieves that were commonly known as "the choke and rob men" who used to follow people who had jewellery and suspected of having money. Their practice was to put their arm around their victim's neck, choke them and demand their jewellery and/or money.

These men were extremely dangerous, they were known criminals who showed their victims no mercy, and were known to carry weapons. They were almost all of African origin, and preyed almost entirely on Asian people, mainly women who generally worn jewellery, and would seldom fight back. Asian men, who went into the city to do business, would carry knives themselves and would invariably resist being robbed, unless they were intoxicated.

We pawned the jewellery, paid Mr Barsatie for completing the passport form, went to a photographic studio with five of my sisters and my mother and had our photo taken. It was sad that my sister Dede was not allowed to accompany us to the studio. My father was too sick to travel, so he was not in the photograph. So we secured my passport from the British High Commissioner and returned home surrounded by all these gorgeous females who have and continued to play a major part in my life. Friends and neighbours were very generous and I secured all I needed to start my journey to the mother country.

The few days before my departure were hard for both of us. My sister tried to persuade my mother to wear a pair of sandals to go to the airport but she refused. Ma had never owned a pair of shoes, nor did she ever turn on a light switch in all her life. When I kneeled down and kissed my mother's feet minutes before departure, I felt I would never see her again. I then stood up, cuddled her and whispered, with tears streaming down my cheeks, that I would be back to take care of her.

Ma returned to the family home

I kept in contact with my mother through my sisters who would read my letters to her and write to me on her behalf. Her health deteriorated further and she returned to live permanently in the family home, but separately from my father. I understood from various members of my family that she had become a very difficult person to live with and had regular disagreements with my sister Julie. Ma created a small living area in a room on the ground floor that we had formerly used as a storeroom. Whenever I could afford it, I sent her money via British Postal orders, without getting any verification that she had received them. Her health deteriorated further and, by 1966, she was very unwell. I desperately tried to make the journey back to Guyana to see her during her sickness but it was not possible due to lack of finance. In 1967, Ma died. She was only fifty four years old. Ma died only a few months after my step father. Later that year, my grandfather, Sakla, also died. These deaths within such a short period in time left me devastated.

So my poor mother died a lonely and miserable death, of cervical cancer, after many months of severe pain. When the telegram arrived at my house telling me of Ma's death, I immediately secured a small loan intending to attend her funeral. I discussed the situation with my wife and friends and we decided that, since I was unable to book a flight for several days and would have missed her funeral anyway, it would be better to send some money to my sister Julie to help with the funeral arrangements and to support the family instead, which I did. My employer, London Transport, was also reluctant to grant me extended leave to attend my mother's funeral.

1967 was a year of mixed blessings for my family and me. Although I lost my grandfather, mother and father, my wife Doreen safely delivered a beautiful baby daughter. It was a further six years before I was able to visit Guyana and my Mother's unmarked grave. I was told that she was buried in an area of the open and unkempt cemetery, which was used to graze cattle. My mother was buried near to my father. Unfortunately, none of my sisters were keen to discuss Ma's final years with me. I asked several questions but they were met with silence, or evasion. Julie, who by this time had safely secured herself in the family home as the sole owner, despite the fact that my father had left the property to all of us, made it extremely difficult for me to have any access to the family home except for a few days during my first visit back to Guyana in 1974.

It was left to a neighbour to inform me of the last three years of my mother's life. She was living next door and had full view of what was going on in my father's home. From what she told me, and was corroborated by other neighbours, friends of my mother and people who knew her, it seemed that Ma had suffered from diabetes that was untreated. She suffered from regular anxiety and panic attacks, depression, and ill health. Her life was one of dreadful isolation, poverty, pain and misery. Her physical and mental state troubled my sisters who were struggling to survive and were unable to support her financially as they themselves were poor and unsupported. As a result the relationship between my mother and my sisters deteriorated to the point where my mother was living in a shack on the ground floor where we used to keep chickens. My four sisters lived on the first floor and Julie was the head of the family home. None of my sisters were able to tell me about how my mother spent her last couple of years. I left Guyana in June 1961 and my parents died in 1967, just six years after I arrived in England. I used to send money through postal orders almost every few weeks to my family in Guyana. I had no idea how the money was used. I frequently had begging letters from family members for financial support and I responded the best I could. After getting married in August 1963 my wife and I continued to send small sums to Guyana to support my family. I do not believe my mother benefitted much from this support. None of my sisters told me what had happened to the jewellery my mother had kept and told me in letters written for her that she wanted my wife to have her jewellery when she died. I was never given anything left by my mother to me and my wife. Traditionally the jewellery was given to the eldest son's wife and this would then be given to her eldest son's wife when he got married. I feel dreadfully disappointed that I have nothing but memories to pass on to my children and their children.

According to her neighbour and her friends, she often discussed me with anyone who would listen to her. She longed to see me, my wife and two children and would often say "My son will be coming next month and he will look after me. I am saving my jewellery for my daughter-in-law when she comes." In the end, neither my wife nor I inherited anything from my mother. All I have is one very old photograph of her, and of course, the cherished memories, which have stayed deep inside of me to remind me of her, and I will carry to my grave. Julie to this day will avoid me at any cost. She denies me access to my family home during my subsequent visits to Guyana; she did her best to turn my younger sisters against me who were loyal to her as she brought them up after the deaths of our parents. I have admired Julie for taking care of my younger sisters who were also helped by Dede and Doreen, when they could sneak some support for them without their husband's knowledge.

Sadly, my wife or children never met my dear mother, father or grandfather. I know that my parents and grandfather would have loved them and enjoyed meeting them. I hope by reading this book all my family will have some understanding of the influence my parents, especially my mother had on me during my life as a person and as a husband, father, brother, uncle and grandfather. My mother is the reason why I have always hated the ideological concepts and practices associated with unrestricted capitalism and its associated 'so called' democratic political system, which condemned hundreds of millions of people under colonialism, rampant capitalism, globalisation and neo-colonialism. The western capitalist nations, especially the Western Europeans, that dominated Africa, South America and Asia, colonised and enslaved the indigenous people for centuries have a lot to answer for the poverty, misery, insecurity, unfairness, inhumanity and brutality they used to dominate and control them, even to this day.

For the first few years after her death, I saw my mother regularly in my dreams and for at least the last twenty years, I have felt terribly guilty for not supporting my mother a great deal more during her last five years of life. I was unable to do more for her as I was struggling myself with the financial commitments towards a young family and a home. I still think of my mother in a fond and loving way. She did her best to put food into our bellies at any cost to herself, her reputation or her safety. She was fiercely independent and someone who really operated outside the box. She hated conformity, injustice, exploitation and domination. I really admired her commitment to social justice, anti-colonialism and stance against rampant capitalism. In a strange way I admire my mother *because* of all her faults. She certainly lived an unusual life in a setting grossly influenced by culture, tradition, history and religion. As a smoker of pure black tobacco roll-ups she was highly unusual, although modest drinking of alcohol was not so unusual as many poor women struggling to make ends meet and to feed their families had the odd tipple from time to time, ostensibly to calm the nerves, and forget their problems, albeit temporarily. What was most unusual was her desire to have her own space and do her own thing, even if it meant leaving her husband and family, returning with someone else's child and expecting to carry on as though nothing significant had happened.

My mother could be described as either an "unconventional woman", "a victim of circumstances", "a fighter for equality and liberation", or even "a feminist", Was she a victim, a survivor, a pioneer, a challenger of traditional values or someone with serious health problems? I believe she was all of the above to varying extents. To me she was my Ma, my role model in terms of politics, social consciousness, the fact that she was a fighter, fiercely independent and not afraid to challenge and be different. Yes she enjoyed her roll ups, discreetly drank local Demerara rum with her few selected friends, yes she had a number of relationships with men who exploited her, but for me she never failed to care for her children the best she could.

She was certainly no angel, nor did she ever pretend to be above criticism. For me, she was a person who has been attached to my heart from childhood and will remain so forever. As I look across the years I still sometimes see myself, barefoot, with torn clothing trotting beside her, and hanging on to her dress, on the hot and dusty roads along the coast of Demerara, in rain and in sunshine. I have felt her emotions, been conscious of her pains, cried when I saw the silent tears rolling down her bony cheeks and asked God to help her and to alleviate her suffering. Feeling guilty, inadequate and regretful has become a permanent feature of my character when I refer to my parents. The fact that I never had the opportunity to take her in my arms as an adult, cuddle her, whisper to her how much she meant to me, shower her with things to make her comfortable and to see her smile and then laugh aloud with joy, means that these dreadful feelings are likely to remain with me as long as I live.

The time I spent with my mother was much too short. The dream I had as an immigrant returning to my homeland with my wife and children and seeing my parents with my sisters and their families greeting me on arrival at the airport in Guyana was never realised. Had this been the case I would have kissed her feet with the same emotions I did when I last saw her alive at the tiny Atkinson Airfield when I left Guyana in 1961, aged seventeen. I am now seventy years old and yet I have such strong feelings for my dear mother nearly fifty years after her death.

On many occasions during writing this book, sitting in front of my computer alone in my large detached office; I felt that maybe mother was sitting beside me throughout the years. It was extremely difficult to write this book. Every time I started to write about my mother, my father and eldest sister Dede, I ended up in tears and had to stop writing. Sometimes it took me up to 6 months or longer to feel comfortable to return to writing this book, which took the best part of ten years. On one particular occasion I left my office in distress, at around 2.00am after writing part of this chapter and I saw my mother sitting on the step leading to my office. I am not a believer in ghosts, but I swear it was my mother sitting there. I frequently feel her presence around me especially when I am feeling distressed and have been forced to endure pain and suffering.

Circumstances, the prevailing environment and individualism shaped my mother's view of herself, her family, society and life. My mother was born before her time. She was a woman who would let nothing stop her from providing for her children and for whom she would defy the accepted norm, in order to support them. Although she had limited means, she was creative in the way she she made ends meet. She was clearly a woman before her time. Ma was the Germaine Greer of her time, a feminist, when most did not know what the word meant, a little naughty, by the standard of these days, and a seeker of unconventional fun. She would have fitted in seamlessly with the 21st century woman. I am confident that if my Mother was alive today she would be proud of my life and achievements. She might even say to me, "You're a chip off the old block, my son; it's in the genes you know".

Top – Bottom
Wife Doreen with 2 eldest sisters Dede and Doreen
Jim and Datsie
Jim and Dede, eldest sister

Chapter 3:

My Seven Sisters

My sister Dede

My second eldest sister, who was the first surviving child from my biological parents, was legally named Yomatie, also commonly called Betya by everyone in the village, but, was known to all her sisters and myself – the only brother – as Dede. She was born in 1937, six years before my birth. I believe Dede is a Hindi word for elder sister. All of us addressed her as Dede and she addressed me as Bud, short for Budya – a Hindi word for brother. Dede was like a mother to all her sisters and myself. We spent most of our time with her before she got married and left the family home, in 1954. Doreen, my second eldest sister and I were left in Dede's care when we were under school age, whilst my mother and stepfather were at work.

Our parents worked six days each week when paid employment was available on the plantation. They worked from early morning until late in the evening. Dede took care of us with all the love, dedication, affection and care of a mother. Her caring responsibilities meant that she never had any schooling, and she remained illiterate until her death in 1992. I have always loved Dede with all of my heart as long back as I can remember. She was truly a gift to my heart, a friend to my soul and an important part of my childhood that will never be forgotten.

As the only brother I was much cherished by all of my sisters. Dede's love and attention meant a great deal to me. We looked very much alike and it was easy to recognise us as sister and brother. Dede used to take my second sister Doreen and I to cut and fetch firewood or to catch fish and shrimps in the canals near our house. She also involved us in looking after our couple of cows, our donkey, a few sheep and some chickens. We used to cut and fetch grass for our cows and clean the cow pen each day. The cow manure was used as fertiliser for our small kitchen garden. Dede taught me many useful tasks when I was around six to ten years old. Fetching water for cooking and drinking from the well some two hundred yards away, was also a regular journey with her. My special relationship with Dede lasted until she died. She was a special friend who fulfilled the role of a mother when she was left in charge of us. Life for us would have been even more difficult without Dede's love, affection, sacrifice and commitment to our family. Time spent with Dede will never be lost and will remain in my memory forever.

My sister Doreen was some three years older than me and Dede was three years older than her. She was a very quiet and placid person and had a tendency to do less housework as she used to attend school during the day. Dede and I used to spend a lot of time together. Even during the evenings and at weekends, when Doreen and I used to play with other children Dede used to be occupied with housework. I can never recall her disobeying any instructions from our parents.

Children as young as nine or ten performing domestic duties at home, was a common occurrence on the plantation. They would also, often be taken to work with their parents on the sugar plantation to help them complete their allocated work in the cane field. Sometimes Dede was up in the morning at five o'clock and she was expected to help with household chores before setting out to work in the fields with our mother. Doreen would then stay away from school if it were not school holidays to look after me, and my younger sisters. Even though Dede was illiterate she insisted that Doreen and I did our homework before we went to play or to bed each evening. I recall Dede sitting with us next to a bottle lamp filled with kerosene oil and a wick made of old clothing, which provided the light to enable us to read and write. There was no electricity or gas available for poor people in the village. We even had restricted use of kerosene oil due lack of money for basic goods. I used to play pictures with Dede on occasions when she allowed me to have a break from my school work. We used to open pages at random and guess whether that page contained a picture or not. Parents are the first educators of children and in my case my Dede also fulfilled this role.

Dede started to work on the plantation full-time when she was about fourteen years old. Less than three years later she was married and went to live with her husband some two miles away. Dede's wedding was a traditional Hindu occasion, organised over three days and attended by several hundred villagers. For my mother and us children this was both a happy and sad occasion. We all went into a state of depression after the wedding as we missed Dede very much. I used to walk to where she was living with her husband's family almost every day to see her, and to discreetly observe how she was coping in her new environment.

Her husband and his family were fishmongers and they had their own small fishing boat and a quantity of nets. They fished a mile or so from the Atlantic shore. Very soon Dede was involved in selling fish and shrimps from a handcart which she pushed along the hot and dusty main road. Walking barefoot in the hot sun for hours was common sight for working class women. Dede's life of work from early morning to late at night, seven days a week continued from a child to parent to grandparent, and until her death, at age 54. It got worse when she had her first child, Harry. By then Dede's life was not only characterised by hard work, but also by serious domestic violence. Her husband frequently got drunk and abused her; she suffered physical and mental abuse on a regular basis. Dede's marriage was arranged for her and she accepted her situation despite the many difficulties. Almost everyone who purchased fish or shrimps from Dede did so with credit. She had to make a mental note of the dozens of purchasers, as she was unable to record the purchase in writing. Dede would then collect the money owed to her on Sundays, the day after workers were paid each week. Like our mother she was often short of money because people refused to pay her or, denied ever purchasing sea food from her.

I recall several occasions when my poor Dede arrived at our house crying and covered in bruises. Her husband was most violent when he was drunk, and he insisted on having more money to buy more bottles of rum for himself and his friends. The situation was particularly bad when my sister had no money to give him. He was known to use a strap, a branch from a tree, or his fists to assault her. I was always in tears when I saw my loving sister in such a state. I frequently promised myself, that I would protect her and sort her husband out when I was older. Dede's miserable life, apart from the domestic violence, continued many years after the death of her husband, even though some of her children were married and working and she was better off economically. She was determined to support all her children and encouraged those who were academically inclined to take up professional studies and careers. Dede encountered many disasters in her life and did her best to be dignified and forgiving.

When I left for England in June 1961 I was conscious of the fact that the little protection I was able to provide for my sister against domestic violence would no longer be available. Her husband, who was a tiny person smaller in size than I was, knew that I would challenge him physically if he abused my sister in my presence. There were no other male relatives apart from my sick and elderly father to support my sister and my mother. After arriving in England I kept in regular contact with my parents; sisters Dede and Doreen who were both married to fishermen, and my four younger sisters. They both had to cope with drunken and violent husbands on a regular basis. Dede would often ask her husband to write to me during periods of hardship for financial assistance. I have never denied her any of such requests, even if I had to borrow money to assist her.

Despite Dede's harsh and painful life she was determined that her children went to school to escape the cycle of poverty and helplessness as adults. She understood that a successful career was dependent on high educational standards. Her eldest son Harry, who stood up to his father and defended his mother, sisters and brothers against his aggression was sadly drowned at sea at the age of sixteen or seventeen years, a few years after I left Guyana. Harry was a tall, strong, young man. As a teenager he was training to be a goldsmith. He was handsome and caring towards all of his family and his aunts who loved him very much. Apparently he decided to go fishing with two younger friends to earn money, so his sisters and brothers would have new clothes and books to return to school after the summer holidays. His father had decided not to go fishing that night. This tragedy was the first major problem for all of our family. It shook me badly when I heard of Harry's death. There were several versions of how his death at sea came about. Each of the two young men who went with him to the sea that night and survived the event gave different explanations. It was claimed by the two young boys who accompanied Harry to the sea that night that whilst out at sea, their small fishing boat was struck by a large vessel. Harry was probably struck by something from the offending vessel and died soon after.

Harry was very close to his mother and did all he could, including taking risks by going to sea to support his family. He also protected his mother against his father's excessive and unwarranted bad behaviour which happened less frequently as the children were becoming teenagers. Despite weeks of searching the many miles of coastal areas along the West Coast and the small Islands off the mainland, neither his body nor any item of his clothing were ever found. This was extremely unusual, as it was usual to retrieve the body of anyone who had been drowned at sea within a short period, and certainly no more than a few days. Dede found it difficult to cope with the loss of her loving teenage son and kept his personal belongings neatly stored in a wardrobe I had bought her for many years after his death. She lived in hope that he may turn up one day, just as if he had been rescued alive at sea and had been taken away from his home.

The following three years were no better for Dede as our mother, father and grandfather passed away. However, Dede's second son Geewan had reached teenage years during the early 1970s and he together with his sisters was able to help his mother. I believe the violence against his mother by his father occurred on a less frequent basis because of the intervention by him and his sisters.

The following years witnessed even more tragedies for my dear sister and her family. She lost her third son Mohan who committed suicide by drinking poison after being rejected by the parents of a young lady a few houses away, who he fell in love with. Dede's second eldest daughter Golin who was a qualified teacher also committed suicide. Golin had two young children and everything to live for. Her mother struggled to support her through teacher training college and she was set on a successful teaching career. Apparently, she had set herself alight using kerosene and a match, after a heated argument with her husband. It was alleged that he was having a relationship with another woman. From what I can gather from a number of sources, Golin was suffering from post-natal depression that went untreated for quite some time before the incident. Golin needed support because of her medical condition, but this support was never available to her and her relationship with her husband deteriorated. Golin left two lovely children who have been brought up by her brother Geewan and her sisters. Both children, especially her daughter have achieved academic success in Guyana, Australia and elsewhere.

Dede did her best to cope with the tragedies in her life. She continued to work exceptionally hard until her death from a massive burst stomach ulcer. At the time of her death she was living on her own, with her youngest son Sunil, and an elderly and sick aunt we knew as Powa. During Dede's last few years she was always surrounded by her children and grandchildren when she was not working. Although they assisted her and pleaded with her to work less and take care of herself she ignored their pleas and continued to work very hard and to pay little attention to her personal health and safety. I last saw my dear sister alive in 1991, when I visited Guyana with my wife and children, Mike and Jane. We spent three weeks with my sister three years earlier and we had a great time in her company. My wife and children still miss my Dede very much. During my visits to Guyana I always stayed at Dede's house as I saw her as the head of our family after the death of our parents.

Whenever I visited Dede we would always spend evenings singing old Indian songs, and telling stories about the days when we were children. Dede was a good singer and we would often cuddle each other whilst singing an old song and the rest of the family would be clapping hands or tapping the tables to provide the music that made the occasions more pleasurable.

Leaving Guyana and returning to England was always a seriously emotional occasion. I did my best to support two eldest sisters and their families. My younger sisters were supporting each other and were either working or in full-time education. I supported them also as far as I could. Even so they all had a difficult time due to lack of sufficient income. My sister Julie was quite an independent and strong willed person who assisted Dede and her family even though she had very little herself during the few years after the death of our parents. Julie even physically challenged the husbands of my eldest sister when they abused their wives.

For me, the death of my sister Dede was a major turning point in my life. I felt guilty that I should have done more for my dear sister – even though I did my best to support her in a variety of ways for many years. She would have been able to live a comfortable life, but instead devoted her attention and scarce resources towards supporting her children and grandchildren. During the last few years of her life four of her children were working and doing relatively well and there was no need for her to struggle so much. I opened a joint bank account on my visit to Guyana in 1989 between Dede and me to enable her to access money when times were difficult, but she never used the account. She was a proud person who developed a sense of independence when she became a widow. She left a reasonable sum of money hidden in her bedding that was discovered after her death. Dede lived and died for her family. She would often say to me, "Bud if this is what my life is going to be then I will do my best to live it. I will not give people the chance to say to me look how you left your children and home and ran off like your mother". Her investment was focussed on the success of her children and their families. I only wished her children who were working had been more committed and persuasive in ensuring that she paid more attention to her health.

Dede's' death was a personal tragedy for me. I received a telephone call from Guyana informing me of her death. Within hours I started the long and sad journey to Guyana. I asked her children to delay the funeral until my arrival. Within a few hours of my arrival we visited the undertaker's premises where her body was kept in cold storage. I was accompanied by three of my sisters, my nephew Geewan and a couple of other relatives. As soon as we arrived, the caretaker of the building, wanted some money to buy his breakfast, which included half a bottle of Demerara rum. He pestered me until I gave him some money. This man later drove my sister in her coffin with my nephew and I, from Georgetown, the capital of Guyana, across the bridge which spans the Demerara River, then along the West Bank of the river, and finally down the West Coast of Demerara. We arrived at my sisters' home in Leonora an hour later. I felt sick throughout the journey and my mind was in total turmoil and reflection.

The incident which tormented me the most was when the caretaker opened the part of the storage in the mortuary where the bodies were kept. He showed us my sister whose appearance was rather strange. There were several bodies, males and females, stored naked on top of each other in these large freezer boxes. It appeared that my sister had been, prior to our visit, placed in a pile with another body placed on top of her. They then removed the body and placed it in another box so my sister was on top of the pile when we saw her. Her face was somewhat distorted with the pressure of the other body on top of her when she was placed in the freezer. Her nose was flattened and she looked so peaceful but different. Equally distressing was to see my loving sister lying there completely naked. I cannot recall ever seeing my sister naked previously and I deeply regretted visiting the mortuary. I held onto my sister Datsie and my nephew Geewan, who were equally distressed, to stop myself from falling over.

My sisters and the relatives present did a brave and tremendous job. They gave Dede a bath, washed her and dressed her all in white. My sisters took the headscarf, dress and all the garments to the mortuary. Dede's' hair was neatly combed and her white headscarf neatly surrounded her head. I kissed my sisters forehead and stroked her hands before the lid of the coffin was placed over her.

We arrived home with the body and we were greeted by a large crowd, many of them crying and screaming. The body was kept overnight in her house in a room upstairs. Family, neighbours and friends took turns to look at the body and to pay their last respects. My other sisters, family and friends along with Dede's children stayed downstairs during the cold and windy night resting for brief periods on sheets and using other sheets to cover ourselves. Dede was buried the next day after a ceremony by the local Hindu Priest.

Dede was well respected in our village and many people visited her home to see her for the last time. The coffin was kept open for a period and I felt compelled to speak, after being invited by the Priest to say a few words. After speaking I kissed my sister on the forehead for the last time before the coffin was sealed for the final journey. We went to the burial ground to lay Dede's body to rest. I watched the local builder, Brother Harold sealing the concrete structure after placing the coffin in its final resting place. I turned away knowing that I would never see, touch or sing with her again. It was a sad and difficult time, for me and all our family. She was a peaceful, loving, respectful and hard working woman and will always be so in our hearts. I took some photographs of Dede as she lay in her coffin before the lid was sealed. I cannot bear to look at them since returning to England from the funeral. I still have the photographs, showing my dear sister resting so peacefully.

I returned to England totally shattered and depressed. I think of my sister always with a mixture of love, regret and guilt. My love for Dede was as great as my love for my mother. I felt guilty for not insisting more on her taking care of her health and regretted at not doing more for her when she most needed help. On several occasions I pleaded with Dede to seek medical help, but she was a fatalist who believed in, "what will happen, will happen anyway". I even encouraged her to visit me in England so I could secure medical help for her, but Dede was never one to travel outside of her functional and recognised environment.

A few days after Dede's funeral, I was told that her youngest child, Sunil whom she spoilt somewhat terribly, as he left school well before he was 10 years old and followed his mother during her work as a mobile fishmonger, was also involved in some bad company. I was told that he would frequently accept shots of rum from older boys and men, who took pleasure in watching him behaving badly when he was drunk. I was also told that he was interested in a young woman in a similar position to him, whose parents were poor and she had very little education. I was well aware that Sunil and Dede were living together at the family home, as all his sisters and his only remaining brother, Geewan were married and living away with their families. I asked my sister's children whether they would help me to get Sunil to England, but none of them seemed to support such an idea, which I had suggested several times previously. So we decided to ask Sunil if he wanted to marry this young lady who was pretty and slightly younger than him. He told me that he would like to get married as he was worried about living alone in the house. Sunil had a reputation as a difficult person, especially when he was drunk and none of his family wanted to have him living with them. I saw the parents of the bride to be and we all agreed that a wedding would be good for Sunil and the young lady. Within two weeks, before I returned to England, the wedding took place and the couple seemed very happy together. They had a lovely baby girl who has grown up to be very intelligent and successful in life. Much of this success is due to Geewan and his family as well as the support of Dede's other children.

Ten years later Sunil who was by then estranged from his wife, died in a car accident, whilst he was a pedestrian on the main road late one night. I believe the car never stopped after the accident. Sunil left his wife and a daughter behind. His funeral was well attended by local people and top politicians, as Geewan was by then a senior Minister in the Guyana government. I believe the President of Guyana, Bharat Jagdeo, whom I met when he was the Finance Minister, also attended the funeral.

Dede lost three of her children before her death and a fourth died after she had passed away. Four of Dede's children are still enjoying life and are very successful people. Geewan who is still a senior Minister in the government, Anjanie, her eldest daughter is living most of the time in New York, America, but returns to Guyana where she owns two large properties. Romanie, her next daughter is a very successful, professional woman with a leading role in government and the civil service in Guyana; she graduated in Guyana and America. Romanie has a very supportive husband, Madray and two mature children who are graduates. Dede's youngest daughter, Sally is also a very successful businesswoman with shops in the city and a massive modern house in Leonora. All of Dede's surviving children are extremely successful. None of them will ever have to worry about economic problems. All of Dede's children and grandchildren are doing very well and will never experience the difficult life their parents, grandparents and great grandparents had to endure.

The death of my sister Dede changed my life. I became a diabetic, due to worries, drinking too much beer, being overweight and suffering lots of stress soon after her death. It was indeed a major shock for me and my family. I will be indebted to Dede all my life for her love and sacrifices on my behalf.

My sister Doreen

My sister Doreen is the second child of my biological father and my birth mother. She is three years older than me. Unlike my eldest sister Dede, Doreen was educated at our local school in Anna Catherina. Although Doreen and I spent a lot of time together and for part of the time attended the same school, I was always a great deal closer to my sister Dede. When I left Guyana both Dede and Doreen were married and had children. Both sisters had married fishermen who were notorious for their lifestyles especially for consuming large amounts of alcohol, almost on a daily basis, as long as funds were available to purchase this awful drink. Alcohol consumption in Guyana has always been a common practice amongst men from around the age of eighteen until they die. Alcohol consumption which constitutes part of the Guyanese working class culture and lifestyles has caused untold misery to those who are engaged in this destructive habit. Families have suffered enormously because of alcohol addiction affecting a substantial number of men from poor backgrounds.

Although men consume the alcohol and in many cases are victims themselves due to lack of opportunities, poverty, helplessness and cheap booze, the women and children are also victims. The women, including my sisters Dede and Doreen were in many ways the bread winners in the family who kept the family together through their personal efforts. Doreen had been engaged for most of her working life as a fishmonger and brought up her children against a system of domestic violence, poverty and distress. I saw my sister, as she was in her teenage years, as a beautiful, charming, educated and compassionate person. Some of these qualities remain with her to this day. Doreen has seven children: two boys and five girls. Her eldest daughter Sandra lives in Leonora quite near her mother with one of her two daughters, Marisa who is a graduate of the University of Guyana. Her eldest daughter, Rosanna is living in America with her husband and child. Sandra's husband Gope passed away a couple of years ago. He was a local person who was very hard working and helpful to my sister Doreen and her family. Sandra spent a few years in Canada as an economic migrant with her brother Frankie and his family who settled over there some years ago.

My sister Doreen is a frequent visitor to New York in America where three of her daughters are living. During her stay she often secures part time work and uses the money to support herself and her permanent home in Guyana, where her daughter Annie lives. There are hundreds of thousands of Guyanese living in America, especially in parts of New York, such as Queens, Long Island and the Bronx. Queens is dominated by people from Guyanese and Caribbean backgrounds. Many Guyanese living abroad have the responsibility for caring for the rest of their families living in Guyana, whilst at the same time providing the

Guyanese government with useful foreign exchange currency. Doreen had a shop in Guyana selling a wide range of goods.

Doreen's eldest son Moses is married to Babita who is Gope's sister and they have five children, their eldest daughter is also a graduate from the University of Guyana. Moses is a highly skilled and established Science teacher who has worked in America and in various countries within the Caribbean, where his skills were much valued. He now combines teaching with the running of a grocery and soft drink distribution business in Guyana. I am delighted and proud that I contributed to his early educational achievements, especially when one is reminded that he spent many years during his childhood helping his mother to make a reasonable living for herself and her family. Moses has always been a hard working person from childhood when he used to walk the hot and dusty roads barefoot whilst engaging in the sale of fish and shrimps in and around the villages of Leonora with his mother. Frankie, Doreen's second son, runs a small cleaning business in Canada in which he is assisted by his very supportive and loving wife Sherry and their children. Frankie has always been a hard working person, helping his parents as fishmongers. Unlike Moses Frankie decided to become a trader, purchasing small items from countries including Venezuela, Brazil, Trinidad and Barbados and selling them in Guyana at a small profit. I always admired Frankie's courage and determination and assisted him when I could. I am pleased with Frankie's determination to work hard, to keep in touch with his family and to regularly communicate with me especially during periods when I have suffered from poor health.

I look forward to my sisters and their children visiting me in England. Only my sister Datsie (with her daughter Nancy) have visited me in England and that was many years ago. Doreen's second eldest daughter, Annie, is a lively and determined character. She is married to George and they are currently living at the same address as her Mum. Annie is very helpful to her mother and has always been by her side when she needed her. In 2005 she visited me and my family and spent six months with us, before returning to Guyana to help her mother with their small shop. Doreen's other three daughters are currently living in New York where they are working and studying for further qualifications. They are all very ambitious women and they are very supportive of their mother and the rest of their family. I believe they are also married and are doing well for themselves. Doreen is a great grandmother and is the oldest person in all our family alive.

My sister Doreen, unlike Dede, has never been afraid of air transport or of travelling abroad. She has made several trips to America to visit her children and her other three sisters living there. On one occasion during her stay in America she travelled on her own by bus from New York to Canada to visit her son Frankie. That was a commendable situation for someone who is over seventy years old and not in very good health. During her last visit to America in 2008 I had arranged for her to visit me in England with my sisters Datsie and Petsie, but sadly Datsie's husband, Frank, died a few days before the visit, which had to be cancelled. I stayed with my sister Doreen during my last visit to in 2007, and we spent a few occasions reminiscing about our past, including our childhood experiences and our memories of relatives who have passed away.

Doreen's husband passed away several years ago, after they had separated, and I am pleased to know that after many years of extreme suffering my sister Doreen is able to spend her remaining years in relative comfort and security and with the support of all her children, sisters, brother and grandchildren. She telephones me on a regular basis from America. I hope I can see her once more before either of us passes away. I am reluctant to travel to America or Guyana due to problems with my health. The quadruple heart bypass and kidney operations, coupled with my diabetes, have seriously restricted my ability and desire to travel long distances.

My sister Julie

My sister Julie is three years younger than me. Of all my sisters Julie is the one with whom I have had the least contact, either in writing or in person. When I left Guyana she was fourteen years old and to a large extent she had the responsibility for taking care of our three younger sisters, all of whom were of school age. Julie and my three younger sisters were living at our parent's home with my stepfather and mother. My two older sisters were of course married and living with their own families a short distance away. Both my mother and stepfather had suffered from periods of ill health in the past due to excessive work, poor diet and lack of medical care. Julie's role in bringing up my three youngest sisters was commendable.

It has always been common consensus within all my family, that Julie played a crucial role in caring for, and educating our three youngest sisters, Datsie, Joyce, and Petsie. Of course, I did my best to assist Julie, my three youngest sisters and my parents on a regular basis, as I fully understood their desperate economic situation. Both my parents were ill and were unable to work normally even though they were both relatively young being under sixty years old. My mother was forty eight years old when I left Guyana and my father was a few years older. Both of them appeared much older than their actual age. Guyana was a colony at the time and had no welfare provision to assist either, the sick, unemployed, poor, disadvantaged or those in financial difficulties. So six weeks after arriving in England, finding work and somewhere to live was my first priority. My second most important priority was to regularly send whatever money I could afford to my parents and young sisters in Guyana. I also wrote each week to my family in Guyana to let them know how I was getting on and to assured them of my commitment to support them in any way possible.

Unfortunately, after living in England for a couple of years I was getting some negative feedback from family and neighbours regarding the lack of cohesion within my family. Apparently, the problems started soon after I left Guyana. My two eldest sisters Dede and Doreen were having enormous problems including domestic violence and lack of support from their husbands, whilst my mother and father were having disagreements which resulted in my mother living separately on the ground floor of the family home and continuing to walk the hot and dusty road barefoot selling fish for her living. Julie and Ma were not getting on well for a variety of reasons. My mother was obviously ill and was finding life increasingly difficult. She had become isolated once again. The fact that my mother was working despite her illness, living on her own albeit in the family home, worried me a great deal. On many occasions I wanted to return home to take care of my parents and young sisters, but I had to decide whether it was more beneficial for them for me to go home or for me to remain in England, and to work and support them financially as far as I could, even though I was unable to provide physical help for them. Returning to Guyana before I was married would have resulted in numerous problems, as I had no qualifications and very little savings. I felt I had little choice but to remain in England, pursue my education and support all my family in Guyana the best I could.

By August 1962, just over a year after my arrival in London, I had met and fallen in love with Doreen who shared my concerns for my family. After we were married in August 1963 we both committed ourselves to assisting my family financially as and when we could afford to do so. Doreen regularly ensured that we sent money to Guyana even though we were struggling ourselves. In February 1964 our first child Michael was born and Doreen decided to work as a labourer in a local factory once she had secured a good child-minder a few months after our son was born. We continued to support my family in Guyana by making real and personal sacrifices in our own lives. For example, I chose to walk four miles to work and back, in order to save small sums on transport, which we spent on food or other necessities. Nevertheless we still managed to send small sums of money via postal orders to Guyana to assist my family.

I subsequently discovered that for whatever reason my parents did not receive some of this money which I regularly sent. I kept the receipts for years. So it would appear that my parents and sisters had very little respite from the problems associated with poverty and helplessness. I really do not know what happened to some of the money I sent to support my family in Guyana. The relationship between my sister Julie and my parents worsened and this led to frequent disagreements and quarrels. Julie continued to work hard and to support our youngest three sisters who were doing well in their education. Julie also took responsibility for occasionally defending our oldest sisters from their inconsiderate and violent husbands.

Between 1964 and 1966 Guyana was in a state of dreadful political turmoil, and violence regularly erupted between the two main ethnic groups, consisting of the majority East Indians and the largest minority group from African descent. On 26th May 1966 Guyana achieved political independence from British colonial rule, but the economy remained stagnant and in disarray due to years of political and economic misadministration and neglect. Before leaving Guyana the British helped to install an African dominated government which became increasing sectarian and undemocratic and remained in power for over twenty five consecutive years. Life for Julie and my family did not improve but instead deteriorated due to the death of my father, mother and grandfather in 1967.

Despite the struggle Julie and my younger sisters had to endure during the decade after my departure from Guyana, they still managed to achieve good academic qualifications and two of them became teachers. On my first visit to Guyana in 1974, Julie and my three youngest sisters were living in the family home where I decided to stay during my visit. Datsie was married and her husband was working in America and taking care of some of her needs, whilst Joyce was working as a teacher in Leonora, and Petsie was attending Bishops High School for Girls in Georgetown. Julie had a young daughter, Carol whose father was living in England and had never supported Julie or his daughter financially as far as I was aware. Julie later married a young man called Randolph and she continued to work as a seamstress, a job which she is still doing to this day.

After about a week or so of my first visit to Guyana I had serious disagreements with Julie who I believe felt threatened by my presence because I asked questions about the way she had conducted herself during my absence and in particular the dysfunctional relationship she had experienced with our parents. I also made enquiries about the jewellery my mother had saved to pass on to my wife as it was traditional to do so because I was her only son. Although my parents had made a will which I understand was firstly made out to leave the family home to me, it was later changed to include all the children. Julie decided to pay off my eldest sister her share and Doreen refused to accept any payment. I also refused to accept any payment and insisted on building a house on the land to accommodate all our family including those who were living abroad and would require temporary accommodation during short visits.

Julie refused to give up or share the family home, even when she decided to purchase a home and to live in Barbados and develop her business. The family home, which Julie has greatly improved over the years, has been a source of contention since the death of my parents. Julie spends most of her time in Barbados with her daughter Carol and grandson Jason. I always send all my sisters and close relatives Christmas cards and a detailed letter informing them of key developments within my immediate family during the previous twelve months. Unfortunately, I have never had the pleasure of receiving a Christmas or birthday card from Julie. Her daughter Carol visited my home when she was a student in London. She returned a few years later for a brief visit with her son, who is now a teenager and they spend most of their time in Barbados. I love all my sisters and would welcome a harmonious relationship between all of us.

My Sister Datsie

My sister Datsie has been living in America with her four children and grandchildren for many years. She joined her husband in America after living alone with her children in Guyana. Her husband made frequent visits to Guyana and they had three children during the period when she waited to move to America. Her fourth child, Nancy who graduated from university a few years ago and has a successful career was born in America. Sadly, after many years of being relatively happily married, my sister separated from her husband Frankie, but remained good friends. Datsie who is over sixty years old cared for her husband during his illness prior to his death. Datsie bought a property in Queens, New York and worked very hard as a single parent to support her family. She has improved her skills, knowledge and experience a great deal and has achieved many qualifications in her professional work.

Datsie is employed as a senior care worker. Since arriving in America over three decades ago Datsie has acted as host to numerous members of our family including my younger sisters, and children from our sisters as well as other members of our family. Many of them have settled in America and have their own families and professional interests. There is a relatively large Guyanese community including several members of our family who owe a lot to Datsie for the love and support she has given them over the years. Datsie is a really generous, caring and loving person. She lives with her daughter Michelle and her dog. Datsie is still working and she spends as much time she can spare with her children and grandchildren who are all close to her. She tries very hard to keep in contact with all of family, whether they are in America, Guyana, England or Canada.

My sister Datsie has been one of the great pillars within our family structure. Her love, affection and kindness towards our close and extended family have been a major part of her character. Many family members and friends have lived in the basement of Datsie's home during their induction periods to America. Datsie always goes out of her way to build and support family cohesion, even though at times she does not achieve complete success or recognition for her efforts. Datsie's eldest daughter, Sharon, works as a teacher in New York where she lives with her daughter and her partner. Datsie's son Tony lives in Long Island, New York with his wife and their son. Tony's first marriage was sadly dissolved after several years. His two teenage children are living with their mother who has also remarried. During her career Datsie has been a teacher, a nurse and a care worker. She is in reasonably good health and frequently shares ideas and information over the telephone, on how we could and should, improve the quality of our lives and our health. Datsie and I are both diabetics with related conditions. I was privileged to receive my sister Datsie and her daughter Nancy at my home in England well over a decade ago. It gave me a great deal of pleasure to accompany her on visits to the popular sites in London and also in other parts of England, such as the birthplace and home of William Shakespeare. Unfortunately, many of the photographs we took during their visit were destroyed, due to the breakdown of the printing machine at Tesco.

I am deeply inspired and motivated by the frequent telephone conversations between my sister Datsie, my family and I. I have visited Datsie and my relatives including my two other younger sisters in America on three separate occasions. I have always been inspired and proud of their hard work and achievements. Datsie is very much loved and valued by all of us and we all wish her a long and happy life which she most certainly deserves, as she has had to endure many difficult situations in her life, since she was a young child.

My Sister Joyce

My sister Joyce is ten years younger than myself. She was brought up during her school years by my parents and then my sister Julie who took full responsibility for her total care after our parents died. Joyce was always a quiet and intelligent child. She became a dedicated student and committed herself to education and training. She excelled rapidly during her high school years and later graduated as a teacher. She taught at Leonora Secondary School, and during her teaching years she became interested in research and writing. Joyce married Renold whilst she was a teacher in Guyana. After completing her studies in Guyana, Joyce worked for the Government, including providing close support for a number of Ministers. We kept in regular contact with each other and I was delighted to learn of her strong political convictions closely related to those of our parents and my own. Joyce became very interested in Women's studies and accompanied a number of Ministers during their visits to various Caribbean Islands to discuss and debate issues relating to oppression and exploitation of women, including domestic violence and abuse.

Her interest in this area has grown immensely over the years, and she has produced many documents and detailed reports some of which have had considerable influence in Guyana, the Caribbean and in America. Before she left Guyana like all my sisters Joyce experienced a wide range of difficulties following the death of my parents and the economic situation in which my youngest sisters were left. I take a great deal of pride in the achievements of my younger sisters whose academic success was due to their hard work in difficult circumstances and Julie's guidance. Of course, my elder sisters Dede and Doreen provided help and support whenever possible. I also did my best to assist.

Joyce also worked in a number of senior government positions in America and developed various academic and research interests which led her to further her studies including completing her Doctorate Degree. She worked for many years at the University of Maryland whilst supporting her husband and children through their academic studies in Guyana. Her husband and children later joined her in America and they all continued to achieve academic qualifications and good career opportunities.

Her work during her years with the University of Maryland in America extended her interest even more in politics and human rights. She is the only one of my sisters with whom I can have a detailed and even controversial discussion on a wide range of issues. She has established herself as a prolific and well respected researcher and author over the last decades. Unfortunately, her health has deteriorated over the last few years and I hope that she pays more attention to her health in the future. I believe she has recovered from some of the health problems and she is able to spend time with her children and grandchildren. Both her children are happily married and she was a grandparent for the third time 2013 when her daughter Charmaine had a son. Her son Romain and his wife Amanda had their second child in 2009. Her daughter Charmaine also got married in 2009. None of us from England were able to attend Charmaine's wedding which took place in July, because I was operated on, for a quadruple heart bypass during the same week.

My brother-in-law, Renold is one of the most thoughtful, caring and loving persons I have known. He has been a pillar of strength and support not only for my sister Joyce and their children, but also for other members of my family in Guyana and America. Renold was born in Guyana in a small village named St Laurence. My sister Joyce worked at a school close to his home, and I believe they met each other whilst working in the area. Renold is also a qualified teacher and has taught children with special needs and learning difficulties in New York and in Maryland. Renold's mother, sister and other relatives have visited him and his family in America and they are in regular contact with each other.

My Sister Petsie

Petsie also known as Patsie, or Patsy by some of us, is my youngest sister who was around three years old when I left Guyana. I remember lifting her up and giving her lots of kisses and hugs before I started that long journey from our home in Leonora to England. As the youngest child much love and attention was given to her by all the family. After the death of my parents, Petsie's care was totally dependent on my sister Julie, with some support from her father, our sister Joyce and Datsie. With Julie's hard work and support Petsie excelled at school and later won a scholarship to Bishop High School for Girls. After completing her studies she married Adam and they have three children, who are now all adults, and are living and working in America. Petsie's children have children of their own and I know that my sister Petsie, like all grandparents, adores her grandchildren. Petsie left Guyana to improve her education and career prospects in America.

Petsie has been in America for nearly two decades and has worked extremely hard to support herself and her children, who later joined her in America. Sadly Petsie and Adam separated before she left for America. Adam is still living in Guyana and I believe that there is some communication between him and his family in America. My sister Petsie has been working as a carer for many years, and has secured several professional qualifications associated with her work. She graduated after studying for Doctorate Degree, also in Social Care Work in 2010. I cannot help but to admire the stamina and ambition of my youngest sisters who have achieved so much over the years. During my visit to America in 2006, it gave me a great deal of pleasure to meet my three youngest sisters, Datsie, Joyce and Petsie and to enjoy their company. As it happened, my sister Doreen was also in America at the time of my visit, so it was quite a family get together before I returned to England. I was so impressed with Petsie's knowledge of America and her ability to drive with confidence all over New York. I always feel sad when I leave them to return home, because it reminds me of when I left Guyana and the fact that none of us knew if and when we would meet again. I am very proud of my sister Petsie and I admire her determination and strength very much.

My sister Raj

I had another sister called Raj who had the same father as me but a different mother. I only had occasional contact with her before I left Guyana, but was much better in later years. Raj played a very small part in my life. As there was a certain measure of antagonism between her mother and my mother, it was inevitable that the relationship between my eldest sister Raj and the rest of us would be different from that of my other sisters from my biological father, and later my step-father and my mother. As a consequence, Raj and I had very little face-to-face contact with each other, but on the occasions we met I felt a strong bond between us.

Like all my sisters Raj was a very hard working woman. She had five children, all of whom became successful people within the academic, profession or business spheres. Her youngest son Subass is a successful lawyer and her youngest daughter has a thriving catering and restaurant business. Other children have decided to seek their fortune in America and in England, and as far as I am aware have successful businesses too. Like a number of my other sisters Raj outlived her husband. She took on full responsibility for ensuring the cohesion of her whole family, and its success.

I met two of her sons in London on a number of occasions. One son returned to Guyana and then eventually settled in America. The other son remained in London and has been a successful business man. Sadly, I have lost touched with him and his family.

After arriving in England I did my best to keep in contact with Raj and her family, but with little success. However, on each occasion I returned Guyana I ensured that I visited her and I was satisfied that she was keeping fit and well. On my visit to Guyana in February 2007, I went to visit her as I normally would and I was shocked when I was informed that she had passed away two years earlier. Raj lived about one mile from where members of my extended family lived, yet no one bothered to inform me of her death. I am not certain how long she had lived, but I believed that she was either in her late seventies, or early eighties. I informed two of her children that I would like to visit her graveside to pay my last respects before I returned to England, but for one reason or another visit did not take place. I intend to do so on my next visit to Guyana as I want to rid myself of the guilt I feel for not having the opportunity to be present at her funeral.

A True sister listens to her brother with her heart

I have been fortunate to have so many kind and loving sisters even though we have had a number of interruptions to our relationships. On occasions I have had some disagreements with my younger sisters but I always felt our relationship has been underpinned by genuine love and respect. I have made my will and have decided to leave a sum of money for all my sisters. I am delighted that all my other sisters are getting on well together. Sometimes brothers and sisters are as close as hands and feet, but sometimes they can also be miles apart. For me life is far too short and precious to bear malice or hatred. Peace and understanding are preferable to disagreements especially when such contentious situations linger on for years.

Helping one another is part of the religion of sisterhood and brotherhood. Sisterhood is a powerful force and I am delighted that my sisters frequently look out for each other. There is no better friend and supporter than a sister and I have been privileged, as an only brother, to benefit so much from all my sisters. My sisters contribute so many memories of my childhood that will always be part of me and my life.

Chapter 4:

The journey from
Guyana to London

No turning back

The watchman moved slowly and lazily from the stool in his small cabin situated just outside the gate of the sugar factory on Plantation Leonora and walked towards the huge brass bell which he rang every hour every day of the week. People from up to two miles away and even greater distances had grown accustomed to using this signal to organise their daily lives. It had been known that watchmen had fallen asleep and had, on albeit rare occasions, given an occasional extra ring or failed to register the required number. In any event for the workers living within close proximity of the sugar factory it was the authoritative sound which started the daily ritual of toil, on Plantation Leonora.

One morning in early June 1961 the bell rang four times and my best friend Joseph turned to me and said "Look brother, it is four in the morning, and I must go home and get a couple of hours of sleep before we leave for the airport". I replied "Yes man you must go but remember to be back here at seven sharp so we can be at the railway station for the nine something train." Joe bid goodnight to the dozen or so people who were still awake and were either quietly engaged in conversation or silently preparing food for the journey ahead. Everyone replied in a rhythmic tone "Goodnight Joe see you later".

Joe had been my best friend ever since we had cycled around the West Coast through housing schemes and remote isolated villages trying to attract the attention of girls. Joe's push bike – a Raleigh model made in England and nicknamed Sir

Walter – had completed many thousands of miles with Joe peddling and me sitting on the cross bar. We were not best friends at school because Joe was around two years older than me and we were in separate classes. Joe was always accompanied by his torchlight when he was away from home without his bicycle at night.

As soon as he said goodnight a number of people who lived nearby also said goodnight since it would be expected of Joe to escort them to their homes with his torch to ensure that they did not walk into any ditches or on any frogs or snakes along the grass covered walkways. Equally important was that they would have less difficulty crossing the small streams which had narrow planks across. They had come to share the sadness and the joy of a friend, a relative or a neighbour, as it was traditional in the village to share some time with someone who was about to depart on long and lonely journey. They had bid their farewells and had wished me a happy and safe journey and a good life in England – the mother country. Some people had arrived early in the evening and had left before midnight. It was a dark, chilly and windy night even though it was June.

Members of my family and friends who stayed the night slept on carefully-washed brown colour rice sacks covered with clean cotton sheets and used similar sheets to cover their bodies. Women slept upstairs and men made the best of what was available downstairs which was open apart from shelter provided by the floor of the two bedroomed house built on brick pillars 7 feet high. In the hallway of the tiny house were some twenty people – mainly children, who were fast asleep. Adults were either asleep or continued quiet conversation. Intermittently, there were faint cries from my mother, who would repeatedly tell others of her pain at the thought of her only son leaving her. I could hear her cries from under the house "Oh my son you are leaving me......... my son, my son, I may never see you again............ oh my son may God bless you and keep you safe so you can come back to us".

The plantation bell was struck five times and Jack, the Creole red and black cockerel confirmed the time by crowing repeatedly to remind people if they had missed the bell. Day was breaking and it was time for them to get up. Dede, my oldest sister, calmed her child who was coughing. The child had a permanent cold and chest problem. My first nephew, whose name was Harry, age about seven or eight, like his younger brother, needed medical attention but like so many poor families it was a luxury only available to the people who could afford it. There was only one general hospital in the whole of Guyana situated in Georgetown and difficult to access by the poor people living many miles away.

Whilst stroking Harry's head and with the tears running down her cheeks Dede whispered to him "sleep, my son, sleep, your mamo will leave us today, you must be a good boy and look after your brother when we go with mamo to the airport". Dede's sobbing woke Julie up. Julie said to Dede "I must get up now and start the cooking. Who knows I may be cooking for him for the last time. What is going to happen tomorrow Dede when all of you will be back in your own homes, what is going to happen to us?" cried Julie. Dede said "don't worry us sisters will look after each other and our parents, after all we still have our mother and father".

The cooking had already started well before Jack the cockerel started his noise and the men sleeping downstairs not far from the chicken pen shouted out "put him in the pot". Julie washed her face and hands after taking a cup of water from the galvanised bucket and started to help in the kitchen. The fire was started with small pieces of wood upon which a small amount of kerosene was sprinkled before it was set alight. It was kept going with the aid of a long metal tube from which air was blown from the mouth. We called it a pockney. Gradually people began to wake up and select certain chores for themselves. I replenished the firewood, someone else refilled the water buckets and others made themselves useful in other ways. Julie and the other sisters took charge of the cooking. Mother swept the yard, and little children went to the canal to bathe themselves.

By this time it was bright daylight, with the sun shining and factory workers making their way to work. The field workers had already left for work between five and six o' clock. It was now the turn of those who were working or had to travel to places outside the plantation to make their way to wherever they were going. The small traders hurried along the red dusty road, others waited in small groups along the roadside for the bus to arrive; a few children who had secured scholarships or whose parents were fortunate to be able to send them to one of the half a dozen or so private schools in the city were making their way to the railway station.

There was much activity in my house that Wednesday morning in June. People had emerged from under their cotton sheets and were busy cooking, tidying up or getting ready – washing and dressing. Those who were going only as far as the railway station made less fuss of themselves than those chosen to go all the way to the airport with me. Someone said, "Why don't someone ask neighbour Violet to turn up the sound of her radio so we can follow the time?" as there was no one with a clock or a wrist watch around the house, and with all this commotion they may not hear the factory bell. Then, there was the thought of – what about if the watchman chose on this day, to ring less than the required number of times. I had an old watch which I had bought from a workmate. Although it never worked, I used it for special occasions. It was simply to impress the girls during my regular cycle trips with Joe on his pushbike through the villages. The radio sound was turned up and some people followed the time because they identified their favourite programme. It was Indian Hour, an hour of Asian songs interrupted by news. People went about their chores humming some of the tunes.

Joe had returned looking his best and had already started to take charge of some of the arrangements, especially the responsibility for carrying my grip (suitcase) all the way to the airport. He told me that he hadn't slept well because he kept thinking of the journey and the departure of his best friend. I said to him "Don't worry - it could be your turn next". Joe smiled at the thought and nodded his head in agreement, then went off again to tell everyone to hurry up. The gentle sunshine had become much warmer and some people were already sweating from the heat. Friends and neighbours who had not been present the previous night came to say their farewells. The younger ones smiled, shook hands and said '"take care, be good" or "Have a safe journey and write to us." The older ones invariably thought it appropriate to offer words of advice including; "Be good my son.... you must always keep in touch with your parents, remember you are their only son, remember how your mother suffered to raise all of you....you must come back and marry a nice Leonora girl...don't get involved with them white girls and forget your family,..... God bless you son and life spare we will see you in Leonora in a couple of years' time."

The children were happy because some of them were going to miss school that day whilst others were excited about the journey ahead. The adults who had jobs were conscious of the fact that they would be losing a day's work whilst at the same time having to spend money on travelling and so on. Money was always a problem. When people were working and money was coming in they were conscious of the need to pay off debts so as to ensure their credit worthiness in the future when they would owe the landlord; the shopkeeper; the firewood merchant and their relatives. For the three to four months each year when the sugar factory on the plantation came to a halt for repairs and to enable the white overseers and managers to return to Europe for their annual leave, not many people would find work. In fact very few people would be hired by the plantation bosses.

The majority would have to survive as they had done in previous years by borrowing; selling some possessions; pawning their jewels; accepting hand-outs from other relatives; finding temporary work outside the plantation; helping others with odd jobs in return for a meal, and on the whole trying to make do with less. Those who were fortunate to have a farm or a piece of land to grow rice on would take their friends to help them in return for some provisions. Some women and men would use the opportunity to fish, sell a few items – mainly fruits and vegetables if they had a kitchen garden – or to replace that old outside toilet. Only a handful of people on the plantation, and of course the white plantation overseers, had access to a flush toilet.

I had a shower using a bucket of water drawn from the canal. The water was cold and it sent a tingle through my body. I wondered whether there were trenches and canals in England where people had a swim or fetched water for drinking. What sort of place would this England be? Was it similar to Georgetown except there would be white people instead of black, and would I be able to understand them when they spoke? Would I be nervous when they talked to me, and what about when I wanted to talk with them, to ask them if they have any work for me? Would it happen the same way, as when I got my first job on the plantation, by approaching the white overseer who was sitting in his office on the ground floor with his window open, and after queuing up outside his window for some time and said *"manin bass, bass have you any work? I do anything, anything at all bass me am sixteen"*. The overseer did not speak. He simply scribbled a note, handed it to me and pointed me towards the next window.

I had never had a conversation with a white person. My only communication with them were when I was very occasionally given instructions by them at work, when I had asked them if they had any work or said good morning to them, when they invariably replied with a nod, or said nothing not even bothering to look at in my direction. On a number of occasions my best friend Joe and I had met white people who were friendlier. They used to worship at the Baptist Church opposite my house over the main road and across the bridge on the other side of the canal some three hundred yards away. Before we started to attend the Baptist church and Joe and I became friendly with the Reverend Sokhai and his family, we used to attend the Chinese Church some five hundred yards away near the bend in the road towards the village of Stewartville. Although this big, old wooden building was known as the Chinese Church the villagers never saw any Chinese people using it. Even Mr Albert Loo, Mrs Loo and their son Winston who were the only Chinese people in the village, never attended the church services. Some of the white overseers from plantation Leonora and other plantations would sometimes attend the Protestant church for the main Sunday morning worship. Mr Obediah, who occupied the large house behind the church, acted as caretaker and preacher for the black congregation when there were no white people in the church.

Whenever there were white congregations there was invariably a white preacher. Unlike the other young men in the village, Joe and I were Christians. Whenever white people attended places of worship they sat in the front rows. The white overseers never attended any local Temples or Mosques but from time to time there were white visitors from abroad who perhaps made an occasional visit. I often wondered why I became a Christian when my parents were Hindus. Maybe it was because my mother once told me that it was good for me to go to church because when my time came to seek employment on the sugar estate the white overseers may remember my face. On the other hand, it may have been the feeling of wanting to be different and to be exposed to a different type of worship! When I was about eight years old I was playing in our front garden and I saw a beautiful young lady at least twice my age walking by, she said "why don't you come to Sunday School after the main service, you will get a bun, a drink and a chance to meet other children? I did attend a couple of weeks later and sat next to this young lady who was the Sunday school teacher. I took a liking to her almost immediately and attended regular for a few months, then I left after she got married and left the area.

I returned to the church in Anna Catherina on a regular basis when I started work. Whatever the reason for becoming a Christian, I was happy because I had met and made friends and explored greater challenges and thoughts about people and ideas. Even though I saw myself as a Christian I participated enthusiastically in all of the Hindu ceremonies and rituals within our village. I had even told a number of people, that I intended to study the Christian religion in England and to return to Guyana as a priest. I also wondered why the white visitors to Leonora appeared to be more sociable than the white people on the plantation. Was it because the visitors were missionaries, with the aim to convert local people into the Christian faith, as opposed to the local overseers who were only interested in us as labourers, regardless whether we had souls or not?

I tipped the remaining water from the bucket over my head and then hurried off to get dressed. I had never worn a suit before and wondered whether people would recognise me as I walked towards the railway station. It was a light brown suit made by the local tailor Mr Bangalang who had given me a good price for the job. In any case as the local tailor he felt it his duty to charge only a small fee and the rest of the cost would be his gift to me. I got dressed and waited under the house as it was cooler than the upstairs and more convenient for visitors who had come to pay their respects and to see me off. I also had an opportunity to take a long good look at my surroundings for the last time.

The kiskadi sang

As I stood under the house chatting with my school friends and neighbours I noticed a kiskadi - a bird similar in size to a female blackbird. The kiskadi's back and head was covered with shining black feathers and the rest of the body in bright yellow and black. It was a common bird in Guyana and one which prompted mixed feelings amongst children, because they knew that kiskadis fed on ripe fruits. So whilst the sight of the kiskadi was welcoming it was also a sign that if you did not get in quick the kiskadis would deny you of your share of soft, fresh ripe fruits.

The bird inspected the star-apple tree which overhung onto the roof of the house, and having discovered that the fruits were not quite ripe decided to pay a visit to the jamoon tree with bunches of small black fruits hanging from the branches like grapes. On this occasion it was successful and it sang merrily after gulping each mouthful. I had hardly previously, given any special attention to the birds, trees, flowers, fruits and plants in terms of their beauty. I saw plants and fruit trees as food or nice things to look and the birds as creatures robbing humans of their meagre lot whether it be fruits or grain.

Whilst I was listening to the conversation around me, my mind was focussed on other things. Somewhere, where I knew things were different but was unsure what the actual differences were. My mind wandered backwards and forwards, to and from my childhood and the life I had been accustomed to so far. It was a life that had had a massive impact on shaping my thoughts, actions and behaviour so far. People regardless of their age, are either consciously or unconsciously grossly influenced in their values, fears, feelings, fantasies and behaviour by their childhood experiences. I wondered about the landscape of the new country I was going to live. Would there be trenches and canals in England so if things turned a bit bad I could catch some fish and sell them as I had done, on several occasions in Guyana when I used to bunk off school with my friends; do some farming or if things really turned out bad to chop down some trees and sell the branches for firewood. I had no idea about England, apart from what knowledge I gained from watching films made in Europe and America.

"No", I said, "I am likely to end up sweeping a factory as I have done in Guyana or I might be lucky and get a job in an office where I will be able to learn to read and write proper English; to teach myself mathematics and to learn how to be a good politician. Yes, that is what I want. I want to be a politician so I can come back to Guyana and join the fight for freedom from white rule." Cheddi Jagan, our most important politician, said that Guyana had problems because we were not free; we were governed by white people whose only interest in Guyana was to exploit us. Perhaps like Cheddi I could go to England, study politics, marry a white woman who was bound to have lots of money, like all the white people I have seen on the plantation and in films, and then return to Guyana. My mother would be proud of me since she was one of Cheddi's biggest supporters.

I also thought of the long cycle rides along the coastal areas; the friends in the village and the fun which we had had over the years; the times when we stole fruits and were chased by the owners; the long journeys to catch fish or crabs and the games which we played as boys growing up together in the same village. I looked over towards the house next to the Chinese church to catch a last glimpse of the roadside where I spent many days of my life with friends, playing cards, marbles or just chatting. I also thought about the Muslim girl, Katigan – the sister of my friend Khalid who lived in Brick Wall Street near Anna Catherina – and wondered whether I could send for her after I had saved some money in England. I was beginning to find all these thoughts interesting but also confusing. I then turned to other thoughts such as the reasons why I was going to England; the specific incident in my life which had made me decide to approach my mother and give her an ultimatum that I either go to England or she would not have a son: the overwhelming desire to leave the life of poverty, degradation, squalor, violence, injustice and helplessness which characterised the lives of all poor families in Guyana.

The food prepared earlier in the morning consisted of tea from the lime plant in the yard, coffee, roti, boiled rice, fried vegetables and curried fish. Some of the food was consumed for breakfast and some packed neatly in food containers which contained up to four separate bowls and were called carriers. The remaining food was left in the pots for those staying at home. All packed and ready to leave for the railway station Joe made a loud noise as he signalled to everyone that it was time to leave, by lifting the suitcase on to his shoulders. "Come on", he said, "There is no time for tears – save it for the airport, he will not be going anywhere if you all don't hurry up. "

People were always reluctant to argue with Joe as he was an educated and well respected person in the village not only for his immense strength, but for his strong principles, including his frequent comments that "Guyanese people complain too much: what they need to do is to get off their backsides and help themselves". It was a comment which Joe would often direct at the village men who were frequently drunk or too idle and lazy to care enough for their families. The village drunks, who were unable to find regular work but somehow managed to club together at least once or twice each week to purchase a bottle of cheap rum to drown their sorrows, or to help them to temporarily forget their problems, would sometimes sneer at Joe, a proud Christian. They would often say to Joe "If your God is so good why are we suffering so much"? "Why our children can't go to school because they have no decent clothes, why are there so many poor people, some of them begging for a living after they have worked all their lives"? "Why are the old people and children dying from lack of basic medical attention?"

Joe would reply "It is because of the wickedness of people..., they have sinned..., they refused to follow God..., God showed them what is right and what is wrong, but because of their greed and their desire for material things they have disobeyed God... and the sins of the father will fall upon the third and fourth generation who disobey God... this is what the Bible says". Sometimes the men would tease Joe as they enjoyed his debating skills and the fact that he took things seriously. They would say "hi, Joe man, it is not so, we are poor because we were too rich in our previous lives, we are illiterate because we were too intelligent in our previous lives, and we have no work now because we were much too busy in our previous lives at least this is what the Hindu Bible tells us, this is what re-incarnation is about. It is about people reappearing as opposites each time they die and return to a new life".

The start of a journey of thousands of miles

It was now eight o'clock and it was utter mayhem in and around the house. Everyone was encouraging everyone else to make haste. Mothers discovered that a button was missing from their son's best shirt; there were shoes to be borrowed and cleaned; people queued up to go to the toilet some thirty yards away from the house and documents had to be identified and placed securely in my inside jacket pocket with a safety pin. Joe and I concentrated on packing the small suitcase which was made of compressed paper. The contents were basic and consisted of: three shirts; three pairs of trousers including two pairs of denims; a towel; six pairs of socks; one dozen handkerchiefs; five neck ties; four pairs of underpants; one pair of plimsolls; five or six tie pins made from Guyana gold; two toothbrushes; a tube of toothpaste; half a dozen combs; a large jar of hair cream; two bottles of Demerara rum; a large bag of fried and dried fish and shrimps; some fruits; two jars of pepper sauce and a large parcel for the family of the man from the village who would meet me when I arrived in England. Most of the contents were gifts received from family friends and neighbours. I also had around two hundred Guyana dollars equivalent to less than £60.00. Most of this money was given to me as gifts.

Joe secured the case with a hefty bang from his clenched fist and said "that will stay closed until you reach England". He stared at the dent and the small tear on the case which emerged from under his fist and murmured "These bloody things are too damn weak". Joe lifted the case onto his shoulder and gave the command "come on all of you time to go". The party started off with Joe in the lead followed by me, my parents and then the rest of the family and friends.

Everyone looked smart in their new, borrowed, well starched and ironed Saturday best clothes. Women and children wore brightly coloured clothes and people along the road leading to the station knew that something important was happening. Even my mother was seen wearing a pair of soft shoes something which she had seldom been seen in before, even at weddings. They knew that the party was on their way to a long journey since women and children wore their best clothes mainly on Saturdays or when they attend special religious or social functions like a wedding, for example.

Market day in Leonora was a major attraction. It was pay day for workers employed by the sugar estate. Saturday was market day and people came from all along the coast to sell or to purchase goods from live chickens and crabs to fish, fruits, vegetables, clothing etc. People dressed in their best clothes to shop. The actual market started not too far from the office where people lined up for their pay on Saturdays, if they worked for the plantation. After receiving their wages it was customary for workers to slip a small sum to the foreman who invariably shared it with the overseer responsible for that area of work. This was to ensure preference when limited work was available. Most men would go straight home to give their wives their weekly allowances which fluctuated each week, depending on the amount of work, bonus or overtime. No one except managers received sick pay. It was therefore quite common for people to line up outside the factory with outstretched arms begging. A small number of men would go straight to the rum shops with their friends, and would not leave until they were taken home or staggered home, invariably with little or no money left, to torment and terrorise their wives and children who would be facing a terrible week ahead

My departure was on a weekday, so there were only a few traders along the route we took, which was along the road where the market was situated. The traders wished me well and offered some fruits for the journey. Most people knew that I was leaving as we had had a farewell party the previously weekend. Small crowds came out of their homes and stood in their front gardens or the road waving and wishing me luck on my journey. Others came to the end of the streets to look at the party leaving and some came up to me along the short route to the station and shook my hand or gave me a slap on the back with best wishes.

As we reached the point in the road where it bends towards Anna Catherina on the left with a smaller road branching off towards the railway station just a couple of hundred yards away, I turned to have a last look at my home and my village. This particular piece of road was bad with deep holes and small pools of mud and water every few yards. It was dangerous not only for the people but also for the horses and donkeys which were regularly making the journey to and from the railway station with sacks of rice, huge baskets of vegetables, fruits and other commodities.

The party arrived at the station and someone purchased several return tickets and one single. The Station Master, a good friend of mine, came out of his office to wish me a safe journey. The Station Master, Khamal, and I had been involved with others in the setting-up of an adult education group which met in a room provided by the estate for us through the Welfare Officer, during the evenings. Khamal and the older boys – who were either employees of the plantation, self-employed, working in the city or unemployed – would help me, the youngest, with reading, writing and arithmetic. At the station we met another party engaged on the same mission. A tall, strong young man about four years older than me was also leaving Leonora for England on precisely the same route. His name turned out to be Milton, and we exchanged a few words. We congratulated each other on how well we looked in our new suits, and expressed our pleasure that we were not travelling alone and that we would stick closely with each other throughout the journey. Both families were delighted that Milton and I were starting off together and our respective mothers promised to keep in contact with each other so they would be able to pass on any information as appropriate as and when they received news from their sons after they had arrived in England.

Although the airport was only around fourteen miles away from Leonora, it involved a train journey; a steamer trip across the Demerara River and finally a bus ride from Georgetown to the airport. The flight from Atkinson Airfield was scheduled for early afternoon, but the passengers were advised to be at the airport an hour or so before the actual flight.

I felt my pockets to make sure I had all my documents. The passport and the travelling documents were in my jacket pocket, with the money I was carrying. The money was equivalent to three months average salary for a worker in Guyana. This money was in the trousers pocket that was sewn with needle and cotton. A small sum of money around $10 was placed in my hand by my mother for spending money on the journey to England. All along the station platform people were chatting and smiling with each other. Suddenly the expressions of a number of people changed. The train had announced it presence before it was in sight. Regular travellers were well aware of the signals including the sound of the train some distance away. For some people the pleasant expressions associated with the quiet conversations came to an abrupt end. Those family members and friends of Milton and me who were not boarding the train hastily said their final goodbyes before the train arrived.

The parties boarded the train and we waved at the crowd at the station as the steam train slowly but surely pulled away. The people were waving and smiling, and some were crying at the same time. It was an emotional and painful parting for me for I knew that I was leaving the warmth and security of my family to venture into a journey which even grown-up and intelligent people may fear. Yet here I was, only seventeen years old, a village boy who had no experience of living alone in Guyana, was on his way to a foreign land and a new home.

The journey from Leonora to Vreed-en-Hoop took around thirty five minutes stopping at seven stations en-route. The journey between Vreed-en-Hoop and Parika, the opposite end of the line on the West Coast of Demerara, covered some twenty-one miles in just over an hour. Train journeys were quite exciting especially for those who only used the service occasionally. The sound of the steam locomotive and the smoke rising into the air was a familiar and welcoming scene. There were always first class carriages on the train, generally used by the wealthy, whilst the less wealthy were invariably crammed in the second class carriages. Traders with their large baskets of fruit, vegetables, poultry, eggs fish and snacks would travel in third class. Many traders normally endeavoured to secure a place in the goods carriage but frequently had to squeeze in with other passengers. It was not unusual for live chickens to be carried on the train for sale in the city or for workmen to join the train with their tools such as a forks and machetes.

I tried very hard to refrain from any conversation: my thoughts were wandering backwards and forwards thinking of what I was leaving and what the situation was likely to be in the days and months ahead. I looked at my mother and sisters whilst they sat on the wooden seats as the train sped past the sugar plantation, farms, canals and rice fields. They looked at me and we smiled, each time our eyes met. Each family member understood what the other was thinking. I wondered what would happen, if something terrible should happen to me in England, a strange and foreign land several thousands of miles away. Who would comfort me? Would there be someone to smile at me and to say "You don't worry you will soon be alright", as had happened when I was sick with mumps, ear aches, and occasional stomach aches and my parents and sisters comforted me. The sound of the speeding train blurred out a rhythmic tune and I found myself humming the sound of the train. I wondered whether there were trains in England and whether there was first class for white people and second class for blacks and whether the trains would have soft seats for the rich and hard wooden seats for the poor.

As the train rumbled through the countryside towards Georgetown I saw men, women and children carrying heavy loads on their heads; there were men casting nets in the trenches and canals along the journey and workers in the rice fields working in several inches of water along the villages of Blankingberg, Windsor Forrest, Denamstel and Crane. I wondered whether I was doing the right thing going to England. Then I reflected on the working conditions in Guyana where people worked up to ten, twelve or more hours each day, and sometimes worked throughout the night when the moon was shining. The moonlight was the only light available to the field workers. The cane cutters who harvested the sugar cane would often work until the job was finished. I thought about the labourers including women and young children who would work in the fields despite the rain, and continue to do so when the sun came back and dried their clothes whilst they continued to work. The plantation existed to make profits for the owners and the workers were simply the mechanism for them to do so. Their welfare, wellbeing and lives meant very little to the owners as chattel slavery had long been abolished and replaced by economic slavery that resulted in no financial loss to the plantation owners.

Like beasts that lived in the fields they were exposed to all the elements. Some of them would have left home early in the morning and walked for up to an hour sometimes in pouring rain before they even started their work. Having completed their tasks they would have to walk back to their homes tired and exhausted and thanked God, if they were able to secure a good basic meal. They would dry their clothes during the night and dress themselves in the same clothes before leaving home again early the next morning. There were no fixed hours of work, people worked all hours and generally every day except on Sundays. It was piecework and the price was fixed by the drivers (supervisors) generally in consultation with the white overseers. The rates of pay were so poor that workers worked long hours and some of them regularly took their parents, partners and children to assist them.

At the end of each week there was only one pay packet and the wages were barely enough to keep a family in basic necessities. Yet sugar was king and the plantation owners -the absentee landlords-were doing well back in England. I understood the system well since I was often taken into the fields with my sisters from the age of seven to assist my parents. I hated school because of constant bullying, yet would have gladly missed the work in the cane fields to attend school.

Beside the railway track there were shepherds- mainly young boys, with massive old felt or straw hats on their heads standing with a stick in the burning sun ensuring that their cattle did not stray onto the railway track. Owners of cattle which strayed onto the track and collided with the trains were fined severely even though they had lost their cattle. On a number of occasions when an accident took place involving a cow or a bull the train crew would stop and quickly chop off a leg and chuck it on board. I had never witnessed such a thing but had no reason to doubt such statements either. All along the journey people including children were carrying heavy loads on their heads and either walking next to the railway track or on the muddy roads which crossed the railway tracks at every mile or so. They seldom wore shoes as they made their way to or from work, homes, or farms.

The train arrived at Vreed-en-Hoop terminus and the parties departed from the train and made their way towards the waiting area for the journey across the Demerara River. Young children with baskets of fruits, snacks and sweets tried to entice customers to part with their money. Little boys and girls shouted "Get your nuts, sweets, popcorn here, only five cents a packet". Others shouted "Mangoes, mangoes anyone want sweet and juicy mangoes – only fifty cents for two". Children dressed in rags shouted "news get your news here – get the Chronicle and the Mirror here".

These children were sometimes the only wage earners within their family and they certainly worked hard. Joseph and I went just outside the waiting area and Joe said "How about a beer, or some coconut water, and how about some crushed ice with sweet syrup or even some mauby (local soft drink) with ice? You're not going to get these things where you are going. So you better taste them for the last time before you go". I took Joe's advice and we enjoyed the different things. We even had a glass each of freshly pressed sugar cane juice, with ice of course.

Joe and I re-joined our party which numbered around fifteen in total. The steamer was making its way back from the Georgetown side of the brown and fast flowing river more than half a mile wide at the point of crossing. The vessel was around one hundred feet long and thirty feet wide and had two decks. The top deck was quite small but it provided a lovely view. On a clear day one could see the tall chimneys of the sugar plantations along both sides of the Demerara River which narrowed on its way towards the Interior. Diamond sugar estate, one of the largest in the country, was situated on the East Bank with Wales and Versailles on the West Bank. I had often walked past the Versailles estate which was situated a couple of miles or so from Vreed-en-Hoop when I went to visit my aunt whose name was Tota. Auntie Tota who was my own father's sister was a well-loved aunt and known as Tota Powa. Powa is the Indian/Hindi word for aunt. I also walked past this estate when I visited my step father's aunt and uncle who were strict Christians and lived in a little village called Good Fortune. I and my sisters called the little old lady Agie and the old man with a deep no nonsense type of voice, Aja. Agie and Aja were Indian/Hindi words for grandmother and grandfather. I used to walk to Good Fortune and La Grance from Vreed-en-Hoop instead of taking the bus to save a few cents each way in fares. I would buy a drink and a piece of cake instead.

The party boarded the steamer after the passengers had alighted, some scrambling over the rails and onto the dock, even before the vessel was firmly secured. The older and wiser passengers waited until the steamer was at a standstill and the planks were securely in place before they started to board the vessel. Those who were fit and were not carrying any heavy load hurried and even ran towards the few seats that were available. Others with heavy loads consisting of large baskets of food, fish, vegetables etc. would patiently wait until it was safe enough for them to ask someone for a lift -to place the basket on their heads- and then make their way out of the vessel. Motor vehicles and horse and carts and cattle were usually the last to board, or leave the vessel.

As I stood in the steamer I reflected on the long, hot, sunny and lonely but loving days I had spent with my relatives in La Grance and Good Fortune. My relatives always looked after me and made a lot of fuss of me. I would always return to my home with a new shirt and short trousers and lots of fruits and bits and pieces plus a bit of pocket money for myself and my sisters. Neither set of relatives had any children of their own. So they enjoyed having me with them for short periods.

On the Eastern side of the river there were several large ships from various countries. Some were too large to be actually moored along the wharfs/docks on the river and their cargo was taken to and from them by smaller vessels whilst they were anchored almost in the middle of the river. I wondered what the ship would look like, which I would be boarding in Grenada for my journey to England. I had always been scared of the sea, especially since I was present when the body of a good school friend was rescued from the sea, about half an hour after he went missing during a swim close to the shore. The thought of spending days if not weeks on the surface of the ocean created a tremendous fear in my mind. Then there was the thought of the journey on an aeroplane from Guyana to Grenada. I thought, "Oh God what if something goes wrong with the aeroplane during the flight, and then what would happen if the ship lost its way; caught fire; hit an iceberg like the Titanic or ran out of food? I had seen films at the Roxy cinema showing large ships having difficulties at sea and had heard of the Titanic being hit by an iceberg. I had even read about a man called Jonah who was swallowed by a whale and subsequently survived, and saw the film "20,000 Leagues under the Sea" in which a giant octopus clambered on to a large submarine and created havoc for the crew. I tried to put these thoughts out of my head by talking with

Joe and asking him to keep an eye on my family as there would not be any brother around to take care of them.

A small group of people came over to me and said "Hello England man, please when you get to England say hello to my family in England, and tell them that everybody is alright. Tell them they must write to us. Long time now since we receive a letter from them. Tell them to come over for a holiday". I promised to look them up as soon as I settled down. I asked for their names and they were promptly given but when I asked for their addresses they just said "London, London England just asks for Rabat, Lucko, and Pakal" and so on. I thought: what if London is not like Guyana where everyone in the surrounding villages knows each other? How will I contact them? "Then I thought, well it can't be that bad I'll just have to ask a few more Guyanese people I come across in London to pass the message on."

The steamer arrived and the party did their best to stay together for now we were about to step down onto the streets of Georgetown. This was a place which most country folks feared because of the large crowds around Stabroek Market and Water Street; the pushing and shoving; the heavy traffic; its reputation for pick-pocketing; choke-and-rob and violence. Parents grasped their children's hands tightly as they made their way through the streams of people moving in both directions. The hardened and petty criminals standing on street corners and in doorways along Water Street, Lombard Street and the side roads were experts at spotting people who were infrequent visitors to the City for business such as the purchase of a Ferguson tractor, a large piece of machinery or to purchase a large amount of goods for a wedding, and were likely to carry a sizeable amount of cash with them. The criminals worked in gangs and they had an efficient signalling system. They were always lurking in the background outside the many pawnshops that East Indian women regularly visited to pawn their gold bangles and necklaces in order to pay for medical treatment for a member of the family; purchase food or clothing for their children; finance the cost of a wedding, or purchase a piece of land. The thieves would carefully observe the transactions and as soon as the people left the pawnbroker's shop they would put one arm around their neck and their accomplice would relieve the victim of their money. Hence the infamous act of choke-and-rob.

My mother and I had been always extremely careful whenever we went to the pawnbroker near Lombard Street to pawn her jewellery which she had accumulated over the years since she was a young bride and had had items specially made for certain occasions. We kept watch on the pawnbroker until there was no one lurking around outside who appeared to be a criminal. My mother then went in and did the business and, having quickly and discreetly divided the money into four parts we hurried back to do our business before catching the steamer from Georgetown to Vreed-en-Hoop. The money some $300 or £125 had been divided into four parts with one part placed in my mother's pocket; one in her bra; another in her underwear and the other part in my pocket. Presumably the strategy was to protect our money if we were set upon by the choke-and-rob fraternity.

The Bus terminus was only a couple of hundred yards away from the dock and I made sure that my money was safely tucked away in my pocket. I made sure that the people around me were all friends or relatives. We boarded the bus, an old yellow and brown vehicle with the capacity to seat about thirty people. The luggage rack was actually on the roof of the bus. Joe insisted that he was not going to have the suitcase on top of the bus, and that the party would prefer to take another bus if the conductor a pretty, young, fair skinned woman in a light khaki blouse and brown skirt didn't give way to Joe. The rest of the party boarded the bus and in a short while we were at the airport. There were terrible scenes at the airport with women weeping, fainting, revived with bayrum (a highly scented liquid) daubed on their forehead and the small bottle held to their nose. Women – mothers and sisters would weep and sometimes scream "oh my son, my son is going away from me", and sisters would weep, "My brother, you must come back and see us". Male relatives would appear to be less emotional and in more control of themselves. They would weep quietly and discreetly. In any case it was more painful for a mother, or a sister to see a brother depart because a son or a brother was more likely to defend his mother and sister from the oppression and violence from anyone.

Arriving at the airport

At the airport there were families from all the three counties of Guyana - Berbice, the cattle, timber, bauxite, sugar and farming county; Demerara, the sugar, rice and food producing county and Essequibo, the county famous for rice, coconut, gold and timber production. The airport was quite small with a couple of light planes situated at the border of the airfield. About an hour after I and my party arrived at the airport an aeroplane taxied up towards the airport main building. It stopped at around sixty yards from the terminal building.

The aircraft appeared small but inviting to me. It was the closest I, and, indeed, any of my family, had been to an aeroplane and I wondered whether this small noisy little thing would be safe to travel in through the clouds and over the Atlantic ocean: the thought of such technology and the fact that I was going to the country where such inventions were created made me feel good. During my school years I had constantly been reminded, via the textbooks, that the white races were superior to the dark races. The Europeans were the great inventors. They were the most civilised, intelligent, creative and powerful people on earth. They had the most powerful war machines and weapons of destruction the world had ever seen. Britain had conquered and colonised more than half of the world, populated by black and brown people, at the time of my birth, and had even defeated the armed forces of a number of European Countries according to the books which I had read, published by Thomas Nelson & Sons in England. I thought that if the white people were so powerful, then God must be a white person. I was totally unaware of the great civilisations, armies, inventions, buildings and material things long before the Europeans were conquered by the Romans nearly two thousand years ago.

From time to time I glanced at the small aircraft and wondered how such a small craft would be able to take off with some dozen passengers and their luggage. I wondered whether it was all happening for real. My thoughts were moving rapidly from one situation to another. One moment I would be thinking about the journey ahead, and then suddenly I would look at my family and wonder how they may suffer because of my absence. I would then have a vision of myself returning with lots of money, education and power to assist the people of Guyana. Every remaining moment was becoming more and more precious and I was becoming more anxious. I wanted to say so many things to my family before departing from my country of birth but because of my emotional state I decided to wait a little longer before approaching each member of my family to say a few final words to them. By that time someone was bound to say it was time to board the aircraft.

It was a bright sunny day, a typical day, when the temperature was at least 85-90°F. A welcoming light breeze caressed my cheeks as my eyes wandered around the airport building exploring and examining what was taking place around me. The blue sky, layered in parts with varying thickness of white clouds, provided an inviting background for an aircraft to navigate towards. The sun and the breeze rapidly dried the tears and sweat from around my face as I stood beside my friend Joe, a short distance away from my family.

A few men in different colour uniforms were in charge of various tasks in connection with the flight, and the airport management and functions. The small airport building constructed from the famous Guyanese timber known as greenheart was painted brilliant white. The green grass separated by strips of tarmac added to the resemblance of the well-kept gardens at the Overseers Compound in Leonora. The large white painted wooden building and the surrounding facilities were more than adequate for the few aircraft which transported the few passengers to and from the Caribbean and England. Air transport was almost exclusively used by colonial administrators; Europeans working as managers, overseers, and technocrats on the sugar plantations, bauxite mines and businesses; politicians and professional people travelling to and from Guyana and the Caribbean. These people had the resources, power and confidence to use these aircrafts, which appeared as huge mechanical birds floating in the sky after leaving the ground at high speed and amidst tremendous noise.

However, an increasing number of ordinary working class people had started using air transport for at least part of their journey to the Caribbean, America, or England in search of work or education, or both. For most people of all classes, travel for the first time in an aircraft was quite a unique and daunting experience filled with apprehension and fear. Within a few years of my departure, the airport at Atkinson Airfield became inadequate to accommodate the larger aircraft and the increase in the volume of air traffic as economic migration and business journeys grew substantially. A new airport at Timehri was opened to facilitate this growth.

It was getting close to the time to board the plane, and friends and relatives were saying their last goodbyes. The atmosphere was very tense and distressing for all concerned. Those who were leaving were as distressed as those relatives who were seeing them off. My family, friends and I characterised a typical group at the airport. Each person leaving was surrounded by approximately a dozen people consisting of parents, brothers, sisters, close relatives and a couple of friends. Some of the male members of the party were doing their usual thing such as knocking back a few shots of rum. Each shot of rum was followed by some water. Paradoxically, rum was traditionally used as a stimulant to encourage excitement and happiness, and also for the purpose of overcoming sorrow and grief. It was used during happy and unhappy occasions. The female members were standing around me offering advice on how I must look after myself and write home regularly. My best friend Joe kept by my side throughout the journey and our time at the airport. My step father Jokhan stood in silence near the family.

My two eldest sisters, Dede (Betya) and Doreen were at the airport. The other sisters Julie, Datsie, Joyce and Petsie stayed at home. Dede and Doreen were very upset because their only brother was leaving them and they were vulnerable. On numerous occasions they had to endure severe brutality, abuse and suffering from their husbands. Though quite young, I, as their brother, had given them support and had tried to retaliate on their behalf. Now that I was about to leave Guyana they were afraid of their future. Both sisters were comforting our mother whilst their husbands were slowly getting drunk.

Joseph was around nineteen years old. He was a strong young man of red complexion and well built. Joe had already built up a reputation as a tough guy. Most men of his age would think twice before upsetting him. As a Christian he was heavily involved in the local Anglican Church where we both worshipped. Joe was a person with strong and rigid principles coupled with a very bad temper. He was never inclined to turn the other cheek even though he was a devoted Christian. Joe hated injustice and unfairness. He often defended people against aggression and abuse from others. At five feet eight inches tall with a good physique and weighing some eleven stones, compared to my weight of only eight stones, he was quite a fearful character when he was angry. On many occasions he had defended me against aggression from other young men.

People began to get in line towards the exit of the airport, and it was clear that the time for departure was very close. Suddenly there were lots of hugs, kisses and the soft whispering of advice all around. An atmosphere of melancholy pervaded most of the airport among the gentle smiles. I hugged and kissed each member of my family with special and prolonged hugs for my mother, father and elder sisters. I also kissed their feet as a mark of respect. They all appeared to be most distressed at my departure. I then turned and shook hands with my friends saving Joe for last. We hugged each other and Joe said, "Come on, it's time to go, I will carry the case up to the counter for you". I asked Joe to keep in contact with my parents and my sisters and to do his best to protect them. Joe promised to do his best for them and I promised to write regularly to Joe. The last few minutes before departure were most distressing for everyone. Everywhere people were emotional. Mothers were wailing, sisters crying and fathers were doing their best to hold back their tears. Friends smiled and shook hands wondering if it may soon be their turn to leave.

Despite all the commotion and mayhem the bosses maintained their routine. Passports and other necessary documents had to be carefully scrutinised and approved with the correct stamp of authority. The departing passengers quickly lined up by the exit and the customs officer diligently and unemotionally performed his duties. The rope across the door was unhooked and passengers were told to board the aircraft. I wanted to say a few more last words to my relatives but I was too emotional. I really wanted to cuddle my mother again and tell her that I would be back to look after her at her time of need; to tell my father that soon he would be able to take things easy as I would be sending money home for the family, and to tell my sisters that when I returned I would be a big strong man and their husbands would be afraid of me and would desist from abusing and humiliating them. But this was never to be.

Whilst walking to the aircraft, I kept turning around half smiling with tears and perspiration dripping down my face. Milton and I were amongst the last ones to board the plane, which was probably a Dakota, and as the passengers made their way to the aeroplane, they frequently turned and waved towards their relatives and friends.

Up, up and away

As the door closed I knew that there was no turning back. I looked out of the small window as I sat in what appeared to be a very small and crowded plane. I continued to wave to the crowd in the airport building who were also waving. The passengers were told to sit still in their seats and secure their straps. I continued to look out of the window at my family huddled together at the airport. The pilot said a few words before taking his seat. Soon after, the plane took off on its journey to Grenada in the Caribbean. I sat in the plane with my eyes closed thinking about the people and country I was leaving behind. I thought of the things I had seen and done; my childhood and adolescent years; the suffering of my family and of the promise I had made to my parents and to myself. I was adamant that I would return educated, and with enough money to provide a comfortable life for my family. One thing I definitely had in mind to do on my return to Guyana was to instruct my parents, particularly my mother, to stop paid employment immediately, and to spend her time supporting her children and grandchildren. Her suffering was too much for me to bear, but I could at the time do very little to relieve her of her burden. I understood my mother's plight and was convinced that her suffering would not be for very much longer. At least no more than three to five years.

The noisy aircraft with its passengers firmly secured in their seats; doors firmly secured and engine gathering momentum started its journey. With a terrific accumulation of speed it quickly became airborne, but not without a struggle it would appear, as it climbed towards the blue sky. I held on tightly to the back of the seat in front of me, whilst at the same time looking towards the airport which was rapidly disappearing on the horizon below within a few seconds after take-off. I was the youngest passenger on board and probably the most frightened. I sat beside Milton who was also drying his tears and sighing heavily. We looked at each other and spoke about our families, each of us saying how hard it had been to say goodbye to our loved ones.

Throughout the journey I reflected on the plight and vulnerability of the family I was leaving behind. I was concerned for the health of my parents and grandfather and the safety and security of my sisters. I was leaving for the unknown, a journey that I could hardly imagine. I had never been separated from my family before, except for short durations to stay with people whom I knew and trusted. I was on my own on this journey to a strange land with different people and culture some thousands of miles away.

Surprisingly, within a few minutes everyone started to appear quite cheerful and was heavily engaged in conversation. People were smiling and even laughing. It was such a strange feeling. Perhaps minds were beginning to focus more on the future and less on the past. The tension which appeared to have gripped those who were in an aircraft for the first time was beginning to subside and to give way to a variety of questions and comments. The aircraft continued its journey through the clouds and intermittent turbulence. Milton and I commented to each other about the splendid and fascinating view from the aircraft. Most of the passengers, especially those who had had little or no sleep during the last twenty four hours were fast asleep after about thirty minutes in the air. For most, if not all of the passengers, who were economic migrants to Great Britain, and had spent their last night in Guyana at home with family and friends, celebrating their departure with mixed feelings. The farewell party would probably have started at around seven o' clock the previous evening and finished in the early hours of the morning. My family and friends had arranged for a cottage prayer meeting where some members of the Christian Church, where I worshipped, sang a few hymns; read passages from the Bible, and said at least one prayer; wishing the would-be traveller a safe journey and a beneficial trip abroad.

Reverend Harrichand conducted the proceedings with commitment and vitality. Children and adults from the neighbourhood gathered to participate in the cottage meeting; preparing and participating in refreshments and to genuinely join in the occasion to give me a good send- off. In those days people simply did what they thought was expected of them. Unlike modern times individual neighbours and friends were not formally invited. The women and men would simply come and get involved and assist in any way possible with the preparations. A few people brought gifts, such as gold tie clips; shirts; ties; cakes and fruits. In fact most of the clothing and items I was wearing during the flight had been given to me as farewell gifts. Friends bought the material for the suit; the first and only suit I had had in my entire life so far. Mr Bangalang, the tailor converted the light brown material into a decent jacket and a very baggy pair of trousers. The owner of the local general store; Deo Mahadeo had presented me with a long-sleeved cream Windsor shirt, and my mother had bought the pair of black shoes. The handkerchief was presented by my fourth eldest sister, Datsie; the tie was a present from Joe; the tie clip was a gift from my eldest sister Dede; the wallet from the second eldest sister Doreen, and the socks were a gift from the third sister Julie. Some of the money in the wallet represented small gifts from several people. After around four hours from Georgetown the aircraft was flying over Grenada. The island of spice; white sands; coconut palms and surrounded by blue seas was in sight. The aircraft flew alongside some tall mountains and gradually descended into a rather bumpy but safe landing.

Grenada, Island of spice and sunshine

The aircraft arrived in Grenada around three hours after setting off from Atkinson Airfield in Georgetown. It was a journey full of anxieties, sadness, adventure and hope. The flight from Guyana to Grenada was petrifying at times, especially as I had always been afraid of heights. I was worried throughout the journey about arriving safely Grenada without me being sick. The small aircraft dipped, swayed and trembled in the air and each time I opened my eyes, all I could see was, the Atlantic Ocean, mountains and frightened passengers. I also silently prayed for part of the journey, which lasted about three hours.

The landing was bumpy and somewhat scary, but satisfactory. My companions and I were pleased that we were back on land. The small island looked picturesque from the sky and it was equally charming on the ground. Grenada, which is part of the Winward Islands, is undoubtedly a beautiful place with lush vegetation, waterfalls and spices. The capital, St George's, is situated in a magnificent hilly setting of nicely painted concrete and wooden buildings. The walls of the houses were painted cream or light yellow, with either red or green roofs. The streets were clean and the gardens were pretty with an abundance of colourful flowers and fruit trees. The population was mainly people of African descents, with a sizeable number of mixed race and Asians. It was a friendly and welcoming place where people appeared far more relaxed than in Guyana. Grenada is quite a small island, just over one hundred and thirty square miles, compared to Guyana, which covers eighty-three thousand square miles. In those days the population was less than one hundred thousand. The common language was English, but many people also spoke patois and French. It was an island with many small mountains and large hills, and some lovely sandy beaches surrounded by blue, warm water. We were fortunate to spend a couple of hours on Grand Anse Beach with our host.

After landing at the airport my friends and I were separated into small groups of two or three to spend the three days in Grenada with employees of the travel company involved in arranging the journey from Grenada to England on the passenger liner, the Ascania. My friend Babulall and I were taken to the home of the most senior employee who was a very pleasant person. His house was a couple of miles from the capital St George's. It was a modern building with all the comforts which were so alien to me and Babulall. For both of us it was the first time sinks, showers and flush toilets were actually available in the house and could be used without any difficulty during the night. Babulall and I reflected on the fact that if we had reason to use the toilets during the night in the countryside in Guyana it was often a risky business. It was not unusual for someone to step on or over large frogs commonly known as crappos on the way to the toilet. One would often have difficulty walking in the dark and on wet grass or on slippery pieces of wood to and from the toilets situated some fifteen to twenty metres away from the house. Apart from the frogs there were occasionally other dangers such as rats, snakes and even stray dogs to cope with during the night.

Babulall and I were determined to make the most of the pleasant environment in Grenada. After settling ourselves in at the beautiful house having sampled the bed, which was so much different from the mattresses we were accustomed to back home and which were filled with straw and contained numerous species of blood sucking pests, we decided to sample all the other facilities available to us. Within a few minutes we were ready for a meal which we knew would be available as the smell was very enticing. The meal, consisting of rice, meat, fish, bread and fruits, was delicious and so different from the eating arrangements at home.

Everyone sat around the table to eat and there was more than enough for everyone. The occasion provided a good opportunity for Babulall and me to practice eating with knives and forks and spoons; a practice which was not common on the sugar plantations of Guyana. Picking food up by hand from the plate was quite common for us, especially if we were eating fish or meat. Chewing the bones and sucking the fish heads would soon become a thing of the past for us.

Getting lost in Grenada

After a very tasty meal we decided that we ought to have a good look around the streets. We informed our host that we would like to take a short walk into the capital, St George's. We were given instructions on how to get to the capital and also on how to conduct ourselves. The owner of the house was a little concerned about letting his two guests wander around on our own as it was not uncommon for strangers to be robbed by the locals. He then took us for a brief tour of the city and surrounding areas by his car. The conducted tour was very enlightening. It confirmed the beauty of the island. On returning Babulall saw a building which resembled a typical Guyanese rum shop. He immediately requested the driver to let us out. He persuaded both me and the driver that we would be safe, and after a look around we would walk the mile or so home before it got too dark. I believe Babulall was desperate for a few glasses of rum. He was a country person who lived and worked in the countryside in Guyana, a long way from any urban area. He was also very partial to a few glasses of rum. Within an hour of us spending time at the shop Babulall was obviously intoxicated.

Babulall was a simple person who had had no more than four years of total formal education in his life. He had spent most of his thirty years as a labourer working for the rice farmers in Berbice. Berbicians were often seen by people in Georgetown as being uneducated but hardworking farmers with a great pride in themselves. Babulall was a short man weighing around eight stones. He was extremely talkative becoming argumentative after a few glasses of rum. He had a slight speech impediment which became more pronounced with each glass. After we were dropped off Babulall led me straight to the bar. Babulall was the kind of person who could sniff out a drinking den with his eyes closed. There were a number of Trinidadian and Grenadian construction workers in the bar who were having the kind of discussion common to any such setting in Guyana and the Caribbean. Arguing loudly and over emphasizing small details characterised the conversation which everyone wanted to dominate.

Babulall bought a beer for me and a quarter bottle of rum for himself. He assured me that we would have only a couple of drinks before making our way home. Within a couple of minutes of purchasing the bottle which was served with a jug of water, Babulall was heavily involved in the debate taking place between the Trinidadians and Grenadians. He ignored every bit of advice to mind his own business and to keep out of the argument. It was simply too difficult for him to keep his mouth shut. The argument, which had started off quite politely and at normal voice levels, soon became a rowdy and disagreeable affair. The argument centred on a statement made by a fair-skinned Trinidadian who had spent some time as a student and a worker in England after the War of 1939 – 1945. For him life in England was very lonely; the people were hostile to blacks; the place was too cold and it was not a nice place to spend too much of your life.

However, there were opportunities for someone who wanted to work long hours in factories and on public transport. There were opportunities to save some money; return to the Caribbean and start a business. He had done this himself. In fact he was a road building contractor and the others in the discussion were his employees. The Grenadians were not prepared to accept that life was hard for black people in England. They had difficulty accepting that black people were picked on purely because of their skin colour. Even though Grenada was populated by people from many countries including Asians, Africans, mixed races and Europeans the legacy of slavery, imperialism and colonialism was much in evidence. Skin colour was not only crucial for advancement in England but it was also a key determining factor for prosperity in the Caribbean. Social class; status; power; culture and lifestyles were greatly influenced by skin colour.

Stratification on the basis of skin colour was common in Guyana and the Caribbean. Life on the plantations was highly regulated stratified and differentiated through skin colour. Babulall told the men in the bar what he would do if someone tried to tangle with him in England. He would just "Give them two cuffs and curse them until they could take no more." However he agreed that the contractor had done exactly what he wanted to do – to return to Guyana with lots of money to purchase his own rice fields and cattle.

After our discussions and arguments with the men at the bar, we decided to walk back home in the dark. By the time the argument had ended Babulall was really and truly intoxicated. Neither he nor I had the name of the host or the address of the house where we were staying. Babulall was drunk, confused and angry with himself for staying out so late and for having difficulty getting home. So, slowly and with some trepidation, we set about trying to walk home. It was indeed a beautiful journey along the hills and valleys under a cool and dark sky. The lights from the houses on the hillside and down the valleys appeared very attractive from a distance. We continued the conversation about life in England as we started our journey. Soon it was difficult to be certain about the best route home, even though we had had a clear idea about the return journey a few hours previously. We remembered a great deal about the interior of the house; the large dining table; the soft bed and the inside toilet but could not remember the house number; street name or, any special exterior features. It was a large house, some one hundred metres from the lane which branched off from the main road, but there were so many lanes along the road. The large houses were very much alike with red tiled roofs, cream painted walls and immaculate gardens with beautiful flowering shrubs and plants typical of middle to upper class district in the Caribbean.

After asking a few pedestrians for assistance and receiving a lot of sympathy we were beginning to get worried. Continuing along the road, which we recognised as being an area which we had been through at least twice, we met two young African men who appeared extremely helpful. They genuinely appeared pleased to meet us and assured us that they knew the area well and it would only be a few minutes before we were at home. We followed the two men who took us through areas with which we were unfamiliar. Babulall was very angry with himself and he talked to himself throughout the ordeal. The young men were clearly heading back towards the city. Suddenly, they came into contact with a policeman who was making his way home in an old Land Rover vehicle. He stopped to enquire who these strangers were and where they were going.

The young men informed the police that they had found these two who claimed to be from Guyana and on their way to England. The Africans informed the police that these two men were probably lying about their situation and the likely story was that they were Trinidadians who were illegally in the country and were looking for work. They also enquired as to whether they were entitled to a reward as they were escorting the two men to the police station. The policeman told the young men to clear off and took us to the police station. On the way Babulall, who was exhausted, confused and furious to the point where he was almost incoherent, wanted to know why he was being taken. The policeman assured him that everything would be alright as he had an idea where the house was and who owned it.

By the time we reached the station the policeman had had enough of Babulall's shouting, swearing and racist remarks about Africans and Grenadians. Within minutes of arriving at the station Babulall and I found ourselves in a cell. This infuriated Babulall even more and he continued his anger until he fell asleep.

Apparently there were some criminal fugitives – Indians from Trinidad – who took to hiding in Grenada to avoid capture at the time. Babulall and I, both Guyanese, ended up spending most of the night in prison. After quite a few hours, the prison officers managed to locate the person we were staying with and he promptly collected us.

Throughout all this problem and commotion I remained calm but scared. I said very little but thought a lot about it. My main concern was that we may be attacked and robbed, and I had been pleased to see the policeman. After a few hours the policeman informed Babulall and I that a Mr Brown, commonly known as "Red Man" was at the station and that he had spent the last couple of hours looking for us. He had decided to call at the station to seek assistance in locating us. It later transpired that Red Man had telephoned the police station earlier in the night and had given them a brief description of his two guests. So the police were well aware of whom we were and they only decided to detain us at the station because of Babulall's behaviour. Red Man was not happy to say the least. However he was sympathetic to travellers, especially Guyanese of Asian origin, who were often distressed and needed a drop of rum to calm their nerves during such a stressful situation.

The next day, having overcome the trauma, Red Man informed us that he would prefer if we stayed at home until he returned from his office in the afternoon. He would then show us around the island. We could not remain in the bungalow for too long after breakfast, so we decided to walk around within a short distance from the house. It was a delightful morning and the scenery was beautiful. We stood on the hill overlooking the blue sea and explored the neighbourhood. After returning to the house we were informed by the house maid that other Guyanese who had stayed at the house had similar experience to ours including being drunk and getting lost. She told us that she was also thinking of going to England to seek a better life. We promptly gave her the names and addresses of the friends in England and asked her to make contact with them on arrival in England. Babulall even opened his suitcase, took out a bottle of Demerara rum and offered the young woman a drink which she accepted. She was in her late twenties; of fair complexion and attractive personality and she was happy to talk about herself and her native island.

After lunch Red Man took us visitors for a long drive. We visited the beautiful Gran Ants beach with its white sands and dwarf coconut trees and other interesting tropical plants. The beaches were hardly used by foreign tourists as the trade in foreigners was almost non-existent at the time. The locals would normally visit the beach on week-ends or during holidays. During the evening Red Man shared his experience with the us regarding his trips abroad including other Caribbean islands, England and North America. Babulall and I were very impressed and wished that we had travelled widely ourselves, instead of having only experienced travelling to the city – Georgetown on a few occasions and along the coastal areas of Demerara and Berbice. However, we were on a journey which would take us to a number of countries before arriving in England.

The following day we were taken to St George's Harbour to wait for the SS Ascania which would take us across the Atlantic to England. We met the rest of our countrymen at the Harbour around mid-day and naturally we all had a lot of information to exchange. We felt good about our stay in Grenada and we were ready for the next stage of the journey. Music and drinks were constantly available and the vendors would often stop trading to have a break and to dance to the constant calypso tunes from the Mighty Sparrow and Lord Kitchener, who were famous calypsonians in the Caribbean at the time. The some two hundred people waiting to board the ship joined in the dancing, drinking and eating. Someone pointed out to Babulall and me that the large fortress type building on Richmond Hill overlooking the Harbour was the island's prison. Babulall soon went into a tirade of insults, abuse and condemnation of the Grenadians and particularly the Afro-Grenadians. On their way to the Harbour Babulall and I recognised places which we had seen during our first night on the island. Each one blamed the other for taking the wrong turning and for getting lost.

At around six o' clock SS Ascania could be seen gradually and majestically gliding along the blue waters towards St George's Harbour. The sight of the ship was greeted with tremendous cheers and jubilation by those waiting and local residents alike. The picturesque setting of the Harbour with its blue/green water lashing along the hilly coastline; the blue sky and the Ascania moored some couple of hundred yards away would have made a lovely postcard. The ship was anchored for a couple of hours before the passengers were ferried in smaller vehicles to board it. In the meantime incoming passengers had left the ship and the vessel took on board lots of supplies for the journey ahead. The situation changed from the beautiful sunshine, blue skies and the waves of blue/green and clear water kissing the side of the ship to a much duller evening by the time the ship was ready to depart. My friends and I, though delighted to be aboard, were very nervous of the prospects ahead for us. We were familiar with the fate of the Titanic and only hoped that we would not meet such a fate ourselves. We boarded the massive and beautiful ship, the Ascania, an Italian vessel, with at least three hundred other passengers, ultimately bound for our next stop on our way to Southampton, England.

Journey across the Atlantic

After leaving beautiful Grenada, we sailed to a number of West Indian islands including St. Lucia, Dominica and Jamaica, while collecting more passengers. We spent about four hours on land when the ship docked in Jamaica and took on supplies and passengers. Jamaica is a much larger Island than Grenada, with nearly eleven thousand square miles and a population of around two million people. Like Guyana, Jamaica was a British colony and was invaded by the Spanish through Christopher Columbus in 1494. It was captured by the British in 1655, and remained a colony until it achieved independence on 6th August 1962, exactly a year after my 19th birthday. It is the fifth largest island in the Caribbean, with a population of more than 2.3 million people at the time, around seventy five per cent originated from the African continent. The indigenous people, the Taino called it Xaymaca, in Arawakan, meaning "The Land of Wood and Water, or the Land of Springs". Guyana was also known by the native inhabitants as "The Land of Many Waters", a similar name to early Jamaica.

Jamaica – Land of Wood and Water

It is very sad that during my life in Guyana we were taught more about Britain and Europe than about our neighbours in South America or the Caribbean. In fact we were taught more about the so-called savages in Africa and how the colonial powers civilised them, brought them out of the darkness, out of cannibalism and saved their souls by converting them to Christianity. It was clearly in the interests of the colonial masters to keep the colonies isolated from each other in trade, culture and economic interaction.

During our short stay in Jamaica, Babulall and I went for a stroll not too far away from the ship. We had learnt our lesson from getting lost in Grenada. Within an hour we were robbed, whilst browsing at the goods for sale at an open market quite close to the harbour in Kingston. I had a gold ring and this Jamaican trader asked my friend and me whether we would like to sell our gold rings. We were not interested in selling our rings. He then asked us to let him have a quick look at our rings, as he was interested in Guyanese gold. He passed the rings to his assistant who admired the rings which were normal design and nothing fancy. We were distracted by the trader who showed us a tray of gold rings. He returned the rings to us and we continued with our sightseeing tour. We both subsequently discovered a few days later that it wasn't our original rings the trader had returned, but gold plated rings instead, which quickly lost the outer surface and revealed a mixture of metals underneath the gold plated surface. Babulall and I blamed each other for getting caught in this swindle. The presence of the Jamaicans on board changed the atmosphere on the ship a great deal, not only because of the large number of new passengers, but also the general attitudes and behaviour between the different groups from other countries. The Jamaicans were far more westernised and accustomed to life in urban areas, than the average Guyanese. The capital, Kingston, had a population of well over 600,000 people at the time. Almost all the Jamaican passengers were strong young men; a few had already been to other Caribbean Islands, America or Britain.

Sailing across the ocean wasn't at all nice. The ship packed with over one thousand people, was very crowded and the food was so different from what we had been accustomed to. Most of us experienced seasickness and felt quite bored and depressed after a couple of days. I was very apprehensive about what lay ahead of us, and was often pre-occupied with fear of the sea and possible disasters before arriving in England. The group of us from Guyana became very friendly throughout the journey and everyone tried to assist me in every way possible as I was the youngest and appeared to be most vulnerable amongst some of the tough-looking passengers.

The atmosphere on the ship changed considerably, not only due to overcrowding in the bars and on the deck, but also because of the aggressive and loud attitude of some of the Jamaicans. There were several arguments between the passengers from Grenada, Dominica and other islands and the Jamaicans. There was stereotyping and jokes directed against the people from the smaller islands by the Jamaicans. Before long there was self-imposed segregation on board the ship, with each group sticking closely to the people from their respective countries.

During the journey I befriended a young lady from St. Lucia who had joined the vessel with a group of some forty people. They all appeared to be Christians and to know each other; they spoke some broken French and a kind of Patois language. I believe that they were trying to take my mind off the problems, which I was encountering during the journey. I had been away from home for well over a week and was missing my family. I had overcome my sea sickness and was feeling quite low. This young lady was also feeling miserable. She was with a large group who assembled each morning after breakfast on deck and held a Christian service, which included singing of hymns and reading of the Bible. I stood a short distance from the group and listened to their service which I enjoyed. I almost fixed my attention on this young lady and she regularly turned towards me and smiled. She was the youngest person in the group, about two years younger than I was. We made friends very quickly because the older men from our group told her how much I admired her and wanted to talk with her. We met regularly and discreetly in the cabin I shared with three other Guyanese men. It was the first time I had had such a close relationship with a female. It was a very enjoyable experience, which lasted for just over a week, before we landed in Southampton.

The Ascania was a beautiful ship, staffed mainly by Italians. The food was different from what we had been accustomed to in Guyana and Grenada. Guyanese loved their rice, chapatti and curry dishes, we were accustomed to fresh fish, vegetables and fruits. We never had spaghetti or food cooked without salt and pepper. The Jamaicans also missed their rice and peas and curried chicken or meat. They made their dislikes quite clear to anyone amongst the crew who would listen. There were some pleasant distractions on board, especially during the evenings and nights with free drinks, including alcohol available and pleasant live music and singing. I believe the ship owners and the captain were not fully aware of the social, cultural, dietary and lifestyles of the people from the Caribbean, even though they did their best to please the passengers.

There were some lovely scenes during the crossing of the Atlantic, I recall seeing groups of dolphins swimming and playing alongside the ship. We sometimes saw large merchant vessels in the distance that appeared to be gliding past in the opposite direction. Each day we enquired as to how far we were in our journey and how many more days we had ahead, before landing. We all knew that once we were near England it would only take a few minutes to pack our few belongings in our cases and be prepared to land.

The Ascania, having safely crossed the Atlantic Ocean, was making its way through the English Channel in the darkness of night. All the passengers were excited, but also aware of the social, cultural and economic differences which characterised the dissimilarity between people from the colonies and those who resided in Britain. For example, Guyanese and Caribbean's were either educated or indoctrinated into a system which was based very much on the English system but suitably adapted to maintaining the unequal relationship between the "mother country" Britain, and the Colonies which constituted the British Empire. The subtle conditioning experienced by generations of Caribbean's through the education system; films and contacts with Europeans, had done little to prepare us for our lives in England. We heard stories from a few men on board the ship who were returning to England having served in the British Air Force, Navy and Army during the Second World War – 1939-45. They were reluctantly returning to Britain as their previous experience in the "mother country" had been far from positive. Many of us were well aware that we would not be treated equally in England, in the same way the Europeans treated us in our own countries. We were also well aware that we were from the colonies that the Europeans, mainly Britain had ruled for generations, and were regarded as lesser beings than the Europeans.

Late one night we were told that the shores of England would be visible by daylight. The tensions and anxieties were pushed aside by excitement and vision of good and great things to come. Most passengers had a mental picture of life in Britain, built up over many years of education in their country of origin, for their role as second class citizens in the "mother country". The notion of superiority based on skin colour; geographical location; wealth; power and religion were well ingrained in our minds, attitudes, expectations and behaviour.

The hierarchy of various ethnic groups, especially between White Europeans and Black people from Africa, Asia and the Caribbean based on skin colour was well understood. White was generally accepted as superior and Black as inferior. The education system; the media – especially films such as Tarzan – and the economic and political systems re-enforced the notion of superiority and inferiority. And so many of the passengers had a mental image of a very beautiful, rich, prosperous, highly sophisticated, intelligent and benevolent society with lots of opportunities, even if it meant doing the menial jobs which were considered too low in status for white workers. In any case most of us were confident that our stay in Britain would be relatively short and that we would be back in our country of origin to re-join our loved ones within a few years, having saved a small fortune to be invested in a business back home.

Most of the passengers had had a fairly restless night. We were well aware of the importance of the next twenty four hours and were anxious to catch the first glimpse of the shores of England. The packing had to be done and apart from that the mental and physical preparation for the next day was extremely important. Many of the passengers who had by now become close friends – some of them too close – did their best to enjoy each other's company during the last evening/night on the Ascania. Apart from some, people had to frequently vacate their cabins to provide some privacy for someone who wanted to spend time with their friends alone, it was relatively a quiet night filled with reflections and a few drinks between friends. My friends and I spent most of the night sharing thoughts about our homeland; our friends and relatives; the journey so far and plans for our future in Britain. Of course all these conversations took place whilst the bottles of Demerara rum were being consumed. Only those with more than one bottle left were encouraged to share. We were all well aware of the problems someone who landed at the home of a fellow Guyanese in Britain would face if they turned up without at least one bottle of rum and some pepper sauce. So those with one or part of a bottle were encouraged not to betray the expectations of their hosts.

My friends and I had a great time on the last night aboard the Ascania. The group of us Guyanese who had bonded since leaving Guyana took turns to comment on Babulall's many idiosyncrasies since leaving Guyana. He had no rum left to pass around on the night because he had quietly drank his two bottles of Eldorado, five year old XM rum, yet he was the first to get drunk and to start various harmless but heated arguments. Someone said to Babulall "What will you do if there are no rum shops in England"? He would reply "Shut your mouth. What do you know about England? The white men are bigger drinkers than us; I have seen it in the films. They love their whisky…that's what I am going to drink – lots of whisky."

The group of eight became a group of around twelve as each person who had a friend invited the person to join the group for the last breakfast on the ship. Breakfast was served early and before the English shoreline was visible. Soon after breakfast there was a big cheer as land became visible. Within three hours passengers were preparing to leave the vessel. The men changed into their light coloured suits generously cut to accommodate the very baggy trousers and loose jacket. This was the first suit most of them had ever worn and had been made especially for the journey. The few women passengers wore beautiful dresses brightly coloured with flowers, colourful patterns with equally attractive hats, handbags and shoes. These colourful and relatively light garments worn by the women and men were so different from the generally dark and dull clothing worn by British people at the time.

Landed at Southampton

We arrived in Southampton early in the morning in July 1961. It was so interesting to see the buildings and skyline as we sailed towards the docks. The Ascania docked at Southampton and we all last stepped on to English soil with a mixture of excitement and anxieties. We were very happy to have safely completed the journey so far without any major problems. At least the most hazardous and predictable part of the journey was very near to completion. The final part of this outward mission was full of apprehension and unpredictability. All the passengers wondered whether our friends or relatives would be there to meet us on our arrival. We were not certain where and what time we would land given the distance of the journey. Many of us were under the impression that we would land in London and not miles away in Southampton. However, the travel company had arranged everything well for us including a train from Southampton to Waterloo. We all hoped that we would be met at the railway station by a fellow country man or woman whose address we had carefully guarded since leaving home. A few passengers were fortunate to have had more than one address and therefore had a wider choice in terms of settlement. The system of "chain migration" had been well established by Black people who had settled in Britain. Newcomers would invariably settle – at least initially – as near as possible to the person who received them on their arrival. It was not surprising therefore that there were pockets of

Jamaicans, Guyanese, Barbadians and other groups from Africa, Asia and the Caribbean in certain towns, cities and streets in Britain.

Safety, security, friendship and help in adjusting to the new and strange environment were of paramount importance to the newcomer, and the greater the number of previous settlers the more comfortable the newcomer felt. Of the eight men who left Guyana together, and were by now close friends, two were destined for London; two for Nottingham; one for Birmingham; one for Bristol; one for Liverpool and one for South Wales. Other passengers were similarly bound for the large cities which have traditionally acted as hosts for several migratory chains involving other Europeans, Irish, Welsh, Jews, Africans, Asians and now the Caribbean's. Almost all the passengers knew the addresses of their hosts off by heart.

My friends and I gently, and in an orderly manner, stepped down the gangway with our single suitcases. No one was in any great rush. The passengers were assured that there was enough room for everyone on the steam locomotive train specially scheduled to transport us London. The immigration formalities were very basic as everyone living in the colonies had a right of entry to Britain. Britain wanted workers. The government encouraged immigration and workers were generally welcomed by employers, especially within the public sector. However, antagonism against Black people and the opposition to further entry by the average indigenous adult was gaining momentum. Expressions of opposition to Black immigration by politicians, trade unionists and people who were living in inner cities and opposed to Blacks living in their neighbourhoods were quite vocal through the local newspapers. The national newspapers were constantly running stories which portrayed Black people as dirty; lazy; carriers of disease; creators of slums; adversely affecting the education of British children in schools; putting pressures on the health service; living on unemployment benefits and corrupting young white women.

However, until the restrictions imposed by the Commonwealth Immigration Act, 1962, Black and Asians – children of the Empire – were coming to Britain in great numbers during the 1950's and 1960's. Between 1955 and 1960 some 211,600 Caribbean's and Asians had arrived in Britain. Of these arrivals 33,070 were from India; 17,120 from Pakistan – including Bangladesh; 96,180 from Jamaica and 65,270 were from other parts of the Caribbean. Between January 1961 and the implementation of the Commonwealth Immigration Act 1962 (1 July) a further 191,060 people from the Caribbean, India and Pakistan had arrived. Many of them started their journey to Britain earlier than planned in order to arrive before I July 1962 and therefore to "beat the ban". Despite the fact that the total Black population in the early 1960's was less than 1 per cent of the total population many white people and large sections of the media expressed forceful concerns about being "overrun by Blacks" and "swamped by people of an inferior culture and lifestyle".

My friends and I were unaware of the often intense debates about immigration and the concerns and fears expressed by the indigenous population; the experience of overt, covert, individual and institutional racial discrimination, and prejudice against Black people in Britain. We were equally unaware of the racial disturbances in Notting Hill, London and in Nottingham during the summer of 1958, and the many other racially motivated incidents which were becoming increasingly common as unemployment in many areas began to increase followed by increasing racial tensions and intolerance.

So, we were now in Britain and totally unaware of the problems associated with securing accommodation and a job; little did we know that we would soon be seeing notices in newspapers saying " Room to let - sorry no blacks, Irish, children or dogs...Labourers required – sorry, no blacks", or that we would encounter both direct and indirect racial discrimination. As far as we were concerned we felt that our presence would be welcomed since we were quite prepared to do any job regardless of its status, as long as we were able to save a little after paying our bills, educating ourselves and helping our families and relatives back home. Friends or relatives who would be receiving us later that day never really discussed their real fears, concerns, and problems with people back home. It was true that they described in detail their experience of the British weather, and in particular, the cold, foggy and harsh winter months; walking in the snow; rushing home from work in the dark; staying indoors by the fire during the night and having to boil the water in the morning before they could wash themselves.

Apart from the weather very little other information was conveyed so accurately. For many Black people did not reveal their true feelings about their lives in Britain to their families or friends back home, ostensibly, because they "did not want to worry the family back home". Many of them either had considerable difficulty expressing their real feelings in the written word, or had chosen to accept things as they were with the hope that it would not be long before they returned to their country of origin, and therefore, they were prepared to tolerate their disappointments, feelings of loneliness and racial prejudice. On the contrary, quite a number of Black immigrants exaggerated their situation and informed their people back home that they were very happy; that they were in very good, clean and well rewarded jobs; that they were living in good areas and were enjoying themselves.

The Journey in to London

Having landed firmly on the outskirts, the passengers dressed in colourful garments, were gradually making their way to the heart of the mother country. Many were already experiencing a number of culture shocks within this strange environment. For example, they were surprised to see white porters pushing barrows and offering to carry their suitcases; to see white men and women doing what they regarded as menial work at the dock and at the railway station. Even more surprising for them was to be addressed as sir or madam by White people. More culture shocks and transformations were waiting for them along their journey and in almost every area of activity during the coming months.

The straggly line of people waiting to process their documents was quickly organised and recognised as a well accustomed British phenomenon – the queue – moved quietly and speedily through the minimum of immigration formalities. Hundreds of passengers destined mainly for London, Birmingham, Liverpool, Nottingham and Cardiff, were expected to board a train already waiting for them. In any event these were children of the Empire coming to the mother country in which they were legally entitled to settle.

We quickly cleared customs and made our way by train to London. I believe the train arrived at Waterloo station where our friends from Guyana that were living in England, were waiting for us. The small sum of Guyana dollars I had with me was converted to sterling at Southampton; it was just about enough to purchase the rail ticket and to leave me with the equivalent of less than ten pounds sterling.

Almost every passenger had a single suitcase, commonly known as a grip, in which we had secured our most precious belongings for the journey. The small sum of local currency; letters from friends or relations in England, the address of their hosts and their passports were safely secured in their pockets or handbags. Little winter clothing was taken on the journey as the new comers arriving at the height of the British summer were either expected to purchase such garments later in the year or, were assured that such clothing would be made available through their friends and relatives. In any event winter coats, pullovers and scarves were unavailable in the hot, sunny Caribbean. Nevertheless we felt the difference in temperature from the Caribbean, directly that we landed in Southampton.

The passengers gradually boarded the train. Everyone wanted a seat by the window so that they could survey the scenes along the journey to London. It was a beautiful journey. The steam engine pulling the crowded carriages sang its repetitive tune as it made its way towards London.

Considerable excitement was generated aboard the train as it rumbled through the small towns, villages and open spaces. Passengers pointed towards unusual and large buildings. Those destined for London were most excited as they knew their journey would end there, as opposed to those who had to travel well beyond London. They knew they would soon be arriving at Waterloo, and hopefully, their contacts would be there to receive them, and to take them to their lodgings, or in few cases their own homes. Most Black people in Britain during the 1950s and 1960s had not managed to secure their own accommodation in the private, or public sectors, due to relatively high cost of home ownership, difficulty in securing mortgages, vendors refusing to sell their property to black people, local councils refusing to house black immigrants before local people, or others from Ireland. Racial discrimination in housing, education and employment was well known and documented in research material and publications.

Many sellers who sold their homes to black people requested a higher price for their property. Estate agents were often reluctant to sell homes to black people either because they did not want to "get a bad name for doing business with blacks", or the seller was reluctant to entertain a Black buyer, because the neighbours would normally view a Black owner as someone who would cause the price of properties in the street to decline. Blacks were seen as the least desirable neighbours because of the well-established stereotypes about them. Building Societies were invariably reluctant to provide mortgages for Black home buyers, and it was reported that some of them charged higher interest rates and asked for larger sums in deposit. As far as public sector housing was concerned most local authorities' Housing Departments discriminated against Black applicants. They applied all sorts of indirect discrimination such as points system, length of residency; length of time on the waiting list and even downright direct discrimination, by refusing to house black immigrants.

Blacks were often unaware of the procedures for securing council accommodation, and they were often placed at the bottom of the list; kept on a separate file, or ignored when it was their turn to be housed. Those who were fortunate to secure a house or a flat were often housed in areas generally reserved for families who were regarded as 'problem families'. They were invariably behind with their rent; had caused problems in their previous accommodation; were despised by their neighbours or regarded as criminals. They were re-housed in certain areas because the type of property was least desirable. Of the few Black people who had managed to secure council housing, many were experiencing abuse, harassment and even violence from their neighbours.

The journey through the English Countryside with its farmland carefully separated by neat hedgerows, and in between acres of barley, wheat, potatoes and other crops portrayed some familiar sites: from a distance wheat could easily be mistaken for rice fields. Also common along the countryside were herds of cattle, flocks of sheep and miles of grazing land. Some of the passengers no doubt contemplated the possibility of working in agriculture. However, because of the mechanisation of farming few workers were to be seen in or around the fields. At least the miles of countryside with a variety of crops and animals certainly brought back memories of home for me and my friends as the majority of Guyanese lived and worked in the countryside.

The passengers took a keen interest in almost everything they saw along the journey. They were particularly interested in the size and design of the homes and factories which they saw along the route. The greenness and rationality of the countryside was easily identified and accepted, unlike the somewhat long, dull and dreary buildings with small chimneys on top of them. This sea of roof tiles, red bricks, grey concrete and neatly laid out buildings were stared at through the windows of the train as it journeyed through the urban areas along the route. The curiosity of the passengers reached enormous heights when they realised that some of the long buildings with chimneys from which smoke was being released were in fact houses. Families actually lived in them. Although they were grossly different in structure and size, they were very similar in principle to the rows of houses called logies built by sugar plantation owners to accommodate workers on the estates. Some people were not convinced that the terraced buildings were homes. They were convinced that they were factories. Others felt that the smoke was coming from firesides (clay ovens) which were very common in Guyana, but some felt that firesides could not cause so much smoke.

For some people who lived on the sugar plantations it reminded them of the logies and they were convinced that people lived in the terraced properties. However, they wondered as to whether these houses had running water, electricity, or toilet facilities, unlike the logies on the plantations back home. The neatness and uniformity of the landscape through the countryside and towns was the subject of much debate and discussion. The English countryside in the height of summer is a lively and pleasant site. Cattle, crops, cottages and plants projected colour, contrasts, vitality and life. The green and pleasant countryside prompted some passengers to think that there may be job opportunities in farming for them. Some people talked about their preference for finding work, and living in the countryside. Others were less keen to engage in any kind of farming, having recently escaped from labouring in the plantations, paddy fields, farmlands or shanty areas in their native villages and towns back home. For most people they knew that they would be residing in large urban areas and working in factories and offices. Very few had contemplated working in public transport such as the railways and buses. Many were unaware of the limited range of jobs that would be available to them when they started to look for work. Few were aware that they would ended up in the public sector including transport and the health service, and the more sought-after public sector jobs such as communications, water supply, electricity, gas, the civil service and even local government would refuse to employ black workers, because of direct and indirect discrimination, despite the fact that they were public services under the control of the government.

In reality, few if any, black people found jobs on the land or in the private service industries such as retail, banking, hotel and catering. Instead they were destined to fulfil manual occupations in the public services and large private sector manufacturing companies which many white workers had vacated for better paid occupations.

The massive train driven by steam locomotives finally entered the Greater London area. The buildings were larger, and only small patches of green areas could be seen. Tension, excitement and worries became obvious as each person adjusted their garments; checked that they had all their belongings and attached themselves to their suitcases in anticipation of meeting their hosts at Waterloo Station, or preparing themselves for the rest of their journey on their own. Those bound for London, were contemplating the possibility of someone not being there to receive them, or that they may have problems recognising each other. The skyline of London grew larger and larger whilst the heartbeat of the passengers grew faster and louder through excitement and anxiety.

Friends and families were at long last re-united at Waterloo Station. My friend Hakim was there to receive me and so was Milton's friend. Those destined for outside London were busy seeking assistance on the journey ahead. So here I was, in the heart of the "Mother country" and looking forward to life ahead.

Top – Bottom, L-R
Jim with; Pakistani cricketer Intikhab Allam
West Indies fast bowler Joel Gardener
Former England cricket captain David Gower
England fast bowler Fred Truman
Drinking with West Indies captain Clive Lloyd

Chapter 5:

Discovering London

On the dole

My friend Hakim met me at Waterloo and took me to his home where he was living with his partner Anga – a woman from Guyana – and they were very kind to me. The rail journey through London underground from Waterloo to Shepherd's Bush was educational but also frightening; it was my first time to travel underground. I kept an eye on the doors which opened and closed automatically and wondered what would happen to someone if they were caught between the doors. As we walked the five hundred yards from the station to Fritville Gardens, Hakim told me that a few black people from Guyana shopped at the local Shepherd's Bush Market on Saturdays. "Great", I thought, "I'll make sure that I visit the market the next Saturday." Shepherds Bush is in West London and was given the name because the area was used by shepherds as a resting place with their livestock on their way to Smithfield Meat Market in the City of London. It was also the home of the BBC Television Centre, one of the largest studios in the world, which opened just over a year before my arrival. The famous White City Stadium was also nearby.

I stayed with Hakim and Anga on the first night and on the second day Hakim took me to see a landlord near where they were living. It was a good fifteen minutes' walk away and quite close to the Hammersmith Apollo, where many great and famous stars such as Duke Ellington, Louis Armstrong, Johnny Cash, Ella Fitzgerald and Count Basie performed in the early 1960's. This landlord who let me a room had provided accommodation for Hakim when he first arrived in England, so they knew each other well. The landlord and his wife were a white retired English couple. They rented most of their three storey property, except a couple of rooms on the ground floor, which they kept for themselves.

Hakim and his partner Anga were very good to me, and did everything possible to help me: I was delighted to be taken care of in England by my much respected friend. Both Anga and Hakim helped me a great deal to familiarise myself with the new environment. I spent the first couple of days with Hakim and Anga in the two-bed roomed second floor flat owned by a fellow Guyanese who had settled in England before my arrival. Hakim helped me to register with the Labour Exchange Office in Hammersmith.

Very few newcomers were able to support themselves with the money they had brought with them from Guyana and after having to exchange some of what was left after arriving in Southampton, at least to pay for the train journey, very little was actually left for any sustained living costs. The Labour Exchange was not far from Luxembourg Gardens where I was living. For most newcomers signing on at the Dole Office as soon as possible after arrival was essential since Guyanese dollars were almost worthless in England.

During the first few days Anga prepared breakfast for herself, Hakim and me. It consisted of scrambled eggs with baked beans, lettuce and bread. It was delicious. The evening meal consisted of a mixture of Guyanese and English food and these were really tasty. Even after I moved into the room in Hammersmith I would often return to Hakim's place for my meals. Anga introduced me to English food and explained a great deal about shopping and cooking to me. The first few days living on my own, I felt dreadfully lonely, living in this small room with no one around even though there were many tenants in the house. I walked back to my friend's house as often as I could, so I could talk with Anga and Hakim. Both of them worked during the day, so I waited until the evening to see them.

After one day of living on my own I walked around the area and saw lots of notices for vacant jobs, but I was very shy and lacking in confidence to apply. I plucked up enough courage the following day and made enquiries at a number of security gates at the entrance to the factories, but was either informed that they were no vacancies, or they were not "employing coloured people". In those days, employers were very reluctant to employ black, Asians and visible minorities. Sometime they also discriminated against Irish workers. I wondered why they called England the "Mother Country"; as surely, no decent mother would discriminate against her offspring because of the colour of their skins or ethnic origins! The next day I tried a few local employers without success and also called in at the Labour Exchange.

I noticed that many employers would only employ black people in jobs for which they could not readily recruit white workers. They wouldn't employ us in white-collar jobs or professional jobs, but jobs, which involved working long and unsociable hours, low pay and poor working conditions. The major employers in the public sector such as health, railways and transport had experienced difficulty in recruiting indigenous British workers and had, during the previous decade, organised recruitment campaigns in the Caribbean to fill public sector manual jobs in transport and the NHS. Many white workers saw us as cheap labour and either resented, or reluctantly tolerated our presence; they felt that we had degraded the status of their jobs and saw us as competitors. Unlike the white workers, we were keen to work overtime and to work during our rest days, as the public services operated seven days each week and in some cases such as the NHS and public transport twenty four hours each day.

The Exchange found me a casual job as labourer in a warehouse which was part of a famous store in Kensington. I worked there for less than two weeks. About a week later I had started work for London Transport as a trainee bus conductor. I turned up with Hakim, at London Transport Recruitment Centre in Marylebone, London and joined the queues, consisting of almost all black Caribbean men and women, and a few Irish people waiting to be interviewed for work. Hakim gave me directions on how to make my own way back home. I hung about feeling quite nervous and anxious about taking an exam and having to be interviewed by a white person as I had never sat face to face with a white person in a room. We were conditioned never to look at an adult in the eyes when they asked you questions, let alone a white person. I was well aware that the workers on the plantation where I had previously worked often used to appear humble in the proximity of a white overseer by taking their hats off and shuffling out of the way when the overseer was coming towards them on his mule, jeep or motorbike. Apparently, due to the pressing need for workers, the interviews and exams were quite short and friendly. Anyone who was unsuitable was asked to leave during the training period.

An Asian man who looked quite like me approached me and asked me where I was from; I told him I was from Guyana. He then told me 'you will never pass the test as they use different money in England, let me have your papers, you wait nearby for me and I will take the test for you'. A few minutes later he appeared smiling and gave me a letter inviting me to attend the London Transport Training Centre in Chiswick, London the following Monday for training as a bus conductor. I thanked the person for his help and paid him ten shillings as agreed. I spent the next couple of days finding out about using sterling and familiarising myself with London.

The rent for my room was 27 shillings (£1.35) per week, and with the £3.25 I received from the Dole Office, I managed to survive reasonably well. I was even able to send a 30 shillings (£1.50) postal order to my parents only three weeks after my arrival in England. This was a nice little sum in Guyana. Such transfers through the use of money orders from post offices were a common practice for me, as I was well aware of the impoverished situation my family was experiencing in Guyana.

The landlord (Mr Smith) was a white man aged around seventy with a long white beard. His wife was a small white woman about half his body weight. Mrs Smith, like her husband who was retired, was a charming English person who always appeared with a turban and apron. She spent most of her days cleaning, pottering around the house and small garden, and cooking and fussing with her husband when she was not watching the television. Although Mrs Smith was a very discreet woman when visitors and tenants were around she was quite assertive and forceful with her husband, when no one else seemed to be around. I recall an occasion when I thoroughly annoyed her after flushing the toilet at 4.30 am one morning and apparently woke up the entire household which consisted of Mr and Mrs Smith and most of the tenants who occupied the eight rooms in the house which consisted of three floors.

As a busman I worked unsocial hours and often had to leave home between 4.30 and 5.30 am when I was on early shift. On returning home at around 3.30 p.m. one day, I was aware of some upset I had caused to Mrs Smith and some of the tenants earlier, because the expression on Mrs Smith's face was quite severe when she saw me, as I entered the house. She did not respond to my greeting of hello on this occasion but immediately informed Mr Smith that I had arrived. I anticipated that a visit from the landlord may take place later in the day as I had overheard a heated conversation between Mrs and Mr Smith from my room which was directly above the Smiths' living room. Mr Smith tried hard to pacify Mrs Smith who was adamant that I had to conform to house rules or leave. Mr Smith was generally more sympathetic to all his tenants and was normally the person who dealt with awkward situations involving tenants.

Mr Smith, who was about thirteen stones, nearly twice the weight of his wife and two feet taller, had rosy cheeks; an intelligent-looking face; thinning white hair on his head and a large white beard, greeted me in my room and with a wide smile asked about my welfare in a sympathetic and gentle manner. He asked me if I was well, had I heard from Guyana?, was I coping all right and so on before asking me whether I had flushed the toilet at 4.30 am before leaving the house. I confirmed that this was the case and apologised for any noise I had caused. Mr Smith, who was a grandfather-like figure with enormous tact and patience accepted my apology and suggested that in future I should be more careful about making any noise before 6.30 am.

The Smiths occupied part of the ground floor including the living room which was directly at the opposite end of the front door. One would invariably see Mrs Smith or her husband when one entered the house as the door to the living room was always slightly open to enable someone to have a discreet glance towards the front door whenever someone had entered. Mr and Mrs Smith were both English and had visited India. In fact Mr Smith was a loyal supporter of a Hindu Temple somewhere in East London and made regular journeys on Sundays to worship there. The Smiths were clearly liberal minded people who were to some extent sympathetic to the problems faced by black people in England and around the world. However, they were also very mindful of the impact Black tenants were having on their business as landlords, and therefore sought to limit the number of black tenants to no more than one or two at any given time. The Smiths had no children of their own but were often visited by two teenage children from next door who used the gate between the two properties to communicate with the Smiths when they were in the kitchen. The youngsters, a boy and a girl, had a dog which they played with a lot in their garden. I was able to observe the activities in the gardens from my room and often reflected on my own childhood; my relationship with my friends and family in Guyana and my own little garden which performed a functional role in supplementing the family meals.

I was very shy and lacked confidence and was unable to communicate effectively with either Mr or Mrs Smith. Mrs Smith had told me off on several occasions for the foul smell after the use of the toilet; using the toilet late at night and early in the mornings; flushing the toilet and waking her and other tenants up, walking around the room and having the lights on in the room all night and for not closing the front door quietly on entering or exiting.

The room was around nine feet long and seven feet wide with a single bed and wardrobe and a window overlooking the rear garden. No cooking facilities were available or allowed and Mrs Smith did not like her tenants staying in during the day. She wanted to be able to clean the rooms, have a good look around to ensure that no one had brought any visitors, left any lights on or was using any electric fires or paraffin heaters.

I was afraid of Mr and Mrs Smith in a strange way even though I liked them both and was grateful for their help in providing me with accommodation The fear I felt was the same as all young black people have of white people within a colonial setting. Such fear was motivated by ignorance; culture; power relationships; and lack of contact and interaction between black and white people, especially in rural areas around the colonies.

Apart from me, all the other tenants were white Europeans who were single people with no children. I was extremely surprised at the lifestyle and relationship of the tenants and the landlord. The relationships were very business-like and formal. People kept themselves to themselves and the unwritten house rules were generally respected. The rules were basic and included few visitors if any; returning home before 11.00 p.m.; no slamming of doors or playing loud music; no queuing up outside the bathroom or toilet; no cooking in the rooms; no smell of "foreign" food as tenants were expected to have their meals elsewhere; wiping of feet before and after entering through the front door; no conversations in the landing; cleaning the sink and bath after use; not disturbing the landlord with requests for shillings for the gas or electric meters, and, most important, rents must be paid promptly on Saturday morning each week in cash, at ten in the morning.

A London busman

Within a week in London I was beginning to find my way around. Having been taken to the Job Centre to register for benefits I had secured a couple of week's casual work as a labourer at a large store in Kensington about twenty minutes' walk away from my accommodation in Shepherds Bush near Hammersmith. Within a couple of weeks I was actively involved in the trade union. I was coming up towards my eighteenth birthday and I wasn't able to read and write English as fluently I needed. I could write simple letters, but even those contained a lot of grammatical errors. I had no formal qualifications except a bundle of recommendations, which did not impress any employer. I was in a new country, with a vastly different culture, lifestyle, and structures and I felt isolated and lost. In addition I was bullied and attacked by some white racist young men at work.

This was a bitter experience for me. I was racially abused, tormented and attacked by three older white young men who stuck my head down a toilet on one occasion and then flushed it. I was regularly bullied and insulted. I left soon afterwards. I could not understand why they took a dislike to me simply because of the colour of my skin. I was unaware of the dynamics of racism, colonialism, cultural diversity and power relationships. Despite the white skins they were part of the working class, similar to me, so I was amazed that they rejected me. I felt we should have all been united against the employer and supported each other.

There was a mature black African man from Jamaica, who worked in the same building, but in another warehouse, and was a member of the Communist Party at the time. He didn't say much to me at work but coming home on the bus each day, he would engage me in conversation about racial prejudice. He took me to a meeting one Saturday and I met other members of the Communist Party. They welcomed me to the meeting and the white and black people present really made me feel special. The language they spoke was very much the language the trade union and political activists, including my parents, spoke in Guyana. During the regular Saturday meetings at Farringdon Street which I attended after work, they talked about colonialism, imperialism, poverty, trade unions, racism and so on.

Things began to trigger thoughts of home and I quickly realised that working people everywhere were concerned about pay, conditions at work and a decent home life for themselves and their families. I also realised that to change the unjust and exploitative conditions, which I left in Guyana, I had to campaign for better conditions and justice for workers in England and the world. I was inducted into international solidarity and the fact that there is only one race –

the human race. My trade union and political ambitions and career in Britain therefore started with my involvement with the Communist Party.

I reported at the London Transport Training Centre bright and early and joined one of several groups of people, almost all black and male, awaiting instructions. We were asked to enter one of the training rooms where we received lots of information about London Transport, conditions of our employment, rules and regulations and how to use the ticket machine. The training lasted two weeks, and included practical training on a bus inside the Centre, followed by more training on the road, a tour of several parts of London and reading different fare charts. The first week of training was mainly in an office environment, familiarising ourselves with the British money, use of the ticket machine, and use of emergency tickets; reading fare charts; identifying familiar places in London and customer care. Please, thank you and hold tightly please, and mind how you go, had become standard vocabulary for the some eighty trainees mainly Caribbean's at the Centre. After some in-house training we were driven around London on a special bus to familiarise ourselves with the names of places and sites; to experience standing on the bus platform (entrance to the bus); requesting the driver to stop; actually issuing tickets to fellow trainees who were pretending to be passengers and engaging in various role playing situations. A couple were regarded as unsuitable and were asked to leave before the end of the training.

On the first day of training we were issued with a bus pass, so a number of us decided to pair up and to use our free pass to explore London. We were given several maps identifying places of interests and famous places frequented by visitors to London. I was quite popular with fellow trainees at the Training Centre. I was a fan of Elvis Presley and I fashioned my hair similar to his. My nick name was Elvis as I had developed a technique of cracking an egg and using the white part to put on my hair so I could comb my hair forward and then back, creating a lovely hairstyle which remained rigid throughout the day. I even adopted the Elvis walk and even planned to purchase a guitar and practice singing like Elvis. A few months later I did purchase a Spanish guitar, which I have to this day, but never to play a tune or sing any near like the "King." I even tried to walk like him. I also had a bit of a reputation for chatting up young ladies when I was in Guyana. I made friends with a young African woman from Barbados about my own age, much to the envy of the other trainees. We discovered that the best way to get a good view of London was from the top of a double decker bus and we made good use of our passes every evening. Unfortunately we were posted to different garages after the training and I lost contact with her.

The training was pretty basic but functional. It was a real problem to wear the uniform, especially the peak hat; it just didn't go with my Elvis Presley's hairstyle. So, I carried the hat around in my hand until I was instructed to wear it. Each trainee strapped on the ticket machine and was equipped with a leather money bag with a long strap across the shoulder for depositing coins and a fare chart for calculating individual fares. It was very difficult at first to simply walk the bus without holding on or falling over when the vehicle braked suddenly. The trolley buses with overhead electric cables were the worst for being erratic. The route-masters were a lot better. After a while I managed to walk around the bus collecting fares whilst it was moving. London traffic at the time ensured that most vehicles moved relatively slowly especially during peak hours. Very soon after receiving my uniform I went to a photographic studio in Hammersmith Broadway and had my picture taken in my uniform, cap and overcoat. I promptly sent a copy to my relatives in Guyana so they could see that I was working and a bus conductor's job was perceived at the time by people back home as a relatively decent and steady job.

After the training, I was placed at a depot in Chelverton Road, Putney in South West London. A number of very busy routes were located in this depot. For the overwhelming majority of people in London, travel to and from work and recreation activities were carried out by bus and underground rail. Few workers travelled to and from work in private vehicles. I had training on several routes including the 37 route which operated between Hounslow in Middlesex and Peckham in South West London. This was a very diverse route which went through, Richmond, Putney, Wandsworth, Clapham and Brixton. Other routes included number 30 and 74 which went through South West, Central and North London. Brixton, Clapham and Peckham were difficult as far as collecting fares and dealing with passengers was concerned. The queues were invariably disorderly, the passengers aggressive and reluctant to pay their fares and jumping on and off the bus in between stops. Most of the passengers described above were young men of various ethnic groups, and people who were intoxicated especially night and weekends when the pubs had closed. My pay was less than £8 per week, working forty-four hours and six days each week. Now that I was working my family naturally anticipated regular transfer of money back home to help them.

I met a number of young women black and white, at the depot and on the various bus routes. I worked every day I could, including my rest days so I had little time to keep up friendship or to make new friends. I needed the money to support my family, even though I only had four hours break in between shifts. Chelverton Road depot was some three miles away from my residence in Hammersmith. Since the buses were in service from five 'o' clock in the morning to beyond midnight, getting to and from work was problematic for me, even though staff buses were available. The weekly shifts rotated between early, middle and late duties on a forty eight hour week. Days off known as "rest days" were staggered throughout the week to provide a full seven day service for passengers each week. Like others I worked my rest days which were paid at extra rates. It was not uncommon for busmen to work for months without having a day off. Earning between £10.00 and £15.00 per week with overtime was a regular feature for me. Many of us worked double shifts or shift and a half on certain days. By this time I had infrequent contacts with my friend Hakim. I had made friends with people from various parts of the Caribbean who worked on the buses, including young women from Barbados St Lucia and Grenada. Despite the fact that I was very popular at work, had many friends and was beginning to feel more confident and happy, I nevertheless missed home and wished I had close contacts with fellow Guyanese in London.

My friend Milton, who was a travelling companion on the Ascania, settled in Sudbury near Wembley, Middlesex and was living at the same address as three single men from Guyana including the landlord Freddie, and a man called Raj who also came from our village. Freddie was estranged from his wife and he decided to rent out four of the 5 rooms in his house. Room charges varied between 25 shillings (£1.25) and 60 shillings (£3.00) per week. Cooking facilities were available. Coins had to be inserted in the electric meter for electricity.

I had kept in contact with Milton and it was arranged for me to visit him and to ask the Landlord to let me have a room when one became available. Sudbury Town is around a mile from Wembley and about the same distance from the Alperton Bus depot. I thought that it would be great to transfer from Chelverton Road depot to Alperton if only a room could become available in Fred's house. I would be amongst my countrymen and my friends Milton and Raj who were from my village in Guyana. Wembley was quite famous for the Stadium and the Empire Pool. The complex was opened in April, 1923 for the Football Association Cup and in 1924-5 was the venue for the Britain Empire Exhibition.

Shortly after my visit to Milton a room became available and I subsequently secured a transfer from Chelverton Road, in Putney, London to Alperton depot in Wembley. I occupied the small box room at Fred's house at £1.25 per week rent. Soon after moving to Sudbury, I registered at Harrow Technical College for courses in English, Economics, British Constitution and Book-keeping. I purchased a three piece suit and bought a leather briefcase to carry my books and material. Within a year I passed a number of GCE 'O' Levels and I felt quite confident in pursuing my education in England. I had a vision long before I left Guyana. I wanted to be a professional person, preferably a politician or an adult teacher, so I could empower others to change society for the better. The experience I had accumulated working on the plantation and growing up in poverty, exploitation, discrimination and religious hypocrisy made me bitter, even though I was a Christian and a regular church goer. The suffering of my parents and their parents as well as us children under the capitalist sponsored colonial system was degrading, inhuman and contrary to God's teaching. At Alperton Garage I worked on the number18 bus which went into the heart of London, and to many of the famous areas I was by now familiar with. I spent a lot of my spare time using my free bus pass exploring London.

Exploring sixties swinging London

By the summer of 1962 I had lived in London for a year. I had made full use of my free bus pass and visited as many places as I could during my days off. London seemed a strange, but fantastic city to me, coming from a village background in Guyana and having only made a few visits to Georgetown, the capital of Guyana. It was quite frightening in many ways to find myself in a highly developed country where its history, customs, values, culture, infrastructure and lifestyle were so alien to me. My first impression of the centre of London was much as I had expected, having seen films, and read the history books about this great historical city. I was of course amazed by the large buildings; bright lights, entertainment, busy shops and streets, and density of the population and buildings. The easily accessible transport, education, health, welfare, and the judicial system were also impressive.

On the other hand I was disappointed because I never envisaged so much poverty within a mile of the City of London, in areas such as East London. I could not believe that a country that had ruled about half the world on different occasions, with highly sophisticated and developed economic, political social and industrial developments would have such inequalities. At school we were told to read about the country that gave birth to the industrial revolution; that had an empire; that was so rich in wealth, influence and history and had, apparently civilised the world and saved Europe from German Fascism, could have such high levels of poverty, poor housing and class divisions. In fact many white working class people were relatively as poor as some of the people in Guyana, Africa or Asia. I was surprised to see the long terrace houses, which were quite dilapidated in certain areas, especially within the East End of London, still had several families living in them. I quickly realised that the streets of London were not paved with gold.

By the end of the summer in 1961, the year John F Kennedy took over as President of America, on 24 January, and the USA entered into the Vietnam War, I was familiar with many sites and places in London. It was the year after the female birth protection pill was first available, and the birth of the swinging sixties, characterised by the mini skirt, hippy culture, sexual revolution, teddy boys and music from Elvis Presley, Cliff Richard, Chubby Checker, the Beatles and Dusty Springfield. London was seen as the fashion and musical capital of the world. On the other side of the free love, loud music, youth rebellion and a vibrant youth culture, there were other serious sides of London that were equally fascinating for me, and I took full advantage of the opportunities to observe, explore and participate. Having a free bus pass every day, seven days a week was a gift, which I made good use of in my spare time.

Apart from visiting famous places like, the London Zoo, in Regents Park, St Pauls Cathedral, Buckingham Palace, Madame Taussauds, Trafalgar Square, Piccadilly Circus, the British Museum, Houses of Parliament, the Royal Albert Hall, the Tower of London and many other places, I spent a great deal of time at Hyde Park Corner, also known as Speakers' Corner. For me Speakers' Corner had a particular attraction as it reminded me of the days and nights when I walked alongside my mother with our hand torch to attend highly charged and emotive political gatherings, listening to speeches from members of the Peoples Progressive Party (PPP) led by the great anti-colonialist and Marxist Dr Cheddi Jagan. In many ways I modelled my views and beliefs on my mother's, but my charismatic speech making, political values and commitment to that of Cheddi Jagan. I listened to several speeches of Cheddi, his American wife Janet Jagan and members of his Party including a Mr Ramkarran who led the Guiana Agricultural Workers Union (GAWU). My parents were active members of both the PPP and GAWU and I was a committed supporter.

The speeches at Speakers Corner were always challenging, ambitious, provocative, and charged with much emotion. The fact that you could heckle, interrupt, challenge the speakers, or even get on your own 'soap box' was quite an experience. This part of London attracted many good and great people who used the ostensibly right to free speech in Hyde Park to expound their theories, ideologies, philosophies and prejudices. Amongst the great people who have spoken at Speakers Corner included Karl Marx, Vladimir Lenin, George Orwell, C L R James, Marcus Garvey, Kwame Nkrumah, Walter Rodney – my countryman, Lord Donald Soper, Lord Bertrand Russell and many others whose politics I admired. There were also many great and gifted speakers from other parts of the world including Africa, Asia, Europe and the Caribbean. They were always inspiring and motivational. You either agree or disagree with them, they were in many ways uncompromising and well organised in their thoughts. The speeches that inspired me most were those about anti-colonialism and anti-imperialism, as well as speeches against wars, poverty, injustice, exploitation and inequality.

The failed American CIA sponsored invasion of Cuba, that was led by Fidel Castro, Che Guevara and other revolutionaries, who defeated the right wing Army General, Fulgerncio Batista who ruled Cuba until he fled on 31 December 1959, was a major topic. The incident known as the 'Bay of Pigs' invasion epitomised the approach the Americans were taking towards the growing revolutionary struggles in South and Central America, which they regarded as their 'backyard'. The Vietnam War and the Cuban Missile Crisis which almost brought about a nuclear war between the USA and the Soviet Union was also a major topic for speakers as well as the anti-colonial struggles, that resulted in Ghana gaining Independence from Britain in 1957, followed by Jamaica and Trinidad and Tobago joining the Commonwealth as Independent nations that had shaken off British colonialism in 1962. The success of the first person in space, the Russian Yuri Gagarin who completed an orbit of the earth on 12 April 1961 in his Vostok 1 spacecraft was seen as a tremendous success for the Soviet Union and the many liberation struggles around the world that were sympathetic to towards the communist regime in the Soviet Union that was engaged in what was described as the 'Cold War' between the East and the West. At the same time the building of the Berlin Wall which started in 1961 was also a burning topic. I enjoyed every minute I spent at Speakers Corner and I learnt a great deal from what I heard.

I remember many incidents on the buses which still stand out in my mind today. For example, there was an occasion when I was assaulted by a white male and then on a second occasion by a black male. Both events took place within a few months of each other and on each occasions I was defended by white middle aged men. It does goes to show how irrational it is to stereotype people on racial grounds. I also remember when a posh middle aged woman, with furs and gloves used to get on my bus early in the evening in Hyde Park Corner and travel to Fulham. On several occasions she put the fare on the seat and asked me to place the change and ticket on the seat next to her. On one occasion I thought I would disobey her and place the change and ticket into her hands. So after picking up the two shilling coin from the seat I decided to put the change and ticket into her hands by holding her left hand with my left hand and placing the change and ticket into her hard. She screamed with anger and shouted racial abuse at me. On several occasions I made friends with young ladies my own age and older before I met my wife. For a few months when I was on the 187 bus I used to have a relationship with a young lady in Kilburn who worked in a laundrette, opposite where the bus terminus was. Whenever we had a few minutes to spare especially during the evenings I used to see her in the laundrette before we started off on our next trip. My driver was very jealous and so was the Inspector who forever kept asking me to see whether I could introduce him to the young lady. I did introduce him and I later understood that he had married her. I sometimes used to carry my guitar on the buses and tried to learn how to play it, a skill I never managed to conquer. I have the Spanish guitar to this day and my grandchildren often play a tune on it.

Discovering London's life

I had arrived in England in the summer of 1961, so it was good to be able to move around without the fear of being too cold or dark. However the dreaded winter gradually emerged. As the winter became apparent I discovered a very different England in terms of lifestyle, dress and the environment. London was full of smog and smoke; you could hardly see five yards ahead of you. The first winter was very cold and I felt quite uncomfortable but like everyone else I managed. I often had to get up at between four or five in the morning for early shifts on the buses. I usually walked to the bus depot nearly 2 miles away and started work on a cold bus with no doors, to protect us conductors from the elements. I managed to get through my first winter. Little did I know that the winter of 1962 was going to be one of the worst for over a hundred years, including the really bad winter of 1947. The early morning shifts during the winter on buses without a door were most uncomfortable. It became more bearable when I discovered long woollen underwear. On one occasion during the winter of 1962, the snow was thick on the ground for several weeks and the fog was also dense, even during the day. One day I had to walk in front of the bus with a flare so that the bus could crawl behind me back to the garage. Both the bus and I ended up on more than one occasion in the wrong road and almost entered a cemetery.

Even during the winter months London was and still is a great city. It was quite an experience to travel around London and to visit museums, historical sites and places of interest. Naturally, I had pictures taken of myself outside many of the great sites, which I sent back home to my family. People worked hard regardless of their race, colour, age or gender. It was not the England I had anticipated. I could not help reflecting that, far from being a land of milk and honey, it was quite difficult for most working class families, a life of hard work extreme and difficult conditions, to earn a reasonable wage. I learnt a great deal by touring Inner and Outer London from the top deck of the red buses during the day and evenings. I visited The British Museum in London, it was established in 1753 and first opened to the public in 1759, and considered to be one of the world's greatest museums of human history and culture. It was a popular destination and I visited it several times. The museum's permanent collection, numbering some eight million works, was amongst the finest, most comprehensive, and largest in existence. The collection originated from all continents, illustrating and documenting the history and story of human art, cultural achievements and inventions from the beginning of life on earth. The museum also reflected the British colonial footprint and the acquisition of priceless exhibits taken by various means from countries during the colonial era. I read a great deal about British history, politics, trade unions and socio-economic issues. I also learnt a great deal from watching television and listening to people at work, at public meetings, trade union and political meetings, as well as the radio.

However, there were lots of opportunities for learning new skills and I was determined to fulfil my dreams to become educated and return to Guyana with wealth and ambitions to become either a top politician or a charismatic trade union leader, but most of all to help my family and others out of poverty. I tried very hard to develop my skills and abilities to ensure progression in employment, education and training, but it was not easy. Working long hours to support myself and my relatives in Guyana was quite a struggle. I worked every bit of overtime that was available to me, whilst taking full advantage of education and training opportunities.

Becoming a trade union and political activist

I had had a keen interest in trade union and politics since starting fulltime work at a young age in Guyana. I was a trade union member before I was fourteen years old in Guyana and I joined the Transport and General Workers Union (TGWU) at Alperton and became a member of the TGWU Branch Committee at the age of twenty. The TGWU, like the other public sector unions such as the National Union of Railwaymen (NUR) and the Association of Locomotives, Engineers and Firemen (ASLEF) were not very sympathetic to black workers. Whilst they generally welcomed their financial contributions through membership they were more supportive towards their white members.

Black workers were disproportionately represented in the public sector especially transport and the Health Service. White workers generally perceived the influx of black workers as undesirable and threats to their positions and status. Black workers were replacing many white workers in jobs characterised by unsocial hours of work; low pay and least desirable by white workers, many of whom were either promoted, or had left for more desirable jobs in other sectors of the economy. Prejudice and racial discrimination were common in most workplaces in Britain and practised regularly by business people, managers, workers and even trade unions in certain circumstances. I tried to leave the buses on many occasions but it was difficult to find a job in an office, or even a factory. So I stayed on the buses. I joined the Labour Party whilst I was on the buses and became active both in the unions and the Party which were almost inseparable at the time as the Trades Union Movement had given birth to the Labour Party as their political arm in Parliament. I very soon became active in speaking against racism in Britain and within the workplace and the Labour Movement.

Race relations in Britain were at a relatively low point. The flow of black immigrants from the Commonwealth increased substantially until the ban on free entry to Commonwealth immigrants in 1962, through the Immigration Act. The increasing flow to "beat the ban" was matched by the increase in tension between Black and white workers; deterioration in race relations; alarming media reports and racist comments and behaviour from white people. Despite this racial tension and racism within the unions I was determined to become involved and to support the struggle for workers' rights. The Labour Party, born out of the deliberations of the Trade Union movement in their desire to secure Parliamentary representation in order to procure the status and improve the advancement of workers, was closely linked at all levels to the Labour Party. I began to participate in both Trade Union and Labour Party activities and represented the TGWU on various committees. Alperton garage had a multi-racial workplace and some busy and diverse bus routes.

A number of the bus routes passed through areas with relatively high numbers of Commonwealth immigrants. For example, the 187 bus on which I regularly worked passed through Acton, Harlesden, Kensal Rise, Kilburn and Park Royal. Harlesden and Park Royal had massive industrial areas engaged in manufacturing. The Jubilee Clock was a well-known landmark for picking up and dropping large numbers of black immigrants who worked in the neighbouring industrial estates. On Sundays Alperton operated some buses on the number 18 route from Sudbury Town to London Bridge. The number 18 bus route was quite challenging particularly along the Harrow Road, Harlesden and Stonebridge Road areas. There were a sizeable number of Irish and black men who frequented the Prince of Wales Public House and other pubs along the route who were extremely difficult, particularly after closing time due to intoxication and high spirits. Black bus conductors and even drivers were by far more vulnerable to this undesirable behaviour, which often resulted in assaults, harassment and abuse.

As a country boy whose culture, understanding and experience were rapidly changing, I was on the whole, happy with my life in England so far. Each day I would reflect on my country of origin; my family and my life in this strange environment. I occasionally met a newcomer from Guyana on the buses and we would exchange addresses and catch up with the latest news about home. We did not have access to a telephone and frequently lost such contacts with people. The different Caribbean accents were by this time familiar to me. I could identify the Bajans (Barbadians) Guyanese, Trinidadians, St, Lucians and Jamaicans. I could also broadly identify the Irish, Scottish and Welsh accents. This was useful because I was able to select the sort of people I would befriend during and after the training sessions. As fellow economic immigrants to London we understood and empathised with some of the issues and concerns about living a long way from home. It was easier to make friends with the Irish, Welsh and Scottish than with the English who were much more reluctant to accept black people as friends.

It was quite common then, to see notices in shop and front room windows stating "room to let, sorry no blacks, Irish or dogs or children". Different versions of such advertisements were openly displayed.

I was also surprised at the level of discrimination, antagonism and prejudice amongst the various immigrant groups from Africa, the Caribbean and other parts of the world. The experience of colonisation with its "divide and rule" tactics created a situation where people from each Caribbean country had a relatively negative impression of people in other Caribbean countries. The people of Asian and African descents were sometimes antagonistic towards each other. People from the larger islands such as Jamaica had little time for, or anything good to say about the people from the smaller islands. People kept very much to their own ethnic, cultural, religious and geographical group.

During my first year in London most of the older colleagues I worked with, were always telling me about the Second World War – 1939-45, how Britain won the war, almost single handed, as the 'Americans arrived late on the scene; the Soviet Union were not quite on our side; the French were cowards for allowing the Germans to occupy their country: the Italians were Fascists and supported Germany. None of the men who boasted about Britain's role and their individual involvement in the War ever talked about the two million black and Asian soldiers and civilians who were casualties in the War, and fought on behalf of Britain and the British Empire. No one mentioned the involvement of the men and women from the Caribbean, Africa, Asia and America who were stationed in Britain and fought on the frontline in Europe against fascism. Many of the black and Asian soldiers, who were involved in the army, air force, navy and in civilian jobs experienced racism not only from the local white population, but also from their comrades in the armed forces. The racism that existed in America followed the white soldiers to Europe. After a while, I was able to respond to these men with confidence, because I did my best to read as much history I could as well as listening the people at Speakers Corner, I was able to explain that the Soviet Union played a major part, and lost more people in battle and in the civilian population than Britain, France, and America put together. The battles against the German elite forces on Soviet soil resulted in the loss of nearly ten million people, over twelve times the size of the British casualties.

Despite the sometimes heated arguments mainly between Englishmen and black workers, there were many occasions when genuine friendship developed between us. We got on a great deal better with people from Wales, Scotland and Ireland, especially with the Catholics from the Northern Ireland and the Republic of Ireland. Many workers who were not English developed a special relationship with black workers, probably because we were all economic migrants to England and were experiencing some of the irrational and stereotypical perceptions of outsiders from different cultural, racial and religious backgrounds. There was a fair bit of common and shared feelings, attitudes, experience and behaviour amongst these various ethnic groups who had left their homeland and had arrived in England in search of work and betterment. Inter-racial and inter-ethnic friendship developed to the point where people ended up getting married or living as partners and raising families.

As a busman I was constantly aware of the level of racial prejudice against the non-white busmen. There were often disagreements between black and white workers and the situation was no better in other public and private sector occupations where some white workers perceived black workers as threats. It was common knowledge that Britain wanted workers. The government encouraged immigration and workers were generally welcomed by employers, especially within the public sector. However, antagonism against black people and the opposition to further entry by the average indigenous adult was gaining momentum. Expressions of opposition to black immigration by politicians, white trade unionists and people who were living in inner city areas with poor housing, services and environment opposed black people living in their neighbourhoods. They were quite vocal through the media. The national newspapers were constantly running stories which portrayed Black people as dirty; lazy; carriers of disease; creating slums; adversely affecting the education of British children in schools; putting pressures on the health service; living on unemployment benefits and corrupting young white women.

Centuries of Black presence in Britain

Britain has always been a mixed society made up of immigrants. If we go far enough back into history, we could argue that everyone who lives in Britain today had his or her origins elsewhere. From the Bronze Age and the Neolithic migrants who travelled to North West Europe 40,000 years ago, to the various armies including the Romans, Saxons, Vikings, and Normans, to the waves of immigrants and refugees from France, Ireland, Russia, Eastern Europe, Africa, Asia, and the Caribbean; the fact is that most people in Britain today are either immigrants or descendants of immigrants. It is correct to say that at some time in European history all the inhabitants were people with black and brown skins. Black people actually discovered Europe long before it was populated by people with white skins, blond hair and blue eyes.

Europeans, especially Britain, given its long colonial past, including its involvement in the Trans-Atlantic slave trade involving Africans for centuries, has benefited from immigration and ethnic diversity throughout its history in all areas of social, economic, cultural, scientific, and recreational activities. Each group of immigrants has helped to enrich the life and progression of British society.

I was very interested in the historical insight into the presence of Black people in Britain, their backgrounds and experience, the way in which they have been portrayed, and the contributions that they have made to British society over the centuries and, in particular, over the last 400 years.

Most people know about the Black and Asian immigrants who arrived in Britain during or after the Second World War (1939-1945), which began in Europe and claimed the lives of over 20 million people. Very few people are aware of the fact that there were Black people before 400 AD. Septimus Severus, a Romanised

African commander, who became the Emperor of Rome in 193 AD, led many Roman soldiers into Britain. He arrived in Britain in 196 AD and was stationed in York. Among the Roman soldiers stationed in Britain were hundreds of Negroes who, under the command of Severus, "restored the Hadrian Wall and helped to save Britain from the barbarians" (from Roman Britain, by R. G. Collingwood, pp. 38-9). Some historians believe that black people were present in Britain even earlier than this.

What is certain, however, is that Black people had established sizeable permanent settlements in parts of Britain by the late 16th Century. In 1555, it was reported that, "the five Africans who visited England were stared at very hard indeed by local inhabitants … along with the 250 elephant tusks, 36 casks of maleguetta pepper, and over 400 pounds of 22 carat gold [from their country]" (from Staying Power, The History of Black People in Britain, by Peter Fryer, p.7). These Africans were slaves brought to England by John Locke when he returned from Guinea. He educated them and trained them to act as interpreters for traders.

Africans were brought to Britain when British merchants and explorers journeyed into Africa with imperialistic and colonial ambitions. Sir John Hawkins, who was among the first Englishmen to benefit from the lucrative triangular trade in slaves, took at least 300 Africans from the Guinea Coast. These Africans were either captured by his men or sold to him and transported to Haiti and the Dominican Republic. Hawkins sold his cargo of men to the Spaniards for £10,000 worth of pearls, hides, sugar, and ginger. Having realised a profit of some 12 per cent on the venture, Hawkins was financed by Queen Elizabeth I to make a second slave-hunting journey in 1564 on the 600-ton vessel, The Jesus of Lubeck, and a crew of 300 men. Hawkins' coat of arms included a portrayal of three black men shackled with slave collars and another black man bound with rope.

During the decades following Hawkins' journeys to Africa, many more slave traders and merchants set sail from Plymouth to engage in the triangular trade. As a consequence, many Black people were brought to Britain to be sold as slaves or servants. The growing population of Black people in Britain caused considerable concern among some people, prompting Queen Elizabeth I to sign an order to repatriate Black people.

On 11 August 1596, the Queen's Privy Council instructed the Lord Mayor of London and the sheriffs of other towns that:

> "Her Majesty understanding that there are late divers blackamoors brought into the realme, of which kind there are already too manie, considering how God hath blessed this land with great immense of people of our owne nation ... those kinds of people should be sent forth of the lande."

The Queen's attempt to rid England of Black people did not succeed. In 1601, she issued a further proclamation in which she declared:

> "[The Queen is] highly discontented to understand the great numbers of Negars and Blackamoores which are crept into this realm ... who are fostered and relieved here to the great annoyance of her own people that want relief which these people consume as also for that the most of them are infidels, having no understanding of Christ or his Gospel. The Queen had therefore given 'especial commandment that the said kind of people should be banished and discharged out of the Her Majesty's dominions."

As the slave trade intensified and its connection with the triangular trade consolidated, the Europeans and, in particular, the British used the enormous profits from the trade to develop the industrial revolution and to build rapid prosperity at home. The colonisation of most of Africa, North, Central, and South America, and the Caribbean provided opportunities for Europeans at home and abroad. It enabled Europeans to control world trade and development through brute force and economic and political arrangements carefully designed to serve the interests of the European economies. In 1788, the Committee of the Company of Merchants trading with Africa declared, "The effects of this trade to

Great Britain are beneficial to an infinite extent ... there is hardly any branch of commerce in which this nation does not derive some advantage from it."

> "In 1788, the manufacturer, Samuel Taylor told the Lords of Trade that the value of goods supplied each year to Africa from Manchester was about £200,000, of which £180,000 was for the sole purpose of buying black slaves; about 18,000 men, women, and children were employed in this manufacture, which had a capital of at least £300,000. Our trade with Africa is very profitable to the nation. In general it has this advantage, that it carries no money out and not only supplies our plantations with servants, but brings in a deal of bullion for those that are sold to the Spanish West Indies ... The supplying of our plantations with Negroes is of the extraordinary advantage to us that the planting of sugar and tobacco and carrying on trade there could not be supplied without them; which plantations ... are the great cause of our treasure proceeds chiefly from the labour of Negroes in the plantations." (From Staying Power, The History of Black People in Britain, by Peter Fryer)

For over 150 years, black slaves were bought, sold, abused, and exploited. Torture, sexual abuse, starvation, exploitation, and degradation characterised their lives. Children as young as six years old were abused and tormented by their masters. The rich and powerful – from the nobility to the politicians; merchants, manufacturers, and clergy; - gained enormous wealth and influence through the enslavement and exploitation of Africans. One man wrote in 1745,

> "If we have no Negroes, we can have no sugars, tobacco, rice, rum, and other commodities. Consequently, the public revenue, arising from the importation of plantation produce, must be annihilated. And this will turn many hundreds of thousands of British manufacturers into beggars ... The Negro trade therefore ... may be justly esteemed an inexhaustible fund of wealth and Naval power to this nation."

The slave trade was "the first principle and foundation of all the rest; the main spring of the machine, which sets every wheel in motion."

Between 1630 and 1807, British slave merchants netted a profit of about £12 million from the trade of at least 2.5 million African people (*from Staying Power, The History of Black People in Britain*, by Peter Fryer).

In 1764, someone wrote to the Gentleman's Magazine complaining about the presence of Negro servants in London. He claimed that some 20,000 Negro servants were causing concerns, albeit that there were only 676, 250 people living in London at the time. No mention was made of the free Negroes who were part of London's life.

"The practice of importing Negro servants into these Kingdoms is said to be already a grievance that requires a remedy and yet it is every day encouraged insomuch that the number in this metropolis only is supposed to be near 20,000. The main objection to their importation is that they cease to consider themselves as slaves in this free country, nor will they put up with the inequality of treatment, nor more willingly perform the laborious offices of servitude than our own people and if put to do it, are generally sullen, spiteful, treacherous, and revengeful. It is therefore highly impolite to introduce them as servants here, where that rigour and severity is impracticable, to make them useful." (*From London Life in the Eighteenth Century*, by M. Dorothy George).

According to writer, Henry Mayhew, "It is only common fairness to say that Negroes seldom, if ever, shirk work. Their only trouble is to obtain it. Those who have seen many Negroes employed in Liverpool will know that they are hardworking, patient, and often underpaid."

Not a great deal has changed over the centuries, as Black people have always been grossly over-represented in unemployment, disadvantage, and poverty statistics. Black people in Britain, Europe and in the colonies have been exploited, abused and discriminated against because of their skin colour and lifestyles. As a result Black people in Britain had to make the best of their lives. The majority of Black people in Britain during the 15th to 18th Centuries were forcefully brought here as human cargo to be bought and sold and engaged as servants in dismal and abusive conditions. Some bought their freedom by employing themselves as entertainers, domestic labourers, apprentices, traders, sailors, and businessmen. The majority of those who arrived in the 20th Century were economic migrants, encouraged to settle in Britain because of the shortage of workers in certain key areas of public services such as transport and health services.

It was estimated in the 2001 census that around 1 in every 5 people living in London is from a visible ethnic minority background. About 60 per cent of all non-white people in Britain are in London.

Before the restrictions imposed by the Commonwealth Immigration Act, 1962, black and Asians – children of the Empire – were coming to Britain in small, but constant numbers during the 1950s and 1960s. Between 1955 and 1960 some 211,600 Caribbean's and Asians had arrived in Britain. Of these arrivals 33,070 were from India; 17,120 from Pakistan – including Bangladesh; 96,180 from Jamaica and 65,270 were from other parts of the Caribbean. Between January 1961 and the implementation of the Commonwealth Immigration Act 1962, which took effect on 1 July 1962, a further 191,060 people from the Caribbean, India and Pakistan had arrived. Many of them started their journey to Britain earlier than planned in order to arrive before 1st July and therefore to "beat the ban". Despite the fact that the total black population in the early 1960's totalled less than two per cent of the total population, many white people and large sections of the media expressed forceful concerns about being "overrun by blacks" and "swamped by people of an inferior culture and lifestyle". Racism in Britain goes back a very long way, at least since the invasion of Britain by the Roman Emperor Julius Caesar in 55 and 54 BC. The Emperor Claudius would have also encountered, during his successful invasion of Britain in AD 43, the tribe described by Caesar as people with 'black skins and curly hair', whose ferocity was a stumbling block in securing victory for Caesar.

For most people in Britain, black immigrants began to arrive in Britain, in noticeable numbers with the landing of the SS Empire Windrush, which arrived in Tilbury Docks, London in June 1948, with 493 paid passengers mainly from Jamaica. The debates about the presence of black people in Britain for many centuries have been associated with unwelcome aspects associated with immigration. Waves of white and black immigrants to Britain have suffered from prejudice, discrimination and negative stereotyping, and the situation was no different for black people, except that they were easily identifiable in skin colour, cultural and religious lifestyle and practices. White immigrants were hardly noticeable after the second or third generation. The fears expressed by the indigenous population against black immigrants, has hardly changed after third and fourth generations. The reasons given for such resentment and fear have always been the same. Blacks have always been accused of increasing the population of Britain which is such a small over-crowded Island; they are a burden to the state and the socioeconomic system, through accessing benefits, burdening the National Health Service and the education system; adding to the problems of unemployment; being part of the problem of housing shortages; being more likely to commit crime and engage in terrorism; being unpatriotic; engaging in drugs, prostitution and illegal activities; and exploiting the welfare state.

Part 2

Chapter 6:

Marriage and family life

Before I met Doreen

I had a number of casual relationships with young women from various Caribbean Islands and Britain, before I met my wife Doreen. I had a special relationship with Cynthia, from Jamaica who worked in the bus canteen in Alperton Garage, before pursuing her career as a nurse, at Papworth Hospital in Cambridge. Cynthia was three years older than me, and she gave birth to our son, Richard, which interrupted her training. She was an experienced mother who had two children before she left Jamaica for London. She also had her children's father in Jamaica who was waiting to join her in London at some stage. Neither of us wanted children, nor did we have plans to stay together. Cynthia always talked about getting together with her children's father and uniting her family after she finished her studies. It was convenient for us to live together at the time, as it was difficult to secure accommodation in London for Black people and indeed most immigrants. It was the period when notices would appear in shop windows, newspapers and in private homes – "room to let, sorry no colours, Irish, children or dogs". The most common one was "sorry, no colours. Few people used the word Black in those days. Cynthia and I started off sharing a room and a bed in Kilburn. We designated our particular side of the bed and at first promised to respect the unmarked divide between us. The rent was around £3 per week, for one room on the upper floor. We had a paraffin heater which we used for cooking, heating drying clothes, boiling water for tea and washing ourselves. There was a communal bathroom and toilet, but no kitchen available to us. The landlady was a fierce looking Cockney who had other tenants. She wore a turban and aprons all day and spent a lot of her time standing behind her net curtains in the ground floor of her four bedrooms, terraced house. We used to call people like her curtain peepers; they followed every movement that took place outside their homes.

After Cynthia started her training in Cambridge we kept in touch with each other and saw each other occasionally. Cynthia found a full time child minder for Richard who was discovered to be severely disabled mentally with autism and a number of other illnesses, which prevented him from being able to read or write, and even at the age of fifty he requires twenty four hour care. Soon after Richard was born, I had very little contact with Cynthia, she was determined to complete her studies and to start a nursing career in America. I started to have casual relationships with different young women until I met Doreen on a 187 bus on her way home from grammar school one evening, in July 1962, and she later became my wife on 23 August 1963.

Cynthia was a person with a strong, no nonsense personality. Although she was very loving and caring, she missed her children badly. They were staying with her mother in Jamaica and she was sending money to support them. There were lots of disagreements with her children's father who was living in Jamaica but only rarely seeing their children. He was hoping to join her and bring the children when it was possible. Unfortunately he didn't seem to feel able to wait as long as was needed; he started a relationship with someone else. The presence of Richard did not help matters for Cynthia. During her training in Cambridge Cynthia started to write to me almost daily, I could see that her plans to set up home with her children and their father was falling apart. I was unprepared for marriage of taking on responsibility for Richard and his siblings.

The last time I saw Cynthia was when I told her that I was not interested in continuing a physical relationship with her. I also asked her to make arrangements for me to see and support Richard. She refused any support or, to let me know who was looking after Richard and whether I could visit him. I also told her that I had met a student whose name was Doreen, and we were very serious about having a steady relationship. I did not see or hear from Cynthia after this meeting for more than five years, when I met her at a friend's house in Wembley.

All attempts to contact Cynthia directly or through her sister Merzel, who ended up marrying my friend Milton, from Guyana, and living in Wembley, completely failed. Cynthia had informed Merzel and Milton not to let me have details of her or Richard's address, or telephone number. Cynthia got married to a Jamaican man and they had at least more two children, before moving to America. She brought her mother and her first children to America to be with them too. The next time I saw Cynthia and Richard was in 2007, when I visited her in her comfortable home in the Bronx, in New York. Richard was forty five years old, still mentally disabled, but physically quite fit and well. Cynthia was retired and separated from her husband. I am so pleased to have renewed my acquaintance with my son Richard. Cynthia and Richard have kept in close contact with Doreen and me since 2007 and we send financial support to help Cynthia with Richard's care from time to time.

Cynthia, although retired from work is busier than ever as not only Richard is severely mentally ill, but another son conceived with her last husband also suffers from precisely the same problems, and cannot read or write and requires constant care. Clearly, there is a genetic inference from Cynthia's end that affected two of her four children. Her sister also had a son who suffered from a lesser form of this illness, but he overcame this illness in his teenage years.

One of my biggest worries is how would I find a way of helping with Richard, should Cynthia die before me. My wife and I have set aside a substantial sum for Richard when I die. Cynthia is aware of the contents of my will. Although Richard was born in England, he does not have a valid British passport, something which I have asked Cynthia to secure for him. I would like to visit him a great deal more, but this is not possible due to my deteriorating health. Doreen and Cynthia have been friends for some time and Doreen always remind me to send support for Richard and Cynthia. I am so pleased that we have a friendly and open relationship between us.

Meeting Doreen

I first met Doreen in the summer of 1962, shortly after her seventeenth birthday and after Cynthia and I had become estranged. Doreen was living with her parents in Greenford less than two miles from where I lived in Sudbury, near Wembley. She was a pupil at Willesden County Grammar School and she boarded my bus number 187 one evening after school. I had seen her on a few occasions before on the bus with lots of other passengers. She was very good looking and she caught my eye more than once, but I never had a chance to talk to her own her own. On this particular evening she boarded my bus after kissing her boyfriend goodbye. She decided to sit on the upper deck in the back seat so she could wave to her friend after the bus had departed from the stop at Harlesden near the Jubilee Clock. Doreen was the only passenger on the upper deck of the bus for a large part of her journey home, as the bus route between Harlesden and Greenford contained a lot of industrial activities.

I checked her bus pass and started a conversation with her. I told her that I had seen her on my bus on previous occasions in the company of other people, and I wanted to chat with her, but was unable to do so, because she was always with other friends. Doreen used to live in Kensal Rise, a short distance from her school, but her family moved to Greenford some five miles away soon after she started Grammar School. After checking her pass and having a brief chat with her, I asked her if I could see her one weekend and we could go to the pictures. To my surprise and delight she readily agreed. We decided to meet at the bus stop, near the cinema in South Harrow, a short distance from her home a week later. We went to the cinema, sat at the rear and had a few kisses and cuddles. Doreen was quite forward and I got the impression she had had a number of boyfriends prior to and possibly after meeting me. I believe that it was not the intention of either of us to have a serious relationship, even though we agreed to meet again soon.

Doreen was quite a charming and bouncy young lady who was full of life and energy. I was five feet six and a half inches and weighed around the same weight as her, around nine to ten stones. She was of course highly intelligent, and had lots of teenage friends. The next time we met it was at a fancy dress party where I met lots of her friends who were quite a lively bunch. I met her best friend Barbara and her boyfriend John who had a motorbike. Doreen was dressed in a skirt and a white shirt borrowed from her father. She had long brown hair and seemed to enjoy life. Doreen grew up as an only child in her family, although she had a much older sister, Joan who had lived in Canada with her family since Doreen was an infant. Her parents were also very mature and typically working class when I eventually met them.

The party was very lively and some people were drinking alcohol quite freely. Doreen was not keen on alcohol, but enjoyed a cigarette. I felt somewhat out of place as I was the only non-white person at the party, even though they were all very friendly. I felt a sense of differences not only in race and class, but also in intellectual and academic achievements. I did not see Doreen for a couple of weeks after the party, and decided to leave it to her to contact me if she wanted to do so. I was two years older than Doreen and although I had a couple of casual girlfriends at the time I took a strong liking to her after our first few dates. I was a reasonably popular teenager whose nick name at the garage was Elvis. I was a keen Elvin Presley fan and I used to copy Elvis' hairstyle. I used to break an egg and used the white parts to rub into my hair, which made is possible for me to have the Elvis hairstyle. I used to comb it forward, then backwards and it used to be stiff all day. Elvis was the King of Rock 'n' Roll and adored by women and men. I bought a second hand guitar, which I still have to this day, but have never managed to play a decent tune on it. I even copied the Elvis walk and was able to do some of the Elvis movements on the dance floor. I continued to see other casual girlfriends, although I felt attached to Doreen. I subsequently discovered that her parents were not keen on my relationship with her, for a number of reasons.

They were very committed to their daughter's education and career, as she wanted to be a teacher, and did not want anyone to frustrate her career plans. In addition, I was from a visible ethnic minority background, and people with my skin colour were seen by the British people as inferior due to centuries of indoctrination, associated with slavery, imperialism, colonialism and stereotyping. I was also a manual worker and not quite the type of person they had wished their daughter to spend her life with. Doreen's father, Joseph Cash, was a fierce and bigoted person who hated Black people. He totally rejected mixed relationships, especially one involving his daughter. Mr Cash was born in a large Southern Irish family who had settled in England and lived in Suffolk and London. Her mother was much less racially prejudiced than her father, but equally committed against a mixed relationship involving her daughter. I believe Doreen felt tormented, uncertain and apprehensive about our relationship, but was drawn towards me the more pressure her parents put on her to break off our relationship.

Mixed relationships between people from different visible ethnic minority backgrounds were very uncommon and met with almost universal disapproval by the British and indeed white people in general. Such relationships were illegal in a number of countries such as South Africa, and were subjected to enormous social, cultural and economic rejections in Britain, Europe and America. Mixed couples were often met with stares, verbal abuse, harassment, bullying, discrimination and even physical violence. White women associating with black men were labelled as prostitutes, traitors to their race and people of low moral standing. Such attitudes, behaviour and perceptions were common in Britain despite the fact that black people had lived here for many centuries. I believe Doreen had assured her parents at some stage that she had ceased our relationship and that she had another boyfriend who was English and white. She gave them the impression that she saw him regularly, especially on Sundays, when she was supposed to be attending church with him, but was seeing me instead. Doreen became my one and only, and special girlfriend within a couple of months after I checked her bus pass that evening in September 1962.

I was warned by a number of people to stay away from Doreen and "white girls" and that I was totally unsuitable to have a relationship with Doreen. On several occasions I tried to avoid seeing Doreen, and on a couple of occasions she turned up at the garage and waited for me to finish my shift. One day she suggested to me that we should run away to Gretna Green in Scotland as soon as she was eighteen to get married, her parents' consent would not be required. I was terribly confused at the time, as I was trying to work as many hours overtime as possible, send money home to my family in Guyana; worrying about Cynthia and Richard and also trying to study at Harrow Technical College during the evenings. Doreen would often write to me, sometimes twice each day and would call round to my address to see me. I could see that she was desperately in love with me and I was with her. I was concerned about her education and that she was unhappy at home. She also bunked off school on a couple of occasions so we could be together.

It was around November 1962 that I was invited to meet Doreen's parents and her father giving me very long, passionate and tense lectures on British history, identity, way of life and the glorious and generous history of the British Empire. He also told me a great deal about the 1939-45 War and the role he played in defending Britain. Much of what he told me was fabricated. He used to go on at length about Britain's long standing burden and commitment towards civilising the rest of the world, especially Africa, Asia and the Caribbean. He boasted about the wealth, influence and power of Britain, and also enlightened me on the determination and reasons why it was essential for Britain to keep foreigners out as it was a small island that had very little resources for its own people, let alone accommodating foreigners with undesirable habits and customs, who were unwelcome as settlers. I was pleased when he told me that I would be allowed to see her on occasions, but I was not allowed to distract her from her studies and her career. I was terrified of Mr Cash and promised him that I would obey his wishes.

It was very difficult for me to either interrupt him let alone disagree with him. I felt that this angry white man, nearly six feet tall and a great deal stronger than I was could not bring himself to listening to me, or to simply find out about me, as a person. He saw me as an uneducated, foreigner who was totally unsuitable for his daughter. To make matters worse I was a Black man that would not be acceptable in racist Britain and his daughter would forever suffer as a result. Doreen's mum, like many working class women stayed at home, not only because she was disabled, but because she saw her role as supporting her husband as the bread winner and to look after all his needs. In those days, men were generally seen as the boss of the household and it was not the darn thing for wives to be independent minded, or to overrule them. Her name was Edith and she was much friendlier towards me, especially when her husband was not around. She was a marvellous cook, who also kept herself busy by making clothes, and doing active tasks around the home despite her disability caused by problems with her spine. I remember spending Christmas Day 1962, at her home and I was treated to a great deal of her hospitality.

It was in many ways quite strange and also challenging for me to be a guest in the home of an English family. It was a social, cultural and racial experience I had never previously felt would happen, coming from a rural peasant, colonial background. As a child up to sixteen years old I felt like the rest of the Guyanese population that the white race was grossly superior to the darker races, and that God had created such a hierarchical situation. The superiority of the white race was as natural as any phenomenon accepted by non-white people. In fact we thought that as God made us so different and placed the white race in control of us, it was natural that God was indeed a white man. We had seen photographs of Jesus Christ, his mother Mary and father Joseph with blond hair and blue eyes and had accepted the history of the world as it was described by the slavers, imperialists, colonialists and modern day rulers of the world, as our superiors in every respect. We questioned ourselves about our past, our history and our civilisations and we were convinced that we had nothing in our past or history that we could claim to be positive, glorious, innovative or civilised. This is the legacy of centuries of domination, exploitation, indoctrination, conditioning and misinformation

Our glorious history in Africa, Asia, South and Central America was deliberately distorted to persuade us that the darker races had contributed nothing of significance to language, science, architecture, medicine, literature, philosophy, art, manufacturing, commerce, engineering, education, political structures, transport, communication or anything useful. We were in darkness, ignorance, squalor, helplessness, and in a permanent state of war with our neighbours as we were too uncivilised to create wealth, opportunities, and resources, social, economic, cultural and political structures to procure the status and increase the advancement of our respective nations throughout our history. Of course none of this is true and it was the darker races that had given the modern world all the things necessary to advance themselves. There was ancient civilisation outside Europe thousands of years and long before the ice-age which covered Europe in thick ice. There were also modern civilisations in Africa, Asia, North and Central America comparable to anywhere in Europe before the Europeans including, Christopher Columbus set sail in 1492, to discover distant lands that were already populated by people who had had sophisticated civilisations for hundreds, if not thousands of years. My relationship with Doreen and her parents forced me to take a long hard look at myself, my environment and everything on this planet earth that were connected to human existence and civilisation.

I saw Doreen when I could. We were both dreamers, not recognising that love alone can never breakdown all the barriers, nor would it secure a life that we would wish to have during a lifetime together. Doreen did concentrate on her studies and did reasonably well, despite all the personal baggage and uncertainties she was carrying. Doreen and I were writing to each other regularly almost every week. We used to telephone each other using public call boxes in the streets. I was unable to see Doreen during the evenings when I was on afternoon and late shifts on the buses.

1963 – A special and memorable year

In January 1963, the North Vietnamese, Communist Viet Cong won their first major battle against the South Vietnamese regime supported by America. I took a lot of interest in this war and even wrote to the North Vietnamese government offering to join their army and fight their enemy. I received a letter thanking me for my support and suggesting that I could support them by collecting money and goods and sending it through the support network in Britain. Incidentally, I also offered my support to the revolutionary leadership in Cuba in 1962, which met with a similar response. On 14 January, George Wallace, a racist Southerner became the Governor of Alabama, a State in the USA with a large number of black people many of whom were the descendants of African slaves going back to at least the 18th Century. Black people in America were for most white Americans, not seen as equals, and segregation in schools, colleges, universities, public places and services. Although Blacks were able to vote at political elections, many of them were too afraid to do so, especially in the South due to, racist intimidation assaults and even murders.

In his inauguration speech Wallace declared 'segregation now, segregation tomorrow and segregation for ever'. On 16 April 1963, Revered Dr Martin Luther King Junior wrote a number of letters from prison, calling for civil rights for black people. It also appeared that Africa as a continent was beginning to work towards unity, by setting up on 25 May the Organisation for African Unity. Race and racism was on the international agenda and there were a number of new organisations set up by black people in Britain to combat racial discrimination, including attacks, police brutality and exclusion from many areas of social economic and political life. In the summer of 1963, John Kennedy, the President of America made an important speech on 11 June supporting civil rights for all Americans, regardless of race or colour. This was followed on 28 August 1963, with a historical speech from Dr King, 'I have a Dream'. This speech came just five days after Doreen and I were married at the Willesden County Register

Office. Of course many other great events took place that year which included, for example, the news that the first woman, Valentina Tereshkova, from the Soviet Union was involved in a space flight on 16 June. Betty Friedman, an American author launched her famous book,' Femine Mystique', which re-awakened the women's movement. The radical women's movement has supported to a large extent the struggles of black people for equality in Britain. CLR James and other black activists were very involved in the suffragette movement and worked closely with Emeline and Sylvia Pankhurst and others, in the early 19th Century, for women's emancipation and the right to vote, which was achieved partly in 1918 and fully in 1928. Despite Kennedy's speech both the racists and the ant-racists stepped up their campaigns and on 15 September 1963, white racists bombed a Baptist Churched used by black people in Birmingham, Alabama that killed four people and injured twenty two others including children. A popular black American singer and his band were arrested for trying to register at a 'white's only hotel' in Louisiana. The worst event in my view took place in Dallas Texas, when J F Kennedy, the President of America was gunned down, on 22 November 1963 whilst driving in an open top car with his wife and others. Unlike the majority of black people in Britain, I got very involved in the civil rights movement in London. I wanted to be part of the change I dreamed of, but circumstances saw the decline of my direct involvement with the black liberation struggles in London and my regular visits to Speakers Corner.

Getting married and moving to Luton

The year 1963 was a very special and memorable year for me. Not only did I get married to Doreen on 23 August, but also became a home owner, moved to Luton from London and was confirmed as a father whose child was due in February the following year.

One Sunday morning Doreen informed her parents that she was going to church, but instead she came to see me. I had a single room at my address, which I shared with three other men from Guyana who were all older than I was. So whenever Doreen came to see me we would go up to my room in this three-bed roomed terrace house have some tea and play some records. On this particular day she informed me that she had missed her period for three months and she was concerned that she was pregnant. I was in a state of shock and I had no relative to turn to for support, or advice. I believe she informed her parents of her concern and she was taken by her father to see the doctor, which was almost at the end of my road, near Sudbury Town Station. Doctor Cree confirmed that was pregnant and had probably conceived in June 1963.

Directly after the confirmation of pregnancy, Doreen telephoned me and told me that she was pregnant, and her father told her to tell me that I 'would have to marry' her. I was summoned by Doreen's father, through her to see him at her home. I was petrified about this encounter, but nevertheless plucked up enough courage to see the family. Mr Cash was a lot calmer than I had expected and he welcomed me without any violence, sat me down and explained what he had in mind for Doreen and me. We sat before him in silence, like two very naughty children, about to be severely disciplined by a scary head teacher. We sat on the settee and he sat on a chair in front of us. He told us we had to get married, and then move out of London as soon as possible and not to return to his house, after Doreen had moved out. For him, Doreen had destroyed the future he had planned for her – to complete her studies, at Grammar School, enter teacher training and build a professional career as a teacher. It was also what Doreen had wanted. We both accepted his instructions and we set about making arrangements for our wedding. It was during the summer holidays and Doreen had already taken her final GCE Advanced Level examinations and had left school. She was now just eighteen and I was three weeks away from my twentieth birthday. Doreen had a part-time job at Sainsbury near Greenford and I used to visit her at work. Each time I entered the shop when it was quiet, Doreen was nowhere to be seen, and she would then emerge from under the counter where she was busy eating cheese, biscuits and other bits of food, claiming that she was eating for two.

It was not uncommon for young people to get married in their teenage years during the sixties. I was asked by a number of girlfriends if I would consider getting married, before I met Doreen, but I always declined. My relationship with Doreen was an intensely loving one. I was madly in love with her; I could not get her out of my mind. I wrote to my parents in Guyana and told them about her and, I told them that I wanted to marry her, and they gave me their blessings. This was long before we knew she was pregnant. They told me to take her to Guyana later on so we could have a Hindu wedding and invite the whole village. My mother would have pretended to be a Queen for that day, sadly, it never happened that way. Even though I was committed to marrying Doreen I still had some difficulty envisaging mixed relationships that would last long into the future. A white person having a relationship with a black person and living a normal life was generally seen as problematic, not only by parents, relatives and friends, but also by the general public. Therefore all the mixed relationships I had before getting serious with Doreen were casual ones. There were also very few black or Asian teenagers in London around my age, as most of the non-white immigrants to Britain were men and people much older than myself.

So Doreen and I decided that we would get married at Willesden Registry Office on Saturday 23 August 1963 at eleven o' clock in the morning, having made all the necessary arrangements. I took the Saturday off work and we arranged to meet at the bus stop near her home outside the Greenwood Public House. We travelled on the 187 bus with our documents to the Registry Office and followed the instructions. We were informed that we needed a couple of witnesses and the couple waiting next on the list to get married kindly obliged to be our witnesses. After the wedding, we held hands, did some window shopping, bought some fish and chips to eat on the bus and made our way home to my room, in Central Road, Sudbury. We told everyone in the house that we were now married and they congratulated us.

After a couple of hours together contemplating our future, I walked Doreen to the bus stop, kissed her goodbye and waved as the bus disappeared in the distance. I returned to my room wrote a long letter to my sick and elderly parents, explaining what had taken place and begged them to forgive me for not involving them in one of the most important days in my life and theirs. In my view marriage is not simply an arrangement between two people, but a bond between families, as they can often be the key to a successful marriage. I do not believe that happiness in a marriage is entirely a matter of luck or chance; instead it is a valuable institution which creates the best framework to build and sustain a family. I had often thought of getting married with all my family and friends around me, to receive blessings, embrace them and thank them for helping me to prepare for the next stage in my life.

Doreen was eighteen and I was twenty years old, when we got married. We had very few possessions between us. We had nowhere to live together and little money. Between us we had a couple of old pots and pans, cups, plates, knives, forks, spoons and a few ornaments given to Doreen by her parents. My father-in-law took me to an estate agent, Rutherfords, in Ealing Road, Wembley, and they kindly helped me to complete a mortgage application form under the Greater London Council Overspill Scheme, that encouraged people to leave London due to overcrowding. Naturally, I was encouraged to lie about my age, claiming that I was twenty one years old and earning fifteen pounds each week as a panel beater instead of the less than ten pounds I earned as a busman. Mr Cash acted as a guarantor for us and helped us to raise the ninety five pounds deposit which included legal fees.

The agents agreed to drive us all the way to Luton and show us several properties. The first property was in Brook Street, an area known as the red light district then and still is to this day. We were showed an old property which the agent described as totally suitable for us, as there were couple of other black tenants nearby and only two minutes' walk to the heart of the town Centre. We rejected this property, after the woman next door approached us and asked us if we knew what had happened at that property, she went on to tell us that a murder had been committed in the property a few weeks earlier. The agent then took us to a property in Sundon Park, and we liked it straight away. It was number 16, Epping Way, with a small but nice front garden and a much larger rear garden. We were the first mixed race couple in Sundon Park for quite some time. The property was only a couple of years old. It was a modern semi-detached three bedroom house with a nice garden and a long driveway. The only problem was that the property was almost four miles from the town centre where I worked as a busman, on the London Country buses. The property was priced at £2,300 and the monthly repayments were £15.55 pence. This was around the average price for a modern property. Wages were low, but so were prices, as a loaf of bread cost only six or seven pence at the time.

About three weeks later Doreen and I set off from London carrying all our possessions with us in my suitcase and two large bags. We changed buses on four occasions on a journey lasting the best part of half a day. By this time I had accumulated a few books, personal belongings and a typewriter. Doreen also had some books, personal possessions, school certificates and mementoes, some clothes and everything else we owned was squeezed into the cheap, old-fashioned suitcase which had previously carried my even fewer possessions all the way from Guyana to England just a couple of years previously. What we were unable to carry in the suitcase we crammed into two large bags.

We arrived at our home and discovered that the outgoing family had left us a few bits of battered furniture and utensils. We had no heating except facilities for a coal fire and an electric heater. We had no beds, but a blanket and a couple of sheets of linen Doreen brought with her from her room. Doreen was over four months pregnant and we decided that she would stay at home and I would work all the hours I could as we now had a sizeable financial commitment. Having settled in our new home with our meagre possessions and expecting our first child in five months' time, we knew that life would be tough for us. We made a commitment to assist my sick parents in Guyana, and my four younger sisters who were all living in poverty in Leonora. Sending small sums to Guyana via postal orders on a regular basis caused us a lot of financial hardships. I often had to walk the four miles to and from work, as I was unable to pay the few pence fare on the local green buses, run by The Eastern National Bus Company that rejected my application for a job with them, even though I had a full public service licence and they were short of staff. The Luton Corporation that ran the red busses also rejected my application for work.

Doreen was very careful and she often purchased the cheapest goods. We occasionally could afford cheap cuts of meat, and bought clothes, shoes and household items only when they were absolutely necessary. The winter of 1963-4 was a nightmare for us as we relied entirely on the small electric heater which we carried from room to room.

Soon after moving to Luton I became involved in the Civil Rights Movement. I met many Black American, African, Caribbean and British activists, including supporters and leading lights of the Black Panther, Martin Luther King Junior, Malcolm X, The Anti-Apartheid Movement, Irish and African nationalists. On 4 April, 1968 Martin Luther King Junior, age 39, was gunned down in Memphis, which provoked riots in many town and cities in America, leaving forty-six people dead. Cassius Clay, the world heavyweight champion joined in the black struggle by refusing to fight in Vietnam and on 25 February, he was renamed Muhammad Ali, by Elijah Muhammad, head of the Nation of Islam. Couple of months later the assassination of Robert Kennedy, who was a friend of the Civil Rights Movement, took place on the 5th June 1968. The CIA and the various police chiefs in several American cities colluded to act violently against the rising militancy of blacks who were demanding equal rights despite the fact that the Supreme Court had agreed that everyone black and white had equal access to voting in local and federal elections. After the death of Martin Luther King I got much closer to the politics of Malcolm X, who changed his name from Malcolm Little. Malcolm was assassinated on 21 February 1965 at a meeting in New York. The assassination was carried out by a black man on the instruction of the Nation of Islam, after Malcolm separated from them. He was only forty years old and had captured the attention of black and white radicals around the world.

The world was changing fast in a number of ways, and on 20 July 1969 the Apollo spacecraft landed Neil Armstrong on the moon, just three years after the first person Russian Yuri Gagarin made history by being the first human into space. The various Civil Rights Acts passed in America in 1964 and 1965, as well as the Race Relations Acts passed in Britain in 1965 and 1968, demonstrated the success of black radicalism and struggles. I became a member of the Race Today Collective and several other organisations and met and photographed with Jessie Jackson, Kwame Ture (formerly Stokely Carmichael, who led the student non-violent, struggles before joining the Black Panther Party and became a strong advocate for the Black Power Movement). Black people must recognise that it is good to be Black and beautiful, but better still to be Black and powerful. Unity amongst Black people is essential to secure real equality and respect. Historically there have always been too many Black people in the prisons, mental institutions, living in poverty, being forced to join American military due to lack of job opportunities. Institutional racism has pervaded the lives of Black people since they arrived in large numbers in America in the 17th Century as slaves. To this day, Black Americans are still grossly and overwhelmingly represented in the negative aspects of American life from unemployment, poverty, crimes and imprisonment, poor housing, low educational achievements, and in many other areas. They make up thirteen per cent of the American population, yet their numbers in prisons, poverty and deprivation are by far much greater, several times their numbers per cent wise. The struggle for equality for Black Americans goes on despite, the election of a Black man, Barak Obama to the Presidency of America for a first and a second term in office.

The 1970s was a crucial decade for the Labour Movement. The Labour Government moved considerably towards the right of British politics as strikes, unemployment and political tensions and disagreements increased. Labour was defeated by the Tories, having won both the 1964 and 1966 general elections, following a period of national strikes, economic recession and bitter disagreements on race, the economy, policing and Trades Union rights. Edward Heath defeated Harold

Wilson in 1970 and started to attack the trade unions. By then I was working in the post office and was an active in my union at local and national levels. I joined the post office in 1969 from the country buses.

Our two children, Mike and Jane

Our son Michael was born at home during the early morning. I remember, whilst trying to assist the elderly midwife with the provision of hot water, clothing and so on, I suddenly fainted. I fell beside the door at the sight of blood and my son being born. The midwife had to step over me to get to and from the kitchen, as my wife was giving birth in our front room. This was because the hospital did not accommodate mothers who were not perceived to have any complications during the birth. It felt great to be a father and to have a family of my own. Michael was a lovely child, and three years later our daughter Jane was born. She was also born at home and on this occasion I decided not to be present at the birth. I was quite good in assisting the midwife throughout the process until I was told to leave when the birth was imminent.

My son Michael was born on 8 February, 1964 and daughter Jane in January, 1967. They both went to Cheynes Infant School in Sundon Park, and then Kinross Junior School and Lealands High School. They were amongst the first couple of black children in the three schools in Sundon Park and they had quite a difficult time on occasions, but also made some good friends and I believe they enjoyed their education despite the obvious problems of bullying and racial harassment.

As young parents we had very little social life. My wife worked in offices when she could to supplement the family income. There were many occasions when we were short of money for food which was only about ten pence old money. My wife was tremendous in bringing up our children and working for most of the time, and of course when she wasn't working she was a student doing her teaching certificate. Contrary to what her parents and family had said Doreen did fulfil her dream of becoming a teacher. They were all wrong when they claimed that 'she would have no future or career, having married to a black man, who would have her on the streets before long'.

She initially started as an infant school teacher and then moved on to Challney High School for Boys where she worked until she retired at age sixty. I will tell you a lot more about Doreen and how she influenced and changed my life over the fifty years since we got married in later chapters. Not only did she prove her parents wrong, when they told her that she would never be a teacher, marrying someone like me, but also ended her teaching career as an Assistant Head Teacher in a large High School for Boys. She could have been promoted to a headship, and was encouraged to apply, but declined to do so as she enjoyed the classroom too much. She was a gifted, dedicated and much loved teacher and her pupils always remember her to this day with much love, respect and fond memories.

Our son Michael Thakoordin went on from Lealands High School to an apprenticeship in the motor industry, and then went on to university and trained as an agricultural engineer. He did his Masters of Science in Agriculture at Silsoe College, which is part of Cranfield University. He is a Chartered Engineer and he is presently working for Ford Motor Company in Basildon, Essex as a senior manager. He is married to an African Guyanese lady Vivienne and they have a son Elijah who was born in Luton in August 2000. They also have a gorgeous daughter, Sarah, a real Essex girl, born in 2004 in Southend General Hospital.

Our daughter Jane Thakoordin went on from Lealands High School to Luton Sixth Form College and on to Lancaster University, and the University of Glasgow. She is a Senior Social Work Manager with Birmingham City Council and a visiting University Lecturer, as well as an established artist and businesswoman. Her husband Paul is an Irish Catholic whom she met whilst at University in Glasgow. Their daughter Rohanie was born in March, 1996 and she started further education in 2012. Their second child Aoife was born in October, 2002. We have four lovely grandchildren who have given us so much pleasure and hope in our lives. We see them as often as we can and we love them dearly. We have set up trust funds for them so they can each maximise their educational and career potential.

During the first ten years of marriage I continued to work at the London Transport, Country Bus Depot in Park Street, which was opposite the old Whitbread Brewery. They used to brew beer in Park Street, opposite Luton College, which is now The University of Bedfordshire, formerly the University of Luton where I was a member of the Governing Body. There was of course Luton Market where the massive Arndale Centre now stands.

I worked on the Green Line buses 321 and the 714 coaches from Luton to Dorking until 1968. I tried on a number of occasions to work for the Luton Corporation buses and the Green Eastern Counties buses but on each occasion I was told that they "will not employ black people". I then moved to the Post Office and very quickly I became the branch secretary, as I had been at Park Street Bus Depot. I will provide much more information about our children and four grandchildren in later chapters.

Bitter memories
following several deaths in our family

The year 1967 started off with a lot of expectation, as our second child was due in early January. Doreen and I were so happy to have a girl and we named her Jane. She arrived on 10 January. Since moving to Luton I either joined or formed several organisations, such as the West Indian Association, National Association for Multi-Cultural Education, the Labour Party and for a short period the Communist Party. I missed London and the regular visits to Speakers Corner and the large political and trade union rallies, as well as the many black campaigning groups. Nevertheless I took a lot of interest in my family in Luton and in Guyana.

I kept in contact with my parents and grandfather through my sisters who would read my letters addressed to them. They were in poor health and Doreen and I did our best to support them financially when we could. Their health deteriorated and, by 1967 I had lost both parents and my grandfather. I desperately tried to attend their funerals, but was unable to do so because of lack of money and time off work to travel to Guyana. These deaths occurred within such a short period and left me shocked, devastated and feeling a lot of guilt as the only son in our family. On each occasion I secured a small loan, when first my father died, followed by my mother and then my grandfather. The money I sent was to assist with the funeral arrangements. On each occasion I was unable to attend the funeral. I discussed the situation with my wife and friends and we decided that, since I was unable to book a flight for several days and would have missed the funerals anyway, it would be better to send some money to my sisters to help with the funeral arrangements and to support the family instead. My employer, London Transport, was also reluctant to grant me extended leave to attend my mother's funeral. During this period Doreen was extremely supportive to me. She did everything she could to support me and my young sisters.

Doreen's mother also died in May 1967 and we were pleased that she was able to see both her grandchildren. I do not believe Doreen's family ever came to terms with our relationship and few of her family ever tried to contact or visit us. Her mother was pleased to see us and she made a few trips to Luton with Doreen's father to see us. We continued to see Doreen's father, who moved to Worthing in Sussex, after the death of her mother. Doreen and I did our best to take care of him until his death in February 1997. I have never held any bad feelings towards Doreen's parents and always treated them with utmost respect. Her father was a regular visitor to our home, especially during holidays such as Christmas and the summer. He lived to see Doreen graduate from university and promoted to a senior teacher before he died.

1967 was a year of mixed blessings for my family and me. Although I lost my grandfather, mother and father later in the year, my wife gave birth to our daughter Jane in January. It was a further six years before I was able to visit Guyana and see my parents and grandfather's unmarked grave. I was told that they were buried in an area of the cemetery which was used to graze cattle.

From letters I received from Guyana, I was informed that my mother often discussed me, with anyone who would listen to her. She longed to see me, my wife and two children and would often say "My son will be coming next month and he will look after me. I am saving my jewellery for my daughter-in-law when she comes." In the end, neither my wife nor I inherited anything from my mother. All I have is one very old photograph of her, and of course, the memories which have stayed deep inside of me to remind me of my love for her.

Sadly, neither my wife, nor children ever met my dear mother. They would have loved her and she would have enjoyed meeting them. I hope by reading this book they will have some understanding of the influence she had on me during her life, and as a husband, father and person. She is why I have always hated the ideological concepts associated with unrestricted capitalism and its associated so-called democratic political system which condemns a large part of world's seven billion populations to poverty, misery, insecurity, unfairness, injustice, exploitation, violence and brutality. I admired the Marxists and revolutionaries such as Che Guevara who was captured and executed in Bolivia on 9 October 1967, aged just thirty nine years, and Ho Chi-Minh, the Leader of the North Vietnamese who fought and defeated the Americans, but died on 3 September 1969, before the Americans finally accepted defeat on 23 April 1975.

After the loss of my parents I developed a much broader and critical view of my life and environment, committed myself towards the struggle for political and trade union advancement for working people. I became very active in the Trade Union and Labour Movement and I developed a strong commitment towards Socialism. I felt closer to the Marxist and revolutionary-based parties, especially those fighting colonialism, imperialism, globalisation and exploitation of poor countries by Western capitalism. Doreen and my family; especially our daughter shared my passion for justice and equality.

My family regularly took part in evening and weekend meetings, demonstrations and campaigns. Doreen's support and understanding enabled me to spend more time in Trades Unions and political struggles than with my family. The 1960s and 1970's were characterized by various protests including the anti-Vietnam war movement; trade union militancy; the return of a Labour government; the politicization of students; rising unemployment; debates on immigration; and the rise of right wing racist and fascist political parties in Britain. My family and I were involved in many of these activities to secure fairness and justice for working class people. In 1967 the racist and fascist National Front was officially launched in Britain, it was the same year when the first heart transplant took place in South Africa, by Professor Christian Barnard, using the heart of a Black man to save the life of a white man. In America the Civil Rights Movement was generating a lot of interests in Britain and worldwide.

Working as a Trade Union Officer

This was a significant position accompanied by a good salary, flexible working hours, a brand new Ford Capri car and generous expenses allowances. My family enjoyed this new status and the rewards associated with being part of the Labour Movement. They all supported my politics, lifestyle and public recognition as a regional and national activist. I was often in the local press, and often featured in the national media. My children and Doreen helped me to distribute leaflets when I was trying to become a local councillor. Doreen helped me to write political speeches, encouraged me to stand as a Labour Parliamentary Candidate in 1982 and helped me produce several pamphlets and key documents on Race Relations, poverty, policing, politics and Industrial Relations. I relied a great deal on Doreen's English language skills, not yet having brought mine up to the required standard necessary for written work.

Life for our family was going very well. We had moved from Sundon Park to a lovely detached bungalow in a small village, with nearly half an acre garden, just three miles from Luton Town centre. We all worked hard and improved our new home, almost double its size within a few years. We had enjoyable holidays around England, in Europe and in America.

Mike was, by now, a really handsome young man in his early twenties and Jane had just turned twenty. Doreen was in her early forties and a much loved and well-respected teacher. Both Mike and Jane completed their University education and matured into responsible, professional people. They both enjoyed relationships and Jane was the first to settle down with Paul and start a family. Mike returned to Guyana in his thirties to work as a chartered agricultural engineer and returned, after a few years, with a Guyanese wife.

We missed being present at Mike's wedding which took place during school term time so we were unable to attend. Mike settled in Luton, where we had helped him to purchase a modest home. It was here that his first child, and our only grandson, Elijah, was born. Mike's work then took him to Rayleigh in Essex with his family. Jane moved from Scotland, where she had been studying, and settled in Birmingham with her husband and children.

Doreen's health and lifestyle

Around the year 2003, Doreen, took a liking to sweet sherry following a cervical cancer scare which was successfully treated at our local hospital. As the years passed, her taste for the dreadful alcohol increased and so did the tension and arguments after forty years of marriage. By this time I was seriously diabetic and suffered from a series of heart minor heart operations. I was taking up to a dozen tablets each day and the impact was both positive and negative, as I frequently suffered from high bold pressure, angina, anxiety and panic attacks. I was not the most rational and supporting person I should have been. This dependence affected Doreen's professional as well as emotional life and seriously impacted on our relationship. My health worsened from being a diabetic with serious heart problems to having kidney disease and feelings of insecurity, even though I lived a very active life within the community, politics, trade unions, and the media and at work as a self-employed Training and Management Consultant, which started in 1994. I continued to work a full fifty to sixty hours per week as well as seriously taken up writing and publishing books, despite my relatively poor health. I felt compelled to occupy my time usefully, if not earning then doing voluntary, community, Trades Union and political work. Any time that was left over was spent in my huge, lovely garden. It is always uplifting to me to see how the one hundred-plus shrubs, two dozen fruit trees, conifers and dozens of colourful trees and flowers brighten our garden throughout the four seasons of the year.

Disagreements between Doreen and I continued to worsen, especially when the issue of alcohol came up. She retired in 2005 and we decided to buy a holiday home in Leigh-on-Sea in Essex, near Rayleigh where Mike and his family live. Our retirement home is within walking distance of the sea and a short, convenient bus ride from the main town, Southend. Leigh has a small, beautiful sandy beach where I spend a lot of time with my grandchildren, even during the winter months. I take great pleasure in watching my grandchildren enjoying themselves on the beach or in the shallow water, watching the sailors and fishermen going to and fro and purchasing fresh fish and seafood from the Fishermen's Co-operative. Leigh-on-Sea is a quaint little town with lots of things to see and do to pass time.

Doreen enjoys her time in Leigh-on-Sea in the flat which she has beautifully and tastefully furnished. She spends as much time as she can there, but most of her time is spent with me in our home in Woodside. She uses her time in Leigh to chill out and to see our grandchildren. Still, it was in Leigh that she wrote her first book, 'Jolly Hockey Sticks' in 2007.

My health seriously deteriorated in 2008 with heart and kidney problems causing much concern. My diabetes, diagnosed in 1995, probably three years too late, affected my eyesight with a result of glaucoma and cataracts. All these problems resulted in operations to my kidneys and heart and had an impact on my ability to drive at night or for long distances. In July, 2009, I underwent a quadruple by-pass operation; a major operation and a strange experience.

I was almost certain I would not survive this major operation, partly because I was feeling quite pessimistic, tired and fed up with married life. 2006 – 2009 were difficult years for our marriage. Even though we had both committed occasional indiscretions which caused some stress on our relationship due to feelings of betrayal and disloyalty, these incidents were nothing compared to disagreements associated with alcohol consumption and associated behaviour. I learnt a great deal about the impact of alcohol on people who may have number of social, medical or psychological concerns. Alcohol seldom, if ever, resolves such difficulties although it may provide temporary relief from other worries.

July to November 2009 was important for my recovery from heart surgery. Apart from experiencing some of the usual complications associated with major surgery, I had to cope with one of the most difficult periods in all my forty-six years of marriage. The pressure caused by my total dependence on Doreen during the first couple of months after the operation expressed itself in some awful altercations between us.

However, my recovery during the first six months after the operation continued slowly but continuously. During this period I experienced the pain of gout, problems with drainage in my right leg from which the vein was taken to repair my heart and regular periods of anxiety, panic attacks, depression, loneliness, isolation and serious worries about the quality of my future life.

2010 appeared to be a welcome turning-point for our family relationships. Doreen and I felt that we needed to make some serious changes to our lifestyles and the way we live. I also re-established a reasonable relationship with my daughter-in-law and son. Mike and I have never been great communicators with each other, although we have always loved and respected each other. I was disappointed with Mike for only visiting me twice in the first four months after my heart operation – once at the hospital a couple of days after the operation and then once almost four weeks after the operation. Sadly, my daughter-in-law never communicated with me for five months after the operation even though they live only 63 miles from our home in Woodside. On the other hand, our daughter Jane, made regular visits to the hospital and our home, this lifted my spirits a great deal. I needed someone to share my physical, mental and family concerns and having my daughter and granddaughters by my side on a regular basis gave me the hope and will to face present and future challenges.

Although I have five sisters, three in America, one in Guyana and one in Barbados, I didn't see any of them during one of the most difficult years of my life. Four of my five sisters kept in touch by telephone, but of the seventeen nieces and nephews, only a few bothered to either write to me, or telephone me during my illness. Several of these nieces and nephews benefitted enormously from my support when they were young and their parents were struggling to make ends meet. I suppose this is the way the world has changed. Family values and gratitude have no place in a self-centred, materialistic world.

Nevertheless, I am happy to live to see all my sisters doing so well, unlike our parents and our childhood which was characterised by poverty and helplessness. My nieces and nephews are doing even better materially and financially and I hope their children will remember that their success is due to the sacrifices made by their parents and grandparents who laid the foundations for their success. I am so grateful for the occasional telephone calls and e-mails from my four sisters and my nephews and nieces Frankie, Tony, Anjanie, Sharon, Nancy and Charmaine.

I do not believe that there is any better source of support, bond, love, care and recognition than the family structure. Sadly, this structure has been constantly eroded over the decades even in cultures where families have traditionally bonded together with generations living under one roof and caring for each other through thick and thin. The extended family has become fragmented in an age of market capitalism, the welfare state, migration, materialism and individualism.

I love my wife and all my family equally and will always do my best for them. I have never been a perfect husband, father, brother, uncle or grandfather but I have always strived to be loving, honest, respectful, caring, and a source of support.

Doreen – my best friend always

My wife and I met each other when we were teenagers and we were married in our teenage years. We did our best to raise our children, look after our extended family and helped them the best we could. We have been married for over fifty years and like all marriages we have had our ups and downs. On the whole I feel we have been very loving and caring towards each other. Many marriages in Britain tend to be difficult to sustain for long periods, as Britain has one of the highest divorce rates in the world. All marriages can hit rocky patches at times and ours is no exception.

We have had our share of difficulties apart from having to compromise in terms of cultures, lifestyles and backgrounds. When we got married mixed relationships between indigenous people and people from Asian and African backgrounds was very rare. It is now quite fashionable for some people to engage in mixed relationships. In fact some twenty five per cent of all marriages in Britain are between people of different cultural or religious backgrounds.

Mixed relationships between black and white people can often start off with difficulties because of resentment and prejudice by some parents and relatives. I am very satisfied with the relationship I have had with my wife over the years in terms of how we have organised our lives and supported each other. I love her dearly and always will. Both our children have mixed relationships too. It has been difficult at times in some ways to sustain a completely loving relationship, but we have managed it for over fifty years. I am hoping that we will spend the rest of our lives together, enjoying the things that we have worked so hard to achieve, such as our home, a caring and loving environment, our children and grandchildren, and the things we have around us.

Yes, we have put aside some savings for our old age. We are still very active in our paid and community activities. My wife may have retired 2005, but she keeps herself busy doing some part-time teaching and spending time with our children and grandchildren. I am still heavily involved in trade unions, politics, community work, fighting racism, writing books and supporting people less fortunate than myself.

During many periods of my life my wife has been a tower of strength and support. I could not have sustained my studies as a mature student at Ruskin College, Oxford, Essex, London and Warwick Universities and the University of Hertfordshire, without her moral, financial and academic support. My wife worked and kept the home and kept the children and helped me out financially. I hope that I have been as supportive to her during her studies as a mature student. Her encouragement and support throughout our relationship have been extremely valuable, especially during the difficult periods in my community, voluntary, political and professional involvement. My wife has always been there to support the ideals I have strongly fought for and advocated despite the backlash from opportunists, bigots, and racists. I have been the subject of persistent bias and unfair reporting by the local media especially the newspapers, which only give coverage to black people when they have either committed crimes or betray their communities.

Doreen has helped me in every political and trade union campaign. She played major roles in supporting workers and unemployed people against low pay, poverty, injustice and oppression. We have campaigned together with our children against cuts in public services, racial prejudice, and attacks on trade unions, workers' rights and civil liberties. We have been involved, not only in local and national struggles, but also in supporting workers abroad and in the struggles by people in Africa, Asia, Vietnam, South America and elsewhere against apartheid, racism and exploitation by colonialists, imperialists, capitalists and militarism. We stood side by side supporting the Vietnamese against American militarism as we did against white oppression in South Africa. Equally we marched and demonstrated against racism and fascism in Luton and elsewhere when many black people and so called white radicals stood back and allowed the racists to attack our communities. Without Doreen's love and support over the last fifty years I would not have the academic qualifications, positions within the trade union and Labour movement or the skills and confidence to pursue a successful career. Together, we have achieved a great deal for ourselves and our children, despite the institutional and personal challenges and set-backs. We have consistently fought discrimination, prejudice, jealousy and stereotyping associated with mixed marriages, and bringing up a multi-racial family.

Doreen has changed a great deal over the last few years, especially since 2010, when she decided to give up alcohol and to spend more time with our grandchildren, who all love her dearly. She is a loving, caring and a very generous grandmother. We have been saving for all our grandchildren since their birth and we will be handing over a five figure sum to our eldest granddaughter, Rohanie when she becomes eighteen in March 2014. Sadly, our son and his wife are contemplating divorce proceedings as I am writing this book in 2014. We are of course very concerned about our grandchildren who are well aware of the breakdown in relationship between their parents and the associated tensions that surrounds the family. Doreen is very supportive to our only son and our grandchildren and we have assured both parents of our financial and family support. It is our wish to remain at good terms with both parents and to support our grandchildren aged 13 and 9 in every possible way.

Returning to Guyana

Before I left Guyana, I promised my family that I will return within three years with enough money and education to support all my family. I promised my elderly parents who were in poor health that I would return and take care of them. I would marry a local woman and they would have lots of grandchildren. I would defend my sisters against domestic violence and help them to realise their full potential. I felt it was my duty as the only son and brother to undertake such a responsibility. I did not expect to spend the rest of my life in England. I kept in close contact with my parents until their death in 1967. I also kept in contact with my sisters through letters. I helped all my family when my parents were alive and after their death the best I could, despite having my own family to support. I would have done a lot more for them had I had the resources at the time.

I was unable to attend the funeral of my parents and grandfather who died within four years of my arrival in England, due to lack of money and difficulties in securing transport at short notice. By 1972, my wife and I had accumulated a small amount of savings, and we agreed that it was time for me to visit my country of origin. For this visit I had saved up my annual holidays for 1972 and 1973. I arrived in Guyana in 1973 for the first time since my original departure in 1961. The visit lasted six weeks and I missed my family very much. Doreen managed everything extremely well during my absence and I was so pleased to return home after a very difficult but interesting visit. During my stay in Guyana, I stayed with my sister Dede and her family. I was so upset when I saw Dede and she told me about the impact from the loss of her eldest son Harry. He was such a strong and loving son who would have protected his mother from domestic violence and abuse. He was a teenager when he died at sea, during a fishing trip to earn money, so his brothers and sisters would have new books and clothes at the start of the school year.

I met all my sisters and I had some serious disappointments because of the differences between my sister Julie and me. Julie occupied the family home with my three youngest sisters, Datsie, Joyce and Petsie. Julie did her very best for them and for her daughter Carol. Unfortunately, I was forced to leave the family home from which I departed from for London twelve years earlier. It was our family home that was left to all of us as children, but before I had arrived Julie had bought out the shares of four of my sisters and she felt that I was going to show an interest in the house, which was not my intention. So I left the family home and stayed with Dede. I felt bitter and disappointed by being forced to leave and never to returned to the house again, even after I made the further three visits to my village. My last visit was in 2005, which is likely to be my final visit. It distressed me enormously to see some of the undesirable changes within my family, my village and the country.

Then in 1987, I visited Guyana again but with my wife and children this time. My family in Guyana, apart from my parents, grandparents and eldest nephew Harry were not present, as they had passed away many years previously. I was so happy that my remaining family, friends and people who knew my family were so pleased to see us. We all had a wonderful time. Doreen and my children found out a great deal about my background, and I felt my family understood me more as a person following this visit.

We spent most of December, 1987 and the first week of January, 1988 visiting many parts of Guyana and meeting close and distant family members, school friends and village elders. On Christmas day we had at least five or six Christmas dinners, as everyone wanted us to visit their homes. For most of the people it was the first chance they had had to entertain a white person in their home. Though Doreen, Mike and Jane were excited and honoured at all the fuss and compliments, it was quite an effort to share a meal with everyone, especially when the meals were so similar. Curried chicken or duck, rice, roti and fish were popular dishes for most people.

Even those people who were so poor they could hardly provide a meal for themselves were determined to provide us with a small meal, consisting of the very basic chicken curry and rice. Aunty Mary, who was a friend of my mother and was in her late seventies and living alone, had somehow found the money to purchase a tin of sardines imported from England to eat with the small portion of boiled rice. She thought that, being an Englishwoman, Doreen would prefer something from England even though it cost Aunt Mary more than she could reasonably afford.

Doreen's lifestyle attracted some attention, especially when she greeted some traditional Hindu activists on their way to a wedding by waving her hand holding a bottle of strong local beer above her head while smoking a cigarette at the same time. Local women would not dare smoke or drink alcohol in public.

The visits to the Interior were spectacular. Lakes and canals, though full of brown water and populated by alligators, snakes, piranhas and other creatures did not deter my family from enjoying themselves and taking precarious-looking speedboat rides. The local food was always fresh and tasty. Fish, meat, fruits and vegetables were brought fresh to the local market each day. The biggest problem was sanitation – or lack of it. Most people had outdoor toilets consisting of an open pit surrounded by old, galvanised zinc sheets or wood. Mosquitoes were a major problem in the villages. They somehow targeted Doreen more than the rest of us, and she had to have medical attention due to infestation. Drinking water was also of poor quality. However, Doreen and the children were determined to spend time in the villages with the local people. For this, I was so proud of them. So often, Guyanese returning to their homeland pretend to be too delicate, special or high and mighty to spend time with poor villagers and prefer the comfort of the city hotels.

The journey from Gatwick to Guyana involved changing planes in Trinidad after a ten-hour flight. Then the flight from Trinidad to Guyana took just over an hour and a half. Once actually inside the country, there was always a struggle to get through customs and immigration, unless passengers were prepared to offer bribes or gifts to the officials.

Two large barrels of presents, household gifts and clothing that we had sent by surface mail eight weeks before we were due to arrive was only released to us a few days before our departure from Guyana and then only after a lot of hassle by and bribery of customs officials.

Before leaving Guyana, we gave away almost all our clothes and personal possessions and preferred to return with dried fish, shrimps, fruits, chutneys, pepper sauce, arts and crafts and gifts. Even then, we had to bribe the officials at the airport to allow our luggage on to the plane. At boarding time, my family was asked to board the plane whilst I was detained in a small office by officials who wanted more bribes. On this occasion, they wanted British money, not local currency. I ended up being the last person to board the plane after being separated from fifty pounds which delighted the officials as they wished me "a pleasant journey back home".

On reflection, we all had a great experience in Guyana and enjoyed most of the time there. Doreen, Mike and Jane were upset about the level of cruelty to animal life, and equally disturbed by the level of poverty, domestic violence, corruption, lack of health care and sanitation throughout most of Guyana. Trips across the Demerara, Berbice and Essequibo Rivers, which separate the three regions of Guyana, were memorable. We travelled all along the coastal belt by car, ferry-crossings and mini buses with Indian music blaring out, to the satisfaction of the passengers crammed in to the worn-out seats, sweating in the Guyanese sun. It was good to get back home to Luton to our boring but normal lives.

On returning from Guyana after my first visit there, I had the intention of building a career within the Trades Union and Labour Movement. The poverty, inequality and post-colonial legacy I saw in Guyana made me ask a lot of questions, that I felt unqualified to provide with answers. My position as an active trade's union representative within the Union of Post Office Workers enabled me to access education and training through the Trades Union Council (TUC). I immediately applied for a TUC Scholarship to Ruskin College, Oxford, and won a place starting in October, 1974. It was quite an exciting time to be a student at the age of 31 in such an historical context, Oxford being one half of the bastions of education in England, with Cambridge making up the other half.

A better world for young people and families

I re-joined the Labour Party in 2013, after resigning in 2010 after forty-six active years, as well as increasing my involvement in the trade unions. I have been elected to several committees associated with the Trades Union Congress (TUC), my own University and College Union National Executive and several local and national political, civil and human rights and community campaigning groups.

I have also increased my involvement and writing, in fighting racism and fascism, which is the responsibility of all of us. Black and white people must unite and fight racism and fascism otherwise we will all lose out in the end. It is a shame that the economic crisis in Europe and the USA has resulted in the de-stabilisation of the economies of many countries and there is a real crisis in Greece, Italy, Portugal and elsewhere. Britain has been undergoing severe financial and austerity measures since 2010 and the situation is likely to get worse before it gets better. The European Union (EU), which involves twenty seven members, are experiencing enormous turbulence economically and politically, as stability in both areas is inter-dependent on the success of each other. The austerity measures taken by countries within the European Union has created mass unemployment especially amongst young people, cuts and privatisation of public services, reductions in living standards. Massive increase in poverty, attacks on immigrant workers and collapse of large parts of the banking and financial institutions. Millions of workers across the EU have been engaged in strikes and demonstrations and have encountered some of the worse policing practice in modern times. On top of this tragedy, the right wing forces with racist and fascist tendencies have made enormous gains within the democratic process across the EU. Many countries have governments formed with well-known fascists and racists as coalition partners.

Alongside this social, political and economic turbulence in Europe, America and elsewhere there is a great deal of loss of trust and confidence in politicians, governments and financial institutions. One of the worrying features of this crisis is the increase of support and representation of supporters from the far right political parties and groups across Europe, and in other countries. This is a major concern not only for Doreen and I and our multi-racial children and grandchildren, but also for everyone who are opposed to racism and fascism. Doreen and I have worked together for several decades to combat racism and fascism. Our children and our grandchildren have also joined in this struggle.

We have some cherished photographs of our granddaughters Rohanie and Aoife carrying placards and banners on demonstrations against racism, cuts in public services and supporting the struggles for women to secure equality and justice.

Jim Family Life, wife, children grandchildren
Top – Bottom, L-R
Doreen at retiring from teaching
Doreen speaking at Jim's 70th birthday and 50th wedding anniversary
Jim Doreen and Michael
Jim Doreen Jane and Mike
Jim and Doreen with grandchildren

Top- Bottom, L-R
Doreen with Rohanie, eldest grandchild
Doreen with father and Rohanie
Doreen with her parents Edith and Joseph Cash
Doreen with Mike (son) Jane (daughter) Rohanie, and her father

Chapter 7:

Our children and grandchildren

Our grown-up children

Our son Michael is over fifty years old and our daughter Jane is three years younger. I never believed that I would be around, given the state of my health, to see them reach such landmarks in their lives. I admire their maturity, professionalism and family commitment. Our son Mike has developed a much closer relationship with us and his sister since he started to have serious disagreements with his wife. We love him and his children dearly and I certainly forgive him for not showing more commitment towards his family a few years after he got married. We are also pleased that our grandchildren are in frequent contact with each other over the telephone and Skype.

My wife and I are so fortunate to have four beautiful and outstanding grandchildren who have given us both so much pleasure and love. All my grandchildren are each different, unique, loving, caring and close to me. They are all very bright and above average in their achievements at school. Apart from the massive influence and support from their parents, especially from their mothers, they have benefited from the commitment towards their educational success by the consistent and targeted support from us, especially their Nanny. Having been a teacher for thirty five years and ending the career as an Assistant Head teacher at our local High school Nanny has been in a position to provide guidance, advice, resources and encouragement.

Our four grandchildren:

Granddaughter Rohanie

Rohanie, our eldest was born to our only daughter Jane and her husband Paul in March 1996 in Glasgow, Scotland. Being grandparents for the first time was not only a unique and historical landmark for our family, but also a time for reflection, joy and celebration. Neither Doreen nor I were present at the hospital to witness the birth. The first time we knew that we were grandparents was when I took a telephone call, with someone saying "hello granddad". It was of course our daughter's voice which sounded so different from her normal voice. I suppose motherhood has the capacity to change a woman in numerous ways, from her physical, mental and her personal characteristics to her voice, appearance, and even the way she sees and interprets the world.

Jane had met Paul, from Dungannon in Northern Ireland, who was a fellow student, in Glasgow. Paul has always been respectful, supportive and caring towards our whole family. We could not wish for a better person to be the father of our first grandchild. Although, like many fathers there were times when I felt that my only daughter deserved the best amongst the very best for a husband. We are nonetheless very proud of Paul and have had the privilege of meeting his parents, sisters and brother and other members of his family.

It has been a unique experience and one full of pleasure, excitement, hopes and dreams since we heard of Rohanie's birth. I remember after receiving the call from Jane "hello granddad" I in turn phoned Doreen at work saying "hello nanny". I wept for joy and for the future of our family. It was a significant time for all of us. Our lives have constantly changed with the arrival of our dear Rohanie. Seeing Rohanie, holding her in our arms, touching, kissing and having conversations – albeit only one-sided – with her was a wonderful experience. We saw Rohanie for the first time when she was a couple of weeks old. There have been very few days in the lives of Doreen and me when we have not had a conversation about our grandchildren. Every birthday, meeting and get together gives us grandparents an opportunity to celebrate and to thank God for being blessed with such remarkable, fit, loving and intelligent grandchildren.

Seeing Rohanie and her parents has become a major part of our lives and our routine. I am convinced that the arrival of Rohanie and the love and affection her presence generated helped Doreen and I to consolidate and strengthen our own personal relationship even further. From our point of view we were so pleased when our daughter and her family moved from Glasgow, which we discovered ourselves and loved, to Birmingham, in England, a mere ninety five miles away by car from our home town in Luton. We used to enjoy the short air flight from our local airport in Luton to Glasgow. However being able to see our granddaughter in Birmingham was so much better for us. The children in the local school as well as the teachers were curious about this beautiful and cuddly little girl with a deep Glaswegian accent. Rohanie has always been a charming person and her mother has always encouraged and embraced diversity, which our granddaughter has inherited and accommodated. Birmingham has become one of the most multi-racial, multi-cultural and diverse cities in the United Kingdom and our own daughter and her family have reflected this fact.

Rohanie started her college in October 2012 with much commitment, determination and style. At sixteen years of age she is the tallest in her family including Nanny and Granddad. This beautiful young woman with her hairstyles, which have included several colours, including black, brown, orange, white and blue tipped, headed off to college with confidence. As her loving and faithful grandparents, Nanny and I have pledged our full support to see our granddaughter through her academic career, and deeper, into her adulthood. Our love and best wishes for a successful career and life will always be with her, hopefully throughout her life, from child, to adulthood and through the journey of parentage, into being a grandparent and beyond. I have spent much of my working life campaigning for a better world for all the children in it.

Rohanie has always treated us and her relatives with the utmost love and respect. Watching her growing up over the years and following her progress at school, in her home and the wider community has rewarded us with so much pride, satisfaction and hope. Her examination results in 2012 were excellent, with four A stars, four A's and a B in her GCSE results. To us this confirmed her commitment to learning, academic achievements and success through hard work. She is now thoroughly committed to her studies at college and hopefully will move on to university and a successful career of her own choice. Soon after her birth we opened a trust fund for her educational aspirations. This fund now contains a healthy balance, as indeed do the other trust funds for all our grandchildren.

We spent time with our daughter Jane and her family in the first few days of 2014. It was a memorable occasion to be with our grandchildren and discussing their aspirations and plans for their future. Rohanie is hoping to undertake a Foundation Year Course after her studies at college, before hopefully securing a place at university. She has in mind to apply for a place in a Scottish University, as well as a number of universities in England, probably to study art, language and or social studies. Rohanie is one of the most beautiful, charming and hardworking young person we know. Our grandchildren are our future as indeed all grandchildren and children are the future of our world.

Grandson Elijah

Elijah, our next grandchild was born in the year 2000. Our daughter in law, his mother, Vivienne was born in Guyana, some eleven miles from where I was born and where I lived until arriving in London, aged seventeen. Elijah's father, our son Michael was our first child. I was so pleased to have a son for our first born child, since I myself am the only son from the eight surviving children my mother had. It was therefore a pleasant surprise to see Elijah, our first grandson. All our children are different but equal. My daughter much to my surprise and gratitude kept her maiden name after marriage, along with her husband's surname.

This honour was even extended to all four of our grandchildren who all share my surname. Elijah was born in the Luton and Dunstable Hospital and both his Dad and Nanny were present at his birth. Having a grandson only five miles away from us was wonderfully handy, and we made the most of the opportunities to see him. Unfortunately, for us, a year or so later our son and his family moved to Wales, which is well over one hundred and fifty miles from us. He moved due to his career development with Ford Motor Company. We saw our grandson a couple of times before his family moved again, to Essex, this time again as a result of Michael's further promotion with Ford's. Our son relocated in Raleigh, about ten miles from his workplace in Basildon. Elijah settled in nicely to the local nursery and primary schools, just a few minutes' walk from his home.

Elijah is a loving, caring and honest young person who loves life and works hard at his education. He is always polite, respectful and full of energy. He has developed a special relationship with his Nanny. For his Nanny he can do no wrong and is more than entitled to have anything he desires. So far I believe his Nanny has never ever rejected any of his requests, not as far as I know. He is not however a greedy or demanding child. On the contrary, I find him to be quite a modest child with a great commitment to learning about different religions, cultures, civilisations, history, science and current affairs. He is of well above average intelligence for his age. We often engage each other in a variety of issues of both national and international levels.

Elijah is committed to many of the issues I have been involved with for half a century. Issues such as world poverty, human rights, abuse of power, peace, justice, socio economic and political issues too. Elijah started grammar school in 2011 and his grasp of current affairs as well as international issues has increased enormously. It is my sincere hope that he will become involved in national politics after pursuing a professional career. Despite his relative smallness in size, being possibly the shortest person in his school class, he has managed to hold up his end admirably. He can well defend himself, both physically and verbally against the bullies who are much taller and older than he is. His Nanny is forever referring to Elijah as "my boy, the best boy in the whole world". This is something Elijah always seeks to extract from his Nanny by using his natural charm and winning smiles. Like his father, he can be quite reluctant to spend his own money. He often discusses with Nanny and Granddad his future plans for spending the quite considerable sum we have saved for him in his trust fund. When he is eighteen he will take possession of that fund. I cannot believe my only grandson is now only a few years away from this great day.

Elijah and his nanny Thakoordin seems to have a very special relationship, which is so obvious when they are together, and when she refers to him. He loves and milks as much attention he can attract from his nanny. We are so proud of Elijah and all that he has achieved so far. Of course we know there are many more surprises and happy years to spend with our precious grandchildren, and we fully look forward to this.

Granddaughter Aoife

Our third grandchild Aoife was born to Jane and Paul in October 2002 in a Birmingham hospital. Initially she looked exactly like Rohanie at birth and for the following few months. Like her sister Rohanie, Aoife was a beautiful baby who brought much joy to all our family. Being a second child Aoife grew up very quickly with her elder sister, six years older, supporting all aspects of her development. She has always been very active and close to us. From the age of three Aoife's distinct and independent lifestyle was noticeable in contrast to our other grandchildren. Each child is unique and responds to their environment differently. During our visits to Birmingham Aoife invariably took it upon herself to add her special welcome and to assist with practical things, such as, who sits where at the dining table and who pulls the first cracker at Christmas.

Over the years I have developed a unique and special relationship with each of my four grandchildren. At her primary school Aoife befriended a disabled Asian boy in her class who was wheelchair bound, his name is Yash. She used to help him get his meals and do other things to make his life at school more comfortable. She also befriended other children from a wide variety of ethnic, national, cultural and religious backgrounds. Aoife was my first grandchild to inform me that she "would look after me" when "you are very old". She carefully examined the numerous scars on my body, resulting from various heart, kidney and other operations without any fear or apprehension.

Whenever we visited our daughter and her family in Birmingham Aoife always made us feel very welcome. We usually slept in her bedroom. Both girls would often sleep in together to create space for us. Spending time in Birmingham would always result in Aoife and me taking a trip to Poundland as well as the local coffee shop. When she was younger we would also go to Sainsbury's, where it was convenient for her to reach the sweet shelves without leaving her pushchair. Aoife has always been generous and caring. She is always full of fun and likes to be at the centre of things. Teasing her elder sister is a well-practiced feature of their relationship. In comparison to Rohanie, Aoife is likely to be much shorter and plumper. Her physical appearance is likely to be more similar to her mother rather than her father. On her tenth birthday Aoife invited seven young girlfriends for a sleepover on the Saturday night. It was quite an occasion. Like their mother, both Aoife and Rohanie have taken part in both political and trade unions demonstrations. There have been photographs taken of them, carrying banners with a range of political slogans. I am so proud of my daughter and all our grandchildren are special with different personalities, ambitions and preferences. Aoife is quite a forward and outgoing person with a strong, determined and independent personality. She has been involved in numerous challenges and activities including dancing, playing the piano, sports and even gymnastics. She also has a very caring aspect to her personality. Aoife has had lots of thoughts about pursuing a career through university, including being a Carer, a marine biologist and a vet. We are so pleased that Aoife has taken a special interest in her cousins, and spend lots of her time on Skype chatting to them.

Granddaughter Sarah

My youngest grandchild, Sarah celebrated her eight birthday in June 2012. She was born to Vivienne and Michael in 2004. From a young age I started to address her as "my Pincess". Not "Princess" which she has always welcomed. Sarah is quite tall for her age and enjoys school despite the difficulties that she and her brother have had to endure. Their beautiful braids, brown complexion and attractive features, especially in primary school, with very few non-white children, made them vulnerable to racial taunts, harassment and bullying on occasions. Despite the occasional incidents my Pincess and my grandson have managed to do well at school and to have friends from various ethnic, national and cultural backgrounds.

My "Pincess" and I often discuss school issues and explore all sorts of related issues. Unlike Birmingham, which is one of the most diverse and multi-racial communities in England, Raleigh and South End in Sussex are much less diverse. Sarah is very close to her brother. They share a lot of ideas and experiences and have supported each other at school and at home. I remember one occasion when my "Pincess" took part in a fight at primary school where they were both pupils. She did not hesitate to charge in and defend her brother physically against two boys who were attacking him. She is quite strong and from an early age we used to practice fighting, including attacking and defending. I have discovered in my own life that bullies are also cowards and that running away from them is not the answer. As someone with much experience in karate, keep fit and confronting racists I am pleased that my grandchildren stand up for themselves. The grandchildren spending odd nights with us in Leigh - on Sea and part of the school holidays with us in Luton has given me so much pleasure and has really helped me to cope with my illnesses for many years. My "Pincess" would often inspect my many scars resulting from several operations, many of which had become quite prominent, due to the scars becoming keloid. After her examinations she would remind me "don't worry Granddad, I will look after you when you get older and I am a lot bigger".

My darling "Pincess" is so obviously loving and caring at times that it has made me quite emotional as a result. She is a cuddly person despite the fact that she enjoys a good fight. Once when her Nanny told her "girls don't fight", her response was "this girl does". My "Pincess" loves cooking and she regularly helps her father cook the Sunday roast dinner. It is her who prepares the vegetables, the pudding and lays the table. Other things we both have in common are that she loves gardening, wildlife and reading. I think of all my grandchildren every single day. My "Pincess" features prominently in my thoughts and in my conversations with her Nanny. With her being born in South End General Hospital, she has a real Essex girl accent, which I love. We spent 5 days with our son and his two children over Christmas 2013, and we enjoyed every minute of it. Our "Pincess" was the number one tea maker and pastry cook. She is full of humour and fun. She will be ten years old in October 2014.

Top- Bottom, L-R
Jim with family at daughter Jane's wedding ceremony
to renew vows
Grandchildren
Jim and Doreen with Jane and Mike

Chapter 8:

Becoming a full-time student

On occasions, I felt dreadfully guilty leaving my wife to take total responsibility for the home and children, while holding down a full-time teaching post. Doreen was marvellous, even though she knew of my extra-curricular activities in Oxford. Doreen and the children (Mike, who was about 11, and Jane, who was about 8) visited me at Ruskin and enjoyed the Ruskin facilities as well as the city of Oxford. Doreen had her own car (a tiny, green Mini) and I had my little Morris Minor, which I used to transport up to five other students to and from political and social events. I will forever be grateful to Doreen and my children for allowing me eighteen months away from family life to pursue this course.

After finishing the course at Ruskin I had the opportunity to continue my studies at New College, Oxford but decided to do this instead at Essex University, an establishment well-known for student politicisation and militancy. The break from Ruskin in July 1976 provided me with an opportunity to re-establish close and loving relationships with all my family. From what I gathered, Doreen was no angel herself during my time at Ruskin. However, I was in no position to criticize her, given my own conduct.

Moving on from Ruskin to the University of Essex was exciting as well as challenging for me and my family. I wanted more time and space to further my interests in Socialism, Marxism and various other political systems. I was also keen to explore issues such as class, power and race relations. Essex was ideal for me and I enjoyed the course on Comparative Government and Sociology.

Although I was heavily involved in student militancy and politics, I decided to spend more time at home with my family. So, I would leave Colchester on Thursdays in my Morris Minor, and return late Sunday night or early Monday morning. University terms were relatively short and the six 8-9 week terms went quickly. During the holidays and some weekends I worked as a lorry driver for the Luton Knitting Company delivering parcels and collecting materials from London and the Home Counties. I also worked as a labourer through various employment agencies.

During my studies at Essex, I started a part-time M.A. Degree at the University of Warwick, as they ran a course for potential Trades Union Officers. I later started a teacher training course at Garnett College in London. I graduated from the B.A. Honours course at Essex in the summer of 1978 and graduated from the PGCE Teachers' course in the summer of 1979. I decided not to submit my final piece of work for the M.A. at Warwick as I had secured a Regional Education Officer's post with the London Region of the GMB Union. Fifteen years later I completed an MBA course in Business Studies at the University of Hertfordshire.

Ruskin College, Oxford

I arrived at Ruskin College, Oxford, on 11 October 1974 the day after the Labour Party won the second general elections within eight months with an overall majority of only three votes. Ruskin as an institution was closely linked with the Labour and the trade union movement. I won a trade union scholarship to Oxford, having been active in the movement for several years. It was a period of great political discussions and activities within the trade union and Labour movements. Labour was the largest party in Parliament after the general election on 28 February, 1974 but short of thirty three seats to have an overall majority. I arrived in Headington Hall, Oxford with my green Morris Minor plastered in Labour posters and stickers.

Labour had defeated the Conservatives after thirteen years of consecutive rule in 1964, but had a small majority of only four seats. Harold Wilson the Prime Minister decided to call a general election 1966, a period of great industrial strife, including strikes and economic problems. Labour won the election with an overall majority of ninety eight seats, but lost to the Conservatives, on 18 June by thirty eight seats, due to worsening industrial disputes, decline in manufacturing and rising cost of living in a period of economic and financial austerity, as well as serious divisions within the Labour movement.

The 1970's, and indeed the 1960's, were periods of great industrial strife and political agitation. Trades union power was at its highest point, in terms of membership numbers and militancy. The manufacturing base in the Britain was a great deal stronger than it is today and several unions were led by members of the Communist Party and socialists involved in the Labour Party. There were also many radical and socialists members of Parliament who won their selection and consequently their places in Parliament. The unions and their radical supporters inside and outside Parliament and the Party were competing for the soul and direction of Labour. This competition and conflict caused Labour and the unions to lose a great deal of public support even amongst traditional Labour supporters.

The Conservative Prime Minister had a difficult time managing the economy and his term of office was characterised by strikes including a coalminers strike, power cuts, industrial action by nurses, public sector workers and an oil crises, leading to a 3-day working week and a cap on pay. The Labour Party in opposition was always more radical than when in power, so the Labour Movement was a strong opposition to the Conservative government. The Prime Minister was also increasingly undermined by a number of right wing conservatives including one Mrs Thatcher who was Minister for Education and became notorious for taking away free school milk from all school pupils.

I had arrived in Oxford, having worked hard to secure this Labour victory. I had secured long term leave to attend Ruskin College from the Post Office, where I was postman and the union organiser. I was thirty one years old, married with two children, my son aged ten and daughter aged seven. My wife Doreen, who was a teacher, made a lot of sacrifices to take care of the family and the cost of keeping our home. She even gave me some pocket money on occasions.

Ruskin College was founded in 1899 as an independent education institution for adults who have had little or no formal education, and are lacking in academic qualification. It was named after John Ruskin, who was a great philanthropist and socialist. The main college site was situated in the heart of Oxford city centre, in Walton Street, with a secondary annex in Headington, Oxford, and two miles away. Ruskin provided university standard education for working class people, men and women; with association in the Labour movement. Although Ruskin was not part of the formal Oxford University set up, it nevertheless enjoyed all the facilities, such as Ruskin's students could attend lectures at any of the Oxford universities, could use the Bodleian Library and have membership of the Oxford Union Debating Society. Naturally, I made use of all the facilities. The final assessment of the students work was assessed in conjunction with academics from Ruskin and Oxford University.

I arrived in Oxford dressed quite modestly in jeans, t-shirt and a black leather jacket, bell bottom trousers, shoes with three inches high Cuban heels and long hair, resting on my shoulders and a Mexican type moustache. It was really good to be with fellow students who had similar experiences to mine. We continued to celebrate Labour's victory for a few days and to engage in heated and often sectarian, but good humour debates on politics, race, class, gender, sociology and unions. I was ready for learning in this trendy historical city. The city centre appeared to be swarming with students and almost separate from the rest of Oxford and its beautiful countryside, except for those of us who quickly established links with the trade union, especially in the motor industry at Cowley, home of the Morris cars.

Some months before my arrival in Oxford, my wife had given me a copy of a book called Jude the Obscure, written by Thomas Hardy. I read this book with great interest, it described a young man, Jude, from a working class background, who had aspirations and ambitions for learning and had arrived in Oxford from his humble residence in the Wessex countryside. Sadly despite many attempts by Jude to secure a place at Oxford University, and to further his education, it all ended in dreadful disaster. In my mind, I thought I would not make the mistakes that Jude had made, and that I would come out of Oxford with distinction, commitment, and a bright future.

I found Oxford to be a great city for learning and for student life. The historic buildings built during the Middle Ages were overwhelming. The architecture was stunning, and so was the lifestyle of the students and lecturers. There were students of all ages and ethnic and racial origins. However, they were overwhelmingly middle class, who were enjoying the great privilege in the bastion of bourgeois and radical education. It was easy to reflect on the history of Oxford as one walked along the cobbled streets and alleyways. It was easy to feel the history of this marvellous place of learning. During the 12th and 13th Centuries, Oxford was a manufacturing town, noted for clothing and leather trades. Manufacturing declined during the next two centuries as more universities were opened and students were attracted to this city.

So gradually the focus moved from goods to services, especially services for the university staff and students, there had always been some conflicts between the local people and the students. In 1209, there were conflicts between local people and students; a local woman was killed, and the town folk ended up hanging two students. This tension existed for over a 150 years, and in some cases, it was apparent when I arrived and got involved in student politics in the city, and outside the city, in the car parks where trade unions was at its peak, at the Morris car part manufacturing centre.

When Oxford was granted a city status in 1542, the population was a mere 3,500. A hundred years later it had grown by another few thousand. In 1651, the first coffee house in England was opened in Oxford, and Oxford was recognised as a market town for a number of centuries. In 1708 a charity school for boys, The Bluecoat School was founded and during the next three centuries, Oxford grew at a fair rate in population and status. In 1913 a business man named Morris started producing cars not far from the city centre, followed by other manufacturing companies, many of which supported the local motor industry. Many workers arrived from wide and far to seize opportunities in the motor trade and in manufacturing and a number of estates, public and private houses were built to accommodate workers and their families.

During my stay at Oxford, I made full use of the university facilities and had pleasure in visiting a number of the universities such as: New College Oxford, founded in 1379; Balliol, New College; Maudlin College; and others founded between the 14th and 16th Century, and that have educated many prime ministers and presidents around Europe and the Commonwealth. I took a particular interest in the prestigious Oxford Union debating society that was founded in 1823. It was a place where students with political ambitions had an opportunity to test out especially amongst their peer groups their political interests and debating skills.

Once I had settled down, and made friends, I took some interest in the other colleges that were not as ancient as the ones mentioned above. For example, there were a number of colleges and halls that were built for female students, as women were not allowed to attend lectures in Oxford University until 1884. Some were allowed to attend the university but were not awarded degrees until 1920, so colleges like Lady Margaret Hall built in 1878 and Summerfield College in 1879, and Saint Hilda's College in 1893, were for female students only. Colleges and halls were extended to accommodate students as they were not allowed to live with local townspeople after 1410 students attending Oxford University until 1854 had to belong to the Church of England in order to gain entry to the university.

So here was I, a country boy, aged 31 in the heart of the British educational system and the bastion of bourgeois education, forty-three miles from home, missing my wife and children, and having to change my life seriously in many ways. Coming to terms with life in Oxford was exciting, challenging and interesting. But there were also other aspects which troubled me a great deal. For example, I had little experience of essay writing, reading a book from cover to cover within a week, engage in high levels of analysis, conceptual thinking, and spending time alone in a small room, mixing with adult and mature students on a daily basis, questioning life and society values and engage in serious debates about national and international issues. The institutions and the environment in the city were at times extremely overwhelming, yet very interesting.

In my year at Ruskin College there were students from various parts of the world - Africa, Asia and the Caribbean, - but most of the students were British. The first week in Oxford enabled us students to get to know each other, our tutors, and the college facilities, as well as getting to the town and the local facilities. At the first meeting of students I was elected the house chairman. I was one of few students who had experience in negotiating with management. I was excited about this role as it seemed an extension of my trade union work and seemed certain to keep me busy, and in the limelight of course. I soon made friends with quite a number of characters. A few of them still linger in my thoughts, when I think of Oxford and Ruskin College.

I lived in Headington Hall during the first year, but spent most of the days and evenings in Oxford city and in Walton Street at the main college centre. I made contact with local trade unions at the Morris plant and in the businesses in the city centre; I consciously wanted to retain my working class and trade union tradition and background. I was partially accepted by a number of trade unionists who were highly suspicious of students getting involved in their union activities My style of dressing in black shirts, denim trousers, black leather jacket, long hair, bits of metal around my wrist and my neck, and often speaking the language of the shop floor caused a few concerns amongst the comrades. However, they were aware that Oxford was a great centre for radical student politics. There were all types of organisations, from the Red Mole, to the Black Dwarf; The Socialist Worker's Party; The Fourth International; The Communist Party; Labour, and many other fringe political organisations. It was such a different environment from which I had been used to. Getting away back home during most weekends brought me back to reality.

The 1970's were also characterised by a number of major disputes in the car industry, the miners' strike, the three day week, and a rise of fascism and racism, and right wing politics in Britain. I recall attending a number of meetings at the Oxford union debating society addressed by Enoch Powell, Keith Joseph, and other controversial Conservative Party characters on the right of British politics; most of the time I was outside with the ultra-left groups. However, I did join them and other radical groups, picketing the Oxford Union and trying to prevent these people from entering to advocating their racist and right wing philosophies. Most University students were from privileged middle and upper class backgrounds whose parents were probably mostly Conservative supporters, many of them were interested in politics and therefore were somewhat sympathetic to the right wing philosophy.

I met many politicians and presidents from around the world, including Julius Nyerere and other statesmen from Africa and the Caribbean who have had association with Ruskin College. I also met many political exiles from pre-colonial and post-colonial African countries, especially from South Africa, Zimbabwe, Angola and Ghana. International politics and relations was a popular subject for African exiles and there were regular meetings and discussions on colonialism, imperialism and the role of Britain in world politics. I was always welcomed at these discussions even though I was not an African. Having been brought up and worked in a British colony I was able resonate with their fears and hopes.

Meeting Benazir Bhutto

Student life in Oxford was very free, easy and enjoyable. Students from the various universities mixed together particularly during the evenings and weekends and frequented the bars and clubs in the city. I enjoyed many sessions in the Picketers bar, in Ruskin College, which was the place for intoxicated students to change the world, at least in theory. I also met one famous student visitor at Oxford, one Benazir Bhutto, the daughter of the famous prime minister of Zulfikar Ali

Bhutto (1928-79) of Pakistan who became President of Pakistan in 1971 and Prime Minister in 1973. He was also founder of the Pakistan's People Party which was also led by Benazir after he was killed by the military government in 1979.

Benazir Bhutto was a student at Lady Margaret Hall after completing her studies at Harvard University in America. Benazir was stunningly beautiful and intelligent. Naturally she was interested in politics and took part in debates at the Oxford Union of which she became the President. Benazir was ten years younger than I, having been born in June 1953. She was a very active student and enjoyed a good political debate. Benazir arrived at Oxford a year before I did in 1974. Benazir gravitated towards politics and later became Chair of the People's Party in Pakistan and the first woman Prime Minister elected in Pakistan, a Muslim state. In 1988, age 35, she was removed from office by the President, but returned as Prime Minister in 1993.

She was in office until 1996 when she was again removed from office and later went into exile. Sadly Benazir, who was the original Iron Lady in Politics, was killed by a bomb after returning to Pakistan and taking part in a political campaign, in preparation of the 2008 general election. Benazir was addressing huge crowds from her car on 27th December 2007 when she died. It was an election that Benazir would certainly have won had she survived. Nevertheless, her husband Asif Ali Zardari led the People's Party and later became the President. I met Benazir in London during her period as prime minister of Pakistan, and she gave me a signed photograph of herself which I still have.

Ruskin students were perceived as more radical than most other students at the university; clearly because many of us came from a trade union and political background, and we were far more mature than the average Oxford student. A number of us took part in local trade union and political activities, mainly anti-racism activities, and we were labelled "Ruskies". We took part in strikes supporting workers at the Churchill Hotel, and also at the Blackwell's Bookshop and I believe the local paper gave us the nickname of "Rent a Ruskie" because we were always on the picket lines supporting local people in trade union disputes.

Sinking the Oxford Boat

There were lots of interesting and enjoyable moments whilst I was at Ruskin College, apart from befriending a number of young ladies from Summerville and other colleges and engaging in a lot of and fun and excitement. On one occasion in March 1975, my friend Mick Bloombury and I were on the River Thames, in a punt with two young ladies when we saw the Oxford team in their boat practicing. They were some distance away from us, both Mick Bloombury and I had a pole each, and we were trying to steer the punt away from the direction of the Oxford boat, coming towards us at high speed. In our clumsy attempt to do so, we ended up placing the boat exactly sideways in their direction. There was this guy on the bank of the river, riding a bicycle and had a loudhailer, like a funnel, screaming at us to "get oorf the Riivaar!" in this posh voice; and there was this Oxford boat a few weeks before the famous boat race between Cambridge and Oxford, heading towards us at full speed.

We didn't have a clue what to do, we certainly weren't going to jump out of the punt into the river, and so the boat eventually crashed against our punt. The guy riding along the bank with a bicycle and a loudhailer ended up in the river himself, and there was a young female Cox on the boat who was shouting "come on stag 1, 2, come on stag 1, 2,", was still in the boat and all the males rowing towards us did not know what to do. There were some shouting and fist waving towards us, and some clumsy attempts to row away from us. A couple of them jumped out of the boat, whilst the majority stayed as the boat eventually took in a lot of water. No one was hurt and they eventually took the boat next to the river bank, extremely angry and abusive towards us.

Mick Bloombury was from a travelling family in London, and thus quite a tough guy, he naturally screamed insults back at them. I had to restrain him from swimming ashore to engage in fisty cuffs with them. The two young ladies in our punt were amused at the whole incident. We returned to Ruskin College later that afternoon and the students were lined up outside the canteen, cheering us for sinking the Oxford boat as we went in for dinner. It was seen as an action of working class against the snobs. I don't think it was the main boat that they normally use for the race, it was probably a practice boat; nevertheless, the Ruskin students thought it was a great feat for Ruskin College.

There were other occasions such as when I took a part time job at the Churchill Hotel, washing up dishes, and pots and pans, and I was amazed at the amount of food that was wasted, I salvaged the large chunks of beef, pork, chicken and turkey, and sometimes half a salmon and I took it back to Ruskin although I shouldn't have done this, it wasn't allowed, but I was quite shrewd, and I managed to take this food back to the college, and we would have a tremendous feast.

It wasn't all play of course, because work had to be done, and for me it was quite difficult having had little schooling and attempting to learn at age 31, it wasn't easy. My grammar was poor, but I was able to conceptualise and analyse in a reasonable way, and I was quite diligent. But writing an essay wasn't a very pleasant thing for me; I would enjoy reading the books, I enjoy reading about Marxism, socialism, working class history, politics and civilisation; but to put the words together in a very logical way was always difficult for me, so I used to prepare my essays and the tutors used to give me red marks almost covering the whole pages and say "this is not English" and then they would get to the point of "this isn't English" so my essays were poorly marked. So what I did, I used to bring my essays back home and my dear wife used to type them for me, and of course, being an English teacher, she corrected the grammar and introduced some of her own thoughts to me. I used to take my essays back and secured very high marks and I used to sell some of them in the picketers bar. I used to run an essay bank, where I charged 50p for my essays with more than 70 per cent marks. I had a nice little business going which, at least it paid for the beer and the crisps in the Picketers bar at Ruskin College.

Being a mature student in Oxford with a Morris Minor car, I felt quite privileged and I made friends quite easily, especially with the opposite sex. Many young ladies were missing a male in their lives; they were probably away from their homes, their villages and towns for the first time in their lives. Being a mature person and one who was able to sit and listen to them, apart from flogging them my essays, I was reasonably popular. Sometimes there were up to five or six of us in this little Morris Minor going around Oxford or in the outer lying villages including Woodstock having fun.

I did also have a relationship with a woman who worked for Ruskin College, a lady more my age, and I missed that relationship when I finished Oxford. Her name was Anne. I hope she is still around and in good health. She was a single parent with a young son at the time, and I hope they are both well. One couldn't avoid getting into a relationship in Oxford because it was such an informal atmosphere compared to what was known before.

Leaving Ruskin and heading for Essex University

Despite my lack of initial academic background, I did reasonably well and I secured credits in a number of subjects, once I was at Ruskin. The college had a very good relationship with other colleges within the university. Ruskin students, especially those from working class and trades trade union backgrounds, used to argue that when we finish at Ruskin College, we should all go back to the shop floor and help the workers and their unions. Others wanted to become trade union officials, members of Parliament or involve in radical and revolutionary activities. A number of others would argue that we should use the opportunity to progress to university especially Oxford.

Funnily enough, it was quite interesting to see the number of students who initially opposed to us progressing into university, but they themselves were desperate to secure places there after completing their Ruskin College course. I was in two minds about what I would do after leaving Ruskin College. But I was so overwhelmed by life in Oxford I decided to seek entry into New College Oxford, because they had a history of taking Ruskin students from the days of George Woodcock, the General Secretary of the TUC who was an ex New College student years earlier.

On average around a dozen of the one hundred students passing out each year ended up in Oxford University. When I was interviewed by the Principal at Ruskin, he asked me what I wanted to do after leaving Ruskin. I informed him that I wanted to be a trade union officer. He asked me whether I had given any thoughts of entering university. I informed him that I knew a close friend who was a student at Somerville College and I would consider a place there. He informed me that it was an all-female college and there were no chance of securing a place. He also informed me that Margaret Thatcher a well-known Conservative politician was educated at Somerville. However, he informed me that the admission arrangements for Oxford Colleges were changing and they were committed to doing away with single sex colleges in an age of equal access and against sexism in the selection process. I decided I was not the right person to break such a mould and agreed to apply elsewhere. I applied for New College, Oxford, Essex and the University of Sussex and I received acceptance at all three universities.

After being accepted at New College Oxford, I boasted to my left wing colleagues, that I had made it; but I was surprised when the colleagues who I was hanging out with, mainly the Socialist Workers Party and the Communist Party were against me going to Oxford and suggested that I accept a place at Essex or at Sussex. I was closer to the Left of Labour politics, even though I was a member of the Labour Party. However, the Labour Party was totally ineffective in taking a stance against racism and engaging in demonstrations or supporting black students who were the victims of racism at Oxford. Labour was moving away from its working class roots and I was disappointed with the level of racism and lack of acceptance in the Party due to my race and politics. Labour wanted ethnic minorities to vote for the Party, but not to share power with them. They were seen as electoral fodder for mainly white male politicians, even in areas with large number of non-white immigrants.

I found myself in a difficult situation. I wanted to stay in Oxford as I had many friends there. But I also wanted to leave as my wife had found out about a number of relationships I had had whilst I was there. So I thought it may be better for me to leave Oxford and go to Essex which was on not only a university with a radical reputation, but was also favoured by my left wing colleagues. Also, it was reasonably accessed using my famous little Morris minor. It was cheaper and more convenient for me.

I sometimes regret getting carried away with left wing politics and not accepting the place at New College. At age thirty three, I should have known better. I should have discussed my options with my wife as well. I regret being persuaded not to go to New College Oxford but instead to go to Essex, a red brick university with the worst record for student's militancy and disruption. I knew I would be involved in more radical students and political campaigns and agitation at Essex which also had a Trades Union Unit that attracted many mature students.

So like Jude in that Thomas Hardy book, Jude the Obscure, who never made it to Oxford University and ended up having a sad and difficult life, I also never quite got to the university, although I was satisfied that Ruskin College qualifications were recognised by the university and to most people as an Oxford degree was even more sought after than one from one of the mainstream Oxford colleges. I had made many friends from all parts of the world, especially a few friends from South Africa who were either exiled or refugees and were studying in Oxford. I supported them a great deal and I recall us marching from Oxford to Banbury, which must be over twenty miles, and back to raise money for the Anti-Apartheid Movement which was committed towards the liberation of South Africa, the release of Nelson Mandela and for majority rule.

Looking back, my time at Ruskin College was a great experience. It prepared me for my life in politics and trade unions, even though it made me extremely critical of the political policies and structures of the Labour Party, which I have been a member for forty six years until my resignation in 2010, and also very cynical of the trade union bureaucrats. I was a Labour Councillor for over Thirty years, a Parliamentary candidate in Milton Keynes in 1983 and a London Regional Trade Union Official for eight years.

I left Ruskin College a far more radical person than when I started, but was also able to read and write, and to enjoy doing so, and to discover myself as a person, my life, and my environment, and to understand reasons why there was so much poverty and suffering in the world, which people who are in control of the world's resources, and care very little about working people and their needs.

I still keep in touch with some ex-Ruskin students, thirty years and more after we have met. Quite a few Ruskin students have gone on to become members of parliament, including Dennis Skinner, John Prescott, Richard Marsh and others. Many others have achieved very high status from General Secretary of trade unions, to ambassadors for Britain, diplomats and senior civil servants.

I also recall an occasion when I was house chairman of Ruskin College, and we used to invite speakers on a regular basis to our meetings, and we once invited one Neil Kinnock, who later became leader of the Labour Party. In 1974, he was quite a left wing radical person, opposed entry into the common market and was also a darling of the trade union left wing comrades. After the meeting, which went down very well, we took Neil out to Oxford city centre to the bars to have a drink, and we all enjoyed that, then we all came back to the Picketers bar in the basement of Ruskin College and we had a tremendous sing song. I have a picture of Neil and I with our arms around each other, singing our hearts out, in Oxford city centre.

Chapter 9:

Universities

University of Essex

After leaving Oxford, in around July 1976, I decided not to pursue my academic career at New College Oxford and to do so instead at the University of Essex which was quite notorious for radical student activities. I had a short break for two weeks to enjoy my family in the summer and to have holiday with them in Worthing. My children were growing up, my son was a teenager and we endured the teenage antics that all parents had to put up with. Our daughter was always as close to me as our son was to his mum. My wife continued to play a major part in our lives, working as a teacher and at the same time taking care of the children and the home. I found it difficult to find work as by now I was on the various employers' list of people who were seen as left wing and politically motivated trade union activists. There were two right wing organisations in England that kept national records on people who employers should not employ. This national database of radicals and militants was added to and supported by many employers and the special branch of the Police. However, I did manage to find a part-time job as a heavy goods vehicle driver delivering parcels in London from a warehouse in Luton until I started at Essex.

So on 7th October 1976, off I went to the University of Essex in Colchester in my Morris Minor. I once again re-kitted and restyled myself to suit the radical Essex crowd. So with my bell bottom trousers, Cuban heels, lots of iron around my neck and wrists, hair down to my shoulders, and my black leather jacket I settled in a small room on the 13th floor of one of the famous tower blocks. I soon discovered that a student committed suicide by jumping out of the same floor just before final examinations

Within a few weeks of arrival I became heavily involved in student politics, I became a volunteer in the student union shop, serving behind the student bar, joined several radical groups and took part in demonstrations against soldiers based at the Colchester Barracks who had entered campus and assaulted a couple of black students. This incident soon elevated me from a humble first year student studying Comparative Government and Sociology to a recognised student activist. I was given a year off from a 3-year course due to my excellent academic results with several credits from Ruskin. Essex University was described as one of those red brick universities with massive student discontent, and a history of militancy. Most of the militants were in the Comparative Government and Sociology Department. Many of the lecturers were also known nationally as radicals who attracted likeminded students to Essex.

I met a Professor Lockwood who interviewed me a few years earlier for a famous book – *The Affluent Worker*. This book was largely based on the notion that the traditional working class life and culture was changing as society became more prosperous and affluent. Luton being a large manufacturing base with large multi-nationals such as Vauxhall Motors, Commer Cars, Bedford Trucks, SKF Ball Bearing, Electrolux and other heavy engineering companies were expanding during the 1960's and were unable to recruit sufficient labour to sustain their growth. So there were more jobs than people and the local authority had built large council estates to accommodate workers resettling in Luton as part of the Greater London Overspill Scheme. The same Scheme under which my wife and I secured our ninety five per cent mortgage and settled in a house in Sundon Park, four miles from the Town Centre where I worked. I renewed my acquaintance with Professor Lockwood and informed him that Luton was still a prosperous town with workers coming from all over the UK, Asia and the Caribbean to work in Luton.

As a mature student, I was able to interact with several professors and Senior Lecturers, in ways that other younger students were unable establish. So I enjoyed conversations, debates, tutorials and arguments with the university lecturers and professors during lectures and meetings of the academic board. By this time, I was feeling very confident about my ability to speak and debate in public. I often addressed hundreds of workers on strike in Luton and in other parts of the County. I became the secretary of the Luton Trades Council and I contributed to the work of the Trade Union Unit at Essex. My first year at Essex was quite academic and relatively peaceful. The University of Essex, located outside the town of Colchester was so different from Oxford. Colchester was historically a Roman town and in modern times a Barrack town with a strong army presence.

Colchester was clearly a town where students felt they couldn't go out at night to frequent the pubs and clubs due to fears of confrontation with soldiers. It was so different from Oxford at night. There were frequent incidents with soldiers and students bumping into each other. The disciplined soldiers took a dislike to certain students, who were portrayed in the Colchester Evening News as long haired, left wing, dope smoking, anti-establishment people, whose education was a waste of public funds. Students in higher education were I believe unfairly labelled in Britain and Western Europe as irresponsible radicals who spent too little time learning and too much time engaging in national and international political issues, wars, social and class issues, and the ruling elites. In order to avoid confrontation with soldiers and members from the racist National Front who would frequently harass us in the town centre, or on the university campus, when we organised discos and cultural events, we set up a group of stewards to keep these people out of the university events. I was naturally, elected as the Co-ordinator of this group.

For most of the time I was in Colchester, we took part in a variety of internal political, social, trades union and cultural activities organised mainly within campus. Of course we made full use of the bar facilities and engaged in unending debates about race, internationalism equality, trade unionism politics and internal university democracy. I used to enjoy coming home at weekends, chasing through the Essex and Hertfordshire countryside in my Morris. I would often return home on Thursday evening and leave early Monday morning to attend lectures at nine o'clock. I would make my way back in my little Morris from Bedfordshire, through Hertfordshire and into Essex to my accommodation in one of the tower block, flat thirteen, commonly known as "Suicide Tower", because a number of students had jumped out after being high on drugs, or frightened about the outcome of their examinations.

By the end of the first academic year I had seriously got involved with the student politics again, even though I had become involved in Labour Party and trades union activities as well as doing part-time work during weekends and holidays. My radical activities at the university took off in a high profile way after the Labour Prime Minister; James Callaghan made a major speech in Colchester on education. He outlined specific changes relating to funding of higher education, some of which would have detrimental financial and access implications, especially for foreign students. The Secretary of State for Education in the Labour government was Shirley Williams – later became Baroness Williams, after resigning from Labour with three other ministers to form a break-away political Party, called the Social Democratic Party. Essex University had a large per cent of overseas students from Africa, Asia and the Caribbean. During the 1960's and 1970's there were always vicious and sectarian debates in the media and political parties about the problems associated with black immigrants and the need to reduce the number arriving in Britain. It was a period of massive racist reporting, growth of right wing extremist political groups committed to "repatriation of blacks" and blaming them for all the problems of British economic, social, financial, racial, and domestic issues.

This was a period of strong and bitter discussions about overseas students and immigrants exploiting the British state and the indigenous people. There were strong disagreements and bitter confrontations within the Conservative and Labour Parties, with Labour showing the country that they were as tough on immigration as the Conservatives were, even though the overwhelming number of black (non-white) immigrants voted Labour at national and local elections. The universities in England wanted the income from overseas students, but were reluctant to charge them much higher fees than home students. This was an issue that made me extremely angry with Labour, as education was so close to my heart and my beliefs that working class young people would break out of the poverty and disadvantages experienced by their parents, and would achieve this through higher education. So I became very involved with the fight for equal access to education for everyone. I was very involved in lots of debates, demonstrations on campus, in London, at other universities and campaigns against increases in fees, especially disproportional increase in overseas student fees.

A large number of students supported by the Student Union at Essex decided to occupy the university. Occupation wasn't as unfamiliar as some students felt, because students as Sussex and other red brick universities had engaged in similar occupations. It was a period of massive growth of working class students in higher education, participation in politics and anti-establishment protests, stemming from the 1960's with the anti-Vietnam war and the growth of what was described as American imperialism. The failures of the British economy, resulting in cyclical unemployment, de-stabilisation of traditional values, coupled with the fact that many students enjoyed studying political theory, comparative politics, sociology and that kind of subjects, which gave them a sense of internationalism and solidarity with the victims of oppression. Students placed themselves as a vanguard in the class struggles spreading across Western Europe, the failure of the political class and financial elites to deliver the promises of growth, equality and opportunities. They felt resentment against the excesses of capitalism and the divisions caused by wars, poverty, racism, sexism and unemployment amongst qualified students. I must emphasize that the majority of students did not participate in radical or even in any type of action within or outside the universities. I was determined before the increase in fees were imposed on students, because I wanted to have a different from what I had in Oxford, so I came home on a regular basis and got involved in a local trade union and political issues as well as participating in anti-racism activities in Luton, London and the Home counties.

However, I was voted Chair of the Essex Occupation Committee and we promptly occupied various parts of the University. During the students' occupation, a helicopter flew above the university, and we thought that the helicopter was full of police officers coming to arrest us. So a number of us got onto the roof of the university to stop the aircraft from landing. Whilst running along the roof, I stepped onto a skylight and fell into a room. I had to be rescued by fellow students. The room contained large number of cabinets and files which were ransacked by students looking for any records kept by the university about students. As a consequence of this and other actions later on, about 30 of us students were disciplined for criminal damage and a whole range of other issues identified during the occupation. The university managers regarded me as one of the ringleaders, so I was singled out for serious punishment. The occupation lasted for a few days only and I was involved in the negotiations surrounding the occupation with the Bursar and his team. Sadly, we did not succeed in our resistance to increase in fees, nor did the Labour government led by James Callaghan, after the sudden resignation of Harold Wilson. Labour lost the general election after a prolonged period of industrial strife and economic decline. Mrs Thatcher was then elected as Britain's first woman Prime Minister.

The Disciplinary Committee of the university carried out various investigations and introduced disciplinary action against the main activists during the occupation. Many of the students decided that they would not oppose their punishments and would welcome expulsion because, for them it was a big statement in their lives and they didn't care very much about acquiring qualifications. For me, a mature student with a family and the prospect of building a career in the unions or in politics I was worried and it certainly brought me to my senses. My poor wife was working so hard to assist me and there was I, a mature man who should have known better, taking part in this type of activity to the extent which I did as a leader of the students, and getting myself in such a pickle that I could very well leave without securing my honours degree.

The student union decided to hire legal support to represent the students, and I was one of the few who decided to use the appeal system. So I had to appear before a Professor, who was a professor of politics at the time I was there, to Chair the Disciplinary Committee. I decided to accept the assistance of the Student Union solicitor and we jointly prepared my defence. I did not want to get expelled from the university, I wanted to really complete the course and return home with a degree. I wanted to secure a job and to start to live a normal life. The solicitor said to me "do you really wish to appeal Jim"? I said "yes I am serious". He said "what are your grounds"? I said "I don't think the Professor could really hear my appeal because there were rumours that he has an association with a government Minister closely associated with the increase in fees". I really don't know how true this was, but it was rumoured by students that this was the case. The solicitor said to me, "Is this your defence"? I said "yes", and he said "well, I don't know what I can do, but I'll see what I can make of this information you have given me" then he said, "you are playing a bit dirty Jim", and I said "what do you expect, I am a trade unionist. I am quite sharp and I will do anything to defend myself and to get myself out of this pickle".

Anyway, he asked to see certain members of the Disciplinary Panel with a Professor of Politics from my Department who was also my personal tutor and agreed to support me. After this private discussion in my absence, there was an adjournment, before we were called before the Panel. I pleaded guilty to the charges, expressed regret for my actions and gave a promise of good conduct during my remaining few weeks at the university. I was delighted when the outcome was, that I was suspended from the university, but they had deferred the suspension until after I had completed my examinations; so the suspension was a suspended suspension. So I was happy with the result. I was told by a professor that I was in line for a first class degree, but no one convicted for the occupation would achieve more than a 2.1 degree. I also decided to that this university game was no longer for me and I need to concentrate on practical things such as finding a job. After leaving the University of Essex, I desperately tried to find work, but despite lots of applications I was never offered any employment apart from casual manual work on a temporary basis.

I was not prepared to be unemployed or inactive, so I decided to organise against racial attacks and harassment in the work place and in the community. The National Front was building its profile across the country, and were agitating against black people in Britain. Racial attacks and harassment as well as racism within the police service and the judiciary were common place. The media was also agitating against immigrants and blaming them for taking the jobs of white workers; being a liability to the British economy, exploiting benefits, abusing the public services and responsible for housing shortage, high levels of crime and so on. The economy was not as prosperous as in previous years, and clearly whenever there was a down turn in the economy, there were increased agitation against black immigrants who were blamed for everything that was unacceptable. The National Front had set up an office in Luton and was quite active. Robert Relf had lived in Luton and was notorious for putting a notice outside his house in Coventry, saying "house for sale, but no blacks". So he hit the headlines in a number of newspapers and when he came to Luton as a bus driver, he organised a local National Front group.

University of London

I was quite active in community relations in Luton, I used to also be the secretary of the Luton Trade Union Council, and I had a regular feature in the newspaper, writing on industrial matters. The Labour government was in fairly serious trouble and had to secure large loans from the IMF to bail Britain out of debts. Mrs Thatcher as Leader of the Conservative Party promised to break the power of the trade unions, restore Britain to prosperity, reduce unemployment and strikes and introduce a wide range of right wing policies if elected in 1979. I could see there were troubles ahead and I desperately wanted to start a profession career. I was offered some evening work at Barnfield College teaching Sociology, Politics and Economics. I was congratulated by my senior tutor, a fellow trade unionist and Labour Party member for the success achieved by my students. He suggested that I should complete a Further and Adult Education Teaching Course (FEATC) evening course, and I should also apply for a full-time teacher training course at Garnett College, part of The University of in London, where he had been a student a few years earlier. I followed his advice and succeeded in completing both courses before I secured a job with the GMB Union as the London Regional Education, Training and Public Relations Officer.

I also enrolled for a part-time Masters of Art course in Industrial Relations at The University of Warwick, whilst I was at Garnett Teacher Training College, in order to increase my career options. After securing the job with the GNB union I decided to drop the Industrial Relations course at the University of Warwick. Having a job with the trade union movement meant I had to make a number of changes to my lifestyle and trade union activities in Luton. I would describe my work in the trade union movement in another chapter.

University of Hertfordshire

It is true to say that no one is too old to learn, and that learning is for life. So I have experienced a fair number of years in the University of Life and in proper universities. So at the age of 50, after eight years as a union official and a number of senior posts in local government I decided to go back to full-time learning, and I was fortunate to have financial support from the Local Government Management Board where I had previously worked as a Senior National Advisor to Local Government in England and Wales, to undertake a master in business and administration course (MBA) at the University of Hertfordshire.

It was a one year course starting in October 1994 and finishing in September 1995. I found this course extremely boring and so whilst I was at university in Hertfordshire I used to come home very regularly and I used to get involved in local issues, but I also studied for a counselling course and I did other short courses at Barnfield College. The MBA was very interesting but it was very much business orientated something which was never close to my heart, because I was more on the side of working people.

I was probably one of the oldest students on the course and I was interested to see these young people who had gone to school, then on to Sixth Form College or the local college of further education, then straight onto university. Naturally before the end of the course they had almost all secured lucrative employment. The only ones having problems in finding any type of employment were the few African students on the course.

After the course I started self-employment as a Trainer and Management Consultant on Employment Law, Equality and Diversity, Strategic Management and Managing Change. I named my sole trading company 'Working for Equality", and designated myself as the Director. I have retained this company right up to the present day.

Part 3

Chapter 10:

Involvement in governance of public bodies and agencies

A happy board is not necessarily an effective one

"The practice of governing is mainly different from managing: It is not about managing [organizations] but confirming they are well run. It is less about doing and taking action than reflecting and learning. The key principles are that of prudence, acting in good faith, stewardship, duty, openness, transparency and integrity. These are the real building-blocks of excellence in corporate governance and the inclination actions for an effective board."

A happy board is not always effective

During my forty five years in public life, through my involvement on health boards, trustees of several local, regional and national voluntary, community and charitable organisations as well as local and national government agencies government, I have gained significant knowledge and experience on how quangos, bureaucracies, institutions and boards operate. All these organisations share a common culture, management style and mind-set, to varying extents. I have always felt it my duty to be an active participant on boards whether they are school, university, local government, health or, government agencies to hold the executive directors to account. Openness, transparency, accountability, performance measurements, leadership, honesty and monitoring are essential prerequisites for good governance. Organisations spending public money must be held accountable to ensure "value for money", democratic and effective outcomes. Quangoes are now accountable for over £200 billion of public expenditure involving the NHS, education and dozens of central government agencies, yet in my view, many of them have fallen short of the essential requirements, due to poor governance, management and leadership.

The people who are either nominated or elected to these boards to protect the public interests are often ill equipped through lack of training, experience, skills, and ability to understand the dynamics, culture, process and mechanisms associated with the organisation. Most of these people in top boards have secured their positions through patronage by local and central governments, institutions and organisations. Few are elected through competitive arrangements. Most of these people are paid small sums or are entitled to claim expenses, whilst a minority are paid massive sums, especially if they belong to more than one board, which is not uncommon.

Most of these top boards are packed with men and some women. I have served on numerous boards, especially between 1970 and 2000, where I was the only Black person. What made matters worse for me is that I was expected to smile a lot, say very little, being loyal to the directors and desist from making any criticisms of staff or fellow board members. Such behaviour was seen as not being a team player. Being intelligent, having several university degrees, always ready and willing to ask searching questions and challenging reports and strategies often created tensions and discussions that would seldom occur had I not been present. Even when there were boards with mixed gender and ethnic minority members, I invariably stood out because of my style of working and the way I contributed to the deliberations as well as challenging issues I felt concerned about. I always seek to work within a strategic and professional framework and never challenge unless I have done my homework, have alternative ideas to offer and be prepared to argue my position in a professional way. For most of the directors, senior managers and board members, they operate within a culture of consensus, approving reports, strategies and policies with very little challenges, as meetings are organised in such a way where key decisions are often made within a short time span. Directors and managers are invariably in control of the agenda, process, reports and presentations. Board members are frequently given enough time to question, challenge and suggest alternatives. Therefore the culture of boards is to endorse the recommendations, say as little as possible and enjoy the refreshments. Most board members and directors are seldom tolerant of people like me, who are accused of pro-longing meetings, having too much to say, and denying others the chance to contribute. The problem is that too many board members ask questions and dwell on trivial issues that are not the least strategic or dynamic, whilst keeping silent on key policies, practices, procedures and strategies. I believe in Nelson Mandela's view that "The time is always right to do right." I discovered that exposing weak performance to public scrutiny is a remarkably effective way of challenging public sector managers who are often complacent, arrogant and manipulative. Too many people try to be good in organisations only because they fear being challenged and for reward. I have always stood by directors, managers and board members when they stand for what is right, honest, and in the public interest.

I am not bound to win, but bound to be true

Between 1980 and 2003, as a part of my involvement as a County Councillor, Chair of the County's Education Committee and an activist within the Labour Party and trade unions, I was nominated at various times to represent these organisations on governing bodies of universities, colleges and several charities and government agencies. I welcomed these opportunities to influence institutions to create the change they aspire to realise their aims and objectives. As a mature student and someone who acquired qualifications later than normal in life, I was keen to ensure that education was the key to redressing the level of inequality, unemployment, poverty, skills, confidence and abilities that characterised the lives of millions of working class people. I wanted equality for women, ethnic minorities, disabled and older people. So I gave a great deal of attention to ensuring that our educational establishments were fit for purpose. I believe I did manage to assist in a small way towards this direction, despite being in a minority and having to work in an environment with regular cuts in public expenditure and austerity.

The 1980's saw massive changes in the provision and restructuring of post-16 education. The return of the Conservative Government led by the Prime Minister Margaret Thatcher, in 1979, introduced many changes in every aspect of our lives, including education, housing, trade unions and the economy. Education went through many changes designed for:

- Improving the standard of education;

- Linking further and higher education achievements, performance and standards with the dynamics associated in improving the economic and competitive success of the British economy;

- Upgrading a range of academic institutions such as polytechnics into universities

- Increasing the number of students in higher and further education, especially females;

- Decentralising funding and governance of education;

- Introducing greater accountability and involvement by local stakeholders in the governance and direction of educational institutions

I welcomed some of the Thatcherite changes, because I believed many institutions were complacent, lacking in vision and were stuck in ideas and practices that were re-enforcing the divisions and inequalities within British society. My concerns were to the following:

- Under achievement of working class pupils, especially boys;

- Stereotyping of learning and opportunities for females, males and learners from ethnic minority backgrounds;

- Females selecting careers which led them into traditional opportunities in areas dominated by their gender such as retail, childcare, hairdressing, nursing, teaching and public sector administration;

- Males were equally channelled in stereotypical career opportunities;

- Black, Asians and visible minority ethnic pupils were amongst the lower achievers, apart from Indians and Chinese;

- Stereotyping of race, class, gender disability and achievements within the pre and post 16 education systems.

To my amazement and disgust, I found stereotyping deeply embedded within the school, further and higher education systems. Many working class children were grossly underachieving, and were leaving school with very few sought after academic or personal qualifications. Many had difficulty with reading, writing and arithmetic. Personal confidence, motivation and inter-personal skills were also lacking, which placed them at a disadvantage in securing good career opportunities and employment. I was determined to do my best for these learners. But it was too difficult to challenge the institutional culture, power of the head teachers and senior management teams.

Effective governance means the board does not accept what it is told without question

As a trained teacher and experienced lecturer with several years of experience as a full-time London Regional Officer for a large trade union, and lectured in schools, colleges and universities I was familiar with the institutional culture and decision making process. I was also involved in the design, delivery, and evaluation and supporting of a wide range of courses for adults from various educational, social, cultural, religious and ethnic backgrounds. This experience provided me with lots of useful transferable skills and knowledge relating to teaching and learning within all areas of education. My wife was also a senior who shared her professional experience with me. We also supported two mixed race children through the education system. I had decades of experience in chairing boards of governors in primary and high schools for many years, as well as serving on boards of colleges and universities.

For a period of four years I was a member of the funding council, which funded and reported on further education in England and Wales. This involvement was very useful and it provided me with a great deal of ideas on financial, academic and performance management within schools and colleges. For much of my professional life serving on public bodies and government agencies, I was either the only black or non-white person who was prepared to take my role seriously and participated fully at all meetings. I always tried to focus on outputs, outcomes, added value, quality, standards and other strategic issues.

Unlike most participants, I was always prepared to read all the documents challenge the status quo and make critical and objective strategic interventions as and when I felt appropriate. I frequently questioned suggestions and recommendations and often tried to introduce change by expressing views even though they may appear to initially represent the position of a minority of participants. Influencing the outcomes and decisions making process is important for people representing the public interest.

This professionally challenging style which I generally used at meetings of governing bodies resulted in a wide range of response from the paid bureaucrats and those who were opposed to my professional or political views built around accountability, transparency and democracy. For many members of governing bodies, trusts and committees, they feel that they are expected to be nice, supportive, polite, and agreeable as far as the bureaucrats are concerned. Pleasing the bureaucrats does not necessarily ensure successful management which benefits all the stakeholders.

Public bodies and government agencies too often puts the interests of staff, especially at senior level before the consumers or service users. It is therefore essential that members ask the appropriate questions, challenge the status quo as necessary and seek to shape and direct outcomes even if it sometimes conflict with what is recommended by the bureaucrats. All the key stakeholders in schools were well aware that they were failing large number of children, parents, employers and the nation, yet they were often complacent, inclined to blame the students who were perceived as low achievers because of their social class, race, English not being their mother tongue or generally low achievers. Teachers at all levels, the teaching unions and governors were sensitive to criticism from any source and continued to led down large numbers of learners.

As a school governor for over thirty years, including chairing the governing bodies of two high schools for over eleven years, I had to work very hard to convince the Heads and other teachers as well as the unions and governors that the school could and should achieve greater success. As a result I often found myself isolated, marginalised and even hated by teachers and fellow governors. On a number of occasions, head teachers, unions, governors, the local education authority and fellow councillors contrived to remove me from senior positions, or from governing bodies altogether.

I have suffered a great deal during my involvement as a councillor due to my style, which can be described as interventionist, challenging, questioning, and being pro-active, critical, directional and strategic. My role has always been influenced by my commitment to equality, equality, diversity, equal access to learning and opportunities, maximising use of human physical and financial resources, accountability, openness and transparency, performance management and value for money, added value and thinking outside the box.

These are the very values and styles which terrify bureaucrats who are not inclined to be open or accountable. As a consequence they tend to be intolerant of people like myself. In general bureaucrats in educational institutions are no different from those in the wider public sector and government agencies. Not only do they oppose any challenge or disagreements to their performance or management practices, but they also have a large capacity to enhance and consolidate their position and influence amongst board members or governors, in order to shape the work and opinions of those around them. Governors are expected to support the school, the staff and the Head. Even being a critical friend can be seen by some school managers as threatening on occasions. They prefer total and uncritical loyalty from governors, parents and the local education authority.

To a large extent I believe governors and board members have failed many pupils, parents and the public because of their failure to question, challenge and hold institutions to account in the interest of all the stakeholders.

Governor of Dunstable and Barnfield Colleges

"The route to education is bitter, but the fruit is sweet. " – Aristotle.

I enjoyed my work as a governor with Dunstable College. The college had some difficulties during the 1980's due to cuts in funding and increased demand for courses and support for students. I played a large part in issues associated with strategic management, managing change, equality and diversity and opening access to wider range of students from working class and black minority ethnic students. I worked closely with a fellow county councillor Ms Shepherd, commonly known as Sam. Sam was an old style member of the Conservative Party who had lived in India for a while and was a well-known councillor from farming background in rural Bedfordshire.

She was fiercely independent and like myself often displayed tendencies associated with being a no- nonsense and difficult person to control by the bureaucrats. Sam was quite a stout lady in her sixties. She was a typically British middle class woman and also a typical member of a rural Conservative Party County Councillor. Sam was never reluctant to express her views on any subject including controversial issues such as feminism, equality, race, racism, immigration, class, religion, unemployment, crime, Britishness or multiculturalism. People who were often referred to by Sam as being "work shy" "living on benefits" "unwelcome immigrants" or the "deserving poor". She had no time for trade unions, feminism, the Labour Party or people who failed to "integrate within British society".

Despite her straight talking and us being at the opposite end of politics, Sam and I worked well as fellow governors on Dunstable College and Luton College of Higher Education. I recall an occasion when Sam and I attended a conference on race and education in Bradford. Her comments caused severe chaos after she stated that "Asian immigrants were coming to Britain, working all hours of the day and night living on bananas and saving up enough money to buy up all our news agents and corner shops.

Sam was very verbally attacked mainly by women, from all races and backgrounds. I had to intervene a great deal to save her from abuse and derogatory name calling.

On another occasion we were part of a recruitment panel for a head teacher. The interview took place in County Hall and was attended by the chief Education Officer and other senior advisors to advise and support the panel on equality and fair selection issues. At the start of the meeting the recruitment panel was present in a large room except for Sam. As the Chair of the panel I decided to find Sam who was having an afternoon post lunch nap in her favourite settee within the members lounge.

I woke Sam up and led the way to the interviewing room some twenty metres away. Sam decided to pause outside the room, to inform the five candidates sitting around a large coffee table that she "intends to select the successful candidate in the same way as I select the Barton beauty queen each year". Sam was totally opposed to equal opportunities or any other arrangements associated with positive action or "political correctness". Together we made a lot of changes within the college, including replacing the principal and number of senior managers. I even persuaded Sam to appoint a black person to the senior management team.

In 1993 I decided to resign from Barnfield College's governing body, to accept a part-time consultancy part manager of Equality Diversity and community liaison. During my period as a governor of the college I did my best to promote equality, diversity and widen community representation and within the college. Barnfield was a relatively small further education college located on a single site on the outskirt of Luton, some two miles from Luton town centre and the Luton College of higher Education where I also served as a governor. Barnfield College had grown to become one of the largest and most successful Colleges in England and have extended its sphere of influence and control to local High Schools that were amongst some of the worst achieving schools in the County. The previous Principal, Jim Horrocks MBE and the then Principal, Peter Birkett have created a number academies and have massively increased the resources, performance and achievements of tens of thousands of learners in Luton schools and Barnfield College.

During my period as a governor of Barnfield College I frequently raised issues on equality, diversity, community involvement, marketing of courses within the black and minorities' ethnic communities, people living on estates and poorer areas. To fulfil all these commitments, the college had to grow substantially. As a councillor and a governor I was able to support the college financially to enable substantial extension of the buildings, the number of students on and off college sites, and diversity of courses within the College and the community.

I also assisted in putting into place a number of policies and procedures and strategies for marketing the courses and facilities to the wider community especially in the areas identifies as being disadvantaged. At Senior Management Team meetings and at meetings of the governing body I was encouraged by Fintan Donohue, the Vice Principal, to raise several issues and requested a range of reports in order to promote progress on policies and strategies designed to inform future strategic planning and performance. This discussion created a lot of resentment from college managers and fellow governors and I was challenged by fellow governors who were generally happy to enjoy both the hospitality and status afforded to governors, but reluctant to challenge the senior managers. They were on the whole happy to leave the decisions to the principal and staff.

I took the view that as large sums of public money were allocated to the college and there should be accountability, probity, transparency and value for money. The college also had a duty to empower and support all sections of the community equally and fairly, as well as providing high quality courses for everyone. I wanted the courses and students to reflect the make-up of the local population and to increase the number of staff from the diverse community.

After a difficult meeting of the governing body the principal said to me "Jim you criticised us as college managers on many occasions how about joining the college management team and help us to address these issues?" I reply "you offered this to me before and I declined because this would mean I have to leave the governing body because of conflict of interest". However, I informed him that I would seriously consider his offer and get back to him.

A short while later I was offered early retirement at the age of fifty with a substantial lump sum and fifteen years enhancement in my pension which was accessible as soon as I signed the contract. About 3 weeks later, I signed the contract and took up the post with the college. I kept my position with the college for nearly twelve years and during this period I was involved in many strategic and practical changes in many areas of the college and community life. I was frequently praised by the principal and more so the by the vice principal to whom I am grateful for allowing me to contribute towards the following:

1. Massive expansion of the college from one to five large sites;

2. Barnfield identified as one of the largest and most successful college in the region;

3. The college identified as one of the most successful and diverse institutions in England in terms of courses, achievements, students, staff and community involvement;

4. Extensive decentralisation of a number of courses delivered within the community

5. Increased involvement in the college by members of the diverse community

6. Clear and extensive policies, procedures and guidelines on equality and diversity, employment rights, staff training and development, recruitment and selection, progression of employees and students;

By the time I left Barnfield I felt it was a very useful experience and the changes I contributed towards would have substantial impact on future college plans.

Luton College of Higher Education and University of Luton

I joined the college in 1981 when I was elected as a County Councillor and a member of the Education committee. Prior to 1993 colleges were funded by and accountable to local Education Authorities. My inclusion on the governing body was welcomed by the principal and some governors and senior managers. Not all of them welcomed me as I was often portrayed in the local media as a champion of race equality, trades union rights, general equality and diversity, empowerment of working class people and challenging institutions, public bodies and service providers. Many governors and managers had pre-conceived ideas about my politics and my styles in articulating the issues I felt strongly about.

I was often labelled in the local media as the "Tony Benn, Ken Livingstone, or Red Jim of Bedfordshire". I was even portrayed in the media as the "four B's – Bedfordshire Black Bully Boy". I was identified with the leading Left wing characters that were very prominent in national politics of the Labour Party. I was associated with being radical and extreme with strong working class, socialist principles and values that threatened the conservative establishment. During my years of political and trade union work at local, regional and national levels I had extensive contacts with people like Tony and Ken Livingstone, Dennis Skinner, Neil Kinnock and radical trade union leaders.

The college Principal anticipating my potential to make waves within the governing body tactically decided to occupy my time by asking me to work with the Vice Principal to develop the college's Equal Opportunities policies, practices and strategies. I was always very vocal at meetings of the governing body, as I was on all the other governing bodies I served on. For almost all of my time on governing bodies, Trustees, or Board members of various institutions such as the NHS, Manpower Board, National Charities and Universities, I was invariably the only non-white member.

My willingness to contribute at meetings and to articulate my views supported by careful research findings and analysis generated considerable resentment against me. The principal was aware of this and he frequently re-affirmed his support for my style. He often praised me for asking questions and requesting feedback from managers on issues associated with equality, diversity of students, community involvement, academic achievements and support for students. On a number of occasions he informed me that I "should not change my style" as it kept him and his senior managers focussed on the need to be well prepared for information dissemination, challenges and question at meetings.

I was also involved with my colleague Sam Shepherd in the appointment of the new Principal and Chief Executive who eventually led the successful application for the college to be designated a university. The college was struggling financially due to cuts in funding and demand for courses during the 1980's and early 1990's. The governors explored several possibilities of merging the college with a number of other educational institutions including Bedford College and Hatfield Polytechnic. I was one of the governors who argued against merger and for full university status.

University of Luton

Planning for University Status was both enlightening and challenging. At the outset I made my position clear should we succeed with our application that the university should reflect local interests and identity as far as possible.

I wanted local people, businesses and communities to positively identify with the university and to access the benefits of such an institution located at the heart of our town. It was essential that the university positively target black, Asian and minority students, females and unemployed people as well as mature learners. Many Asian parents were reluctant to encourage their daughters to access higher education especially if it involved leaving home. The university would be well placed to attract Asian woman, disabled people, those with caring responsibilities and mature learners who would not require residential accommodation. The university would help to create a range of opportunities for jobs, services, cultural and social events. I decided that the university should be named the "University of Luton" for the above reasons and proposed this at relevant meeting. Other names such as "University of Chilterns" and "University of Bedfordshire" were proposed. I managed to persuade at least two fellow governors, one of which was the Bishop of Bedford, who were quite cynical about my choice of name as they felt the "University of Luton" would be see as a joke because the image of the town which characterised it at the time. We manage to persuade the governors to agree with us.

Celebrating University Status

At last, University status was granted by the Queen who endorsed the decision with her personal seal. This occasion clearly warranted an organised celebration which was duly arranged for the summer of 1993 at the Putteridgebury Management Centre. The Centre was in a lovely rural setting some three miles from the main University site in Park Square, Luton. All the Governors and their partners were invited to this formal occasion together with many local and national distinguished representatives, guests and senior members of staff. At first most people felt that given Luton's image at the time, naming the new institution the "University of Luton" would put lots of students off from applying to the university. The University later changed its name to the University of Bedfordshire and has proven to be one of the most successful post-1992 Universities in England.

Unfortunately my wife, who was a senior high school teacher at the time, decided not to attend the celebration with me, and decided that it would be better to celebrate a Friday evening on her own as she had done for some time, accompanied by some background entertainment from Bob Dylan. So, there I was, all dressed up in my bow tie and best suit attending an important function on my own.

Naturally, the occasion was marked by good food, fine wines, vintage port, grand speeches and lively entertainment. There were about fifteen tables with a dozen guests sitting around each one. As a senior member of the Governing Body and Chair of the County Council Education Committee, I was placed among some distinguished guests and given the task of ensuring that they had enough food and drink, and an entertaining evening. The event was scheduled to close at 11:30 p.m. but went on until nearly midnight.

During the evening, there were many toasts to people such as the Queen, other members of the Royal family, the High Sheriff of the County, the Vice-Chancellor, and many others. By the end of the toasting sessions we had all taken quite a bit of liquid. For those like me, who toasted with wine, it was inevitable that we would exceed the legal drink and drive alcohol limit. It is quite easy for a fifty-year old man on his own at such an event to get somewhat carried away.

After the speeches and toasts, the entertainment started while I was in conversation with a very attractive lady a few years younger than me. She told me that she was a teacher who had previously given up her job to support her children, but they were now at University and she would like to return to her profession. I empathised with her position and, being a County Councillor and spokesperson for the County's education provision, I took her details and promised to pass them on to the Teacher Recruitment Team.

As I was taking her details, her husband asked her if she would like to dance. She replied, 'Can't you see I am having a conversation with Councillor Thakoordin?" He disappeared and, a few minutes later, the lady asked me for a dance, a request to which I promptly accepted, even though I have two uncoordinated left feet and could not dance to save my life. However, the dance went reasonably well, no doubt because of the alcohol stimulating the movements in my two left feet. So, we had a couple more dances before returning to our seats. Her husband returned and promptly asked her for a dance. Again, she refused his offer but, a few minutes later, she and I were dancing again. During this dance with this charming and attractive lady, I kissed her neck and complimented her on her appearance. At the end of the social event we all parted in fairly high spirits.

My good friend and fellow Governor of the University, who later became a Labour M.P., offered to give me a lift home but I decided that I was able to drive myself. After a mile or so, I felt I was being followed. So, I decided to pull in to the main University car park, some three miles from the event, wait a few minutes, and then complete the journey home. Half way through this leg of the journey, I clipped the kerb and ended up with a punctured tyre. I decided to walk the rest of the way home but, after a few yards, a police car pulled up beside me.

I was asked where I had been, where I was going, and whether I had consumed any alcohol. Having replied to the questions I was then invited to blow into a bag and was promptly informed that I was marginally over the drink-drive limit. I was taken to the police station just after midnight and I believe that the Chief Constable was informed that a member of the County Council and an ex-member of the Police Authority had been arrested. I also believe the Chief had told the police officer to charge me and to treat me with the utmost respect by processing the charge quickly, not putting me in a police cell and taking me home as soon as possible.

I decided against accepting a lift from the police and telephoned my wife, requesting that she come and pick me up from the police station. She was naturally very angry and gave me a hard time at the police station, followed by more verbal abuse and threats when we got home: this lasted until late the following morning. After discussing the matter with my solicitor who had quite a reputation for pleadings amongst magistrates, he told me he would get me off this charge.

My solicitor suggested I should claim that someone had spiked my drink and, as I was only very slightly over the limit, I had not consumed excess alcohol. I gave the lawyer the telephone number of the woman I had been dancing with at the social and, instead of acting as a favourable witness for me; she told the lawyer that she believed someone she knew had alerted the police before I had started my journey home on the night in question. I have often wondered who that person was, even though I believe I knew his identity.

I did not go along with my solicitor's advice and appeared in court on my own. The local press, having been alerted of this misdemeanour by an insider, naturally gave prominence to this shameful act by a high-profile local politician who should have known better. This incident resulted in a hefty fine, twelve months driving ban and a serious lecture from the Chair of the magistrates who knew a great deal about me. In fact the case had to be postponed on at least two occasions as they had difficulty finding a group of magistrates who were unfamiliar with my political, trade union and community work. So for a whole year I had to use public transport, scrounge lifts from my wife and friends or engage local taxis. This incident also damaged my political career to some extent.

The humiliation of having to live with the stigma of a criminal record for life has changed certain aspects of my social life for good. I quickly and discretely resigned from the governing body of the University and also from the Court of Governors at the University of Cranfield.

Institutional inertia and management failings

My overall experience of governance in the public sector has been disappointing despite the vast sums spent on further and higher education. The massive expansion on management and leadership training, through the numerous short and specific courses, to longer ones, including Masters in Business Administration (MBA) and qualifications in Public Management Administration has so far not stemmed the severe criticisms of management in the public sector. Printed below are some recent comments relating mainly to the National Health Service that has been criticised for serious and tragic failures almost on a daily basis by the media and members of the public.

"Many trust board members cannot be sure that their hospital is operating within the law." Audit Commission, 2009 (Taking in on trust)

"Most readers will be well aware of the recent furore regarding mortality rates and NHS regulation. According to an article in the Health Service Journal (HSJ – 3 December 2009) NHS Confederation policy director Nigel Edwards said "Inspection is hugely burdensome. Regulation should be a backstop – the foundation stone is board and professional accountability."

"Effective governance is not a 'one-off' event, but rather a continuous process of vigilance. It is the duty of any NHS Board to systematically and rigorously hold the organisation to account for the achievement of its objectives. It should do so by scrutiny of evidence and the exercise of judgement on a constant, iterative basis." Richard Leblanc and James Gilles –'Inside the Boardroom: How boards really work and the coming revolution in corporate governance'– p251 June 2010.

"In the twenty first century most doctors and nurses still haven't got much of a clue about the quality of care we're providing, the effect we have on you, what happens to you after you're discharged, whether we've made your life better or worse or even if we've killed or cured you. We operate and consult in a vacuum, with virtually no feedback,

just muddling through and hoping for the best." Dr Phil Hammond, 2002. Trust me, I'm a doctor. *Metro Publishing, London*

Despite the many, constant and varied criticisms about the NHS, the majority of patients and users of the services are happy with it. The NHS helps millions of people every week. By committed and caring staff. I blame many of the problems associated with the NHS on cuts in budgets, inadequate resources, constant political interference and re-organisation, poor quality senior managers and directors as well as ineffective boards.

It is the same scenario in the other public bodies as far as I know. Our public sector democracy whether it is local government, the NHS, Police or Fire Authorities has been undermined by weak managers and those appointed by the public to oversee these bodies. Many of these people are well established Quangoes who were subjected to political appointments and are very keen to promote their status, interests and opportunities to secure financial benefits as appropriate. For example, a councillor in local government would be entitled to a general allowance, plus responsibility allowances, plus a sizeable sum for being nominated to a local Fire, Police or Health Authority as well as running their own business, or being in employed.

The public is either too passive or forgiving of public bodies, even though they do grumble about poor services and practices on occasions. Too often the public and governors hey have failed to hold managers in public services to account. The framework established to do so through the governance system has also grossly failed the public. We have been informed of large numbers of unnecessary suffering, abuse, maladministration and deaths in hospitals, care home, prisons, children's homes and detention centres. The elderly, disabled, ethnic minorities and vulnerable people have suffered most due to incompetence, racism, stereotyping, poor management and lack of discipline and accountability. Billions of pounds have been spent by the NHS, the police and schools in compensation for poor services. This money could have been better spent on improving efficiency and greater access to quality services.

I have been vigilant in all my public life to promote better added value services of high standard equally accessible to everyone. I have challenged decision makers, institutional incompetence and discrimination, poor decision making, inappropriate cultural values and practices. Sadly, for most of the time I was on the side of the minority and not the majority, my comments were often taken up by managers in private; they seldom formally acknowledged me for my contributions in public. I am aware that most people feel that few individuals have the power to change society, or the world, but I know that each one of us is capable of creating a tiny ripple in an ocean, that collectively have the capacity to realise significant and lasting changes for the benefit of everyone.

Top- Bottom
Jim with the Queen in 2005 at opening of
Luton and Dunstable Hospital extension
Jim chair of Governors. Doreen at work at Challney High School for
Boys where Jim was the Chair of the Governing Body.

Chapter 11:

Health, wellbeing and our NHS

The greatest wealth is health

My first serious health problem occurred when I was three years old. I was with my family on Plantation Leonora in Guyana at the time. An older boy was peeling a coconut with a machete and I was chasing about in the yard and according to the older boy, I walked into the accident. The cutlass came down on my left foot and almost sliced through the whole ankle area, leaving it hanging by the skin. I was rushed to the only general hospital in Guyana in the city. It was pinned and stitched back together and I made a total recovery. However, I have felt some weakness in this leg which has got worse as I grew older, especially during the winter season.

Growing up in Demerara, especially in rural areas, was always a substantial health risk, due to lack of easily accessible local healthcare facilities. Infant mortality rate, premature death, disability and disease were common as they were in all countries under colonial administration. Accidents were very common, especially amongst young boys who often had accidents from climbing trees, walking barefoot and using cutlasses for domestic use, or assisting the family in the fields. Adults working on the plantation and using sharp equipment and tools also experienced a high level of accidents. My friends and I used to climb coconut trees up to 15 metres high, when we were barely teenagers. Fruit picking and collecting firewood added to the scars on my body.

Apart from the normal cold or flu, having measles, mumps, ear and stomach aches as a child, I did not have any other serious health problems until I was about thirteen years old. I had quite a serious unintentionally self-inflicted wound to my left foot one day when I was helping my mother and my older sister in the rice fields. We had been working for many days in the fields to prepare for rice planting season. My sister Doreen who was three years older and I were fed up with this hard work; working from early in the morning until late at night. Our mother was an extremely hardworking woman, she was also a very strict no nonsense person, who was angry if she caught us wasting time or slacking in our work. Life was hard for all of us, and my sisters and I felt that we had to make our contributions. On this particular day, we had been working from early morning and we were tired and fed up. We had stopped for lunch, what little we had to share between us. After lunch, my mother sharpened the three machetes, for each of us and we were having a general chat. I sat in the hammock and placed my machete under the back of my knee. The hammock shifted and I ended up with a severe cut in my left foot.

Naturally before my mother tended to my leg, she gave me a couple of slaps round the head because she thought I had deliberately done this in order to avoid the work. We were about at least three or four miles from home and many more miles to the nearest hospital. So like on many previous occasions, my mother prepared a potion made up of various leaves and barks which she chewed in her mouth and placed it on the wound. After the bleeding was stopped, she tore a piece of her petticoat and bandaged the wound. My sister and mother returned to work and I joined them about half an hour later.

I had a few more accidents during my early teens because my father was disabled and mother had to do everything she could to keep us. In Guyana we did not have the privilege of having a welfare state. Nothing was free, there were no hand-outs except if you borrowed from a neighbour or a member of your family and they would of course expect the same in return if they were short. So no work meant no income; and no income meant very little or no food in the house. Even as young as eight I was frequently seen beside my mother working in the cane fields, or in the small plot where we farmed privately to supplement our food requirements.

If I was not helping my mother, I was trying to earn an independent source of income; I used to climb very tall coconut trees, cut down the branches, I used to clean the branches and use the centre stems to make brooms which people used to sweep their homes and their yards. This would often cause injury to me. On many occasions I would strain myself fetching large bundles of firewood to take home, sometimes carrying the firewood for a mile or two. I would also catch fish in the canals and streams, moving around barefoot, and have accidents because of broken bottles or glass which I accidently stepped on. Although I often had accidents, through cuts, bruises, and sprained ankles, most of these accidents were treated at home by my parents or friends. We could not afford hospital treatment and what little medical treatment was available on the plantation dispensary was quite basic.

As the only son and having a disabled father who I believe was an undiagnosed diabetic, I felt almost forced by circumstances to perform as an adult to assist my mother as a husband would. So during harvest season or working on a small plot of land where we grew bananas, plantain, cassava, eddoes, yams and sweet potatoes, I would carry heavy loads in baskets for long distances which would often end up in me having stiff necks or sprained ankles, having had to jump across drains and stumble over stumps of wood. During the rice harvesting season I sometimes used to carry up to sixty kilos of rice in large sacks. It would often take two persons to help me to lift the sack onto my back. I would carry this to the cart or the truck to be taken the rice mill. I loved my mother and my family, and I always wanted to do my best for them, even though it meant taking risks with my health.

My father worked, when work was available. When there was no work available, he didn't get paid and there were no other benefits coming in to help us. My mother was always a creative woman and always found a way of finding some kind of activity which enabled us to have food in our stomachs. Even when my parents were both working and my sisters and I were helping them, it was still difficult for us to eat what one would describe as a balanced meal because my parents had to repay the loans and their debts to the shopkeeper that they had incurred when times were really hard. When I was not helping my parents in the fields or in and around our home and village, I was working as a labourer on the sugar plantation.

Life is not only to be alive, but to be well

The next serious illness I had was when I arrived in England, aged seventeen. Within two weeks of arriving in England I caught chicken pox. I was living alone at the time in a small bedroom in Fritville Gardens, Sheppard's Bush. The house I lived in consisted of three floors and about eight or nine bedrooms. The landlord and landlady, a couple in their sixties, rented out most of the house except for a couple of rooms on the ground floor where they lived. I was lucky to have this room at the total rent of seventeen shillings and six pence, but I had to find my own food and I had to put money in the electric meter and gas meters if I needed to do any cooking or use any light. The landlord and landlady and all their tenants were white and I was the only non-white person in the house. I was told not to make myself too noticeable and to keep myself to my room when I was in the house. I was not allowed to use the garden or any communal areas. I felt like a chicken in a coop. It was so different from Guyana where I spent lots of my childhood outdoors.

Having chicken pox was a frightening experience for me, the landlord and landlady told me that I must not leave my room whilst I had the chicken pox. They also told me that there was no point seeing a doctor or to seek treatment because it was a natural thing and it would take its own course. I felt dreadfully lonely, isolated and miserable. These spots, I have never experienced this before, all over across my face and my body, itching all the time and making me so uncomfortable. I was advised not to leave the house, or mix with other tenants and so the landlord and his wife would often put a bottle of milk outside my door and any spare food they had and I would retrieve the food and the drink after they had gone. I spent about eight days in this room on my own, which seemed like a lifetime. On many occasions I wished I was back at home with my family around me. I had no family in England, just a friend who had received me when I had arrived and who had arranged this accommodation for me.

Soon after the experience with the chicken pox, I was advised to register with a local doctor, which I duly did. This seemed quite a privilege for me, as in Guyana there was only one main hospital; so, decent healthcare was not easily accessible and was expensive. Since my family were never able to afford healthcare, we treated ourselves even when injuries were quite serious. Serious injuries and very poor health and sickness were regarded as natural and that we had to suffer through this process either because it was our fate, or it was God's Will. In reality, good healthcare was only available to the rich and the privileged. Guyana was under British colonial rule and under colonialism life was cheap, nasty and brutish. No one cared very much about the health and safety of the people throughout the centuries of slavery or Asians brought to Guyana through indenture ship. The plantation owners cared about profits; people and their health were not a priority.

The effects of racism in England in the 1960's made me felt lonely and depressed at times. I missed my family. It was insulting and demoralising to see notices in the newspapers, in windows and on notice boards "room to let – sorry no Blacks, no dogs, no Irish". It was equally distressing to make enquiries in factories where vacancies were displayed only to be told "we don't hire Blacks here". On top of this racism I found it extremely difficult to go around on my own. I was barely eight stone; could hardly speak good English; and was unable to defend myself against the racist skinheads, teddy-boys and others who would shout racist remarks and abuse at me. When I did find a job as a porter, I experienced several bouts of physical attacks and abuse. I bear some of these psychological scars to this day.

For nearly thirty five years after arriving in England, I had reasonable health, and apart from a few minor injuries whilst doing do-it-yourself work around the garden building up a vegetable patch, or gardening, or working around the house,

I have not had any serious injury or health concern. However, when I was about fifty years old, I began to feel very lethargic and tired on a regular basis. I visited my doctor for about a period of six to ten months and explained my condition to him, and he would say to me "Jim, your problem is that you are working too hard, you are a County Councillor, you do a lot of voluntary and community work, you have a demanding job" and "What do you expect – a person of your age?" I got on well with my doctor and we addressed each other by first names. I had recruited him to the Labour Party as an active Labour councillor and full-time trade union official; we shared some common values and views about politics and trade unions. He was very interested in the Labour Party and also interested in trade unions, because he was active as a representative of his colleagues in the medical profession. So, we would often have a moan about the government of the day and other socio-economic and political issues. We would spend very little time discussing my health. I told my doctor on several occasions that I was feeling very tired throughout the day, very lethargic, and that I often took a litre bottle of water with me to bed at night, and would get up two or three times to use the loo. He continued to tell me to "take life easier and don't work as hard". I believed him of course, but I continued to work the long hours, doing both paid and unpaid work.

On one occasion, I was sitting as a member on an Employment Tribunal case that was listed as a case of racial discrimination, where a senior nurse had complained against her hospital management for failure to promote her due to her racial origin. The case was listed for seven days. The nurse turned up at the Tribunal with her trade union official representing her and the hospital management turned up in force, including the Chief Executive and several Senior Managers as witnesses for the employer. At the start of the hearing, the Respondent to the case (being the hospital management) objected to my presence on the Tribunal, stating that at some time in my past political career I was a non-executive member to the Hospital Board. They objected to my presence even though I had resigned from the board many years earlier. The Chairman informed them that if they wished to object to my presence the case would have to be postponed and rescheduled for another occasion as they could not secure another member to replace me at short notice. The respondent decided to withdraw their objections to all and the case could continue.

After about one and half hours into the case, I felt very dizzy and I told the Chairman I was feeling unwell. The next thing I knew, I woke up in a small office, probably the first aid room in the Tribunal building, and I wondered "what has happened to me?" I was later told that the Tribunal staff, after the Chairman had dismissed the Tribunal, had escorted me to this room and left me there with a drink, for a couple of minutes to recover. I was later informed that the Tribunal members that the Chairman had asked the party from the hospital, which consisted of several doctors and nurses, if they could assist, but basically they did not want to get involved. We did not resume the case that day, but we did the following day. On hindsight I discovered that I must have had a diabetic attack even though I was not aware of being, or diagnosed as, a diabetic.

A few weeks later I was at work at Barnfield College where I was employed as an Equality Consultant for a number of years, and I met a colleague in the gents. He said to me "Jim, why are using the gents so often"? I said "the same reason as you". He said to me, "well, I am a diabetic and for this reason I have to use the gents on a regular basis." I said to him, "What do you mean, being a diabetic?" He then explained what the effects diabetes had on such sufferers. He said "you're probably a diabetic and you don't know it" I can't really recall talking about diabetes previously in my life. However he said to me, "I'll bring something in with me to work tomorrow which you could use to test your urine and it would tell you whether you are diabetic or not".

The following day he gave these few small paper sticks and I followed his instructions and urinated in a plastic cup, I dipped these little sticks into it and it showed dark straight away. My colleague said to me "Jim you are seriously diabetic, you need urgent help. If it was greyish to dark then you would be mildly diabetic, and if it remains green then, you would not be a diabetic at all. I tested my urine again a few minutes and it reached the darkest colour again. I went home and explained the situation to my wife and she said to me "you need to go to the doctors straight away", which I did. I told the receptionist I did not want to see my normal doctor, but to see another doctor. I saw a female doctor, and I explained to her the situation, she said to me "from what you have said, you are a diabetic. However, let's check". So I performed the same task in the doctor's surgery; I provided a sample and used the dipstick which went black almost straight away. She confirmed that I was a diabetic and that I should go to the hospital diabetic clinic as soon as possible.

I arrived at the diabetic clinic a few days later and was told some very sad news. Firstly, not only was I seriously diabetic, but I had been a diabetic for at least two or three years without recognising it, and as a result, the diabetes had affected my eyes and feet. I was suffering from glaucoma, high blood pressure and possibly other problems. So in 1995 I was diagnosed as a type two diabetic. I have been taking Metformin starting with 350mg and gradually rising to the present state of 850mg three times a day. Naturally, the number of tablets for various symptoms and effects of diabetes increased over the years. I also have to have regular eye drops daily since being diagnosed a diabetic. These tablets will continue throughout my life.

My bodyweight increased from eight stones in 1961 to fifteen in 1995. The doctors told me that as part of my treatment for diabetes, I needed to lose weight. I was lucky that within six months I lost nearly two stones. My health was reasonably well controlled until 1998.

On a lovely summer's morning I made my way from my home to a Tribunal in London, and on my way I felt slightly ill and with a little bit of stiffness and pain around my chest. I arrived in the Tribunal office safely and the Tribunal case started with me as a member, but just before the parties were invited into the room, I felt a dreadful stiffness in my chest and I felt as though I was drowning.

I recall saying to the Chairman of the Tribunal, "I feel ill. I think I am going to faint. Please call my wife and this is the telephone number of the school where she is a teacher". I cannot recall anything else until I woke up in University College Hospital, London, and a few minutes' walk from the Tribunal office. I was told by the Tribunal staff that I had passed out in the Tribunal room when the Regional Chairman of the Tribunal was trying to comfort me. I was having breathing difficulties and it was suggested that I should be taken to the first aid room and allowed a few minutes to recover, as the Tribunal had to continue. I was also told that a person waiting outside the Tribunal room informed the staff of the Tribunal escorting me to the first aid room that "that gentleman was having a heart attack and someone should call the ambulance quickly". Thank God they took this person's advice, and called the ambulance.

Later in the day at the University College Hospital, the ambulance crew came to see me and told me that I was a very lucky person and that they had feared for my life while transporting me from the Tribunal office to the hospital because they thought that they would lose me. It was a very serious case. I spent three days at University college Hospital and then returned home. I was diagnosed with heart failure and heart disease brought about partially because of my diabetic condition. So I now had diabetes, angina, prone to heart failure, glaucoma, hypertension and possibly other health problems.

Later in 1998 I had an angiogram, which is an exploration of my heart and its condition. I was told that I had some minor arteries partially blocked and that I would need angioplasty, which happened a year later. I was very worried, but I was in good hands, at Harefield Hospital, with a great reputation for successfully treating heart patients. I was given clear instructions after the angioplasty about having to live a different lifestyle, which included regular exercise, weight loss, dieting and avoidance of stress. A couple of years later I suffered another mild heart attack and had to have further angiograms and angioplasty.

I was a senior councillor on Luton Borough Council at the time of my first heart attack and whilst I was in hospital I said to my wife "separate my post please", because I used to get up to thirty letters each day. Most of the letters were in brown envelopes, but more personal and interesting letters were invariably in white ones and frequently hand written. These basically came from friends, relatives, or ordinary folks asking for my support and assistance. I said to my wife "make two piles, put the brown envelopes on one pile, and the white ones on another". I later realised that there was also an article in the local newspaper about Councillor Jim Thakoordin having a heart attack. It was common knowledge, not only among my colleagues on the Council, but also amongst the general public.

When I returned from hospital and settled down at home, I said to my wife, "I am now prepared to look at those letters, the white ones first". There were a few, from friends and family wishing me a speedy recovery, and expressing regret at my health condition. But sadly, there was not a single letter or message from any of my fellow councillor colleagues. A few days later, I had letters from the Liberal Democrat and the Conservative Leaders expressing regret and wishing me a speedy recovery, but nothing from my Labour colleagues or its leadership. There were a few letters from members of the public but the majority of the letters were seeking my help and support. I then realised that flogging me for the best part of thirty five years in politics, trade union and community work meant little to anyone. For years, I took it for granted that people appreciated my work and I was recognised as a hardworking and conscientious person giving my time voluntarily for the good of the public. What a shock this was for me.

In 2003 my heart condition worsened and so did my diabetes. The number of tablets I had to take each day increased to nine. I became short of breath again and had to have another angiogram and an angioplasty resulting in a number of stents placed into my arteries because of partial closure. This offered me some respite for another couple of years, and then in May 2005, I was sitting on a Tribunal case again and I told the Chairman, "I can hardly stand up or walk". I was feeling quite tired and lacking in energy. I couldn't climb the stairs and had to sit in the Tribunal room and eat my lunch. He said to me "are you joking?", and I said "no, I am serious". He said "look, you are not well; we will terminate the Tribunal as soon as we can, and you need to go home and see your doctor". So I drove home, told my wife what had happened and we went to see the doctor. The doctor discovered that my pulse rate was only twenty nine beats per minute, instead of seventy. She informed me that I was in serious difficulty, and I should be taken to the hospital straight way. I was admitted within an hour, and I was told during the evening I was either tachycardia or brachycardia. On a couple of occasions I passed out for brief moments and had to be revived. After a couple of days at the local Luton and Dunstable hospital, I was transferred to Harefield hospital, familiar grounds, having been there twice before for operations and after about four days I had a pace maker inserted in my chest and attached to my heart. I then had normal a heartbeat, around 65 to 70 beats per minute.

By this time I was over sixty two years old, and was feeling quite uncomfortable and worried about the future. I had four beautiful grandchildren and I wanted to see them grow up. During each of my operations in hospital I thought of my grandchildren and one little one in particular, called Aoife who was very, very close to me. I focussed on her face and her love prior to each operation, and thank God I survived the operations.

My next serious encounter health wise occurred in February 2006 on my return from America. During my stay in Harefield hospital the previous year, I thought if I survive all this, I would like to visit my disabled son Richard and three sisters in America and also to visit my homeland in Guyana as soon as I am able to do so. I felt it may be my last opportunity to see some of my family abroad. By this time the number of tablets had increased, and I am sure that because of the number of tablets I was taking they were causing me many side effects. For example, I would often have stomach ache, blood in my urine, feeling quite anxious and depressed and also suffering from anxiety attacks and high blood pressure.

I visited America and saw my family, but on the return journey I became seriously ill again. I went to the toilet first thing in the morning and I discovered that my urine was totally white; as white as milk and as thick as cream. I called my wife's attention to this. She brought me a jug which I soon filled up with this white thick cream. We both had a laugh and a joke about it, not realising the serious implications behind it. Within a few hours I had filled a two litre Tesco milk bottle with fluid, and my wife and I agreed that it was not a passing situation; it was much more serious and I should see the doctor. Neither of us had had any experience of this condition before. When I saw the doctor and explained to her my condition, and presented her with this litre of fluid, she was amazed. She could not think what it was, or what had caused it. The doctor offered no treatment, or information as to what the problem was. I felt the doctor could have given some more attention to my condition because later, after using the internet, I researched into this condition, which although not common, is well recognised amongst urologists. The doctor sent a sample of this white thick urine to the hospital for examination and asked me to return within two or three days. She told me to drink a lot of water, which I did. I returned to the doctor the following day as the liquid became thicker and thicker. I was having difficulty passing any water. The following day I could not pass any water and I was in severe pain.

My wife contacted the doctor and I was told to go to the hospital accident and emergency. I did as the doctor instructed, and attended the Accident and Emergency Unit and explained my condition, carrying a two litre carton of thick white fluid with me. The doctors and nurses were not convinced that I had really passed the contents I had shown them.

The staff could see I was in dreadful pain and agony. I wanted to pass urine and was unable to do so. I was crying and screaming in pain. I waited in the Accident and Emergency ward for about three hours before someone helped me. In the meantime I was asked to keep drinking more water to help to flush the system. My wife held my hand and tried to calm me down, but I was becoming increasingly distressed. A bed was then made available for me after a long wait and I was transported to a ward at around 11.00pm at night, after waiting on a trolley in the corridor on a Sunday night.

The nurse in charge of the Ward felt that she could not do anything for me without prior consultation with a doctor. As there is generally a shortage of doctors especially at weekends, I had to wait in severe pain for hours. I was seen by two doctors, a male and a female at around midnight. They managed to insert one of the largest catheters they had and drained me of two litres of thick, white lumpy fluid that was preventing me from passing urine. It was such a tremendous relief. The doctors had the most unique experience in their careers, as they had never treated someone with my condition. As they inserted the catheter the fluid went up in the air and splashed all over their hands, white coats and other parts of their bodies. They decided to keep me in for a number of days to carry out tests and to monitor my condition. After about four days in hospital, I was told that I had a glandular malfunction.

I stayed in hospital for a further six days until the urine got back to normal. I was given very little information about my condition or about the diagnosis. A few months later I experienced a similar situation and the white thick urine lasted a few days and then it became clear again. I saw my doctor and further samples were taken and it was confirmed that the thick fluid consisted of eighty five per cent blood and fifteen per cent fat and blood. By this time, having taken aspirins and numerous other tablets for my diabetes and heart condition, my stomach lining was in a poor state and was subject to constant bleeding. I was later told by the consultant urologist that this was associated with my illness, which was then described as Chyluria, a rare disease, most common in the South Asian subcontinent that affects Indian and Chinese people. The urologists at Luton and Dunstable hospital had only experienced one patient before with such a condition. I was also told that I would need further examination of my lymph gland and an operation which had only been performed once at the Luton and Dunstable hospital before by the present team. They wanted to trace the connection between the lymph gland and the kidneys. By now I was dreading hospital life and treatment and after the previous experience, spending ten days in hospital, I was in a state of fear and apprehension.

Health and Intellect are two blessings in life

Most of the treatment I received in hospital was very good, but some of my time as a patient was very disappointing. The food was extremely poor and unpalatable; portions far too small; poorly cooked and unseasoned and nothing like what I had been used to all my life. Some of the nurses were very caring and compassionate, but others were cruel, callous, uncaring and I felt should not be in that type of occupation. It did not matter what nationality, ethnic or racial origin they were. There were good and bad amongst all groups. A number of foreign nurses told me that they were working full twelve hour shifts each day, four days a week and the other remaining three days they worked as bank nurses. So they had very little chance to sleep and to replenish their energy. They were chasing money because working on a single bank shift was equivalent to more than a fortnight's earnings in their country of origin. They were committed to work as hard as possible and to save as much as possible for invest in a property when they returned to their country of origin. Also many of them had to support extended families abroad. They decided that it was in their interests to work all the hours available. Clearly, not only the foreign nurses did this, some British nurses did the same. But whilst they were busy making money and working long hours, they hardly had the energy or inclination to give the patients the individual care they needed.

During my stay in hospital, I often had to feed older patients whose meals were brought to them, sometimes placed outside their reach, but because of their condition they were unable to feed themselves or were not interested in eating. Some had no visitors at all and I did my best to assist against the instructions of some nurses. The toilets were often filthy, with occasional queues waiting to use the facilities. I remember on one occasion I said to the cleaner there is no light in a particular cubicle washroom, and she said "don't worry, I will sort it out".

The following day I reminded her that it was still dark; on the third day I saw the manager and complained to her, and she said it would be seen to but it was several days before it was sorted out. After the cleaner had been around the toilets would soon become filthy again. I often informed the cleaner that the toilets were dirty, she would say "I have cleaned it once today", not accepting that many patients were sick, disabled, elderly and needed regular use of the facilities.

There were numerous occasions when I was in pain and I begged for pain relief tablets. I was frequently told by sisters that "we don't prescribe pain killers anymore; it has to be done by a doctor". Hours later you would be told there were no doctors available, although you were in constant pain and agony. I felt like ripping the tubes out of my body, throwing the catheter on the floor, screaming my head off, or opening the window and jumping out. I was on the fourth floor. It was hell for me on occasions. It appeared that the more you complained the worse treatment you received. I asked to see someone to express my concern on several occasions. Someone would come and see me days later claiming to be senior and independent, take notes of what I said, and nothing would happen. I have had these experiences each time I stayed in most hospitals.

Harefield hospital was a different matter. It was a great deal better. But also, there were occasions when there were problems due to staff shortages. I remember on one occasion after having my pacemaker fitted, I was wheeled out of the operating theatre and placed in the corridor half conscious, but I could recall the doctor ringing up the ward and saying to the sister in charge "your patient is ready" and I assumed the sister had agreed to come and collect me. Yet over an hour and a half later I was fully conscious and still waiting in the corridor. Other patients had come in and had operations and had gone out again, until one of the doctors decided to ring the ward again, to remind the sister to come and collect me. Although I felt quite good at Harefield, on occasions it was a bit disconcerting. On one occasion, a patient next to me had open heart surgery involving several bypass, and yet just after forty eight hours they were thinking of sending him home. On the third day after this major operation, having been open from his neck to his stomach, I saw a person sitting with his bag waiting near this bed, for this man to go home so he could settle in for his operation the next day. Clearly the hospital would argue that you would get better care at home, but even if this was the case, it would still worry some patients. I wondered what care one would get at home and how that could be better than care in a hospital, where the experts are on hand, and readily available if something goes wrong. I discovered that there were real and substantial inequalities in health care and better care was available if one could pay for it. Also the elderly, disabled and those with poor communication skills were frequently neglected by the system. I returned from Harefield, and felt that I wouldn't be going there again; little did I know that the following year I was directed to Harefield with further heart problems.

Following this Chyluria disease and the malfunction of the lymph gland my kidneys needed further attention. The urologist at the Luton and Dunstable hospital decided they would carry out a keyhole operation. They would insert a tube through my urethra to my bladder then up to my kidneys. I was told that they would remove a lot of debris from my left kidney and clear the areas where there were blockages. So it was back for another stint at hospital, and again I experienced some dreadful difficulties. For example, I was on a bed, with a catheter, and there was blood on the floor. I wanted to step out of bed after I had recovered within twenty four hours, but I couldn't because of the blood on the floor. I said to the nurse, "could someone please clean that blood away so I can step out of bed and sit on the chair"? She said to me "it's not my fault, it's not my problem, and I will get a cleaner". I thought "My God". The cleaner then swept all round the blood and did not clean it up. I pointed it out to a nurse, she then told me to have a word with a sister, whom I did, so it was about four hours later someone cleaned up the blood on the floor. What I saw in the hospital was clearly poor management.

The sister in charge was very busy, but other nurses were less so. Senior nurses appeared reluctant to closely supervise staff when they are not up to scratch, which is a dreadful shame. I notice that when certain patients complain, the nurses and the sisters would gang up and make the patients feel they were unreasonably moaning, being grumpy and dissatisfied, or they were making unfair demands. I saw on many occasions' people ringing the red buzzer, especially at night, would have to wait long periods for attention. I had to go to the work station on several occasions to inform nurses chatting away that the buzzer was ringing. Staff shortages were a common response to poor care and attention. After turning the lights off at around nine at night they seem to huddle in a group in the reception area and you could hear conversations going from what's on the television to personal relationships, cooking and all sorts of things and it was dreadfully sad. On many occasions I complained that my catheter was full and needed emptying and later on I needed a utensil to urinate in and you could be there waiting for hours and reminding them and still waiting. Patients who were regarded by nurses as "troublemakers" were frequently identified by derogatory names or labelling.

So after a year of the first kidney operation, age sixty three, the chyluria came back with a vengeance and I was seriously ill again. By then the doctors knew the routine, so when I went into accident and emergency (A&E) by ambulance, I went equipped with notes and my previous records. I tried to explain to the doctors in the accident and emergency unit that I was in dreadful pain. I had been unable to pass urine for two days. I was in tears and screaming for attention. The A&E unit registered me and I was given a bed. The nurse, who seemed to be either from the Philippines or in that part of the world, said to me "what's the problem?" and I explained to her. She said, "We need to consult a doctor". An Indian doctor came and saw me about half an hour later and said to me "I think I know what it is. Your lymph gland is not functioning. Don't worry we will drain you out and we will find you a place in the ward".

I felt a bit of relief but still in dreadful pain, so he instructed the nurse to look after me because there were lots of other emergency cases waiting. This nurse then proceeded to put the smallest catheter she could find through my urethra to drain the chile, which is this white, creamy, thick liquid that had blocked me up. The tube was not large enough to drain the fluid. I explained to her that the largest catheter had been advised to be inserted and one can syringe it out as well. I had to wait another hour in dreadful agony, with my wife holding my hand for comfort, and then another nurse appeared. I was later told that the previous nurse had completed her shift and left. I explained it all to the new nurse and then she said to me "there is nothing I can do, I haven't got all the equipment, I haven't got the larger catheter insert, and the best thing to do is to get you off to a ward". So I was then wheeled off to a ward, by that time I had been in accident and emergency, screaming in pain, for five hours with my wife by my side throughout.

When I went up to the ward, my wife went home. On the ward, I was screaming and I begged the nurse for pain killers and pleaded for somebody to do something for me, I was crying and screaming. They left me alone to cope. At ten o'clock that night I phoned my wife from my mobile phone and said, "I can't cope with this anymore, I am either going to jump out the window or can you please come and collect me to take me home. I have begged them for pain killers but they wouldn't give them to me". The sister heard my telephone conversation with my wife. My wife then came, at about half ten and they tried to convince my wife that it was my fault; that I didn't ask for painkillers, and in any case there wasn't a doctor available because they were too busy in the accident & emergency department. They then gave me something that made me fall off to sleep, and my wife informed me later that as soon as I was asleep, she left the hospital again.

When I woke up a couple of hours later I was in pain again. Two doctors, a male and a trainee female, both young doctors came to see me. They prescribed stronger pain killers and inserted a large tube through my penis. They told me that according to the notes I was drained earlier in A&E which was not true. They said, "You have already been drained once, earlier in the afternoon". I said to them "that's not true". They said "well the nurse said when you came in that they had drained two litres of fluid from you" and I said "that nurse is lying because she never did drain me. She changed shift and went home". I was amazed that the nurse had told such a lie. Nevertheless, these two doctors then inserted the tube; I should have warned them because as soon as this tube reached the area where the fluid had been built up, the horrible creamy and smelly fluid shot right up into the air and splashed both doctors. Both had a dreadful shock because they had never seen anything like this before. I thanked them and cried with relief then went straight to sleep.

I then spent some time in hospital and I must say on this occasion, things were slightly better. By then I had made friends with a nurse called Brenda, a very senior nurse, who seemed to be a trouble shooter and worked across departments, but she always seemed to be around the urology department. She was tremendous. She gave me her bleeper number, her personal number, her mobile number, and all sorts of information. She did drawings for me so I could present it to the hospital if this happens again. She was just tremendous. Mr Alam the urologist was also extremely kind, and he explained things to me. He was very good indeed. Mr Alam, the Consultant urologist informed me that I would need another keyhole kidney operation soon; because the chile was being built up again and perhaps the duct to my kidney was being blocked.

I was then called to the Luton and Dunstable Hospital for yet another kidney operation and I was told on this occasion it would not be too long, possibly forty five minutes and that it would be keyhole surgery. So I turn up with my wife, I believe it was in the early afternoon and they had prepared me for surgery. My wife waved me off as I was wheeled into surgery, three hours later. I was still in surgery after a couple of hours and my wife was getting worried, wanting to know what had happened, and she made enquiries. An hour later she had enquired again and she was told I was still in surgery. An hour later she enquired again. By now she was convinced that I had died. She was getting very worried. I believe I came out of the surgery about an hour later. Apparently, the keyhole surgery did not go as planned and they had to carry out open surgery instead. Much to the relief of my wife I was wheeled out of surgery after a four hour operation.

When I came round, and still partially conscious, I heard the nurse who was cleaning me up telling another nurse that "it was touch and go", he had bled a great deal". The seven inch wound on the left of my stomach took some time to heal. I was in hospital for another seven days, and on this occasion I tried to keep myself busy, I met a couple of patients who were in the ward with me before, so we supported each other. I also took a lot of reading material with me and I started to write this book, which I had put off for a little while. The nursing care did not improve, nor did the food or anything else at the hospital. So I was desperate to get home. My wife brought food to the hospital sometimes twice each day which I shared with others.

Prior to this final kidney operation there was an operation to my lymph gland, one of the most difficult glands to access. They wanted to put some fluid in this gland to trace it into my kidneys and out of my kidneys to see whether there were particular blockages. That was also an extremely painful operation, the doctor had not performed an operation of this type before, and she had invited several doctors to join here for an operation which should have lasted no more than an hour, but instead lasted for eight hours. Again, my wife was beside me, holding my hand, and I was conscious all the time. They actually cut right across both of my feet, by the toes and tried to insert the dye through a needle. There must have been scores of attempts to do this, and each time they cut it deeper and higher up. I was in dreadful pain. In one instance this senior nurse said to the doctor, "he must feel dreadful; can't you see this gentleman is in such pain, can't you up the pain killer or whatever you are giving him to keep the pain away? This elderly gentleman has been in such distress". So I heard this altercation between this senior nurse who took my part, and the doctor who said, "Oh don't blame me, I have never done this before and I was invited to do this. I will try to complete this and do my best". So that was a very painful exercise.

After this major kidney operation, I felt that I may not live much longer and I really wanted to go to my country of origin, Guyana, and to see my relatives perhaps for the last time. So in 2007 I went to Guyana alone, I met my relatives, had a great time. Before I arrived in Guyana, on my way there, we stopped in Trinidad for a few hours, because there was no direct flight, and then continued the flight to Guyana. When I got to Trinidad I felt great. At home I had been hardly able to walk for more for more than a hundred yards without much discomfort, but when I stayed over in Trinidad I was able to walk around the shops with no difficulty and to purchase presents and so on. I felt good in the hot sunshine, so I asked my niece, to build a nice house on a piece of land with a shack on it which I had bought way back during my first visit to Guyana in the 1970s. I wanted to have a retirement home to spend the winter months away from England. Sadly this dream has never been realised.

My wife Doreen, retired in 2005 as Assistant Head teacher of a local boy's high school, we had some difficulty in terms of our relationship. We agreed to purchase a property in Essex, not too far from where our son, his wife and our two grandchildren live, only about three miles away. We enjoyed being in this retirement home in Leigh-on-Sea for short periods. I continued to live in Luton as I was working and also involved in politics and the voluntary and community sector. During my hospitalisation, and my illnesses, it was quite difficult for me because I never really took time off work or from the voluntary activities I did, and also to continue my role as a councillor and on my union's national executive committee, my union being the University and College Lecturers Union. During the day when I was occupied, it wasn't too bad, but at night it was dreadful. I would often have panic attacks, especially when my wife wasn't there. Doreen enjoyed living near our son and his family so I spent many days on my own coping with poor health.

By then Doreen and I had a number of difficulties, probably due to the demands my health made on her over the years and my refusal to retire and enjoy my life instead of continuing my involvement in work, political, trade unions and community work. So Doreen spent a lot of time on her own in the flat in Leigh on Sea. I remember one occasion when I was very ill having returned from hospital after a major operation and I had to get out of bed to let in the nurse who came to visit me at home and it was such a difficult task. The stitches came apart and the nurse had to re-stitch my wound. On another occasion after the kidney operation and recovering at home, one of the nurses who came to do home visit, pulled up in the driveway next door then crashed her car reversing out after she was told she was at the wrong address. She then came to see me, and I could smell alcohol on her breath. She was extremely rough and she said "I've never done this before" but she inserted a new catheter and to get the tube through my penis and into my bladder caused me a great deal of pain.

Some of the day care nurses that did home visits were great, we had long chats and they made me cups of tea. Living in a large detached bungalow on nearly half an acre of land with fields in front and back and a mile from any village shops made life quite lonely sometimes. On another occasion one of the nurses instead of using the proper water to syringe my bladder and to wash it out used the wrong liquid. She used the sterilisation fluid that was used to sterilise the equipment instead, and then injected my bladder with the wrong liquid. This caused me such dreadful pain because it burned and stung my insides… the nurse couldn't understand why until we discovered that the jug which she used to pour the water in, which was used to syringe me, was full of sterilisation fluid instead. Doreen had used the two litre jug to put the sterilisation fluid in. so it was partially my wife's fault and partially the nurse's fault. The sterilisation fluid was blue and the plain water was clear.

On many occasions I was on my own with no one to talk to because my wife was in our retirement home; our son was having some difficulty in his relationship, and I felt my wife had talked me into buying the retirement home in Essex because she wanted to be near to our son. We have a son and a daughter. Our daughter lives in Birmingham, and our son in Essex; and Mike, our son, was always his mum's favourite. So my wife positioned herself there to keep an eye on her grandchildren and to help out when she could, but I missed her dreadfully. These panic attacks were extremely frightening and if I was on my own, what I would do is turn the radio on, or the television, and that sometimes wasn't sufficient. I would then put my coat on and walk around the garden and talk to myself. On a few occasions I got into my car and drove to the hospital and sat in the A&E department without reporting any problem, but just sat there, with people around me and then I would drive back home. But I can tell you these panic attacks are dreadful things. You really feel so anxious; anxiety creeps in about all sorts of things including suicide, and it is so difficult to describe.

Since 2007, I really discovered within my family who cared about me very much, and who cared very little. My daughter was tremendous, she always took an interest in her parent's welfare and, as I said earlier my son had always got on better with his mum, as my daughter always has with me. Our daughter Jane has always been there for us and her entire family shared her concerns for my health. Jane would enquire about my health on a regular basis, make regular visits, and do her best to care for me, and to give me comfort. My son, perhaps he loved me as much, but he wasn't around as much although he lived only sixty miles away in comparison to my daughter living nearly one hundred miles away, I wish my family altogether had taken a bit more interest in my health. My wife was good, sympathetic and supportive, but on occasions I could see that she had her own issues to cope with and to address. Her own health was not very good and I could not pressure her too much to give me support. I do believe that sick people do need support; especially when they suffer from anxiety and panic attacks and depression. This can put a lot of pressure on partners and families.

In 2008 the chest pains returned and I was unable to cut the grass on my lawns in one go as I always have done, for nearly thirty years. So I would have to stop every five or ten minutes to breathe. I informed my doctor of this situation, and I was sent to Luton and Dunstable hospital to see the cardiologist, who then recommended an angiogram to find out where the weaknesses were. He did so, in early February 2009, and during the angiogram operation, he identified three main blockages in my arteries. He subsequently recommended a triple heart bypass operation. I saw a senior cardiologist and an experienced surgeon who decided on an operation at Harefield. Before the operation they explained to me that the operation was a common and routine event, even for people like me, over sixty five with a pacemaker fitted to my heart and also a diabetic. It nevertheless did not stop me having sleepless nights and fearing the worst outcome. I normally worry over minor health problems, so you can imagine the level of worry I had to endure since I was informed of the operation.

The heart operation took place in July 2009 and since then I have been reasonably well again. It turned out to be a quadruple heart bypass operation which was successful. Once again my daughter was up and down the motorway from Birmingham spending time with me in hospital and at home and supporting all of us. I saw my son once in six weeks after the operation, but he kept in contact about my condition. My family continue to support me, and Doreen and I have overcome our differences. We spend many weekends with our grandchildren in Luton and Essex. We also enjoyed holidays in Cuba, several countries in Southern Africa and Tenerife. We had also made plans to visit India and Spain.

Hospitalised in Manchester

In 2012, just after we decided to go back to Tenerife in January 2013 for two weeks to avoid the horrible winter which started early with heavy snowfall, I had to undergo yet another operation. On this occasion it took place in Manchester over 150 miles from home. I caught the train in Luton with two colleagues who worked at the Luton Law Centre, where I was a Trustee on the Management Board. We arrived in Manchester for the National Law Centre Conference, in time for lunch after five hours of travel by rail and taxi. We had a lovely lunch and soon after I started to feel a dreadful pain in my chest. I recalled a slight pain on the train when we were about to approach Manchester train station, due to a woman accidentally hitting me in the chest, with her suitcase, when she walked past me. She was getting ready to leave the train and she appeared to be in a hurry. We went into the conference and within an hour I felt really ill with severe chest pain. I asked the Hotel Manager to get me a first aider, who was very good. After thirty minutes I felt much worse and requested that he contact my colleagues Gillian Sharpe and the other delegate, who promptly came to my room. I asked them to call an ambulance, but we decided to take a taxi instead to the hospital. Gillian was really wonderful, she stayed with me in the Accident and Emergency Unit, where we waited for well over two hours before I was seen by an Asian nurse who told me that she had to wait for a doctor to diagnose my condition before I can receive any medication. I pleaded with her for some pain killers and after she saw how distressed I was and sobbing with agony, she offered me two painkillers, but asked me not to tell the doctor. The pain was unbearable and I decided to ask for a doctor to see me. Gillian also requested help on my behalf. I eventually saw a doctor after waiting another hour. This doctor asked me a few questions and took me on a trolley to a side room. I explained my medical history to the doctor and pleaded with him to assist me. He left the room and Gilliam came to see me. She was so caring and concerned, but decided that she had to return to the Conference. Another colleague from the Law Centre who was the Chair of the Board came to see me and brought my bag with all my belongings to the hospital.

I was not given any treatment despite my pleading for some pain killers. I was taken to a ward and was told that I would be seen by a doctor. I pleaded with the male Asian nurse for some pain killers and was told to wait for a doctor. I could no longer cope with the pain and I felt suicidal. I was anxious and in a state of panic. No doctor arrived until the next morning. I explained my situation and the doctor told me that it was a problem with my gall bladder. The most likely scenario was that a gall stone had blocked my bladder. He informed me that I would have an X-ray later in the day and he prescribed strong pain killers. It was such a relief after 20 minutes. I took six instead of the three tablets prescribed. I thought I would never return home alive. Gillian had contacted my wife but she was unable to leave home as there were over 6 inches of snow on our drive and our village was cut off due to the weather conditions. Doreen telephoned me in the morning and I asked her not to make the journey, and that I would be home within a couple of days.

Doreen telephoned our daughter Jane who lived in Birmingham, around fifty miles from Manchester. I was so pleased to see my daughter who went out and bought me food, fruits and drinks. My daughter has always been a tower of strength to me and her mum. I cried when she left. I believe we were both in tears. She promised to return, but I asked her not to put herself through the terrible journey in such poor weather conditions. The snow covered many parts of Britain for nearly a month. I talked with my wife and daughter every day. On the fourth day after arriving at the hospital and still in terrible pain, I complained to the sister in charge and two doctors who were visiting the ward. An Asian doctor said to me, "do I know you?" I asked him "why should I know you". He said "I was trained at the Luton and Dunstable Hospital and I believe you were a member of the Hospital Board, and a local councillor. I had seen your photograph in the local newspapers on many occasions." I explained my position to this doctor and we had a long conversation after he had completed his round. He told me that I was in one of the worst wards with a Sister who was one of the worst managers and had the least patients taken into surgery each day. He also discussed with me the ratio of patients who passed away in her ward due to lack of care. He asked me to "keep this information in confidence."

I had recognised the problem with the nursing staff in the ward from day one. I noticed that the nurses made no attempt to feed the elderly patients who slept almost all day. The caterers would leave their meals beside their beds and collect the trays later, knowing that none of the food had been eaten by the patients. I took it upon myself to wake some patients up and to help them to eat. Two patients were unable to swallow solid food and I asked the nursing Sister and staff to let them have soup instead. They refused my request and I later informed the relatives of the patients who told the nurses that their relatives should have soup. One patient's son took my advice and bought some cans of soup for his very frail and elderly dad, who used to talk aloud in his sleep. I believed I helped to save Derek's dad, as many patients were too weak to have their operations and they just passed away. Derek and I are Facebook friends and as far as I know his dad is still alive. I used to ask for milk in my cereal and brown toast, but I was refused on every occasion. Almost all the catering staff, who served the food, was people of African descent. I deliberately identified the staff by their gender and ethnic origin as I have seen good and not so good staff in hospitals from all racial origins and gender.

I had my operation and my gall stone was removed. I felt great. Within 8 hours, I was helping other patients who were much worse off than I was. A few of them were not mobile and I helped them the best I could, especially after the nurses disappeared at around nine at night. The ward was an all-male ward with almost everyone in the eighteen beds being elderly. Those of us using the compressed paper utensil, which collected the urine, would have to wait sometimes days before they were taken away. In fact the utensils placed on top of my cupboard, which contained my clothes and papers, leaked over a period of two days and soaked all my clothes without my knowledge. I only discovered this problem on the morning when my wife was coming to take me home. I complained about this and was told that "nothing could be done about this". I rinsed out my clothes in the bathroom, and asked the staff to dry them for me and they refused. I wrote a nine page report and gave it to an Asian member of staff who claimed to be the person responsible for complaints. Nothing ever happened with my complaints. A typical example was one occasion when a trainee Caribbean Nurse accompanied by a white fully qualified nurse came to my bed at around in the early hours of the morning to give me medication. She pulled my trolley away from my reach, put my lights on gave me an injection, tested my blood sugar and left me uncovered up to my neck, with the lights on and my desk out of my reach. I never saw them again until four hours later just before breakfast. My wife had brought me some warm clothing and together we left the ward. During my six days stay I was never given any of the thirteen tablets I used to take each day for my condition before I went in to the hospital. I asked for tablets, but was told to take the tablets I had brought with me from home in a small box with seven small compartments. I only had enough tablets of my own for four days. I wrote to the hospital, but never received a response. The journey from Manchester to home was difficult. My wife had a taxi waiting for us at Milton Keynes Railway Station. It was an Irish woman who worked for Shamrock Taxis in Luton. She knew us, as we had used her before. Doreen asked for her, and she courageously drove the forty eight miles in the thick snow to and from Milton Keynes to deliver us home safely.

My latest health scare occurred in January and February 2014, after I was asked to attend the Luton and Dunstable hospital for a pre-examination discussion due to excessive blood in two recent stool samples. Doreen and I went to the briefing session and were informed of all the possibilities that could account for the blood in my stool. I was told that it could be a number of reasons from the worse scenario of cancer of the bowels, or colon, to recent diet or, some minor damage in my stomach. We were delighted to learn after the Colonoscopy that apart from detecting and removing a small lump and detecting signs of piles, nothing else was wrong. The booklets I had been given to read on cancer contained useful information, even though the thought of cancer gave me many sleepless nights and involved my wife and my family in some worrying discussions. My wife, who has regarded herself as my carer, since 2009, has been wonderful to me, for which I will always be grateful. I returned home from the hospital to a curry meal previously prepared, as I had been consuming only water with laxatives for two days. I hope this will be my last health scare for a while. I am well aware of the health problems and difficulties older people, especially those over sixty five years have to face, particularly concerns with coronary diseases and cancer. I am so pleased to have; I hope, a few more years to see my lovely grandchildren grow up. I also want to see my children and their family improves their life. It is my mission and duty to do all I can for my dear wife, who I hope will survive me. I want us to relocate and to downsize as our present property and garden is much too big for us and we have far too much possessions accumulated over fifty years.

Happiness is good health

I hope that I will continue to live an interesting life. I have several other books I need to complete, which are only partially completed presently. I am pleased that despite all my illnesses over the years, since 1995, I have maintained full employment, played my full part in society as a councillor, as a community volunteer, as active trade unionist; and hopefully I will continue to help my fellow beings who are less fortunate than myself. I am trying my best to cope with my illness through dieting, regular exercises, and trying to avoid stress. I regularly meditate, and listen to music which I like, and do other things I like, but I gain most pleasure when I see my beautiful grandchildren, Rohanie and Aoife from my daughter's side; and my grandson Elijah and granddaughter Sarah from my son's side. I hope that I will continue to enjoy the pleasure of their company in the future.

Our National Health Service is a wonderful institution. I believe that given a choice most of us will contribute a greater proportion of our income towards sustaining the National Health Service. However I do believe that pouring money into the Health Service is not necessarily the answer in terms of achieving quality and better standards. I have served on various health trusts for over fifteen years in different capacities, and I have given them a great deal of my thoughts and attention and time. Each time I have visited these hospitals I can see major problems, problems of management, of direction, of control, of people taking responsibility. I have seen so many problems in hospitals; I have seen dirty wards; uncaring nurses; doctors who say very little to the patients about their condition; I have seen nurses lie on record about treatment, in a first-hand way in my case. I hope that some government will have the courage to take on these fat cats who are paid enormous salaries to ensure that our hospitals are run appropriately and that the conditions are good. Sadly too many people go into hospital with minor illnesses and end up dying in hospital because their health deteriorated. Too many hospital diseases, too much neglect, and especially neglect of older people, something which worries me a great deal. I have seen old people screaming in pain, starving on hospital wards and people who care very little about them.

There needs to be a change in the culture of our hospitals; a change in attitudes; there needs to be rewards for those who do their job and a decent salary should be sufficient reward; but those who fail in their duty, regardless of their position and their grade or status, ought to be reminded of their obligation and should be dealt with appropriately. We live in a situation where management is afraid to challenge staff, either because of fear a trade union backlash or the fear that they will be accused of discrimination.

For example, if it is a male dealing with a female, of sexism; or equally, a female dealing with male might be also accused of sexism; or a white person dealing with a black person could be seen as racist, or vice versa. This is clearly not helping the services within our hospitals. Hospitals have got to be more accountable to the people they serve. Sadly these trust boards, from my experience having served for many years, are a waste of time. They are appointed under statute as watchdogs of these hospital boards, they are now paid over £8,500 a year for attending half a dozen or so meetings. They have little contact with the public at large; they attend meetings, say very little; invariably thanking the executive board members for the good service they provide; they ignore the complaints from patients or from people within the community; they draw their rewards of £8,000 or whatever; and they say very little.

The present management and service delivery system is not working. We need greater accountability, higher standards and better value for the vast sum of money that is going into the National Health Service. The coalition government led by Conservative Prime Minister, David Cameron and Nick Clegg, the Deputy Prime Minister from the Liberal Democrats have made a serious mistake by passing a Health and Care Bill that will create a two tier NHS. It will privatise much of our NHS service; create longer waiting lists and poorer service for the less well-off that need free and easily accessible healthcare. I believe the poor and the elderly will suffer most from this legislation passed in the Care Bill in 2012. Cuts by central government year on year in the welfare state, grants to local government and others measures resulting in the elderly being hospitalised and cared for in Care Homes instead of living in their own homes, is unacceptable in a civilised very rich country. Far too many elderly people are living in fear, poverty, cold and damp conditions and are subjected to premature death through no fault of their own. On many occasions their homes are being sold to pay for their care, which are often identified as inadequate and expensive. I am an active campaigner for free and accessible quality health care and will continue to do so as long as I live.

Sadly hospitals still have a lot to learn judging by the following quote:

"In the twenty first century most doctors and nurses still haven't got much of a clue about the quality of care we're providing, the effect we have on you, what happens to you after you're discharged, whether we've made your life better or worse or even if we've killed or cured you. We operate and consult in a vacuum, with virtually no feedback, just muddling through and hoping for the best." Dr Phil Hammond, 2002. Trust me, I'm a doctor. *Metro Publishing, London*

"Many trust board members cannot be sure that their hospital is operating within the law." Audit Commission, 2009 (Taking in on trust)

All three main political parties have now messed about with our greatest asset – the NHS. We cannot trust our politicians with our NHS. It is our NHS and we must be prepared to defend it. I would never be alive now without the NHS. I have some thirteen tablets each day and I visit my local doctor's surgery on a regular basis. Friend often says to me, "How are you Jim"? I would often say "I am good. I keep taking the tablets. "

Chapter 12:

Local labour movement activist

Politics are almost exciting as war, and almost as dangerous

I was a member of the Labour Party when I moved to Luton from London in 1963. I joined the Party not because I was concerned about right or left, but because I was committed to put right the things that were wrong. It was a moral duty as I saw it. I quickly discovered that the leaders in both the Labour and the Conservatives Parties were people of principles, but neither Party followed their principles, or kept their promises, when in power. I found the Labour Party in Luton to be racist, lacking in vision and radicalism, sexist and disorganised, given the demographic, industrial and character of the town.

I decided to leave the Labour Party and to join the Communist Party due mainly to the fact that most trades union and politically active people were from the left of Labour. I also found the Labour government that replace the Conservatives after thirteen successive years in government started to distance it-self from its historical working class roots and the trade unions. Labour's readiness to criticise the unions, support big businesses and provide tacit support for the cruel, vicious and dirty war in Vietnam turned me against the Party.

The prolonged war in Vietnam where the richest country in the world, America, was attacking one of the poorest countries in the world was grossly wrong and immoral. After the loss of more than a million lives, especially on the part of the North Vietnamese who fought bravely with much less sophisticated weapons, eventually drove the Americans out of South Vietnam and unified their country. Britain under the Labour Party also contrived with the USA, to deny the majority population in Guyana under British colonial rule, real parliamentary democracy and independence by distorting the electoral process.

I was also disillusioned with the Labour Party on the question of race, race relations and immigration. The Party in opposition campaigned against the 1962 Immigration Act which stopped non-white citizens from the Commonwealth having the automatic right to enter Britain, but in government accepted the Act in full. It also failed to address the everyday problems associated with racism, sexism, poverty, unemployment and poor housing. After campaigning for the Party in the 1964 and 1966 general elections I was disappointed with the direction of the government by 1969. Labour's broken promises were too much to bear. I have since found it difficult to take politicians at their face value, or believe in their promises. I had lost faith and confidence in Labour despite the common feeling that Labour was the friend of immigrants. One Conservative politician even went on record in 1964 to say *"if you want a nigger for a neighbour you should vote Labour"*. I soon discovered that Labour has for thirteen years accused the Conservatives of racism, attacking trade unions and supporting the rich, and now the Part could be accused of the same policies.

By 1968 Labour was in great difficulty. They were faced with lots of opposition from businesses, the media, financial institutions, unions as well as a growing number of industrial disputes resulting in widespread strike and dissatisfaction amongst large sections of the population. Even though I had stopped attending Labour Party meetings I had retained my Party membership, voted Labour and defend the Party when attacked by its opponents. As an active member of the trade union movement I felt disillusioned with Labour's performance but still preferred Labour in power than the Conservatives. It was obvious that most people still had lots of confidence in politics, but there was a shortage of politicians to place our confidence in. Politics was supposed to be the second oldest profession, but I felt that it was not a great deal different from the first. Too many politicians were duplicitous, self-centred and only too keen to look out for themselves.

I decided to contest as a candidate for local elections Communist Party candidate in nineteen sixty eight as a protest against Labour. However I soon re-joined Labour, despite my concerns about its direction, not only on the economy but also on race relations and immigration. The Conservatives had introduced yet a further piece of legislation which was the 1971 Immigration Act which restricted immigrants from the new Commonwealth, and other parts of the world where there was not a connection in terms of a parent or a grandparent born in the UK. This act clearly discriminated disproportionately against Black people from the Commonwealth countries in Africa, Asia and the Caribbean. It favoured white immigrants from Australia, New Zeeland, South Africa and Canada. Labour had agreed to repeal this act, but it continued to its shame to operate this legislation which remains in the statutes to this day. I was never a committed to communism, at least not the kind of communism which operated in the Soviet Union, Eastern Europe or China, so I returned to Labour and attempt to secure a seat on the local authority as Labour Party candidate. I agreed with General Charles de Gaulle that politics was "too serious a matter to be left to the politicians".

Councillor Jim

After re-joining the Labour Party I took an active role in local politics and stood for elections nearly a dozen times for Labour between 1971 and 1981. In 1981 I was elected a county councillor with lots of enthusiasm, commitment and hope. I was by then a full-time London Regional Education and Public Relations Official and a member of the list of possible parliamentary candidates. I represented the Dallow ward in Luton on the Bedfordshire County Council Dallow had a substantial visible minority mainly Asian voters. Prior to 1981 there were very few councillors from Black and ethnic minority backgrounds in Bedfordshire, or indeed in the UK. I was confident that I would enjoy being a councillor and that I had the necessary backgrounds, understanding, commitment to democracy and justice, intelligence, understanding and the level of intellectual coherence and persuasive power to play a significant part in promoting my Party values at

County Hall. It was the first time I had been selected by Labour for a safe seat, unlike the eight previous occasions when I was deliberately kept out of winnable ones as I was seen as someone who not only thinks, but was a socialist, therefore I was dangerous. I landed in a safe seat because the candidate selected for the seat withdrew late the night before the papers had to be submitted to the electoral officer. I was at a meeting when the Chair of the local Party, Kelvin Hopkins, asked me whether I would be prepared to stand. He was and still is a leading socialist and has been a backbench Member of Parliament for many years. Socialists do not get far in the People's Party.

It came to my attention within a short period that the Labour Group was not too keen on people who were seasoned campaigners, with strong commitment to the principles of trade unionism, race equality, justice and fairness, or commitment to working class people, instead they favoured people who would not challenge the leadership, nor raise any challenging questions. I was not given any key responsibilities within the Labour Group, yet I was one of the most vocal members within all the committees I served on. I was often congratulated as a "good, honest and interesting speaker and debater by almost all councillors, although many would say "I do not necessarily agree with you". I was often recognised by senior councillors as very challenging, because I read all the reports, made notes and prepared questions in advance. I was also very quick to respond to issues at short notice. Politics seemed to have a tendency to keep people apart instead of uniting them. The Conservatives on the Council were quite a right wing bunch on the Council, whilst the Liberal Democrats were often open to compromise with either Party.

Many Labour party branches and constituencies felt that putting up Black candidates would be a liability and white voters would be reluctant to vote for them. So even in wards with large numbers of Black people white candidates were put forward by the Labour Party and they expected Black voters to support them as the Party, which was less overtly opposed to Black immigrants. By 1981 I was fairly well known within the region and in certain areas nationally for my work, especially within trade unions and the community relations.

During the mid-1980's, despite the rise of racism and xenophobia and calls for repatriation, and an end to Black Commonwealth immigration, a number of local Labour Parties adopted Black candidates and a sizeable number were successful and therefore partly put an end to the myth that Black candidates were automatically a massive liability for Labour. In 1982 there were four Black and Asian councillors in Bedfordshire, one on the local borough council and three on the county council. For most of my time as a county councillor, which spanned over 15 years, the council was either a hung, which means that no single party had overall control, or through negotiations either the Conservatives or the Labour Party took control with the tacit support of the Liberal Democrats and the Independents. Decision making was therefore quite complex and meetings would often start during the day and ended up very late at night and even after midnight, especially during the making of the annual budget.

I remember an incident on the very first day I entered County Hall. As a new councillor, I felt good, as I drove into County Hall to gain access to the members parking, the caretaker informed me that it was reserved for councillors only. I explained that I was a councillor and he muttered something which I can't remember, but then made enquiries and agreed to let me in. I was one of the first Black councillors elected to the Bedfordshire county council. It was cultural shock, not only for the officers of the council, but also for some councillors. I was well prepared in the art of discussion, negotiation, contracting, reading complex documents, chairing meetings, arguing a case and presenting evidence, as I had been an active and senior trade union activist for many years and had taken part in negotiations and consultations with employers. In addition, I was one of the few councillors with a university degree in government and politics and in trade union studies. I was also a trained teacher, and was working as a full time regional education training and public relations officer for the General and Municipal Workers London region.

As an activist, with radical ideas, and from a trade union background, I was a natural target not only for the Conservatives who were opposed to much of my thinking but also to some members within the Labour Party and indeed amongst Independents and the Liberal Democrats. I was always ready to engage in debates and if necessary, disagree with people. Bedfordshire county council at the time was quite conservative; for example, we started off our meetings with prayers and some councillors even stood up when the county secretary/clerk walked into the room dressed in his dark clothing and gown. I was one of the first who did not stand up, and this practice soon ended.

During my time on the county council I stood out a great deal partly because of my radical politics and partly because of my capacity and propensity to challenge traditions, ask questions and to an extent interrogate officers about their options and preferences for certain strategies and policy matters. I took a great deal of interest in areas such as employment as unemployment increased to nearly three million under Mrs Thatcher's government. Mass unemployment contributed a lot to the pain and suffering for workers and their families throughout the country. At the same time, I was mindful of ensuring that the county council performance was of a very high standard and that officers and senior managers were accountable to us as councillors as representations of the public, for their actions on policy and direction. I also argued for accountability, transparency and efficient use of resources, much to the annoyance of my fellow councillors who invariably rubber stamped much of the decision making at County Hall.

The officers at senior level, including the Chief Executive and heads of departments were highly skilled and professional people; articulate, with university degrees and a lot of experience under their belt on policy matters. They were also good at persuading councillors to follow their decisions. They managed the agenda and provided advice and support to councillors. Many councillors were too close to senior managers and became friends outside of the council chamber. I always felt that as councillors we should keep our distance socially; be professional with officers; ensure that we were there to represent the public interest and not following recommendations from officers without due probity, analysis and exploration of alternatives. Not many councillors wanted this, nor were they able to challenge officers on details, especially on financial matters and alternative strategies. They were mainly retired, people from working class and manual backgrounds or people who were self-employed.

So naturally, within a short period of time I was identified as a bit of troublemaker somewhat by the officers. I was not one of the councillors that would turn up at County Hall with envelopes unopened having not bothered to read their agenda, plan a strategy, or to prepare themselves for the meeting. Instead I was one of those who had read the agenda carefully, and had carefully scrutinized the recommendations. I would often prepare myself to put forward alternative recommendations or to amend recommendations on the agenda placed by officers. I was not regarded as a friend of the chief executive or senior managers and was often told by other councillor colleagues and even officers that, although at times they agreed with me, they were reluctant to say so at the meetings, which were open to the public. I felt that I was a very hardworking and intelligent councillor and that some officers and councillors felt somewhat threatened on occasions by my ability to critically challenge, request alternatives and expose the lack of value for some projects.

Bedfordshire County Council was a council without any Party having an overall majority, so it was quite challenging to get things done without endless debates and discussions. After a couple of years I decided to try and win the trust and confidence of some of my councillor colleagues from Luton end of the county. Having built some support within the Labour group is was then able to become a senior councillor with increased responsibilities.

During my time in the county council I fulfilled a number of roles at one time; I was a deputy leader of the Labour Group and we took control that year of the council. I was also chairman of the education committee was a budget in excess of two hundred million pounds. I chaired a number of important committees including the performance management committee which I thought was one of the most important committees contrary to thinking of my fellow councillors, who did not understand the importance of the performance management and the efficient use of resources or linking performance with accountability and priority. I also chaired the police committee, fire service committee and other working parties and subcommittees. One of the committees I valued most was the committee on looking at special needs but I chaired that working party for the best part of five years.

Bad politicians are elected by good people who do not vote

During my period as a county councillor, I visited many schools, possibly two hundred schools in the county. But I made a point of visiting every special school in the county, some of the experience I had was quite distressing. There were insufficient resources set aside for children with special needs, and our special schools were often in very poor condition, in terms of buildings and facilities. During the 1980's under the Conservative government there was a great deal of cuts in education due to reduced resources from central government to local authorities.

I felt that special education was the poor relation within the education system. Staff working in special needs were often poorly paid, badly resourced and had on balance, less job security. They worked extremely hard in very difficult conditions, and I had a great deal of sympathy for them, and for their students. I saw some very, very distressing situations where the students, who were severely disabled and were suffering a great deal, physically and mentally and their parents and the teaching staff were doing their very best to support them. Again they were trying to do so with inadequate resources. I tried to be creative and to put forward policies such as, parents should be supported during school holidays because the school look after the children for five or six hours during the day, but almost all had to return home during the evenings, be with their parents at weekends and during school holidays without any external support. I felt that there should be at least some resource available to parents outside school. I argued for access to computers, or laptops, games, toys, books and equipment to be made available to parents on loan, but I was never supported by the council. I also wanted some schools to be open during holidays not only for children with special needs, and others, but also parents as well without any success. Politicians as Oscar Wilde once said "knew the cost of everything, but the value of nothing". Many councillors were masquerading as principled champions of the community, but in reality were more interested in their personal status and gains. County Hall was not the place I came away from with any faith in human nature. Politicians are always keen to think of the next election and not very much about the next generation.

Sadly I did not get a great deal of support from my fellow councillors for enhancing the resources for special needs pupils which distressed and frustrated me a great deal. At the same time it seemed that it was always possible to find resources by senior managers for other projects they had in mind including training, equipment, purchase of resources, increases in salary, provision of cars and transport and paying for officers to attend expensive training courses. They often re-engage senior managers who have retired early with large pensions and lump sum to return as consultants at massive salaries. I intervened on several occasions to expose such practices much to the annoyance of my group leader.

I was amazed and disappointed at the level of wastage within the county council. Senior managers were highly salaried and on balance their jobs were often more secure than those who were lower paid, and were providing frontline, necessary services in very difficult circumstances. Very soon after I became a county councillor, I recognise that the common conception that councillors were in charge of local government was clearly a myth. In fact, local authorities were run like the civil service where the permanent senior managers who were in place regardless of changes in politicians or political control. Permanent senior officers had a great deal of advantage over newly elected and poorly informed councillors.

The majority of councillors were decent people who wanted to improve the lives of people within their communities. They were not academics or university trained, but they had a basic instinct of what is right and what is wrong. They were unable on occasions to fully understand the dynamics and strategic significance of how decisions are formulated, implemented, managed and monitored. They would often argue over the pennies and over trivial matters, whilst the millions and important issues are dealt with expediently by officers who knew how to work the democratic process.

The dynamics associated when managing a budget of hundred millions of pounds, or even billions can be quite daunting and challenging, even for experienced councillors. Senior management in local government are quite disciplined, the chief executive of a local authority can expect more loyalty and support from his departmental heads and senior managers, than a leader of a local authority can expect from his or her own group. Officers are far more disciplined, calculated and work as a team to achieve common objectives; in comparison to councillors whose Party consist of a very wide range of opinions, often in direct conflict with each other. Political groupings can be quite dysfunctional, undisciplined and having to compromise on a number of issues because of internal disagreements. It is a reflection of our democracy that people vote for the Party they dislike the least, instead of the best person for job. Too often politicians are elected by people who do not even bother to vote. So it could be said that the public deserves the politicians they have.

Officers on the other hand are unelected, but they mostly control the agendas, write the documents, advice councillors, manage the process and keep the business going, especially in local authorities where no single Party have an overall majority. Being a member of a hung council, with no Party having an overall majority was quite problematic. The only way to make progress is to engage in compromise, for example, no councillor wanted a school closed in their patch and certain councillors have preference for certain types of education and institutions depending on their party leanings. Also each councillor and political party would fight as much as they can for the areas they represent. They would prevent any negative impact in their own backyard and therefore the acronym of NIMBY meaning not in my back yard. So councillors often do deals to save services and facilities that were of common concerns.

During my period as a county councillor I represented the council on a number of international bodies and visited a number of countries in Europe on delegations. I also became an executive member of the association of county councillors and I was for many years the only visibly minority ethnic person on the executive and on a number of committees of the Association of County Councils, or the Local Government Association. Too often I was either defined by my colleagues, by my race, my commitment to equality for everyone and my links with the unions. I often found myself in disagreement and in conflict with the majority of colleagues from all political persuasions, who were invariably white and had very little practical knowledge of the impact of race relations on disadvantaged communities. I recognise the impact of intuitional racism and oppression, very early in my political life.

Who is in charge of local government?

It has been said that *"Some people are in politics because of principles; others shed principles for their Party."* Local government, political parties, major institutions and even minor ones are institutionally racist, not by design but through lack of commitment, understanding, knowledge and awareness of issues and concerns concerning Black and minority people, who have suffered disproportionately from oppression, deprivation, poverty, prejudice and discrimination sine they arrived in Britain many centuries ago. Black people have been part of the underclass in the inner cities and declining industrial areas of Britain. Not only did they experience high unemployment and the worst working conditions when employed, but also, mainly living in over-crowding and poor housing stock, surviving in areas with very poor facilities in terms of education, health inequality, crime, pollution and environmental concerns. Local government has considerable power and resources to changes the lives of local people. For many years and to this day, local governments still fails to deliver appropriate services to ensure that all communities regardless of culture, race, ethnicity, social status, gender or other backgrounds have equal access to resources that are allocated according to needs.

During my time on the council, I tried to work with the trade unions, but we never got on well together because on one hand I was arguing for the efficient use of resources, which meant that management had to be accountable and workers had to provide the highest quality service to the public. Local government at the time and to this day, still experience relatively good working conditions, pay, pensions, holidays, time off for various needs, and other benefits and opportunities in comparison to other public sector workers, especially workers in the private sector. I believed they had a duty to ensure that the services they provide was the best quality and that they were dedicated and committed to their work.

I was alarmed at the high level of absences which included sickness, time off for various activities, large amount of time spent on training and development, fairly generous holidays including having bank holidays off and a day in lieu of a bank holiday which they claimed. Many local authorities paid generous travelling allowances for car use, provided company cars for many managers, reserved car parking facilities and seldom held staff accountable when things went wrong. Local government has always been highly organised trade union wise, and many managers were afraid to raise issues in case they upset the relationship they had with the trade unions. I found a number of staff would very regularly complain about discrimination of one type or another, whether be race or gender, or other types of discrimination, harassment on bullying, when they were held accountable, or challenged by their managers over issues like performance, attendance, sickness, or poor quality work.

I believe that there is a great deal of wastage in local government, duplication of resources has always been widespread and in many cases, the public does not get value for money. I also believe the Audit Commission system of monitoring local government expenditure was a waste of time and did not serve the public interest well.

During my years at County Hall, I was recognised as somewhat of a character, intelligent and smart, but should be avoided if possible, not only by officers but also by councillor colleagues. As councillors we were entitled to expenses and allowances for attending meetings some of them were keen to secure as many places on committees as possible. Meetings lasting that exceeded four hours attracted a much enhanced sum. So colleagues would support me when I during my many interventions, but would quickly wish to silence me after the magical four hours had been exceeded, and therefore we could claim the maximum in expenses and allowances.

So I didn't make many friends by keeping the meeting going for long hours after the maximum allowances had been reached. Between 1989 and 1994 I changed jobs and I was working for the local government management board, where I had written a number of training manuals on various aspects of equality, quality and management issues. I was also involved in training chief officers, senior managers, councillors and other local government employees on a range of subjects, including equality, management change, strategic management and decision making. I was also heavily involved in the Labour Party, being a Parliamentary candidate in Milton Keynes in 1983 and a Member of various policy forums and committees at national levels with many people who later became senior government ministers after Labour was returned to power in 1997. I sat on various local government committees nationally that agreed the strategy on equality, quality and local government reform and my contributions were often critical in determining Party policies.

During my tours of local authorities in England and Wales as a senior management advisor on local government, I would bring back best practice guidelines to Bedfordshire and also to Luton Borough Council. It was never simple, because as I said earlier local government is quite conservative and it would appear that only suggestions that arrived via senior management locally were likely to succeed and become policy. In any case, there have always been too many policies and not enough implementation. In 1994, I stood for the last election as a Luton County councillor. High Town Ward Labour Party rejected me for a candidate for white male candidate in rural Biggleswade some thirty miles away. Nevertheless I secured a seat in a ward by defeating an ex-leader of the Conservative Party on Luton Borough Council. It was a ward in which my wife, Doreen had taught at the local High school and the name Thakoordin was well known. I had also served as a non-executive director of the local Luton and Dunstable Hospital and many hospital workers were familiar with my name. Doreen probably won the election for me on that occasion.

Unitary status returned to Luton in 1998, all the Luton councillors were separated from Bedfordshire County Council. Luton county councillors were part of the transition team which subsequently ended up as Luton borough councillors. Needless to say, Luton borough councillor colleagues did not welcome us because they thought under the unitary borough, us county councillors would obviously have more experience a running education, social services, police, fire and other services previously operated by the County. I had to face another group of councillors who were opposed to me, felt threatened by my knowledge, experience, skills and abilities and my high profile. However, I did secure a position as vice chair of the education committee and play the major part in restructuring the Luton borough council education services. A white Luton borough councillor, who had been a county employee in the youth service, became chair of the education committee, even though I had chaired the Committee at County Hall for seven years.

The Chair of Education was totally depended on the Director of Education who had many years in as a Deputy Director in a county. On occasions I disagreed with both the Director and the Chair on a number of issues especially on the question of who should give leadership in terms of policy matters but in the newly constituted education committee. Being a seasoned councillor on education and other unitary issues, I tried to influence the Luton framework but with little success, and it wasn't long before I had lost my position. During my time in local government I played a very active role in the education services, for example I was a chairman of two high school governing bodies for a total of over fourteen years. Altogether I had been a governor of several schools, two colleges and two universities for a period of nearly thirty five years.

As a latecomer to education I recognised the value of education and how education can change the lives of people at any age. So I was determined that people should have a fair opportunity to succeed on the first chance and if they failed they should succeed on their second attempt or subsequent attempts. They should always be able to access opportunities and to progress. Education is extremely liberating, it is a democratic right of everyone throughout life which helps to support not only the individual but also families and communities.

I was a Luton Borough councillor when I had a mild heart attack, whilst I was attending an employment tribunal in London, as a member. I was taken to the University College Hospital after I passed out in the tribunal room. I spent a few days in hospital before I returned home and spent another few days convalescing at home. I said to my wife, could you please sort out my post for me. I used to get upwards of sixty letters a day as an active councillor who was often seen as challenging, hardworking, controversial and proactive and I would pick up issues for constituents outside my own area and across the country. I was often singled out as a counsellor who would be prepared to take up issues when others would feel that such issues were lost causes.

As a Labour councillor I recognised very early that people would always be looking out for power, status and opportunities and they would deliberately target certain people as friends and would support each other on the basis that you support me for committee places and I will support you. But I never got involved with this bartering for positions as I felt that my knowledge, skills, abilities and commitment would be sufficient to secure me places on committees that I was interested in, and felt I could do a good job.

But local government is not like that; people are out to get what they can for themselves, first and foremost and use every opportunity to enhance their position and status. In doing so, they disregard the needs of some of their constituents. I felt as a counsellor I should be championing the causes of the constituents, and the people who provide the resources to finance local government. People would often contact me with their problems even though they were well aware that I was not their councillor, nevertheless it did not stop them demanding my attention. I was disappointed that most of the Asian councillors appeared to be involved mainly with their own ethnic, cultural or religious groups, and others felt let down by such councillors. I discovered after returning from my heart attack that my fellow councillors were within a few days seeking to take over my committee places. I only had about a dozen letters from people who wrote to me expressing their regret at my poor health. Two of these letters were from the opposition Parties, three from officers and seven from members of the public. Not a single letter from my own Party.

To become the master, the politician poses as the servant

During my time as a counsellor I've learnt a great deal of lessons about politics and people. It was interesting to discover what motivates people from such diverse backgrounds entering local politics. It has been said that "Politics is the art of the possible." For me it seemed at times that it was the art of the impossible, with constant cuts in budgets whilst maintaining increasing statutory duties and expectations from service users. As the Chair of the education Committee on and off for a period of seven years I was forced to make some harsh decisions, in terms of prioritising services whilst ensuring fairness, equal access and high standards. I recall having a mother knocking on my door one day, demanding to see me about her son who was seriously disabled. He was given a place at a special school within the county, but the mother wanted her teenage son to be placed in a school over one hundred miles away from home, that had all the facilities she felt he needed. She wanted him to be in a rural setting with lots of open spaces, horse riding facilities and various other things that were unavailable within the county special schools. It was at a time of serious budget cuts and we were trying to avoid sending pupils out of county as the cost was sometime up to two or the three times the expense for a local place. This mother came to my house with her son and a knife and threatened to kill him in my presence by slitting his throat, if I do not agree to authorised the cost of an out of county place. Fortunately, the leader of the opposition group agreed with me and we were able to place this child in the school of his mother's choice. Bedfordshire County was a hung council for at least twenty five years before it was abolished and split into three separate unitary authorities in 1998.

On several occasions during my time as a councillor I had to face angry crowds who were opposed to cuts in services. On many occasions I was shouted at threatened, abused and harassed, especially by mothers who were determined to secure the place they felt was best for their children. The fathers would generally take a more relaxed approach, but the mothers were far more determined to get the best deal for their children, and would go to any length to do so. I was very upset one day, when I visited a special school for severely disabled children in the county. Some of the children were barely conscious as to where they were and many had physical and mental disabilities. I saw a teacher pushing a young girl, age about twelve, in a wheelchair who wanted to use the toilet. The door to the toilet was taken off the frame to enable wheelchair access, and this had been the case for a long time. I reported this matter to the Chief Education officer the same day, yet it took the best part of a year before this problem was addressed. I wanted all pupils with disabilities in special schools and at home, to have access to a computer, but was told by fellow councillors, this was not possible. Yet the same councillors agreed to have two council departments switching floors at

County Hall and renewing lots of equipment at a cost of over £200.000. One year I was told that the department would have to lose thirty seven teaching and learning support jobs in special education due to cuts in the departmental budget. I decided to meet with the senior officers and we decided to do an audit of the entire spending of the department from the top to the bottom. We discovered several areas that were not as a priority given the severity of the cuts and in the end, instead of cutting thirty seven jobs; we increased the staffing by twelve. Reductions were made in reductions in consultants, many of whom were senior staff that were retired on generous pensions, but were re-engaged on short term contracts. We also discovered that some senior staff was attending professional career development training courses costing up to £600 per day, whilst more junior staff was denied training and development opportunities.

Equality for all

For most of my time at County Hall, I chaired the Equal Opportunities Sub-Committee; the Special Needs Working Party, the Standing Committee on Religious Education and other committees and sub-committees. I specifically targeted equal opportunities, special needs and religious education as all these areas were linked in to access to support and resources for children from poor and religious backgrounds, Luton was and still is one of the most diverse, multi-cultural, disadvantaged and urban towns in England, and I was very concerned about the well below average achievements by poor white and black children, and the even less achievement by children from Pakistani, Bangladeshi and Caribbean backgrounds. The education system during between 1965 and 2005 was inefficient and institutionally racist, despite lots of attention by Labour and Conservative governments. White working class children have always achieved less within the state education system, and the poorer they were the less they achieved. It was not always due to poverty and lack of efforts, the schools themselves did not perform to the highest standards.

In my years as a councillor I saw quite a few incidents that were far from legal. I recall an incident when a crate of alcohol was left on my door step from a company that had done work for the council a few days before Christmas. I took the crate to County Hall, explained the situation and left the alcohol in the building. An hour later it was all gone, because the councillors had helped themselves. I was offered exceptional hospitality on several occasions, but declined them all. I saw fellow councillors and officers of councils accepting all sorts of hospitalities, some of which were quite substantial. The law has changed a great deal since then, and I believe all councillors and officers have to register any gifts and hospitality over a certain sum. On the other hand councillors were given more discretion to increase their expenses and allowances substantially since 2000, as almost all councillors drew relatively small sums in expenses and allowances because they saw their role as willing volunteers who were committed to public services. Some councillors can earn up to £50,000 or more these days and regards their council work as their main source of income.

Pleased to meet you your Majesty

I have many and diverse memories of my time as a Councillor. I was particularly pleased to meet the Queen Elizabeth on three occasions. The first and second occasions were when I was invited to the Garden Party at Buckingham Palace. During the 1990's and the third occasion was when she opened an extension to the Luton and Dunstable Hospital. I received the invitation to the Garden Parties through the Chief Executive of the Bedfordshire County Council. I believe each Chief Executive received a small number of invitations, which are then passed on to the Leaders of the main political groups. The leader of the Labour group on the council could not attend on each occasion, so the invitation was passed on to me as the deputy leader of the group. My wife and I attended the parties and it was quite interesting and reflective. The security system was of course very extensive. There were on each occasion about three or four hundred people in attendance all dressed up and excited to be part of this memorable occasion. I know that some socialist would refuse to attend such a gathering as they would feel some sort of class betrayal, or because they were opposed to the Royal family and all that they represent in the past and at present. I had mixed feeling myself, but decided to attend with my wife for the experience and to see for myself what the day was about. Personally, I am not very keen on the Royal family not only for historical reasons due to their association with colonialism, imperialism and slavery, but also because of the vast sums of public money being spent on a family that is so rich. The Queen is probably amongst the richest women in the world and the cost of maintaining their many properties exceptional lifestyles of the extended family is quite difficult for a socialist to come to terms with, apart from the family being at the top of the pyramid that distinguishes the class system in Britain.

The actual Garden parties started with tea, cakes, sandwiches and soft drinks in the attractive and pleasant garden in the heart of London. It reminded me of Ascot Horse Racing events, where women generally dress up in bright and colourful garments, including fancy hats and stylish shoes. After about an hour in the warm sun chatting to people and exploring the gardens, we were asked to line up along a pathway about sixty metres long and three metres wide in readiness to meet Her Majesty. Our eyes were fixed towards the rear of the large Palace, and we eventually saw the Queen, accompanied by the Duke of Edinburgh and other members of the Royal family making their way slowly towards us. A few carefully selected people were identified well in advance to have a brief word with the Queen, who spent no more than thirty seconds with each of these special people. The Duke and other members of the family kept a few paces behind the Queen and they had brief chats with others in the crowd. On the first visit to the Garden Party, a woman fainted in the hot sun, but she quickly recovered with some help. There were no pushing or shoving and everyone appeared happy, polite and to be enjoying the event. My wife and I visited the large marquees where the refreshments were served and we found the occasion interesting. In any case it was something to tell our grandchildren about. We were not allowed to take pictures once we entered the Palace grounds, so we had to make use of having our photograph taken in front of the Palace. My wife Doreen really looked sweet and charming in her lovely outfit, including hat all bought for the occasion.

The third time I met the Queen was when she visited our local hospital. I was a member of the Hospital Board for many years before meeting the Queen. Sir Stanley O'Dell was the Chairman of the Hospital Community Healthcare Trust of which I was an active member. He kindly invited me to meet Her Majesty and to have a photograph taken with her during the visit. The Queen asked me how I was and we exchanged a few words of pleasantries. We spent about thirty five seconds together and I found her a charming and genuine person who enjoyed her work. The photograph is displayed in our dining room.

I became a Luton Borough councillor after my time with the County Council; the Luton culture was grossly different amongst both the officers and councillors. I was seen as an outsider, especially since I was not living within the Borough. I was not unhappy at leaving the council largely due to my health, having had a heart attack and becoming seriously diabetic. After serving my time as a Luton borough councillor I decided to downsize my political activities, having been involved heavily in local, regional and national politics for a long time. I decided I needed to spend more time with my family: the normal excuse for failed politician. It has been said that "all political careers ends up in failure." I would not argue against such statement. During my career in local government politics I frequently met top national and international politicians, academics, professional and even famous and not so famous people. I met all the Labour and TUC leaders since 1964 including Prime Ministers. I met and interacted with Tony Blair, Gordon Brown, Neil Kinnock, Michael Foot, Claire Short, Harriet Harman, Willy Brandt (Chancellor of Germany), Jack Straw, John Prescott and other Labour and Tory Cabinet Ministers and members of parliament. I met many African and Caribbean political and trade union leaders as well as leaders from Europe. I have had a very diverse and often difficult political life by the time I left Luton Borough Council, so I decided that the time was right to become a parish councillor, which was supposed to be less stressful. But this was not the case.

Racism in rural areas

In 2001 I became a parish councillor and very soon after that, I became the vice chair of the parish council. I chaired the finance committee and the general purposes committee. I also campaigned on issues such as having a parish plan, involving local people in identifying priorities for the parish, seeking to bring additional services such as a library, a dentist, small businesses, community support services and an internet café for young people. Unfortunately, I was unsuccessful in persuading the council to adopt even a parish plan. I campaigned for a parish newsletter which I was successful in achieving and also for greater transparency, accountability and probity, even though parish councils have very little power and very little financial resources at their disposal.

Life as a parish councillor was a great deal different from that of a borough or county council. Parish councils are quite parochial. Parish councillors are people with very deep personal and political interests, but would often claim to be independent minded, non-political and only interested in supporting the local parish. This may be true for some, but it is not necessarily so in many cases. When the chairman of the parish council, who was extremely hard working and well respected, resigned as chair and from the council, I thought that I had gained sufficient experience and support to become chair of the parish council, as I was the vice chair. But it wasn't to be; instead it was the start of a massive hate campaign against my wife and I who were both on the parish council. Although I had lived in the village for over twenty five years I was still seen as an outsider, someone from Luton where lots of black people lived and crime rate was high. This village which borders Luton Borough was very conservative in many ways. Most of the workers in the village earned their living from jobs in Luton; they shopped in the town and enjoyed many of the town's facilities, but felt they were somewhat superior to the average Lutonians, especially those who were black.

I was the second black person to move into the village with my wife, a white Londoner and two teenage children, both born in Luton. There was another mixed race couple in the village and we became close friends. Over the years I had to give a lot of support to newcomers in the village who were Asians and Caribbean's, especially the Asians who took over the two newsagents at various times. A few others who dared to settle in the village experienced similar problems. It is an area with less than two per cent non-white as opposed to Luton with over thirty per cent non-white people. It also appeared that many people were jealous of us, having a lovely large bungalow on a large plot of land; my wife and I, both professional people in senior positions and earning well above average incomes. Although I made many friends in the village of Caddington, I also turned a number of people against me, including members from my parish council. I was the only black person to ever served on the Parish council and I paid a high price for not only being black, but to be an intelligent, articulate experienced, and clever councillor having served on county and borough councils as well as being a councillor for over twenty years and a senior national advisor to local government in England and Wales for seven years. In addition, I had written several books, contributed regularly to newspaper articles and to local radio as well as regional television programmes.

At one stage I upset a number of colleagues on the parish council who had taken all the senior positions I previously had, and was reported to the standards board for local government, for bringing the parish council into disrepute and for not treating my fellow councillors with disrespect. During the hearing of the standards board committee, I was unable to attend to represent myself because I was in hospital recovering from an operation. The board subsequently found there was no case about me bringing the council into disrepute, but there was a case to answer in terms of being disrespectful to my colleagues. Therefore they recommended that I had some training, which I did and it lasted for about three hours from an ex-Tory councillor. The allegation against me was that "I had repeatedly boasted about my experience in local government and in doing so, new councillors found this disrespectful."

After the decision by the standards board it was reported to the local media who made a great story from this situation. The newspapers, as always looking out for gossip and stories, whether true or false, to fill their newspapers, also reported a number of incidents where I had disagreed with a Tory county councillor who moved next door to us and was a regular participant at the parish meeting where we frequently disagreed with each other. This disagreement encouraged him and several other councillors who made several other complaints to the standard board, of which all were dismissed.

An incident which took place when a black family who were moved to the village for security reasons from London, were being harassed and bullied and when the male member of the family retaliated, he was imprisoned for criminal damage and threatening behaviour. I felt the community could and should have done a great deal more to stop the bullying and racial harassment in the earlier stages, and therefore preventing this family from suffering the way they did, the children were attacked at school. Their home was repeatedly attacked with stones and several young people regularly hanging around in the road opposite the house of the victims harassing them. The father was black, mother white and the children were mixed race. Despite my plea on behalf of the family, the police, the local councillors, the local vicar, and everyone else didn't provide any help. In fact the chair of the parish council in Slip End reported me to the Commission for Race Equality claiming that I "unfairly labelled village". This story secured front page coverage in the local newspaper.

Even though I am no longer a councillor since May 2011, I am still a high profile community and political activist who appear regularly in the local newspapers, radio and occasionally on television on issues of local, national and regional significance. This includes education, race relations, trade unions and major economic issues.

I have no regrets over being a councillor and giving so much of my life towards fighting for justice fairness, equality and better services for people, regardless of their age, race, culture, colour or ethnicity. My only regret is that politics and politicians has become so self-centred and lacks the trust and confidence of the vast majority of the public they claim to serve. In my days as a councillor we were given fairly modest allowances which have since changed and some councillors are earning the best part of £50,000 plus, in expenses and allowances. Other councillors could easily earn £10,000, £15,000 or £20,000 by sitting on police authorities, health authorities fire authorities and other guanos, which during my time they were carried out by councillors who volunteered their services to these public bodies and agencies.

However, despite the fact that councillors can earn a fair bit of money for their work in local government, whilst keeping their professional paid jobs at the same time, there are still insufficient numbers of people willing to come forward to be councillors and in many areas at election times, seats still go uncontested in rural areas. I very much regret that politics and politicians have become so grasping and discreditable. I do believe that there are some genuine people who have a strong desire to promote civic matters and do their best for the public they seek to represent. Others have turned politics into a career for themselves. They speak a language which is often alien to the majority of electorates, a language of spin doctoring and often duplicity. They seldom provide straight and comprehensible answers to questions. I am not surprised that politicians, like journalists, are seen as the least trustworthy people around.

As Nikita Khrushchev, President of the Soviet Union once said, "Politicians are the same all over, they promise to build a bridge even where there is no river". Or as Plato stated in ancient times: "Those who are too smart to engage in politics are punished by being governed by those who are dumber."

Top- Bottom, L-R
Jim with; Dennis Skinner MP 2003, before Iraq war
Robin Cook, Foreign Secretary 1998
Gordon Brown in 2004
Ken Livingstone, September 19th 1984, eve of re-election to GLC
Diane Abbott 1990
Jim with Labour manifesto 1983

Top – Bottom L-R
Jim with; Clare Short Blackpool 1984
Neil Kinnock 1984
John Prescott 2004
Harriet Harman and Margaret Hodge in the 1980s

Top -Bottom
Jim with; Barbara Castle 2004
Outside Downing street in 1998 for Labour victory party
Cherie Blair in 1998 for victory party

Chapter 13:

The Labour Party, politics and black struggles

The legacy of British imperialism and colonialism

Any examination of racism in Britain, especially amongst Black people must take into account the historical aspects which shaped race relations for over four hundred years. During imperialism, colonialism, and slavery Blacks were brought to Britain in sizeable numbers. By the 16th Century Blacks had settled in many areas of the United Kingdom especially around the large ports and urban areas such as Liverpool, Bristol, London, Manchester, Cardiff and Glasgow. The Black population in Britain constantly increased during the 16th, 17th and 18th centuries with the continuation of the slave trade until its gradual abolition in Britain, which started with the Mansfield Judgement in 1772. Slavery was not formally abolished until 1834 in the colonies although historians have argued that it continued in some shape or form for many years after formal abolition.

Blacks were brought to Britain between 1500 and 1600 mainly for the purpose of being servants to wealthy families; used as status symbols by the rich; as prostitutes or sexual conveniences for the rich; and as court entertainers. Many Blacks ran away from their owners and masters and lived independent lives as sailors, entertainers or labourers. In the 1570s Queen Elizabeth was shown with a group of Black musicians and dancers entertaining her courtiers and herself. However entertaining the Queen may have found the Black entertainers; she was nevertheless opposed to their presence in her country, arguing that there were enough people in England without blackamoors.

On 11th July 1596, when the population of England was only 3,000,000 Queen Elizabeth sent an open letter to the Lord Mayor of London, and the Mayors and Sheriffs in other towns in the following terms:

> *"Her Majesty understanding that several blackamoors have lately been brought into this realm, of which kind of people there are already too many here….. Her Majesty's pleasure therefore is that those kinds of people should be expelled from the land…."*

In 1601 the Queen issued a proclamation in which she declared herself:

> *"Highly discontented to understand the great number of negars and Blackamoors which (as she is informed) are crept into this realm…. Who are fostered and relieved here to the great annoyance of her own people that want the relief, which those people consume, as also for that the most of them are infidels, having no understanding of Christ or His Gospel" (Peter Fryer "Staying Power – The History of Black People in Britain)."*

From 1621 onwards the trade in Black people as slaves was quite common in the large cities of Britain. In 1770 there were 8,000 Black slaves in London alone, forming some 3 per cent of the capital's population of some 650,000. However, despite various attempts to rid the realm of Blacks they continue to increase in many towns and cities. The gradual reduction of the slave trade in Britain resulted in many freed Black trying to find work to support them. It was extremely difficult for many of them who drifted into prostitution, vagrancy, unemployment and destination.

When the government's attention was drawn to the plight of the freed slaves its response was to repatriate them. It offered free passage and £12 per head for every Black who agreed to be deported to Freetown in Sierra Leone in Africa. 411 Blacks and 60 white prostitutes were bundled off to Freetown in 1786. A hundred years later the number of Blacks in Britain reduced drastically because of fewer newcomers, inter-marriage and those returning to their country of origin.

However, with the growth of colonialism; imperialism; growth in world trade; and the economic and political domination of many African, Asian and Caribbean countries, Black people began to arrive in Britain in sizeable numbers as students and seamen in the late 19th Century.

Slavery, which was linked with colonialism and imperialism, generated the wealth, which was instrumental in the creation of the industrial revolution in Britain. According to Ramsay Muir, "A History of Liverpool" published by Williams and Northgate, 1907.

> "The slave trade was the pride of Liverpool, for it flooded the town with wealth which invigorated every industry, provided the capital for docks, enriched and employed the mills of Lancashire, and afforded the means for opening out new and ever new lines of trade.
>
> Beyond a doubt it was the slave trade which raised Liverpool from A struggling port to be one of the richest and most prosperous trading centres in the world."

The same could be said for all the major towns and cities and the industries which grew from the highly profitable slave trade and colonialism. The cruelty of slavery both in Britain and her colonies; the exploitation, suffering and oppression of tens of millions of the Blacks for centuries; and the exploitation of the natural resources of the countries under colonialism, coupled with economic subordination of the colonies to the British economy, cannot be ignored by either the black or white people in Britain and Europe. I saw myself as part of the product of British colonialism and the gradual increase of black people in Britain since the 19th Century. My parents and my ancestors who were taken from India as indentured labourers by the British to work on the sugar plantations alongside the ex-slaves were also products of the system that was linked to racism and the wealth of the British nation.

Brief overview of political parties
and race relations

The Labour Party was initially formed in 1900, as a centre-left political party by the trade union movement to establish political representation in Parliament. It was seen as a 'socialist' commitment with the original party constitution of 1918. That 'socialist' element, the original Clause IV, was seen by its strongest advocates as a straightforward commitment to the "common ownership", or nationalisation, of the "means of production, distribution and exchange". The Party has been described as a broad church, containing a diversity of ideological trends from Marxists, Christian Socialists, trade unionists and a range of people with various radical ideas committed to transforming society for the good of the many and not just the few. The Party also attracted a sizeable number of people who regarded themselves as moderates or social democrats. The Labour Party overtook the Liberal Party in general elections during the early 1920s and formed minority governments under Ramsay MacDonald in 1924 and 1929–1931. The party was in a wartime coalition from 1940 to 1945, after which it formed a majority government under Clement Attlee, with a massive 145 seats majority. The Party was then in a position to carry out much of the far reaching nationalisation and public ownership programme it had discussed for nearly fifty years. It was during the 19045-1950 that the Party created the National Health Service and brought the public utilities, transport, coal mining, and other industries into public ownership, despite the fact that Britain was in very serious debt and the country was in very poor financial position due to the Second World War, which lasted from 1939 – 1945. The Labour was also in government from 1964 to 1970 under Harold Wilson and from 1974 to 1979, first under Wilson and then James Callaghan. Labour was defeated by Margaret Thatcher in 1979, 1983, and 1987 and by John Major another Conservative leader in 1992. Labour was then returned to power in 1997 under Tony Blair, who won the 2001 and 2005 elections with massive majorities in Parliament, but decided on a political and ideological strategy grossly different from that followed by Clement Atlee fifty two years earlier. Tony Blair who removed Clause IV from the Party's constitution was replaced in the same way Thatcher had been replaced by her Party as the Leader and Prime Minister, in between general elections was succeeded by Gordon Brown, who failed to secure a majority of seats in 2010. The Party has been the Official Opposition in the Parliament since the Conservatives under the leadership of David Cameron went in to a Coalition government with Nick Clegg, the leader of the Liberal Democrats. Labour under Gordon Brown's in one of the worst economic recession for over sixty years which affected much of the western economies. The present government which term will end in May 2015 has been involved in one of the most sustained and prolonged period of austerity, which has taken the Thatcherite policies of de-regulation, privatisation, cuts in public services, changes in employment rights and the entire judicial system, as well as significantly restructuring the welfare state, and allowing real incomes for people below average earnings to fall substantially. Britain is now one of the most unequal, societies in Western Europe, with rising poverty, unemployment, house prices and rents, as well as having much of local and central government and public services outsourced to private companies operating for profits.

The Labour Party The years leading up to the First World War and during the inter-war period saw major race disturbances in both mainland Britain and in its colonial outposts. During 1919, there were disturbances in port areas of Britain with large concentrations of black people. Some of the most serious of the racial disturbances in the UK occurred in Cardiff, Liverpool, and Bristol London in 1905 and again in 1919. Local white males attacked black men in the docks and other poor areas where they were living and forced the black community to either leave the area, barricade themselves in their homes or challenge the racists in the streets, despite the fact that they were grossly outnumbered and the police were not on their side. Black people were not only attacked and ridiculed by self-confessed fascists and racists but were also ridiculed and stereotyped by those who claimed to be radicals, liberals, socialists, trade unionists and feminists. The post-war depression of the 1920's and 1930's made the conditions for black people much worse than the rest of the population. Many blacks lived in terrible poverty and some turned towards the trade unions and radical political parties for support and involvement.

The start of the First World War in 1914 brought about dramatic changes for Black people in Britain. Opportunities were created for many workers British workers, including women and Black workers from abroad. Black labourers were recruited to work in munitions and chemical factories recruited to the merchant navy and replaced white men who joined the army and navy. Many Blacks in Britain and in the colonies joined the war on behalf of the allies and fought in Europe and elsewhere. By the end of the war there were some 20,000 Black people in Britain. During the war regiments made up almost entirely of Black soldiers fought in Europe and Africa. Many were commended for their bravery. Racism was rife in the army and even on the battlefield. Blacks were often referred to by the white soldiers as 'monkeys' and 'apes'. Shortly before the end of the War in 1918 about 2,000 wounded soldiers including some 50 Blacks were brought back to military hospital in Belmont road, Liverpool. The Black soldiers were subjected to regular racial taunts and abuse. On one occasion some 400 to 500 white soldiers went into battle with 50 Black soldiers. The Black soldiers were blamed for the rioting but a War Office enquiry found otherwise, ("The Belmont Hospital Affair"; African Telegraph. 8 December, 1918).

After the war Black people found themselves once again at the rough end of life in Britain. White workers demanded jobs occupied by black workers. Many white workers refused to work with black workers. Black workers were being sacked to make way for White workers in the sugar refineries in Liverpool and in the docks in Cardiff. There were riots in Liverpool, Cardiff and elsewhere in Britain as Blacks were attacked on site. Racial violence was very common. Blacks organised to defend and protect themselves against constant racism. Blacks were often turned out of their accommodation for having no jobs and no money. Even hostels accommodating Black men were targets for the racists. (Peter Fryer,

"Staying Power – The History of Black People in Britain" Pluto Press, 1994, pages 289 –321).

In 1936, black workers in Cardiff formed the Coloured Seamen's Union, bringing together Africans, West Indians, Arabs and Malays to fight against the operation of the colour bar on the Cardiff Docks. Similar actions took place in other cities such as Liverpool, London and Bristol. This move to develop their own black self-organised structures within the context of the labour market was as a direct consequence of the failure of trade unions to effectively take up the specific issues facing black workers at that particular workplace. The period also witnessed the formation of the first independent black self-organised trade union in the UK. The Coloured Film Artistes' Association (CFAA) was established at Elstree studios as a means of attempting to improve the terms and conditions of work for black actors and extras at the site

Asian workers were also active in creating black self-organisation with strong links with the trade union movement. They formed the Indian Workers Association (IWA) in Coventry in 1938. Many other local branches were formed in subsequent years in areas with a high concentration of Indian workers, for example, in Leicester and Southall. Many IWA members had been activists in India and brought with them a strong tradition of militant struggle. The IWA always encouraged trade union activity, but initially its main focus was concentrated on the issue of Indian independence from British rule - this was achieved in 1947.

As a result of this and the fact that there was a big increase in the number of Indians coming to live and work in Britain after World War Two, the IWA focused more on the trade union and anti-racist struggle in Britain. By the 1950s, the various Associations had combined to become the Indian Workers Association (Great Britain). After unifying these local groups, the IWA (GB) quickly became one of the most important Punjabi associations in Britain, with strong connections to the trade union movement and closely involved with both anti-racist and immigration legislation.

During the Second World War there was a substantial increase in the number of Black people in Britain, which included some 35,00 Black American soldiers. Between 1939 and 1945 many regiments, consisting mainly of Black soldiers, fought in Europe once again, on the side of the allies. Racial tensions, harassment and attacks inside and outside the army and other services were commonplace. Many White Americans brought their prejudice and racism with them to Britain. Several questions were raised in the House of Commons and debates took place in the Cabinet about situation faced by the Black soldiers in Britain. Many institutions and organisations were apprehensive about the way they should treat or respond to Black soldiers.

For example, the wife of a vicar in Weston-Super-Mare during a talk to local women suggested a six-point code of behaviour, which includes the following advice:

- White women must have no relationship with coloured men;

- On no account must coloured troops be invited to the homes of white women;

- If she is walking on the pavement and a coloured soldier is coming towards her, she should cross to the other pavement.

Quoted in the Sunday Pictorial, 6 September 1942.

The major General responsible for Administration in Southern Command issued to District Commanders and Regional Commissioners a set of "Notes on Relations with Coloured Troops." According to the author, wherever they lived, however, they possessed certain fundamental characteristics, which had to be borne in mind when dealing with them in a British context:

"While there are many coloured men of high mentality and cultural distinction, the generality are of a simple mental outlook. They work had when they have no money and when they have money prefers to do nothing until it is gone. In short they have not the white man's ability to think and act to a plan. The spiritual outlook is well-known and their nature. They respond to sympathetic treatment. They are natural psychologists in that they can size up a white man's character and can take advantage of a weakness. Too much freedom, to wide association with white men, tends to make them lose their heads and have on occasions led to civil strife. This occurred after the last war due to too free treatment and associations which they had experienced in France." Appendix to Sir James Grigg, Secretary of State for War memorandum for the Cabinet 3 October 1942, WP (42) in CAB 66/29.

After the war Black people in Britain continued to suffer from racial discrimination and racism. A number of soldiers stayed on in Britain after the war and a number of Black people began to arrive in Britain in search of work. The first wave of economic immigrants from British colonies started with the landing of the SS Windrush at Tilbury Dock on 22 June 1948, with 492 passengers from the Caribbean. The 1948 Nationality Act had granted United Kingdom citizenship to citizens of Britain's colonies and former colonies. The British passport gave them the right to come live and work in Britain.

Between 1948 and 1958 Black immigrants from Africa, the Caribbean and the Asian sub-continent grew steadily. In 1948 less than 1,000 Black people arrived in Britain to seek employment. By 1954 some 24,000 Black immigrants arrived from the Caribbean. 26,000 arrived in 1956, 22,000 in 1957 and 16,000 in 1958. By the end of 1958 there were some 125,000 Caribbean's/West Indians and around 55,000 from the Asian sub-continent.

Many Blacks in the Caribbean, India and Pakistan were recruited by London Transport and the Department of Health with full support of the British Government to fill the jobs which many white workers were reluctant to do. These jobs were in transport, the health service and in manufacturing. They were characterised by low pay and unsociable hours.

Post-war Britain needed labour to sustain the growth and development and it was not surprising that immigrant people from the colonies and ex-colonies filled this gap. The cycle had turned a full circle from being unwelcome to Britain and subject to repatriation nearly two hundred years previously to being recruited to work in Britain. However, despite the presence of less than 200,000 black people in Britain there were enormous debates regarding the uncontrolled flow of black people to Britain; and blacks people being responsible for crime and prostitution; slum housing; unemployment; disease and poor environment. Many private employers and even public sector employers apart from the Health Service and London Transport employed black workers only when white labour was not available. Black people were employed in the lower paid and low status jobs, often in unhealthy and unsafe conditions and working different shifts including working at nights, weekends and long hours. Many industries such as banking, insurance retail, administrative, clerical supervisory, management, construction, mining, hotel and catering, gas, water, electricity, telecommunication and local government jobs were generally unavailable to black people. Employers, landlords and providers of services were free to discriminate against Blacks on the basis of skin colour or ethnic origin. Racial discrimination, harassment and marginalisation of Blacks continued almost unchecked for centuries in Britain.

Britain pre-occupied with immigration

In 1958 there were riots in London (Notting Hill) and in Nottingham some 200 miles away from London. By the end of 1958 and the beginning of 1959 open conflicts involving black and white people were common in London and in many large towns and cities in Britain. This led to calls from politicians of all persuasions for an end to immigration. Racial tension and conflicts escalated in 1960's. Politicians, trade unions and the media openly discussed "the colour problem." Black people were seen as the problem. Instead of addressing white racism politicians and institutions and the media pandered to racism. The Conservative Government introduced the Commonwealth Immigration Act

1962, which became operative on 1 July. against opposition from the Labour Party in opposition. Sadly, the Labour Party implemented the 1962 Act as well as subsequent Immigration Acts designed to restrict immigration from the non-white Commonwealth and even introduced a number of anti- immigration themselves. This measure restricted Black immigration to those who had been issued with employment vouchers and dependants of Black people already settled in Britain. At the time of the 1962 Act, which grossly restricted the flow of Blacks in Britain, the Black population totalled only around 200,000 out of a population of over 50,000,000 people.

By 1962 the following arguments were dominant in discussions relating to race, racism and race relations:

- Britain had a colour problem because too many Blacks were here;

- Black people were the source of the problem;

- Good race relations was dependent on the size of the black population;

- Race relation would improve with severe restrictions on newcomers;

- Black people should integrate and assimilate into British culture and lifestyles;

- There were insufficient jobs, housing and health care for the indigenous people let alone foreigners;

- Blacks were lazy, dirty, and were exploiting the welfare state;

- Blacks were not welcome as neighbours, their presence would lower the standard of the neighbourhood;

- Blacks were bad neighbours. They were living in overcrowded houses, and they were noisy, uneducated and much less desirable as neighbours than British people;

- Blacks were taking jobs, houses and health care from British people;

- All Blacks were immigrants/non British even though they had settled in parts of Britain for centuries;

- Blacks were a liability to Britain;

- They were prepared to work for less money and accept a lower standard of living;

- British culture, standards, values and way of life were being swamped by Black people; and

- Britain was a small over-crowded island, and had to have a strict immigration policy.

The 1964 General Election, which resulted in a Labour Government after thirteen years of rule by Conservative Governments, was bitterly fought contest. Race was a major topic of discussion. A conservative candidate Peter Griffiths fought on an openly racist platform: demanding the ending of immigration and the repatriation of "the coloureds." His slogan was: "if you want a nigger for a neighbour vote Labour." Peter Griffiths defeated a senior Labour minister and won the Smethwick seat in Parliament.

The 1960's especially from 1965 onwards were a period of growing politicisation and Black awareness particularly in America, Britain, France, Africa and the Caribbean. Black radicals either formed separate civil rights organisations or attached themselves to radical socialist, or liberal political and liberation movements. Both confidence and militancy increased amongst Black people and their organisations. Many liberal people, including feminists, students and politicians, supported the demands for an end to discrimination and racial violence against Black people. Demands for equal access, rights and justice for Black people were widely debated alongside the arguments by the right wing and racist politicians and people who were arguing for further immigration and repatriation of Black people.

The Labour Government elected in 1964 having initially opposed to the Immigration Act 1962, boldly implemented the 1962 Act having accepted that it was necessary for good race relations, and declared that strict immigration control was a necessary prerequisite to good race relations, racial integration, assimilation and multi-culturalism. Labour also decided to impose further control of Black immigration to Britain by restricting the number of employment vouchers available to potential Black immigrants from 30,000 to 8,500 annually through the 1965 White Paper "Immigration from the Commonwealth. The White Paper was commonly regarded by anti-racists as further concessions to racists. Institutional racism became respectable to some extent. Extremism was increasingly being regarded as 'common-sense.' Of course, the racists would never be satisfied. The numbers game meant little to the racists whose strategy was clearly designed to intimidate the Black population and to reverse the flow of Black immigration. The Labour Government introduced yet another piece of nakedly discriminatory legislation. The Commonwealth Immigration Act 1968 was steam-rolled through Parliament in a record time of only three days of emergency debate. The sole purpose of this legislation was to restrict the entry into Britain of East African Asians who were mainly living in Kenya and were holders of British passports. The British government broke a pledge by previous governments to honour rights of British citizens to enter Britain. This right of entry was removed from East African Asians who were holders of British passports. It did not restrict the right of white British passport holders living abroad for generations to enter Britain.

Amongst the most vocal, respectable, and powerful voices supporting the anti-immigration lobby was the Right Honourable Enoch Powell, Conservative Member of Parliament for Wolverhampton Southwest. On 9 February 1968 he stated:

"There is a sense of hopelessness and helplessness which comes over persons who are trapped or imprisoned, when all their efforts to attract attention and assistance brings no response. This is the kind of feeling which you in Walsall and we in Wolverhampton are experiencing in the case of continued flow of immigration into our towns... Recently those of us who live in the Midlands and in other areas directly affected have been startled to learn that a provision in the Kenya Independence Act and similar British legislation has the unexpected effect that some 200,000 Indians in Kenya alone have become literally indistinguishable from the people of the United Kingdom, so that they have an absolute fight of entry to this Country." *(Smithies B and Fiddick P. Enoch Powell on Immigration, London Sphere Books Ltd. 1966).*

The speech had the effect of panicking the Labour government into passing the 1968 Immigration Act. This legislation together with the 1962 Immigration Act, and the 1965 White Paper, legitimised the notion that Black people were the source of racial tension and conflict, and that they were responsible for what was seen as the "race problem."

The sole purpose of these Acts was to restrict Black immigration and to allow entry to white immigration. The 1968 Act Immigration Act also included the setting-up of a Body to foster good race and community relations through a national and local framework, which established local Community Relations Councils. Many white people including substantial numbers of trade union members were pleased about the further restrictions imposed on Black immigration, but angry at what they saw as appeasement of Black people, by seeking to ban discriminatory advertisements.

Before the 1968 Race Relations Act discriminatory advertisements which included "No Coloured" or, "Europeans Only" were quite common. Whilst the Act stopped such advertisements being openly displayed, it had very little effect in stopping discrimination in practice.

The various official and research documents continued to highlight the severe inequality experienced by Black people in almost every sphere of British society.

Racial discrimination was widely practised by institutions, organisations and individuals in jobs, housing, services and access to opportunities. The PEP (Political & Economic Planning) Reports of 1967 and 1974 explained in detail the extent and implications of the systemic discrimination against Black people which pervaded and transcended every aspect of life in Britain.

During the 1960's the revival and growth of the fascist and racist organisations were met with organised resistance by Blacks, especially those who were proclaiming and projecting Black liberation through "Black Power" and "Black is Beautiful." Throughout the history of the Black presence in Britain there were indigenous people who were supportive to their struggles for equal treatment. These radicals joined with Blacks in marches, demonstrations and at meetings expressing solidarity in fighting racism.

The Immigration Act of 1971 which was introduced by a Conservative government, and came into force in 1973, changed the status of most Commonwealth immigrants to that of aliens. The Act divides people into 'partials' and 'non-partials.' Partials are British passport holders who were born, or whose parents or at least one grandparent were born in the U.K. The Act opens the door to immigration wider than at any time since restriction began, because it grants unlimited rights of entry to millions of Commonwealth whites settled in Canada, America, Australia, New Zealand and Southern Africa. This Act is blatantly racist and has been accepted as such by many politicians and writers on the subject of race, immigration and nationality. The Labour opposition in Parliament bitterly criticised the 1971 Act but as before retained it during their return to power between 1974 and 1979.

During the 1970's racial discrimination, harassment and violence continued. By the end of the 1970's almost half of the Black population living in Britain were born here. Britain was rapidly becoming a multi-cultural, multi-racial society. There were some two million Black people in Britain. The Trade Union & Labour Relations Act 1974; the Employment Protection Act 1975, and the Employment

Protection (Consolidation) Act 1978, passed by a Labour government provided some protection for Black workers in employment. However the most important piece of legislation was the Race Relations Act 1976 (RR Act) which replaced the Race Relations Acts of 1965 and 1968, and passed by a Labour government covers discrimination in employment and training, education, housing, and the provisions of goods and services. The 1965 Act created the criminal offence of incitement to racial hatred, which made it an offence to use speech, written word or illustration in public which were abusive, threatening or insulting, or were likely to stir up racial hatred. The 1976 RR Act transferred this offence to the Public Order Act 1936 and it is now contained in the Public Order Act 1986. The overwhelming majority of people prosecuted under the 1965 Act were Black people. Few white people were prosecuted under the Public Order Act 1936 or the Race Relations Act 1965. The Labour government also implemented the Race Relations Amendment Act 2000, which strengthen the 1976 RRA. Labour also introduced various Equality legislations between 1997 and 2010 which strengthened previous legislation on eliminating racial discrimination. The Conservative and Liberal Democrats coalition government has been busy dismantling and reducing the impact of the various Acts implemented by Labour since the 1970's, under the pretence to reduce the burden on employers and remove red tape and bureaucracy. The net result has been to reduce the rights of all workers.

After fifty years the British people, the media and the politicians are still pre-occupied with immigration, although the concerns gave shifted from black immigrants to those coming from the twenty seven countries within the European Union, especially from the Eastern European countries. Despite the Prime Minister David Cameron making quite an issue of his commitment to reduce the net number of immigrants to Britain, and having to face serious challenges on the subject of immigration from the rapidly growing right of centre United Kingdom Independence Party (UKIP), the net figure has showed an increase of 200,000. Immigration is once again likely to be a major issue as it has been in every general election since 1959 in Britain. The non-white population in the United Kingdom (UK) has grown consistently since the 1960's.

According to the 2011 Census of Population there were over 8 million (8,108,170) Black, Asian and mixed race visible ethnic minorities in the UK, accountable for 12 per cent of the total population, compared to 4.6 million in 2001 representing 7.9 per cent of the population. The estimated figures for the non-white population in the UK in 2014 are likely to be around 9 million or, around 14 per cent including all those who have not secured legal status. There are also nearly 3 million Muslims living in the UK accounting for over 4 per cent of the population. This is the largest and fastest growing of all the non-white groups in the UK and has attracted a great deal of attention since the invasion of the Iraq by NATO forces in 2003. The wars, ethnic and religious conflicts together with the massive publicity and discussions relating to extremism, terrorism and conflicts within Islam worldwide has created considerable tensions within the UK, Middle East, Europe, Africa, America, Asia and other parts of the world. This has worsen race relations in Britain and elsewhere in Europe leading to an increase in the number and popularity of anti-immigrant and racist far right political parties. Many of these parties have become almost respectable and have either secure seats in Parliament and in a number of countries have become part of the government. This trend is likely to continue in the foreseeable future as the immigrant population increases, along with the growth of far right anti-immigrant groups, which has been associated with increasing racial attacks and violence.

Hate crimes and racism

In July 1993, the Minister of State for the Home Office reported to a Home Affairs Select Committee on Racial violence that there might be between 130,000 and 140,000 racially motivated attacks reported each year, and that the "true figure" could be as high as 330,000. In 1992 ten people died as a result of what are believed to have been racially motivated murders.

Hate crimes including racial attacks, has been consistently increasing in Britain with the overwhelming number of victims being Black and mainly from Asian origins. Victims of hate crimes and racial violence include men, women and children from all ethnic groups including number of white people. A racist incident, according to the police, is any incident, including any crime, which is perceived by the victim or any other person to be motivated by a hostility or prejudice based on a person's 'race' or perceived 'race'. In a twelve months period between 2011 and 2012, there were 43,748 'racist incidents' recorded by the police in England and Wales. On average, that is about 130 incidents per day. Of these, 35, 816 were recorded as race hate crime and 1,621 as religious hate crimes. A 'Hate crime' is defined in law as any criminal offence committed against a person or property that is motivated by hostility towards someone based on their disability, race, religion, gender-identity or sexual orientation, whether perceived to be so by the victim or any other person.

Racial violence is largely underreported to the police. According to the Crime Survey for England and Wales (formerly the British Crime Survey), there were about 130,000 racially motivated 'hate crimes' per year in the years 2009/10 and 2010/11. The actual figures are likely to be even much greater in reality. Of those people who said they had been a victim of hate crime (not exclusively those hate crimes motivated by 'race') and not reported it to the police, 55 per cent said that the reason was because they deemed the offence too minor, or that they did not have faith in the police to respond adequately. Of those who did report their victimisation to the police, people thought that the police took the matter as seriously as they should in only 45 per cent of cases. The proportion of adults who had been a victim of racially motivated hate crime varied by ethnic group, with white adults the least likely to have been a victim and Asian (or Asian British) adults the most likely, according to the Institute of Race Relations (IRR), based in London. According to the IRR in 2011/12, the number of defendants who were referred by the police to the CPS for a charging decision for racially and religiously aggravated crimes fell by 5 per cent, from the previous year, to 12,772. The number of prosecutions completed during this year fell by 7 per cent to 12,367. The number of convictions for racist or religious hate crime fell from 11,038 to 10,142 and the proportion of 'successful outcomes' was 84.2 per cent (an increase on the previous year).

According to The Institute of Race Relations that monitors deaths with a known or suspected racial element in the UK. "As of March 2013, our research indicates that there have been at least 105 such deaths in the UK since April 1993." Of these, the vast majority (eighty-five) were in England, with five in Wales, twelve in Scotland and three in Northern Ireland. Within England, twenty-eight murders took place in London. This number has increased to a total of well over 120 in 2014, including deaths of black people in police custody and in prisons.

Poverty, inequality and unemployment

Race and racism has occupied the British economic political, social and cultural discussions at local and national levels for well over fifty years through regular newspaper headlines in the media on all major issues affecting our everyday lives. Although immigration has been one of the most controversial issue, other key issues that received national headlines involving black people, include policing; riots and rebellions, gang crimes and culture; street crimes; rapes; murder; grooming and having sex with underage girls; and racial attacks. Generations of black people have lived through institutional and individual stereotyping, prejudice and discrimination resulting in poverty, inequality, unemployment, under-achievement and lack of equal access to resources. A relatively small middle and upper class section of the black community has made considerable progress despite racism and have achieved high positions in almost all professional areas in Britain from politics, law, businesses, doctors, teachers and entertainers to sports, science, media, new technology and in many other important areas that affects our daily lives. Race relations, racial tolerance and justice in Britain has improved considerably, despite the fact that the majority of black people are either within or just outside the category of the underclass, and lagging behind in wealth, influence, power and control.

Across the UK and especially in England where 15 per cent of the population are from non-white groups the level of poverty is over twice the level of the white population. According to a TUC Report "Ten Years After" produced in 2008 and covered a period from 1997 – 2007, which spans ten years of a Labour government in power and seen as the golden years of economic growth, with rising living standards, employment opportunities and educational achievements, the position of the vast majority of black people were a long way behind the average white population. Black people earned less than 60 per cent of the median household income of white British people. Between 2005 – 2011, 27 per cent of white children were living in poverty. Compared to 50 per cent Asian or Asian British children and 51 per cent of Black or Black British children. In 1996/7 white poverty rate was 24 per cent whilst the black poverty rate stood at 51 per cent. Nearly ten years later in 2005/6 the figures were 20 per cent and 40 per cent respectively. In unemployment rates for white workers stood at 6.7 per cent and fell to 4.4 per cent in 2001, but increased to 4.6 in 2007, but for black workers it was 14.2 per cent in 1997, 11.9 per cent in 2001 and 11.5 per cent in 2007. For black people the living conditions and standard of living during the Thatcher years and right up to the Labour victory in 1997 were up to twice and for some groups within the black community up to three times worse than the white community.

In 2010, nearly three-quarters of 7-year-old Pakistani and Bangladeshi children and just over half of those black children of the same age were living in poverty. About one in four white 7-year-olds were classed as living in poverty. In 2009, the Wealth and Assets Survey revealed that the 'average white household' had roughly £221,000 in assets, black Caribbean households had about £76,000, Bangladeshi households £21,000 and black African households £15,000. Black groups are also more likely to experience homelessness, poor health and poor education. They are on average likely to between seven and ten years younger, where I live in Luton and the black population represents some 40 per cent of the population.

In June 2012, 7.3 per cent of white people, 15.5 per cent of Black (African or Caribbean) people and 17.3 per cent of people with mixed ethnicity, of working age (16-64), were unemployed. In October 2012, 23 per cent of black males aged 16-24 were unemployed; 13 per cent of white males in the same age group were unemployed. In parts of London and the South East where the majority of black people live, up to 50 per cent of young black people are unemployed, even though they have achieved high levels of education and training. In 2011, about one in four black Caribbean and Bangladeshi households did not have a family member in employment. This figure was slightly less for black African and Pakistani households. Of white British households, roughly 15 per cent did not have a family member in employment. The overall unemployment rate for all economically active people aged 16 and over in 2014 was just over 7 per cent, with variation between different ethnic groups. The White ethnic group had the lowest unemployment rate of around 7 per cent and the highest unemployment rate of 17 per cent was found in the Pakistani and Bangladeshi groups. In March, 2014 there were over 31.5 million people economically active in the UK and around 2.5 million registered unemployed. According to government figures around 1 million young people between 16 and 24 years were unemployed and there were less than 600,000 vacancies in the UK. Many workers in employment are unable to earn enough to live on and are only surviving on benefits, debts and assistance from family and friends. There are well over 5 million working poor are amongst the nearly 30 million people in employment in Britain in February 2014, and nearly 4 million children are living in poverty. Black people are grossly over-represented in poverty amongst the working poor and the unemployed.

Struggles within the Labour Party for race equality

For me, my struggle within the Party started just after arriving in Britain in July 1961. I joined the Party as well as the trade union as soon as I started work. I felt at the time, that if I wanted to change the conditions of working people in Guyana, I had to become involved in the trade union and political movement in Britain. The Conservative Party that had ruled Britain between 1951 and 1964 introduced the 1962 Immigration Act in order to placate the British Public and the right wing media that were preoccupied with non-white immigrants to Britain. This anti-immigrant culture in Britain has been kept alive by the media, politicians and trade unions at varying levels of throughout the 20th Century and to the present day. Black workers in Britain have a long history of association with the trade unions and the Labour Party despite that fact that both organisations have openly criticised the influx of black immigrants and have seen them as threats to white British workers and the economy. Black people in Britain have also a long record in building self-organisation and joining unions for protection against racial discrimination.

During the post-war boom of the 1950's and 1960's many British workers did not want to do the kind of manual jobs which they regarded as being unsociable, unhealthy, dirty, low paid or low status; in fact the Conservative government had encouraged immigrants from the Caribbean and Asia to come to England to occupy these least desirable jobs within England both in the private and public sectors. The Labour Party did not repealed the 1962 Immigration Act when it got back into power, between 1964 and 1970, but instead supported further measures to restrict immigration from the Commonwealth. Labour was elected in 1964 and 1966. I was one of those young people who got completely intoxicated, celebrating the election victories, on both occasions.

The 1960's and 1970's were very difficult years for black people in Britain. Racism was rife and it was not unusual to see notices, jobs or vacancies saying that "no Blacks need apply". Similarly, houses for rent or rooms to let "no blacks, Irish should apply". The race riots in Notting Hill in 1959, and other racial disturbances in Nottingham, Liverpool, Cardiff and elsewhere, gave the media and the many racist right wing, and extremist political groups to call for an end to immigration and repatriation of those already here. Black people were blamed for all the things that were wrong in Britain. They were blamed for causing unemployment; being a drain on the National Health Service; being lazy; taking jobs away from white workers; labelled as criminals; being a burden on the welfare state; responsible for poor housing and shortage of accommodation; corrupting white women and have no loyalty to Britain. There were stereotypes of black people in every area of activity, institution and life in Britain. As a result racial discrimination, harassment, bullying and attacks were common especially in inner city and deprived areas where white workers saw immigrants as competitors for jobs, services and resources.

In 1964 the Labour secured a majority of four seats and in 1966, a total of ninety eight seats in the House of Commons. The Labour government introduced the 1965 and 1968 Race Relations Acts and eight years later, the 1976 Race Relations Act, which did reduce the level of discrimination in employment and services. It also addressed direct, indirect discrimination, and victimisation on racial grounds, and less favourable treatment. But as we all know, it is difficult to legislate about people's racial prejudice and abuse of power.

The disagreements between the Labour government and the trade union grew, whilst the economy was in recession, between 1966 and 1970. Industrial action and strikes were common, resulting in severe problems for the economy. I withdrew from the Labour Party for a short period because I felt the Party was not prepared to challenge the capitalist system. The acrimonious disagreements between the Party and the unions, together with economic problems paved the way for the return of the Conservative government. Harold Wilson, the Labour Prime Minister stated in 1966, in a speech to New York Bankers "We have taken steps which have not been taken by any other democratic government in the world. We are taking steps with regard to prices and wages which no other government, even in wartime has taken". He wanted to change Britain and the restrictive practices of the unions. He reminded the unions by claiming that "He who rejects changes is the architect of decay, the only human institution which rejects progress is the cemetery."

The reason for leaving the Labour Party for a short period was partly because of the Vietnam War, the fight with the unions and the economic recession, I felt our Prime Minister could and should have done a great deal more to challenge the capitalist system, work closer with the unions and speak out against the war in Vietnam from escalating, which involved the death of at least a million Vietnamese. The Vietnam War was a dirty war, and the Americans used every device including napalm and chemical bombs indiscriminately in villages and other areas of North and South Vietnam. The mightiest and most equipped army on earth had supported the South Vietnamese politicians against the North Vietnamese, led by communist, Ho Chi Min. I was involved in the 1968 demonstration which turned into a mini riot outside the American Embassy. I was so angry about the Vietnam war, after attending a large meeting at the Royal Festival Hall in London that was addressed by a woman Minister from the Vietnam government, that I wrote to the North Vietnamese Embassy in London to volunteer my services to support their war against the Americans. I received a courteous letter thanking me for my offer of support, and encouraged me to continue to campaign against the war. I. also wrote a similar letter to the Cuban government a couple of years earlier to support them in their struggles against American aggression against their country. The response from the Cuban Embassy was almost identical to the one from the Vietnamese Ambassador.

I renewed my involvement with Labour and worked intensely after Labour had lost power in 1970 by thirty seats in Parliament. The Tories returned with an agenda designed to reduce the powers of the trade unions and in my role as an active trade unionist, I felt that despite my previous disappointment with the Labour Party, all trade unionists should rally around the Labour Party during its period in opposition to protect the gains working people had made during previous Labour governments.

Difficult years for Labour and race relations

Between 1970 and 1974, the Conservative government lead by Edward Heath, gave Margaret Thatcher a prominent role within his government as Secretary of State for Education. I was Secretary of the Trades Union Council in Luton in 1971 and took part against the cuts in public services and the anti-union legislation. Labour regained power in February 1974, but failed to secure an overall majority by thirty three seats. Another election in October 1974 gave them an overall majority of only three votes. Despite trade union legislation introduced by the previous Conservative government, strikes continued at a very high level, both in the private and public sectors. Inflation and prices were extremely high and unions fought to retain their living standards by seeking pay increased above inflation. Between 1974 and 1979 I attended courses at Ruskin College, Oxford, and courses at three different universities as a full-time student, but remained active in the Labour Party and unions. I was disappointed when Harold Wilson resigned as Prime Minister in 1976 and was succeeded by James Callaghan, who lost to Mrs Thatcher, the then Leader of the Conservative Party after defeating Edward Heath in the leadership Contest in 1975.

Labour implemented a wide range of Employment and Equality Acts between 1974 and 1976, including various Employment and Health and Safety provisions, the Sex Discrimination Act 1975 and the Race Relations Act 1976. Labour, led by Jim Callaghan, found itself in deep disagreement with the trade union movement once again during 1975 and 1979. There were numerous strikes, especially in the public sector. The refuse collectors, nurses, teachers, and even the grave diggers were on strike. Britain was characterised by the international media as a country torn apart by industrial dispute with refuse piling up in the streets and bodies having to wait a long time before they were buried. Had Jim Callaghan called an election in 1978, the chances of winning another term for Labour would have been greater, but instead, he decided to continue in power whilst the economic situation worsened. Mrs Thatcher won the support of millions of people in the

1979 general election, because of her policy on immigration, claiming that Britain was being *"swamped by people from an alien culture"* and that she would ensure the sale of council housing to tenants of local authority housing. This was a golden opportunity for people who were living in council accommodation and had been paying rent with no opportunity to ever owning a single brick within that property. So Mrs Thatcher, who promised them an opportunity to purchase their homes at knock down prices, would enable them to accumulate wealth, through rising property prices and also have the choice of leaving their homes to their children and grandchildren.

Mrs Thatcher – The Iron Lady

Mrs Margaret Thatcher won the general election in 1979 and became the first woman Prime Minister in Britain. Mrs Thatcher rule between 1979 and 1990 was characterised by strong ideological commitment, strong leadership, commitment to market forces, reduction in public expenditure, reform of trade unions, sale of council owned properties, privatisation of public assets, deregulation of controls over large businesses and securing victory over Argentina over the war to retain the Falkland Island as British territory. Mrs Thatcher also challenged the powers of the European Economic Community and secured substantial gains for Britain. She was also a significant player with Ronald Reagan, the President of America in pushing back the Soviet Union and helping to re-unite the divided German nation. Mrs Thatcher was a significant world leader who brought back a lot of pride and respect for the British state and people.

The Iron Lady led from the front and once stated that *"I am extraordinarily patient provided I get my own way in the end."* She also stated that *"If you set out to be liked, you will accomplish nothing."* In fact Mrs Thatcher was probably liked and disliked by the British people in almost similar proportions. She was dynamic, populist, energetic, anti-trade union and a campaigning radical Conservative. Mrs Thatcher was at first popular with women and working class people who were grateful to her

unions were closely linked since it was founded in 1900. As a result around twenty five black members were approved by Labour Party to be included on the list for possible Parliamentary candidates between 1980 and 1982. We organised meetings within the Labour Party, mainly in London and called ourselves the Labour Party Black Socialist Society, which we thought would fit into the Party with the various other Societies that were already part of its national structure.

The humiliating defeat of Labour in 1979 was a serious blow for workers, but particularly Black and minority ethnic who were employed in the manufacturing and certain public sectors such as transport, the NHS and local government, where there were disproportionate redundancies. Pay and conditions for these workers were disproportionately reduced due to reductions in pay and cuts in job opportunities. It was at this state when I decided that I should stand for Parliament and I began to seriously organise with other like-minded trade union and Party activists to set up self-organised Black sections within the Party to increase the representation of Black people as councillors and members of Parliament. I worked closely with Bernie Grant, Keith Vaz, Marc Wadsworth and many others to establish key contacts in seats where there were sizeable numbers of Black voters and a number of us were put on the list as Prospective Parliamentary Candidates (PPC). I attended several PPC selection meetings as lost a few by a small number of votes.

Mrs Thatcher's historic and significant leadership ended when senior male members within her own party organised against her, despite the fact that she had won three consecutive elections for the Conservatives; defeated the National Union of Mineworkers and almost destroyed the coal mining industry in Britain; shut out the TUC from their involvement with national government and almost reduce the trade union membership from fourteen to less than seven million; deregulated most of the commanding heights of the economy and privatised almost all of the public services apart from the NHS and the Post Office. She opened up Britain for businesses from home and abroad and together with Ronald Regan as President of America helped to bring about the dissolution of the Soviet

Union. Her achievements were numerous, but there were also many problems at home, with relatively high and persistent unemployment; racial tensions resulting in riots in parts of England; industrial disputes; rising poverty in an atmosphere of greed, selfishness, materialism, individualism and lack of compassion for the less well off. Thatcher's Britain became more right wing, unequal and less as a "one nation democracy". Black people suffered most under Thatcherism with various attacks on immigrants and immigration to mass unemployment and cuts in living standards, and feeling insecure with the rise of racist political groups. She even introduced legislation in 1983, for the first time, children born in Britain to non-British parents were denied automatic citizenship, fostering further racism and discrimination in immigration policy. Mrs Thatcher once said "there is no such thing as society", and set out to prove it by promoting individual greed and competition for everything. Privatisation was the single most massive attack on democracy we have seen until the coalition government between 2010 and 2014 took her policies even further. It destroyed the public's power to determine via parliament the public services and actual cost of such services. The relative wealth of the UK one per cent had been falling steadily for fifty years when Thatcher took power in 1979; since then it has climbed steeply and is almost back to 1918 levels. Britain is one of the most unequal societies in the developed world.

I spent almost every weekend during the Thatcher years attending demonstrations against Thatcherite cuts and austerity, as well as her sustained attacks on trade union shouting - "Maggie! Maggie! Maggie! Out! Out! Out!" When she walked into Downing Street in 1979, promising "harmony instead of discord," only one in seven children were living in poverty and Britain was more equal than at any time in modern history. But within five years, a third of children were poor, a sign of the yawning inequality from which the country never recovered. Thatcher came to personify those ready to push anyone aside to gain power in a man's world and strengthen that world with their ruthless and selfish ambition. Thatcher hated any measure of socialism or left wing radicalism. She opposed sanctions on the racist apartheid regime in South Africa and embraced the right wing almost fascist dictator, General Pinochet, who had violently overthrown the Marxist orientated Allende government in Chile. For Thatcher her time was running out and her own members in Parliament turned against her, after the nationwide uprising against the famous poll tax, which replaced the council rates with the Community Charge (popularly known as the poll tax) was a single flat-rate per-capita tax on every adult, introduced in Scotland in 1989 and England and Wales in 1990. Critics said the shift from a tax based on the value of a house to a tax based on the number of people living in it. This discriminated against the less well-off and especially the poor, who were already suffering severely from her policies. Large numbers of people refused to pay and the tax triggered violent riots, notably the pitched battle between police and rioters in Trafalgar Square on Saturday, 31 March, 1990. I was there and saw the ferocious and frightening charges by the riot police with batons against the demonstrators. Some left wing and anarchists groups confronted the police and were met with much violence. At the end of the day parts of London looked like a battlefield. The hated tax was abolished in 1993. I was not surprised when in November 1990 members of her Cabinet felt, enough was enough and called on her to resign after eleven years as Prime Minister. She had survived the death threats and the bombing of the Grand Hotel in Brighton where she was staying during her party conference, by the Irish Republican Army (IRA) that she so callously attacked, and refused to compromise with the IRA hunger strikers, who starved themselves to death in prison, bur she succumb to defeat at the very hands of the men she appointed into top positions. I once met Mrs Thatcher, it was at the Conservative Party Conference in 1989, when I worked as a senior national adviser for the Local Government Management Board and we were showcasing our work in the exhibition section outside the actual conference hall. She stopped at our exhibition stand and asked me what I was doing and whether I was "a small businessman." She wore a blue suit and was dressed exactly like another woman who walked through the exhibition about twenty minutes earlier, looking exactly like Mrs Thatcher. We were later told that it was a deliberate security exercise, to have a decoy on such occasions. Baroness Thatcher died on 8th April, 2013, age 87. There was lots of bitterness expressed as well as respect for her after her death, as there were during her time as Prime Minister.

I believe that Baroness Thatcher's greatest legacy was forcing the Labour Party further and further to the right of British politics, which ended up with New Labour, led by Tony Blair and his commitment to embrace Thatcherism. Tony Blair, Gordon Brown and their band of opportunists and careerists supporters in Parliament, having won a landslide victory in 1997 understand the significance of Thatcherism and decided during the thirteen years of New Labour rule (1997-2010) not to reverse it, but instead to carry it forward. Their reckless private finance of public investment and services went beyond anything she dared dream of. Baroness Thatcher saw Blair as her legacy and even acknowledged this in public. She was Blair's first guest at Downing Street in 1997 after Blain moved in.

Parliamentary candidate

After a great deal of lobbying members and the trade union branches affiliated to the Labour Party I managed to be selected as the Labour Party PPC for Milton Keynes, which was a new Parliamentary constituency from the previously named Buckingham constituency. We knew from the start that it was not a winnable for us. The Party was losing a lot of support to the break-away Social Democratic Party (SDP), led by ex-Labour Cabinet Ministers from a previous Labour government. The Labour Party was seriously divided between right and left factions and had a manifesto that was described as "The longest suicide note in history". The SDP had targeted Milton Keynes as a possible winnable seat and Labour was hoping that a 3-way split would benefit us. Milton Keynes was a growing city and it was allocated its own seat as part of the re-organisation of Parliamentary boundaries, except that the boundary included many rural villages for miles around the city centre. Had the boundary been limited to the new City areas and Bletchley, it would have probably been a winnable Labour seat. The seat was held at one time, by a well-known newspaper tycoon, by the name of

Robert Maxwell, a Labour Party member, but later occupied by a member of the Conservative Party, Bill Bunyan, who was the sitting Member of Parliament. The 1983 general election was a disaster for the Labour Party. The Party had suffered a great deal from internal divisions since its defeat by Margaret Thatcher in 1979, which led to Baroness Shirley Williams, Lord David Owen and others, leaving to form the SDP. Both the SDP and the Conservatives managed to seriously erode the traditional Labour vote. The right wing mainly conservative media supported the break-away SDP, because they were more likely to damage Labour than the Conservative Party.

My selection was greeted by the media in Bedfordshire and Buckinghamshire with mixed response. I was well known in the counties surrounding Bedfordshire because I was a regular contributor to the BBC Three Counties Radio, Chiltern Radio and the BBC Anglia Television. I was regularly portrayed as a "controversial race and community leader", an "angry and aggressive trade unionist," or a "Black power supporter." I was also labelled as the "Tony Benn, Ken Livingstone, Arthur Scargill, or Ted Knight of Bedfordshire. These men were almost household named that received regular negative reporting by the mainstream media, and were labelled as extremists and socialists within the Party. Local newspaper reported my nomination as a PPC, as "Bid for first Black MP" and "Jim is Labour choice." I was delighted at being selected for the constituency, but wished I had not attended the selection meeting and focused on a more winnable seat instead, as the Conservative held the seat with a 14,000 plus majority. It was an area with a very tiny number of Black voters. Having been selected for a seat, my name was removed from the list of possible candidates. I tried to get selected for one of the two local Luton seats, but did not succeed. One of the Party organisers told me "You have as much chance of winning either of these seats, as someone with one leg winning an ass kicking contest." The Milton Keynes comrades put up a good fight, but the number of workers was far too few. It was a large urban and rural constituency that required a lot of attention and hard work to persuade the voters to support us. I passionately fought the campaign as though we had a chance of winning the seat, but I knew that even in safe Labour seats the swing was against us. It was also a contest between Labour, the Conservative and the rising Social Democratic Party. Apart from our Party Manifesto, the swing against Labour, a massive Conservative majority, a divided local Party, as their local candidate was rejected in preference to me, and the fact that I had some negative response due to my politics, reputation and that I was living outside the constituency did not help our cause. However, we still did reasonable well coming third with 13,046 votes, compared to the SDP candidate securing 16,659 votes and the Conservative candidate 28,181. The night of the counting of the votes, was very strange as I found myself being heckled and abused by the nationally known right wing racist Party that stood a candidate who targeted me and was delighted when he saw that the votes were going against us. I was also involved in an altercation with the right wing candidate and his supporters when I made my speech after the result was declared. I responded to the heckling and name calling with a few choice words, which on hindsight was somewhat inappropriate at the time. I should have been more graceful in defeat. It was such an unusual night that when my wife and I returned home some twenty five miles from the count, we discovered that neither of us remembered to bring our son, Mike, who had been helping us throughout the day, back home with us. He was nineteen years old at the time, so he managed to stay with one of our Party worker until the next day.

In the general election in June 1983, there were eighteen black candidates including six from Labour. No black candidates were elected to Parliament, even though there were black members representing the Labour Party and the Communist Party a few decades ago. The election of Michael Foot as the leader of the Labour Party also turned out to be a disaster; even though he was a great orator and a socialist with a strong commitment towards addressing the needs and concerns of working class people and their families. Michael Foot was unable, even with a moderate and formidable politician, Dennis Healey by his side, as his deputy, to persuade many trade union members and many working class people to vote Labour. What was significant was that Michael Foot's leadership and the Labour

Party were castigated on a daily basis by the British media. The Labour Party was portrayed as being divided and lacking in direction and under the influence of well-known left wing politicians such as Tony Benn and Ken Livingstone. It was also reported by the media that the Labour Manifesto was "The longest political suicide note in history." The Party had taken a severe hammering in the elections with Margaret Thatcher securing an overall majority of one hundred and forty four seats in Parliament and the Labour support had declined substantially, making it one of the worst Parliamentary election performance for many years. It was a bitter lesson and a severe defeat for Labour and the trade unions. The Party held its Annual Conference in October 1983 in Brighton and it was an opportunity for the labour movement to review its entire strategies, including its leadership, policies and past history. The divisions within the Party and unions widened as the right accused the left for being responsible for the historical defeat and the left accused the right wing of wanting to move even further to the centre-right political position, to win back the lost voters. It was a very sad experience for me and the black activists within the labour movement who had campaigned for a return of a Labour government. For me the only positive outcome was the fact that over 80 per cent of black voters voted for the Labour Party, and the fact that once again race was an issue at the election, one can reasonably assume that black voters trusted Labour overwhelmingly trusted Labour on race issues, Various surveys since 1964 has shown that black people certainly did not support the Conservative Party due to their approach on race. The majority of black voters live in urban and densely populated inner city and deprived constituencies that are more likely to return Labour members of Parliament. So the Black activists knew that if we wanted to elect black MPs, we need to target winnable Labour seats within the urban areas, especially the ones with sizeable black voters.

Labour examines its wounds

Having firmly established the concept of self-organisation at work, Bernie and I decided to work within the Labour Party with others to create Black Sections within the structures of the Labour Party at local and national levels. We had already established such sections within the trade unions, especially within local government and the NHS. Our breakthrough came in 1983 at the Labour Party Conference in Brighton when I addressed Conference on my experience as the Party candidate in Milton Keynes, and after examining the voting patterns and disappointments of Black people since the defeat in June. What struck me most during the campaign and afterwards, was the fact that Black voters who always voted Labour by up to ninety per cent felt that Labour had always took their votes for granted. I appealed to Conference to recognise this problem and to urgently take action to empower Black people within and outside its structures. I called for more Black councillors, members of Parliament and the setting up of Black self-organised groups at all levels of the labour movement. During and after my speech which was televised live on national television there were as much cheering as there were heckling. The cameras followed me back to my seat, where I happened to sit next to Tony Benn and I was later interviewed by all the major national newspapers and television networks, including several foreign stations. Other Black candidates also spoke of their own experience demanded that the Party share power with black people and not to see them as voting fodder. The lobbying we had engaged in over the previous three years within the trade union and Labour Party was beginning to be taken seriously. The party had set up various Working Groups to explore greater involvement of Black people at all levels within the Party, but failed to make changes. There were of course other significant speakers from the Party and unions who spoke against creating greater opportunities for Black people through self-organisation, as they saw such arrangements as similar to apartheid; but supported the principle of greater involvement.

During the week at Party Conference almost all the daily newspapers contained part of my speech and speeches from other black delegates arguing the case for more black representation at all levels of the Party. The Sun newspaper on 4th October had a headline with my photograph stating *"Bring in blacks demand"*

and the Daily Telegraph printed *"Labour examines its wounds"* with a sub-heading *"Your Record stinks"* and included a sizeable part of my speech. The Daily Mirror headline stated *"Sharpen that image"* and a sub-heading *"Black slams record on race".* The Morning Star headline stated *"Shake-up of party machine demanded".* All the reports focussed on large parts of my speech, which also attracted attention from Neil Kinnock, who had replaced Michael Foot after the historic defeat. The Party knew for the first time that they were taking the black votes for granted for far too long and that they were facing serious and concerted challenges from black members who were unlike most of their parents and grandparents were, educated, challenging, organised and ideologically committed to fighting racism within the heart of the British institutions and structures. We have endured racism within the Party and unions as well as from the general public, employers, the police and public bodies with very little, or no support from the labour movement. On many occasions we were blamed for our own social, economic and political problems and disadvantages in Britain.

My speech was well received by the majority of black members and labour movement activists, but not by the leadership of the Party, many right wing trade unions leaders and most members of Parliament who saw us as a threat to their seats, which they thought were there for their entire political career. My speech at the Party Conference and at the fringe meeting organised by the Black Sections – mainly Bernie and emphasized the following key points:

- Black people consistently voted Labour at general and local elections. In fact 86 per cent of those who voted, supported Labour according to the Commission for Racial Equality Report

- Black people wants to ensure that Labour remains the 'natural- home' of the black voter

- We support the struggle for Socialism in multi-racial Britain and that means the recognition by the Labour Party that Black people must be allowed to

- organise in the way they choose within the Party, like the special 'Sections' for Women Young people

- We believe that through Black Sections we will be able to effectively articulate our legitimate demands

- Over 1 million black people voted Labour in 1983

- Black people stood by Labour when the white working class including union members abandoned the Party

- The Party must respond to demands from black people for equality in the Labour movement when it comes to policy-making and representation

- Soon there will be well over 100 marginal Parliamentary seats in England where the ethnic vote could decide the outcome

- Labour is not representative of the black people who supports

- It is not enough for the Labour Party to be committed to building a multi-racial society. We must also become a multi-racial party in the town halls and in Parliament

- There is hardly any Labour Party branches that has a black membership in proportion to the local black electorate

- There would be much fewer councillors and MPs without the black vote

- We still have no black MPs, or council leaders We have failed to build links with the black communities

- There is a possibility of some black voters promoting independent black or Asian candidates at elections, rather than continuing to look to Labour for support. This would divide the black vote and allow the Tories in

- Black self-organisation within the Party is the only way of forcing Labour to tackle its own racism

- Most black voters are disillusion with Labour for taking their support for granted

- Margaret Thatcher deliberately courted the racist vote during the 1979 election campaign with her notorious "swamping" statement and the pledge of bringing black immigration to a standstill

- The Labour Party has promised new, non-racist immigration laws, and the Labour parliamentary opposition has promised to repeal the racist Immigration Acts and have never done so

- Labour must address the serious concerns of black people who have remained an underclass in Britain with massive poverty and disadvantages

- Labour must urgently implement policies on tackling racism and race discrimination in employment, education and training policing, crimes and deprivation in our inner-cities

- The Party must commit itself to ending racism and, particularly, institutional racism

- It is not for white activists to dictate the path for the party to follow on empowerment of black members: instead, the Party must listen to black socialists, inside and outside the Party

- The Party must live up to its own policies and promises and empower black members and voters

- Labour Parties and Labour councillors must regularly canvass the views of black members, appoint them to various bodies as Labour representatives, support them and develop strong links with local organisations and communities

- Give high priority to the selection of a black parliamentary candidates in winnable seats

- Provide space for black people to speak for themselves and do not impose white candidates in areas of large numbers of black voters

- Black Section is not divisive, instead it is a system of uniting black people into a cohesive dynamic and powerful group which I believe will change the political colour content and direction of British politics

- Black people in Britain and Europe many of whom ware descendants from slavery, indenture-ship and colonialism and have been oppressed for a long time are now knocking on the door of the white imperialists, and colonialists inside their defences, and stating clearly that they will not tolerate domination any more

- Black people who have been divided for far too long, are developing a new awareness; a sense of purpose and unity to work together as Africans, Asians, West Indians other non-Europeans, women, men, old and young to access and share power in Britain

- The white power structure should not be afraid of black unity, strength and organisation, or losing their own privileged positions

- The Party should not pander to the black middle class and use them as token candidates to pacify the black communities

- Black members are not accepting the view that the "colour blind" approach is credible

- We are not seeking apartheid or separatism within the labour movement, but positive action based on partnership, unity, equality, respect, trust, fairness, justice, democracy and equal access and rights in all aspects of life

- We will fight racism in the Party wherever and whenever it exists through radical working class and socialist strategies

Bernie and I printed and distributed leaflets at the conference; we invited Diane Abbot who was working for Thames Television Network and Marc Wadsworth, who was a reporter with the Voice Newspaper to cover a fringe meeting we had organised during the evening, in Brighton. We also asked Frances Morrell, a Greater London Councillor to the meeting. The media turned up in large numbers and so did many women members who were also working for more recognition within the Party. There were around sixty Black delegates and visitors who gave specific examples of how the Party organisation had kept them out of the selection of council and Parliamentary candidates. We left Brighton with a great deal of satisfaction as well as challenges, as we had identified may supporters within the Party and the unions as well as many key leaders within the movement who were opposed to the concept of Black self-organisation. Amongst the opposition to our campaign were the Party leader and most of the Shadow Cabinet, as we; as the majority of centre-right union leaders. The media continued to report our presence during the next twelve years as our organisation and support within the leadership of the movement, and Black and white activists ensured that there were lots of motions at both Labour and union conferences every year. The Black Sections we set up established roots across the labour movement, but mainly in London and large cities in Britain from Glasgow, to Cardiff, Manchester, Birmingham, Leicester and Bristol. My own local and regional Labour Party were overwhelmingly opposed to our campaign and I had to tolerate a lot of personal criticisms, condemnation and attempt to remove me from being a councillor. By this time I had persuaded over one hundred members from the local Black community, mainly Asian Muslims who were amongst the most disadvantaged people in Luton. The local Party quickly realised that it could use this membership against me. They did this by using some of the Muslim leaders to inform their members at meetings in the Mosques that I was stirring up racial tensions through my involvement as Chair of the Luton Anti-Racist Committee, and an organiser of many demonstrations against the racist British Nation Party and the National Front. The Party and the Police informed the local community organisations that the best way to oppose the racists was to stay away from their activities and ignore them. These racist and fascist groups were meeting in various council properties, including the Town Hall, libraries and in local schools. In 1985, I was deselected as a county councillor in a ward where the majority of the voters were Muslims. The local Party contrived with a group of Muslim men in the ward to de-select me as a county councillor, by using all sorts of tactics, including using a Black African Muslim woman to impersonate a white female student who were abroad on holiday.

The Party turned against me

The Labour Party and unions turned against me in the most vicious and uncomradely way following the Party Conference in Brighton in 1983. I was seen as dividing the Party and the unions through my work for black self-organisation at local and national levels within the entire labour movement structures. I was in the forefront in the media and at conferences making the case for black self-organisation, whilst helping to organise dozens of black groups within unions and the Party across England and Wales. We had established national Black Members Conferences, structures and created a massive within the constituency Labour Parties, the TUC and within the public sector trade unions. At last the tide was turning in our favour, even though the leadership of the Party, and private sector unions opposed us. More black people joined the Party and the unions through the Black self-organised groups and caucuses that threatened the domination of the white male middle aged, centre-right labour movement bureaucrats. Black and women members were networking and making more demands for representation and leadership. There were more Black and female councillors and Parliamentary candidates and black councillors set up their own national structures with annual conferences, constitutions and support networks across the United Kingdom. We issued our own programmes, policy documents and manifestos. The regional,

A greater number of black people totalling more than 50, men and women from African and Asian backgrounds, are now members of the House of Lords, which is the Upper Chamber within the British Parliament.

The question of Black representation continued to play a significant part in parliament and at Labour Party and trade union conferences with black people making gradual progress. The question of Black representation was settled in the party in 1994, when the party finally accepted a compromise position and agreed to recognise a Black Socialist Society (BSS), which later became the Black and Asian Minority Ethnic group. Until 2010, Black MPs elected at general elections had been Labour. The Conservatives however increased their number of minority MPs from 2 to 11 in 2010; so now the Conservatives have 41 per cent of the minority ethnic MPs. No Liberal Democrat MP has ever been elected at a general election. At present there are 27 non-white MPs (16) Labour and 11 Conservatives selected to the House of Commons which is 4.2 per cent of all 650 MPs. If the non-white population were represented proportionally in the House of Commons, there would be around 117 Black MPs. Given that the overwhelming number of black voters votes Labour, the size of the non-white MPs in Parliament is very disappointing.

I continued to plan an active part in the Party as a councillor and a member of the National Policy Forum. I was involved on a number of Committees advising Ministers after Labour was returned to office in 1997. Sadly, I was one of the left wing casualties of New Labour which started with the election of Neil Kinnock as leader in 1983, long before Tony Blair and his close associates took over the Party machine in 1995. I tried to get back on the Labour list of Prospective Parliamentary Candidates after the 1983 general election defeat. Unfortunately despite many attempts I discovered that the Party was determined to ensure that I did not appear on the list. I took part in interviews and written assignments to be recognised as suitable for the official list, but I met with constant rejections apparently for "not reaching the required standard". I was never allowed any appeal, nor was I even allowed to see the feedback from the interviews or a copy of my written work. I sent my CV to lots of constituencies within the South East of England, mainly London and the Home Counties but although I received quite a bit of support and attended at least fifteen short listing interviews, I was never able to defeat the candidate favoured by the Party bureaucracy. I complained on several occasions to The Chair and General Secretary of the Party about being excluded from the Parliamentary List and for an opportunity to be allowed back on it, but to this day I have been unable to be accepted.

I continued my involvement with the Black Socialist Society and had several meetings with three General Secretaries of the Labour Party mainly to revive the Labour Party Black Socialist Society (BSS). The following pages outline some of my concerns and suggestions for change. The Party under Blair's leadership had contrived with a number of leading members of the BSS to keep issues and discussions around race and the Labour Party quiet, as it regarded many of us who had been active on race issues within the movement as "dangerous" and a liability in terms of making race and representation a high profile issue within the Party.

1997 and New Labour in power

Like Mrs Thatcher, Tony Blair was elected as Prime Minister with an overall majority and won three consecutive general elections. Blair swept into office for the first time in May 1997 with a 179 overall majority in Parliament followed by another large majority of 167 in 2001 and a majority of 66 in 2005. Like Thatcher his appeal was declining and supporters of Gordon Brown seized every opportunity to replace him with Gordon, who had a yearning ambition to become the Prime Minister. Blair's biggest political mistake, I believe, was taking Britain into a disastrous war in Iraq with the Americans, even though well over one million British people physically took to the streets in opposition of the war. With the war in Iraq and Afghanistan and the uncritical support of Israel in the Middle East, Labour lost substantial support from the black communities, especially the nearly two million Muslim voters in 2005. This was a turning point for Labour as far as the black voters were concerned. By 2010 the black vote in Britain was divided between the main three political parties, with less than 50 per cent voting Labour. In the 2010 elections only 47 per cent of black voters voted Labour with 13 per cent voted Conservatives and 22 per cent voting Liberal Democrats. The 2015 general election will be one of the most crucial events for all three main political parties as black voters in the marginal constituencies could decide who forms the next government. Black voters have become far more sophisticated and politically aware unlike the past when it was only necessary to court the attention of the black leadership within the various communities. The Labour Party is leading the Conservatives in March 2014 by around ten per cent but the outcome in fifteen in fourteen months' time may very well be different, depending on the economic situation, which has so far disproportionately disadvantaged the black communities.

I never liked New Labour or Tony Blair, in fact I saw him as an infiltrator and destroyer of the Party that I had given nearly fifty years of active support to. I also had little respect for Gordon Brown who always either ignored or failed to answer my questions, by responding to the specific points I had raised. Like Blair, he was New Labour through and through. He was desperate for power and used his enormous talents as a speaker and persuader to get his way. In the end he was unable to improve the British economy to any extent beyond what Blair had done.

I was a member of the Labour Party National Policy Forum (NPF) as one of the four representatives elected by black members at a Conference, so even though I was marginalised by the Party I was still able to attend meetings of the NPF between 1995 and 2004. The NPF was carefully designed to be the policy forum for Labour as the New Labour leadership gradually stripped the Party Conference of its sole policy making forum. Even when the Party Conferences disagreed with the leadership, it made no difference. New Labour had the entire package inside and outside Parliament in their control. The Party's head office, regional offices and every aspect of the structure was under the control of New Labour. Most radical members like me had left the Party and those remaining either went through an open conversion by not disagreeing with the tightly controlled NPF, the national executive, or the leadership at conferences. It was easy for New Labour to manipulate the NPF as most of the Cabinet members attended and had a personal say in the shaping of the policies. Most officers of the NPF and a large number of the forum members were eventually elected to Parliament, appointed to the House of Lords, or appointed to high public positions by the New Labour Government. Several NPF and active New Labour supporters were recruited as advisors and consultants to the government. Cronyism in politics became quite common as the public gradually lost faith and trust in the system. The Party political spin doctors, speech makers, press officers and special advisers grew by their hundreds, whilst the Party's democratic structures were pushed aside.

I made another attempt on 5th March 2000 to secure a place on the Parliamentary list for the following general elections, but was once again ignored. The following letter was sent to the Labour Party with several pages of supporting evidence:

Eileen Murfin
Candidate Liaison Unit
The Labour Party
Milbank Tower
Milbank
London SW1P 4GT

Dear Colleague

National Parliamentary Panel

I acknowledge receipt of your letter dated 29 February informing me "that whilst you were technically competent, your communication skills fell far below the required standard".

I am very disappointed with the decision of the interviewing team's conclusion as I believe that my communication skills are my greatest asset having communicated quite well for a number of years on the National

a short period moved on to other duties replaced Faz. There has been no designated contact at Milbank to work with BSS for over two years.

Unfortunately, due to further staff changes at Milbank no action had taken place to move things on at national, regional and local levels. A number of meetings have taken place since 1997, involving up to 8 Black Party activists. Tom Sawyer, Kamlesh, Faz, Dave Gardner and others were present at the last meeting about a year ago. Since then we have not heard from Milbank about the need to assist the BSS to re-establish itself.

I have raised this issue on several occasions directly and indirectly with Party Officers, and at the National Policy Forum meeting in October 1999.

After raising issues relating to BSS at the National Policy Forum in October, and requesting that the BSS should be re-constituted and/ or re-launched, to ensure accountability, democratic participation, transparency, and effective representation by Black members both Margaret McDonough and Margaret Mythem met informally for a couple of minutes with Gloria Mills and myself. It was agreed that a meeting would take place in the near future and the Chair of the Party would be invited to attend.

It has been agreed that this meeting will take place during the next meeting of the National Policy Forum in Eastbourne on 10/12 December 1999.

It is vitally important that we should all work together to ensure that our Black members and supporters are well aware of our policies and strategies. We have made a lot of progress within the Party and the Labour Movement in general in promoting and securing race equality within the Party and the unions. We have increased the number of Black Members of Parliament, Black Ministers and Representatives within institutions, such as the NHS etc. I am proud of the achievements, which we have made in recent years, and I want us to build on this success.

We should not allow the situation of under-representation of Black members to continue.

I would like to suggest the following action as a possible way forward to address the situation:

a. That the Party convene an urgent meeting with colleagues who are still involved as BSS representatives and other active Black members such as Margaret Payne and others to explore the best way forward for Black people to become involved and represent the Party at all levels, and agree a framework to enable the Party to work with, and win support for its policies within the Black community;

b. That the Party should set in motion the process to convene a meeting within the next 4 months to re-launch the BSS within the constitutional framework which currently exists within the Party;

c. That in the meantime Regional and Constituency Parties should seek to discuss issues relating to Black representation and democratic participation with the Party;

d. That CLP's and Regional Parties implement the constitutional arrangements already agreed by the Party relating to the BSS;

e. That the Party set in motion arrangements to fill the NEC seat reserved for BSS before the next Party Conference;

f. That CLP's and Regional Parties are informed of the involvement of Gloria and myself on the National Policy Forum and that we are prepared to attend meetings to inform CLP's and Regional Parties of our work on the National Policy Forum;

g.   That the Party assists us in reporting to our Black members through the CLP's and Regions of our work on the Forum.

Any suggestions and ideas would be would be much appreciated.

Yours fraternally

Jim Thakoordin

Member – National Policy Forum

I wrote numerous letters to various people within the Labour Party establishment at national, regional and local levels with hardly any response. The Party had by 2000, destroyed the black structure by targeting individual black careerists and opportunists who were sympathetic to New Labour, and they generated a fair share of interests from the aspiring middle class black communities. Below are samples of letters I wrote to the Party between 1999 and 2004, without receiving any response.

20 February 2000

Margaret Mythen
Head of Policy
The Labour Party
Milbank Tower
Milbank
London SW1P 4GT

Dear Margaret

Downing Street Reception – 22 June 1999

I wrote to you when we were invited as NPF members to meet with the Prime Minister, at Downing Street, on 22 June 1999, regarding a group picture with the Prime Minister and members of the National Policy Forum.

You informed me that we should not take our own cameras, and that a photographer would be present who will take pictures as and when the prime Minister meets members of the audience informally.

I felt that the visit was most interesting and I was delighted to make direct contact with the Prime Minister on 2 occasions during the event and the photographer took pictures on each occasion.

I spoke to Chloe soon after the event and I was told that she had some pictures but she was unable to sort them out before going on leave. I wonder whether the photographs have sorted out, and whether it would be possible to have a copy. I would be happy to pay for the cost of the same.

Thank you very much for your assistance, and I look forward to your response.

Yours sincerely,

Jim Thakoordin
National Policy Forum Member
Enclosed:

20 February 2000

Margaret McDonough
General Secretary
The Labour Party
Milbank Tower
Milbank
London SW1P 4GT

Dear Margaret

Meeting with members of the Black Socialist Society

Following my input at the NPF meeting in November 1999, you met Gloria Mills and myself and agreed to convene a meeting between us at the NPF meeting in Eastbourne during 11/12 December 1999. Unfortunately, due to the various pressures you were under it was not possible for you to meet with us. However, we did have brief chats with Margaret Mythem and the Chair of the Party, which were very useful.

I circulated a copy of the attached document to the Black members who were present at the NPF and to Margaret Mythem and the Chair of the Party. The feedback was very positive.

I know that you are still busy and are always likely to be so. However, I would be grateful if you would give some consideration towards a possible meeting, as I am very keen for us to address the following:

a. To involve as many Black and ethnic minority individuals and communities in all areas of the Party;

b. To demonstrate to Black and ethnic minority members the Party's commitment towards involving them at all levels of the Party structures and organisation;

c. To provide a framework to enable the BSS members on the NPF to report to the CLP's, Regions and Branches deliberations of the Forum in the same way as CLP's representatives on the Forum.

I want to assure you that my efforts to involve Black members and members of the Black and ethnic minority communities in the Party at all levels are honest and supportive. As a founder member of the Black Sections and subsequently BSS I have no desire to go back to the bad old days. We need to focus on the positive achievements within the Party and to work in partnership with all others to promote our Party and to win broad-based support to secure a second term in office.

I look forward to your response.

Yours sincerely,

Jim Thakoordin - National Policy Forum Member

C.c Gloria Mills, BSS.

Margaret Mythem, Labour Headquarters.

A group of BSS members met in June 2000 after the Labour Party bureaucracy refused to re-convene the BSS. They decided to call themselves the Black Action Campaign Committee (BLAC) with the view to persuade the Party to reconstitute the BSS. This action completely failed as the Party set up various low profile Working Groups under Black Members of Parliament and others before it handed over a framework to a number of relatively new and more passive black members who were deemed safe as some of them were interested in becoming members of parliament, or being honoured by the Party for their involvement. The many letters sent to the various General Secretaries of the Party were not even acknowledged, let alone addressed.

Black Action Campaign Committee (BLAC) Summary notes of Inaugural Meeting 3 June 2000

1. Present: Linda Bellos, Marc Wadsworth, Jim Thakoordin, Munira Thobani, Simon Hinds, Shahid Malik, Irma Critchlow, Paul Sharma, Bevin Betton and Saul Mullard

2. **Apologies**: Narendra Makanji,

3. Agreed Linda Bellos to Chair meeting and Jim Thakoordin to take notes.

4. Individual opening remarks and statements

Linda:

- "This meeting is long overdue. We need to recruit more people into the Party especially young people. We need to identify the things we agree with and build networks with people we have to work with nationally and internationally.

- We need to identify practical ways forward to build Black leadership within the Party and the community. BSS is only one of many structures.

- We need to address how we are going to broaden this group

- BSS will need to have an inclusive agenda"

Munira:

- "We cannot all be involved politically because of our position in local government. However, I have been working with a range of groups including women and Black groups on a range of community issues. Have also worked with Black and Asian Councillors Network and would like to work on a new agenda for empowering Black people".

Paul:

- "The Labour Leadership has marginalised Black people who have been active in the movement. The Haringey PPC selection was a good example of tokenism.

- Black Socialist Society should use the Party structure to build Black representation. Black workers within the GMB have used the structure to address Black issues.

- We need a radical agenda for the future. The GMB could write to the Party about BSS

- We need to keep in contact with all key Black people in the movement.

- We need a copy of the BSS Constitution. I will get a copy of the BSS Constitution

- We need to get branches to call an AGM".

Simon:

- "We need more Black people in local government and in Parliament, even though I am not certain about the importance of this process for achieving a Black agenda, as some Black people currently in powerful positions are only promoting them. I am interested to know what we can do to develop a structure to promote Black representation".

Marc:

- "The present situation is much different from the 1980's. There is many Black people present who have been involved in the 70's and 80's who have failed to realise their personal agenda, and have started to fight back. It is true to say that we have made progress since the 1980's. There are also a number of Black people in positions of responsibility who are not the enemy even though they are being supported by the Part machine. We need to bring them aboard the Black agenda.

- Black self-organisation have set the pace for progress within the unions, Party and local government, we must build on this foundation. The ARA achieved some success. It was sad the way it turned out in the end. The articles by Trevor Phillips and Diane Abbott provide us with an opportunity to move things forward now. Despite Trevor's motives we should work with him and others ensure that we take the initiative in providing Black leadership within the movement.

- We should also involve Shahid Malik who is a NEC member in the work of BSS. BSS should remain as the Black Socialist Society and should not revert back to Black and Asian Society as this is totally divisive.

- We need a strategic approach to take us forward. We need to work and build support within the unions; the Party and the community. We need a democratic, inclusive framework to promote the Black agenda and not to end up supporting individuals who are only interested in opportunities for themselves.

- We need to convene an AGM of the BSS, and we need to set-up a BSS Steering Committee to prepare for the AGM. The EC members of BSS and the National Policy Forum members should convene a meeting to make arrangements for the AGM.

- This group meeting today could call itself BLAC and act as a broad representative group involving Party members and Black activists outside the Party to advance the Black agenda within the movement".

Bevin:

- "Jim and I have worked to promote the Black agenda within UNISON for years. We have promoted self-organisation only to see a lot of Black people promoting themselves and ignoring the problems within the union. We need to establish a democratic structure to make sure the unions is working for black people. We need a proper structure to deal with racism within the movement. I have made contact with Shahid Malik and would be happy to keep him on board with us".

Jim:

- "We need to reflect on our past to enable us to map out the future. In the 1970's Bernie Grant, Bill Morris and myself were the only Black Trade Union Officials. We recognised the racism within the movement and we made many efforts to represent and support workers across the union movement. We were instrumental in the setting-up of the Black Trade Unionist Solidarity Movement, which gave rise to the concept of self-organisation. Bernie and I printed leaflets and convened a meeting of BUTSM at the Labour

Party Conference in Brighton in 1983. A GLC Councillor, Frances Morrell addressed the meeting and Marc Wadsworth and Dianne as media employees gave us a very good write-up. We then went ahead to form the Black Sections. Marc, Diane and others joined us and we managed to organise within a short space of time to establish Black representation and a universal concept throughout the movement. We had many people within the NEC, Party and Union hierarchy against us but we still succeeded. We were instrumental in securing the election of the original 4 Black MPs. Since then we have more Black representation in Parliament, institutions and elsewhere.

- We need an open, democratic and cohesive framework within the labour movement to promote the Black agenda. Many of us who have been involved for years have lost out on opportunities within the movement or in career progression, but we are still here fighting.

- We have made a lot of progress and we need to organise strategically to continue the progress we have made in promoting effective Black self-organisation and representation within the movement. We should contribute to the changes within the 21st Party consultation process.

- I apologise for not contacting Kingsley because I thought others would have done so

- We need to convene a meeting of the BSS involving Gloria and the Party machine to democratise the BSS and to enable it to function effectively within the Party, the movement and the community

- We will need to be mindful of the timescale as the Party's Constitution could change at the next Conference and we could find that BSS Constitution will become invalid".

- Erma Critchlow and Jim Thakoordin to continue to represent the BSS on the NPF

Temporary officers:

- Linda and Paul to act as Co-ordinators

- Marc and Munira to act as joint Secretary

Next meeting on 18 June at GMB Office, 59 Phoenix Road, and NW1.

Having won the 1997 general election by one of the largest overall majorities for nearly fifty years, Tony Blair and New Labour were very popular with all voters. I was a member of the NPF and I served on the Equality and Education Working Groups. I was invited to join an Advisory Group that worked with the Rt. Honourable David Blunkett who became the first New Labour Secretary of State for Education and Employment. I served as an Advisor for two years. I also had significant inputs on New Labour's Equality strategies that became legislation between 1997 and 2003. I cannot fault New Labour on its commitment to promoting equal opportunities for all disadvantaged groups. The populist success of New Labour continued and in the 2001 general election Labour once gain ended up with a commanding majority of 167 seats compared to 179 in 1997. New Labour felt that the black vote was not an issue as non-white voters would still prefer Labour than the Tories who always laboured the negative side of non-white immigration. Having adopted much of the Conservative policies since 1997, New Labour started to experience serious resentment from large sections of the voters following Blair's commitment to the war in Iraq in 2003. This was a significant turning point for black voters as many of them voted Liberal Democrats and Conservatives instead of Labour being their natural choice. Since the abrupt departure of Mrs Thatcher in 1990, due to divisions within her own Party in Parliament, the Conservative Party went through a depressing period of internal divisions and problems with the economy. Despite this, John Major who succeeded Mrs Thatcher in 1990 won the 1992 election and was replaced by Blair in 1997. Between 1997 and 2005 the Conservative Party had four different leaders, which gave New Labour a considerable advantage between 1997 and 2005. Blair won the 2005 general election by 66 seats in parliament, but was replaced in 2007 by Gordon Brown, who took no interest in reviving the demands for black representation within the Party. By the general election in 2010 the black vote was more divided amongst the three main Parties with Labour securing less than half of the support from Black voters.

In 2004 I was losing a lot of trust and respect for the Labour Party, not only with the policies at home but also with its Middle East and foreign policy in general. I was finally removed from the NPF in 2005. There were no letter or telephone call; I was never invited to any more meetings. I made another attempt to seriously get involved in local politics and gave up any ambition towards Parliament. Again I was blocked by the County Labour Party as demonstrated by the following letter:

2 September 2004

Alan Ollve
Regional Director
Eastern Region Labour Party
97 For Street
Ipswich IP4 1JZ

Dear Alan

County Council Elections 2005

Thank you very much for your letter dated 24 August in respect of the above.

I am interested in being a County Councillor. At the present time I am serving as a Parish Councillor on the list of the Residents Association as the Labour Party does not field candidates for the Parish seats. In fact no Political Party is represented on the Parish.

I have been a County and Borough Councillor for most of the period between 1981 and 1998. I was also Labour's Parliamentary Candidate in Milton Keynes in 1983.

As I have explained to you in previous letter which you choose to ignore my local Labour Party branch has been defunct for more than 5 years and the CLP is doing very little to revive it.

I have made a specific complaint to you about racism and incompetence within the Luton South CLP and again you have decided to ignore my complaints.

I attach copies of previous letters for your attention. I would be grateful if you would respond to my letters.

Yours sincerely,

Jim Thakoordin.

I continued to write letters and make formal complaints directly to the Party's senior staff at Headquarters including the General Secretary, the Chair and several members of the National Executive Committee. The top movers and shakers in the Party ignored me completely, even though I was still a member of the NPF. It was clear to me that no one wanted to address the issues I was raising, or return to the public debates on "Black representation within the Party." Tony Blair and the senior members and staff within the Party saw the issue of black representation as a vote loser, and seen as being problematic within and outside the Party. For them, the best approach was simply too marginalised and ignored the radical black activists like myself, whilst targeting black members who were passive, and prepared to collude with the leadership on race. The tactic was to identify black people they could control and encouraged them into positions within the Party. These black people willingly helped the leadership to stifle discussions on race and were rewarded with positions as councillors, parliamentary candidates and members of public bodies. By 2003, most of the radical black activists who had been actively in the black struggle had either left the Party or joined other black groups, such as The Anti-Racist Alliance.

According to Mao Tse Tung, Chairman of the first Community Party in China, after the 1949 revolution, *"Politics is war without bloodshed, while war is politics with bloodshed."* Tony Blair was a master of both types of politics. I had several encounters with Tony Blair, Gordon Brown, John Prescott, David Blunkett, Jack Straw and other Labour Cabinet Ministers during the reign of New Labour. I remember when Tony Blair decided to support the war in Iraq and he came to Milbank Tower Labour's Headquarters, to address members of the NPF and other senior Labour activists after a much advertised Press Conference. Tony asked us not to show any dissent whilst the press conference was going on, and that he would give us plenty of time to question him on his support for the war. Tony did his press release and we all kept quiet. He was well aware of the Party's opposition to the war and his support for George Bush, one of the most right wing conservative President of the USA for decades. Tony Blair reminded me of the politician who would lay down the lives of many innocent people for what he would describe, as his country. We would all like to vote for the best people in politics, but such people seldom wish to take such lead.

So the media disappeared and Tony took his jumper off, rolled up his shirt sleeves, and stood at the rostrum in his blue jeans and said, "alright, it now your turn to raise questions". He said "I know there will be questions, Jim is here sitting in the front and raring to have a go". At first I thought, I better get in quick before the many others, as there were well over one hundred and fifty people in the hall. So I was the first to raise my hand and Tony pointed to me. I ask him a long question about his decision and I criticised him for agreeing to go to war without the support of the British people. He gave the standard response he had given to the media earlier. The funny thing was that there were hardly any unfriendly questions from the audience who were mainly anti-war, but in the presence of Blair they were not prepared to challenge him. Only a handful of questions were asked and Blair smiled, waved and thanked the audience before he left. We were then treated to a lavish buffet sponsored by a multi-national business, lots of palatable wines supplied by another business supporter of New Labour. During this lunch I did not hear a single person supporting the war. I certainly support the view that politicians like napkins should be changed on a regular basis and for the same reason.

I was one of those people, perhaps the only one who never stood up at Party annual conferences, or any other event when Blair made speeches. On one occasion in Manchester I did not stand up for the eleven minutes standing ovation after Blair's Conference speech. The people on both sides of me and a couple from behind tried to physically pull me up and held me in a standing position whilst shouting abuse at me, even though I explained to them that I only recently had a serious heart operation. The security people later came round and questioned my credentials and my conduct.

On another occasion, at a NPF in Scarborough I was approached by Jack Straw and John Prescott at a small table I was sitting alone having my sandwiches. They asked me about my concerns over the war in Iraq and I told them that "I had a petition against the war with me, but had not collected any signatures so far". They said it the subject will come up later and they were aware that "I would try to co-ordinate support against the war". I was told that the unions were not going to make much fuss about the war and I should "do the same". I was also told in a roundabout way that I was a long standing member of the Party and that the Party had plans for people like me as a reward for loyalty, but I had to change my views on constantly challenging the Party leadership. Examples were given to me of loyal members who had ended their political career in the House of Lords. Of course I continued to criticise the war and the leadership over their economic and political policies that were making the rich richer and the poor poorer, as well as taking the Party away from its traditional roots.

I had another couple of encounters with Tony Blair at 10 Downing Street, the home of the British Prime Minister. I was invited to receptions at number ten on four occasions in various capacities such as being a member of the NPF and an activist. On each occasion I was closely followed by the Party apparatchik who ensured that I was not in any photograph taken at these receptions with Tony. We were told not to take our own cameras, so it was entirely at the discretion of the Party bureaucrats to censure any photos with people like myself who despised him for his politics. Tony ruled the Party like an American President. He changed the Party over the years to ensure control from the top and ignore any policies democratically agreed at the Party conference each year. I wrote to the Party about the photographs and was told "they all got lost".

The most difficult time for me within the Labour Party was the start of recession in 2008, with Gordon having supported the Thatcherite policies of deregulation and applying "a light touch" approach towards controlling the commanding heights of the economy that was dominated by the banking, finance and investment industries, discovered that Britain was heading towards its worst recession since the 1930's. It was clear before 2008 that the British economy was declining and the government was increasingly forced to take drastic measures to reduce the enormous borrowing to balance the economy. Labour had created many changes in equal rights and opportunities, employment law, social security and in public services, but despite all the good things, the poor were poorer and the rich richer since Labour took control in 1997. By 2009, the recession was having a substantial negative impact on working class people. Millions of low paid workers and their families were struggling with declining living standards, rising prices, increases in unemployment and cuts in services. Millions of working class people felt betrayed and abandoned by Labour. On top of this the scandal of MPs fiddling their expenses claims, and using all sorts of financial manipulations to cheat the public of large sums of money, through buying and furnishing second and even third homes; claiming for all sorts of household goods and repairs and even a Labour Home Secretary claiming for the cost of pornographic videos. Most voters lost trust and confidence in the politicians and the political system by 2009.

Resigning from the Labour Party

In May 2009, I decided to resign from the Party. Printed below is a copy of my letter of resignation.

11 May 2009

Rt. Hon. Gordon Brown MP
Prime Minister
House of Commons
Westminster
LONDON SW1 1AA

Dear Prime Minister

RESIGNATION FROM THE LABOUR PARTY

I have been an active member of the Labour Party for over 46 years and have been in the forefront of Black, Community, Trades Union and Political struggles to ensure equality and justice for Black, Asian and working class people in Britain and the world. I have been a County, Borough and Parish Councillor for many years. I have also served on the Labour Party National Policy Forum, various national Advisory Committees and a Trustee on a number of public bodies as a Labour representative. I was also a Labour Parliamentary candidate in Milton Keynes in 1983.

In recent years I have become increasingly disappointed with New Labour because they have:

- enabled the bankers, public utilities and international capitalists to damage our economy, democracy and reduce our living standards

- allowed members of Parliament to develop a culture of greed, duplicity and unaccountability

- grossly reduced our civil liberties and moving us towards a Police State

- alienated working class people and have given indirect support to the BNP

- supported the rich, powerful, greedy and uncaring as opposed to many working and middle class families

- enabled the rich to become relatively richer and the poor poorer

- created a rip off culture in Britain supported by individualism selfishness

- failed to support an adequate house building programme and turned communities against each other

- destroyed the Labour movement organisation

- become besotted with celebrities and personalities

- undermined democracy and increase the lack of trust and respect for politics and politicians

- damaged race relations by restricting black immigration and encouraging white European immigration on a massive scale to keep down wages

- encouraged 24 - 7drinking, pornography and gambling

- enabled more black on black violence because of increasing alienation amongst black youths

- enabled businesses through the media to sexualise more young people under and above teenage years

- attacked the living standards of pensioners

- failed to ensure accountability for the massive increases in public funds allocated to public bodies

I am convinced that New Labour has been responsible for the rise of the BNP because of the disappointment experienced by working and middle class families.

I have decided to leave the Labour Party after 46 years of active membership. I am still committed to Socialism and Labour principles including democracy, fairness, justice, freedom, peace and equality.

I would welcome any response from you. I attach a brief copy of my CV for information.

Yours sincerely

JThakoordin

Jim Thakoordin

c.c General Secretary of the Labour Party.

Looking back, looking forward

After tendering my letter of resignation from the Labour Party, I received a telephone call from the Prime Minister's – Gordon Brown – office asking me to "withdraw my resignation" as I had been "such a long standing and active member." I explained that "it took me a long time to make up my mind and I cannot withdraw my resignation." I had a letter from the General Secretary who also pleaded with me to remain in the Party, but I rejected his request. I felt compelled to swallow my pride and some of my principles and re-joined the Labour Party four years after resigning. I re-joined, because have seen what the present coalition government has done to working class people and the attacks on our welfare state and public services, I could no longer remain outside the political arena. I still have many doubts about the direction of the Party and the way Ed Milliband is seeking to loosen the historical ties with the trade union movement as well as agreeing with much of the current coalition strategies and policies for the economy and the welfare state. I can no longer stand outside the Party and just fight within the trade unions and campaigning groups, I want to add my support to those in the Party who are fighting to defeat the coalition government and to ensure a Labour Party in government reverse the attacks on the welfare state and public services; reverse the privatisation of parts of the NHS; create job opportunities for the unemployed; build large number of social and affordable houses; improve educational opportunities and invest in the environment as well as taking much greater control of the banking and financial sectors of the economy. I want to see a Labour government committed to equality, fairness, justice, equal access to resources for all, a peaceful and equal world, working towards reducing the threats to climate change, attacking poverty at home and abroad, care for the vulnerable and tackling all forms of discrimination. I hope the next Labour Leader will address the concerns over race, gender and class inequality as well as seriously attacking poverty and inequality.

Over the last twenty five years the number of black members of the House of Commons increased to twenty seven, including sixteen Labour and eleven Conservatives. There are also forty two black members in the House of Lords and two black women in the Lords have held positions such as Valerie Amos, Leader of the House of Lords in 2003. Valerie was born in Guyana not far from where I grew up as a child. Patricia Scotland, was the tenth, of twelve children from a family in Dominica, was the first black woman Queens Council, and was appointed by Labour as the Attorney General in 2007. We have had several black Cabinet and Shadow Cabinet Ministers over the last fifteen years, but sadly, they all saw themselves as politicians who happen to be black. There are some exceptions such as Diane Abbot and Bernie Grant, my countryman who stood by their principles as supporters of black self-organisation. Diane is a fighter for equal rights and I was disappointed when she was removed by Ed Milliband as a shadow minister for Health. She stood for the leadership of the Party when Gordon Brown resigned as Prime Minister. I believe she was at last given a position she rightly deserves in the Party, but lost it within a couple of years. All the black members of Parliament are now in the mainstream .and very seldom,. None of them ever, every raise issues of race and racism despite the fact that black people have been grossly and disproportionately disadvantaged for many years in Britain, regardless of the state of the economy. . They are almost all, from middle class and professional backgrounds, with strong career commitments. The Party has indeed changed to the point where all the four candidates for the last Party leadership in 2010, were grades from Oxbridge. We live in a world where political power and control is no longer determined by the majority of people who are entitled to vote, but by those who abstain from the process and those who, like the rich and powerful lobbyists and donators of funds to political parties having a tight grip on political outcomes that governs our lives. The truth is seldom determined by the votes of the majority. As Plato stated many centuries ago: *"Those who are too smart to engage in politics are punished by being governed by those who are dumber"*.

Jim with Tony Benn in 1983

Jim with Guyana Presidents Bharat Jagdeo in 1999 and
Cheddi Jagan in 1989

Top – Bottom
Jim with Michael Foot Labour Leader 1983
Jim with Norman Willis TUC General Secretary 1990

Chapter 14:

Politics, economics and democracy

The American dream

I have completed three score years and ten and have seen and done a great deal since childhood. I have seen enormous changes in every area of human life and activities, including the good; the bad; the ugly and the beautiful. Transport, communication, technology and science have enabled people to land on the Moon; equipment on Mars and surveyed other planets; replace parts of the human body including the heart, kidneys, liver, and other changes that enable us to live longer and healthier lives. Despite the rise in the world's population which stands at over 7 billion and likely to increase to 10 billion by 2050, the world leaders are still stuck in the mind-set of the past. The abuse of our generous and precious planet through over exploitation of our natural resources; greed for greater profits, wealth, power and materialism has done irreparable damage to our environment resulting in serious climate change due to global warming. These changes have already threatens the existence and survival of many countries, town, cities and rural areas with flooding, famine, conflicts over scarce resources and the quality of life for the poor and deprived majority on our planet. Human beings have real difficulties learning from history and therefore continue to repeat past mistakes. The last 400 years have witnessed the greatest holocausts, wars enslavement, and empire building in the history of the world. It has been estimated that around 130 million natives of North, Central and South America have suffered pre-mature deaths due to Western European imperialism and colonial policies rooted in enslavement and ethnic cleansing.

A similar story of holocausts, genocide, enslavement, abuse and ethnic cleansing was carried out by the Europeans in Africa; the largest, richest in natural resources;

and poorest continent with the fastest growing population in the world. It has been estimated that over 110 million Africans and their descendants died pre-mature deaths due to European imperialism, colonialism, neo-colonialism and globalisation. Wherever the Western Europeans colonised they set about over-powering the natives by force, denied them their human and civil rights; seized the lands; denigrated their lifestyles, cultures and customs. This is the case not only in Africa, the Americas, the Caribbean, Australia, and New Zealand and to a lesser extent, Canada. The European powers not only sought to redraw the world boundaries, steal, rape and pillage as much wealth and resources from the four continents of the world originally populated by black people, but also engaged in wars with each other to over these conquered territories and their resources, but also on controlling the colonies politically, economically and in every other aspects. This ideology based on the 'survival of the fittest' the use of violence, brute force and military might was responsible for the two World Wars in the 20th Century and the loss of well over fifty millions lives. The sad thing is that 100 years later, this ideology of might, is right, greed, materialism, excessive profits exist today. Conflicts in Africa resulted in over 20 million pre-mature deaths in Africa including 10 million in the Democratic Republic of the Congo during the last 50 years. Blacks in the Americas, Australia, New Zeeland, and Asia are still the poorest in the world and are subjected to the dominations of the world powers led by America with the mightiest military machine in the world and its European powers within the European Union and NATO. Of course, America and Britain, given the fact that the majority of the white Europeans who invaded and settled in America, Australia, New Zeeland and Canada were British have a special relationship in defending and protecting each other's interests. Not surprising that when American and Britain invaded Iraq, which resulted according to the UN, in the loss of 1 million lives and 5 million refugees, they were supported by NATO countries and their troops.

America either invaded or, sent troops into 22 countries and destabilised over 60 countries resulting in change of government in South and Central America, the

Caribbean, Asia, Middle East and Eastern Europe. Much of this work has been carried out with the active involvement of the unelected, USA secret service, the Central Intelligence Agency (CIA). The same strategy has been in use in Afghanistan for over a decade, and in a more covert way in Libya and Syria. America now has over 830 bases in at least 130 countries in the world and is rapidly building up its military, technological and surveillance resources to encircle Russia, China and to control as much of the Oceans large seas, airspace, media and land space as possible. America has vowed to defend its interest and citizens in any country at whatever cost and have been engaged in the pre-emptive strike strategy around the Middle East, Africa, and Asia, using drones attack, killing hundreds of innocent civilians including women, children and the elderly. At the same time the Americans and some NATO allies have provided protection for some of the most tyrannical and oppressive regimes in the world such as Saudi Arabia that has the world's largest deposit of oil and many of the oil rich Arab states that are ruled by feudal Kings and Princes.

There are many corrupt regimes, some of them led by the military that are under the protection of America because they are important purchaser of American military hardware and goods, in turn supplies America with essential commodities such as oil, minerals and raw materials. The Saudis signed a single contract to purchase $63 billion dollars of military equipment from America. Some of the military equipment the feudal Arab countries purchased from America, Britain and other NATO countries are being used to suppress people campaigning for democracy, civil and human rights. America has a warped sense of democracy, which translates not government of the people for the people, but government of the people by the corporations in collaboration with the political and ruling elites. This is the formula America has been seeking to impose quite successfully, around the world as it perceives its role as the world's policing authority and the only remaining superpower by far in the world presently. By 2018 China is likely to overtake America as the top manufacturing nation in the world and by 2030 may even match America's military capacity. What is certain, is that the American political and moral brands are losing credibility worldwide, due to its support for corrupt regimes; exploitation of sovereign nations; hypocrisy on democratic, civil and human rights; duplicity and complicity in world trade, development and exploitation through large American corporations the IMF and World Band , especially in developing countries.

It is not an accident that all the major world and international organisations are located in America and dominated by America and Western Europe, such as the United Nations, the World Bank and the International Monetary Fund. America. These institutions together with the various treaties, agreements, interventions and strategies dominates world trade, investments, political control and the capitalist ideology, and they have proven time and time again to take any action, including military, economic, political and actions overtly and covertly to manipulate and control the world under the pretence of defending so called human rights, democracy or freedom. America with only 5 per cent of the world's population spends 45 per cent of the total cost of world militarism, spies on every country, businesses and institutions through its National Security Agency (NSA) as revealed by the ex-CIA whistle-blower Edward Snowden and accepted by the President of America. The United States government is now taking legislative steps to deter media reporting of national security leaks, such as the information disclosed by Edward Snowden. Despite its superior military and economic superiority America still feels vulnerable and is prepared to heighten world tensions and global military threats whenever it feels NATO may be losing influence, as in the case of the Russian intervention the Ukraine in March 2014.

America is the richest most powerful country in the world, even though it is in more than $17 trillion dollars in debt and survives financially by printing more money and attracting hundreds of billions of dollars in investment from China and oil rich Arab states. Despite this vast wealth, over one in every seven of its population (45) million are living in poverty. The money spent on militarism in one year would eradicate poverty at home and much of the world if other country follows such example. The USA is home of the mega corporations, and the bastion of capitalism. It is where democracy has been severely undermined by the rich and the large corporations, that finance the main political parties and exercise massive control over politicians and the political as well as the economic and financial process and structures. Politicians are more inclined to listen to the corporations than the voters who generally feel helpless and powerless in influencing governments. These corporations include the media, the arms manufacturing, energy and fuel companies and the giant pharmaceutical, mining, financial and investment businesses. It is also probably the most unequal, segregated and permissive society in the world. In 2013, a Chief Executive Officer in the USA earns up to 475 times that of an average worker, whilst in Mexico it is 46 times, Britain 22 and Japan 11. The top 10 per cent on the rich list owns more than 80 per cent of the nation's wealth.

Our world has become far more aggressive, uncertain and much less peaceful since the terrorist attack on 9th September 2001, in America by Al-Qaeda, organised by Bin Laden. This incident led America and NATO to invade Iraq, Afghanistan, bombing Pakistan, Yemen, and other countries with drones and the massive extension of American military bases around the world. America is using drones in several countries even against the wishes of the national governments, claiming the right to defend its interest in any country, with or without the permission of its government. America and NATO partners are building bigger and more powerful unmanned drones, and weapons of destruction, including robots and systems to wage wars without putting soldiers at risk. Of course Al-Qaeda and Bin Laden were nurtured and supported by America during the period when Russia was involved in propping up a sympathetic communist government in Afghanistan. Bin Laden was employed by the American secret service (CIA). The president, of Afghanistan Hamid Karzai, who ruled the country with his family and friends and supported by America, admitted to getting millions in bags of cash delivered to his doorstep by the CIA, according to the New York Times and many other credible media organisations. President Karzai's brother, Ahmed Karzai, has also been getting cash delivered from the CIA. Ahmed Karzai is also linked to

Afghanistan's opium trade. In fact, the entire Karzai family has almost always been linked to Afghanistan's opium trade. And the CIA inadvertently helped them to create this trade. Afghanistan now produces 85 per cent of the entire world's heroin supply and 95per cent of the world's opium supply. In fact opium production has been increasing in Afghanistan, ever since the US occupation. Afghanistan produced 6,900 tons of opium in 2009, but produced less than 300 tons in 1979. Afghanistan's Minister of Counter Narcotics says foreign troops are earning money from drug production in his country. The UN found that the Taliban actually nearly eliminated the opium and heroin trades in 2001. Hamid Karzai advised an American oil company - Unocal - on a $2 billion Turkmenistan-Afghanistan-Pakistan gas pipeline in 1996. Although it was cancelled right after the USA launched missile attacks in 1999. Karzai was put into the presidency in Afghanistan by the United States. The same way the puppet regime was helped into power in Iraq by the USA, at a total cost of over $4 trillion for both the Iraq and Afghanistan wars. Karzai and to a lesser extent the leadership in Iraq criticised America and NATO for destroying their countries and killing large numbers of innocent people.

This so called war on terror has now reached every continent in the world and America sees itself as a victim, instead of the main country with its NATO allies in Western Europe that gave birth and nurtured Al - Qaeda. Terrorists, fundamental Islamists, secessionists and various nationalist groups under different names now actively creates havoc and mass killings in various countries and continents in the world today based on some of the principles of Al – Qaeda. In January 2002, America set up a prison camp in the Naval Base at Guantánamo Bay, Cuba, which is the oldest existing U.S. military base outside U.S. territory, to hold what they regard as "unlawful combatants," and not "prisoners of war," and their rights under the Geneva Convention are removed. The first 20 prisoners arrive at Guantánamo on 11th January 2002. Hundreds of prisoners have passed through this detention centre which has and is still renowned for some of the most horrific torture of human beings, most of them have never been convicted of any crime by a proper court of justice, and have been held in brutal conditions for years. President repeatedly stated his desire to close the camp, but has still failed to do so after six years in office.

Britain in the world

Britain once had an empire that spanned across the continents of the world. The sun would never set on the empire due to its size and location. America was part of this vast empire along with much of Africa, the Middle East, and much of Asia. It was through the exploitation of the empire and the Trans-Atlantic Slave Trade that Britain secured the wealth and markets to be the leader of the Industrial revolution in Europe. Much of this empire has dissolved into independent nations, have fought and won their freedom after enormous sacrifices from colonial rule. Millions of lives were lost in these anti-colonial struggles, including at least 2 million in the struggles leading up to the independence of Pakistan on 14th August 1947 and India, on 15th August the same year. In Africa, the anti-colonial struggles from Britain and the other European countries, that carved up the continent between them was even more intense, prolonged and cruel, as Britain and the European nations resisted the anti-colonial struggles. Yet despite all the plundering, enslavement, exploitation, and cruelty by Britain and the European colonialists, over hundreds of years, which resulted in the enforced transfer and movements of tens of millions of people and the pre-mature death of hundreds of millions of natives from North, Central and South America; Africa Australia, Canada and New Zeeland and Asia, Britain and Europe are on the verge of bankruptcy, except for Germany and a few other countries. From being the richest country in the 18th Century, Britain is probably now the seventh largest economy, even though it is seriously in debt and has had a deficit in its budget for years. The decline of Britain would continue, and would have declined even much faster, if it was not so closely associated with America, that has not only protected British interests abroad, but has also shared the spoils from wars, neo-colonialism, control of world financial markets and institutions. The growth of corporations through globalisation and manipulation of trading arrangements has ensured the supply of wealth from the ex-colonies to Britain and Europe. Britain claims to be the 4th largest military power in the world, even though it has less just 0.91 per cent of the world population and much less than land space of only 94,060 square miles, which is smaller than the state of Oregon in the USA, Finland, Guinea, or Morocco.

Britain has experienced rapid and extensive changes since I arrived in London in 1961. The changes have been political, economic, social, cultural demographic and lifestyles. For example there are more women in work than men; more in parliament and in top jobs than ever before. Britain is a multicultural society with more diverse cultures, religions, lifestyles and preferences in food and way of life. More people use restaurants, large super and hyper markets, betting shops, nightclubs, charity shops, online shopping, drugs and alcohol, watch pornography, use new technology, go abroad on holidays and have sex with multiple partners during their teenage years. Life in Britain has changed considerably with one in five Londoners being non-white and dozens of towns and cities have between 20 per and 40 per cent non-white populations and people from non-Christian faith groups making up more than 40 per cent of the community. Hundreds of schools and dozens of colleges have either a non-white majority or in many towns and cities almost a totally non-white learning population. This trend is likely to continue as the non-white population is growing much faster than the white population, By 2050 scores of towns and cities will have a non-white majority population, making up more than 20 per cent or 15 million of the British population, of which up to 6 million are likely to be Muslims who will be the largest group of voters in over 70 parliamentary constituencies. These changes will have even greater impact on all areas of life and activities within education, employment, housing, the environment and services.

Gay rights have been extended and weddings between people of same gender will become more common. Young people in Britain are more likely than other Europeans to experiment with illegal drugs, alcohol, sex and sexual preferences from as early as eleven years according to many credible research findings. The nation as a whole is accessing more pornography, including violent and sadistic types; has less interest in God or religion; becoming more individualistic and materialistic; less interested in trade unions and politics and community based activities. Gambling, pornography, violent films, are available in our homes on television and the internet every minute of the day and night non-stop. Young people especially within disadvantaged and impoverished neighbourhoods, towns and cities are more likely to engage in gun and knife crimes, forming gangs, engaging in sexual abuse of young women gang members, use drugs and alcohol and engage in anti-social behaviour. Many young people are accumulating large amounts of debts through student loans even before they start earning wages and salaries. In many cities and towns across Britain young men and women regularly gets drunk on weekends, and end up vomiting and urinating in the streets, engaging in fights, anti-social and criminal damage. Alcohol abuse and illegal drug use causes many of them to end up in police cells or in the accident and emergency units in hospital. Over 33,000 deaths each year are due to alcohol abuse. It has been reported that one third of all women age 18-25, in Liverpool engage in binge drinking most weekends. There were 40,000 binge drinking related incidents in just one year in Liverpool.

Some of these young people are often drunk before leaving home as it is cheaper to get drunk at home, before doing the regular pub crawl later on. It is sad that so many young people are indulging in recreation drugs and sex, alcohol abuse and anti-social behaviour. Women have caught up with men on such conduct and also on liver and other diseases due to alcohol and drug abuse. British people, especially young people who holiday abroad, are frequently identified as binge drinkers with relatively poor behavioural standards. Binge drinking is responsible for the fourth highest cause of death amongst women in Britain. Young people as young as ten and eleven years old are engaging in alcohol, sex, and drug abuse in towns and even in villages within Britain. Many people who regularly abuse drugs and alcohol are likely to engage in crime, prostitution and anti-social behaviour to finance their addiction and are a serious drain on the scarce resources of the NHS. The majority of young people are sensible and are not abusing alcohol, drugs or engaged in recreational sex. Governments and society in general should and must do more to give hope and opportunities to young people through job creation, greater access to education and training and to tackle the parts of the media that does a disservice to people, especially those that are vulnerable.

Over 1 million young people age 16-24 are registered unemployed or, not engaged in education, employment or training and are existing outside the attention of institutions. More young people are living with their parents and fewer people are buying their own homes since the recession started in 2008. Poverty, including child poverty is rising and nearly 1 million people are relying on food banks and charities for their survival. Britain has become increasing polarised with the rich getter richer and the poor, poorer since 2008. Due to rising unemployment, declining incomes and historical drop in living standards; cuts in public spending and the welfare budgets, cuts in public and local government services; phenomenal increases in house prices, rents, fuel and energy as well as a significant reduction in house building when the population has increased by several millions over the last decade.

Amongst some of the most significant changes in Britain are the decline in respect for politicians and the political system, especially since the exposure of politicians across political parties, gender, race, class, status and wealth have been exposed for claiming excessive expenses and in many cases falsifying their claims and having to serve time in prison or, returning substantial sums. Some members of parliament have been claiming for purchasing second and even third homes then selling them at a hefty profit; making claims for small sums of less than £1, as well as refurbishing second homes, or homes owned by their families. It has become a deep seated culture amongst the parliamentary and political class to misuse their positions, by claiming for meetings, they did not attend; expenses they did not incur; accepting money from lobbyists; being rewarded with lucrative financial positions within private companies or within the public sector when they leave parliament. Clearly, the majority of politicians are good intentioned and honest people, but the fact that even those with lots of money, bearing in mind that over 75 per cent of politicians elected in 2010 were millionaires when less than 5 per cent of the general population are millionaires. In addition, these very political classes are implementing cuts and austerity measures that are reducing benefits and welfare payments, pay and living standards; reducing and privatising public services; allowing prices and inflation to increase and rewarding the bankers, hedge funders, corporations and speculators to increase their bonuses, pay, shares and other incomes; whilst at the same time bailing them out and subsidising their profits through the public purse. The British government and more so, the American government has spent large sums by printing money through the method of quantitative easing (QE) to give as cheap loan or purchasing the bad assets and bonds from the very corporations that damaged the economy through fraud, mismanagement, illegal trading, corruption and untruths. America has spent well over $7 trillion and Britain well over £300 billion on QE to assist corporations and businesses out of their financial problems, yet many of them are engaged in tax avoidance and tax evasion at a large scale, some not even paying any taxes on large amounts of profits through international financial and banking manipulations.

Capitalism in crisis

There are many different views about capitalism. Some people say "capitalism is in crisis" and others say "capitalism is the crisis." For example a famous American gangster stated "Capitalism is the legitimate racket of the ruling class." George Bernard Shaw political thinker said Capitalism destroyed our belief on any effective power but that of self-interest backed by force." And according to philosopher Bertrand Russell "Advocates of capitalism are very apt to appeal to the sacred principles of liberty, which are embodied in one maxim: The fortunate must not be restrained in the exercise of tyranny over the unfortunate." Regardless of the virtues or otherwise of capitalism, most people would recognise that western capitalism is in a deep crisis and has been so at least since 2007. For decades the capitalist system has become an integral part of corrupt and inefficient political and economic system. They have failed to regulate, supervise, or exercise adequate management and control over public interests and assets, and ensuring that the financial and banking system were operating within the free market rules that distinguishes the ideology of capitalism. Governments and corporations failed as risk managers, and also failed in the monitoring, regulating and defining the roles and responsibilities for international economic and corporate organisations, that have global interests, systems of accountability and locations. Governments have colluded with crony capitalism to promote growth within the economy and to consolidate their political power base. They compete with each other for trade and internal investment by colluding with the bankers, hedge funders, and financial institutions through financial concessions; manipulating interest rates, loans and house prices; and taking actions to reduce labour costs and increase productivity.

The political and financial elite also took the view that markets needed to function with the least possible government intervention, and that any intervention should be within 'a light touch' framework, which in essence prevented them from identifying and avoiding serious risks including illegal transactions. So the crisis left a disastrous legacy for many countries resulting in high unemployment; cuts in benefits; public services and the welfare provisions; privatisation of public services; enormous fiscal deficits and debts, reaching up to 100 per cent of gross domestic product (GDP); reductions in living standards, and printing large sums of money to bail out the greedy capitalist system. Our ineffective and disgraced political class in Britain are locked in serious discussions with the wide ruling political class within the European Union (EU 28 countries in Europe and NATO) in that are facing similar economic, political and social problems – except Germany – over the crisis of capitalism that so far has resulted in much suffering amongst the population below average incomes. There are over 26 million people unemployed in the EU including 17 million young people and over 20 million under-employed and are living in serious poverty. Unemployment in Greece, Spain and Portugal

budgets to local people, as well as ensuring that businesses are punished for tax avoidance and tax evasion are the kind of initiatives the people would expect from their governments. Instead an ever increasing number of people all over the world, especially in the rich capitalist world are disengaging from the democratic process, which makes it much easier for the corporations and business interests to undermine the democratic process. Again for Pope Francis who also speaks for millions of others who care about humanity and our planet states that "While the earnings of a minority are growing exponentially, so too is the gap separating the majority from the prosperity enjoyed by those happy few. This imbalance is the result of ideologies which defend the absolute autonomy of the market place and financial speculation. Consequently, they reject the right of states, charged with vigilance for the common good to exercise any form of control."

How can a world that claims to be interested in democracy, justice, fairness, the rule of law and equality when over 5 million children each year die in the world prematurely from poverty and ill health before age of five; politicians condoning such massive inequality between the rich and the poor, by ignoring the wishes of the overwhelming majority of the people and pandering to corporations and the rich; supporting a system which condemns half of the world's population to poverty, disease, shortage of basic necessities and pre-mature deaths?

Politicians no longer fear the voters; instead they fear the wrath of the corporations and their control of the media and the financial life blood of the economy. Surely, democracy, freedom , justice and equality means more than the voters having the choice once every three or four years to choose between a small number of no more than two or three political parties that shares broadly the same ideology that props up crony capitalism? No wonder that people are confused, disillusioned, and distrustful of politics, politicians and their broken promises. Many governments in the western democracies are often elected into office by less than 30 per cent of the eligible voters and even less than 40 per cent of the actual voters. Mainstream political parties are funded largely by large interest groups, corporations and rich individuals who are in turn well rewarded by the Party in government with lucrative contracts, patronage, supportive legislations, parts of public services that has been privatised and numerous opportunities to make large profits. The irony in all this is that when these corporations experience difficulties, often due to their own greed, mismanagement and corruption, the state steps in to bail them out from public funds. No wonder many angry, poor and radical people are increasingly contemplating more confrontational tactics such as occupation, civil disturbance and resistance on a mass scale to create the change they want for a democratic, fair and free society, have seen the old and traditional forms of demonstrations and protests being ignored by the political and ruling elites.

Capitalism cannot claim a moral ground when even during the recession which seriously started in 2008, profits have risen twenty times that of wages; trillions of dollars stashed away in off shore tax havens by corporations instead of being invested in the economy; the rich and billionaires operating within a bubble created by themselves with tacit support of governments; and governments using the police, army, security and surveillance services and anti-workers legislation to undermine workers demanding a greater share of the gross domestic product. The crony capitalist system will not change unless there is a seismic change within the democratic process. Too many politicians are sitting too comfortably and are not challenging and holding the government to account, in fear of jeopardising their careers. Far too many parliamentarians are paid full-time salaries, but have more than one or more jobs and financial interests. Instead of these people elected for life, they should be barred from serving more than two consecutive terms. Parliamentarians should be more accountable and accessible to the people they represent and should not be able to use public funds to employ family and friends. Parliament should serve the people and not the interests of the politicians and the grossly overpaid and powerful senior bureaucrats and political advisers spin doctors, media cronies and the lobbyists who have infiltrated the political system. Politics has been reduced to sound bites, slogans, double speaking, hypocrisy, false promises, distortion of the facts, people entering the system to enhance their careers, instead of a commitment to public duties and the betterment of the many instead of the few.

Banks, banksters, gangsters and fraudsters

The financial crisis which became prominent worldwide in 2007–2008, also known as the Global Financial Crisis (GFC) is considered by many people as the worst financial crisis since the Great Depression of the 1930s. It resulted in the threat of total collapse of many large financial institutions with global investments. Governments in America and Europe decided that the financial institutions, mainly banks were so large, and part of the national and global financial system, that the only way forward, in order to avoid the worst recession for 80 years was to bailout the banks and key corporations by printing money through Quantitative Easing (QE). These governments were already running deficits and had substantial accumulated debts through borrowing for many years prior to 2008. America spent over $7 trillion in bailouts in America and Britain spent well over £100 billion by 2013. The American government did not want other banks to go bankrupt as did the Lehman Brothers did in 2008, without any bailout money.

The politicians, businesses and economists either blamed each other, the global market or the public for "living above their means". The truth us that the entire management team of the capitalist system are responsible for the crisis. The politicians and the people they appointed to manage the financial system such as the Federal Reserve Bank in America; the Bank of England; the financial regulation and supervisory bodies; the greedy bankers and hedge funders and the financial institutions are all to blame. According to an article in the Guardian Newspaper, in 2009, the crisis was bought about by 25 key people in America, Britain and other parts of the world. These people, mainly men, with a couple of women and a black male Chief Executive Officer (CEO) were at the heart of the meltdown. These rich and powerful people have made fortunes before and since the start of the crisis. Only one of them; Geir Haarde, prime minister of Iceland 2006-2009, has been found guilty by an Icelandic court in 2009, of helping to cause the crisis. His crime was that he failed to hold emergency cabinet meetings in the run up to the crisis. Haarde fell from power after the country's three biggest banks collapsed, the country's economy went into meltdown, and the government was forced to borrow $10bn (£6.3bn) to prop up its economy. Capitalism was living well above its means for many years and the crunch had to come sooner or later. President Bill Clinton, who was praised for turning around the American economy from the disastrous impact of President Reagan, repealed the Glass-Steagall Act in 1999, which helped to create the "casino banking" culture. Clinton repealed the Act after fierce lobbying from bankers and financial institutions. The U.S. Congress passed the Act in 1993 as the Banking Act, which prohibited commercial banks from participating in the investment banking business. The Glass-Steagall Act was sponsored by Senator Carter Glass, a former Treasury secretary, and Senator Henry Steagall, a member of the House of Representatives and chairman of the House Banking and Currency Committee. The Act was passed as an emergency measure to counter the failure of almost 5,000 banks during the Great Depression, which started in 1929 in America.

This action by Clinton paved the way for a wide range of "high risk" and complex financial products; undisclosed conflicts of interest; the failure of regulators, the credit rating agencies, and the market itself to rein in the excesses of the stock markets and the stock exchanges. The financial crisis was created by the financial institutions which could have been avoided if they were not so greedy and bent on making lots of profits. It was the failure of governments as much as the banks and the regulators in financial and corporate governance. This led to banks being engaged in excessive lending and borrowing; taking too many risks by lending to people and institutions that were unable to repay their mortgages and debts; being secretive, unaccountable and engaging in all sorts of unethical transactions. Banks ended up taking all the profits and the public ended up with the risks through QE. The bankers even acted illegally by predicting financial outcomes because they manipulated the interest rates and financial transactions. They were also fixing the interest rates for money they lend to each other under LIBOR, and lend money to home buyers at 100 per cent loan in order to keep repayments and house prices high. Bankers continue to pay themselves large bonuses, salaries and award themselves lots of shares even if they did not make a profit, or they were partly or mainly publicly owned. Some banks made massive profits by using the public money under QE to restock their capital instead of lending to businesses as requested by the governments.

This defiance by the banks and the fact that they continue to ignore the public good, having survived by public funds is disgraceful, especially since the governments in America and Europe, continue to force working class people to bear so much of the sacrifices to rebuild their economies. Banks create debts, because the bigger the debt the greater is the added value in profits for them. I do not believe it is wrong to accuse the banks of having raped the American, British and much of the western European economies, with the knowledge and support of the political structures and the governing elites. The politicians are forcing the people to pay for the crisis created by the banks, whilst the bankers continued to reward themselves for failure. For many people who are seriously affected financially and are struggling to survive, it would appear that the bankers and the politicians are colluding to create cheap money from the public purse, through QE to continue to bail outs the banks. The banks used the money to restock instead of lending, but when they do lend they charge charges high interest rates, whilst paying savers negative interests, at less than the rate of inflation. To the ordinary saver who have earn their money in difficult circumstances, pay tax and national insurance on their earnings and put aside some money for emergencies, retirement or family reasons, forced to accept below inflation rates of interest, having to pay tax on any income from such savings. This is nothing by legalized robbery of many vulnerable people, especially people like pensioners with fixed incomes.

Bankers, large corporations and the rich, have been bankrolling political parties and candidates for political office especially in Europe and the USA to the tune of billions of dollars for many years. In turn they exercise a great deal of influence over politicians and the political structures, which undermines democracy, freedom and equality. It is not surprising therefore that the banks, hedge funders and financial institutions have been trading illegally for many years, through illegal laundering of money from sale of drugs, fraud, theft by oligarchs, presidents, world leaders from their people, because they know that their businesses will just be fined and they will not be sent to prison for such criminal actions. Many banks and financial corporations have been deliberately selling products that were not credible and have been forced to repay billions of pounds back to customers who have been miss-sold certain products. Some people have even labelled such behaviour "financial terrorism." To add insult to injury, it has been reported in March 2014 that greedy big businesses avoid £35 billion tax on profits in one tax year, which represents around 7 per cent of the total amount collected in tax. The continued avoidance and evasion of tax by corporations each year is disgraceful and requires urgent, drastic and substantial actions by governments to claim retrospectively from the dodgers and evaders the hundreds of billions of pounds owed to the public treasury. Instead governments are committed to impose austerity measures such as the bedroom tax to save just £500 which is causing the much pain and suffering to the poor. Some of these people have been driven to serious illness and even committed suicide because of the fear and concerns over the cuts and austerity measures. Around 600,000 people in Britain today have to rely on food banks to support them, whilst millions of people are forced to choose whether to eat, or heat, starve to feed themselves or their children. This situation is causing much distress, illness, worries and disasters that are leading to increase in suicides, divorce, family breakdowns and anti-social behaviour.

Chapter 15:

My trade union background

"Man is born free, but everywhere he is in chains" –
Jean-Jacques Rousseau

I was a trade unionist long before I joined a trade union; because I saw the bitter struggles workers were engaged in to secure fairness and justice against employers operating within a capitalist system under colonialism. I was born and grew up on a sugar plantation on the west coast of Demerara in British Guiana, later renamed Guyana after gaining political independence from Britain, on 26th May 1966. Most of the people from my village were the descendants of indentured labourers from India who were imported into Guyana by the British sugar plantation owners and the British state, to work on the sugar plantations. Like the overwhelming majority of the population in my village my parents were illiterate and poor. With many children to care for, in a country with no welfare state and hardly any free public services. I grew up in a household with six sisters. I was the only boy and two of my sisters were older than me. Children were expected to follow their parents as field workers: Sugar plantations were the only source of paid, albeit seasonal employment along the West Coast of Demerara that stretches for about twenty one miles along the Atlantic Ocean. The economy of Guyana was very much dominated by agriculture, mainly sugar and related production. There were some relatively small pockets of urban areas where commercial, trading and business interests were conducted such as in capital, Georgetown and some much smaller urban areas on other two counties: Berbice and Essequibo. The population of Guyana has always been scattered, with a few villages built up around each of the some twenty five sugar plantations owned by a few absentee British companies.

My village was named Leonora, and it was one of the larger and most productive plantations with one main road, two schools, two churches, one Mosque, one Hindu Temple, two shops selling rum and beer as well as dry goods, a couple of small general stores and dozen small and medium size retail shops. Market day on Saturday in Leonora was always the busiest day in the week, as workers were paid in cash from early Saturday morning until the late afternoon, allowing for those who worked in the fields to collect their pay on their way home from work. Naturally the market which attracted trades and customers from miles around was situated along the route from the plantation administrative office to the side roads along which workers have to travel to either go home, shop or stop for liquid refreshments at one of the two rum shops. Sometimes these wretched workers would end up spending large sums in the rum shops and had little money left for them to pass on to their family to shop for the week. One of my jobs on Saturdays was to wait outside the factory gates for my father to pass on his pay envelope after removing some for refreshments with his friends at the rum shop on his way home, so my mother (ma) could shop for the week. Ma would make sure that we children were up early on Saturdays, complete our chores, have a bath using buckets of water or using the nearby canal, before getting in our best clothes to accompany ma to the market and the general store. We would also use our pocket money to affect our own tiny purchases, consisting a drink, cakes, sweets or fruits. Leonora market was always a colourful, noisy, entertaining and busy place. Friends, families and acquaintances would meet, exchange greetings and share the latest news. Young boys would use the opportunity to steal a glimpse and a possible quick chat with a girl they fancied, which was always difficult as most of the time the young ladies would be with their mother or other female family members.

Between the age of seven or eight to fourteen years, I used to help my mother on market days at her own tiny stall which was a jute bag about 1.5 metre deep and 2 metres wide with whatever food we could either make at home, or provisions we were able to purchase at a price that we could sell for a profit. I also used to use our donkey and cart to transport goods for other people to and from the market. After we finished at the market, ma and I would shop at the general store for our weekly shopping. On good days ma was able to pay for our goods and even pay off some of what seems to be an unending debt owed to the shopkeeper. On bad days we were unable to purchase all the basic food such as oil, rice, flour, curry powder and potatoes and ma had to endure abuse and insults from the owner of the shop. On special days, such as weddings, cultural and religious festivals we would be treated if our parents could afford it to an item of clothing. As ma stitched clothes for all our family, on our very old (at least 40 years old) singer foot peddled machine, I was always guaranteed a shirt made up from the colourful bits that were left over from the material used for dresses.

Our lives changed when my two elder sisters and I started to earn our own wages as plantation workers. Both of my eldest sisters were working from their early teens until they were married, still in their teens. Our family was also drifting apart at the time and the pressures caused ma to become a diabetic, a condition for which she was never treated medically. This resulted in some irrational behaviour on her part and alienated her from the rest of our family for a while, until she returned soon after I left Guyana in 1961. I worked with my parents at home and in the fields from an early age, and in paid employment as a worker on the payroll at age fourteen.

I was often taken to trade union meetings mostly with ma, but sometimes with my father; they were staunch supporters of the anti-colonial struggles orchestrated by both the Guyana Agricultural Workers Union (GAWU) and the main political party – the People's Progressive Party (PPP). Both GAWU and PPP were led by Marxists and were opposed to the exploitation of workers by the sugar industry. The plantations were notorious for rebellions by workers, way back to the days of slavery, apprenticeship and indenture-ship. There were frequent disputes between workers and the plantation management. Even though I was only a child I understood the feelings of the workers and listened carefully to the speakers who were articulating their grievances at the public meeting which took place beside the railway station in Leonora. For me, the issues were quite straight forward and basic. The white European overseers who managed the plantation, wanted to maximise profits, and the workers wanted a decent wage for their labour. This situation inevitably meant that there will be conflicts from time to time, especially in a situation where there was only one large employer for miles around. I learn my trade unionism from my mother who hated the bosses and their local non-white stooges. These local foremen and supervisions were often more cruel than the white overseers because they frequently demanded bribes and sexual favours from certain women in return for work. Ma was fiercely independent; always ready to strike, protest and join political campaigns. She would organise the village women and criticise the men if they were reluctant to take action.

Women would mainly work in the cane fields, weeding and cleaning between the rows of cane. It was difficult, poorly paid, and painful work, having to bend over most of the day – working barefoot in very hot weather and sometimes wet conditions. They often worked through heavy rainfall, sunshine and rainfall again, wielding a machete and what we would call a grass knife, or sickle, to pull the vines and weeds away from between the rows of cane. These women would often have to cross trenches either by a tiny boat or by walking across canals, up to their neck in water, carrying their equipment and their lunch, if they had any with them above their heads. They would often have to cross the canals when finishing work, and then walk miles back to their homes. On a couple of occasions, whilst helping my mother and sisters in the cane fields, I saw women who either had a miscarriage or had given birth when they were at work. Many worked right up to the signs of labour pain. Pregnant and sick women were always subjected to accidents at work given the nature of their tasks. Women who have had accidents or given birth would often have to prepare meals for young children within hours, unless there were family and friends to help them out.

Member of the Hyman gang

At the age of around thirteen or fourteen – having lied about my age by claiming to be older, I secured a job of my own on the plantation working with a gang of boys known as the Hyman gang. Mr Hyman was the foreman who managed around a dozen of us age fourteen to eighteen. Our main tasks were to keep the factory clean and tidy; transporting waste into areas where they were stored, recycled or dumped; washing, sweeping and cleaning, not only the factory floor, but other areas including plant and machinery within the large factory complex where many tons of sugar cane stems were crushed and the juice processed into sugar and other products. We would assist builders, who were carrying out repairs, by using wheelbarrows, cleaning in between the massive machines that press the sugar cane and process the cane juice from liquid into sugar. This type of work was always dirty and dangerous. We worked six days a week and if there was overtime on Sunday mornings when the engines stopped working, we would go into the factory and clean between the engines and clear up all the waste material.

I wasted no time in encouraging most of the gang to join GAWU. Mr Hyman was seriously alcoholic and frequently abusive towards us boys. He would often misuse his position. He was tall African man, about six feet in height and quite a loud, authoritative and ferocious character. As part of this abuse he would touch some of the boys inappropriately, he would demand bribes from us in money or bottles of rum. Those who gave him bribes or allowed him to touch them were offered lighter jobs and the rest of us would get the worst jobs.

Hyman hated me as I was one of the rebels who opposed his exploitation of the boys. I secretly reported him to the trade's union steward who told him off. I attended all the trade union meetings which were sometimes held secretly, and explain to the men the conditions we had to tolerate, including being pushed and slapped, by Mr Hyman when he was in a drunken state. I decided that this was not the job for me and I wanted to improve my education and opportunities to secure better employment, so I joined an adult education group organised by a number of men who were in white collar jobs, such as administrators, clerks and technical workers. These older men helped me with my learning as I had little formal education having missed school for months on end and left school without any formal qualification.

I applied for a job as a laboratory assistant when I was sixteen, collecting samples from various places in the factory as the sugar cane juice was being processed, and returning samples to the laboratory for examination and assist the chemist in regulating the quality standards of the sugar. I was dismissed from this job before I was eighteen. Within three months of being dismissed I arrived in London, secured a job first as a porter for a few weeks, where I encouraged some boys working with me to join the union, even though they frequently racially abused and harassed me. During my employment with London Transport and London Country Buses I joined the Transport and General Workers Union (T&GWU) and was elected shop steward and then Branch Secretary. I joined the Luton Post Office in 1968 and very quickly became a member of the Branch Committee then Branch Secretary. I enjoyed my union work and I managed to make many friends across several industries and parts of the UK whilst attending conferences, courses and meetings in Britain and abroad. It was through my involvement with the union I won a scholarship to attend Ruskin College, Oxford at age thirty one. I maintained my trade union activities during my five years at three different universities, always supporting workers in struggles locally and across England. I took part in almost all the major regional national industrial disputes since my arrival in London in 1961, either by joining marches and demonstrations or writing letters supporting the workers, or collecting signatures or funds to support their campaigns. I supported many dispute involving black workers in London and the South East, Nottingham, Liverpool, and elsewhere when they were in dispute with their employers; being I spent a lot of time supporting the struggles of black workers involved in the historical strikes at Grunwick in North London in 1976 and 1977, as well as many other workers across the UK who were fighting for better pay and conditions as well as a fair wage. I always believed in the slogan that "Unity is our Strength" and that "An injury to one, is any injury to all." I will always remain loyal to my class and my race until I die. There is only one race, which is the human race. I always felt it was my duty to support those within the human race that were victimised, persecuted, attacked and exploited by powerful interest groups, because of their gender, race, religion, ethnicity, skin colour, age or socio-economic status and lack of power.

Full-time London Region Union Officer

In late 1978 I was offered a fulltime Regional Trade Union Officer's job, with the General, Municipal Workers Union (GMWU, which later became the General Municipal and Boilermakers union GMB). I was only the third black person to be appointed into such a position within the trade union movement, even though black workers were involved in working class struggles in Britain for centuries. It is very likely that there were around one million black members organised within trade unions in 1979. Within weeks of my appointed I started to campaign for more recognition of the needs of black workers as there were numerous investigations and reports over several decades by the TUC, Workers Education Association; Labour Research Department; Commission for Racial Equality; Runnymede Trust; International Labour Organisations and academic institutions, identifying specific concerns about racism not only within the workplace, but also within trade unions themselves. I worked with the GMB, the TUC and several trade unions to set up procedures, structures, processes and training courses specifically designed to address discrimination amongst black, women and your workers, as well as encouraging them to become more involved at all levels within trade unions. I was involved in writing policies, guidelines training manuals and workbooks, leaflets and reports which were used for training of unions officers, negotiators and staff involved in recruitment. I helped to design material produced by the Commission for Racial Equality (CRE) and several trade unions and the TUC as well as designing and delivering training courses within my own union and across several other trade unions. I set up a direct mail list for women, black and young workers and organised an annual conference for each group to advise the union on equal access to services and jobs within the labour movement.

Having involved with the Civil Rights movement in Britain and followed the history of Black Struggles in America for equal rights and access to resources as well as an end to racial discrimination, I started to network with key organisations and institutions, such as the Industrial Society, CRE, Colleges and Universities as well community and anti-racist organisation to speak on race and race relations. In those days trade unions were broadly recognised by governments, employers and workers as an essential part of our industrial and economic life. This was the case until Mrs Thatcher and the eighteen consecutive years of rule by the Conservative Party resulted in the trade union membership being reduced by 50 per cent and unions forced out of any tripartite arrangements between governments, employers and unions. I actively campaigned against the government and its anti-trade union and racist policies throughout the eighteen years of conservative rule and beyond. I combined my trade union work with political campaigning, as the Thatcher era was the great threat to trade unions and working class people. Her years in power resulted in cuts in public services, privatisation and growing inequality amongst the lowest twenty per cent of income earners. It left black people as the permanent underclass. During my work with the GMB I had to confront racism from within the union as well as from workers in general, who felt that I was not as good as the white officials, based simply on the colour of my skin, and the fact that I was an immigrant.

During the 1979, 1983, 1987 general elections, I worked with Lord Larry Whitty, who was a National Officer with the GMB to promote Trade Unionist for a Labour Victory, and other radical groups including women, black and community organisations to boost Labour support. At the same time I worked with the BTUSM and Black Socialist Society to empower more black people in unions, politics and institutions. One of the early successes was the growth of the BTUSM. In 1984, I chaired a Greater London Committee on Race and

Trades Unions. We produced a book entitled; "Racism within Trade Unions" as the evidence was overwhelming that unions were still institutional racist. Ken Livingstone thanked me personally for chairing the committee and for writing parts of the book. He also invited me to address a May Day Rally outside County Hall, with other speakers, including Tony Benn, Neil Kinnock, American Singer Stevie Wonder and himself. It was a large crowd with lots of entertainment. Stalls and fun. The Report which was published as a book was sent directly to all trade unions, and hundreds of trade union activists in England. I was severely criticised by a number of trade unionists from inside and outside my own union. Before the 1987 general election many black trade union and Labour Party activists worked hard to ensure the Black voice inside of Parliament. We were therefore delighted to see four black MPs elected.

My bid to become a trade union leader

Without unions, workers will lose many of the protection previous generations have bitterly fought for against abusive, greedy and uncaring employers. Pay and conditions for all will be depressed, even when profits are at record levels, as we have seen in recent years in the rich western countries. Many large employers deliberately choose to pay workers in the rich country less than a living wage, whilst at the same time, exporting jobs to less developed countries where they pay much less for labour and materials. Outsourcing jobs to Asia, Africa and elsewhere within a globalised world labour market has gained momentum for employers and corporations seeking to maximise profits and productivity minimise labour costs. Labour costs are much cheaper because of very little, if any legal protection for workers in areas such as terms and conditions, health and safety, pensions, abuse, child labour, minimum wage, paid holidays and victimisation. Having been an active trade unionist for all my working life, including a full-time Regional Officer, I decided I had enough experience to make a bid to become the elected head of Britain's third largest trade union; the General Municipal and Boilermakers union

(GMB). The vacancy of General Secretary arose when David Basnett; a much respectable and committed servant of the union movement decided to retire.

I was encouraged by several GMB activists across England to enter the contest for a new General Secretary to lead nearly one million members. At the time of the election, I was 41 years old and had been a GMB officer in London for six years. I was educated within the union movement and had established quite a bit of credibility and a reputation for championing the disadvantaged groups, including women, black and minority ethnic and disabled workers. I had lots of support amongst the radical activists who welcomed the opportunity to vote for the first time ever for a black person to lead a major trade union in Britain. I was given an opportunity like the other candidates to write 1,000 words; why I wanted to stand for the position of General Secretary. I used to opportunity to challenge the white middle aged and middle class leadership of the union and the absence of women and black people as full-time paid officers. Having described the GMB as "a sleeping giant" that was perceived by many members as "undemocratic, bureaucratic and reactionary" and I outlined my ideas for making the union a more strategic, campaigning, democratic, inclusive, accountable and stronger organisation. I was not expecting to win, but to at least create some robust discussions within the membership. Some members from across the different industries and regions of England, Wales and Scotland supported me, but it was far from sufficient to secure a victory. Nevertheless, I did reasonably well, even without the resources to mount a national campaign in the way the successful candidate did. It was a very useful exercise which boosted my confidence and increased my profile within the union movement. The present General Secretary of the GMB, Paul Kenny is someone who I trained as a student on the GMB courses I designed and delivered, when he was a local government worker in London. My wife taught his son who is also a senior GMB officer.

Black self-organisation within trade unions

There were self-organisation within Britain since the 17th Century against racism, oppression and abuse. These activists attached themselves to all the liberation struggles that were involved in the Anti-Slavery campaigns, Christian Socialist groups, radical political groups such as the Chartists, early trade unions, and the Labour Party as well as various Marxists and radical movements. Black seamen and other workers organised amongst themselves in the 19th and 20th Centuries in the dock areas in Cardiff, Liverpool, London and Bristol against racial attacks from other workers. It was during this inter-war period (1936) that black workers in Cardiff formed the Coloured Seamen's Union. This organisation bought together Africans, West Indians, Arabs and Malays to fight against the operation of the colour bar on the Cardiff Docks. Asian immigrants from the Sub-continent formed the Indian Workers Association in the 1930's. Africans and West Indians formed various several groups such as Campaign Against Racial Discrimination (CARD started in 1950 in London) to fight racism in Britain. In 1979 a small group of us including Bernie Grant who later became a Member of Parliament and other Black activists, mainly in the public sector formed the Black Trades Union Solidarity Movement (BTUSM).

By 1984 I was beginning to feel isolated within the trade union and Labour movement. I was disillusioned with the trade union movement for not resisting more strongly the Tories onslaught, on the rights and working conditions of working class people. The defeat of the miners' union in 1984; the turning tide amongst the public against trade unionism; the dis-organisation, lack of confidence, leadership and direction by the TUC made me look at others ways of fighting inequality, racism, trade union and Labour bureaucracy. This was not possible from within. One senior trade union leader told me in 1985, "you are too left wing to progress within the labour movement and you will never progress within the trade union and labour movement as long as you have a hole in your bum". This insult shocked me, and I felt it was time for me to leave the union job, I valued so much. During my work with the GMB and other unions, I saw some rotten decisions that involved compromises with employers that left black and women workers very vulnerable. The unions were more inclined to support craft and skilled workers than supporting low paid and vulnerable women and black workers. There were lots of incidents which were described as "sweetheart agreements between employers and unions" that involved some shoddy compromises relating to unionisation, pay and conditions of workers in certain industries. I also witnessed incompetence, poor management, and unreasonable claims for expenses, and abuse of union resources and lack of commitment from some union officers and members who served on the bureaucratic and male dominated governance structures of several trade unions. I was fortunate to secure a senior job with Islington Council as a Neighbourhood Officer in Islington Council. I managed a large Neighbourhood office with 70, professional, technical, manual and administrative staff.

One of the most successful campaigns I was involved with was the self-organisation of black workers within the public sector, mainly local government, transport and the National Health Service where black workers were disproportionately represented. We started off with the BTUSM in 1979 and developed a large following in local government in England, Scotland and Wales under the banner of Black NALGO (National Association of Local Government Officers, which later became UNISON the second largest union in the UK), much to the annoyance of the wider trade-union movement. At this time I met with Bernie Grant - my countryman from Guyana, where we had a solid tradition of union organisation. We organised a meetings at the Greater London Council (GLC) with the support of activists from Camden Black Workers Group, made up mainly of NALGO activists and other interested trade unionists who wanted to find out more about Black self-organisation. Among the most active Black workers in London local government were Azim Hajee, Judy Bashir, Gulam Mayet, Chris Khamis, John Ohen and John Fernandez. The black self-organised network especially across London and large cities took off with great expectations and enthusiasm. In 1980

I was elected to the NAGO National Black Members Committee and between this committee and the BTUSM we organised a Black Workers' Conferences in Bradford attended by more than 180 NALGO members over 60 activists from other unions which was very successful, even though there were signs of some factionalism and frustration amongst some delegates. We later lobbied the TUC and sought support from several trade unions, such as the National Union of Miners, Fire Brigades Union, T&GWU, GMB, NATFHE, USDAW, NUT and others to support black self-organisation. The TUC had a Race Relation Working Party since 1976 and they held a national Conference each year, as well as regional Conferences on race and gender. We tried to persuade the TUC to support self-organisation without any success for over ten years. The TUC felt like a number of other unions, especially those with centre right leadership, that it would be divisive to have separate sections for women and black workers.

Another significant event which helped self-organisation of black workers took place on 22 November 1981, at the GLC. The meeting was attended by more than 200 workers, representing over 30 trade unions, pledged their support for "*The Declaration on Racism*" within the Labour movement and society at large. They also agreed to reject a proposal for black workers to form a separate trade union and affiliate to the TUC, if the trade unions reject black self-organisation.

The Declaration pledged to:

- Organise a London-based conference of Black trade unionists in 1982 to discuss a programme of action;

- Make links with other Black workers' organisations, with a view to launching a national Black Trade Unionists Solidarity Movement Campaign;

- Work to improve Black participation at all levels of the union and labour movement; and

- Work for changes within the trade union and labour movement to build greater confidence and participation of Black people's in them.

An Annual General Meeting was called in 1982, with more nearly 100 delegates. Unfortunately, it was disrupted by a group of people arguing about the definition of "Black", after a Turkish woman insisted on her right to attend even though she did not see herself as Black. Very little was therefore achieved and it was agreed to convene a further BTUSM meeting in 1983. Sadly, the BTUSM meeting which took place on 29 May at the GLC to approve the BTUSM Constitution was far from productive. At a meeting in June 1984, BTUSM adopted its new constitution, but, there were still frequent disagreements within the organisation, which was funded by the GLC and had full-time workers who were Bernie. The organisation just fizzled out after a violent confrontation between Bernie Grant and another leading committee member, at a subsequent Committee meeting, which resulted in a court case and Paul Boetang, who was a Member of Parliament and a lawyer did his best to resolve the matter. I chaired the meeting, and it was one of the most bitter and divisive meeting I attended. Unfortunately, such divisions and bitterness, often based on the struggle for power and control, funding and grants, leadership, ethnic and regional differences, opportunism and lack of a historical perspective on race, racism and the 'divide and rule' tactics, so frequently used to disrupt the progress of black people. There were also strong generational, ideological cultural, economic, and regional differences amongst the black activists. Young African Caribbean Londoners from South and North London were very angry and vocal at times because of the depth and volume of living with racism throughout most of their lives. After the demise of BTUSM in 1984, the black activists then focussed on the progression of the Labour Party Black Socialist Society, which we re-launched 1983, following the Party Conference in October, in Brighton. I was also a founder member of the Black Socialist Society.

Between 1990 and 1994 considerable progress was made in making black self-organisation a reality in almost all of the TUC affiliated trade unions representing over 80 per cent of trade union membership in the UK. Even the TUC finally gave in and agreed to organise annual TUC Black Workers Conference TUCBWC) in 1993 with full powers to pass motions and to nominate people to the various TUC self-organised groups, including gender and race. Other groups such as Disability, Lesbian Gays Transgender and Bi-Sexual (LGTB) followed. The Labour Party followed in 1994 with a self-organised Black Socialist Society.

The TUCBWC, from the start has been as an advisory body that influences the TUC General Council where there are three reserved seats for black members. At least two black members who served on the TUC General Council have subsequently become President of the TUC and chaired the TUC Annual Conference. Gloria Mills an African Caribbean woman and Mohammad Taj an Asian Muslim held these positions. One issue that occupies the thoughts of some black members is that unlike the TUC Women's Conference where only women can attend as delegates, a number of unions have always insisted on sending black and white delegates. TUC Women's held in Blackpool in 1992 carried a motion to ban men from attending by 142 votes to 129, even though only 20 men out of a maximum of 350 delegates attended, it was the end of a practice that allowed men to attend for the past 62 years.

The following Report highlights parts of the full report on the TUCBWC in 1991 which was attended by around 100 people, mainly black trade unionists:

A Report of the TUC Conference:

Black Workers' Rights in the 1990s on 31st January and 1st February, 1991, At the TUC National Education Centre, in North London.

The conference was the first to cover two days- day one addressed key areas of black workers' rights in the 1990s, and day two addressed black workers' rights in Europe 1992. Eighty delegates attended from twenty-seven unions and five TUC

Regions. It was chaired by David Lambert on the first morning and thereafter by Dipak Ray. Ken Gill was unable to chair through illness and sent his apologies for the conference.

The conference was addressed in the morning session of day one by Paul Boateng MP, and Bill Morris, and in the afternoon session by Gloria Mills. Speakers on the morning of day two were Pauline Green MEP, and speaker from the TUC Equal Rights Department. In the afternoon there was a special presentation by Sue Hastings of the Trade Union Research Unit of Ruskin College, on a research project commissioned by the TUC on the involvement of black workers in trade unions, which supported the concerns of black workers regarding racial discrimination, marginalisation, stereotyping, unequal treatment and negative attitudes towards black workers by white colleagues. It also identifies weaknesses within the policies, procedures, guidelines and organisational aspects within unions, and supported the need for black self-organisation and greater participation. I attended the Conference and made a number of comments.

Thursday 31st January

David Lambert, in opening the conference, said that "The 1990s must be a decade in which all unions committed themselves to the needs of black members. He wanted the conference to look at the priorities of the 1990s, and how we could achieve a blueprint of ideas for action, and ideas of how unions could actually implement policies for black members. He said that day two would address the race equality implications of 1992- an issue which had dominated the race agenda of unions in the past months." David Lambert then introduced Paul Boateng, MP for Brent South, and a Labour Front Bench Treasury Spokesperson, and Bill Morris, Deputy General Secretary of the Transport and General Workers' Union.

Paul Boateng said "As this was the first TUC conference on black workers' concerns to be extended to two days. It was historic, because it marked the latest in a series of conference of black trade unionists which recognised the central importance of black people in the labour trade union Movements. Paul Boateng stressed the fact that black people had not "recently" appeared in the ranks of the Movement. They had always been there, making a significant impact. Historically the work of figures like John Archer and the type of contribution made by black people to the fabric of society and the fabric of the trade union Movement had to be continually stressed, as it gave black people a sense of pride and place. Black people had learned to be self-reliant, a quality which they had taken into the trade union Movement. He congratulated Jim Thakoordin, Bernie Grant and others who were instrumental in raising awareness of the need for the Black Agenda and the setting up of the Black Trades Union Solidarity Movement. Also the work Jim Thakoordin and others in the Labour Party did to establish the Black Sections within the Labour Party against the massive opposition from sections of the Leadership within the Party."

Bill Morris said "While the 1990s were sometimes referred to as the decade "of challenge and opportunities" for many black workers, that opportunity was still little more than a dream- the conference was a way to review progress and to consider the way forward. He gave an account of the inequalities faces by black people in the job market some fifteen years after the Race Relations Act, and how these inequalities could also exist in the community where racial attacks harassment still featured strongly. If trade unions were sincere in their claim to stand against racial disadvantage, then they had to do something about it in their own ranks. But it was the case that unions had not even taken basic steps like race monitoring of their own membership, officers and staff. Black people were rising in the ranks of local authorities, for example, and it was right that similar progress should be made by black people in trade unions. The struggle by Black NALGO members over the last decade has been a tremendous success and has made a number of trade unions having to examine their policies and structures. Black self-organisation has been growing within the trade union movement and activists, such as Bernie Grant and Jim Thakoordin, who have been amongst the first full-time officials in major trade unions, have done a lot of work to persuade the TUC and the Labour Party of the merits of black self-organisation. However, the case for Black self-organisation is not supported by everyone, not even by a large section of black workers themselves."

Bill Morris concluded by returning to the important priorities for black trade unionist in this country - the need for union rules against racism, better representation and service to black members. His final message was "The issues that mattered to black people were not marginal - they were absolutely fundamental for the movement to address. Black people were challenging the notion that "they must contribute as equals but receive as minorities. Black people would bring their enthusiasm, knowledge and commitment to labour movement, and as a result the movement would reap enormous benefits."

There were four workshops and reports were received from each one:

Workshop 1A – dealt with Unions' Progress in Negotiating for Race Equality at Work.

Delegates were asked to identify action points for unions. The points reported back to the conference were:

- Unions had to prioritise three areas when recruiting: promotion and training of existing black staff; recruiting of black staff; tackling racism at work through grievance procedures.

- Unions had to negotiate an agenda for black workers which helped eliminate racism at work, and which negotiated rights for black workers which included a whole range of topics including time off work for courses, extended leave and special religious requirements.

Workshop 1B – dealt with Racial Harassment Policies and Procedures.

Delegates discussed how racial harassment cases were dealt with by unions and employers. The points reported back to the Conference were that:

- More unions needed to negotiate grievance procedures with management and adopt a firm union policy on racial harassment at work.

- More unions needed to inform black members suffering from racial harassment about what they should do in the initial stages- this would come from written information and advice from union representatives

- Unions had to deal more effectively with the fact that too many black members sought advice from RECs and Law Centres rather than their unions. Unions needed to commit themselves to taking more cases and to publicise successful cases so that black members would have an incentive to approach the union.

- Training in taking racial harassment cases should be a priority for white officers in particular, who would have to deal with such cases.

Workshop 1C – dealt with Trade Union Organisation: Union Progress

Delegates discussed what steps unions had taken to overcome barriers to black involvement, what problems had arisen, and what the lessons there were for unions contemplating taking steps to improve organisation in this area. The points reported back to the conference were:

- Some unions had made progress: examples given were NALGO which had a well-developed parallel organisation of black workers groups. Unions like the TWGU had set up formal and informal race advisory structures.

- Concern was experienced that given the current financial problems of unions financial support for race equality initiatives and organisation should not be downgraded.

- Improved training and education for black workers was stressed.

Workshop 1D – dealt with Black Women and Trade Unions

Delegates discussed which action points which would help improve the position of black women workers in unions. In the report back the following points were raised:

- There was a need for unions to encourage more networking between black women workers and trade unionists.

- Trade unions needed to make a stronger commitment to the involvement of black women as full-time and lay trade union officials, and to provide support for black women trade unionists who felt isolated within their organisation.

- There had to be attention paid to the needs of black women workers-they were continually being ignored and caught between attention race issues and women equality.

- A TUC black workers conference similar in structure to the TUC Women's Conference may be in better position to take up these issues.

Gloria Mills said that black women workers had a special place in history of the Movement's struggle for equality- a contribution which should not be neglected.

Black women remained concentrated in mainly low paid, low status occupation and sectors and continued to be exploited as a source of cheap labour. In Britain, the principle source of information on racial equality was the Labour Force Survey by ethnic origin, but the lack of accurate data on black women made it increasingly difficult to determine the true consequences of the economic position and the impact of social and economic policies on them. They were over represented in cleaning, hotel and catering, and in home working, and very often they were exploited and unfairly remunerated. She added that the rise of nationalism and racism and attacks on black people in Europe all required decisive action by a strong trade union Movement.

The second day of the Conference was very useful with black people continue to urge both the unions and Labour Party to address the situation of Black people in Britain and Europe. Dr Dipak Ray opened the second day of the Conference. He said that the theme of the day was Black Workers' Rights in Europe 1992, an issue which had dominated the race equality agenda of the trade union Movement for some time now. The TUC had hailed a Conference in 1992, Freedom of Movement and Race Equality in June of last year and at the 1990 Congress a General Council Statement on Racism and Immigration was adopted. Pauline Green MEP_told us that the Conference was taking place in her own European constituency on London North where the large black community was concerned about race equality implications of 1992. She spoke of the rising tide of racism and fascism sweeping across Europe as we approached 1992. In electoral terms this meant far- right, racist and fascist MEPs elected to the European Parliament. Over seven million people had voted for openly racist or fascist candidates in the last European Parliamentary elections. Behind these electoral successes lay a rising number of race attacks and incidents of racial harassment across the member states. Pauline then turned to the responses of the European Parliament to the increase in racism. She spoke of the findings of the European Parliament Committee of Inquiry into racism and xenophobia chaired by Glyn Ford MEP, which had the active support of the British Labour Group of MEP's.

Report Back on the 4 Workshops: Black Workers' Rights in Europe 1992:

Delegates wanted to see a stronger commitment ion the Social Charter to race equality. Given the minimal reference to race equality in the

Charter it was very important for the TUC and unions to give effect to the Social Charter in any way they could- especially in campaigning for building race equality legislation. The EC Social Action Programme also had to feature a commitment to tackling race equality legislation more effectively. Delegates also raised the question of unions in the UK raising race issues with their European trade union counterparts. The following points on which delegates felt the TUC should address and campaign. emerged from the four workshops:

- Individual unions had to take up the issues with their own black members and overall membership.

- The TUC and trade unions had to continue cooperation and links with the European Parliament and the European Parliamentary Labour Party in their activities on racism and the rise in fascism

- Delegates were concerned that in the rush to take up this issue, the issue of domestic racism may be marginalised even further by unions.

- Delegates asked about funding from the European Commission and European bodies which could be released for use by black trade unionists in this country.

- Delegates asked if TUC information on 1992 and race equality could be made more readily available to black trade unionists.

- The question of wider networks of black groups was raised, with a view to unions getting in touch with organised groups of black workers in Europe and black trade unionists.

- The question of trade union assistance for black Britons suffering from racism in Europe, while for example being detained at airports, was raised.

- It was stressed that in individual unions at branch, regional and national levels should give more attention to the issue.

The 1992 TUC Black Workers Conference Report

The 1992 conference repeated much of the concerns of the 1991 TUCBWC. Around 170 delegates attended from thirty unions and five TUC regions. Demand for places far outstripped the capacity of the venue in contrast to previous years. The conference was chaired by four members of the Race Relations Committee, Gloria Mills, Dipak Ray, Bob Purkiss and Winston Brandt. Eight General Council Members, including the Chair of the Committee attended the conference. The conference was based on keynote speeches and debates around two themes:

i. Saturday, 8th February - Black Workers and Trade Union Organisations

ii. Sunday, 9th February - Europe 1992: Race Equality, Nationality and Immigration.

Full documentation was also provided, including a launch copy of a Report "Black Workers' in Trade Unions"; "TUC guidance notes on Black Women and Trade Unions"; "Race Monitoring of Unions"; "Membership, Union Rules Against Racism, Racial" and "Harassment in Local Authority Housing: A guide for Trade Unionists."

On the evening of Friday February 7, Bill Morris welcomed delegates to the Conference and was joined by Ken Gill and Joe Abrahams, Deputy Chair of the CRE, who both spoke briefly. The CRE hosted a reception for delegates.

The first session of the Conference on Black Workers and Trade Union Organisation was opened by Ken Gill who clarified the general council position on the status of the TUC Black Workers' Conference. He accepted "That only a minority of union had democratic structure for black workers in place. While some were close to this position, there was a need for more unions to have adequate structures to ensure that the conference was truly representative. The increasing interests in and importance of, the conference would be reflected in the recommendations of the Race Relations Committee to the General Council on the future of the conference. The Race Relations Committee would be informed by the debate at the conference. Black members demanded adequate representation by the union, as well as organisational structures which would allow the views of black trade unionist to be heard. That was the thrust of 1990 TUC Congress Resolution on Black Trade Unionists." In questions to Ken Gill, delegates sought further clarification on the status of the Conference. The general concern in the question focused on the points raised in the 1991 Congress Resolution "Black Trade Unionists", and in particular the section of the resolution calling for a conference similar to the TUC Women's Conference, which discussed motions. In response, Ken Gill reiterated that "The future status of the conference would be discussed by the General Council following at the April meeting of the Race Relations Committee which would consider the matter in the light of the discussion at the conference."

Gloria Mills chaired the morning session and after outlining various debates and discussions and the changes black workers were seeking, she introduced Bill Morris who identified the main priorities which needed to be addressed in the 1990s. In a wide ranging speech he looked at the discrimination facing black people in the UK, and the increasing divisions in society over the past twelve years which had made matters worse for black communities. He argued that despite the division and disadvantage, black people were not passive victims- they were resilient and active in tackling the problems. There were increasingly symbols of success in the black community, which gave inspiration to all black people. However, there was a long way to go. This was particularly the case in trade unions where effective black representation was crucial.

Many of us spoke and expressed our frustration at the lack of progress some unions had made in developing structures which would give members a genuine "voice" within trade union. Most contributions focused firmly on the status of the conference. There was recognition that the conference status had increased, but there were calls for an opportunity to debate resolutions and to make recommendations to the General Council. Contributions of delegates also revealed progress in some unions in developing black structures, while other delegates complained that they had experienced difficulties in getting their union to address black issues properly.

The Saturday afternoon session was preceded by a statement read out by John Edmonds on behalf of the six General Council members the presented at the Conference- Bill Morris, Clive Brooke, Donna Covey, Peter Lenahan, Jean Geldart and John Edmonds. Committee chair had had to leave the conference before lunch for another engagement. The statement read:

> "Six General Council members listened to the debate this morning. We heard the enthusiasm but we also heard of the frustration. We heard a clear expression of opinion about the role of the Black Workers' Conference in the future, and about the development of proper structures for black workers in trade unions. We will ensure that these two messages are forcibly expressed to the General Council of the TUC. Our view is that the first step should be the creation of annual Black Workers' Conference, with the opportunity to debate resolutions and to make recommendations to the General Council. We also believe that the TUC should encourage all affiliated unions to establish effective arrangements that give black workers and independent vive in their unions. The TUC should take the lead in ensuring that the best systems developed by black workers in particular unions are used as a basis for TUC recommendations to every union.
>
> These measures will be the best means of keeping faith not only with the words but also with the spirit of the resolution passed by the TUC in Glasgow last September."

Glyn Ford, Leader of the European Parliamentary Labour Party gave the final speech which described the report of the European Parliamentary Committee of Enquiry into Racism and Xenophobia, of which he was the Chair. He argued that "Many of the warnings given in the report were increasingly relevant, with organised fascist and racist activity widespread in Europe and with far-right electoral success in many EC countries. There had also been an acute increase in organised racist attacks. He argued that the recommendations of his report needed to be implemented now more the ever, if there was to be any check on the rise of fascism and racism."

The conference concluded with calls for unions to do more on the question and to get involved with wider anti-racist movements including the Anti-Racist Alliance, and for unions to take the issue of immigration rights seriously.

A First for Black Workers 7-9 May 1993

The 1993 TUCBWC was a historic occasion. It was the first of its kind, a motion based conference demanded by black workers and organised by the TUC. The conference held on the 7-9 May 1993 at Congress House, marked the 125th anniversary of the TUC and set the agenda for future black workers' conferences. Delegates were drawn from all over the country and numerous unions. Some of these unions did not practice self-organisation and some sent white delegates as spokespeople for black workers. These black trade union members felt this to be acceptable, but the majority of others did not. When the time came to vote for black representation conference voted unanimously for black delegates only. Black members felt strongly that they can represent and speak for themselves.

The TUC Race Relations Committees' report was accepted on Friday and Conference moved towards discussing motions. Delegates participated fully in debates and exchanged a great deal of information. When the time came to discuss self-organisation, delegates from those unions where a black self-organisation was not in existence had to be persuaded about the value of self-organisation. I played a major role in highlighting and explaining that black self-organisation was a necessary part of the trade union agenda. The debates were passionate but rational and black delegates took a decisive decision to have a black delegates only Conference.

During Conference several messages of support were read out from various leading trade unionists and the Conference was also attended by the President and the General Secretary of the TUC as well as speakers from France, Spain, Africa and Canada. Speakers from the Bursall strikers in Birmingham and Jackie Burnett-Pitt, a NALGO delegation member (cousin to the murdered Stephen Lawrence) both of whom received a standing ovation. Conference also had a minutes silence for Stephen Lawrence and for other black people who have died as a result of racist violence.

Other motions discussed included, Racial Harassment, Europe, Asylum Bill, Education and Employment and issues related to Health and Safety. Finally on Sunday, within the completion of the motions in the background, delegates got together in groups to discuss self-organisation in detail and how to achieve this practise. There has been a TUCBWC every year since 1993 and I attended every one of them and made passionate as well as amusing speeches.

Decline of the trade union movement

I joined the National Association of Teachers in Further and Higher Education (NATFHE) in 1990 and joined the National Executive Committee in 1999 after many years of active involvement supporting and building up the union's anti-racist strategies and structures as well as its ability to service all members regardless of race, gender or status. I served as Chair of the National Black Members Committee, the Equality Committee and several other national and regional committees since 1990. My involvement continued un-interrupted when NATFHE merged with the Association of University Teachers (AUT) in 2007 to form the UCU. My involvement with the National Executive, and several national committees continued as well as my work with the TUC and several committees as a representative from the UCU. I was also editor of the UCU

National Newsletter for the National Black Members Standing Committee and the Anti-Casualisation Committee for many years up to 2014, and hopefully beyond. At 71 years of age I am still involved in the National Executive Committee and several UCU and TUC national committees. I am also involved in several Regional TUC committees in the South East Region. I am presently the President of the Bedfordshire and Buckinghamshire Association of Trades Councils, vice President of the Luton TUC and Branch Secretary for my local UCU Adult Learning Branch.

I get quite frustrated at times when I see a consistently rising number of workers within the British workforce, which stands at over 30 million and yet the level of trade union members is still only half of what it was in 1979; 35 years ago. The number of trade unions has declined substantially, due to mergers for economic reasons and trade union density stands at around 20 per cent of the workforce. For me the unions are the only real and effective champion of the workers, even though they have failed to defend the pay and conditions of the members since the start of the recession in 2008. Not only have workers' pay declined by nearly 20 per cent in real purchasing power due to rising prices; year on year pay rises well below inflation; cuts in the social wage such as benefits and welfare support; austerity policies that is likely to remain for a further decade due to the over £1 trillion debt burden within the British economy and unemployment remaining at between 6 and 8 per cent for years to come. It hurts me to know that I have given so much to the trade union movement and instead of substantial gains the entire workforce apart from the top 20 per cent earners; the other 80 per cent are facing real problems in maintaining their living standards. In fact over 5 million workers in employment are living on or, near the poverty level with almost 4 million children living in impoverished households. Full-time work has declined, whilst part-time and zero hour contracts are growing as well as rising poverty amongst people who are actually in work.

As a pensioner and a member of the National Pension Convention National Committee I do my best to support and defend the interest of the 12 million pensioners in Britain. Many of whom are suffering due to inadequate state pension; lack of savings; cost of heating, lighting and council tax, as well as massive increases in cost of living, elderly care and reductions in social and community services due to cuts in local government funding, by central government. These cuts have much of the social and community services local government has built over the last 40 years in the provision of elderly care, community support and social services, libraries, day centres, home help, sheltered accommodation and many other services. The continuation of the austerity measures imposed by the Conservative and Liberal Democrat Coalition government since 2010 will continue, regardless of the changes in government as all three main political parties in Britain are committed to the neo-liberal capitalist agenda. This agenda has already created a political class in or out of government that has ensured rising inequality in Britain since the 1970's; growing national debt; rising power of the large corporations; steady increase in the cost of living and an increasingly divided Britain.

It is a sad indictment on the 21st Century that half of the world population are in dire poverty. That the trade union movement that has worked so hard over centuries to combat insecurity, inhumanity, exploitation, and unfairness at the workplace, and in turn gave workers some measure of rights and dignity at work; protection from serious physical and psychological abuses and inequalities have been singled out by governments in Britain the Western world for such harsh attacks. Working people depend on a labour movement strong enough to maintain some balance to the capitalist economy, in order to maintain some fairness, security and essential benefits such as holidays with pay, time off for key family events and civic duties, and compensation for wrong doing by employers. It is essential for all workers to join a union and to support each other against cruel, uncaring and greedy employers who put profits before the very people that create it. Tens of millions of people in Britain and Europe who enjoy the benefits and rewards they have taken for granted should be mindful that men and women have made bitter sacrifices over centuries win decent pay and conditions. Many small and medium size employers are on the whole far more caring, compassionate and supportive of their workers, it is the greedy corporations with their stooges in government that are anti-union and seeks to squeeze every bit of energy from workers, whilst doing everything to keep the wages bill down.

Workers gave been in the forefront of every bit of change and progress in the history of human kind as it is through labour that profits are generated, and it is the same labour that build things, invent and discover new areas of science, medicine, transport and communication. Corporations use profits from labour, money borrowed from people who have saved, or from the public purse to invest in making greater and often excessive profits. Politicians and the media honour and recognise the rich and powerful who accumulated their wealth through manipulating the surplus value which, was created by workers. No democracy can be claimed to be fair, just and equitable if workers, who are the wealth creators and their unions are subjected to attacks and persecution for simply seeking to secure a fairer share of the fruits of their labour. Modern society and its achievements in a; spheres of life is a testimony to the strength and courage of labour. British workers and the government they supported in 1945 was responsible for creating the NHS, public services and the welfare state, much to the opposition of the rich and powerful. Equal pay and equality for women and black workers, as well as the minimum wage were all progresses by the unions even though the rich opposed them.

All workers ought to be proud of the trade unions and those people and institutions that made so many sacrifices over so many years to protect and support people at work and those that cannot work for whatever reason as well as those who have retired. Governments must reflect these basic essentials that mark a civilised, progressive and democratic and fair society. Contrary to what the media, corporations and some governments would like us to believe, unions are not narrow, self-seeking groups. In fact they are on the whole patriotic, progressive and spend a lot of time and resources to make society more humane and fair through collective bargaining and dealing with millions of grievances in order to keep workplaces functional. There are of course extremists in every organisation and institution that can give such organisations a bad name, and unions are no different, when individuals or small groups choose to ignore the rules. I have spent many years of my working life exposing the wrong doing of unions and workers and worked very hard to understand and respect diversity, equality, fairness and Justice. I hope I have given my best to my fellow workers and their families, so we can all have a better life. I would like to leave you with a quote from Dr Martin Luther King, who lost his life in Memphis to a gunman, where he went to support the refuge collectors in their grievance with their employer, on 4 April 1968 - "In our society it is murder, psychologically, to deprive a man of a job or an income. You are in substance saying to that man that he has no right to exist. You are in a real way depriving him of life, liberty, and the pursuit of happiness, denying in his case the very creed of his society."

Chapter 16:

Employment tribunal years

An injury to one is an injury to all

"The only effective answer to organized greed is organized labour".—
Thomas Donahue

I was nominated to the Employment Tribunal (ET), formerly Industrial Tribunal
(IT) service in 1979 after the government invited the Trades Union Council (TUC)
and the Confederation of British Industry (CBI) to nominate more women and
black members to sit on ET, as there were no black members and very few women
in post within the national ET framework. Such nominations were very sought
after as there was a very generous daily fee, plus travelling and subsistence and
no specific retirement age. This was a prestigious public appointment and the
employer was the Department of Employment, later the Department for Justice.
The ET consisted of a panel of three people managed by an experienced and legally
qualified Chair and two lay members, one from the list of CBI and the other from
the TUC list of nominees. Each of the three members that made up the ET had
equal vote in deciding the outcome of each case brought to the Tribunal by an
applicant or multiple applicants. The employer was regarded as the respondent
and the applicant, or worker was identified as the applicant. A single case could
last from less than an hour to several months. The Tribunal has the same status as
a court of law, but in some areas less formal. Tribunals are seen as industrial courts
as opposed to civil or criminal courts. Tribunal judgements are subjected to appeal
in the higher judicial courts and even the European Court of Justice. I served on
the ET service for over 30 years until I was compulsory retired in 2013, on my 70th
birthday. I have many pleasant, sad, memorable and lasting memories of my years
on ET, some of which I will reveal in the following pages.

The ET service has changed significantly since I joined as a member, as employment law by the British and European Parliament expanded and became increasingly complex since the 1970's. The present government has introduces numerous changes within employment that has shifted the balance further away from workers who wished to make a formal complaint to an ET. The government's case for introducing these changes since 2010 has been identified as making industrial disputes between employees and employers less cumbersome and expensive, and at the same time to give employers, especially smaller businesses more protection against frivolous and vexatious complaints. They have extended the qualifying period before a worker can claim employment rights except for cases of discrimination or victimisation from one to two years and have introduced costs against applicants for registering a case and if the application is unsuccessful. There are also many other changes that has reduced the number of applications, levels of compensation awards, Chairs of tribunals sitting alone on a large number of cases and changes in the management and determination of cases. Being in mind that there is no legal aid for applicants and most of them have very little or no resources to engage legal representation, whilst employers are generally covered for legal representation as part of their liability insurance and other arrangements, the burden of financing any complaint as well as any costs is borne entirely by the applicant. This arrangement is far from fair equitable or acceptable in the 21st Century. Workers are at the mercy of the employer; as employers are in a better position to defend their selves financially and in every other way, because of greater resources available to them.

Although the world of work has changed a great deal from the days of the industrial revolution, followed by the First World War, the depression of the 1930's and the gains made by workers after the Second World War (1939 – 1945), there are still some employers in the 21st Century that can make life difficult for workers. Over the last forty years employment protection legislation has introduced measures to protect the health and safety of employees at work and to introduce on incremental basis legislation to combat discrimination, victimisation and unfair practices at work for all workers. Special legislation has been introduced to deal with gender, race, age, religion and belief, sexual orientation and disability discrimination. Workers through their trade unions and the close relationship between the unions and the Labour Party has created a comprehensive framework since 1974 to protect workers and to promote equal pay for work of equal value, maternity and paternity leave, protection from unfair dismissal and a wide range of employment rules, regulations and advisory services. These rights and responsibilities at work were fought for by workers and their unions, with the employer invariably opposed to any extension of rights at work as they inevitably impose additional responsibilities and duties on the employer, especially within the private sector.

Whilst the private sector has been on balance more likely to oppose any additional employment rights, the public sector which employers over 6 million people, or I in every 5 of the working population in Britain tends to be less opposed to such changes. In recent years starting with Mrs Thatcher's historical victory as Prime Minister in 1979, the tide of trade union growth and power has been gradually eroded. Between 1979 and 1999 trade union influence on governments as well as their membership declined, even though the workforce continued to increase year on year due to immigration and population growth. The areas where unions were most powerful, such as the large nationalised industries, including telecommunications, transport, coal mining. Iron and steel, ship building, health and social care, motor manufacturing, and other key industries had very high trade union membership and activism compared to the small and medium sized private companies, where unionisation was relatively low. The larger companies were more likely to be unionised than the small businesses as it was functional for employers and unions to enter into agreements that on the whole ensured relative peaceful industrial relations. Thatcherism and New Labour that followed on from the 18 years of consecutive rule and lasted until 2010 did very little to promote the principles of trade unions. In fact the policies they pursued which included further deregulation, privatisation of public services, and exclusion of the trade unions from playing their role within a tripartite system of governance that operated between government, employers and unions. As a consequence, trade unions has been seen by the majority of present day workers as no longer relevant, especially amongst younger workers. Much of the gains made by the Labour government between 1999 and 2010 have been around the area of equal opportunities and ant-discrimination at work has been substantially reduced since the coalition government took office in 2010.

I saw and participated in many of the politically motivated changes brought about by governments and the battles by unions to maintain their influence, power and membership since 1974. The fortunes of the unions and industrial relations in Britain fluctuate as the cyclical economic booms and slumps influence the behaviour of employers and unions. A trade union tends to make gains during periods of boom and labour scarcity, whilst employers tend to have the balance of power during slumps and recession as well as a surplus of labour. Governments, being a major employer of 1 in every 5 of the workforce are conscious of keep labour cost to the minimum. Conservative governments have proven to be more sympathetic to the private sector than the public sector and have always more likely to support employers in reducing labour costs and increasing productivity. The current recession that has brought about massive austerity measures has impacted on the employment practices and industrial relations in Britain. Most independent observer would accept that the scale of justice has been tipped on the side of the employer.

Employment Tribunals started off quite informal in the early days, when workers themselves or their trade unions would represent their case on the ET. Many workers used their union or the local Law Centre, Citizen Advice Bureau, Unemployed Workers Centres, a friend or local solicitor to represent them, on cases that may last from a few hours to a few days. Many cases were settled through the Arbitration, Conciliation Advisory Service (ACAS), part of the Civil Service resource to avoid cases going to ET by seeking to settle the case between the employer and the claimant. The majority of cases were either settled by ACAS, or through compromise agreements between the employer and the employee, and only a minority of cases reached the ET. Even then many cases were withdrawn for a variety of reasons and the ET had no involvement with them.

Employment statistics

ET statistics (covering the period from 1 April 2012 to 31 March 2013) published by the Ministry of Justice show a rise (3 per cent) in the number of Employment Tribunal (ET) claims, with an overall total of 191,541 claims. The largest sum awarded by the Tribunal in 2012-13 was £387,472 and was awarded in a disability discrimination claim. High awards were also made in unfair dismissal and sex discrimination claims. The highest unfair dismissal award of £236,147 is in excess of the statutory cap of £74,200 but remember that this cap does not apply where the unfair dismissal is for whistle blowing or for raising certain health and safety issues. The number of costs awards made by Tribunals in 2012/2013 has fallen from 1,410 last year to 651. The Average award for successful unfair dismissal cases was £10,127, race discrimination, £8,945, sex discrimination £10,552, Disability discrimination £16,320, Religious discrimination £6,137, sexual orientation £10,757 and age discrimination £8079. This evidence is contrary to the common misconceptions that employees are irresponsible, greedy, frivolous or vexatious. The success rates for discrimination cases are well below 7 per cent on average, so the overwhelmingly majority of cases go against the claimant. Even in unfair dismissal cases the success rate for claimants is less than 10 per cent. Employment law is a risky business and the overwhelmingly majority of workers cannot afford legal representation and there is no legal aid for employment cases.

On 13 March, the UK government published the latest Employment Tribunal statistics for the October to December 2013 period. Significantly, this is the first full quarter of statistics since Employment Tribunal fees were introduced on 29 July 2013. Depending on the type of claim, it can now cost employees up to £1,200 to bring a claim before an Employment Tribunal, and the penalties could be substantially if the claimant lose their case and have to pay costs on top. The impact of the changes brought about by the coalition government can be seen in the headline statistics for three months October 2013 – December 2013. There were 79 per cent fewer claims received (9,801) in October to December 2013 compared to the claims received (45,710) in October to December 2012. The government extended the period for unfair dismissal claim from one to two years in April 2012; there were 75 per cent fewer claims received in October to December 2013 compared to the claims received (38,963) in July to September 2013; 63 per cent fewer age discrimination claims, 58 per cent fewer disability discrimination claims, 57 per cent fewer race discrimination claims, 77 per cent fewer sex discrimination claims, and 65 per cent fewer unfair dismissal claims received in October to December 2013 compared to the claims received in October to December 2012. Of course, the fall in claims may not necessarily be entirely connected to the introduction of Employment Tribunal fees, the burden of costs if the claimant's case is lost, but also to the perception that the balance of power lies with the employer and in many cases the employee is unlikely to belong to a union or have access to representation by charities and the voluntary sector due to closures of voluntary sector organisations. However, it is not all good news for employers. Under the 2013 Employment Tribunal rules, the Employment Tribunal now has the power to require an employer to pay a successful claimant his or her tribunal fee where the claim is successful. This is separate to any compensation that may be awarded to the successful claimant. Furthermore, from 6 April 2014, the Employment Tribunal will have the power to order a losing employer to pay a financial penalty to the government of up to £5,000 in certain circumstances.

Justice for sale

On many occasions I was emotionally upset when adjudicating on ET cases. Not only did I witness discrimination against people because of the gender, race, disability, age, sexual orientation or religion and belief by employers and their witnesses, but also from some members of the Employment Tribunals. Many tribunal members and judges are successful middle class and university graduates who have had very little experience or personal knowledge of the dynamics in the workplace. All of the legal experts sitting on ET as Judges are committed to ensure fairness and justice on ET cases, but the fact that they have to interpret the law and to decide who is telling the truth and who to believe can be quite interesting. These Judges are very careful not to take risks and can often take the side of the employer especially when the case is finely balanced. They know that an employer is more likely to appeal against a judgement against them as they generally have the resources and contacts as well as the inclination to do so, whilst an employee is far more reluctant to appeal for the opposite reasons. Too many successful appeals against a Judge's decision by an employer could raise serious questions on the credibility of the Judge in question. Equally no Judge would relish the label of being biased against claimants. ET cases have become increasingly complicated, lengthily and expensive as many employers, and a number of unions as well as employees are using top barristers and solicitors to represent them because they have either private insurance cover, or lucky to have their own resources, or convince the union to take up their case. Most unions do not have sufficient financial resources to take on even a dozen of actual ET cases each year. It is always sad to see so many claimants sitting in the ET representing themselves or being represented by friends who have no legal training or experience of ET. They do their best to plead their cases with the very limited knowledge, experience, skills, confidence, records and documents available to them without referring to other cases, precedents, points of law or organised witness statements. Their ability to present their own case and worse still to cross examine the employer and their witnesses is also extremely limited and they would often end up in tears; becomes quiet or aggressive; give up; overwhelmed by the whole process or simply dry up and unable to cope.

Cases are won not on necessarily on the merit of the case, but how the case is presented. Discrimination cases are often complex and difficult to prove as no employer will own up to being a sexist, racist or homophobic. They would defend themselves using the best arguments and legal representatives they can secure. The ET have to infer from the evidence provided as to whether the employer was able to prove that on the balance of probabilities they were telling the truth and that they had not discriminated against the employee. In the case where the employee is claiming discrimination they have to provide the evidence and persuade the ET that they had acted within the law, by bringing their claim in time and their evidence is relevant and within the period in question; and that they have provided sufficient facts and information by which the ET can infer certain acts have or, have not taken place. ET are properly constituted industrial courts, even though the proof, does not have to be beyond all reasonable doubts, but on the balance of probabilities. I have seen so many cases where a disabled person trying hard to represent themselves, conduct their case, preparing their documents and statements with little or no help from anyone, and have to compete with a well-resourced employer and their legal representation as well as the company in-house legal and human resource department and a list of current employees will and paid time off to give evidence. The employee have no such resources and although the ET will often try very hard to see that justice is seen to be done, especially when the claimant is representing themselves, by explaining the process to the claimant and help them to clarify their case as well as assisting with framing some questions to the employer and their witnesses, this help is nevertheless very limited. Not all ET will go out of their way to help a claimant, even with some basic information on rules, procedures and presentation, in case they are perceived by the employer or their representatives as being biased in favour of the claimant. I have seen many claimants with mental and physical disabilities struggling to represent themselves and feeling helpless in the face of challenges and detailed questioning from the employer and their representatives. Many of these claimants have suffered a great deal, having lost their jobs and livelihood, in deep state of financial, mental, personal, family and other distress trying to compete with a legal expert within an ET environment, with invariably little success. They do not only have to bring the case to the ET, but must be able to convince the ET that their version of the events and facts are more credible that the employer's. I frequently left the ET office in tears and having to spend time in the office, or more often in my car before setting off on my journey home. I have been upset for weeks because I have seen cases being lost by the employee when it was clear to me that they deserved to win.

On many occasions I was convinced that the claimant had proven their case, but the majority of the three ET panel members including the Judge disagreed with me. The ET structure allows a majority decision to prevail and for the minority judgement to be recorded in the judgement. During my years at the ET I held the record for the number of minority decisions I have recorded. What is even more interesting is that on several of these cases, where I gave a minority judgement in favour of the claimant, I was proven to be right at a subsequent Appeal Hearing. I always gave a minority decision if I cannot persuade my other two colleagues to support my views on the case. I have had many successes in persuading the other colleagues to support my views after long and sometimes quite challenging discussions in private. Most of my colleagues would be very reluctant to disagree with the Judge and would go along with the Judge's decision even though they may not agree. Some Judges would try to pressurise and even bully me to support their views as they disliked minority judgements against them. I have had long delays, in concluding the discussions and agreeing on a decision; a few instances when Judges get quite angry and one Judge even threatened to lock me in his office until I decide to explain in substantial legal jargon as to why I disagreed with his judgement. His manner only changed when I informed him that I would telephone his boss, the Regional Judge to explain his behaviour. During my ET career I sat in several ET regions and offices in London, Bedford, Watford and Nottingham. I believe I gained a reputation as a "member of the awkward squad."

The areas in which I disagree with my fellow ET colleagues were on cases dealing with race, sex and disability discrimination. Until the year 2000 almost 80 per cent of ET Chairman, later changed to Judges were white middle aged legally trained upper middle class men. It was rare to sit with a woman and even much rarer to sit with a Black Judge. Over the last decades I have had the experience of sitting not only with a Black Judge but with another colleague that is also Black. We often wondered how a claimant, or an employer, whether they are white or black feels about an all-Black ET panel, especially if the judgement goes against them. I have even given minority decisions against Black Judges and an all-Black Panel. These colleagues would plead with me to go along with their judgements, but I never compromise my position regardless of the race or gender of the Judge or panel. Most dissenting panel members would change their minds and agree with the Judge, especially when the Judge asks them to submit their minority view in writing and bearing in mind there is a need to focus on the legal reasons for dissenting. For me this was not a problem, I would readily do so as I always make extensive notes and underline the key legal points as the case is being processed. I also read all the documents – up to thousands of pages – carefully, so I would readily construct my judgement in writing or ask the Judge to give me a day or two to do so when I get home to consult the reference books on case studies. Judges and panel members will always try to think and act rationally and within the legal parameters, however, they are also human beings and are subjected to some measure of prejudice, based on their own lives, culture, backgrounds, gender, race and experience. In fact the legal profession is well known for dissenting and decisions taken by lower courts are overturned by higher courts. No two cases are precisely the same and it is not unusual for three people sitting on a case may end up with different conclusions about the outcome.

Some strange Employment Tribunal incidents

I have had some very strange experience as an ET member, some of which I would like to share with you. Perhaps one of the most lasting experiences was when I disagreed with an ET Judge over quite a serious case which involved an African man who was accused of a very serious assault on a vulnerable mental health patient under his care, and was subsequently dismissed from his job. He was giving his evidence and every couple of minutes he would break into tears and sobbed profusely. In situations such as this, the Judge would normally adjourn the hearing for a few minutes to allow the witness to have a drink of water, stretch their legs and allow them to relax, before continuing with their evidence or cross examination. I looked at the Judge after this witness was in some difficulty composing his-self and was expecting the Judge to adjourn for a few minutes. This happened on at least two further occasions and on the following occasion I whispered to the Judge that "it would be best for us to adjourn for a couple of minutes". The Judge ignored me. I was somewhat surprised at this response, and it brought back memories of a previous incident, a year or so earlier, with the same Judge. On this occasion I had concerns about a case involving an African claimant who I believe, at the time, was not given a fair chance to conduct his case by the Judge. The brief altercation made me feeling angry and concerned about the procedures being applied fairly to both the claimant and the respondent. However, I was not happy with the way my concerns were addressed which I later raised with the Judge in private. Regarding this latter case, I waited until the lunch break and raised my concerns with the Judge who immediately left the tribunal room, asked the other member to make a note of the incident and proceeded to make a formal complaint to the Regional Judge. The Regional Judge was someone who I had a great deal of respect for and had worked together for many years without any problem. The Regional Judge tried unsuccessfully to resolve the matter between myself and the case Judge, as I had also made a complaint to the Regional Judge to give my side of the story. Several months went by and the dispute was still unsettled despite great efforts by the Regional Judge and the National Judge who was Head of the ET service in England. There were a number of threatening letters involved, which caused my wife and I many worries and concerns. A year later, the matter was referred to the Lord Chancellor for his consideration, as it was discovered that there were no formal rules and procedures for ET members to process formal complaints between ET members themselves, and members and Judges. The National Head of the ET services, did not want to deal with the complaint as he personally knew both the Judge and me, so he referred the case to his boss: the Lord Chancellor, who could not adjudicate as he knew me personally when we were both involved in the Labour Party, on a Working Group looking at issues associated with Justice in Britain.

The matter was then referred to a High Court Judge who carried out an investigation lasting several months and produced a report which basically concluded that the ET process was a tripartite system of decision making and management of the proceedings and that the Judge should have listened to my concerns and not to assume that he had total responsibility for the management of cases, and therefore had to listen to the non-legal member. It was resolved that the ET should have recognised procedures in place to deal with internal complaints between ET members and members and Judges. After around a period of nearly two years the report was made available to all parties and rules and procedures were in place to address complaints. So, I could claim this outcome as part of my legacy to the ET service which I served for over thirty years.

The most worrying situation was when I ended up having a heart attack in the ET room in London, a few minutes before I was due to sit on a case. I felt ill walking the half a mile from St Pancras Railway Station to the ET Office in Upper Woburn Place, a couple of minutes' walk from Euston Station. I felt severe chest pain after leaving the train, but managed to make it to the ET office. I informed the Judge that I was feeling unwell and I gave her my wife's workplace telephone number in case there was a need to call her. The next thing I vaguely recall was me lying flat on my back, on the floor and the Judge holding me down. I was having difficulty breathing and some people who were waiting for us to hear their case intervened and told the Judge that someone should call an ambulance as I was "having a heart attack". I was told later by an ET Clerk that the Judge was going to ask a first aider to escort me to the First Aid room so I could recover as the Judge wanted us to hear the case later on. Someone did call an ambulance and I was taken to The University College Hospital a couple of minutes' drive away from the ET office. I have no recollection of the journey to the hospital. Twenty four hours later the ambulance crew came to see how I was doing and we had a brief chat whilst I was sitting up in bed with various instruments attached to my body. They told me that I was "…lucky person, because another couple of minutes of delay would have been fatal." They also told me that I had "lost consciousness" and they thought I "would not survive the attack". I thanked them and the NHS for saving my life.

On another occasion I was listed to sit on a race discrimination case brought to the Tribunal, against an NHS hospital where I had served on the Board of Governors for many years. The nurse, a Black woman was represented by her trade union and the hospital by a qualified legal representative. There were several senior hospital staff present in the ET room, including the Chief Executive who was a qualified nurse and several witnesses who were also qualified medical practitioners. The NHS representative informed the Tribunal Judge that they had concerns about me sitting in judgement on the case as I was known to several witnesses including the Chief Executive. This sort of challenge is not uncommon within ET as there could be conflict of interests that may affect someone's judgement because of prior knowledge of the people involved in the case. The Judge gave the employer to choice of continuing the case with me as one of the three people hearing the case, or adjourned the case for a hearing some months later. The Chief Executive of the Hospital agreed to proceed with the case and within a few minutes of the hearing I felt ill. I informed the Judge that I was unwell; he then adjourned the case for a few minutes and asked the parties to leave the ET room. My condition got worse and the Judge asked the ET Clerk to find me a spare room so I could rest for a few minutes. I fell asleep on the large couch and woke up about half an hour later to be told that the case has been adjourned anyway. I was also informed by the Clerk that the senior nurse whose case we were dealing with and the and the other hospital employees did not offer to check me out, or suggest that an ambulance should be called to take me to the hospital, less than a mile away. I later drove home, but stopped on my way at the Accident and Emergency Unit at the very hospital in question, and was diagnosed with food poisoning, caused by a fish supper I had the night before the Tribunal.

I really hope for the sake of justice, fairness and rights of workers that the next government will redress this dreadful imbalance and unfairness within the ET system. Far too many workers are denied their natural and legal right to justice, simply because the present government made up of Conservatives and Liberal Democrats have decided to reduce the responsibilities and duties, placed on employers through responsible and essential employment protection and rights at work. The changes resulting in the delays in qualifying for employment rights; having to deposit fees and to lose such fees if the claimant loses their case; compulsory arbitration; reductions in compensatory awards and changes in the tribunal rules and procedures to allow Judges sitting alone, instead of a panel of three, on unfair dismissal cases, in order to save the cost within the ET services cannot be justified in my view. The odds against the claimant looks pretty grim with falling number of complaints being submitted to ET and many complainants withdrawing their case due to fear of financial penalties, if they lose cannot be justified in a so-called civilised, fair, or equal society.

This government has implemented a whole range of legislation that affects people on low wages, benefits and without savings adversely. Britain is amongst the top five most unequal society in the developed world. The poor has been getting poorer and the richer, richer under this government. Cuts in benefits, the welfare state, pay and conditions have created a situation where over 5 million people in work are living in poverty and are relying on some form of welfare payments and benefits for their survival. Millions of children are growing up in impoverished households, where nearly 1 million people are relying of free food from food banks to supplement their food intake. This is the most uncaring, class ridden, divisive, ideologically motivated, and anti-working class government, of the rich, and for the rich, I have experienced in all my 53 years as a worker in England.

Part 4

Chapter 17:

Guyana - My Ancestral Home

Guiana – land of many waters

Guyana, formerly British Guiana, lies on the east shoulder of the South America continent. It borders with Suriname to the East, Venezuela to the West, Brazil to the South, and the might Atlantic Ocean to the North. The Atlantic sea coast stretches some 270 miles to the north and connects with the massive Demerara, Berbice, Essequibo and Corentyne Rivers. Around 90 per cent of Guyana's 750,000 people live along the flat coastal belt which lies up to five feet below sea level at high tide, and along the banks of the main rivers for up to 40 miles in land.

Guyana has a land space of 214,969 square kilometre (83,000 square miles), compared to, Suriname with 163,820 square kilometre, Venezuela, with 912,100 square kilometre and Brazil with 8,511,963 square kilometre. Guyana is over eighteen times the size of Jamaica, and almost the size of the United Kingdom of Great Britain and Northern Ireland with 244,100 square kilometres. It is drained by several large rivers including the Amazon, Orinico, Demerara, Berbice, Essequibo and Corentyne. The population of Guyana in 2013 was 739,903 – less than one million, and only 5 per cent of the land space developed. There are probably as many Guyanese and their descendants living abroad, mainly in North America and Britain than those living in Guyana. A good Guyanese friend once said to me "there are only two kinds of people in this world; those who are Guyanese and those who wish they were." I left my country as an economic migrant fifty-three years ago and I still feel more Guyanese than British.

Guyana had been peopled for thousands of years before Europeans became aware of the area some six hundred years ago. The first people to reach Guyana were nomads who made their way gradually from Asia, through Central and South America some 35,000 years ago. Although great civilizations later arose in the Americas, the structure of the native Amerindian society in South America and the Guianas remained relatively simple. At the time of Christopher Columbus's voyages, Guyana's inhabitants were divided into two main groups, the Arawak along the coast and the Carib in the interior. There were also Wario and Taino people in the area. It has been suggested by historians that the Arawak and Carib in the South American gradually migrated northward, and settled in the Caribbean islands.

The word 'Guiana' probably comes from the Arawak words wai ana which means "(land of) many waters". Guyana's first sighting by Europeans was by Alonzo de Ojeda and Amerigo Vespucci in 1499. Christopher Columbus did not visit Guyana until his third voyage of discovery which started in 1498. The coastline of the country was first traced and settled by Spanish sailors in 1499 and 1500; and again during the 16th and early 17th centuries, the search for the fabled city of El Dorado with lots of gold encouraged explorers like Sir Walter Raleigh who explored the region in 1595.

The Dutch began exploring and settling in Guyana in the late 16th Century, it is very likely that they encountered some small settlements of Spaniards, followed by the British. The Europeans began trading with the Amerindian peoples upriver. The first known Dutch expedition to coast of Guyana, led by Captain A Cabeliau, took place in 1598. They established their first settlement on the Pomeroon River in 1581. The settlers were evicted by Spaniards and Indians, probably in1596. The evicted settlers retired to Kyk- over-all (Look over everything) on the Essequibo River, where the Dutch West Indian Company established a fort in 1616-1621 in what they called County of Essequibo.

In 1627 a settlement was founded in the Berbice River by Abraham van Pere, a merchant, and held by him under a licence (issued 12 July 1627) from the Company. Some historians believe that van Pere was a member of a Portuguese

Jewish refugee family. He sent 40 men and 20 boys to settle at Nassau, about 50 miles upriver. Van Pere had a good knowledge of the territory since he had apparently been trading with the Amerindians of the area for a few years before 1627. He later applied his trading skills when he was contracted by Zeeland Chamber to supply goods from Europe to the Dutch settlements in Essequibo.

At Nassau, where Fort Nassau was built, the settlers planted crops and traded with Amerindians. African slaves were introduced shortly after the settlement was established to cultivate sugar and cotton. The situation was very peaceful until 1665 when the settlement was attacked by a few prospective English settlers who were forced to leave by the other European colonists. Between 1675 and 1716 all the cultivations on lands in Guiana took place upstream. Finding the soil on the coastlands more fertile, the settlers gradually moved down river. In 1741 English settlers from Barbados and Antigua began to build river dams and drainage sluices in the Essequibo River Islands, and later tried to reclaim the fertile tidal marshes in Demerara. Until 1804, there were estates Sandy Point and Kierfield, now forgotten, on the seaward side of the present seawall of Georgetown. As attempts at settling inland failed, the Europeans were forced to settle on the coast in the mid-1700s, where they created plantations worked by African slaves. The main crops were coffee, cotton and sugar, the last of which soon become the main crop. The soil quality was poor, however. The slaves, led by Cuffy, (Guyana's national hero), revolted in 1763 in what became known as the Berbice slave revolt.

The British rule in Guyana

The first English attempt at settlement in this area was made in 1604 by Captain Charles Leigh on the Oyapock River but this attempt failed. A second attempt was made by Robert Harcourt in 1609. Lord Willoughby, who also had interests in Barbados, also turned his attention to Guyana, and founded a settlement in Suriname, in 1651, which was captured by the Dutch in 1667, and later recaptured by the British, it was ceded to the Dutch at the Treaty of Breda, (July 31, 1667), a treaty between England and the Dutch Republic. The Dutch was allowed to keep their control of Suriname and Britain took New York from the Dutch. Between the 16th and 19th centuries the European colonists, including the Dutch, Spanish, Germans, Belgians, France the Scandinavian countries engaged in wars with each other to share out the colonies in South, Central and North America as well as Africa and the Caribbean. In this process Guyana was controlled by different colonial powers at various times.

Britain took the region from the Dutch in 1796. The Dutch took it back in 1802, before being ousted again by the British in 1803. Immediately after the British took possession of Essequibo – Demerara and Berbice they began to implement changes in the administration of the colonies with the aim of removing the strong Dutch influence. In 1806 an Act was passed in the British Parliament to reduce the slave trade. The Abolition of the Slave Trade Act came into force on 23 March, 1807 when it received the Royal Assent, abolishing the slave trade in British colonies and preventing British ships from transporting slaves. The Act did not ban slavery; it only addressed the transportation of slaves. Slavery was officially abolished in most of the British Empire. The Slave Abolition Act received Royal Assent on 28 August 1883 and came into operation on 1 August 1834. In real terms, only slaves below the age of six were freed in the colonies. Former slaves over the age of six were re-designated as "apprentices", and their servitude was abolished in two stages; the first set of apprenticeships came to an end on 1 August 1838, while the final apprenticeships were scheduled to cease on 1 August 1840. The 1833 Act provided compensation for the slave owning British planters to the cost of the public at £20 million. Amongst the many hundreds of the recipients of this compensation were people of high social, political, economic and cultural standing, including Lords, Earls, Bishops, and government ministers. Henry Lascelles, 2nd Earl of Harewood received £26,309 for 2,554 slaves on 6 plantations and Henry Phillpotts (then the Bishop of Exeter), with three others (as trustees and executors of the will of John Ward, 1st Earl of Dudley), was paid £12,700 for 665 slaves in the West Indies. The British establishment that was at the heart of the lucrative Trans-Atlantic slave trade for over 200 were now engaged in the suppression of slave trade, which continued for many years. Many captains of the slave ships that were in danger of being captured by the Royal Navy, ordered the slaves to be thrown into the sea to reduce the fines they had to pay. Between 1808 and 1860 the West Africa Squadron captured 1,600 slave ships and freed 150,000 Africans, many of whom were resettled in the Caribbean. The slave trade was abolished in Guyana, in 1834, but this did not stop the system of plantation slavery well beyond until 1834.

The colonies of Essequibo, Demerara and Berbice were officially ceded to the United Kingdom in the Anglo - Dutch Treaty of 1814 and at the Congress of Vienna in 1815. In 1831 they were consolidated as British Guiana. A further rebellion by ten to twelve thousand slaves in Demerara in 1823 resulted in the trial and execution of thirty-three slaves and the trial and conviction of missionary John Smith. Despite the recruitment of West Indian, African and Portuguese and other European labourers, this did not help very much to ease the labour shortage of the 1830s. After the West Indian islands placed restrictions on emigration, the sugar planters in Guyana began to look further afield to obtain a large labour force. One of them, John Gladstone, the father of the British statesman, applied for permission from the Secretary of State for the Colonies to recruit Indians to serve in Guyana for a five year period of indenture. Gladstone's request was granted and he, Davidson, Barclay and Company, Andrew Colville, John and Henry Moss, all owners of sugar plantation in Guyana, made arrangements to recruit 414 Indians.

When slavery was abolished in 1834, the African Guyanese refused to work for poverty wages, and many scattered into the bush. This forced many plantations to close or consolidate their plantations. They also entered into arrangements with the East India Company to transport hundreds of thousands of indentured labourers mainly from India, but also from Portugal and China to Guyana to replace the African slaves.

The Indian connection

According to oral history, handed down to us from our maternal grandfather, who was born on the Hesperus, which sailed from India in 1838, stated that his parents had received a message informing them that his sister who was married to a man living in a village several miles away was abusive towards her. So his parents gathered a number of men from their village and they set out on bullock carts to rescue his sister. They arrived at a major cross road and were greeted by several Indian and English soldiers from the occupied British Army, who kidnapped them and forced them to march for three days before arriving at the Coast. They were then, like dozens of others who were given similar false messages were forced to put their thumbprint on a document, which stated that they had willingly agreed to sign up as indentured labourers, to work on sugar plantations for a minimum period of seven years, in various parts of Guyana and the West Indies. On completion of their seven years indenture-ship they would be entitled to a free return journey to India, if they wished to do so. All the labours were promised gainful and enjoyable employment on the sugar plantations.

Queen Victoria's accession to the British Throne on 20th June 1837 was just a year away from the beginning of indentured labours moving from India to Guyana and the Caribbean. Indian labourers along with labourers from China were necessary to replenish some of the African slaves who abandoned the plantations after the abolition of slavery in 1834 and 1840. Like slavery, indentured labourers were used to satisfy the expanding British colonisation of Guyana. Indenture-ship provided huge profits to the plantation owners and to Britain. There are several views on how the indenture-ship system started and whether Indians willingly offered themselves into such a system which was tantamount to slavery and experienced by African slaves imported from Africa since the 16th Century. Their descendants also experienced the cruelty of enslavement for centuries. The abolition of slavery led to many African Guyanese refusing to work for poverty wages, and many scattered into the bush. There were also several major rebellions and resistance by the slaver during the 19th Century in various parts of Guyana. This situation forced many British plantations to seek new sources of cheap labour from other British colonies in the Caribbean, Asia and Portugal.

Despite the recruitment of West Indian, African, Portuguese and other European labourers, this did not help very much to ease the labour shortage of the 1830s. After the West Indian islands placed restrictions on emigration, the sugar planters in Guyana began to look further afield to obtain labour. Gladstone's proposed venture was supported by a number of other sugar planters whose estates were expected to obtain some of the Indians. By this time Indians were being taken by the Royal British East India Company to Mauritius to work on the sugar plantations, and they were proving to be very productive. Gladstone's request was granted and he, Davidson, Barclay and Company, Andrew Colville, John and Henry Moss, all owners of sugar plantation in Guyana, made arrangements to recruit 414 Indians. Of these 150 were "hill coolies" from Chota Nagpur, and the remainder were from Burdwan and Bancoorah near Calcutta. (The word "coolie", a corruption of the Dravidian word "kūli", referred to a porter or labourer).

To transport these Indians, two ships, the SS Whitby and SS Hesperus were chartered. The Whitby sailed from Calcutta on 13 January 1838 with 249 immigrants, and after a voyage of 112 days, arrived in Guyana on 5 May. Five Indians died on the voyage. The ship immediately sailed to Berbice and 164 immigrants, who were recruited by Highbury and Waterloo plantations, disembarked. The ship then returned to Demerara and between 14–16 May the remaining 80 immigrants landed and were taken to Belle Vue Estate. Of the total of 244 Indians who arrived on the Whitby, there were 233 men, 5 women and 6 children.

The Hesperus left Calcutta on the 29 January 1838 with 165 passengers and arrived in Guyana late on the night of the 5 May, by which time 13 had already died. The remaining 135 men, 6 women and 11 children were distributed between the 8-10 May to the plantations Vreedestein, Vreed-en-hoop, in Demerara and Anna Regina, in Essequibo. My ancestors were on the Hesperus and transported the ten miles from Vreed-en-Hoop to plantation Leonora, West Bank of the Demerara River, where I was born. Other relatives were transported to the East Bank. Chinese labourers were imported to Guyana by the planters. By 1899, the British forcefully marked the Guyana borders with respect to Venezuela. It included some lands that Venezuela still claims up to this day.

The British stopped the practice of importing labour in 1917, by which time around 250,000 people had settled in Guyana. Many of the Afro-Guyanese former slaves moved to the towns and became the majority urban population, whereas the Indian Guyanese remained predominantly rural. A scheme in 1862 to bring black workers from the United States was implemented.

Indenture-ship – a new form of economic slavery

According to Parliamentary Papers (PP), L11 Nos.180, 232, 1837-38. MF41.413-14, PP, XXX1X No. 463, 1839. MF42. 266-67and PP 77, 1840. No. 58 the indentured labourers were from South India including Calcutta, Bihar, Utter Pradesh and Madras (Chennai). The people, Gillanders, Arbuthnot & Company who organised the labourers and shipped them through the British East India Company (1600 – 1874 and operated on a Royal Charter) admitted that those who were transported on the SS Hesperus, the SS Whitby and other ships, from 1837, included:

> *"Hill tribes, known by the name of Dhangurs, are looked down upon by the more cunning natives of the plains, and they are always spoken of as more akin to the monkey than the man. They have no religion, no education, and, in their present state, no want beyond eating, drinking, and sleeping; and to procure which they are willing to labour. In sending men to such a distance, it would of course be necessary to be more particular in selecting them, and some little expense would be incurred, as also some trouble; but to aid any object*

of interest to you, we should willingly give our best exertions in any manner likely to be of service"

The system of indenture-ship lasted up to 1917 and millions of Indians were transported to various parts of Asia, Africa, South America and the Caribbean during this period. Like the Transatlantic Slave Trade, the system of indenture labour was sanctioned and approved, by the Queen Victoria and her Parliament - the Lords and the House of Commons; the Christian Churches and the ruling establishment. Many of the landed and commercial ruling elites including Prime Ministers, Lords, Knights, Barons, Mayors, and the merchants who made money from the slave trade also enjoyed the benefits from indenture-ship. A copy of the contract printed below and bearing the thump print from these illiterate people transported to Mauritius was a standard one used for those transported to Guyana, the Caribbean and elsewhere up to 1917.

Copy Form of Contract

Between the undersigned _____ acting on behalf of _____ of Mauritius, and the natives whose names are hereunto affixed, the following agreement has been entered into by the several parties binding themselves to the observance of the conditions thereof:

1. *The natives agree to proceed to the Isle of France, to work as labourers there, upon a sugar estate, the property of _____ and to remain there, if required, for the time of five years.*

2. *The passage of the natives to the Mauritius shall be paid by _____ who shall also provide a passage again to this country, at the end of five years, for each native who may then wish to return; but if any individual, from any cause, should be discharged or leave the employment of before the expiration of five years, such individual shall have no claim on him for a passage.*

3. *The pay of the natives shall be fixed at the rate of five rupees per month for each man. The labour required from them will be that of digging holes, weeding canes, working in the sugar-house, repairing roads and bridges, or otherwise making themselves useful, according to their ability, as may order them; the quantity of daily labour required from each to be fixed by the manager of the property; the pay of one sirdar shall be fixed at seven rupees per month, and that of one mate six rupeess, and boys at three rupees per month.*

4. *As _____ must be responsible to government that the nativess shall not be a burden to the colony, in the event of their being discharged or leaving their employments, one rupee per month shall be retained from the pay of each individual, until there shall be a sufficient sum to provide a passage for each to Calcutta; should no such contingency take place, the money shall be restored at the end of five years.*

5. *In addition to the pay as above fixed, food and clothing shall be supplied to each as follows -- Fourteen chettacks of rice (about 2lbs.), two ditto of dholl*, two ounces of salt, and some oil and tamarind, daily; and annually for each, clothing as follows; two dhooties, two blankets, one jacket, and one cap.*

6. *Each individual shall receive six months' pay in advance, for which he shall give an acknowledgement here; their pay to commence from the date of their going on board the ship.*

7. *The nature of this agreement (which shall be registered at the police) is such that each native is individually responsible for the observance of its conditions by every one whose mark it bears; and it is further agreed, that while in hospital, from sickness or any other cause, the pay is stopped during such time.*

* Something like dried split peas

SOURCE: **Parliamentary Papers**, *LII No. 180, 1837-38. MF41.413-14*

The conditions suffered by the indentured labourers in Guyana were far from satisfactory as the following document testify:

From the British Emancipator of the 9 January 1839

"I See the British public has been deceived with the idea that the Coolies are doing "well;" such is not the fact; the poor friendless creatures are miserably treated, at least I can speak confidently of plantation Bellvue. On this estate they have made two attempts to escape, as they say, to go to Calcutta. In the first, 22 succeeded by night to cross the river, landing on the opposite shore; they attempted to explore the woods, but after undergoing much fatigue and hunger, they were retaken at the back of plantation Herstelling, and conveyed again to the estate. In the last attempt they were discovered by the watch of the night, and driven back. I saw a gang of them last week in custody of the police, who were taking them to the public buildings; their offence I did not learn. I inquired of Mr. Berkeley, who is a teacher on the place, respecting food; he said they had enough of rice, and I think "fat" or lard. Deaths, he said, more than ten have died on this place, Bellevue, and the manager (Russell) refuses to give a rag of clothes to bury them in. I had one of these Coolies in my own place, who is capable of saying a few words in English; he told me, "Russell no good; Coolie sick salt, salt no more." He was all but naked; and a friend present gave him a few old raiments, which seemed highly to please him. They are paid here with the Company's rupees, five rupees a month. Is not this scandalous? They have been offered by the merchant's two bits a piece for them. I do not believe they can get its value in the colony. Ought not the planters to be compelled to give their value in Demerara silver currency? I have also heard that two from Gladstone's estate escaped through the bush, and were captured by Captain Falant, at Fort Island, in the Essequibo River, and brought back to the plantation. Surely these things are far from being "well;" the one alluded to above told me, "Calcutta better."

*SOURCE: **Parliamentary Papers**, XXXIX NO. 463, 1839. MF42.266-67*

"In fact, in many cases the situation was much worse with regular beatings; starvation, abuse, ill health, and non-payment of wages were common on the plantations. However, it did not stop those who endorsed slavery as well as indentured labourers writing a pack of lies to justify their evil actions against helpless human beings. (The word "coolie", a corruption of the Tamil work "kuli", referred to a porter or labourer).

Further evidence printed below shows some of the lies that were told and written to disguise the cruelty my ancestors endured:

Copy of letter from John Gladstone, Esq. to Messrs. Gillanders, Arbuthnot & Co.

Liverpool, 4 January 1836

Dear Sirs,

"I met with an accident here about three weeks ago, which confined me to the house, from which I am now recovering, and hope in a few days to be able to return to Edinburgh; this will account to you for using my son's pen for writing in place of my own.

I observe by a letter which he received a few days ago from Mr. Arbuthnot that he was sending a considerable number of a certain class of Bengalees, to be employed as labourers, to the Mauritius. You will probably be aware that we are very particularly situated with our Negro apprentices in the West Indies, and that it is a matter of doubt and uncertainty how far they may be induced to continue their services on the plantations after their apprenticeship expires in 1840. This to us is a subject of great moment and deep interest in the colonies of Demerara and Jamaica. We are therefore most desirous to obtain and introduce labourers from other quarters, and particularly from climates something similar in their nature. Our plantation labour in the field is very light; much of it, particularly in Demerara, is done by task-work, which for the day is usually completed by two o'clock in the afternoon, giving to the people all the rest of the day to themselves.

They are furnished with comfortable dwellings and abundance of food; plantations, the produce of the colony, being the most common, and preferred generally by them; but they have also occasionally rice, Indian corn, meal, ship's biscuits, and a regular supply of salt cod-fish, as well as the power of fishing for themselves in the trenches. They have likewise an annual allowance of clothing sufficient and suitable for the climate; there are schools on each estate for the education of the children, and the instruction of their parents in the knowledge of religious duties.

Their houses are comfortable, and it may be fairly said they pass their time agreeably and happily. Marriages are encouraged, and when improper conduct on the part of the people takes place, there are public stipendiary magistrates, who take cognizance of such, and judge between them and their employers. They have regular medical attendance whenever they are indisposed, at the expense of their employers. I have been particular in describing the present situation and occupation of our people, to which I ought to add, that their employment in the field is clearing the land with the hoe, and, where required, planting fresh canes. In the works a portion are occupied in making sugar, and in the distilleries, in which they relieve each other, which makes their labour light. It is of great importance to us to endeavour to provide a portion of other labourers, whom we might use as a set-off, and, when the time for it comes, make us, as far as it is possible, independent of our negro population; and it has occurred to us that a moderate number of Bengalees, such as you were sending to the Isle of France, might be very suitable for our purpose; and on this subject I am now desirous to obtain all the information you can possibly give me. The number I should think of taking and sending by one vessel direct from Calcutta to Demerara would be about 100; they ought to be young, active, able-bodied people. It would be desirable that a portion of them, at least one-half, should be married, and their wives disposed to work in the field as well as they themselves.

We should require to bind them for a period not less than five years or more than seven years. They would be provided with comfortable dwellings, food, and medical assistance; they would also, if required, be provided with clothing, or wages to provide themselves, which, for the able-bodied, would not exceed four dollars per month, and in that proportion for females and their children as they grow up; a free passage would be given to them to Demerara, where they would be divided, and 20 to 30 placed on one plantation. I do not know whether the class referred to are likely to be of a particular caste, and under the influence of certain religious feelings, and also restricted to any particular kind of food; if so, we must endeavour to provide for them accordingly. You will particularly oblige me by giving me, on receipt, all the information you possibly can on this interesting subject; for, should it be of an encouraging character, I should immediately engage for one of our ships to go to Calcutta, and take a limited number to Demerara, and from thence return here. On all other subjects I refer you to letters from the house; and always am,

Yours truly

John Gladstone. "

Between thirty three and fifty per cent of those transported from India died before their period of indenture-ship of five years expired. In addition there were regular conflicts between the African slaves who became apprentices on the plantation after the abolition of slavery in 1834. The term apprenticeship meant that they were bound to the plantation owners for a further six years doing the same work under the same conditions. The Plantation owners received £20 in compensation for each freed slave but the slaves received none of the compensation. Of the 249 labourers including six children and five women transported to Guyana on the SS Whity from Calcutta on 13 January 1838, - a journey which took 112 days, 18 died on route and many others were in very poor physical and mental condition, but had to start work straight away. Indenture-ship of Indians lasted for over eighty years, instead of five, and was only terminated after the government in London and India expressed serious concerns, that the indentured labourers were being treated as harshly as the slaves they were replacing. This trade in human beings from India to South America totalled over 500,000 and continued throughout the reign of Queen Victoria from the time she inherited the Crown on 20 June, 1837, to 22nd January 1901 and beyond.

The British and other European colonialists did not cease the slave trade and the enslavement of people because of purely moral or, humanitarian reasons, but because of economic and others reasons. It was no longer economically beneficial to own slaves and having to provide for them, even though some owners actually worked their slaves death, by extracting every bit from their labour and spend as little as possible to keep them alive. Their wives and children were also slaves and were bought and sold as the master wishes. Slave rebellions and insurrections, followed by sabotage and attacks on their masters and oppressors were also instrumental in the abolition of slavery. The growth of America; the industrial revolution; wars in Europe and America, and the expansion of trade across the continents also influenced the abolition of chattel slavery, but ironically, ensured the transformation of chattel slavery to economic slavery which still impacts on the lives and status of most of the descendants of those that were forced to suffer under imperialism, colonialism, slavery and indenture-ship. Economic enslavement under globalisation; world financial institutions such as the IMF, World Bank and the global banking and finance systems ensures the source of cheap labour and the exploitation of the descendants of the ex-colonies.

Western political manipulations

The British ruled Guyana for over 150 years with the strategies and commitment of a typical colonial administration. The extraction of wealth by any means necessary including the exploitation of the population, the raw materials and mineral resources. For most of the time the population were not allowed to form free and effective trade unions, political parties or campaign for democracy. A Governor was stationed in the colony to consolidate continuous British rule. Profits from the economy were channelled to the British economy and there were very little investment in the infrastructure, the wider economy, housing, education, sea defence, roads, airports or communications that were not linked to the extraction and maximisation of profits. There were no social or welfare arrangements anyway near to what existed in Britain, except to the minimal healthcare, education protection to enable the population to serve the colonial power without impacting too much on the surplus made by the economy.

After the Second World War, Guyanese, like some other people under colonial rule set up independent political parties and trades unions as part of their anti-colonial struggles and fight for independence. The independence of India on 15 August 1947 encouraged the independence movement in Guyana and in other British colonies. The colonial administration made some limited concessions and allowed a measure of self-government without full independence, under a renewed Constitution in 1953, for Guyana.

In 1950 Cheddi Jagan, an Indian Guyanese and his white American-born wife Janet Jagan, who were both Marxists and were seen as a threat by the British interests, joined with Linden Forbes Burnham, an African Guyanese Lawyer, to form the People's Progressive Party (PPP), with a goal of gaining independence for the colony. The PPP was launched on 1 January 1950 with Jagan as Leader and Burnham as Chairman. In 1953 the colony was granted a measure of home rule, and Cheddi became its first prime minister. The PPP won 18 of the 24 seats in the House of Assembly and Jagan became Prime Minister, and the government made up of the main ethnic groups. In the short-lived PPP government that followed, Burnham served as Minister of Education.

The People's Progressive Party (PPP) was established as the political vanguard of all working class people and to establish a socialist society. Although the PPP was originally guided by Marxism and its political ideology which has substantially changed since independence in 1966, it maintained certain allegiance and commitment to varying degrees of socialism, and radical centre left ideology. It has also maintained since independence a commitment to democracy, freedom, equality, racial and ethnic harmony, diversity, human rights and social justice. The British government with strong influence from various American administrations took a range of economic, legal and political actions to ensure that Guyana did not become a Marxist country on the mainland of South America and so close to the Caribbean. These areas were described as Americas' backyard. President Dwight Eisenhower and John F Kennedy of the USA and the British Prime Ministers, including Sir Winston Churchill (1951-1955), Harold McMillan (1957-1963 and Harold Wilson (1964-1970), colluded through various political structures and parties to ensure that power was transferred to a government that was not opposed to Western capitalist interests.

In 1952, Burnham became the president of the party's affiliated trade union, the British Guiana Labour Union, in 1952. In 1955, there was a split in the PPP between Burnham and Jagan. As a result, Burnham went on to form the People's National Congress (PNC) in 1958. The PNC entered its first election in 1961. PP won three consecutive elections in 1953, 57 and 61 and would have won in 1964 if the electoral system was nor manipulated and changed to favour the pro-Western opposition of the PNC and other minor parties. The first elected government, formed by the People's Progressive Party (PPP) and led by Cheddi Jagan, seemed so pro-communist that the British suspended the constitution in October 1953 and dispatched troops. The constitution was not restored until 1957. The PPP split along ethnic lines, leaving Jagan with a party of predominately people from Asian backgrounds and Burnham with people from mainly African backgrounds. From 1953 to 1966 the political history of Guyana was turbulent to say the least.

I am an economic migrant

The British plantation owners and Canadian Bauxite Company that controlled Guyana's economy with other external interests colluded to inflame a serious split within the PPP on racial lines. Between 1953 and 1961 the CIA and British Intelligence MI5 systematically destabilised the Guyana Government and created divisions within the PPP. The March for freedom against colonial rule and imperialism Asia, Africa, South America, the Caribbean between 1940 and 1980 resulted in enormous efforts by British intelligence MI5 and the CIA with the acting support of the Foreign and Colonial Office staff working in harmony with UK and US Multi-national companies to destabilised progressive governments and radical political parties. Divide and rule on racial political and class were key factors and successfully in used the destabilisation process in many countries opposed to colonialism and imperialism. The Americans were determined to strangle any political movement or government that supported Marxism or socialism.

I left Guyana for England in July 1961, having spent several years of my childhood campaigning and demonstrating with the PPP and the Guyana Agricultural Workers Union (GAWU) against British colonial rule. I carried much of the political, social and economic frustrations and concerns with me, which forced me to become a political and trade union activist within days of my arrival in London. In the 1964 elections, while Jagan's PPP won the highest per cent of the vote (46 per cent to the PNC's 41 per cent), but it did not win a majority. Burnham was able to form a coalition with the United Force (TUF) which won the remaining 12 per cent of the votes and became premier of British Guiana on 14 December. On May 26, 1966, British Guiana became an independent country and was renamed GUYANA. For much of Burnham's rule, Guyana was seen by most countries as a police state, ruled by a dictator with the support of a minority within the country and the collusion of the USA and the British state. The Western powers had imposed a system of proportional representation in

Guyana, which disadvantaged the PPP, but at least found in Burnham, someone acceptable to them.

The Destabilisation Philosophy of the CIA and M15 was also successful not only in India but also in Guyana, Dominica in 1965, Brazil in 1964, Chile in 1973, Jamaica in 1980 and Grenada in1983. During this period numerous African countries had experienced similar process resulted in the death of millions of the most able and productive section of the population. The imperialists within the USA and UK, supported by international capitalists were determined to destroy any socialist or Soviet inspired political movement anywhere in the world. Winston Churchill UK Prime Minister supported US President Harry Truman in suppressing popular anti-colonial and imperialist struggles around the world. It was the start of the cold war between the Soviet bloc and the Western NATO powers.

Sir Winston Churchill was Prime Minister and a major proponent of the "Cold War" against communism and socialism. He called for the strangling of the "Bolshevik infant in its cradle" decided to send British troops to Guyana in1953 to stem the successful of the Marxist PPP and the popular government of Guyana. The people of Guyana rejected this intervention which was carried out by both the Conservative and Labour governments.

Harold Wilson who later became a Labour Prime Minister of the UK described the Conservative Party plan for Guyana as "a fiddle constitutional arrangement" – a changed voting system – to replace the third time, popularly elected government in Guyana and install in power L.F.S Burnham who further incited the population on racial grounds and manipulated the democratic process for more than two decades and ruled before the democratic process was restored after his death, on 6 August 1985. The PNC continued to rule under the Presidency of Desmond Hoyte until 1992. Hoyte's first two goals were easily accomplished. The new leader took advantage of factionalism within the PNC to quietly consolidate his authority. The December 1985 elections gave the PNC 79 per cent of the vote and forty-two of the fifty-three directly elected seats. Eight of the remaining eleven seats went to the PPP, even though the PPP had the majority of votes from the Indian Guyanese who made up the substantial majority of the Guyanese population. The PPP opposition boycotted the December 1986 municipal elections. With no opponents, the PNC won all ninety-one seats in local government.

Former U.S. President Jimmy Carter visited Guyana to lobby for the resumption of free and fair elections, and on 5 October, 1992, a new National Assembly and regional councils were elected in the first Guyanese election since 1964 to be internationally recognized as free and fair. Cheddi Jagan of the PPP was elected and sworn in as President on 9 October, 1992, reversing the monopoly Afro-Guyanese traditionally had over Guyanese politics. The poll was marred by violence however. A new International Monetary Fund Structural Adjustment programme was introduced which led to an increase in the GDP whilst also eroding real incomes and hitting the middle-classes hard. The PPP won the following elections in 1997, 2001, 2006 and 2011.

When President Jagan died of a heart attack in March 1997, Prime Minister Samuel Hinds replaced him in accordance with constitutional provisions, with his widow Janet Jagan as President. She was then elected President on 15th December, 1997 for the PPP. Desmond Hoyte's PNC contested the results however, resulting in strikes, riots and one death before a Caricom mediating committee was brought in. Janet Jagan's PPP government was sworn in on 24 December having agreed to a constitutional review and to hold elections within three years, though Hoyte refused to recognise her government.

Janet Jagan resigned in August 1999 due to ill health and was succeeded by Finance Minister Bharrat Jagdeo, who had been named Prime Minister a day earlier. National elections were held on 19 March, 2001, three months later than planned as the election committees said they were unprepared. There were fears that the violence that occurred during the previous election may occur, so this led to monitoring by foreign bodies, including Ex-President, Jimmy Carter from the USA. In March, incumbent President Jagdeo won the election with a voter turnout of over 90 per cent. In December 2002, Hoyte died, with Robert Corbin replacing him as leader of the PNC. He agreed to engage in 'constructive engagement' with President Jagdeo and the PPP. In May 2008, President Bharrat Jagdeo was a signatory to The UNASUR Constitutive Treaty of the Union of South American Nations. Guyana has ratified the treaty. The present President is Donald Ramotar an Indian Guyanese and the Prime Minister Samuel Hinds, an African Guyanese. The PPP have always ensured ethnic and gender diversity in government.

The uniqueness of Guyana and its biodiversity

The interior, which lies behind coastal belt stretches for about 450 miles, consist of dense rain forest, rivers, open savannah country and mountains. Mount Rorima is the highest point at 9,094 feet and the Kaietuer Falls on the Potaro River has a drop of 226 metres - 741 feet, nearly five times the height of Niagara Falls. Much of the interior is under-developed, sparsely populated. Inhabitants of the interior consist mainly of Amerindians, the original inhabitants of Guyana, who are engaged in the extraction of minerals including diamond and gold, timber logging, farming, fishing and cattle rearing.

Amerindians make up some ten per cent or, around 75,000 of the total Guyanese population of around 740,000 people, compared to around 340, 000 Indian Guyanese; 230,000 African Guyanese and 124,000 mixed and other ethnic groups. The majority around 55 per cent of the population are Christians, 30 per cent Hindus, 9 per cent Muslims a 6 per cent other faiths. Just over 40 per cent of the population lives in the urban areas and the working population stands at around 455,000.

During the last four decades the interior, and indeed Guyana has changed considerably, with growing exploitation and destruction of the rain forest. Increasing mechanisation in mining, extraction of timber by foreign companies and people choosing to settle in areas which has become less remote through improved transport and communication have created new opportunities and challenges for Guyana. The Guyanese economy during the centuries of colonialism was dominated by agriculture. Sugar and related products dominated the economy, followed by farming including rice, animal, ground provisions, bananas, fruits and vegetables. Mining of bauxite was also a sizeable activity.

The economy has become much more developed and diversified since independence in 1966 and it is involved in the mining of gold, alumina, production and export of rum, molasses, rice, fish timber and a greater variety of agricultural products. Guyana has been transformed from a colonial economy, designed in almost every area of economic, social, political, cultural community and educational activities to serve the need of the white absentee colonialists and their metropolitan economic and political advancement, to serving the people of Guyana. Guyana has also recently discovered oil and it is developing the tourism industry by showcasing its many and unique attractions.

Guyana has one of the largest unspoiled rainforests in South America. It has been described as one of the most 'spectacular places on the planet' with hundreds of undiscovered species of animal, birds, insects and plants. Much of Guyana's rainforest is unspoilt, unprotected and under threat from logging, land grabs and mining. The rich natural environment, biodiversity and history of Guyana has been explored and described by early and recent explorers including, Sir Walter Raleigh, Charles Waterton, and naturalists such as Sir David Attenborough, Gerald Durrell and others. In 2008, the BBC ran a three-part programme called Lost Land of the Jaguar which highlighted the huge diversity of wildlife, including undiscovered and rare species of mammals, plants, birds, amphibians and other surprises. Guyana has a spectacular number and diversity of flora, fauna, plants, mountains, rivers, and creatures which are unique to its borders. Guyana has one of the highest levels of biodiversity in the world. Guyana, with 1,168 vertebrate species, 1,600 bird species, boasts one of the richest mammalian fauna assemblages of any comparably sized area in the world, with over 70 per cent of the natural habitat remains pristine.

Amongst the uniqueness of some of the species are the giant otter, spiders, snakes and amphibians; the harpy eagle – one of the largest in the world; the giant leather back turtles, up to 1.5 metres long; several species of caimans; the giant arapaima fish, which is the largest freshwater fish in the world; the flesh eating piranhas fish; the Jaguar; the scarlet macaws; the ocelot; the giant anteater; the tapir; bush dogs; capybaras; the golden frog; the tropical greenheart hardwood trees up to 30 metres high; the saki, squirrel and six other types of monkeys; and the black caiman crocodiles over four metres long. Guyana also has four very long rivers, such as, the Essequibo at 1,010 kilometres (628 mi) long, the Courantyne River at 724 kilometres (450 mi), the Berbice at 595 kilometres (370 mi), and the Demerara at 346 kilometres (215 mi). Guyana is a land full of giant wildlife and sceneries, yet so few people have seen these wonders.

The Corentyne River forms the border with Suriname. At the mouth of the Essequibo are several large islands, including the 145 km (90 mi) wide Shell Beach lies along the northwest coast, which is also a major breeding area for sea turtles, mainly Leatherbacks, and lots of other wildlife. The climate in Guyana is tropical and generally hot and humid, though moderated by northeast trade winds along the coast. There are two rainy seasons, the first from May to mid-August, and the second from mid-November to mid-January.

Guyana is fortunate to have more around 80 per cent of its land still covered by forests, ranging from dry evergreen and seasonal forests to lowland evergreen rain forests. Around 90 per cent of the Guyanese population lives on the long thin coastal belt. This only makes up some 4 per cent of the habitable and cultivated area of land. Guyana's tropical climate, unique geology, and relatively pristine ecosystems support extensive areas of species-rich rain forests and natural habitats with high levels of endemism. Approximately eight thousand species of plants occur in Guyana, half of which are found nowhere else. The rain forests in Guyana are home to more than 1,000 species of trees, plants and birds.

Guyana seeks World Heritage Status

Sadly, despite all the uniqueness of Guyana and the efforts made by the government over a long period to achieve recognition of its environment, biodiversity and natural areas, no part of Guyana has yet been declared a World Heritage Site. In February 2004, the Guyanese Government issued a title to more than 1 million acres (4,000 km) of land in the Konashen Indigenous District declaring this land as the Konashen Community-Owned Conservation Area (COCA), to be managed by the Wai Wai tribe on native Guyanese. In doing so Guyana created the world's largest Community-Owned Conservation Area.

This important event followed a request made by the Wai community to the government of Guyana and Conservation International Guyana (CIG) for assistance in developing a sustainable plan for their lands in Konashen. The three parties signed a Memorandum of Cooperation which outlines a plan for sustainable use of the Konashen COCA's biological resources, identifies threats to the area's biodiversity, and helps develop projects to increase awareness of the COCA as well as generate the income necessary to maintain its protected status. The Smithsonian Institution has identified nearly 2,700 species of plants from this region, representing 239 distinct families, and there are certainly additional species still to be recorded. The Konashen COCA forests are also home to countless species of insects, arachnids, and other invertebrates, many of which are still undiscovered and unnamed. There are over 400 species of birds within the Guyanese rain forests.

The Konashen COCA is relatively unique in that it contains a high level of biological diversity and richness that remains in nearly pristine condition; such places have become rare on earth. This fact has given rise to various non-exploitative, environmentally sustainable industries such as ecotourism. Many countries interested in the conservation and protection of natural and cultural heritage sites of the world accede to the Convention Concerning the Protection of the World Cultural and Natural Heritage that was adopted by UNESCO in 1972. Guyana signed the treaty in 1977, the first Caribbean State Party to do so. In the mid-1990s, Guyana seriously began the process of selecting sites for World Heritage nomination, and three sites were considered: Kaieteur National Park, Shell Beach and Historic Georgetown. By 1997, work on Kaieteur National Park was started, and in 1998 work on Historic Georgetown was begun. To date, however, Guyana has not made a successful nomination.

Guyana submitted the Kaieteur National Park, including the Kaieteur Falls, to UNESCO as its first World Heritage Site nomination. The proposed area and surrounds have some of Guyana's most diversified life zones with one of the highest levels of endemic species found anywhere in South America. The Kaieteur Falls is the most spectacular feature of the park, falling a distance of 226 metres. The nomination of Kaieteur Park as a World Heritage Site was not successful, primarily because the area was seen by the evaluators as being too small, especially when compared with the Central Suriname Nature Reserve that had been nominated as a World Heritage Site in 2000. The dossier was thus returned to Guyana for revision.

Guyana continues in its bid for a World Heritage Site. Work continues, after a period of hiatus, on the nomination dossier for Historic Georgetown. A Tentative List indicating an intention to nominate Historic Georgetown was submitted to UNESCO in December 2004. There is now a small committee put together by the Guyana National Commission for UNESCO to complete the nomination dossier and the management plan for the site. In April 2005, two Dutch experts in conservation spent two weeks in Georgetown supervising architecture staff and students of the University of Guyana in a historic building survey of the selected area. This is part of the data collection for the nomination dossier. Kaieteur Falls is the world's largest single drop waterfall by volume.

Meanwhile, as a result of the Kaieteur National Park being considered too small, there is a proposal to prepare a nomination for a Cluster Site that will include the Kaieteur National Park, the Iwokrama Forest and the Kanuku Mountains. The Iwokrama Rain Forest, an area rich in biological diversity, has been described by Major General (Retired) Joseph Singh as "a flagship project for conservation." The Kanuku Mountains area is in a pristine state and is home to more than four hundred species of birds and other animals. There is much work to be done for the successful nomination of these sites to the World Heritage List. The state, the private sector and the ordinary Guyanese citizens each have a role to play in this process and in the later protection of the sites. Inscription on the UNESCO World Heritage will open Guyana to more serious tourists thereby assisting in its economic development.

There are also many other places and buildings worthy of attention to the tourist in Guyana and have been included in submissions for World Heritage recognition. These include:

- St. Georges Anglican Cathedral, one of the tallest wooden buildings in the world, after the Todaiji Temple in Japan. submitted in (1995)

- Fort Zeelandia (including Court of Policy Building) in (1995)

- City Hall, Georgetown built in 1889 (1995)

- Shell Beach (Almond Beach) Essequibo Coast (1995)

- Georgetown's Plantation Structure and Historic Buildings, including the Law Courts, built in 1887, the National Assembly built in 1833 and Stabroek Market built in 1880 and submitted in (2005)

Guyana also has some other notable landmarks such as: the world's fourth-longest floating bridge; the Caribbean Community (CARICOM) Building, Houses the Headquarters of the largest and most powerful economic union in the Caribbean; the Providence Stadium situated at Providence on the north bank of the Demerara

River and built in time for the ICC World Cup 2007, it is the largest sports stadium in the country. It is also near the Providence Mall, forming a major spot for leisure in Guyana; the Guyana International Conference Centre, Presented as a gift from the People's Republic of China to the Government of Guyana and Queen's College, Guyana's top secondary school.

Many Guyanese have become distinguished professionals in the legal, medical, artistic, political, publishing, writing, teaching and other areas:

- Leona Lewis, X Factor winner, father Aural Josiah, from Guyana, mother European

- Rihanna, entertainer, born Robyn Rihanna Fenty, mother Monica from Guyana, father Ronald from Barbados

- John Agard, poet

- Baroness Valerie Amos, British politician and ex Leader of the UK House of Lords

- Deborah Cox, music artist born in Canada from Guyanese parents

- E. R. Braithwaite, writer of the novel *To Sir, With Love*

- Shakira Caine, former Miss Guyana and wife of actor Michael Caine

- Jan Carew, writer and educator

- Martin Carter, writer and poet

- David Case, the highest ranking black officer in the British Armed Forces

- Shivnarine Chanderpaul, professional cricketer for the West Indies cricket team

- Bernie Grant, ex British politician and Member of Parliament

- Eddy Grant, musician

- Melanie Fiona, music artist, born in Canada from Guyanese parents

- Wilson Harris, writer (*The Palace of the Peacock,* 1960)

- Roy Heath, writer

- Ezekial Jackson, professional wrestler

- Cheddi Jagan, president from 1992-97

- Rohan Kanhai, former West Indies cricket captain

- David Lammy, Politician, Guyanese parents

- Trevor Phillips, Politician, born in London from Guyanese parents

- Mike Phillips, writer, Guyanese parents

- Clive Lloyd, former West Indies cricket captain

- Edgar Mittelholzer, author

- Grace Nichols, poet

- CCH Pounder, an Emmy-nominated actress and activist

- Walter Rodney, a Pan-Africanist and social politician

- Ivan Van Sertima, an Afro-centric historian

- Mark Teixeria, MLB American baseball player

- Shridath Ramphal, Commonwealth Secretary

- Rudy Narayan, Barrister

Personal memories of Guyana

I have some very pleasant as well as bitter memories of Guyana as a child. I was lucky to see so much of the diversity of the wildlife and way people lived. I visited the three counties that made up Guyana, explored some of the remote areas and enjoyed the delicious fruits, vegetables, fishes, and local hospitality. Guyanese culture, lifestyle and festivities are very diverse and colourful. I still have many family members living in Guyana.

On my first return visit to Guyana after spending some thirteen years in England I tried to locate my mother's, father's and grandfather's graves, but sadly it was difficult to do so because the area where they were buried had become open pasture for animals to graze. Their headstones were removed and used for building. It was impossible to locate the precise area. It was typical of the plantation owners to treat people worse than they treated their animals whilst they were alive, and to show total disrespect for them after they had passed away. The white overseers and their families were taken to their country of origin if they were seriously ill, or if they had passed away. Local people were not valued or respected by the plantation managers. Sadly, there have been only marginal improvements in various aspects of life and the environment in Guyana since independence, due to lack of money, foreign debt and many highly skilled people leaving the country for a better life abroad. I have returned to Guyana on several occasions since my first returned visit in 1973, and on each occasion I discovered that despite independence from colonial rule, there is still relative poverty and inequality. My wife and children visited my relatives and toured Guyana. My son Michael worked as an Engineering Consultant and Chartered Engineer in Guyana and married an African Guyanese woman, and they have two children age thirteen and nine.

I tried very hard to build a modern house on a plot of land I bought in 1973, but despite several attempts to persuade my family in Guyana to supervise the building of a four bedroom concrete property, for which I secured planning permission, this never occurred. It is one of my greatest disappointments not having a nice house in Guyana near my family where I could escape the harsh British winter with my wife. I wanted a building that could be used by all my family as and when they needed it. It was designed to accommodate two floors with four bedrooms, two kitchens, and a prayer room, a small outbuilding for a watchman, a small swimming pool, a garage and a large veranda. A dream that will never come true.

Top-Bottom L-R
Jim with Jesse Jackson 1984
Neville Lawrence, father of Stephen Lawrence 2010
Bernie Grant Member of Parliament 1989
Muhammad Ali 1984
Jim with Lord Bill Morris, first Black Trade union leader in Britain 2007

Top – Bottom

Jim with Daniel Cohen Bendt – Student Leader who almost brought
revolution to France in the 1970s

Jim with Lord Scarman QC – Author of the Report on the Brixton Riots in 1981

Top – Bottom L-R
Jim with Frank Dobson, Minister for Health 1997
Jim with Arthur Scargill – Leader of the National Union of Mineworkers 1981
Jim with Jack Jones, ex-General Secretary of the TGWU
and Pensioners Leader 2003
Jim with Gloria Mills, first Black Woman President of the TUC 2009
Jim with Len Murray, General Secretary of the TUC 1975

Chapter 18:

Save our planet

We are all in this together

It is my sincere wish to leave this world a tiny bit better for my children, grandchildren and future generations, even if my contribution causes no more impact than throwing a tiny stone into the Atlantic Ocean. Each one of us who has been nurtured and sustained throughout our lives, by mother earth, has a responsibility to give something back, before we die. Hundreds of millions of people are going to die in the remaining 85 years of this century due to climate change; global warming; rising poverty and inequality; scarcity of resources including food, water and fertile land; floods, hurricanes rising sea levels; wars and conflicts. All these problems are inter-linked and are determined by human behaviour. None of these outcomes can be blamed on "natural disasters" as they are all shaped by human neglect, greed, poor governance, and disrespect for each other and putting profits before the needs of people.

Global warming and climate change is the result of the self-inflicted wound human beings have imposed on our plant over the last 5,000 years, but more so during the last hundred years. For too long nations have denied, minimised or argued against the impact of climate change by human behaviour, despite the overwhelming evidence gathered through credible, substantial and sustained scientific investigations. The United Nations Report of the United Nations Conference on Sustainable Development in Rio de Janeiro, Brazil 20–22 June 2012 produced nearly 300 detailed recommendations to address global warming and climate change.

The conference committed to address some of the concerns expressed below:

All across the world, in every kind of environment and region known to man, increasingly dangerous weather patterns and devastating storms are abruptly putting an end to the long-running debate over whether or not climate change is real. Not only is it real, it's here, and its effects are giving rise to a frighteningly new global phenomenon: the man-made natural disaster. **Barack Obama, President of the USA**

America has not led but fled on the issue of global warming. **John Kerry, Secretary of State, USA**

"The danger posed by war to all of humanity - and to our planet - is at least matched by the climate crisis and global warming. I believe that the world has reached a critical stage in its efforts to exercise responsible environmental stewardship. A deal must include an equitable global governance structure…. All countries must have a voice in how resources are deployed and managed…. Entire nations could be wiped off the face of the Earth by rising sea levels if the global warming trend is not reversed…. Coastal flooding and crop failures would create an exodus of "eco-refugees," threatening political chaos." **UN Secretary General Ban Ki-moon**

While human-induced global warming is not going to turn present-day Earth into present-day Mars, global warming is dire enough that our most distinguished scientists recently concluded that as many as 1 million species on the planet could be extinct by 2050 if affairs do not change. **Jay Inslee**

I want to testify today about what I believe is a planetary emergency - a crisis that threatens the survival of our civilization and the habitability of the Earth. **Al Gore, former U.S. Vice President**

I'd say the chances are about 50-50 that humanity will be extinct or nearly extinct within 50 years. Weapons of mass destruction, disease, I mean this global warming is scaring the living daylights out of me. **Ted Turner**

The sad thing is that despite the thousands of reports, hundreds of conferences and scores of serious warnings by the United Nations (UN) Heads of governments, scientists, politicians from all shades of political opinions, the attempts to combat the increasing dangers of Climate Change (CC) and Global Warming (GW) worldwide are far short of what is required to reduce the problem, let alone dealing with the cumulative impact over many centuries. The UN and governments as well as the major world institutions and corporations are saying some of the right things, but in practice are doing the opposite of what is necessary. America, which is the world's largest polluter and soon to be overtaken by China, are determined to build their economies on growth, similarly the other rising world economies such as India, Brazil, the European Union, Russia, Japan and Indonesia as well as the developing economies in Africa, Asia Europe and South America are all following a pattern of growth that will damage our planet.

At a time of such blatant hypocrisy and lack of commitment from the top managers of our governments, corporations and institutions, it would appear that unless billions of people engage in mass acts of civil disobedience, civilization as we know it; is going to die within a few generations. This is not an extremist view, it is the predictions of international institutions and governments backed up by the majority of scientists engage in GW and CC. Lack of urgent and sustained action worldwide may well kill hundreds of millions later in this century, and growing poverty and resource scarcity will plunge billions more into abject squalor and misery, and the only response of the political financial and ruling elite in the rich western world, especially the NATO countries is to promote globalisation; neo-liberal capitalism; a return to neo-colonialism across Africa and South America; and military expansion and antagonisms between America, Europe and their allies against Russia, China and countries that are considered to be unfriendly towards the western nations that dominates the world economy and order. America with only 5 per cent of the world's population consumes 20 per of the world energy and spends 45 per cent of the world's expenditure on militarism and sustains over 800 military bases across 140 countries has been and remained one of the greatest threats to our planet. How long should this world tolerate this neo-liberal insanity, which is built on inequality; undermining of democracy; destruction of our rain forests; promoting globalised greed, individualism and materialism, resulting of destruction of the global environment; promotion of and sustaining conflicts around the world; and misusing substantial sums of the world wealth to make the rich richer and the poor, even poorer? It has been reported that just 5 per cent of the richest people on earth owns 50 per cent of the total wealth. Just imagine if this wealth could be used to address, poverty and inequality, peace, GW and CC, world health, education; and environmental changes!

Our fragile planet –mother earth

13 billion years ago the "big bang" took place and started the formation of the galaxy from a single atom that could fit into the palm of one hand. The matter and anti-matter collided that created the "big bang". Planet earth was subsequently born some 5 billion years ago. It was formed from grains of dust, particles and clouds made up of debris from dead stars that spun like a disc around the sun and gradually became a planet. As the earth was forming the debris and particles that came together were bound together by the heat from the sun's explosion that started the solar system. Earth grew over a period of time and the temperature gradually reduced from up to 2000 degrees Fahrenheit. Earth's formation was a violent and unique process. Much of it was covered in oceans with no oxygen and little life. Life on earth gradually evolved to the point where human beings started to share the planet some 500 million years ago.

The world population has grown considerably over the last 3000 years. At the dawn of agriculture, about 8000 B.C., the population of the world was approximately 5 million. Over the 8,000-year period up to 1 A.D. it grew to between 200 to 300 million, with a growth rate of under 0.05 per cent, per year. A tremendous change occurred with the Industrial Revolution during the 18th Century: whereas it had taken all of human history until around 1800 for world population to reach one billion in 1804, the second billion was achieved in only 130 years (1930), the third billion in less than 30 years (1959), the fourth billion in 15 years (1974), and the fifth billion in only 13 years (1987). In 2011 it was reported by the United Nations that the world's population had reached 7 billion in October 2011, and this will increase to 8 billion by spring of 2024. During the 20th Century alone, the population in the world had grown from 1.65 billion to 6 billion. In 1970, there were roughly only half as many people in the world as there are now. Because of declining growth rates, it will probably take over 200 years to double again, according to the most recent United Nations estimates. Just two countries, China and India, have over 2.7 billion or over 30 per cent of the world's population. More than half (56.3 per cent) of the world's population lives in Asia. Africa which is seen as the poorest continent has the fastest growing population with well over 1 billion people representing around 15 per cent of the world's population. Europe with around 750 million representing 10.4 per cent and North America with 355 million representing 5 per cent of the world's population, between them has most of the world's wealth and power to transform the key institutions in the world to respond positively to climate change.

Despite the large growth and rising demand for resources, planet earth has managed to provide reasonably well, even though human beings are engaged in serious abuse of the planet every second of every day. The needs of those that are in desperate shortage of food and basic resources can easily be met if only the rich countries would stop spending such massive sums on weapons of war, destruction and wastage on food and household goods. Far too much wealth and power are concentrated in possession of too few people. Population growth has been associated with poverty, uncertainty and scarcity of resources as well as religious and cultural influences. Such rapid growth is probably the most lethal factor in GW and CC. To tackle GW and CC the entire world, especially the rich industrialised ones that are responsible for GW and CC have to quickly adopt a new mind-set that will result in extraordinary human behaviour. The survival of earth depends on all of us. We can all survive or perish together. Our planet is at serious risks now. It cannot go on sustaining life for millions of years.

Global warning has melted much of the polar ice caps and increased the Arctic temperature; raised the levels of the oceans; flooded large habitable areas; caused numerous storms, hurricanes and droughts; threatening human, plant and animal life; responsible for extreme climatic changes; brought about widespread conflicts over scarce resources; and threatening the survival of millions of species of plant, animal, insect life and many human communities around the world. Yet, those responsible for perpetuating GW and CC continue to defend the very behaviour and structures that are threatening our world through excessive and shameful inequality in daily life with over half of the world's population living in or below poverty levels, millions dying prematurely every year; stockpiling of over 22,000 nuclear weapons; regularly testing nuclear weapons; supporting wars and conflicts; failure to invest in education and health; and destabilising communities, leading to genocides and holocausts. The United Nations Conference on Sustainable Development, which took place in Rio de Janeiro, Brazil on 20-22 June 2012, produced a Report containing 283 clear, specific and practical measures for implementing sustainable development, whilst tackling climate change.

Recommendation 190 states:

> "We reaffirm that climate change is one of the greatest challenges of our time, and we express profound alarm that emissions of greenhouse gases continue to rise globally. We are deeply concerned that all countries, particularly developing countries, are vulnerable to the adverse impacts of climate change, and are already experiencing increased impacts, including persistent drought and extreme weather events, sea-level rise, coastal erosion and ocean acidification, further threatening food security and efforts to eradicate poverty and achieve sustainable development. In this regard we emphasize that adaptation to climate change represents an immediate and urgent global priority."

Recommendation 191 states:

> *"We underscore that the global nature of climate change calls for the widest possible cooperation by all countries and their participation in an effective and appropriate international response, with a view to accelerating the reduction of global greenhouse gas emissions. We recall that the United Nations Framework Convention on Climate Change provides that parties should protect the climate system for the benefit of present and future generations of humankind on the basis of equity and in accordance with their common but differentiated responsibilities and respective capabilities. We note with grave concern the significant gap between the aggregate effect of mitigation pledges by parties in terms of global annual emissions of greenhouse gases by 2020 and aggregate emission pathways consistent with having a likely chance of holding the increase in global average temperature below 2° C, or 1.5° C above pre-industrial levels. We recognize the importance of mobilizing funding from a variety of sources, public and private, bilateral and multilateral, including innovative sources of finance, to support nationally appropriate mitigation actions, adaptation measures, technology development and transfer and capacity-building in developing countries. In this regard, we welcome the launching of the Green Climate Fund and call for its prompt operationalization so as to have an early and adequate replenishment process."*

This assertion was re-enforced in December 2012 when a leaked early draft of the UN's latest climate change study shows human activities to be responsible for climate warming that will take centuries to reverse, even if greenhouse gas emissions were to stop right now. "Many aspects of climate change will persist for centuries even if concentrations of greenhouse gases are stabilised. This represents a substantial multi-century commitment created by human activities today,".... "For scenarios driven by carbon dioxide alone, global average temperature is projected to remain approximately constant for many centuries following a complete cessation of emissions,".... "Thus a large fraction of climate change is largely irreversible on human time scales, except if net anthropogenic greenhouse gas emissions were strongly negative over a sustained period" according to the draft report by the UN's Intergovernmental Panel on Climate Change. So saving the planet cannot be a quick fix. It will take several generations to stop, let alone reversing this travel to destruction. Instead of the rich and most polluting countries working together to deal with the most pressing issue on our planet, they are set to continue and even resurrect the worst excesses of the cold war over the civil war in Syria, the Middle East and the Russian intervention in the Ukraine.

I have listed below some of the key incidents related to Global warming and climate change since 2004:

- Arctic sea ice shrunk to the smallest area for 12,000 years (September 2011)

- Serious droughts in parts of America, Australia, and Asia followed by severe floods

- Destructive winds and severe floods in parts of England

- The hottest year (2012) in the USA since record, resulting in serious and sustained wildfires

- Several earthquakes in the USA and other parts of the world

- Earthquake and Tsunami in Fukushima, Japan (2011) causing major Nuclear disaster

- Deadly 5.6 magnitude earthquakes in Iran and 7.1 in the Philippines with many deaths (2013)

- 6.8 magnitude earthquake in Peru

- 9.0 earthquake triggered a tsunami in the Indian Ocean, that killed more than 226,000 in 12 countries and left millions homeless, making it the deadliest tsunami in world history (2004)

- 7.9 earthquake killed over 40,000 people and injured thousands more in the Sichuan, Gansu, and Yunnan Provinces in western China (2008)

- Dominican Republic and Haiti hit by torrential rains that overflowed the Soliel River, causing floods and mudslides, destroying villages, and killing more than 2,000 people (2004)

- South Asia: annual monsoons left 5 million homeless and more than 1,800 dead in India, Nepal, and Bangladesh (2004)

- Extreme winter weather including cold, snowfall, avalanches, and flooding in Afghanistan, India, and Pakistan killed more than 800 people. A record 37 in of rain in a 24-hour period and a week of monsoon rains left 1,000 dead in western India (2005)

- Flooding of several rivers in southern and eastern Ethiopia killed more than 800 people

- Monsoon rains and flooding left 660 people dead, and more than a million stranded in West Bengal, India (2007)

- Cyclone Nargis hits the Irrawaddy Delta and the city of Yangon, Myanmar, killing about 78,000 people. Most of the deaths and destruction were caused by a 12-foot high tidal wave that formed during the storm (2008). Cyclone Nargis is the worst natural disaster since the tsunami in 2004.

- The worst flooding in Southern China in 50 years killing over 60 people and destroying 5.4 million acres of crops (2008)

- Typhoon Morakot caused a mudslide that buried schools, homes, and at least 100 people in southern Taiwan (2009)

- At least 2,828 people are killed due to record flooding during the (2011) monsoon season in the Philippines, Thailand, Cambodia, Myanmar, Malaysia, Vietnam, and Laos

- An extreme rainy season causes flash flooding. At least 72 people are killed and thousands are left homeless in Nigeria (2012).

- Five months of rain falls overnight causing massive flooding and killing 172 people in Russia. Nearly 13,000 homes are damaged. Most of the damage happens in the city of Krymsk (2012)

- Flash floods around Boulder, Colorado in the USA caused massive damage, cutting off highways, destroying hundreds of homes and killing at least six people. More than 800 people are unaccounted for in Boulder and Larimer Counties. The flooding is due to heavy rains producing record levels of rainfall.

Earthquakes and tsunamis can be devastating to populations and parts of the planet. An earthquake is a trembling movement of the earth's crust. These tremors are generally caused by shifts of the plates that make up the earth's surface. The movements cause vibrations to pass through and around the earth in wave form, just as ripples are generated when a pebble is dropped into water. Volcanic eruptions, rock falls, landslides, and explosions can also cause a quake. A tsunami (pronounced soo-NAHM-ee) is a series of huge waves that occur as the result of a violent underwater disturbance, such as an earthquake or volcanic eruption. They are sometimes mistakenly referred to as tidal waves, but tsunamis have nothing to do with the tides.

What is to be done?

With billions of humans engaged in highly destructive behaviour towards nature every day causing pollution; spread of toxic chemicals on land and in the oceans; releasing millions of tons of CO2 emissions; abusing plants, animals, wildlife and fertile land; creating billions of tons of waste; and burning tens of millions of fossil fuels, it is no wonder our planet is reacting with such turbulence. The acceleration of natural disasters and radical climate change will continue to destroy the planet's environment and ecosystems that will severely impact on human populations, resulting in famines, infectious diseases, hundreds of millions of pre-mature deaths, wars and scarcity of essential resources for our survival.

Positive things each one of us can do to reduce climate change and global warming includes the following:

- Use less energy as well as less fossil fuel. Organise a home energy audit

- Reuse, reduce and recycle and encourage others within your family, friends at work and in your community to do so

- Promote less energy waste by turning down heating appliances and use energy saving light bulbs. This could save up to 2000 CO_2 annually and save you money

- Eat less and more sensibly as well as avoiding waste of food

- Use your car less especially for short journeys. Share transport and use public transport where possible

- Stop wasting water. Use less hot water. Recycle and use rain water as much as possible. Turn off any unused electrical equipment when not in use

- Eat less animal flesh. Eat more vegetables. Grow your own in tubs if you do not have your own garden space. Share excess vegetables with friends and neighbours

- Plant trees as they absorb CO_2. Just one tree can absorb up to one ton of CO_2

- Make better use of second hand household equipment and repair them instead of replacing them. Buying more energy saving equipment

- Insulate all homes against the cold

- Use less heating, air-conditioning, electricity, gas and petrol

- Keep fit through dieting, regular exercise include walking and swimming

- Spread the word on saving energy and lead by example

Positive things governments and corporations can do to reduce climate change and global warming includes the following:

- Promote the UN common vision on climate change (CC)

- Support sustainable development nationally and internationally

- Use far less energy and fossil fuels

- Always think and act globally to save energy

- Make more use of efficient and clean technology

- Promote public awareness on CC global warming (GW) recycling and reuse

- Carry out energy saving audits regularly support more energy conservation

- Issue guidelines on energy savings. Train staff to save energy

- Avoid wastage through excessive and unnecessary packaging and transport

- Better transportation, cleaner environment, more recycling and reuse of materials

- Less use of chemicals, pesticides, and harmful substances

- Oppose dumping in the seas and oceans. Impose heavy fines for environmental abuse

- Promote conservation of plants and living creatures as well as the rain forests

- Impose carbon rationing. Oppose harmful international trade and exploitation

- Tackle poverty and increase healthcare and education

- Promote gender equality and rights of women to education, training and commerce and politics

- Introduce CC and GW in schools curriculum and award certificates for achievements to pupils and schools. Issue Charter Marks for achievements in CO_2 reductions

- Support peace initiatives, oppose wars and conflicts

- Support land reform and oppose confiscation and appropriation of land from peasants and farmers

- Support fair trade nationally and internationally

- Promote international co-operation and sustainable development globally

- Support human and civil rights, as well as freedom from exploitation and economic enslavement. Support freedom and justice for all around the world

- Spend less on militarism and more on peaceful resolution of conflicts

- Use local products, recruit local staff, pay a fair wage

- Avoid exploitation of workers and work in partnership with local communities

- Promote health, happiness and fitness at work

- Turn off unused equipment and recycle, reduce and reuse as much as possible

- Share research and development as well as new technology with less developed countries and work to increase income and protection of workers

- Respect natural and national cultures, civilisations, rights of indigenous people

- Involve workers, trade unions, women and young people in sustainable development and economic management as well as in the political structures

- Guard against exploitation of poor countries by global institutions and corporations, including the World Bank, International Monetary Fund, cartels, monopolies and financial mercenaries and gangsters

We live or perish together

Delusion is no solution for the pollution and rape of our planet. Urgent local and global actions against GW and CC are well overdue. The rich are far too preoccupied in getting richer at the expense of the poor. This phenomenon applies to individuals, nations as well as economic and political blocks. The discussions around CC and GW are linked to some strange bedfellows. For example, the socialists and left leaning radicals are blaming the rich capitalists and corporations for abusing and polluting our planet in the cause of making profits at any cost to the environment and adopting a short term strategy. They would argue that it is suicidal to continue policies that promote the increased production of fossil fuels -such as the $1.9 trillion of annual subsidies, according to the IMF, that goes towards supporting the industry. And without these subsidies, alternative energies such as wind power, which receive far less financial support, would be competitive with fossil fuels in just a few years, depending on the country. The IMF concludes that just removing these subsidies would reduce waste and result in a 13 per cent reduction in CO2 emissions, with many other positive impacts of reduced demand for carbon-based energy, according to the Paris-based International Energy Agency. The radicals claim that there is a lack of political and financial will by governments and organisations such as the IMF, World Bank and large fossil fuel corporations with enormous power and influence to find alternative sources of energy sue to the high profitability of oil, coal and gas production. For example Exxon-Mobil, for instance, with sales of $428 billion in 2012, has a larger turnover than the GDP of all except the richest twenty seven countries. Also that the largest 100 corporations in the world are responsible for are responsible for over half the world's GW.

Capitalism in a neo-liberal economic period is blamed for destroying small and medium size businesses and concentrating unimaginable wealth and power in the hands of a tiny number, of no more than two per cent of the world's businesses. The owners and controllers of the large corporations and financial institutions are locked into a structural profit making process upon which hangs the compulsion for growth and massive capital accumulation. Hence the wealth of the top 200 billionaires is probably more that the wealth owned by around half of the world's population. These billionaires have accumulated their wealth though exploiting the poor as well as mother earth, as their activities extends beyond the boundaries of nation states, or individual corporations. The capitalist-class worldwide rule over the global economy and they have the power to make and break governments that seeks to regulation the corporations, not only because many political parties and governments are financed by big businesses, but also because the financial interests of the politicians are tied up with the success of the corporations. Some will argue that governments themselves are essentially tools of the capitalist and class system. Politicians may be elected under so-called democratic systems but in reality their campaigns and economic strategies are financed, supported and decisively influenced by the economic power of the capitalist class, which reduces "democracy" to no more than a farce. Therefore, it will be extremely difficult for the capitalist class, the governments that are under their influence to solve the GW and CC crisis, as they and their system are the problem and not the solution. For the radicals on the left it will fall on the working class, those within the tiny section of the capitalist class and the corporations to address the crisis associated with GW and CC.

Fighting global warming
and climate change together

Despite the criticisms of the capitalist class and corporations by the radical left, there are increasing signs that some well-known and extremely rich capitalists and corporations as well as politicians are linking up with the struggles to fight GW and CC. Billionaire George Soros, via his Centre for American Progress, which he funds to the tune of $27 million a year, is a major player in this fight. George Soros also funds several other environmentalist causes and projects totalling billions of dollars. Jeremy Grantham, billionaire co-founder of Boston-based asset management firm Grantham Mayo van Otterloo (GMO), supports Britain's most influential environmental project; the Grantham Research Institute and the Grantham Institute for Climate Change. Several wealthy charitable foundations such as the Rockefeller Foundation, the Esme Fairbairn Foundation, and the Pew Foundation, have political affiliations in the green movement and elsewhere. Other rich and famous people are also joining the fight against GW and CC. Robert Redford; Yoko Ono; Leo DiCaprio; Cate Blanchett; Edward Norton; Brad Pitt; Pierce Brosnan and many others are committed environmentalists. Barak Obama, Hillary Clinton, Al Gore and other influential politicians are, at least in theory committed to fighting GW and CC, not only as a means to create millions of new jobs, but also to address the concerns of the public. Some people may argue that the super-rich capitalists that made billions on the misery of working people and degradation of the environment wants to put some of the money back either because of guilt; wanting to be liked; peer group pressure or, simply have a genuine change of heart. I certainly welcome their interests regardless of their motives.

The cost of fighting CC and GW has been and will continue to be even more expensive as the problem gets worse. According to the World Bank, the costs of "natural" disasters have risen from $50 billion per year in the 1980s, to $200 billion per year in 2013, is likely to cost a total of $3.7 trillion. By 2050, it's estimated the annual requirement will rise to $1 trillion. Underlining that no country is immune, the U.S. had to allocate $100 billion in 2012 as a result of Hurricane Sandy and several other extreme weather, flooding and drought disasters for disaster relief measures. More money will have to be spent on rebuilding flooded cities; building sea defences; financing irrigation projects; mitigating pollution; coping with the spread of wars, famine and diseases; supporting agriculture and refugees; are all things that will add to the financial burden, especially amongst developing countries. According to the UN's Environment Program report, by 2020, Africa will have to find an additional $7 billion to $15 billion to cope with climate change impacts such as increased droughts, flooding, and crop and infrastructure damage. This is quite a burden for the world's poorest continent with the highest population growth, especially during a decade where so-called "war on terrorism", globalisation, neo-colonialism, wars and neo-liberal capitalism has done so much to destabilise our planet and the natural world.

Having taken over the manufacturing, financial and corporate world, the capitalist system is taking over the social, technical, media, communication, transportation, information and marketing world. This fact reinforces the need for activists to get together and to unite across the world to take social, economic, political and ecological action into building one global movement, as all these issues are interlinked in the struggle to combat GW and CC.

The problems associated with GW and CC has been largely caused by the rich countries going back to imperialism, colonialism, slavery, the industrial revolution and capitalist wars and invasions. So far the poorest countries have paid $550 billion on principal and interest to Western financial institutions, on a total debt of $540 billion over the last 30 years. Yet they still manage to owe $523 billion. For every dollar received in grants and aid the developing world commits $13 to debt repayment and purchase of Western goods.

Poorer nations in the developing world have been growing the coffers of the rich nations in NATO, the EU and institutions such as the IMF, World Bank and other Western financial empires and corporations. The Western rich nations and their banking and financial institutions have been draining funds from desperately needed projects in the developing countries, to address poverty, education, health and social welfare due to the lack of infrastructure development, investment capital, agricultural facilities and their ability to adapt to climate change. The rich nations should immediately cancel all "Third World" debt, just as the U.S. and European governments spent several trillion pounds and dollars of public funds bailing out the banks and corporations through quantitative easing (printing money and buying debts as well as keeping interest rates artificially low for years), since the 2008 financial crash. Moreover, governments in the rich Western countries have held down the pay of the overwhelming majority of workers; encouraging privatisation of public services; reduce welfare and public spending; allowing prices of food, fuel, energy and accommodation to increase at a time of reduced living standards and increase debts of poorer people around the world through domestic and global financial and political actions. As a consequence our world has become less caring and compassionate; more unequal, turbulent and dysfunctional; more violent, and disunited due to wars, conflicts and sectarian violence and racism; more people enslaved by unemployment poverty, people trafficking, and helplessness. For example the insanity of political decisions made in Washington, USA – the richest and most powerful country in the world – to cut back on the funding of food stamps for the 45 million impoverish and starving Americans is indeed a shameful indictment on the cruelty of the capitalist and corporate class system.

For the capitalist and corporations, it is more important to achieve higher profits and productivity, lower cost of production, growth and the reduction in the strength of workers and their unions that to tackle, inequality, poverty, the impact of GW and CC, world peace and sustainable development. We must not allow the rich countries to pay lip service to GW and CC, or accuse the poorer countries that will bear the brunt of the problems, for focussing on the destruction of our planet, simply to receive grants from the rich world. Within 18 months of the Rio Conference in June 2012, the rich countries were seeking to reduce their moral, political and financial commitment listed in the 283 recommendations of the Conference to tackle GW and CC. The latest round of international climate negotiations – known as COP 19, for the 19th annual Conference of Parties – held in Warsaw, Poland in November 2013, saw major governments retreating even further from taking real action to curb global warming. The Western nations have bankrupted themselves through lack of regulations within the banking and financial sectors; the financing of wars and conflicts; failure to collect taxation from the rich tax evaders and tax dodgers; failure to invest in manufacturing; failure to tax the rich and super rich who stashed away trillions of dollars in tax havens and bogus investments; failure to reach international agreements on tax dodging; failure to invest in people and creating a much fairer and equal society and failure to defend democracy against the mercenary corporations and financial gangsters. We must not let them continue to abuse us and our planet.

I fear for my family, especially my children and grandchildren and my country of origin, Guyana, which will be one of the first to submerge under the rise of the water in the Atlantic Ocean. I fear for all the 7 plus billion human beings and the 8.7 million species that inhabit our fragile, but still generous planet.

Chapter 19:

People I admire and those I don't

In this chapter I want to pay tribute to a number of people past and present, who I admire because they have had a lot of influence in my life. They have inspired, motivated, and helped me to find meaning, direction and satisfaction. I have already paid tribute to my wife, children and grandchildren who have given much love happiness and reasons to live and to fight for the kind of society and world I want for everyone. I will briefly comment on others who have been part of my personality, character, role model and mentor through the lives they have lived; their legacy to humankind and the lasting inspiration I have gained from them. The first person that comes to my mind is my mother. I really wish I had spent more time with her and to repay her for at least some of what she gave for nearly eighteen years. She was a feminist, a great mother and teacher, a socialist, someone who broke all the traditional rules, lived a diverse life and brought up seven children; sometimes in the most unorthodox way. She did all this without being able to read, write or sign her name. If she was not taken away from us at such an early age, and at a time when I was struggling financially thousands of miles away from her, I would have certainly carried out my plans for her and my father who died within a few months of each other. I would have built her a nice self-contained bungalow with a lovely garden, ensured that there was running water from a tap within the house, a flushed toilet, electricity and all the modern equipment and aids to make her comfortable. I would have also ensured she had enough money to live on. All these things she never had in her lifetime. If only she had lived just ten more years, and not died within six years of my departure from her arms. I have gained a great deal from my mother and I very often felt her presence during the many late nights I spent alone in my large modern dethatched office, three meters away from my bungalow, over the last four years writing this book alone.

Francis O'Grady - first woman TUC General Secretary

I have met many people during my fifty years in trades union and politics, some of whom I have a great deal of admiration and respect. Others, I met have never impressed me, but I nevertheless admired them for standing up for their beliefs. I have met every General Secretary of the Trade Union Council (TUC) since 1961. The position of General Secretary was formed in 1921, when the Parliamentary Committee of the TUC became the General Council. The position of Secretary has been a permanent, full-time position in the TUC since 1904. Before that, the Secretary was elected annually at Congress. Although I met George Woodcock who was General Secretary from 1960-1969, I did not have a personal conversation with him. I did have several chats with his successor Vic Feather, who had a lovely North of England accent. He was in many ways a traditional trade unionist who enjoyed a debate. Len Murray took over from Vic Feather in 1973 and stayed in the job for exactly 10 years when he was replaced by Norman Willis. Len Murray was much different from Norman in a number of ways. Len was more reserved and thoughtful, very similar to a senior civil servant, whilst Norman was quite bouncy, always liked a laugh and chatty. Norman interviewed me for a job at the TUC in 1984 as the Race Relations Officer, but I was not successful. His Assistant John Monks took over from him in 1993 and left in 2003 for a job within the European Trade Union Movement. John also interviewed me for the same position that became vacant at the TUC, during his time as the General Secretary. Again I was not appointed and I decided to make a formal complaint to the Employment Tribunal for discrimination. I later withdrew my case on the first day of the hearing in London as I was not legally represented and the TUC lawyer really gave me a hard time.

John Monks was a long serving staff at the TUC long before he was appointed to the position of General Secretary and I knew him well. His successor, Brendan Barber; now Sir Brendan Barber and Head of the Advisory, Conciliation and Arbitration Services (ACAS) after retiring from the TUC after 10 years, in December 2013. Brendan was replaced by Francis O' Grady the first woman to become General Secretary during the nearly 150 years of the TUC. Brendon's departure was reported in the right wing newspaper, the Daily Mail which made quite a story of the head of the TUC leaving after 10 years with £100,000 golden goodbye and £62,000 inflation proof annual pension. In addition he was within a short period he was appointed to a top national position by the Conservative Government.

Francis O'Grady is a person I admire. I have known her for a long time. She was the Assistant General Secretary at the TUC after being involved in various key positions within the TUC national structure. She was named as the 11th most powerful woman in Britain by the BBC Women's' Hour Programme in February 2013. I met her several times and we took a photograph together at the TUC Black Workers Conference on 11 April 2014. Francis is a charming, as well as a radical person, who will be a great leader for years to come.

The rise and fall of King Arthur

Arthur Scargill and I were arrested on the same day by the police, when we were pickets at the Grunwick dispute: an industrial dispute involving trade union recognition at the Grunwick Film Processing Laboratories in North London, The two-year strike between 1976 and 1978 was one of the bitterest industrial disputes during my union involvement. During the dispute Arthur who was the leader of the National Union of Mineworkers (NUM) brought a couple of coach loads of miners to support the Grunwick workers. I was on the picket line one quiet day when the police were taunting the mainly women strikers about only a few people being at the picket line. Suddenly, we saw the miners with their banners marching towards us and the police started to call for more support in desperation. They knew the miners were tough people from their own strike action a few years earlier. Arthur Scargill is a person I really admire for his radicalism, courage, anti-racism and great speeches at demonstrations and conferences.

The Grunwick dispute became a cause célèbre of trade unionism and labour relations law. At its height, there were thousands of Trade Unionists and police in confrontations, with over 550 arrests on the picket line and frequent police violence. The arrests made during the strike was at the time, the highest such figure in any industrial dispute since the General Strike of 1926. The dispute was reported nightly on the national television news, depicting the often violent clashes between the strikers and the Metropolitan Police's Special Patrol Group. Grunwick was the first time that this paramilitary police unit had been deployed in an industrial dispute. The mostly female, immigrant, East African Asian strikers – dubbed "strikers in saris" by the news media – were led by Jayaben Desai, whose membership of the union was later suspended following her hunger strike outside the Trades Union Congress (TUC) headquarters in November 1977. This was also the first dispute where the majority of strikers were from an ethnic minority and still received widespread support from the labour movement. Mrs Desai, a tiny traditional Hindu woman displayed the courage of a giant. It was amazing to see this fearless lady who passed away in retirement in her native India confronting hundreds of these 6 feet tall white police officers with helmets, shields and batons for over a year. This is a woman I really do admire. She reminded me so much of my mother, who would have done the same in the circumstances.

Arthur was a well-known union militant from Yorkshire, England, he was a great trade union organiser who managed to mobilise over 15,000 engineers to walk out of their workplace in Birmingham to support the miners who were involved in a union dispute in Saltley Gate, in 1972. Arthur was the inventor of the "flying picket" which the Conservative government outlawed. Scargill led two thousand miners to the Birmingham plant to try to force the closure at the Saltley coke depot. It was the first time controversial "flying pickets" had appeared in such large numbers away from the coalfields. Arthur was the strategist as during one of the bitterest miners' strike in Britain in 1974, which had far reaching effects on a Conservative government that was voted out of office a few months later. He was elected President on the NUM in 1981, and led the miners' strike in 1983-1984. This was by far the most bitter and controversial as well as violent dispute in which the Conservative government, under Margaret Thatcher, used the police in their thousands against the striking miners. There were thousands of arrests and injuries during the dispute. My wife and I demonstrated with the miners and we sent money and food to support the striking miners. Sadly, Arthur lost the battle, which encouraged Mrs Thatcher to seriously defeat not only the miners, but indeed the entire trade union movement. The miners lost their jobs by the thousands and the union membership of the TUC declined from nearly from nearly 14 to less than 7 million during the Thatcher years. Arthur was right when he told the nation that the government was determined to destroy the coal mining industry in Britain.

Sadly, King Arthur lost his power base as the NUM leader, which did not help his career in the trade union or labour movement. He was loved by the radicals and hated by the social democrats, liberals and conservatives within and outside the trade union and labour movement. He made a serious mistake by not having a ballot before he called the national miners' strike, something even some of his supporters criticised him for. I admire Arthur and his commitment to fighting racism within the unions and in society, we addresses several meetings together over the years in London. On many occasions, the media in my county referred to me as either, the Arthur Scargill, Ken Livingstone or Tony Benn of Bedfordshire. Mrs Thatcher who took on Arthur Scargill and his thousands of miners, fighting for their jobs and their communities is one of the politician and Prime Minister I most disliked since I arrived in London in 1961. She was serious and committed class warriors whose administration caused much pain, suffering and anxieties to tens of millions of working class and poor people during her time as Prime Minister. The policies she put in place which reduced the power of the unions, deregulated the commanding heights of the economy, privatised the public services, selling off council houses and boosting the individualistic and materialistic aspirations of most of the British people are still haunting the economic, social, cultural and political consciousness in Britain today, even though she passed away in 2013.

Tony Benn

I was inspired a great deal politically by Tony Benn since I joined the Labour Party in 1961. I first met him in the late 1960's when he was Post Master General. He was appointed by Prime Minister Harold Wilson, whom I met on a couple of occasions. I admired Wilson a great deal more than any Labour Prime Ministers since his departure. I disliked Tony Blair more than any other Labour Prime Minister since Ramsay MacDonald who was Prime Minister in 1923. Prime Minister Gordon Brown came second on my dislikes. I met Tony when he visited the Luton Post Office where I was the Branch Secretary. He met the managers and he insisted on meeting the workers and their union representatives. So I had the pleasure of taking him in to the large office where the workers were at 6.00am sorting out their letters before embarking on their delivery rounds. He was very pleasant, interesting and we had a cup of tea together. I became a fan of Tony as he pursued his left wing radical political career. I met him on several occasions since the1960's. He was a regular supporter of the Anti-Apartheid Movement having been the first Member of Parliament to table a motion opposing apartheid in South Africa, and he also first MP to introduce a Human Rights Bill on the use of nuclear weapons and to encourage nuclear disarmament and militarism. Tony was a regular speaker with Michael Foot – leader of the Labour Party, who never became Prime Minister – at the Campaign for Nuclear Disarmament (CND) Marches and rallies in London.

The next time I had a prolonged conversation with Tony was when I interviewed him for over 30 minutes in 1983 for an article as editor of the GMB union Newspaper. He invited me to his home in London for the interview. We started off with a cup of tea, of course and we drank tea throughout the interview. I recorded the interview on a tape and he also kept a recorded copy. Tony was so kind and relaxed. He genuinely appreciated the fact that I was interviewing him for a relatively centre right union which never supported his political ambitions. A photograph showing Benn holding a previous copy of the newspaper appeared on the front page. It was well received by the activists within the union. During his long political career having born on 3 April 1925, and died on 14 March 2014, and served as an MP for 47 years, Tony was a mature, honest and a conviction politician. He followed his father in to Parliament and his mother Margaret was, like his father a strong Labour Party supporter with a lot of commitment to fairness, justice and equality. My wife and I met Tony on several occasions and we always supported him and his politics. My daughter Jane also admired Tony especially for his commitment towards equality for women and his support for anti-racism campaigns as well as rights for workers.

I have never been ashamed being associated with the views of Tony Benn, or labelled a Bennite by the media and people who opposed my political and trade union views. Tony always supported the under-dog; the victims of oppression and injustice, even if it meant he was risking his career. I was heavily involved in the Campaign for Labour Party Democracy (CLPD), which Tony supported. He was opposed to these members of Parliament having selected for a parliamentary seat remained as the MP or, the prospective MP until they retire. Most of these Labour MPs were right wing, lazy and did very little to actively promote peace, justice, fairness, equal rights for women, social justice and workers' rights. They were primary concerned with their own careers, and maintaining all be status and perks of being an MP. Tony Benn challenged them and they disliked him. Tony was one of the few British politicians who become more left-wing as he grew older. He was passionate about peace and rejected the propaganda carried out by Tony Blair and his Cabinet which led to the invasion of Iraq, with the loss of 1 million lives and several millions of people becoming refugees. For Tony the three successive parliamentary victories by Mrs Thatcher were handed to her by the failures of successive Labour leaders because of their failure to build the Party on the radicalism of the working class. For Tony "Our loss to Thatcher was surrender rather than a defeat". Tony had the foresight that the Labour Party since the 1960's was incrementally shedding its radical past, especially during 1945-55 and at the same time creeping up towards the Conservative electoral middle ground. This process has brought the Labour Party to power in 1997 and it maintained this rightward shift until 2010 when Labour was replaced by a Conservative and Liberal Democrats coalition government. Thatcher once said that her greatest legacy was "Tony Blair and New Labour".

The British media never ceased to condemn Tony and labelling him an "extremist" or a member of the "Looney left" because his political and economic views were in many areas the opposite of Thatcherism. Tony was a great socialist, a person with a lot of compassion and love for the human race worldwide. He was the best Labour leader we never had; a person with commitment to radical change; peace and justice for all and not just the few; a believer in public services being publicly owned; introduction of legislation to regulate the commanding heights of the economy; a world free from colonialism, imperialism, militarism and exploitation by corporations. Thatcher was a calculated monster who ended up de-regulating and privatising as much as she could, and as a result created much suffering, misery, inequality and unfairness in Britain and abroad. She destroyed the unions, community spirit and the life chances of many working class people. She enjoyed punishing the poor and demonising them. Tony Benn was the opposite. The saddest thing was that the careerists, opportunists and reactionary right wing leadership within the Labour Party and trade unions denied Tony his rightful place in British and international politics. I am confident that we would have had a more caring, compassionate and peaceful world if Tony was supported by the true comrades in the Party. He would have followed with the changes made by Clem Atlee and Nye Bevan. Instead, we were lumbered with Wilson, Callaghan, Blair and Brown who have all been political pigmies, compared to Atlee. The last time I saw Tony was when my wife and I attended the annual

---

Tolpuddle Martyrs rally in Dorset in July 2013. His last words to us were "See you again next year comrades".

Tony was a great parliamentarian who by the end of the 80s characterising Britain as a state in which the extra-parliamentary struggle had to be supported because democracy was not working. In 1981 he told a Labour rally that Labour was "under attack by the Pentagon, Brussels, IMF, the House of Lords and the SDP". After the US invasion of the tiny Caribbean island of Grenada in 1983, by President Reagan, he told Tribune that America might seize control of the UK if British governments did not do its bidding. The following year, he defended the right to revolt against the "oncoming" totalitarianism of the Thatcher governments. In 2003 he argued and demonstrated against the war in Iraq and Afghanistan and continued to oppose American and NATO aggression in Libya from the rule of Muammar Gaddafi and strongly opposed any intervention in the conflict in Syria by outside powers. He was also passionately about defending the NHS, our public services and welfare state. By the end of his life many of his positions on anti-imperialism and anti-western intervention had become main-stream on the British left. He had become a respected elder statesman of the anti-war, anti-US, anti-intervention generation of radicals. Many people who did not agree with some of his political philosophy were nevertheless convinced that what he said made sense and that his views were rational and sincerely held.

Benn's socialism was definitely non-Marxist. He did not arrive at his worldview through historical materialism as much as through the Bible. What he lacked in knowledge of political economy or revolutionary theory he always more than made up for with energy, charm and honesty. Benn did not consume alcohol: he was assiduous and obsessive with keeping records. He left 11 large diaries covering all major events over at least the last 50 years. Much of his work and thinking were made up of deep and sincere moral fervour that underpinned everything he did, which came from his nonconformist conscience. For him, life was a process of self-improvement, preaching the issues that matters most to ordinary people struggling to live a decent and reasonable life. He saw his career as a duty towards humankind. He never stopped preaching through any programme that would have him, and was a resident on radio's Any Questions and television's Question Time for decades, becoming in time more comfortable with forums in which he could communicate directly with the public – "people at home". He was a great public speaker and a great parliamentarian. Benn was convinced that the role of the Parliament in scrutinising the executive was being undermined by the concentration of power in Downing Street, first by Margaret Thatcher and then by Tony Blair.

Millions were inspired by Benn's principles, his commitment and his unswerving support for many campaigns. He was president of the Stop the War Coalition right up to his death and helped initiate the People's Assembly in opposition to government policies of austerity and inequality. Far from having little influence on politics and change, Tony was in the forefront of opposing wars, apartheid, racism and sexism. In this he was often in advance of establishment opinion, but equally often in agreement with public opinion. He was loved precisely because he did articulate views shared by many outside the corridors of power. We have all have lost a great champion in Tony Benn. His political legacy will inspire many people in the years ahead.

Fidel Castro

Fidel Alejandro Castro Ruz was born on 13 August, 1926. I was born on 6 August 1943. Fidel is better known as a Cuban revolutionary communist politician who overthrew the United States-backed, corrupt military junta of Cuba, President Fulgencio Batista. After serving a years' imprisonment in 1953 after a failed attack on the Moncada Barracks; Castro travelled to Mexico, where he formed a revolutionary group with his brother Raúl and friend Che Guevara, the 26th of July Movement. Returning to Cuba, Castro led the Cuban revolution which ousted Batista in 1959 through a popular armed rebellion. The famous Argentinean revolutionary, Ernesto Che Guevara and a small band or armed rebels secured a historical victory that inspired many revolutionary movements across, Africa, Latin America and elsewhere. Castro became the first Prime Minister of Cuba after the revolution: a position he occupied from 1959 to 1976, and President from 1976 to 2008. He also served as the Commander in Chief of the Cuban Revolutionary Armed Forces from 1959 to 2008, and as the First Secretary of the Communist Party of Cuba from 1961 until 2011. The Americans were furious at the removal of Batista and the governments of President Dwight D. Eisenhower and John F. Kennedy unsuccessfully attempted to remove him, by economic blockade, assassination attempts, counter-revolution and dirty work by the CIA, as well as the Bay of Pigs armed invasion of Cuba in 1961. In order to counter the American threats, Castro formed an economic and military alliance with the Soviet Union and allowed them to place nuclear weapons on the island, sparking the Cuban Missile Crisis in 1962, which almost started the Third World War.

Politically a Marxist-Leninist, Castro under his administration the Republic of Cuba became a one-party socialist state; industry and businesses were nationalized, and socialist reforms implemented in all areas of society. Internationally, Castro was the Secretary-General of the Non-Aligned Movement, from 1979 to 1983 and from 2006 to 2008. Through his actions, struggles, politics and his writings Castro has significantly inspired and influenced millions of revolutionaries, radical individuals and groups across the world. He was a close friend on Nelson Mandela, Hugo Chavez and scores of revolutionaries across South America, Africa and Europe.

In 1961 Castro proclaimed the socialist nature of his administration, with Cuba becoming a one-party state under Communist Party rule; the first of its kind in the western hemisphere. Socialist reforms introducing central economic planning and expanding healthcare and education. The revolution transformed the lives of the vast majority of Cubans and provoked serious backlash from supporters of Batista and those who were opposed to the end of capitalism and private profits. Large numbers of Cubans have left Cuba since the revolution and settled mainly in America. Many of these people are opposed to the Cuban government and are supporting the Americans in their continual blockage of Cuba, despite many resolutions from the United Nations asking America to lift the blockade. Having visited Cuba and travelled extensively as well as asking many questions and speaking to people I recognise that there is state control of the media and the suppression of internal dissent against the regime. I am pleased that the Cuban government has loosened up some of the central planning, state control and encouraging enterprise, investment and trading despite the American blockade.

I admire Castro and the Cuban people for building a much fairer and equal society as well as providing one of the best healthcare and education system in the world. The relentless propaganda and attacks against Cuba by the American establishment and their stooges around the world is disgraceful and President Obama should be ashamed of prolonging the isolation and attacks on Cuba. It is not surprising that a large number of Americans do not see Obama as a Black President. I admire anyone who stands up against American imperialism and militarism.

For me, one of the significant policies of the Castro regime is to support foreign anti-colonialist; liberation struggles and revolutionary groups in Africa, Central and South America as well as in the Caribbean. Thousands of Cuban lives have been lost in these battles, especially in Africa. Unlike America and NATO Cuba has to foreign bases or armies based permanently outside of its own borders. In fact America still has a base in Guantanamo in Cuba, where they illegally imprison and torture people without trial in the most inhuman conditions. Cuba has always responded positively at time of world crisis and natural disasters by sending aids, doctors and specialist help as appropriate and where possible. Unlike the western powers that seek to topple the Cuban regime, Castro has been kind and altruistic to poor and oppressed people around the world without seeking to exploit them in return which is what the so-called foreign aid by America and Europe is all about. For every dollar in aid the donor extracts up to seven dollars in return through trade, interest, raw materials, investment opportunities and political support.

Nelson Mandela

Nelson Rolihlahla Mandela: 18 July 1918 – 5 December 2013 was a South African anti-apartheid revolutionary, politician, and world statesman who served as President of South Africa from 1994 to 1999. He could have gone on as President until he died, but instead declined to serve a second term, something very rare in politics. Mandela was South Africa's first black and democratically elected President. His death was reported and mourned throughout the world. He is one of the most famous and well known African and world politician. He was a socialist with tens of millions of followers all over the world. Mandela served as President of the African National Congress (ANC) from 1991 to 1997. He was committed to world peace and justice for all. Internationally, he acted as mediator between Libya and the United Kingdom in the Pan Am Flight 103 bombing trial, and oversaw military intervention in Lesotho. Mandela was bitterly opposed to the Iraq war and he made his position clear to the world. Mandela served 27 years in prison, initially on Robben Island, and later in Pollsmoor Prison and Victor Vorster Prison. An international campaign lobbied for his release for decades. I took part in several marches and demonstration through the Anti-Apartheid Movement calling for his release, recognition of the ANC and an end to apartheid in South Africa. The American and British right wing politicians supported the right wing racist regime. Thatcher, Reagan, and other European and NATO leaders regarded him as a terrorist and not a freedom fighter that he was.

On 5 August 1962 Mandela was arrested after living on the run for seventeen months, and was imprisoned in the Johannesburg Fort. Three days later, the charges of leading workers to strike in 1961 and leaving the country illegally were read to him during a court appearance. On 25 October 1962, Mandela was sentenced to five years in prison. While Mandela was imprisoned, police arrested prominent ANC leaders on 11 July 1963, at Liliesleaf Farm, Rivonia, and north of Johannesburg. Mandela was brought in, and at the Rivonia Trial they were charged by the chief prosecutor, Dr Percy Yutar, with four charges of the capital crimes of sabotage (which Mandela admitted) and crimes which were equivalent to treason, but easier for the government to prove. They were also charged with plotting a foreign invasion of South Africa, which Mandela denied. The specifics of the charges to which Mandela admitted complicity involved conspiring with the African National Congress and South African Communist Party to the use of explosives to destroy water, electrical, and gas utilities in the Republic of South Africa.

In his statement from the dock at the opening of the defence case in the trial on 20 April 1964 at Pretoria Supreme Court, Mandela laid out the reasoning in the ANC's choice to use violence as a tactic. His statement described how the ANC had used peaceful means to resist apartheid for years until the Sharpeville Massacre. That event coupled with the referendum establishing the Republic of South Africa and the declaration of a state of emergency along with the banning of the ANC made it clear to Mandela and his compatriots that their only choice was to resist through acts of sabotage and that doing otherwise would have been tantamount to unconditional surrender. Mandela went on to explain how they developed the Manifesto of Umkhonto we Sizwe on 16 December 1961 intent on exposing the failure of the National Party's policies after the economy would be threatened by foreigners' unwillingness to risk investing in the country. He closed his statement with these words:

"During my lifetime I have dedicated myself to the struggle of the African people. I have fought against white domination, and I have fought against black domination. I have cherished the ideal of a democratic and free society in which all persons live together in harmony and with equal opportunities. It is an ideal which I hope to live for and to achieve. But if needs be, it is an ideal for which I am prepared to die."

All those on trial, except Rusty Bernstein were found guilty and sentenced to life imprisonment on 12 June 1964.Mandela was imprisoned on Robben Island where he remained for the next eighteen of his twenty-seven years in prison. Prison conditions were very basic. Prisoners were segregated by race, with black prisoners receiving the fewest rations. Political prisoners were kept separate from ordinary criminals and received fewer privileges. Mandela describes how, as a D-group prisoner (the lowest classification) he was allowed one visitor and one letter every six months. Letters, when they came, were often delayed for long periods and made unreadable by the prison censors. Whilst in prison Mandela undertook study with the University of London by correspondence through its External Programme and received the degree of Bachelor of Laws. He was subsequently nominated for the position of Chancellor of the University of London in the 1981 election, but lost to Princess Anne.

He was released in 1990, during a time of escalating civil strife. Mandela joined negotiations with President F. W. de Klerk to abolish apartheid and establish multiracial elections in 1994, in which he led the ANC to victory and became South Africa's first black president. He published his autobiography in 1995. During his tenure in the Government of National Unity he invited other political parties to join the cabinet, and promulgated a new constitution. He also created the Truth and Reconciliation Commission to investigate past human rights abuses. While continuing the former government's liberal economic policy, his administration also introduced measures to encourage land reform, combat poverty, and expand healthcare services. Away from government Mandela became an elder statesman, focusing on charitable work in combating poverty and HIV/AIDS through the Nelson Mandela Foundation.

A person of courage and conviction

A Xhosa born to the Thembu royal family, Mandela attended the Fort Hare University and the University of Witwatersrand, where he studied law. Living in Johannesburg, he became involved in anti-colonial politics, joining the ANC and becoming a founding member of its Youth League. After the South African National Party came to power in 1948, he rose to prominence in the ANC's 1952 Defiance Campaign, was appointed superintendent of the organisation's Transvaal chapter and presided over the 1955 Congress of the People. Working as a lawyer, he was repeatedly arrested for seditious activities and, with the ANC leadership, was unsuccessfully prosecuted in the Treason Trial from 1956 to 1961. Influenced by Marxism, he secretly joined the South African Communist Party (SACP) and sat on its Central Committee. Although initially committed to non-violent protest, in association with the SACP he co-founded the militant Umkhonto we Sizwe (MK) in 1961, leading sabotage campaign against the apartheid government.

Despite the fact that the capitalist nations in the west saw Mandela a controversial figure for much of his life and denounced as a communist terrorist, he nevertheless gained for his courage and political conviction. He received more than 250 honours, including the 1993 Nobel Peace Prize, the US Presidential Medal of Freedom, and the Soviet Order of Lenin. He is held in deep respect within South Africa and the world, where he is often referred to by his Xhosa clan name, Madiba, or as Tata ("Father"); he is often described as "the father of the nation".

Nelson Mandela was the foster son of a Thembu Chief and raised in a traditional tribal culture during his childhood as part of the Thembu ruling family in the Transkei where he herded sheep and learnt to plough. His first name was Rolihlahla; the Nelson was added later by a primary school teacher. Nelson's boyhood was peaceful until the death of his father landed him in the care of a powerful relative who was the powerful Thembu Chief. From his Methodist school he went on to study at the missionary Fort Hare College, but was suspended for organising the students. He was involved in organising protests against white colonial rule of the College. To complete his studies and to avoid a threatened arranged marriage he went to Johannesburg where he met Walter Sisulu – a self-educated fighter against apartheid in South Africa. Sisulu arranged for Mandela to study law. Through his work in the law firm he saw at first hand the suffering of the African people. Being Black under apartheid meant that life for Africans was cruel, unequal, harsh and miserable. Mandela was opposed to apartheid and the associated cruelty and injustice. He committed himself towards the struggle for justice and freedom of the Africans and was prepared for the suffering and sacrifices, which he would encounter in the road towards personal and national liberation.

Mandela's childhood and early life was shaped by centuries of colonial rule which had concentrated all political, military and economic power and control in the hands of a white minority. Access to education, health, employment and freedom was severely controlled and restricted. The wealth of the country was owned overwhelmingly by the white minority. The great mass of the non-white population had been humbled and humiliated into submission by racism, which pervaded the whole of society. For Mandela the options towards liberation were few given that Africans did not have the vote or power to determine their future through the democratic process. Mandela decided to go along the non-violent route as a strategy. As someone who was born and grew up under British colonialism my views about life, liberty and humankind was shaped by my childhood experience and that is why I would rate Mandela as one of the top five people I admired most who have lived during the last 250 years.

The young Mandela became the first member of his family to attend a school, where his teacher Miss Mdingane gave him the English name "Nelson". When Mandela was nine, his father died of tuberculosis, and the regent, Jongintaba, became his guardian. Mandela attended a Wesleyan mission school located next to the palace of the regent. Following Thembu custom, he was initiated at age sixteen, and attended Clarkebury Boarding Institute. Designated to inherit his father's position as a privy councillor, in 1937 Mandela moved to Healdtown, the Wesleyan college in Fort Beaufort which most Thembu royalty attended. At nineteen, he took an interest in boxing and running at the school.

After enrolling, Mandela began to study for a Bachelor of Arts at the Fort Hare University, where he met Oliver Tambo. Tambo and Mandela became lifelong friends and colleagues. At the end of Nelson's first year, he became involved in a Students' Representative Council boycott against university policies, and was told to leave Fort Hare and not return unless he accepted election to the SRC.

Later in his life, while in prison, Mandela studied for a Bachelor of Laws from the University of London External Programme.

After leaving Fort Hare, Mandela relocated to Johannesburg and found employment as a guard at a mine. The employer quickly terminated Mandela after learning that he was from a well-known family. Mandela then worked as an articled clerk at a Johannesburg law firm, Witkin, Sidelsky and Edelman, through connections with his friend and mentor, Walter Sisulu. While working at the law firm, Mandela completed his B.A. degree at the University of South Africa via correspondence, after which he began law studies at the University of Witwatersrand, where he first befriended fellow students and future anti-apartheid political activists Joe Slovo, Harry Schwarz and Ruth First.

In 1944, when he was 26, Mandela joined the African National Congress (ANC) and with Sisulu and Oliver Tambo helped to form its Youth League. Mandela, with his determination to rid the people of a sense of inferiority after years of oppression, was elected its General Secretary. Mandela and the ANC became involved in passive resistance against the pass laws of the apartheid regime, which helped to control the non-white population and keep them in servility. By 1949 the League had persuaded the ANC to adopt a more militant programme of strikes, boycotts and civil disobedience.

After the 1948 election victory of the Afrikaner-dominated National Party, which supported the apartheid policy of racial segregation, Mandela began actively participating in politics. He led prominently in the ANC's 1952 Defiance Campaign and the 1955 Congress of the People, whose adoption of the Freedom Charter provided the fundamental basis of the anti-apartheid cause. During this time, Mandela and fellow lawyer Oliver Tambo operated the law firm of Mandela and Tambo, providing free or low-cost legal counsel to many blacks who lacked attorney representation. Mandela was heavily influenced by Mahatma Gandhi philosophy of non-violence, even though he no hesitation in joining the armed struggle to liberate his people. He later took part in the 29–30 January 2007 conference in New Delhi marking the 100th anniversary of Gandhi's introduction of Satyagraha (non-violent resistance) in South Africa.

On 5 December 1956 Mandela and 150 others were arrested and charged with treason. The trial lasted from 1956 to1961 followed, with all defendants receiving acquittals. The ANC leadership then decided to bolster their position through alliances with a small number of White, Coloured, and Indian political parties in an attempt to give the appearance of wider appeal than the more militant African political activists. On 26 June 1955 at Kliptown 3,000 people adopted the Freedom Charter of the ANC. There, Mandela and other members went out of their way to include everyone in their vision: "South Africa belongs to all who live in it, Black and white". But the government did not like the growing support of the ANC and its ability to attract a mass membership. In 1956 Mandela and 155 others were arrested and charged with treason – an alleged Communist-inspired coup. After an investigation taking four and a half years, the Treason Trail failed; nothing was proved. It was during this time Mandela met and married Nomzamo Winnie Madikizela, a social worker. Despite the fact that for most of their married life, Mandela was either forced into hiding or in jail, she herself was subject to frequent restrictions and house arrests by the government. Winnie Mandela is also a person of enormous courage and conviction. She was also severely criticised by the western media and politicians. From then on the government played cat-and-mouse with Mandela – imprisoning him for his politics, outlawing him, forcing him to go underground and into exile. "I found myself restricted and isolated from my fellow men, tailed by officers of the Special Branch wherever I went.... I was made, by the law, a criminal, not because of what I had done, but because of what I stood for."

The Sharpeville Massacre a turning point

The Sharpeville massacre in 1960 was a watershed in South African politics. The ANC realised that peaceful protests were not enough. In 1961 Umkhonto we Sizwe (Spear of the Nation), the armed wing of the ANC, was created and

Mandela became the leader. Once again, he had to go into exile. He returned to South Africa and, in 1962, was captured and charged with inciting Africans to go on strike. He used his time in court to make political speeches which he knew would be conveyed not merely to his own people, but across the world. And at the famous Rivonia Trial in 1963 he spoke for four hours in his own defence. "The ANC has spent half a century fighting against racism. When it triumphs it will not change that policy… It is a struggle of the African people, inspired by their own suffering and their own experience. It is a struggle for the right to live…"Mandela and seven other activists were sentenced to life imprisonment. He coordinated sabotage campaigns against military and government targets, making plans for a possible guerrilla war if the sabotage failed to end apartheid. Mandela also raised funds from abroad and arranged for paramilitary training of the group. Fellow ANC member Wolfie Kodesh explains the bombing campaign led by Mandela: "When we knew that we were going to start on 16 December 1961, to blast the symbolic places of apartheid, like pass offices, native magistrates courts, and things like that … post offices and … the government offices. But we were to do it in such a way that nobody would be hurt, nobody would get killed." Mandela said of Wolfie: "His knowledge of warfare and his first hand battle experience were extremely helpful to me."

Mandela described the move to armed struggle as a last resort; years of increasing repression and violence from the state convinced him that many years of non-violent protest against apartheid had not and could not achieve any progress. During the 1980s the ANC waged a guerrilla war against the apartheid government in which many civilians became casualties. For example, the Church Street bomb in Pretoria killed 19 people and injured 217. After he had become President, Mandela later admitted that the ANC, in its struggle against apartheid, also violated human rights, criticising those in his own party who attempted to remove statements mentioning this from the reports of the Truth and Reconciliation Commission.

Mandela's influence nationally and internationally, continued to grow during his time in prison. His vision for a just and democratic South Africa – as expressed in his speeches and writings – became widely circulated around the world. During his imprisonment his release became the focus for the international anti-apartheid movement. Many student organisations, trade unions and radical political groups and Parties around the world did their best to keep alive the vision of Mandela and his comrades in prison through demonstrations, protests outside the South African Embassy in London and providing financial and practical support for the banned ANC.

Free at last

On 2 February 1990, State President F. W. de Klerk reversed the ban on the ANC and other anti-apartheid organisations, and announced that Mandela would shortly be released from prison. Mandela was released from Victor Vorster Prison in Paarl on 11 February 1990, age 71 years. The event was broadcast live all over the world. I was attending the Labour Party Local Government Conference at the time and I sat next to Neil Kinnock watching the events on the television. We both wanted to go to the toiled, but forced ourselves to delay this, in case we missed the first glance the world would have had to see Nelson walking out of prison, hand in hand with Winnie. We both ended up in tears and laughter as we and the rest of the conference cheered amidst the tears. On the day of his release, Mandela made a speech to the nation. He declared his commitment to peace and reconciliation with the country's white minority, but made it clear that the ANC's armed struggle was not yet over when he said "our resort to the armed struggle in 1960 with the formation of the military wing of the ANC (Umkhonto we Sizwe) was a purely defensive action against the violence of apartheid". Mandela made a dignified return to the political arena. In 1993 he shared the Nobel Peace Prize with President F. W. de Klerk who helped to dismantle apartheid and white rule after centuries of domination. In 1994 his lifelong ambition was achieved when South Africa became a country in which blacks and whites had equal political freedom.

South Africa's first multi-racial elections in which full enfranchisement was granted were held on 27 April 1994. The ANC won 62 per cent of the votes in the election, and Mandela, as leader of the ANC, was inaugurated on 10 May 1994 as the country's first black President, with the National Party's de Klerk as his first deputy and Thabo Mbeki as the second in the Government of National Unity. As President from May 1994 until June 1999, Mandela presided over the transition from minority rule and apartheid. Mandela became the oldest elected President of South Africa when he took office at the age of 75 in 1994. At his inauguration as President of the new regime in 1994 he said: "Let there be justice for all. Let there be peace for all. Let there be work, bread and salt for all. The time for the healing of the wounds has come". Through the Truth and Reconciliation Commission, he tried to get those responsible for apartheid's atrocities to admit to their past mistakes. Mandela in a massive demonstration of faith, hope, charity and forgiveness even invited his jailer to his inaugural ceremony as President.

A person of peace

Since retiring from the Presidency and despite his age and the fact that he was no longer a leader of a country Mandela continued to influence world affairs on health, investment, conflicts and wars. He described America as a threat to world peace and condemned the invasion of Iraq by America and Britain. Mandela had strongly opposed the 1999 NATO intervention in Kosovo and called it an attempt by the world's powerful nations to police the entire world. In 2002 and 2003, Mandela criticised the foreign policy of the administration of US president George W. Bush in a number of speeches. Criticising the lack of UN involvement in the decision to begin the War in Iraq, he said, "It is a tragedy, what is happening, what Bush is doing. Bush is now undermining the United Nations."

Mandela stated he would support action against Iraq only if it is ordered by the UN. Mandela also insinuated that the United States may have been motivated by racism in not following the UN and its secretary-general Kofi Annan on the issue of the war. "Is it because the secretary-general of the United Nations is now a black man? They never did that when secretary-generals were white". General Colin Powell, the first of two African-Americans appointed by Bush to the position of US Secretary of State, presented to the United Nations Assembly the case for the war in Iraq and overthrow of Saddam Hussein. Prior to the war in Iraq Mandela telephoned President George Bush to warn him against the invasion of Iraq. The President refused to take his call which was answered by Colin Powell, Secretary of State. Mandela then telephoned Bush senior who had led America during his time as President in the first invasion of Iraq more than a decade ago to dissuade his son from attacking Iraq.

Mandela urged the people of the US to join massive protests against Bush and called on world leaders, especially those with vetoes in the UN Security Council, to oppose him. "What I am condemning is that one power, with a president who has no foresight, who cannot think properly, is now wanting to plunge the world into a holocaust." He attacked the United States for its record on human rights and for dropping atomic bombs on Japan during World War II. "If there is a country that has committed unspeakable atrocities in the world, it is the United States of America. They don't care." Mandela also condemned British Prime Minister Tony Blair and referred to him as the "foreign minister of the United States".

Unfortunately, Mandela was not successful in persuading the American government against attacking Iraq with the loss of up to 1 million lives according to the UN. George Bush had the audacity to attend Mandela's funeral, when he and Blair should have been in prison for war crimes. Since his retirement from active politics Mandela has supported numerous important causes for peace and for better quality of life for the poor, the sick and the exploited. He has severely criticised the Americans who dominate international economic, financial and political affairs, being the only super-power with its mighty army and control over international financial structures. Mandela stated that "they [the Americans] think they are the only power in the world. They're following a dangerous policy. One country wants to bully the world". Despite his age Mandela is actively seeking to shape world affairs. Many politicians and leaders can learn a great deal from this giant of the second half of the 20th century. His speeches and writings have been published in a book called 'The Struggle is My Life' and his autobiography called 'Long Walk to Freedom' is also available. Until July 2008 Mandela and ANC party members were barred from entering the United States – except to visit the United Nations headquarters in Manhattan – without a special waiver from the US Secretary of State, because of their South African apartheid-era designation as terrorists.

Mandela's 90th birthday was marked across the world on 18 July 2008, with the main celebrations held at his home town of Qunu. A concert in his honour was also held in Hyde Park, London. In a speech to mark his birthday, Mandela called for the rich people to help poor people across the world. Despite maintaining a low-profile during the 2010 FIFA World Cup in South Africa, Mandela made a rare public appearance during the closing ceremony, where he received a rapturous reception. In November 2009, the United Nations General Assembly announced that Mandela's birthday, 18 July, is to be known as "Mandela Day" to mark his contribution to world freedom. Nelson Mandela's 'long walk to freedom ends' as he was buried and laid to rest at 11.13 am (British Time) on Sunday, 15 Dec 2013, after 10 days of mourning. He died on Thursday 5 December after a prolonged illness. Tens of thousands of people in South Africa had a last glimpse of the great man and many tears were shed as well as expressions of joy for what he has given the world. He was laid to rest in his village in Qunu.

Goodbye and rest in peace great one. The world thanks you Madiba for all you have done.

Mao Zedong

Mao was born on 26 December 1893 and had a long, controversial and interesting life. He died on 9 September 1976. He was the Chinese communist leader and founder of the People's Republic of China with a quarter of the world's population. He was responsible for leading the Great March, the Great Leap

Forward and the Cultural Revolution that shocked the world and like the Russian Revolution resulted in the deaths of tens of millions of people on the process. He was naturally criticised by the western capitalist nations, particularly America and Britain that themselves were responsible for the loss of hundreds of millions of natives of Africa, Central and South America as well as tens of millions of native lives in Australia, New Zeeland, India and elsewhere during colonialism, slavery and wars against indigenous people over 400 years. During the First World War between 1914-18 and the Second World War 1939 – 1945 which were started in Europe by fellow capitalists and colonial powers, nearly 100 million people lost their lives.

Mao was born into a peasant family in Shaoshan, in Hunan province, central China. While Mao attended a small school in his village when he was 8 years old, he received little education. By age 13, he was working full-time in the fields, growing increasingly restless and ambitious. At the age of 14, Mao Tse-tung's father arranged a marriage for him, but he never accepted it. When he turned 17, he left home to enrol in a secondary school in Changsha, the capital of Hunan Province. In 1911, the Xinhua Revolution began against the monarchy, and Mao joined the Revolutionary Army and the Kuomintang, the Nationalist Party. Led by Chinese statesman Sun Yat-sen, the Kuomintang overthrew the monarchy in 1912 and founded the Republic of China After training as a teacher; he travelled to Beijing where he worked in the University Library. It was during this time that he began to read Marxist literature. He was inspired by the writings of Karl Marx, Lenin and other Marxists and communists who were opposed to capitalism, enslavement of the working class and using militarism to defeat and colonise nations across the world. In 1921, Moa became a founder member of the Chinese Communist Party (CCP) and set up a branch in Hunan. In 1923, the Kuomintang (KMT) nationalist party had allied with the CCP to defeat the warlords who controlled much of northern China. Then in 1927, the KMT leader Chiang Kai-shek launched an anti-communist purge. Mao and other communists retreated to south east China. In 1934, after the KMT surrounded them, Mao led his followers on the 'Long March', a 6,000 mile journey to northwest China to establish a new base.

China has a recorded history of over 5,000 years. More than a million years ago, primitive human beings lived on the land now called China. About 400,000 to 500,000 years ago, the Peking Man, a primitive man that lived in Zhoukoudian southwest of Beijing, was able to walk with the body erect, to make and use simple tools, and use fire. Six to seven thousand years ago, the people living in the Yellow River valley supported themselves primarily with agriculture, while also raising livestock. More than 3,000 years ago these people began smelting bronze and using ironware. In China, slave society began around the 21st century B.C. Over the next 1,700 years, agriculture and animal husbandry developed greatly and the skills of silkworm-raising, raw-silk reeling and silk-weaving spread widely. Bronze smelting and casting skills reached a relatively high level, and iron smelting became increasingly sophisticated. The Chinese culture flourished, as a great number of thinkers and philosophers emerged, most famously Confucius. China gave the world many creations and inventions, which enabled Europe to start the industrial revolution in the 1th century.

In 221 B.C., Qin Shi Huang, the first emperor of the Qin Dynasty, established a centralized, unified, multi-national feudal state. This period of feudal society continued until after the Opium War in 1840 with Britain, through which, China became weak and conquered. During the last 2,000 years, China's economy and culture continued to develop, bequeathing a rich heritage of science, art, philosophy, education, manufacturing and technology. The great inventions of ancient China - paper-making, printing, the compass, gunpowder, trade and commerce, have contributed enormously towards worldwide civilization. Chinese civilization peaked at Tang Dynasty (618-907) when Tang people traded with people all over the world. In 1840, anxious to continue its opium trade in China, Britain started the Opium War against China. After the war, the big foreign powers forcibly occupied "concessions" and divided China into "spheres of influence"; thus, China was transformed into a semi-colonial, semi-feudal society. Much of its achievements culturally, economically and materially were destroyed and the people divided and impoverished.

In 1911, the bourgeois democratic revolution (the Xinhai Revolution) led by Sun Yat-sen abolished the feudal monarchy, and established the Republic of China, therefore starting the modern history of China. China had established great civilisations despite the fact that it was under constant attacks by the Japanese and other invaders. In 1918, Mao Tse-tung graduated from the Hunan First Normal School, becoming a certified teacher. That same year, his mother died, and he went to Beijing, but was unsuccessful in finding a job. He finally found a position as a librarian assistant at Beijing University and attended a few classes. He was aware of the successful Russian Revolution in 1917, which established the communist Soviet Union. In 1921, he became one of the inaugural members of the Chinese Communist Party.

In 1923, Chinese leader Sun Yat-sen began a policy of active cooperation with the Chinese Communists, who had grown in strength and number. Mao Tse-tung had supported both the Kuomintang and the Communist Party, but over the next few years, he adopted Leninist ideas and believed that appealing to the farming peasants was the key to establishing communism in Asia. He rose up through the ranks of the party as a delegate assemblyman and then executive to the Shanghai branch of the party. For the next 12 months, more than 100,000 Communists and their dependents trekked west and north in what became known as the "Long March" across the Chinese mountains and swampland to Yanan, in northern China. It was estimated that only 30,000 of the original 100,000 survived the 8,000-mile journey. As word spread that the Communists had escaped extermination by the Kuomintang, many young people migrated to Yanan. Here Mao employed his oratory talents and inspired volunteers to faithfully join his cause as he emerged the top Communist leader.

In July 1937, the Japanese Imperial Army invaded China, forcing Chiang Kai-shek to flee the capital in Nanking. Chiang's forces soon lost control of the coastal regions and most of the major cities. Unable to fight a war on two fronts, Chiang reached out to the Communists for a truce and support. During this time, Mao established himself as a great military leader. With the Japanese defeat in 1945, Mao Tse-tung was able to set his sights on controlling all of China. Efforts were made by the United States and its European allies to establish a coalition government, but China slid into a bloody civil war. On October 1, 1949, in Tiananmen Square, Beijing, Mao announced the establishment of the People's Republic of China. Chiang Kai-shek and his followers fled to the island of Taiwan, where they formed the Republic of China.

The Communists and KMT were again temporarily allied during eight years of war with Japan (1937-1945), but shortly after the end of World War Two, civil war broke out between them. The Communists were victorious, and on 1 October 1949 Mao proclaimed the founding of the People's Republic of China (PRC). Chiang Kai-shek fled to the island of Taiwan. Mao and other Communist leaders set out to reshape Chinese society. Industry came under state ownership and China's farmers began to be organised into collectives. All opposition was ruthlessly suppressed. The Chinese initially received significant help from the Soviet Union, but relations became strained during the 1960,s. However, the Chinese, like the Soviet Union did support the communists in the Korean War in the 1950's and the Vietnam war against America in the 1960's and 1970's. Mao started to innovate and experiment with a different type of communism from the Soviet Union. Mao launched the 'Great Leap Forward' in 1958 aimed at mass mobilisation of labour to improve agricultural and industrial production. He famously said that you "cannot grow crops on a blackboard" and encouraged the middle class to become more agricultural focussed. Unfortunately, the experiment failed resulting in a decline in agricultural output, which, together with poor harvests, led to famine and the deaths of millions. The policy was abandoned and Mao's position weakened.

Mao then launched the 'Cultural Revolution' in 1966, aiming to purge the country of 'impure' elements, he described as "the capitalist roader" and tens of millions of young people took to the cities and countryside with their little 'Red Books' to promote and revive the revolutionary spirit. This resulted in the death of 1.5 million people and the destruction of much of the country's cultural heritage. Mao's wife was also behind the Cultural Revolution. I attended a couple of counter demonstrations in London to give the Chinese moral support as there were daily reporting by the British media attacking the Chinese, when very little was said about the massacres that was taking place in Vietnam by America and its South Vietnamese puppet regime, using chemical weapons, bombs and all sorts of killing methods against the brave Vietnamese communists. I certainly bought and read a copy of the Red Book, and I still have my copy today. Mao eventually restored order in the country with the help of the massive army, which exists today. America was eventually kicked out of Vietnam after invading not only Vietnam, but surrounding countries like Laos and Cambodia, leaving millions of dead and disabled people. The North Vietnamese with the help of China and their great leader Mao ended up victorious, but his health was deteriorating. His later years saw attempts to build bridges with the United States, Japan and Europe. In 1972, US President Richard Nixon visited China and met Mao; Nixon was instrumental in stopping the Vietnam War and for opening up positive relationships with China. Mao also set the scene for China to adopt a more 'Open Door' policy on trade and international issues. Mao died on 9 September 1976. Mao Tse-tung died from complications of Parkinson's disease on September 18, 1976, at the age of 82, in Beijing, China. He left a mixed legacy in both China and the world as a genius, a great statesman, a political thinker and strategist, and a great military leader, as well as the savoir of the Chinese nation. His successor turned China as the world's top manufacturing company which is likely to surpass America in production, wealth and influence within the next few years.

How hypocritical it is that America and its allies saw Taiwan; this tiny Island of just 12,456 square miles and a population of less than 24 million as the legitimate state of China for several decades, America and NATO still protects Taiwan and in many ways regard this Island as the Chinese nation despite China covering an area of 3,705,386 square miles and having a population of 1,385 million people. The western powers kept China nearly 20 per cent of the world's population out of the world major institutions including the United Nations for many decades. I want to end this section with some quotes from Chairman Mao:

- "An Army of the people is invincible."

- "Women hold up half the sky."

- "Politics is war without blood while war is politics with blood."

- "To rebel is justified."

- "In waking a tiger, use a long stick."

Thomas Hardy

I admire Thomas Hardy, OM (2 June 1840 – 11 January 1928) an English novelist and poet 1840- 1928. Hardy was influenced by other great writers such as Dickens, who I admired enormously. My wife who studied English Literature and taught English for nearly 40 years introduced me to his books. I read several of his novels, including Far from the Madding Crowd (1874), The Mayor of Casterbridge (1886), Tess of the d'Urbervilles (1891), and Jude the Obscure (1895). Jude the Obscure had a profound influence on me and it was this book more than any other that encouraged me to seek a scholarship to Ruskin College, Oxford in 1974. Most of his novels were fictional and were set in the semi-fictional region of Wessex. They explored tragic characters struggling against their passions, desires, social class and circumstances, as well as their dreams.

Hardy's Wessex is based on the medieval Anglo-Saxon kingdom and eventually came to include the counties of Dorset, Wiltshire, Somerset, Devon, Hampshire and Berkshire, in southwest and south central England. Reading Jude the Obscure and The Mayor of Casterbridge reminded me of my childhood background in rural Guyana. Thomas Hardy was born in 1840 in Higher Bockhampton a hamlet in the parish 0f Stinsford to the east of Dorchester in Dorset, England. He lived for a while in London and worked in the excavation of the graveyard of the St Pancras Old Church near St Pancras Mainline Railway Station. I travel past the Old Church several times each year on the number 214 bus on my way to my trade union meetings, at the union (UCU) headquarters in Camden, in North London. Hardy never felt at home in London, because he was acutely conscious of class divisions and his social inferiority. He returned to Dorset and decided to dedicate himself to writing and I am glad he became a writer. Jude the Obscure, is a great book, I shed much tears reading about the tragic life of Jude and his family. His life in Oxford was very depressing and whilst I was a student, I used to picture Jude working on the university buildings. Jude life was a failure, not because of any weakness or neglect on his part, but because of the rotten, evil system that existed during his lifetime. Reading about Jude gave me strength, hope and determination to succeed in Oxford and in my life beyond academia.

Sitting Bull and other Native Americans

Chief Sitting Bull born in 1831 and murdered on 15 December, 1890, was a great Chief and warrior; a Hunkpapa Lakota holy man who led his people during years of resistance to United States government policies. He was killed by an Indian agency police on the Standing Rock Indian Reservation during an attempt to arrest him at a time when authorities feared that he would join the Ghost Dance movement. And continue to shame white America for the in human treatment of his people and the Native Americans. Sitting Bull led numerous war parties against Fort Berthold, Fort Stevenson, and Fort Buford and their environs from 1865 through 1868.

Before the Battle of the Little Bighorn, Sitting Bull had a vision in which he saw the defeat of the 7th Cavalry under Lt. Col. George Armstrong Custer on June 25, 1876. Sitting Bull's leadership motivated his people to a major victory. Months after their victory at the battle, Sitting Bull and his group left the United

States for Wood Mountain, Saskatchewan, where he remained until 1881, at which time he surrendered to U.S. forces. A small remnant of his band under Chief Wa⊠blí ⊠í decided to stay at Wood Mountain.

After working as a performer, Sitting Bull returned to the Standing Rock Agency in South Dakota. Because of fears that he would use his influence to support the ghost dance movement, Indian Service agent James McLaughlin at Fort Yates ordered his arrest. During an ensuing struggle between Sitting Bull's followers and the agency police, Sitting Bull was shot in the side and head by Standing Rock policemen Lieutenant Bull Head (Tatankapah) and Red Tomahawk (Marcelus Chankpidutah). His body was taken to nearby Fort Yates for burial, but in 1953, his remains were possibly exhumed and reburied near Mobridge, South Dakota, by his Lakota family, who wanted his body to be nearer to his birthplace.

By early 1868, the U.S. government desired a peaceful settlement to Red Cloud's War. It agreed to Red Cloud's demands that Forts Phil Kearny and C.F. Smith be abandoned. Chief Gall of the Hunkpapas (among other representatives of the Hunkpapas, Blackfeet, and Yankton Dakota) signed a form of the Treaty of Fort Laramie on July 2, 1868 at Fort Rice (near Bismarck, North Dakota). Sitting Bull did not agree to the treaty. He continued his hit-and-run attacks on forts in the upper Missouri area throughout the late 1860s and early 1870s. The European invaders constantly made treaties with the native Indians only to break them when they wanted to steal more of their lands. These very natives who fist welcomed the Europeans to America were massacred by the greedy and cruel Europeans by the millions over hundreds of years. The history of the Europeans in America is one of serious disregard for human rights; enslavement of millions of Africans and natives; genocide of many ethnic and tribal groups; and using brute force of unimaginable proportions to satisfy their lust for materialism, power and wealth.

Leaders of the native Indians such as Sitting Bull's and their band of warriors fought to defend their people against the migrating Europeans who systematically killed their people and stole their lands. The genocide against the natives worsen in the 860s and 1880's when the Northern Pacific Railway conducted a survey for a route across the northern plains directly through Hunkpapa lands, it encountered stiff Lakota resistance. The same railway people returned the following year accompanied by federal troops. Sitting Bull and the Hunkpapa attacked the survey party, which was forced to turn back. In 1873, the military accompaniment for the surveyors was increased again, but Sitting Bull's forces resisted the survey "most vigorously. The Panic of 1873 forced the Northern Pacific Railway's backers into bankruptcy. The natives fought ferociously to retain their land and their culture. They halted construction of the railroad through Lakota, Dakota, and Nakota territory. After the discovery and new wealth from gold in California, other Europeans rushed to explore for gold in the Black Hills. In 1874, Lt. Col. George Armstrong Custer led a military expedition from Fort Abraham Lincoln near Bismarck, to explore the Black Hills for gold and to determine a suitable location for a military fort in the Hills. Custer's announcement of gold in the Black Hills triggered the Black Hills Gold Rush. Tensions increased between the Lakota and European Americans' seeking to move into the Black Hills. Custer was acting for the greedy land grabbers and speculators as well as the greedy European settlers. Although Sitting Bull did not attack Custer's expedition in 1874, the US government was increasingly pressured to open the Black Hills to mining and settlement. It was alarmed at reports of Sioux depredations (encouraged by Sitting Bull). In November 1875, the government ordered all Sioux bands outside the Great Sioux Reservation to move onto the reservation, knowing full well that not all would comply. As of February 1, 1876, the Interior Department certified as "hostile" those bands who continued to live off the reservation. This certification allowed the military to pursue Sitting Bull and other Lakota bands as "hostiles". The divide and rule tactics by the European settlers to conquer the natives was also very successful as they deliberately manufactured conflicts between the various native tribes.

During the period 1868–1876, Sitting Bull developed into the most important of Native American Chiefs. After the Treaty of Fort Laramie (1868) and the creation of the Great Sioux Reservation, many traditional Sioux warriors, such as Red Cloud of the Oglala and Spotted Tail of the Brulé, moved to reside permanently on the reservations. By this time the native population was serious depleted and vulnerable as well as demoralized, defeated and were largely dependent for subsistence on the US Indian agencies. Many other chiefs, including members of Sitting Bull's Hunkpapa band such as Gall, at times lived temporarily at the agencies. They needed the supplies at a time when white encroachment and the depletion of buffalo herds reduced their resources and challenged Native American independence.

The brave and courageous Sitting Bull's refusal to adopt any dependence on the white man meant that at times he and his small band of warriors lived isolated on the Plains. When Native Americans were threatened by the United States, numerous members from various Sioux bands and other tribes, such as the North Cheyenne, came to Sitting Bull's camp. His reputation for "strong medicine" developed as he continued to evade the European Americans. After the January 1st ultimatum of 1876, when the US Army began to track down Sioux and others living off the reservation as hostiles, Native Americans gathered at Sitting Bull's camp. The chief took an active role in encouraging this "unity camp". He sent scouts to the reservations to recruit warriors, and told the Hunkpapa to share supplies with those Native Americans who joined them. An example of his generosity was Sitting Bull's taking care of Wooden Leg's Northern Cheyenne tribe. They had been impoverished by Captain Reynold's March 17, 1876 attack and fled to Sitting Bull's camp for safety. The Hunkpapa chief provided resources to sustain the new recruits. Over the course of the first half of 1876, Sitting Bull's camp continually expanded, as natives joined him for safety in numbers. His leadership had attracted the warriors and families of an extensive village, estimated at more than 10,000 people. Lt. Col. Custer came across this large camp on June 25, 1876. Sitting Bull did not take a direct military role in the ensuing battle; instead he acted as a spiritual chief and had performed the Sun

Dance, in which he fasted and sacrificed over 100 pieces of flesh from his arms, a week prior to the attack.

Custer's 7th Cavalry advance party attacked Cheyenne and Lakota tribes at their camp on the Little Big Horn River (known as the Greasy Grass River to the Lakota) on June 25, 1876. The U.S. Army did not realize how large the camp was. More than 2,000 Native American warriors had left their reservations to follow Sitting Bull. Inspired by a vision of Sitting Bull's, in which he saw U.S. soldiers being killed as they entered the tribe's camp, the Cheyenne and Lakota fought back. Custer's badly outnumbered troops lost ground quickly and were forced to retreat. The tribes led a counter-attack against the soldiers on a nearby ridge, ultimately annihilating them. The Native Americans' victory celebrations were short-lived. Public shock and outrage at Custer's death and defeat, and the government's knowledge about the remaining Sioux, led them to assign thousands more soldiers to the area. Over the next year, the new American military forces pursued the Lakota, forcing many of the Native Americans to surrender. Sitting Bull refused to surrender and in May 1877 led his band across the border into Saskatchewan, Canada. He remained in exile for four years near Wood Mountain, refusing a pardon and the chance to return.

Also while in Canada Sitting Bull met with chief Crowfoot, who was a chief of the Blackfeet, long-time powerful enemies of the Lakota and Cheyenne; Sitting Bull wished to make peace with the Blackfeet Nation and Crowfoot. Being an advocate for peace himself, Crowfoot eagerly accepted the tobacco peace offering. Sitting Bull was so impressed by the Blackfeet chief that he named one of his sons after him. Sitting Bull and his men only stayed in Canada for 4 years. Due to the smaller size of the buffalo herds in Canada, Sitting Bull and his men found it difficult to find enough food to feed his people, who were starving and exhausted. Hunger and desperation eventually forced Sitting Bull, and 186 of his family and followers to return to the United States and surrender on July 19, 1881. Sitting Bull had his young son Crow Foot surrender his Winchester lever-action carbine to Major David H. Brotherton, commanding officer of Fort Buford in the parlor of the Commanding Officer's Quarters in a ceremony the next day. He told the 4 soldiers, 20 warriors and other guests in the small room, that he wished to regard the soldiers and the white race as friends but he wanted to know who would teach his son the new ways of the world. Two weeks later, after waiting in vain for other members of his tribe to follow him from Canada, the Army transferred Sitting Bull and his band to Fort Yates, the military post located adjacent to the Standing Rock Agency, which straddles the present-day boundary of North and South Dakota. Sitting Bull and his band of 186 people were kept separate from the other Hunkpapa gathered at the agency. Army officials were concerned that the famed chief would stir up trouble among the recently surrendered northern bands.

On August 26, 1881, he was visited by the census taker William T. Selwyn, who counted twelve people in the Hunkpapa leader's immediate family. Forty-one families, totaling 195 people, were recorded in Sitting Bull's band. The military decided to transfer him and his band to Fort Randall, to be held as prisoners of war. Loaded onto a steamboat, the band of 172 people was sent down the Missouri River to Fort Randall (near present-day Pickstown, South Dakota on. There they spent the next 20 months. They were allowed to return north to the Standing Rock Agency in May 1883. In 1885, Sitting Bull was allowed to leave the reservation to go Wild Westing with Buffalo Bill Cody's Buffalo Bill's Wild West. He earned about $50 a week for riding once around the arena, where he was a popular attraction. Sitting Bull gave speeches about his desire for education for the young, and reconciling relations between the Sioux and whites. The historian Edward Lazarus wrote that Sitting Bull reportedly cursed his audience in Lakota in 1884, during an opening address celebrating the completion of the Northern Pacific Railway. Sitting Bull stayed with the show for four months before returning home. During that time, audiences began to consider him a celebrity and a romanticized warrior. He earned a small fortune by charging for his autograph and picture, although he often gave his money away to the homeless and beggars.

Murder of Sitting Bull and the genocide of the Native Americans

Sitting Bull returned to the Standing Rock Agency after working in Buffalo Bill's Wild West Show. In 1890, James McLaughlin, the U.S. Indian Agent at Fort Yates on Standing Rock Agency, feared that the Lakota leader was about to flee the reservation with the Ghost Dancers, so he ordered the police to arrest him. On December 14, 1890, McLaughlin drafted a letter to Lt. Henry Bullhead that included instructions and a plan to capture the chief. Around 5:30 a.m. on December 15, 39 police officers and four volunteers approached Sitting Bull's house. They surrounded the house, knocked and entered. Bullhead told Sitting Bull that he was under arrest and led him outside. The camp awakened and men converged at the house of their chief. As Bullhead ordered Sitting Bull to mount a horse, he explained that the Indian Affairs agent needed to see him and then he could return to his house. Sitting Bull refused to comply and the police used force on him. The Sioux in the village were enraged. Catch-the-Bear, a Lakota, shouldered his rifle and shot Bullhead who, in return, fired his revolver into the chest of Sitting Bull. Another police officer, Red Tomahawk, shot Sitting Bull in the head, and the chief dropped to the ground. A close-quarters fight erupted, and within minutes several men were dead. Six policemen were killed immediately and two more died shortly after the fight. Sitting Bull and seven of his supporters lay dead, along with two horses. Sitting Bull's body was taken to Fort Yates to be placed in a coffin (made by the Army carpenter and for burial. In 1953 Lakota family members exhumed what they believed to be his remains, to be reinterred near Mobridge, South Dakota, his birthplace.

The population of the United States prior to European contact was greater than 12 million. Four centuries later, the count was reduced by 95% to less than quarter of a million. The white European invaders and settlers in America quickly implemented policies of slavery and mass extermination of the natives. The same atrocities were carried out against the Taino population of the Caribbean. Within three years, five million were dead. As a result of the cruelty inflicted upon the indigenous population: hanging them en mass, hacking their children into pieces to be used as dog feed, and other horrid cruelties. The Europeans colonisers engaged in mass genocides against the natives for hundreds of years. The "Indian Removal" policy was put into action to clear the land for white settlers. Methods for the removal included slaughter of villages by the military and also biological warfare, starvation and forced marches to relocate the Indians. The Removal Act of 1830 set into motion a series of events which led to the "Trail of Tears" in 1838, a forced march of the Cherokees, resulting in the destruction of most of the Cherokee population." The concentration of American Indians in small geographic areas, and the scattering of them from their homelands, caused increased death, primarily because of associated military actions, disease, starvation, extremely harsh conditions during the moves, and the resulting destruction of ways of life. It is estimated that the genocide in North, Central and South America by the Europeans were the greatest holocaust, in terms of number in the entire human history with over 100 million natives died prematurely, due to colonialism and deliberate acts of cruelty, disease, murder, genocide, starvation, enslavement and abuse.

During American expansion into the western frontier, one primary effort to destroy the Indian way of life was the attempts of the U.S. government to make farmers and cattle ranchers of the Indians. In addition, one of the most substantial methods was the premeditated destructions of flora and fauna which the American Indians used for food and a variety of other purposes. We now also know that the Indians were intentionally exposed to smallpox by Europeans. The discovery of gold in California, early in 1848, prompted American migration and expansion into the west. The greed of Americans for money and land was rejuvenated with the Homestead Act of 1862. In California and Texas there was blatant genocide of Indians by non-Indians during certain historic periods. In California, the decrease from about a quarter of a million to less than 20,000 is primarily due to the cruelties and wholesale massacres perpetrated by the miners and early settlers.

By the end of the nineteenth century, the American Indian people had been decimated. United States military records show a minimum of 1,470 official incidents of Army action against Indians from 1776 to 1907. Treaties were made, regularly broken, frequently altered, or, more often than not, completely ignored. The federal and state governments often re-acquired land designated for reservations if it was found that the land held significant economic value. Such was the case of the Treaty of 1868 with Red Cloud, which assigned South Dakota's Black Hills as part of the great Sioux reservation. The subsequent discovery of gold, and the ensuing gold rush, however, led to the loss of the Black Hills by the Lakota people. The treaty was ignored and the Indians remanded to less desirable reservation lands. Embittered Plains Indians of the Dakotas, Wyoming, and Montana made last-ditch efforts at protecting their lands and rights. I admire all the Native Americans and their leaders for showing courage against the European invaders who they first welcomed to their land; gave them food and assistance, but the greed of the Europeans turned them into murders which resulted in the greatest holocaust against humankind that lasted for over 400 years.

Ho Chi Minh

Ho Chi Minh, born in 1880, was the communist leader of the North Vietnamese when the Americans invaded the southern part of Vietnam led by a puppet regime. The Vietnamese had defeated occupying French colonialists and wanted to re-unite their country under a single leadership.

The majority of the Vietnamese who lived a life of poverty in stark contrast to the French elite, who governed their country as part of the French Empire, were opposed to the French control of their country. By the time Ho Chi Minh was a teenager he shared his father's views – that Vietnam had a right to govern itself free of colonial rule. Ho's sister worked for the French army and she used her position to steal weapons that would be required in any future nationalist struggle against the French. She was caught and sentenced to life imprisonment. Ho Chi Minh parents and family were all bitterly opposed to colonial rule.

Despite having strong nationalist views, Ho Chi Minh attended a French school. Both Ho and his father believed that knowledge of the French language, while an affront to their nationalistic principals, would serve a purpose when the struggle against the French began.

For a short time after his education had ended, Ho became a teacher. After this he became a sailor and travelled to many places in and around the Far East. He soon realised that other regions in the Far East were also under French colonial control. These areas also had one other thing in common – the abject poverty of many within the population.

In 1918 Ho lived in Paris. During the talks that led to the Treaty of Versailles, Ho tried to convince the American delegation to speak out for the cause of the Indo-Chinese people but he was not successful. While in Paris, Ho converted to communism after spending his time reading the works of Karl Marx. Ho became one of the founder members of the French Communist Party – founded in December 1920. In 1924, he visited Russia and while in Moscow he wrote to a friend that all communists were duty bound to return to their country of origin and they had to "make contact with the masses to awaken, organise, unite and train them, and lead them to fight for freedom and independence."

However, Ho could not return to Vietnam without risking arrest by the French authorities. Ho therefore decided to live in China, near to the Vietnam border. Here he helped to organise the 'Vietnam Revolutionary League' – a group made up of other exiled Vietnamese nationalists living in exile.

French authority in Vietnam was swept aside by the Japanese in World War Two. Ho Chi Minh used this as an opportunity to free Vietnam from French rule. Along with others, Ho created the Vietminh. The Vietminh were not prepared for Vietnam to be freed from French rule – only to see this replaced by brutal Japanese rule. The Vietminh took part in guerrilla warfare against the Japanese. Vo Nguyen Giap controlled the military side of the Vietminh. Supplied by the

Soviet Union and, after Pearl Harbour, the Americans, the Vietminh learned a great deal about guerrilla warfare.

In September 1945, Ho Chi Minh announced the creation of the Democratic Republic of Vietnam. However, France wanted to re-establish control over Vietnam. France refused to recognise Ho's republic and both sides quickly engaged in fighting in 1946. Despite the experiences learned during World War Two, the Vietminh found the fighting hard as the French were better equipped and the supplies that had come from both the USSR and USA had dried up. The Vietminh were helped when Mao Zedong's Communist Party was victorious in China. Giap cold now train his soldiers in the safety of China before they crossed into Vietnam to engage the French. Wounded Vietminh soldiers could also be better treated in China. Ho was the accepted leader of the Vietminh and when the French suggested terms to end the fighting, it was Ho who persuaded other leaders in the Vietminh that the French could not be trusted. The Battle of Dien Bien Phu (1954) led to France pulling out of Vietnam.

The victory was a huge boost for Ho and did a great deal to cement the reputation of Giap as a very effective military leader. At Geneva, it was decided to divide Vietnam at the 17th Parallel with the North governed by Ho Chi Minh and the South by Ngo Dinh Diem. Some members of the Vietminh did not accept that Vietnam should be divided and it was left to Ho to persuade then that the division was only a temporary one. He, like them, wanted a united Vietnam but in 1954 it was prudent, according to Ho, to go along with the division.

Ho Chi Minh had few doubts that the people of Vietnam wanted a communist government – even the American President at the time, Eisenhower, believed that 80 per cent of the Vietnamese population were behind Ho Chi Minh. Ho did declare, however, that he had authority over the whole state and he encouraged the Vietminh resistance movement in the south. From 1963, Ho ordered that the Vietminh should be supplied with arms by the north via the Ho Chi Minh trail. In 1965, Ho sent in regular North Vietnamese troops to help the Vietminh when the US sent her military in to back up their puppet regime. The ensuring war which involved the Americans and supported by President John Kennedy lasted for over 10 years and resulted in the death of over 3.1 million people including some 60,000 Americans and over 500,000 civilians. The Americans used 18.2 million gallons of chemical Agent Orange in Vietnam, Cambodia and Laos, which killed nearly 450,000 people, mainly civilians and left 500, 000 children born with serious defects caused by the American chemical warfare. In a single battle during the Tet Offensive 45, 267 people, mainly Viet Cong from North Vietnam were killed and in the Easter Offensive in 1972 up to 75.000 mainly Viet Cong and South Vietnamese were killed. It was a bloody ideological war that was supported by several American Presidents.

Ho's authority in the north was never challenged. He maintained control of the north and the North Vietnamese remained loyal despite the American bombing campaign, which resulted in vast numbers of bombs being dropped on the North. It could be argued that the bombing made the people even more fiercely loyal to Ho. Ho Chi Minh died in 1969. Ho's army defeated the mightiest army on earth, which dropped more bombs on Vietnam than all the bombs used during World War 2. After Saigon fell in 1975 and the American hurriedly departed from Vietnam, the city was renamed Ho Chi Minh City in his honour.

I admired Ho and his soldiers and the entire population who sacrificed their lives to liberate their country against American imperialism. The Americans and their South Vietnamese puppets committed numerous in humane acts and atrocities against the Viet Cong and civilian populations. Mutilation of the enemy bodies was quite common. Black Americans represented up to 40 per cent of the American soldiers in Vietnam even though Black people made up only 12 per cent of the American population. Martin Luther King, Malcolm X and Muhammad Ali all opposed the war and Ali refused to fight in Vietnam. He refused to kill Vietnamese who he claimed never did Black people in America any harm, He was title of World Boxing Champion was subsequently removed from him. I admire all these men enormously for opposing American racism, imperialism and cruelty in America and around the world.

Hugo Chávez

Hugo Chavez was born in Venezuela, on July 28, 1954; he was one of seven children born to working class teachers in Venezuela. He died on 5 March, 2013, at age 58, following a long battle with cancer. Like me Chavez was born in a village that had no electricity during his childhood, and the family struggled to get by. In one moving account, little Hugo was turned away from his first day at school because his grandmother couldn't afford to buy him a pair of shoes. I also attended school barefoot and in torn clothing. He learned resourcefulness from his elders, selling candies at school that his grandmother made, to bring home some money. His childhood life imbued in him an enormous spirit of passion, solidarity, generosity and commitment towards his people, especially the most oppressed. As president, one of his very first acts was to provide free school lunches for hundreds of thousands of poor children. School attendance shot up dramatically as a result. He improved education, housing, job opportunities and healthcare for his people. Chavez attended the Venezuelan military academy and served as an army officer before participating in an effort to overthrow the government in 1992, for which he was sentenced to two years in prison.

Chavez won the Presidential elections in February 1999, and again re-elected in July 2000 under a new constitution for a six-year term. He won another election in 2006. In 2007 he last a referendum to run indefinitely for President, but in 2009 he won the vote to that lifted the term limits on elected politicians and went on to win the election in February 2012 for President. He was a charismatic and dynamic leader who was committed to using Venezuela's oil wealth to empower the working class through social and economic reforms. Early into his presidency, he created a new constitution for the country, which included changing its name to the Bolivarian Republic of Venezuela. He later focused his efforts on gaining control of the state-run oil company, which stirred controversy and led to protests, strained relations with the United States and other capitalist nations that demonise him throughout his Presidency. His opponents with the help of foreign powers briefly removed him from power in April 2002, but he returned after just two days. His actions included selling oil to Cuba and resisting efforts to stop narcotic trafficking in Columbia. In 2006, Chavez helped create the Bolivarian Alternative for the Americas, a socialist free-trade organization. In June 2011 Chavez reveals he was being treated for cancer, and in February 2012 he had further operation in Cuba, and won the Presidential elections in October 2012 for a further six-year term, but died less than a year later. During his time in office he upset the rich and their allies abroad. He also antagonised the church leaders after criticising them for siding with the opposition, defending the capitalist system and the rich, whilst neglecting the poor.

Chavez was someone I admired and respected for his commitment towards the poor and transforming his country towards becoming more equal, fair, radical society. Despite a great deal of covert and clandestine operations, as well as open hostility against him by the American administration under George Bush and Obama Chavez managed to retain the support of the working class in Venezuela and around the world. The American and large corporations with eyes on the Venezuelan economy and oil wealth spent billions of dollars to back the Venezuelan right-wing elite in one plot after another to try to overthrow him and the Bolivarian Revolution.

He accused the Bush administration of "fighting terror with terror" during the war in Afghanistan after 11 September 2001. He made clear his hatred of capitalism and American imperialism, not only around the world, but especially in South and Central America, which divided many nations within the region. Chavez used his country's oil resources to help many nations in South America and the Caribbean, including Cuba where he developed a very close relationship with Fidel Castro and the Cuban people. He established economic links with China, my country of origin (Guyana) Angola and other developing countries. In

2006, he helped create the Bolivarian Alternative for the Americas, a socialist free-trade organization joined by Fidel Castro, president of Cuba, and Evo Morales, president of Bolivia. Chavez was also an active member of the Non-Aligned Movement, a group of more than 100 countries, including Cuba, Iran and several African nations.

In the first hours that Chavez laid in state, 2 million grief-stricken Venezuelans bid their beloved Comandante farewell, in a line that stretched for up to five miles. Countless vigils were organised by people who admired and supported his brave and revolutionary spirit and life.

The massive outpouring of grief and sorrow in Venezuela after the death of Chavez was not just an expression of deep sentiment for a much loved fallen leader, but also for the loss of an era in which Chavez provided hope for a better continent. The cries of "We are Chávez!" and "Chávez Vive!" were a resounding commitment by the people, the masses who brought him back from the grip of a U.S.-sponsored military coup in 2002. Today, they are more determined than ever to defend the Bolivarian Revolution, despite the determination of the CIA and American imperialists to destabilise Venezuela by pouring large sums of money to finance the right wing opposition, which is responsible for the sustained demonstration against Chavez successor Nicolás Maduro in various parts of Venezuela during 2014. The majority of the Venezuelan people and the struggle have been dealt a major blow with the loss of this great leader and visionary. I am confident that the social and political revolutionary movement that he catalysed will continue to grow and others like Chavez will emerge in the coming years to lead the Venezuelan revolution he started to a final victory. Hopefully, America as position as the world bully and aggressive militaristic and imperialist power will be something of the past.

E P Thompson and Peter Fryer

Edward Palmer Thompson's book "The Making of the English Working Class" (MEWC), first published in 1963, still sits on my shelf with either notes or parts underlined in red ink during the last 45 years. It was a book that played a significant part in my education and awareness of class and the class structure of Britain. This book includes mush reference to the thoughts and writings of Karl Marx, Frederic Engels, Thomas Paine, and Thomas Hardy and many other great philosophers and writers whose writings I have so admired, and have inspired me over the last 45 years. This 958-page book on working class history resonated with me, because it reminded me so much of my childhood in rural Guyana under British colonialism.

The working class is a universal class that shares similar experience of poverty, exploitation, oppression, abuse and ridicule by the rich and powerful and the corporations that influence governments. Some significant change has occurred since the early 18th Century that has shaped the lives and behaviour of the working class, which includes the media replacing religion as "the opium of the people," as Marx once stated. Other changes include liberal democracy; great strides in literacy; the welfare state; great achievements in science, technology, communications, transport, agriculture, manufacturing and people living longer and healthier lives. MEWC sits beside one of my other great book: "Staying Power – The History of Black People in Britain," first published in 1984 (632pages). Staying Power is recognised as the definitive history of black people in Britain, an epic story that begins with the Roman conquest and continues to this day. In a comprehensive account, Peter Fryer reveals how Africans, Asians and their descendants, previously hidden from history, have profoundly influenced and shaped events in Britain over the course of the last two thousand years. These two books should be on the shelf of every historian, scholar, trade unionist, socialist, politician, teacher and journalist.

I had the privilege of meeting both these great socialists who lived great lives and contributed a great deal to working class history in Britain and in many ways to that of the world, as Britain was one of the greatest Empires which lasted for over 300 years until the 20th Century. E P Thompson was born and grew up in Oxford on 3 February 1924. He attended Corpus Christi College at the University of Cambridge. Thompson who died on 28 August 1993 was a member of the Communist Party, a socialist, a writer, and peace campaigner. He was a fierce critic of the Labour Party that failed to deliver a radical programme whilst in government for 11 years between 1964 and 1979. I met Thompson and Peter Fryer on several occasions at various conferences in London. Thompson was employed by the Universities of Leeds and Warwick for many years. Fryer was born on 18 February 1927, in Hull; the home of the great William Wilberforce who campaigned for the abolition of the Slave Trade. He worked as a Journalist on the Daily Worker, now the Morning Star and he was a writer and Lecturer. Fryer was a socialist and a committed anti-racist. He died on 30 October 2006 at the age of 79.

Thompson and Fryer proved themselves as popular and exciting historians. They produced a body of work that was original and hugely influential. Both writers brought to the surface new and exciting material that was hidden from history for such a long time. Their work opened up new thinking and enthusiasm for Black and working class history. Thompson and Fryer were radical socialists with a great deal of passion for equality, peace, freedom and justice. Yet they were never conventional historians, they analysis and personal beliefs and values transcends their writings. Through a patient and extensive examination of local as well as national archives, Thompson had uncovered details about workshop customs and rituals; failed conspiracies; trade union history and development; the role of women and children during the growth of the industrial revolution; the dynamics between the workers and the bosses; popular songs, and union club life and a huge insight on the hardships facing the working class during the time of the glorious Empire.

Fryers work also gave a lot of comfort and knowledge to large number of Black people who discovered so much history of the struggles of their ancestors who lived in Britain for 2,000 years. Both of these books provided me with lots of material for a number of books and documents I have written over the last 25 years. "Staying Power – The History of Black People in Britain," showed that racism did not end with the abolition of slavery, it continued to this day as a useful tool to divide and weaken the working class. Fryer recorded the lives and the battles of Black people in Britain over centuries to defend them against institutional and white working class racism. Even the participation of Black people in both World Wars and becoming increasingly accepted into British life and society, the ugly face of racism continues to surface, especially during times of recession. Fryer recorded the events that led up to and during the various race riots in Britain over the centuries and how the police, politicians and bureaucrats institutionalised racism.

Fryer's book has no equal as a social history about the lives of Black people in Britain; not only because of the immense detailed historical material, but also the fact that is so easy to read, digest and refer to as far as the average reader is concerned. I also try to write my books in a language and style that anyone can read and understand. Fryer also showed that ordinary black and white working class people have been the victims of the capitalist system, even though black people suffered a great deal more in the drive by the employers to maximise profits and productivity, at the expense of people and their lives. Black people are here to stay and the size of the black population is likely to double every 10 to 20 years, especially in London and the South East as well as in the Midlands and large cities in Britain. The need for black and white working class people to organise and fight for a more equal, just, fair and harmonious society has never been greater as successive governments have enable the rich to become incrementally richer, and the poor, poorer since the late 1970's.

Marx, Engels and Lenin

These three men are significant people whose thinking on politics, economics, governance, democracy, history and society has been well documented over the last 150 years. I have been influenced by all of them whose theories, philosophies, and writings I have admired. I am well aware of how different politicians and political theorists have adapted various aspects of the writings and involvements of these men, especially Marx who started it all off with the Communist Manifesto in 1848. For the purpose of this book, I intend to restrict my comments to just a few paragraphs as readers will have ample access to find out thousands of publications and billions of words written about them through the internet. I will focus almost entirely on the specific influences Marx have had on me as a trade unionist, a politician and an anti-racist activist.

Karl Heinrich Marx was born on 5 May 1818, in Trier in the Prussian Rhineland, Germany. His family were wealthy middle class Jews who converted to Christianity in 1824 in order to avoid anti-Semitism. Marx was a German philosopher, economist, sociologist historian journalist and revolutionary socialist. Marx's work in economics laid the basis for the current understanding of labour and its relation to capital, and has influenced much of subsequent economic theories since he published the "Communist Manifesto" in 1848. He published numerous other books during his lifetime, including Das Kapital (1867–1894). Marx is probably the most influential, yet controversial character in human history. His influence has reached every continent and almost every corner of the world.

Marx studied at the University of Bonn and the University of Berlin, where he became interested in the philosophical ideas of the Young Hegelians. After his studies, he wrote for a radical newspaper in Cologne, and began to work out his theory of dialectical materialism. He moved to Paris in 1843, where he began writing for other radical newspapers and met Friedrich Engels, who would become his lifelong friend and collaborator. In 1849 he was exiled and moved to London together with his wife and children where he continued writing and formulating his theories about social and economic activity. He also campaigned for socialism and became a significant figure not only within the trade union and in the International Workingmen's Association, but also within the debates and conflicts that were prominent in Europe since the 1840's. I would link the life and work of all three men and the socialist women such as Konstantinovna Krupskaya who became, a prominent revolutionary and wife of Vladimir Lenin throughout Lenin's political life, as well as Rosa Luxemburg, (1871-1919); a Marxist theorist, philosopher, economist and revolutionary socialist of Polish Jewish descent, who became a naturalized German citizen, All these socialists were part of the Marxist theorists who contributed to the success of the Russian Revolution which gave the impetus for other socialist revolution in China and elsewhere. Marxist theories and revolutionary actions changed the world. It played a major part in the overthrowing of the worst excessive of capitalism, colonialism, slavery, and the birth of various types of socialist societies across the world. Socialists have always opposed to slavery, colonialism, racism, fascism and xenophobia. I never regarded Stalin, Khrushchev, or Yeltsin as socialists, and had no respect or admiration for their political and personal views.

Martin Luther King, Malcolm X and Muhammad Ali

I have written brief biographies of Martin Luther King Jr., Malcolm X and Muhammad Ali, Bob Marley, Angela Davis, Kwame Nkrumah, Claudia Jones, Franz Fanon, Gamal Abdel Nasser and Mahatma Gandhi in two previous books. These are all men and women for whom I have the greatest of admiration. They all happen to be socialists, anti-racists and anti-fascists and anti-colonialists. Martin Luther King, Jr. (January 15, 1929 – April 4, 1968) was an American pastor, activist, humanitarian, and leader in the African-American Civil Rights Movement who inspired millions across the world to campaign for civil and human rights. King is best known for his role in the advancement of civil rights using nonviolent civil disobedience based on his Christian beliefs and his support for the views of Mahatma Gandhi. Martin Luther King died as he lived; fighting for his dreams of liberation for his people in America and the world. He was opposed to racism, exploitation, injustice and wars. He won the Nobel Peace Prize in 1964 and was posthumously awarded the Presidential Medal of Freedom and the Congressional Gold Medal. Martin Luther King, Jr. Day was established as a holiday in numerous cities and states beginning in 1971, and as a U.S. federal holiday in 1986. Hundreds of streets in the U.S. have been renamed in his honour. In addition, a county was rededicated in his honour. A statue on the National Mall was opened to the public in 2011. King was one of the most famous people in the 2th century.

Malcolm X (1925 – 1965), born Malcolm Little and also known as El-Hajj Malik El-Shabazz was a revolutionary African-American Muslim minister, a human rights activist and one of the most courageous fighter for civil and human rights as well as freedom for all African Americans and indeed all descendants of Africans worldwide. He was an internationalist and a freedom fighter who took a more radical and at times militant position in relation to Martin Luther King. Many white people and those who benefitted from institutionalised racism accused Malcolm of preaching racism and violence. He has been called one of the greatest and most influential African Americans in history.

Malcolm X was effectively orphaned early in life. His father was killed when he was six and his mother was placed in a mental hospital when he was thirteen, after which he lived in a series of foster homes. At age 20, Malcolm went to prison for larceny and breaking and entering. While in prison he became a member of the Nation of Islam, and after his parole in 1952 quickly rose to become one of its leaders of which he was the most well-known. He was opposed to integration, white supremacy, and all aspects of institutionalised and organisational racism. His books, speeches and sermons were inspirational and he had a worldwide following. In September 1960, at the United Nations General Assembly in New York, Malcolm X was invited to the official functions of several African nations. He met Gamal Abdel Nasser of Egypt, Ahmed Sékou Touré of Guinea, and Kenneth

Kaunda of the Zambian African National Congress. Fidel Castro also attended the Assembly, and Malcolm X met with him as part of a welcoming committee of Harlem community leaders. Malcolm travelled widely in Africa, the Middle East, and Europe and across America. Malcolm was killed by members of the Nation of Islam after falling out with the Group and setting up his own ministry. Malcolm was a revolutionary socialist as well as an African Nationalist. He addressed meetings of the Socialist Workers Party in America and the Organisation of African Unity. He was committed towards a unified and radical African continent free from American influence. Malcolm visited the United Kingdom and spoke at the Oxford Union Society on 3 December 1964; a place familiar to me when I was a student in Oxford. He returned to the UK on 5 February 1965 and addressed the Council of African Organisations in London, as well as visiting Smethwick, near Birmingham on 12 February 1965 before returning to America. On 21 February, 1965, Malcolm X was preparing to address the Organization of Afro-American Unity in Manhattan's Audubon Ballroom when someone in the 400-person audience yelled "Nigger! Get your hand outta my pocket. As Malcolm X and his bodyguards tried to quell the disturbance, a man rushed forward and shot Malcolm X once in the chest with a sawed-off shotgun. Two other men charged the stage firing semi-automatic handguns. Malcolm X was pronounced dead at 3:30 pm, Malcolm X just like Martin Luther King died just under 40 years old. The 1960's witnessed the murder of several famous and powerful world leaders including J F Kennedy President of the USA murdered on 22 November 1963; Malcolm X 21 February 1965; Martin Luther King Jr. 4 April 1968 and Robert Kennedy Democratic Presidential Candidate on 5 June 1968.

All these great people were assassinated because of what the stood for. I admired all these people who had they lived until natural death, would have changed the world for the better. I do not admire some of the right wing American Presidents, including Richard Nixon, George Bush, George W Bush, Ronald Reagan, or what I have seen of Barak Obama since 2008, even though he is a democrat. I believe

George W Bush and the British Prime Minister Tony Blair should have been tried for war crimes for their involvement in Iraq.

Muhammad Ali (born Cassius Marcellus Clay, Jr.; January 17, 1942) is an American former professional boxer, generally considered among the greatest heavyweights in the sport's history. Ali remains the only three-time World Heavyweight Champion; he won the title in 1964, 1974, and 1978. He is probably the most recognisable and loved living person on the planet today. I met Ali on two occasions when he visited London and Birmingham in the 1980's. He is one of the most loved, respected, principled and famous sports person over the last 100 years. Ali has been recognised worldwide not only for the skills he displayed in the ring as a boxer, but also for the values he exemplified outside of it in his support for religious freedom, racial justice, freedom, peace and social justice for all. At the age of only 22, he won the world heavyweight championship in 1964 from Sonny Liston .shortly after that fight, Ali joined the Nation of Islam and changed his name. In 1967, three years after winning the heavyweight title, Ali refused to be conscripted into the U.S. military, citing his religious beliefs and opposition to American involvement in the Vietnam War. The U.S. government declined to recognize him as a conscientious objector, however, because Ali declared that he would fight in a war if directed to do so by Allah or his messenger (Elijah Muhammad). He was eventually arrested and found guilty on draft evasion charges and stripped of his boxing title. He did not fight again for nearly four years.

In 1971 his conviction was overturned on a technicality by The Supreme Court. Ali went on to become World Heavyweight Champion on two more occasions. Nicknamed "The Greatest", Ali was involved in several historic boxing matches. Notable among these were the first Liston fight, three with rival Joe Frazier, and one with George Foreman, where he regained titles he had been stripped of seven years earlier. Ali not only revolutionized the sport of boxing by sheer power and magnetism of his personality, charm and good looks, but also became the hero of the Black struggles after the assassinations of Malcolm X and Martin Luther King.

He transformed the role and image of the African American people and people of African descents around the world. His wits, charm, intelligence, pride and humour and his commitment to racial and social justice antagonized the white establishment in America. I have written biographies of Ali in two of my books on Black History, "Memories of the 20th Century" and "Our Lives, Our History, Our Future."

Pope Francis, Bishop Tutu and others I like and dislike

I was born into a Hindu family and over the years some of my siblings followed me into becoming Christians. For me becoming a Christian started when I was invited by a beautiful young Sunday school teacher to attend the Anglican Church opposite our home. I was only about 8 years old and I took a liking to her. So I plucked up courage, dressed in my Sunday best, but with no shoes attended the School. I enjoyed sitting next to her and enjoying her sweet perfumed smell. At the end we were all given a bun and a glass of homemade squash. I became a regular church goer and continued this when I first arrived in London. My parents were staunch Hindu and later one of my sister was a Muslim. I saw myself as an internationalist as far as religion goes. I basically support the good things in all religions. It is so sad to see so many millions killed by inter religious or conflicts between different religions during my life time.

However, I want to declare my respect and admiration for the present Pope – Pope Francis, who I believe is the most caring, compassionate and radical Pope in my lifetime. I have seen so many religious leaders closing their eyes to mass killings, exploitation, genocide, holocausts, ethnic cleansing and even supporting fascist dictators and racist organisations. But Pope Francis is really special. His comments on Capitalism and exploitation are sincere and relevant today. I list below some of my favourite Pope Francis quotes as I believe the speak volumes that are relevant to today's world:

- "Men and women are sacrificed to the idols of profit and consumption: it is the 'culture of waste.' If a computer breaks it is a tragedy, but poverty, the needs and dramas of so many people end up being considered normal. ... When the stock market drops 10 points in some cities, it constitutes a tragedy. Someone who dies is not news, but lowering income by 10 points is a tragedy! In this way people are thrown aside as if they were trash." (General audience, June 5, 2013).

- "...we must also acknowledge that the majority of the men and women of our time continue to live daily in situations of insecurity, with dire consequences. Certain pathologies are increasing, with their psychological consequences; fear and desperation grip the hearts of many people, even in the so-called rich countries; the joy of life is diminishing; indecency and violence are on the rise; poverty is becoming more and more evident. People have to struggle to live and, frequently, to live in an undignified way. (5/16/13)

- "I encourage the financial experts and the political leaders of your countries to consider the words of Saint John Chrysostom: "Not to share one's goods with the poor is to rob them and to deprive them of life. It is not our goods that we possess, but theirs." (5/16/13)

- "Man is not in charge today; money is in charge, money rules. God our Father did not give the task of caring for the earth to money, but to us, to men and women: we have this task! Instead, men and women are sacrificed to the idols of profit and consumption: it is the "culture of waste." (6/5/13, Environment)

- "...men and women are sacrificed to the idols of profit and consumption: it is the "culture of waste." If you break a computer it is a tragedy, but poverty, the needs, the dramas of so many people end up becoming the norm. (6/5/13, Environment)

- "I believe that, yes, the times talk to us of so much poverty in the world and this is a scandal. Poverty in the world is a scandal. In a world where there is so much wealth, so many resources to feed everyone, it is unfathomable that there are so many hungry children, that there are so many children without an education, so many poor persons. Poverty today is a cry. We all have to think if we can become a little poorer, all of us have to do this. How can I become a little poorer in order to be more like Jesus, who was the poor Teacher?" (6/7/13 Jesuit Schools)

- Bishop Tutu is another person for whom I have great admiration. He is someone I would love to meet and have a conversation with. I admire his sense of humour; his style of preaching and his love for all humans and living things. He is a brother and a Saint in my view. It is so sad that Jacob Zuma; the South African President and his cronies in the ANC have chosen not to listen to Mandela and Bishop Tutu as well as the cries of the African people and decided to betray so much of Mandela's vision for the South African poor. Below are some Bishop Tutu's quotes I admire.

- "When the missionaries came to Africa they had the bible and we had the land. They said, Let us pray." "We closed our eyes. When we opened them we had the Bible and they had the land."

- "If you are neutral in situations of injustice, you have chosen the side of the oppressor. If an elephant has its foot on the tail of a mouse and you say that you are neutral, the mouse will not appreciate your neutrality."

- "We must not allow ourselves to become like the system we oppose. We cannot afford to use methods of which we will be ashamed when we look back, when we say, '...we shouldn't have done that.' We must remember, my friends, that we have been given a wonderful cause. The cause of freedom! And you and I must be those who will walk with heads held high. We will say, 'We used methods that can stand the harsh scrutiny of history.'"

- "What is black empowerment when it seems to benefit not the vast majority but elite that tends to be recycled?"

- "I am not interested in picking up crumbs of compassion thrown from the table of someone who considers himself my master. I want the full menu of human rights."

- "Freedom and liberty lose out by default because good people are not vigilant." "We who advocate peace are becoming an irrelevance when we speak peace. The government speaks rubber bullets, live bullets, tear gas, police dogs, detention, and death."

There are so many people I admired and who have shaped me as a person over the years, unfortunately, I do not have room to write about all of them in this book. However, I feel compelled to mention just a few more:

I have always admired **Sir David Attenborough**, the English broadcaster and naturalist. I enjoyed watching many of the natural history programmes he has made over several decades. I watched much of the nine Life series he made, in conjunction with the BBC Natural History Unit, which collectively form a comprehensive survey of all life on the planet earth. I learnt a lot about our planet and the great and not so great creatures that share the world with us cruel, destructive and inadequate human beings. Attenborough is credit to journalism and broadcasting and a national treasure in Britain, although he himself does not like the term.

Thomas Payne was also a great person, whose book – "The Rights of Man" which informed me on the issues about liberty, freedom and human rights. He was born on 29 January, 1737, Thetford, England. In 1774, he met Benjamin Franklin in London, who helped him immigrate to Philadelphia in America where he turned to journalism and attracted attention in 1776, after he published his book; "Common Sense", arguing for a strong defence of American Independence from England. He later published "The American Crisis" (1776-83), He supported the American Revolution and then he returned to Europe and in 1791-92, he wrote The Rights of Man in response to criticism of the French Revolution. This work caused Paine to be labelled an outlaw in England for his anti-monarchist views. He would have been arrested, but he fled for France to join the National Convention. By 1793, he was imprisoned in France for not endorsing the execution of Louis XVI. He returned to America and died on 8 June 1809 at the age of 72 in New York City. I read all three of his books and I admired him for his support of working class people and for his opposition to slavery of Africans and Native Americans.

Harriet Tubman (1822 – 10 March 1913) was an African American abolitionist humanitarian, and spy for the Union Army during the American Civil War. As a child in Dorchester County, Maryland, Tubman was beaten by masters to whom she was hired out. Early in her life, she suffered a severe head wound when hit by a heavy metal weight. The injury caused disabling epileptic-type seizures, headaches, and powerful visionary and dream experiences, which occurred throughout her life. In 1839 she escaped to Philadelphia, but she returned to Maryland to rescue her family, friends and others to escape. She made at least thirteen dangerous missions to rescue approximately seventy people from slavery, by using the network of antislavery activists and safe houses known as the Underground Railroad to freedom in Canada. She later helped John Brown recruit men for his attacks on the slave masters. Brown was later captured and hanged by the slave masters.

Tubman worked for the Union Army, first as a cook and nurse, and then as an armed scout and spy. The first woman to lead an armed expedition in the war, she guided the Combahee River Raid, which liberated more than 750 slaves in South Carolina. After the war, she retired to the family home in Auburn, New York, where she cared for her aging parents. She became active in the women's suffrage movement in New York and recruited many African women who were ex-slaves into the struggles for equal rights, freedom and democracy. Tubman lived to age 90 and when she was too ill to continue the struggle she moved into a home for elderly African Americans that she had helped found years earlier.

Black women such as Harriet Tubman are women of real substance and not those who have colluded with systems that oppress people to save their own skins or, to become rich and famous as singers, dancers and entertainers playing largely to white audiences.

Chapter 20:

Corruption, Corporate media and democracy

Is there such thing as a 'free' media?

"The current state of the news media is partially to blame for the public's general lack of information vital for responsible citizenship in a democracy. The news media has become an aspect of show business, offering merely infotainment. It has evolved into an entity that tends to function as a public relations agency for wealthy and powerful multinational corporations, members of Congress, the current Presidential Administration including the administrations that preceded it. The news media is being utilized as a political tool of suppression and propaganda by those in power, and propaganda is psychological in nature. Full and half-truths and utter misinformation, it's an arrogant and very commercial strategy that is implemented because it appeals to emotions, fear of being the main one relentless talk of national security, personal and community safety, can trigger childhood insecurities and indoctrinated views of authority." – *Tesesa Stover quotes*

Whatever anyone thinks of the media, one can be assured that there are a multitude of views, assumptions and ideologies surrounding the value, impact, status, effectiveness and functional aspects of the media. As our world has become a small village, in terms of communication, travel, interaction and control; with a small number of corporations, financial and political and elites controlling almost every aspect of our lives, we are increasingly seeing ourselves and everything within our planet from the sounds and images that are directed to us by the media. Some people would say that the media corporations own us and they exercise the greatest influence on our lives in terms of attitudes, culture, behaviour and beliefs. What is certain is that the media in the western world has become so large, dominant and powerful that it is difficult to separate them from all the other social, economic, political, ideological and major decision making process across the globe. The media corporations have become mega giants, operating in a global field and have become increasingly powerful with the advancement of technology, science and accessibility through a combination of gadgets that is readily and easily accessible even in the remotest parts of the world. Regardless of one's opinion about the media, what is certain is that we cannot avoid its impact and influence on the entire planet and everything that is present in it.

I have seen some reports that claim that they media corporations own everything; they own all the important land; they own and control the corporations; they have long since bought and paid for the politicians who occupy the political, economic, structures; the people who runs the town and city halls; the judiciary and the big media companies, because they control just about all of the news and information we have access to. Neither politicians, business corporations, the one hundred richest people and institutions that owns the majority of the world's wealth; the rich, famous and powerful who feeds off the media, are all gullible to media influence and control. Politicians, governments and corporations spend hundreds of billions of dollars every year on advertising, lobbying, persuading, indoctrinating, brainwashing, and misinforming the public through the multiplicity of channels including newspapers, books, television and social media. I have seen in my lifetime the growth of the media and its impact on our lives. I have been a victim of racial abuse by the media and have been unfairly stereotyped from being a "Community Leader" to a "Bully Boy", a "Maverick" and a "Looney Leftie." On many occasions I have criticised the media for misrepresenting my views, for unfairly attacking the trade unions and the Labour Party, and for demonising good people who were working for their communities, genuine values and beliefs. The fact that the power of the media is so strong and pervasive that even people with lots of wealth and power can become victims of the media. It has the power to make and break people, groups and institutions. There are very few, if any government that have the courage to introduce even mild control, supervision, moderation, monitoring or censorship of the private media.

The media, together with the political class and the corporate elites don't want a population of citizens capable of critical thinking, understanding and knowledge of the dynamics associated with the level of power, control and influence of the decision making process and the consequences of such decisions. It is quite common for the political elites and the corporate leaders to be led by the media instead of the other way round. The media is largely unaccountable, uncontrolled, undemocratic and often unpopular, yet they shape almost all aspects of our lives. All day long 34/7 the media is beating us over the head with the stories and alleged facts they want us to believe; to shape what to think, feel and want; what and who to support; what is good for us and what to acquire. This constant process of controlled and calculated information must radically impact on public perceptions of how politics, businesses, so-called democracy, power, freedom, justice, militarism, aggression and institutions work. Given this situation the danger corporate and media power presents to democracy, and the extent to which it has compromised and corrupted the political, economic, social and cultural structures across the world must be a concern for every person concerned about the state of our world, with rising inequality, militarism and institutions that are much bigger and powerful than nation states.

There is no doubt that the media is not all bad and dishonourable, all the time, it can be quite challenging and extremely useful in promoting openness, accountability, transparency and even democratic and human values. It can and often does act as a champion for the underdog, the victims of abuse, those fighting to protect lives of people and the environment, as well as exposing those politicians, bureaucrats, bankers and institutions that are corrupt and incompetent. The case of the corrupt and cheating politicians; the corruption and inadequacies of the Metropolitan police service and its under-cover operations; the unprofessional and corrupt links between the media and the police right up to senior levels; the hacking of the telephones of victims of murder as well as the unacceptable culture that exists amongst the overpaid bankers and top public sector bureaucrats are all excellent examples of good journalism that is good for a healthy democracy. I have been fortunate for being invited to participate in numerous radio and television debates and discussions on some of the issues mentioned above, and I believe the media should be more accessible to people with different views and perspective from that which is seen as dominant. The media like the banks and corporations is far too big and powerful and should be more fragmented and regulated, not through self-regulation, but by statute that ensures accountability, professionalism and public scrutiny.

Money making media

Private media businesses are primarily concerned in making money by any means necessary, which is of course the whole purpose of the capitalist economy. Apart from making money, the media relies on ensuring the maximum number of users of its services, which in turn attracts advertisers and people who are prepared to suck up to the media in return for mutual benefits. Politicians are even more gullible than journalists for fame, fortune and freebies. Most popular media have deliberately set out to target the largest group of people who are seen as the core target audience. This audience is then fed a regular diet of the same messages in slightly different forms to keep the core audience on board. This diet could include a combination of various shades of nationalism, racism, sexism, anti-trade union and anti-socialist propaganda. As almost all of the popular media are in business to make money, they invariably support the capitalist ideology with some variations. It is in their interests to grow their businesses and to attract maximum advertising, attention, influence and power to enable those like-minded people to want their endorsement. I remember a newspaper front page article that appeared the on the day of the general election in Britain; stating something like "The last one leaving Britain - turn off the lights." This was in reference to a possible victory by the Labour Party. I believe this newspaper was the Sun, which is owned by the Murdock Empire. A few years later (1995) Rupert Murdock flew Tony Blair, the then leader of the New Labour Party and his wife flew first class to Australia, at Murdock's expense, as Murdock was reasonably confident that Blair would be the next Prime Minister of Britain. The double dealing and hypocrisy of the media barons will never cease. Rupert Murdock then having dropped his support for the Conservatives decided to endorse Tony Blair and stating that "Mr Blair has vision, he has purpose and he speaks our language on morality and family life."

Mr Murdock and his media Empire spans America, Europe and Asia. He is well known for his right wing political views. In fact the private newspaper, radio and television are on the centre right of the political spectrum, and very few left of centre media are supportive of the unions, the Labour Party and people, who for various reasons depends on the welfare state and public services for their survival. Apart from the Morning Star newspapers, which is owned by its readers, all the other national British newspapers are committed to maintaining and promoting the capitalist ideology and in doing so denigrate any other ideologies or movements that are opposed to capitalism. Even some centre left newspapers such as the Daily Mirror and the Guardian are seen as centre left liberal minded newspapers are often very critical of trade unions and workers who are engaged in securing the best price for the labour and to defend the gains made by previous generations of workers. The Daily Mail, Telegraph, Express and Independent are committed supporters of the centre right political camp. Television is even more grounded in the centre right of politics and so are most national radio stations, despite the common misconception that the BBC is on the left of centre.

The media is at the centre of attention in all western countries, especially in the bastion of the capitalist camp, which are the USA and its satellite NATO partners within the European Union (EU). A recent comment by a well-known right wing columnist - Janet Daley stated in an article in an edition of the Sunday Telegraph that "British political journalism is basically a club to which politicians and journalists both belong," she wrote. "It is this familiarity, this intimacy, and this set of shared assumptions ... which is the real corruptor of political life. The self-limiting spectrum of what can and cannot be said ... the self-reinforcing cowardice which takes for granted that certain vested interests are too powerful to be worth confronting. All of these things are constant dangers in the political life of any democracy." This could be said of the media within the USA and the EU. Almost all mainstream political parties in the western countries shares a set of similar core values that appeals to the centre ground of politics. So it is not surprising that much of the media in the western countries have positioned themselves in the centre as well. Together the media, politicians and corporations have de-politicised and alienated a sizeable section of the voting population who are living on incomes or benefits or both, that puts them below the poverty level, which is below 60 per cent of the average income. The least well of the American and European population which could be up to 40 per cent of the total population have become the most disillusioned, apathetic and alienated voters who are more likely to opt out of the democratic process by not voting. By not voting these people are in reality supporting parties that are very likely to ignore their interests in favour of their core middle class voters. This is where the radical parties on the left are losing out in the power struggle, as working class and the poor are less likely to engage in the political structures, campaigns and struggles on a consistent and determined way. Many have been brainwashed by the media to vote against their own interests by not voting or voting for parties on irrational issues, such as racism, anti-immigration and nationalism.

Most national media engages in corrupt practices. The mainstream American media is broadly supportive to the centre right political views and many of the owners of the media corporations as well as some journalists will not hesitate in colluding with the politicians, the CIA and other agencies and institutions to distort the facts, misinform the public, fabricate the news, or ignoring key news items in the interest of patriotism and the broader American interests. The news is framed in such a way as to reflect certain political views and vested corporate interests. Too many journalists reporting on international and foreign issues are on the secret payroll of the American and European national and international secret services. There ought to be a Hippocratic Oath for all journalists. Not enough journalists are engaged in critical, independent and investigative journalism similar to people like John Pilger who is an internationally known and respected journalists. The media barons are embedded, immersed and intertwined in the society, beliefs and culture of the people they are meant to hold to account. They are fascinated by power struggles among the political, corporate and ruling elite, but have shown very little interest in the conflicts between the ruling elite and those they dominate through their wealth and power. They give much attention to the few at the top and ignore the many at the bottom, who are the real wealth creators, by applying their skills, labour and time to ensure that the wheels of the society are forever working to support the nation in every way. Instead of holding those who hold large amounts of power, influence and resources to account for their actions and inactions media simply ventriloquizes the expressions, concerns and interests of the powerful elite. It is commonly accepted that the media proprietor appoints editors in their own ideological image, who would in turn impress their views on their journalists. So there is hardly a truly independent, unbiased or ideologically free media, where reporters, commentators, journalists and editors think and act independently. It is a lie that the media represents the voice of the people as so many of them claims to do in Britain. The truth is the capitalist media is consistent and pre-occupied in representing the views and interests of those who own control and advertise their services in the media.

Culture, ideology and opium of the people

Much of the so-called free media around the world is predictable, ideological, biased and right wing. The right-wing papers in Britain run endless exposures of benefit cheats, scroungers, illegal and exploitative immigrants, people falsely claiming benefits for disability and various illnesses when they should be at work and petty criminals who are threatening the social cohesion of society. Yet the same media largely ignores the thousands of daily criminal and illegal activities that are depriving the public of billions of pounds and dollars in taxation; financial manipulation and frauds; creative accountancy and banking transactions and siphoning off money into offshore tax havens instead of investing in businesses and social enterprises at home. The rip off culture by the corporations, hedge funders, banking and financial institutions, investors in the housing markets, greedy and wasteful supermarkets, corrupt politicians and police officers, overpaid and under-performed bureaucrats and the money lenders are not receiving anywhere near the media attention they deserve.

This very bunch of right wing media are always ready to denigrate and savage the trade unions, the Labour Party and people campaigning for animal rights, for actions to protect the planet from climate change, to promote social justice, peace and equality. They also lambast the regulations that restrain corporate power, and those people and organisations campaigning for even tighter regulative arrangements to curb the excessive profits of the corporations and cartels, and abuse of the earth's resources. Parts of the media is pre-occupied with the culture of celebrities; sex and sexualisation of younger people; creating a culture that is rude, aggressive, violent, pornographic, individualism and materialism. They have created a culture that is destroying many of the functional and traditional values, whilst at the same time promoting alcohol and drug abuse, and addictive and obsessive types of so-called entertainment programmes. Television programmes such as Big Brother, Reality Television and Talent Shows, game shows, 24/7 gambling and pornography channels available to children and adults and an abundance of crude, violent and abusive films and game shows. The media makes money from marketing its resources. It has become far too intrusive, and invasive in our lives. Much of the media is based on trivialising and dummying down or distorting real and important issues. Television has become so important to millions of people that it has become part of their personality and culture. I know that there are many interesting, entertaining, clean and informative channels and programmes each day on the television, but the public is so taken in by the worst parts of the media that the really good programmes on science, education, nature, politics, animals, the environment, civilisation, history and culture are not as popular as the common trash that have become the standard viewing for tens of millions of people. I often wonder where the demarcation is between entertainment and indoctrination and whether the majority of the public are consciously aware of their addiction to certain programmes.

It is difficult to argue that the media is always fair, neutral or free from the power to shape views and opinions, when so many people spends so many hours viewing or actively engaging in the media. A number of recent reports linked the Arab uprising in many countries in North Africa and the Middle East to the power and influence of the social media, namely face book and twitter. One could easily argue whether it is the people that shapes the media or is it the media that shapes the views, attitudes and behaviour of people. The reality is that the media has become the all-powerful, all inclusive and multi-purpose easily accessible mode of communication, information, viewing, researching, sharing of ideas, participation and voice for various individuals, communities and interest groups, that it is necessary for governments to exercise at least independent and reasonable control and monitoring of all aspects of the media through regulations, in the interest of the general good of the nation and the world.

Many American adults believe the federal government, corporations or both are involved in conspiracies to cover up important information on health caused by genetically modified foods, fracking, and drug abuse by the pharmaceutical companies, the use of cell phones and use of a wide range of chemicals on food crops. The American public is also concerned about the conspiracy between the American government and the large corporations such as Monsanto to misinform the public and foreign countries about the negative aspects of these activities on public health and the environment. Yet the media either ignores such concerns or simply distorts such impacts, leaving some people confused. Much of the media reporting, or failure to report certain issues are due to the direct or indirect influence of the government or corporations or both. The regular rigging of financial markets, trading arrangements and exploitation of poorer countries of through so-called aid, trade and economic development and the intervention by the World Bank and International Monetary Fund (IMF) as well as the growing militarisation of Africa by America and the extensive land grabbing strategy by large western corporations has hardly been reported by the mainstream media. Instead we see articles about how generous the western powers are in providing aid and protection for African and poorer countries around the world. Very little if any, is debated in the media on the re-colonisation of ex-colonies, exploitation of cheap labour involving children and women in Asia and Africa who are indirectly and directly in supplying the western corporations with cheap goods. These are important issues that are ignored by the media. The media was well aware of the impending recession and the financial greed and excesses which were fuelling the recession well before 2007, but decided to collude with governments and corporations and not reporting the truth about the dirty financial transactions the large banks were engaged in across America and Europe. This dishonest collusion in fixing interest rates and taking exceptional risks by the banks ended up with the public having forced spend trillions of dollars, pounds and Euros bailing out the corrupt and dishonest banking and financial institutions. Such failures by the political class the media and the corporations have resulted in forcing tens of millions of people into poverty in America and Europe as well as degrading the status of democracy and democratic institutions in countries such as Greece and Spain.

The corporate media is a gigantic global enterprise that seeks to protect western values and exploitation of working class people below average earnings whilst the small elite increase their wealth and power. The right wing Tea Party movement in America, which claims to be a spontaneous rising of working and middle class Americans against the ruling elite, was founded with the help of the billionaire Koch brothers and promoted by Murdoch's Fox News. Instead of championing the victims of capitalism and exploitation and holding the ruling elites to account the media corporations has been re-enforcing corporate power and values by blaming the weak and defending the strong who have caused the number of people living in poverty in America and Europe to steadily increase over the last six years. The media barons sometimes allow governments to promote the interests of the poor to a very limited extent, but they are always committed to defending the interests and the values of the rich and powerful.

What is to be done?

If the media collusion between the media the political elite and the corporations continue, what is left of democracy in America and Europe would be transformed into hypocrisy, as is evident in the discussions, reporting and deliberate misinformation presented to the public across the world by the American and European governments, NATO and the EU. The USA, EU and NATO that are clearly the aggressors, who encouraged, financed and inflamed the dissention in Ukraine, which culminated in terror gangs, right wing and fascists mobs using weapons, bombs, violence, illegal occupation, criminal damage, arson and murder to overthrow a democratically elected government, have denied any association with these activities or the leaders, and instead portraying themselves as the victims and defender of democracy and freedom in Ukraine. They seek to blame Russia as the aggressor and for being responsible for the violence and chaos, whilst all along the hidden agenda for NATO was to expand their influence into Ukraine and on the borders of Russia.

American and European politicians and bureaucrats wasted no time in joining the rioters in Ukraine, making speeches and holding meeting with the rebel leaders including fascist's leadership that eventually illegally staged a coup against the elected government. The NATO leaders, bureaucrats, politicians and the media corporations shared the same script in the news bulletins and reports that portrayed the west as the victims and Russia as the aggressive undemocratic nation that broken international laws, invaded a peaceful and democratic country for no good reason and are now responsible for re-igniting the 'cold war'; the arms race and world tension. It is so pathetic to see Obama, John Kerry, William Hague, and the European and NATO leaders turning the truth on its head on every occasion they were accommodated by the media to blame the Russians and to portray themselves as the peace maker and the victims of Russian betrayal, aggression and illegal actions. They even condemn the peaceful election by nearly 90 per cent of the voting population in the Crimea to seek federation status with Russia, when Obama, Cameron, Hollande and Merkel themselves did not secure even 50 per cent of the votes that elevated them to power.

Because of the very serious threat the media and its cosy relationship with the political class, corporations and financial elites, which presents a real threat to democracy, fairness and justice, the solution must be to restrict the size and power of the giant media corporations; to introduce statutory regulations and to dismantle the cosy relationship between the elites. To introduce a system that would discourage the media from telling lies, abusing their power, misrepresenting the facts, distorting the truth, hacking people's telephones, corrupting already corrupt politicians even further, and abusing certain members of the public because of their gender, race, social status or, religion.

I doubt very much whether the media culture would change any significant way by the present crop of politicians as they and the media feeds off each other, even though they do have their moments of falling out at times as they did, over the politicians fiddling their expenses and paying them large salary increases whilst expecting the poor to suffer disproportionately for a recession that was not of their making. Readers and viewers as well as shareholders must also become more pro-active in challenging the media, corporations and politicians and forcing them to be more accountable and act more responsibly towards their constituents, readers/viewers and customers. Journalists, reporters, interviewers and newsreaders must also organise within their unions and to sign up to a recognised framework that supports balance, fairness, accountability, openness, the truth and recognising conflicts of interests, avoiding double standards corruption and ideological indoctrination.

The media can be a beacon of hope for the poor and disadvantaged in society; for those who have suffered from institutional abuse, neglect and wrong doing;

for victims of injustice and cruelty; for people who are working to save our planet and everything in it; for those who are seeking to create a more peaceful, loving, democratic, equal and safe world.

Ownership is the key to the corruption and shortcomings of the media. No corporation should be so large as to exercise excessive power over the masses. Ending such large media corporations is a democratic necessity. In recent months we have witnessed a situation involving a senior politician who was involved in handing over a controversial and extremely lucrative relating to the full control of the satellite broadcaster BSkyB to Rupert Murdoch. The Tory MP who was the culture secretary and secretly lobbied with cringe-making enthusiasm for the takeover by Murdock and insisted that he had abandoned all partisanship the moment he was put in charge of adjudicating the bid.

In 2011, following public outcry about the abuse of the media the Prime Minister David Cameron announced that a public inquiry under the Inquiries Act 2005 would be chaired by Lord Justice Leveson on 13 July 2011. The press release on 14th September 2011 stated that the Inquiry would be addressing:

- "The culture, practices and ethics of the press, including contacts between the press and politicians and the press and the police; it is to consider the extent to which the current regulatory regime has failed and whether there has been a failure to act upon any previous warnings about media misconduct."

- "The extent of unlawful or improper conduct within News International, other media organisations or other organisations. It will also consider the extent to which any relevant police force investigated allegations relating to News International, and whether the police received corrupt payments or were otherwise complicit in misconduct."

In 2007, News of the World royal editor Clive Goodman and private investigator Glenn Mulcaire were convicted of illegal interception of phone messages. According to the News of the World, this was an isolated incident, but The

Guardian claimed that evidence existed that this practice extended beyond Goodman and Mulcaire. In 2011, after a civil settlement with Sienna Miller, the Metropolitan Police Service set up a new investigation, Operation Weeting. In July 2011, it was revealed that News of the World reporters had hacked the voicemail of murder victim Milly Dowler. The Inquiry published the Leveson Report in November 2012, which reviewed the general culture and ethics of the British media, and made recommendations for a new, independent, body to replace the existing Press Complaints Commission, which would be recognised by the state through new laws. The Enquiry revealed that there were extensive collusion between the media, politicians, the police and others, some of whom were paid to spy illegally on people.

Not only has the backdoor lobbying and elite back scratching been laid bare at the Enquiry, while Murdoch executives, journalists and police officers have been arrested and charged. But Murdoch's mythology that he has "never asked a prime minister for anything" and leaves editorial policy to his editors has also been mercifully disposed of. Ex-Prime Minister John Major reported that the media baron demanded he change government policy on Europe or his newspapers wouldn't back the Tories at the 1997 general election, while the former Sunday Times editor Harold Evans has described how Murdoch dictated coverage on everything from the economy to foreign policy. The hearings have thrown a gruesome light on the dalliance between press and politicians, and there are dangers for David Cameron in what might still emerge. But as the circus goes on in an atmosphere of deferential chumminess of its own, it shows clear signs of turning into the establishment safety mechanism of many other such inquiries before it.

It is unlikely that the politicians are going to introduce any meaningful statutory role in press regulation and whether any changes will go beyond a slightly more independent body than the ineffective Press Complaints Commission. The court case against the editors of the defunct News of the World is currently taking place in the High Court and it is very likely that some people will be convicted of perjury and other illegal acts that may result in some redress for victims of illegal media intrusion, misrepresentation falsification of details. Crucially, it is essential that the media becomes significantly more responsible, accountable, open and democratic, as well as less contriving with the politicians and corporations. The days of dominance of the corporate ownership of the press and media – and News International's dominant share of the market, which was given to Murdock's Empire by Margaret Thatcher and reinforced by Tony Blair must be tackled. It is essential to avoid mafia-like grip on politics that shaped the media's reporting of everything from the so-called fight against terrorism since 2001, the invasion of Iraq and Afghanistan to the crisis in Ukraine and the need to regulate the financial and corporate powers and control of the banks, media and corporations. Ed Miliband's declaration to set limits to cross-media ownership and the share of the newspaper market controlled by one proprietor represents a significant break with two decades of political class deference to the media monopolists and cartels.

The western media has long been plagued by monstrous proprietors. In recent times, its owners have been particularly noted for their criminality, from Robert Maxwell to Conrad Black who served time in prison to the bunch of editors and newspapers who are currently on trial for illegal media actions. But whereas press barons always tried to influence politics, that extended in recent years to rewriting media regulation in their commercial interests. And when it comes to the content of their papers and websites, the same sort of approach has translated into selling advertisers the right to incorporate their "messages" and "brand themes" into unlabelled news reports. The extension of on-line information, social media networks and 24/7 access to news, views, information and materials will create more concerns and demands for the media to respect people's privacy, show some moral courage by making for example pornography in accessible to children; protecting the vulnerable from cyber bullying and others who use to social media and internet to commit across the globe.

Corporate corruption of the media has shown itself to be a threat to free expression, democracy and to public and social life. The media is driven by privatisation, profits, and market share, which has made them even more corrosive in recent years. The fact that people like Tony Blair, George Bush and others can waltz around the world from being Prime Minister, President, senior politicians and civil servants making tens of millions in contracts and consultancy fees through a revolving door regime that hands ex- politicians, ministers and civil servants lucrative positions in financial and world affairs should be exposed by the mainstream media. It is unacceptable that nearly 150 politicians including several Cabinet ministers have interests in companies involved in private health care that is the result of privatisation of the NHS. I think we're at the most dangerous time in our political history in terms of the balance of power in the role that the media plays in whether or not we maintain a free democracy or not. The media has become uncontrollable and there is too much nepotism, back scratching and convergence between the political and financial elites that has given them far too much control and influence in our social, political, economic and daily lives. A major problem in the western countries is that there is no border between state interest, corporate and commercial interest. The duties of the state, as a result of privatization, contracting, lobbying is fuzzed and blurred out into the edges of companies, media and parliament. It is part of that mesh of corporate, commercial and state interests that seamlessly blurring into each other. The revelations by Philip Snowden, Julian Assange and others have shown the American, Britain and other states and their top politicians and security personnel and institutions colluded with the corporations and commercial interests to not only spy on the general public, but also on governments, politicians, corporations and commercial interests across the world.

An increasing number of people are beginning to challenge the power and ability of the media to tell the truth, to be impartial and to represent all sides within the nation. Recent events that has been reported by the media – which shows that good and factual journalism and reporting can be good for the nation- has encouraged people not to accept much of what they are exposed to through the media as being correct, honest, factual or unbiased. They also reject the notion largely presented by the media that the world is dominated by human failure, crime, catastrophe, corruption, wars, greed, helplessness and tragedy, and that is the natural way on how the world operates, which is far from the truth. The world despite the media distortion has many great qualities which are not given the prominence that are necessary for us to understand what is going on and how we can improve everything around us. It would be good for the media to focus more on ways in which we could all contribute towards a more peaceful, equal, happy, fair, healthy, and harmonious world, instead of so often justifying greed, wars, conflicts, inequality, and crimes committed by the state and corporations and defending a corrupt and unfair capitalist ideology.

Chapter 21:

War on poverty long overdue

"Poverty is not an accident. Like slavery and apartheid, it is man-made and can only be removed by actions of human beings." – Nelson Mandela

One of the most distressing things I experienced as a child was to go hungry. I felt the pain of hunger, witnessed the distress of my poor, illiterate and helpless parents doing all they could to put basic food in our bellies. I felt ashamed, inadequate, frustrated and angry at a system which required people to work six and seven days each week in the burning sun and pouring rain from dawn to dusk, and yet did not earn enough to reasonably feed and clothes themselves and their families. My parents spent almost all their lives without wearing shoes; drawing water from a tap; turning on an electric light; using a flushed toilet; having a bank account; owning a radio, telephone, car or a television; or not worrying about being sick, unemployed and poor. We lived on a sugar plantation owned by an absentee landlord from England. For many miles it was the only employer and naturally the employer paid the lowest wages they could get away with. It was a colony and it was protected by the British State and the British Army intervened when workers took action on to improve their pay and conditions. Fear of poverty was the main driving force that led me to become an economic migrant to England, as well as the experience of living in impoverished conditions as a child.

I witnessed my parents struggling on a regular basis with debts incurred when times were hard and they had to do their best to cope. Life improved for us when I started to work and to receive my own pay envelope each week, but for my sisters who were married and had children their lives and that of their families continued to suffer until their own children were earning and supplementing the household budgets. We were no different from the majority of the population who were poor in colonial Guyana. In fact it was the case for most of the world's population as well over half the world was under colonial rule, whilst those countries that were not colonies also had large numbers of people living under severe poverty. The well off people owned and controlled the economic and financial structures as well as being responsible for the political institutions, controlling the political, legal, security and all other institutions associated with the state. Over the decades life has become relatively more bearable for most people in the world, due to improvements in science, health, mass food production, education, transport, communication, travel and general economic progress. However, the inequalities that existed during my childhood in Guyana have hardly changed across the world, even though we are better off than previous generations. Western nations and indeed other countries that were previously under colonial rule, such as China, India, Nigeria, Saudi Arabia and others have made enormous progress in wealth creation, but have failed to share out such wealth any way near equally amongst its population. Humankind have achieved such greatness since I was born seventy years ago, but so much has been spent on militarism, wars, trips to other planets in the universe and on destroying our environment, which has left insufficient resources to tackle world poverty and equality. We live in a world that is becoming richer each day, but the riches are unevenly shared out and those who are already rich get richer, and the poor gets relatively poorer.

Of course poverty, hunger, powerlessness, inequality and injustice are all part of the same symptoms of capitalism and the process of globalisation that ensures the survival of the richest and the fittest. If you are poor, the chance of you being unemployed is very high; you are likely to experience poor health, housing and security; little or no education; living in a poor environment with little if any, supporting and accessible resources, and an early death compared to the well off. You are likely to be exploited by everyone in power and authority from landowners, politicians, the bosses, businesses and large corporations and international trade and financial systems that guarantee rising systematic and institutionalised inequality between the rich and poor. This state of oppression and powerlessness characterises the lives of more than half of the six and a half billion people on our over-exploited and fragile planet. Nearly two billion people, around one third of the world's population, are in dire poverty and severely under-nourished, at a time of plenty when billions of tons of food are wasted and destroyed by large corporations to keep prices high and by consumers who can afford to purchase more than they need. This is calculated on a basis of people earning 1.5 dollars per day. This calculation is extremely low and ought to be at least even 5 dollars to accurately define poverty. World poverty has increased severely, especially since 1995 - from around 750 million to over two billion in 2014 - and the situation is getting worse, as austerity measures fuelled by the global recession is taking place across the world. Even in the richest countries in Europe, North America, China, India, Russia and Brazil, the poor are getting poor, and the rich, richer, with rising child poverty and the working poor. Instead of spending $2 trillion dollars on wars each year this money should be spent on attacking poverty and building a peaceful and equal world.

The rich getting richer at the expense of the poor

If you take a measurement of people earning less than two dollars a day, then there are nearly two billion people, living in poverty and suffering from severe hunger and shortage of the basic necessities. Even in the richest country in the work, the United States of America (USA) with a population of just over 300 million people, around 50 million are living below the poverty line. Yet this nation spends ten times more on the military than they spend on addressing poverty. They have spent trillions of dollars on wars abroad and yet the Obama administration and Congress has decided to cut spending on food stamps to support the poor, despite one in every four children in the USA living in poverty. According to a United Nations (UNICEF) Report in 2011, Romanie had the highest rate of child poverty at 23.6 per cent, followed by America at 23.1% and around an average of 15 per cent in the rest of Europe. The USA which sets itself up as the world's policeman on democracy and human rights spends in 2011 $739 billion on the military, which represents 45.7 per cent of the total expenditure spent on the military by the rest of the world, according to the International Institute of Strategic Studies. The USA spends ten times as much as China on the military, and yet sees China as a threat. It is the country with the greatest inequality in pay and wealth, with 80 per cent of the wealth owned by less than 20 per cent of the population and the three richest people in America has more wealth than the total gross national product of the poorest forty eight countries in the world. Arch Bishop Desmond Tutu was correct when he stated that "Because there is global insecurity, nations are engaged in a mad arms race, spending billions of dollars wastefully on instruments of destruction, when millions are starving. And yet, just a fraction of what is extended so obscenely on defence budgets would make a real difference in enabling God's children to fill their stomachs, be educated, and be given the chance to lead fulfilled and happy lives." Professor Peter Townshend was also correct when he stated that "Poverty is not something people impose on themselves for want of effort and community organisation. It is constructed by divisive and discriminatory laws, inflexible organisations, and acquisitive ideologies of wealth, a deeply rooted class system and policies which serve privilege in the short term and destroy society in the long term."

A recent Report *"Working for the few"* produced by Oxfam in 2013 showed that the eighty-five wealthiest people in the world owns as much wealth as the 3.5 billion poorest people in the world. And just one per cent of the world's families now possess 46 per cent of the world's wealth, whilst seven out of ten people live in countries where economic inequality has grown in the last three decades. As laid out in the report, the rigging is made possible by this fantastic "ill-gotten" wealth ($110 trillion for the top 1 per cent alone), which creates "political capture": the ability of elites to influence lawmakers to enact policies favourable to their interests. And that leads, in turn, to "opportunity capture," in which the best of everything, from healthcare to education, flows to the wealthy and their offspring. Then the cycle begins again. President F D Roosevelt was correct when he stated that "In politics nothing happens by accident. If it happens you can bet it was planned that way."

The poorest people are in the developing countries; over 600 million are in South Asia, with nearly 430 million in sub Saharan Africa and 350 million in East Asia and The Pacific. So around the world, at least half of the world's population, well over 3 billion people, live in desperate poverty and hunger, and earning less than 2.50 dollars a day. The gross domestic product (GDP) of the forty one most heavily indebted poor countries totalling nearly 600 million people is less than the wealth of the world's seven richest people combined. Around a billion people entered the 21st century unable to read a book or sign their names. Less than one per cent of what the world spends every year on weapons was needed to put every child in school by the year 2014. The rich world spent $ 1,735 billion on the military and wars in 2012, yet it would only take $200 billon each year for about three years, to wipe out world poverty. Over one billion children live in poverty which is almost half the world's children. 640 million live without adequate shelter, over 400 million have no access to safe water, nearly 300 million have no access to health services and around 11 million die every year before they reach the age of 5, which is around 34,000 children per day, which is equivalent to around one child dying every 3 seconds, about 20 children dying every minute - around 8 million children dying every year and nearly 100 million children dying between 2000 and 2012. Poverty, hunger, deprivation and carelessness vary across the world. According to the UNICEF, the world's premier children's organisation which is part of the United Nations:

- Half of the world's nearly 7 billion people were living in poverty in 2013.

- Over 2.5 billion people lack access to improved sanitation

- 1 billion children are deprived of one or more services essential to survival and development

- 148 million children under five years old in the developing regions are underweight for their age

- Over 125 million children are not attending primary school

- Nearly 30 million infants are not protected from diseases by routine immunisation

- 2.5 million die prematurely each year each year due to lack of immunisation

- 12 million children worldwide died before their fifth birthday in 2010

- Over 4 million new-borns worldwide are dying in their first month of life

- 2.3 million children under 15 are living with HIV.

- 18 million children orphaned due to HIV AIDS

- More than 80 per cent of the world's population lives in countries where income and inequality are widening. The poorest 40 per cent of the world's population accounts for 5 per cent of the total global income, whilst the richest 20 per cent accounts for three-quarters of the world's income.

- 72 million children of primary school age in the developing world were not in school in 2010; nearly 60 per cent of them were girls. Less than 1 per cent of what the world spends every year on weapons was needed to put every child in school by the year 2015, but this will not happen. Instead trillions of dollars will be spent on wars, armaments and weapons of destruction.

- Every year there are up to 500 million cases of malaria, with over one million fatalities. Africa alone accounts for 90 per cent of malarial deaths and African children account for over 80 per cent of malaria victims.

- Over 1.2 billion people in developing countries have inadequate access to water, whilst over 2.6 billion lack basic sanitation. Almost two in three people, lacking access to clean water, survive on less than two dollars a day, with one in three living on less than one dollar a day.

- More than 670 million people are living without sanitation and 385 million of these people earn less than one dollar a day. 85 per cent of people, mainly in the developed world, have access to clean, piped water, yet only 25 per cent of the world's population has access to clean, piped water.

- 1.3 billion of the 2.8 billion children in the world are living in poverty

- Two 2 million children die every year as a result of diarrhoea, caused mainly by water-related illnesses. Nearly half of all people in the developing world suffer at any given time from problems related to health caused by lack of and poor water and poor sanitation. Tens of millions of women in the developing countries spend many hours each day collecting water, firewood and whatever they can find to make their lives better.

- There are some 2 billion children in the developing world; of these nearly 7 million are without proper shelter; over 400 million have no access to safe and clean water; nearly 300 million with no access to basic health services and over 125 million are not attending any form of education.

- Around 2.3 million children die each year because they are not immunised; over 15 million children are orphans due to HIV/AIDS. This is similar to the total population of children in Germany or the United Kingdom.

- In 2005 the wealthiest 20 per cent of the world's population accounted for 76.6 per cent of the total private consumption; the poorest 5th consumed just 1.5 per cent.

- Over 1.6 billion people mainly in the poor countries do not have electricity; this includes 706 million in South Asia, 547 million in sub Saharan Africa, and 224 million in East Asia and in other areas 101 million.

- The GDP of the world in 2006 totalled 48.2 trillion dollars; the world's wealthiest countries, totalling about 1 billion people, accounted for 36.6 trillion dollars or 76 per cent in 2006.

- The world's billionaires, just 497 people, who account for 0.0000008 per cent of the world's population, were worth 3.5 trillion - over 7 per cent of the world's GDP. Now the world's poorest people totalling 2.4 billion accounted for just 1.6 trillion of the GDP totalling 3. 3 per cent. 0.13 per cent of the world's population controlled 25 per cent of the world's financial assets in 2004.

- For every one dollar in eight to developing countries, the donor country receives over 25 dollars in return for payment on debt or other sources. The wealthiest nations on earth such as America and Europe have the widest gap between rich and poor of the industrialised countries. All across the world, the rich are getting richer and the poor poorer.

- In 1960 20 per cent of the world's population in the richest countries had 30 times the income of the poorest 20 per cent; in 1997 this had risen to 74 times. Less than half the amount of money spent on militarism and armaments by the United States of America and Europe every year could help to eradicate global water and sanitation problems, provide basic healthcare for everyone and ensure that every child has a place in school.

According to a Report produced by the London based charity –Save the Children Fund - with projects in 120 countries, and published in 2014 (SavetheChildren.org):

"In 2012, 2.9 million babies died within 28 days of being born: two out of every five child deaths. Of these, 1 million babies died within 24 hours, their first – and only – day of life".

"This report also reveals that the crisis is much bigger than we might think. In 2012 there were another 1.2 million tragic losses: stillbirths where the heart stopped beating during labour. In 2102, 40 million

of people in the last decade. In the face of massive poverty, globalisation, hunger and inequality many governments within the poorer countries see themselves as powerless in finding enough resources to improve the conditions of their people.

Children and poverty

For me having worked as a child on a sugar plantation with my parents in Demerara, I have seen high levels of poverty and the damage such poverty can cause to families and communities. If I had one wish in this world, I would wish that poverty be eradicated. I've seen and felt this suffering of domestic violence of men turning to women, attacking and abusing them quite often because they were addicted to alcohol and feeling that they were no longer in control. They had no job, no money to support their family; they were distressed, ill, abusive, violent and irrational. I've seen children bedraggled, undernourished and in a state of hunger, due to no food in the family home, wandering and begging in the streets. Many of these children around the poor world are often ill-treated by their families, forced into all sorts of domestic chores and even paid employment, selling newspapers or vegetables and fruit, doing work for others who are exploiting them physically and sexually, just for a meal. There are hundreds of millions of children around the world today that are suffering from such situations. Women are often abused, tortured, belittled, having forced to have large families as security for then in their old age. Lack of accessible family planning, birth control, healthcare and welfare facilities for mothers and poor families are causing tens of millions of mothers and babies dying at childbirth.

As a parent and a grandparent, I would like to see my children and grandchildren grow up and indeed all children and grandchildren and all elderly and indeed everyone grow up in a world where our basic needs are met; we are treated with respect, people come before profit, people have a real say in how their governments are run, how their economies are planned and how their lives are shaped. Poor, hungry, powerless people seldom think of overthrowing governments or fighting for democracy - that is very much carried out by the middle classes and aspiring middle classes who are fighting for a slice of the power and control from one group or another that has the power and the control and very often abuse that power and control.

The world would have expected that the excesses that involved the exploitation of hundreds of millions of women and children from the age of four years, labouring in the cottage home industries, the mills, farms mining and agriculture during the period of the industrial revolution would have ended, at the latest by the end of the nineteenth century. Instead, such exploitation which characterised the lives of the poor in Europe and North America during the industrial revolution exists today in the developing would. In many parts of Asia, Africa and South America, young women and children are substituting mature workers, because they are cheaper and easier to manage and control.

Millions of children are set to work as soon as they could wield a stick or a knife, fetch and carry. Most of these children are illiterate, living in shanty towns, and subjected to long workers for little or no pay. They are often punished, abused and have very little or no possessions. These young people who are often the sons and daughters of immigrants from rural areas to who were forced to live in shanty towns on the outskirts of cities, are abused by families, bosses, older workers and the state institutions.

There are those, including Western politicians who argue child labour is necessary in many countries; they even try to make it seem unreasonable to oppose such cruelty. But child labour is part of neoliberal economic policy to undercut adult labour, particularly organised union labour at home. The period of neo-liberalism, that we are experiencing today, is simply rampant and unfettered deregulated capitalism in its most deranged, dangerous, inhuman and barbaric stage. Many of these children are working in a cigarette and clothing factories and in buildings in places like Bangladesh, Pakistan and India, where working conditions involve poor ventilation, exposure to dust, fumes, chemicals and environmental conditions, which causes many severe health problems including respiratory, skin diseases, deformed and pre-mature birth and early death. Children and young women in the poor world are sometimes bought and sold as cheap labour, or as sexual objects in today's world. They are working in mining, agriculture, domestic service, sex trade, factories and on the streets as traders and beggars. Many of these poor children are working in toxic conditions, around pesticides, contaminants, dangerous tools, near livestock and in fields as well as in cities. This is a form of barbarism akin to slavery and should be stamped out, but is condoned by large corporations and multi-national businesses that use such profits stained by the sweat, blood, tears, damaged lives and early deaths of those that created such wealth for the rich.

Many rich, famous, patriotic business tycoons and politicians who run the world have no scruples about using children as miners, garment workers, farm workers, or sex slaves because of the economic compulsion to drive down the collective and organised power of adult labour. Racism is also a fundamental component of poverty, exploitation and child labour, which is an intolerable scourge for humanity and modern society worldwide, and must be actively opposed in every shape and form. It children are the hope of the future; then there must be an end to child labour and poverty. The neo-liberal economic, financial and ideological terrorists who plunder the world in search of bigger and easier profits must be held to account, and so should the governments and institutions that prop us and facilitate such cruelty through inaction, collusion with capital or corruption by corporations.

Most people in the Western world are unaware of the extent of child labour in their own rich countries. They believe such practices are a problem in the poor countries populated by non-white people. In fact millions of children in America and Europe are engaged in child labour. Most Americans may feel that such practice is illegal in the USA, but in 2011 the Obama administration removed legislation to protect child farm workers from the violence of agricultural business. There are an estimated 800,000 mostly Mexican and Latinos children, as young as eight and ten years old working with pesticides, dangerous tools, livestock and criminal adults. The Obama administration even made it illegal to even monitor such labour practices in the agribusinesses. In addition there are there are well over 1,000,000 children working in the hidden economy of USA sweatshops, street and sexual exploitation industry within the richest nation on earth. The multi-national agribusiness based in America with tentacles in the poorer countries around the world, that have a controlling stake in the world's food supply are indirectly and directly responsible for much child labour and poverty.

The rich creates the recession and the poor gets the blame

We live in an unfair and an unequal world. I have spent almost all my adult life fighting for justice, freedom, fighting against poverty and exploitation not only in Britain, but around the world. An injustice to anyone on our planet is an injustice to all of us and we are talking about injustice of massive proportion of millions of people, children, women, sick people, poor people living in fear of hunger, poverty, disease, helplessness. Yet much of the rich world spends so much of the resources, often generated by its relationship with the poorer countries of the world, on personal, materialistic and selfish desires. The rich world is rich because the poor world is poor and the poor world is poor because it spends a great deal of its resources, human and material, supporting the needs and desires of the rich world.

The rising middle classes in China, India, Brazil, Russia and elsewhere in the developed countries are improving their situation quite often at the expense of the poor. There is a large army of billions of poor people around the globe whose daily lives are characterised by hunger, poverty, squalor and powerlessness. Many of these vulnerable people are in employment, whether in agriculture, manufacturing, or services are there to provide cheap labour, raw materials, clothing and other goods for those who are better off in their own countries and abroad. The rich people of the world and the rising middle class owe their wealth and their lifestyle to the sacrifices made by the poor across the globe. We live in an unfair world where most of humanity lives in poverty, squalor and deprivation while the richest nations of the world, can access whatever they choose without paying much attention to those who are the creators of such resources. Hundreds of millions of working poor are employed for a pittance that could hardly keep them alive in reasonable surroundings.

The rich nations, especially America and Europe, talks about democracy, human rights, freedom, justice and liberty, but these are hollow words when it comes to international trade and development. Democracy means in its truest sense - government for the people by the people and that should surely mean that everyone is treated equally and have equal access to resources, but clearly this is not the case, either within or outside the rich countries. For the Western nations democracy means that these countries must open themselves up to foreign capital, embrace capitalism, globalisation and the free market, which inevitably means that money should rule and wealth becomes more important than people. So the western democracy is all about making money; it is allowing the privileged to rise to positions of power and the poor to be satisfied with their condition and not to rebel against the system which serves the rich and powerful. The wealthy nations of the world, especially America and Europe, are prepared to invade these countries and to protect the ruling elite against their people, providing they support the capitalist system and democracy as defined by America and Europe and of course the financial institutions that are often greater and more influential than governments on the world stage.

During the recession which started in 2008 in America and Europe, many countries have turned towards severe austerity measures, resulting in change of governments and in many cases replacing radical governments with right wing and/or military administrations. As a result we have seen racism, fascism and right wing politics taking root, in Europe and America and in countries where the Western nations have supported or enforced regime changes. Many of these countries tacking the austerity created by the bankers, corporations, ineffective governments and the ruling elites, have been taking a wide range of measures to reverse the effects of the recession. These include, reducing public services and welfare spending; privatising public services; restricting pay, conditions and rights at work, reducing living standards, charging for further and higher education and public services; increasing the pensionable age, and forcing people to work for poverty wages, and sustaining high levels of unemployment, whilst allowing house prices, rents, food prices and the cost of utilities to increase, These measures have contributed to massive increases in poverty, stress, misery and uncertainties for the poor, in and out of work, as well millions of children, retired and disabled people. Even the Archbishop of Canterbury and dozens of Bishops in the Christian Churches felt compelled to publicly criticised the government for punishing the poor and forcing hundreds of thousands to seek the support of food banks across Britain by signing letters sent to the media in February, 2014.

Whilst the poor in the Western economies in America and Europe are forced to endure austerity measures to rebuild their economies massive sums of public funds are poured into the very same institutions responsible for the recession which would have bankrupted their economies. These people were rewarded for their own failures. According to the Bloomberg Report of 2011, The Federal Reserve secretly lent banks a substantial amount of funds in addition to the known bailout program, bringing the total to an astonishing $7.77 trillion. This information was obtained under the Freedom of Information Act. The Federal Reserve made emergency, low-interest loans during the financial crisis, dwarfing the controversial $700 billion "bailouts" made under the Troubled Asset Relief Program in 2009. The Bloomberg report is particularly critical of the way lawmakers were kept out of the loop. Congress was largely uninvolved; with House Financial Services Committee chair Barney Frank telling Bloomberg that while he was aware of emergency efforts, he "didn't know the specifics." According to Bloomberg reports the "Lawmakers knew none of this. "They had no clue that one bank, New York-based Morgan Stanley, took $107 billion in Federal loans in September 2008, enough to pay off one-tenth of the country's delinquent mortgages." To secure access to documents detailing the plan, Bloomberg went to court against the Clearing House Association LLC, a longstanding banking association representing many of the world's largest banks. In trying to withhold the records, the Federal Reserve's position was that the information would create a stigma against institutions that had taken out emergency loans. A sum of $7.77 trillion, the authors note, constitutes more than half the value of everything produced in the United States in 2009. On a single day in Dec. 2008, the banks required a combined $1.2 trillion in bailout funds, according to the documents. The real consequence of the largest bailout in United States history, according to Bloomberg the "taxpayers paid a price beyond dollars as the secret funding helped preserve a broken status quo and enabled the biggest banks to grow even bigger." Similar deals were done in Britain where it is estimated that up to £300 billion of public funds were spent on propping up the failed banks, and even to rescue them by taking them into public ownership, through majority shareholding.

There are numerous causes of poverty which does include some lack of individual responsibility, but mainly poverty is caused by bad and corrupt government, exploitation of people by global and local businesses with disproportionate power and influence over governments and nations. For many countries, war, famine and conflict have led to increasing violence against children, women, disabled people, the elderly and the poor. The largest arms manufacturers which include America, Europe, especially Britain, China, Russia and other countries are not committed to any global policy on the arms trade. There are restrictions about trades; trade concerns almost every commodity from banana to sugar or manufacturing goods, yet there is hardly any control over the flow of armaments and the sale of weapons of destruction, even to very poor countries which are characterised by famine, disaster, inequality. The arms trade is responsible for a large part of the impoverished people in the world, as governments are setting the wrong priorities. Instead of seeking to feed and improve the quality of life for their population, many of these countries are engaged in civil wars protecting the elite from any resentment from the poor or fighting unnecessary but costly wars in terms of money and lives with their neighbours. These countries are often supported by the western powers with the arms and the technical assistance to enable them to engage in prolonged war, lasting for decades. As a result, tens of millions of people have died. At least 10 million people within the Republic of Congo have died through internal conflicts, with marauding armies equipped with the latest weapons, robbing, pillaging, killing and raping women and children.

The wars in Iraq and Afghanistan have left millions of people destitute; hundreds of thousands of people died. The sanctions against the Saddam regime over a decade resulted in over half a million children dying because of malnutrition and lack of healthcare. For the west it would appear a reasonable price to pay to ensure that Iraq and Afghanistan return to democracy, as interpreted by western nations. There have been millions of people, refugees seeking shelter from military conflicts and poverty, yet governments still choose to resolve conflicts through the use of armaments and the casualties are invariably the poor.

We have enough food to feed everyone on our fragile planet, yet billions of people are starving. It is not a production problem, it is one of distribution and it is one of global need and global requirement. There is a need for global planning in order to avoid hunger and starvation and famine. Africa and Asia have very fertile land; much of the land is not used to support the people and in recent years multi-national companies have been buying up large sections of land in Africa, Asia, South America and elsewhere as investment, because food has increasingly become a weapon by which nations can by subdued. The richer nations will use food as a bargaining power for countries that are experiencing drought, starvation and lack of basic food.

Poverty in 21st Century Britain

The Poverty and Social Exclusion [PSE] project, led by academics at the University of Bristol and funded by the Economic, publishes its first report '*The Impoverishment of the UK*' on 28 March 2014. According to the Report, 33 per cent of the UK

Time-use surveys indicate that people are spending more time working and looking after their own children than some decades ago, squeezing time for community and recreational activity. When loneliness is combined with material deprivation, the result is toxic. A cycle of workless-ness, indebtedness and depression is so much harder to escape. Professionals such as health visitors need to focus efforts not only on social groups traditionally most likely to be associated with social exclusion – those on low income, teenage mothers – but also those identified as having poor social networks. Welfare policies need to be designed in such a way as to ensure claimants are more likely to benefit from the support of their wider family. When allocating social housing, councils could take more into account proximity to family and close friends. Equally, policies such as the removal of the spare room subsidy need to be reconsidered where they disrupt familial support, for example the provision of overnight childcare by grandparents. Strong social networks are an important part of the battle against poverty."

Given this situation it is not surprising that the government plans to change the way child poverty is calculated. According to the Department for Work and Pensions, in 2011-12, 2.3 million UK children (17 per cent) lived in homes with substantially lower than average income.

This rises to 27 per cent (3.5 million) if measured after housing costs are paid. Children's campaigners say the true figure is higher and that 300,000 more children live in poor homes than in the previous year. This is because there are two accepted ways of measuring poverty - relative and absolute. The government prefers the measure of relative poverty - defined as when families have a net income that is below 60 per cent of "median net disposable income" - as does Labour. This amounts to £250 a week or less at the moment. Using this, there was no change on child poverty and the number and proportion of working-age adults in relative poverty also remained at about the same level. But the number living in absolute poverty is higher and on this measure, one in five children in the UK lives in poverty - a total of 2.6 million in 2011-12. On this measure, 300,000 more children fell below the poverty line compared with the year before, and the number has raised to nearly 1 in 4 children living in poverty in 2014. The proportion of working-age adults living in relative poverty is also about one in six (5.6 million) if income is calculated before housing costs are paid - the government's preferred way of measuring relative poverty. This rises to one in five (7.9 million) if the other measure is used.

A similar proportion of pensioners were living in relative poverty in 2011-12 - 1.9 million.

Working target:

• The coalition government has made a pledge to end child poverty by 2020. Between 1998 and 2011-12, the number of children in relative poverty in the UK fell by about one million.

• Work and Pensions Secretary Iain Duncan Smith said the government's aim was to get children out of poverty by getting more people in to work.

"While this government is committed to eradicating child poverty, we want to take a new approach by finding the source of the problem and tackling that. We have successfully protected the poorest from falling behind and seen a reduction of 100,000 children in workless poor families," he said.

"Today's figures underline the need for better measures of child poverty that are not so heavily dependent on where we draw the poverty line."

But children's campaigners say the true picture is worse than the government figures suggest and that the children moving in to the poverty bracket are in families where people are working. Fiona Weir, head of the single-parent charity Gingerbread, said "It was alarming to see one in three children with a single parent who worked part-time was living below the poverty line. Government claims that work is the best route out of poverty are simply not ringing true,"

Food banks will be to the decade what hunger marches were to the 1930s. But they are not dramatic places. You don't see queues of distressed people waiting by their doors. The food banks are discreet. The Churches and charities that run them show their kindness by doing nothing to draw attention to their clients' poverty. For all their unobtrusiveness, food banks might do as a symbol of our times too. As the recession grew, the wealthy were finding new ways of encouraging poverty by keeping the poor on zero-hours contracts whose average hourly rates were 40 per cent below the "normal" earnings for the work. Not just oligarchs it is easy to despise as cruel foreigners, but even the British monarch and head of state employ her staff on zero hours contracts.

The right wing politicians, employers and the media have had a great propaganda success in blaming poverty on fecklessness of the working class. It is not only Conservatives and UKIP voters who believe the poor and the unemployed sit at home laughing as they hoard their benefits, but many Labour supporters too. The recession destroyed the belief that financial markets were best left to regulate themselves and sent the property-owning democracy into retreat. Prime Minister, David Cameron thought the great recession would encourage a "big society", where people help one another. He did not know, and no one had the nerve to tell him, that hard times destroy altruism. In 2005, 44 per cent of people in England and Wales offered unpaid time to help others. By 2010, only 37 per cent did, and the amount of time they were prepared to sacrifice had fallen too. I am personally disappointed that more people, including the millions of poor people, the unemployed, those on low pay, students who are in debt; disabled people and pensioners are not taking to the streets in large number to protest against the nasty policies of this government. The government of the rich for the rich is full of millionaires, they have allowed the rich to become richer by pouring over £100 billion into the coffers of the rich bankers, city financiers and corporations, whilst continuing to penalise the poor, through cuts in welfare services, encouraging high rents, lower interest rates on savings and keeping wages down. At the same time pass laws to weaken the organised strength of working people through changes in employment law.

Globalisation equals global exploitation

Globalisation was almost forced upon the poorer countries by the rich nations, without any consideration on the impact this will have on the social, economic and political structures of poor and vulnerable countries. Globalisation is managed, financed and controlled, largely through large corporation, the World Bank and the International Monetary Fund that are unsupervised by governments on a systematic basis. Individual governments have little, if any control over globalisation or poverty created substantially through the global trading process. Climate change and rising population are encouraging those with money to invest not necessarily to feed the population, but to have access to land which could be converted to resources at a later date, whilst local people are forced out of the countryside because of lack of access to land and facilities for them to grow their own crops and take care of themselves. Instead of poor countries addressing the high level of poverty, many are forced into receiving and accepting further loans from the IMF or the World Bank and richer countries that in the end force them to use much of the gross national product to repay these loans. Also many of the loans are at extremely high interest rates and are often frittered away on projects that are not useful to the recipient countries, yet the poor are often squeezed to repay these loans.

The rich countries themselves are often active in corrupting the leadership of the poorer countries and are supporting projects that are sometimes not the best in terms of resolving poverty and hunger. The richer countries, especially America and Britain, have a lot to say on giving aid to poorer countries. In 1970 the world's richest countries agreed to give 0.17 per cent of the gross national income as official international development aid on an annual basis. Since then billions have been given each year, but rarely have the rich nations actually met their promised target. For example the United States is often the largest donor in dollar terms, but ranks amongst the lowest in terms of meeting the stated *0.7 per cent* target.

In 2011 the United States gave over 30 billion dollars in aid, much less than 0.7 per cent of its gross national product; Germany came next. Germany contributed about 14 billion dollars and the United Kingdom about 13; France came next with about 11 and Japan at 10 billion dollars, with The Netherlands at 6 billion dollars and Sweden at 5, Canada at 5 and Norway at 4; Australia, Spain and Italy at the same level. The nations that came closest to meeting the 0.7 per cent of gross national product in international aid were Sweden, top with just over 1 per cent, Norway slightly less, Luxembourg with about 0.98 per cent, Denmark around 0.9 per cent, Netherlands 0.7 per cent and the United Kingdom came at around 0.55 per cent; Belgium, France and Ireland around 0.45 per cent; the same for Switzerland and Germany 0.4 per cent, with Australia at 0.38 per cent, Canada 0.35 per cent, Spain 2 per cent and other wealthier countries such as Japan at just under 2 per cent; Italy with just around 2 per cent. Many of these countries that owned colonies and exploited the continents over centuries have failed to reach the target they set themselves. It is amazing that the Scandinavian countries, Sweden, Norway and Denmark have come out amongst the top five of donors of international aid.

Further aid is not necessarily the solution to the problem of poverty and hunger, because it often comes with a price of its own for the developing countries receiving the aid. Foreign aid has often resulted in corruption of governments, displacements of local industries through dumping of goods and material. Aid often displaces the local infrastructure and trading arrangements and it can also be quite difficult for those working at subsistence level. Food aid for example could be dumped in countries that could displace the local agricultural framework and instead of the aid being helpful; it could create more poverty and uncertainty amongst the rural population. Aid is often associated with protectionism, trade deals and other arrangements which frequently open markets for the donor country and their products. Aid is often used as a lever to expand globalisation and infiltration by foreign national and multi-national companies into local economies. Governments often use foreign aid to engage in grand strategic projects to boost their own image and their own reputation and often use much of this money, which has been siphoned off, for their own interests and projects and to benefit the ruling elite through corruption and mismanagement. Governments and charities have also created a global structure with hundreds of thousands of people regarded as Non-Governmental Organisations (NGO's) that are often seen as part of the problem, and not the long term solution, as charities, hand-outs, tied aids linked to purchase of Western military equipment and goods are not the answer to solving world poverty. Neither are arm conflicts, civil wars, foreign intervention and corporations using their strength to exploit poor countries, are the answer to mass poverty.

There are also many other inter-related issues which are responsible for hunger, poverty and famine. Many of these are related to economics and other factors such as the denial of land rights and ownership to poor people, the diversion of land use to non-product use and are also often used to develop export-orientated agricultural produce, which can cause a great deal of inefficiency and waste in agricultural practices and processes, causing even further conflict and resulting in wars, famine, drought, over-fishing, poor crop yields and destabilisation of large numbers of people from the countryside, who often gravitate towards the city or urban areas in search of work.

Unequal shares

The world produces enough food to feed everyone. World agriculture produces 20 per cent more calories per person today than it did 30 years ago, despite a 70 per cent population increase. This is enough to provide everyone in the world with at least a reasonable amount of calories per person per day, according to the most recent estimate of the Food and Agriculture Organisation of the United Nations, (FAO) based in America. The principal problem is that many people in the world do not have sufficient land to grow, or income to purchase, enough food due to massive increases in food prices. Poverty is the principal cause of hunger. The causes of poverty include poor people's lack of resources, an extremely unequal income distribution in the world and within specific countries.

The principal underlying cause of poverty and hunger is the failure of the economic and political systems in the world, primarily because of lack of control and distribution of resources and income. Wealth is based on military, political and economic power that typically ends up in the hands of a minority, whose main interest is to grow more wealth and avoid paying taxes, whilst the majority at the bottom barely survive, whether they are in or, out of work. Conflicts around the world are a major cause of hunger and poverty; with tens of millions of people fleeing from wars and major man-made catastrophes, resulting in refugees, starvation and deaths of large numbers.

By the end of 2013, the total number of refugees under United Nations High Commission for Refugees (UNHCR) mandate exceeded 13 million. The number of conflict-induced internally displaced persons (IDPs) reached some 36 million worldwide at the beginning of 2014, according to the UNHCR. Poverty causes hunger and hunger causes poverty, and together they are responsible for poor health, low levels of energy, and even mental impairment, hunger can lead to even greater poverty by reducing people's ability to work and learn, thus leading to even greater hunger. Climate change is increasingly viewed as a current and future cause of hunger and poverty. Increasing drought, flooding, and changing climatic patterns requiring a shift in crops and farming practices that may not be easily accomplished, but can be seriously addressed, if expenditure from wars, military hardware, and sustaining conflicts can be diverted to dealing with climate change, famine, hunger and poverty. Progress in reducing the number of hungry people in the world has been slow and at times stood still, and even went backwards. The target set at the 1996 World Food Summit (WFS) was to halve the number of undernourished people by 2015 from their number in 1990-92. The (estimated) number of undernourished people in developing countries was 824 million in 1990-92. In 2010, the number had climbed to 925 million, and it could be well over 1 billion or more people in 2015. So, overall, the world is not making progress toward the world food summit goal.

Wasting precious resources in a world of poverty

The Swedish Institute for Food and Biotechnology commissioned a report on. *Global food losses and food waste found that,* every year, consumers in rich countries waste almost as much food (222 million tonnes) as the entire net food production of sub-Saharan Africa (230 million tonnes). Fruits and vegetables, plus roots and tubers have the highest wastage rates of any food. The amount of food lost or wasted every year is equivalent to more than half of the world's annual cereals crop (2.3 billion tonnes in 2009/2010).

The report distinguishes between food loss and food waste. Food losses, occurring at the production, harvest, post-harvest and processing levels are most important in developing countries, due to poor infrastructure, low levels of technology and low investment in the food production systems. Food waste is more a problem in developed and industrialized countries, most often caused by both retailers and consumers throwing perfectly edible foodstuffs into the bin. The large supermarkets are amongst the worse culprits. The per capita waste by consumers is between 95-115 kilograms a year in Europe and North America, while consumers in sub-Saharan Africa and South and Southeast Asia each throw away only 6-11 kg a year.

A recent report claimed that in 2008, the total generation of waste in the European Union consisting of 27 (EU27) countries waste products, mainly food amounted to 2.62 billion tonnes. This was slightly lower than in the years 2004 and 2006 where the EU-27 total amounted to 2.68 billion tonnes and 2.73 billion tonnes respectively.

Total per capita food production for human consumption is about 900 kg a year in rich countries, almost twice the 460 kg a year produced in the poorest regions. In developing countries 40 per cent of losses occur at post-harvest and processing levels while in industrialized countries more than 40 per cent of losses happen at retail and consumer levels.

Food losses during harvest and in storage translate into lost income for small farmers and into higher prices for poor consumers, the report noted. Reducing losses could therefore have an "immediate and significant" impact on their livelihoods and food security. Instead of giving farmers in poor countries aid to expand production, such support would be better spent on storage and processing. Many rich countries use food as aid to poorer countries, which can often destabilise local markets and reduce the effectiveness of local farming. Food loss and waste also amount to a major squandering of resources, including water, land, energy, labour and capital and needlessly produce greenhouse gas emissions, contributing to global warming and climate change.

The rich countries and groups of countries such as the EU27, often impose either directly, or indirectly sanctions, tariffs and protectionist measures, which serves exclude exporters from poorer countries to sell their goods to the rich countries. In addition millions of tons of perfectly good food are wasted due to **over-emphasis on the appearance of products.**

At retail level, especially in supermarkets, large quantities of food are also wasted due to quality standards that over-emphasize appearance. Surveys show that consumers are willing to buy produce not meeting appearance standards as long as it is safe and tastes good. Customers thus have the power to influence quality standards and should do so, the report said.

Selling farm produce even in rich countries, closer to consumers through farmers' markets will make a vast difference not only to prices, but also to wastage. Governments of course, are reluctant to encourage this process due to pressures from the owners of large supermarkets and multi-national corporations involved in growing and marketing food products. Good use for food that would otherwise be thrown away should be found through charitable organizations and even small retailers, or co-operatives to collect, and then give to deserving people, or sell at a much reduced rate. We are beginning to see some of this activity as countries in Europe is faced with mass unemployment, deterioration in living standards, increase cost of living and rising poverty. There are over 150 Food Banks in Britain and growing due to massive increase in poverty since 2010. We all have a duty to work towards **changing consumer attitudes towards food, distribution, consumption and poverty.**

Consumers in rich countries are generally encouraged to buy more food than they need. "Buy three, pay two" promotions are one example, while the oversized ready-to-eat meals produced by the food industry are another. Restaurants frequently offer fixed-price buffets that spur customers to heap their plates. Consumers often fail to plan their food purchases properly that means they often throw food away when "best-before" dates expired. Education in schools and political initiatives are possible starting points to changing consumer attitudes. More control and encouragement is desperately needed to avoid food waste and to discourage obesity. Western governments are reluctant to impose stricter regulations due to "free market capitalism" ethics, where profits are more important than people.

The single largest producer of food waste in the United Kingdom is the domestic household. In 2007, households created 6,700,000 tonnes of food waste – accounting for 19 per cent of all municipal solid waste. Potatoes account for the largest quantity of avoidable food disposed of; 359,000 tonnes per year are thrown away, 49 per cent (177,400 tonnes) of which are untouched. Bread slices account for the second food type most disposed of (328,000 tonnes per year), and apples the third (190,000 tonnes per year). Salad is disposed of in the greatest proportion - 45 per cent of all salad purchased by weight will be thrown away uneaten.

Rich countries often import food from poor countries through cartels and they more often than not fail to pay the real market values for the food which could be used to feed local people. The trading between the rich and poor countries is seldom if ever, a "fair trade", although there is a growing awareness in the rich world in relation to "fair trade". People, especially school children around the world, should be taught that throwing food away needlessly is economically, morally and ethically unacceptable. They should also be made aware that given the limited availability of natural resources it is more effective to reduce food losses than increase food production in order to feed a rising world population. Wasting 1.3 billion tons per year inevitably means that huge amounts of the resources used in food production are used in vain, and that the greenhouse gas emissions caused by production of food that gets lost or wasted are causing damage to our fragile planet.

Eliminating the millions of tonnes of food thrown away annually in the US, UK and the EU, could take more than a billion people out of hunger worldwide. Government officials, food experts and representatives of the retail trade brought together by the Food Ethics Council argue that excessive consumption of food in rich countries inflates food prices in the developing world. Buying food, which is then often wasted, reduces overall supply and pushes up the price of food, making grain less affordable for poor and undernourished people in other parts of the world. Food waste also costs UK consumers £10.2bn a year and when production, transportation and storage are factored in, it is responsible for 5 per cent of the UK's greenhouse gas emissions.

The vast sums spent in reducing the total greenhouse gas emissions could be better spend supporting food production in poor countries and educating people in rich countries to eat more sensibly. Food is a powerful weapon in a world with rising population, famine, uncertain and destructive climate change, local and regional conflicts and water shortages. Many large companies are buying up land in poor countries as future investment and in doing so are depriving local poor people of opportunities to grow their own food and take control of their own environment and lives.

In a globalised food system, where everyone are buying food in the same international market place, means the rich countries are simply taking food out of the mouths of the people in the poor countries. Hunger of 1.5bn people could be alleviated by eradicating the food wasted by British and European and American consumers and retailers, food services and householders, including the arable crops such as wheat, maize and soya to produce the wasted meat and dairy products. Production of wasted food also squanders resources, and said that the irrigation water used by farmers to grow wasted food would be enough for the equivalent domestic water needs of 9 billion people. So it is not the case that not enough food is produced, but too much of this precious food is wasted.

Food waste costs every household in the UK between £250 and £400 a year, figures that are likely to be increased annually. Producing and distributing the 6.7m tonnes of edible food that goes uneaten and into waste in the UK also accounts for 18m tonnes of CO_2.

All across the world, people are fighting back against the wastage of food, the fact that food is used as a political, ideological and economic weapon to influence and even dominate poorer countries. People are getting better at organising and shaming the large food corporations that operates globally, despite attempts by governments to protect and even defend multi-national food producers and retailers that are partially responsible for massive increases in obesity, resulting in poor health and demand on precious health and care resources.

I believe that the following quotes sums up the section above quite well:

"But the poor person does not exist as an inescapable fact of destiny. His or her existence is not politically neutral, and it is not ethically innocent. The poor are a by-product of the system in which we live and for which we are responsible. They are marginalized by our social and cultural world. They are the oppressed, exploited proletariat, robbed of the fruit of their labour and despoiled of their humanity. Hence the poverty of the poor is not a call to generous relief action, but a demand that we go and build a different social order."

*- **Gustavo Gutierrez***

"A pacifism which can see the cruelties only of occasional military warfare and is blind to the continuous cruelties of our social system is worthless. There's enough on this planet for everyone's needs but not for everyone's greed. Poverty is the worst form of violence."
- **Mohandas K. Gandhi**

"The problems we face today, violent conflicts, destruction of nature, poverty, hunger and so on, are human-created problems which can be resolved through human effort, understanding and the development of a sense of brotherhood and sisterhood. We need to cultivate a universal responsibility for one another and the planet we share."
- **14th Dalai Lama**

"If poverty is a disease that infects the entire community in the form of unemployment and violence, failing schools and broken homes, then we can't just treat those symptoms in isolation. We have to heal that entire community."
- **President Barack Obama**

"Massive poverty and obscene inequality are such terrible scourges of our times -- times in which the world boasts breath-taking advances in science, technology, industry and wealth accumulation -- which they have to rank alongside slavery and apartheid as social evils."
- **Nelson Mandela**

"Overcoming poverty is not a gesture of charity. It is an act of justice. It is the protection of a fundamental human right, the right to dignity and a decent life."
- **Nelson Mandela**

"In this new century, many of the world's poorest countries remain imprisoned, enslaved and in chains. They are trapped in the prison of poverty. It is time to set them free. Like slavery and apartheid, poverty is not natural. It is man-made and it can be overcome and eradicated by the actions of human beings."
- **Nelson Mandela**

"We have ancient habits to deal with, vast structures of power, indescribably complicated problems to solve. But unless we abdicate our humanity altogether and succumb to

687

fear and impotence in the presence of the weapons we have ourselves created, it is as possible and as urgent to put an end to war and violence between nations as it is to put an end to poverty and racial injustice. It is a tragic mix-up when the United States spends 500,000 for every enemy soldier killed, and only 53 annually on the victims of poverty."
- **Martin Luther King, Jr**

"Being unwanted, unloved, uncared for, forgotten by everybody, I think that is a much greater hunger, a much greater poverty than the person who has nothing to eat. We think sometimes that poverty is only being hungry, naked and homeless. The poverty of being unwanted, unloved and uncared for is the greatest poverty. We must start in our own homes to remedy this kind of poverty. Our life of poverty is as necessary as the work itself. Only in heaven will we see how much we owe to the poor for helping us to love God better because of them. Loneliness and the feeling of being unwanted is the most terrible poverty."
- **Mother Teresa**

Imagine no possessions
I wonder if you can
No need for greed or hunger
A brotherhood of man
Imagine all the people
Sharing all the world".
- **John Lennon**

"In a country well governed, poverty is something to be ashamed of. In a country badly governed, wealth is something to be ashamed of."
- **Confucius**

PART 5

Chapter 22:

Jim's legacy
and what people say about him

Mohammad Taj – President of the TUC

I have known Jim for many years. I often referred to him as 'my brother from different parents.' Like Jim I was also a busman and actively involved in the trade union and labour movement. I am the current President of the Trades Union Council (TUC 2014-2015). I am also honoured to be the first Muslim President of the TUC and I have to thank a number of people, including Jim for the work they have done for such a long time to enable activists like myself to occupy such leading positions within the movement. People like Jim who challenged the system for over 50 years to open up to diversity and involve black people, women and younger people in the structure and decision making process of the unions, have often sacrificed their own careers, so others can have equal access and opportunities to contribute to the movement. Many of us stand on the shoulders of people like Jim, whose record in the trade union struggle cannot be matched by any other person today. At age over 70, he has just been reelected to the National Executive of his union for two more years. I have also been re-elected to my union (UNITE) NEC, so we will continue to work together in the future.

Jim is one of the most consistent, brave and charismatic speakers within the movement.

He always entertains the audience, however large or small, with his wit, charm and sense of history. He has done almost every job within the trade union movement apart from being a general secretary. He did try to lead the GMB in 1985, but did not succeed. Jim was a union official, editor of a trade union newspapers and he has written several books on trade unions, politics and Black History. Jim is one of the most recognized Black trade unionists in Britain who never misses an opportunity to have his say on all sorts of subjects. He has inspired many activists in his own and in the present generation, and I know future generations will benefit from his work and his publications.

The TUC recognized Jim's service with a Silver Badge and hopefully he will qualify for a gold badge for over 50 years of trade union activism. Apart from his trade union work, Jim and a few others have helped to open up the Labour Party to Black members through the formation of the Labour Party Black Socialist Society in the early 1980's. There are now 27 Black MPs and hopefully more to follow in the 2015 election. Jim and his small band of trade union colleagues developed the Black Self-Organisation within the trade union during the 1970's that has taken off to the present day where every major trade union and profession now have Black Self-Organised groups operating within their structures and workplaces. We now have Black Lawyers, Black Teachers, Social Workers, Police, Doctors and many other Black groups.

Whenever Jim chooses to retire from the movement, his legacy will continue. I believe activism and working class politics is in Jim's blood. He has been a fighter for justice and fairness since he was a labourer as a child. Jim's achievement since he arrived in London age 17 in 1961 has been incredible, having put himself through several universities as a mature student; held many senior national positions as a professional and always maintained his trade union and political commitments.

Jim has been a credit to the trade union and labour movement and we all wish him many more years of involvement as we know how much his life revolves around working class struggles. I am proud to write these few words to honour Jim as a friend and a comrade.

Mohammad Taj
President of the TUC 2014-5

Gloria Mills

Jim Thakoordin has had a formidable presence in the British trade union movement for the past four decades. His campaign, energy and passion for a better world continue to bewilder most of his colleagues who have long given up the fight for equality and social justice.

What marks him out is his continuing commitment to realise his vision for all oppressed people. His commitment to education as a pathway out of poverty has shaped a lifetime of his campaigning work to help others to realise their ambition and aspiration.

I first met Jim – at a conference organised by the Black Trade Union Solidarity Movement (BTUSM) in the early 1980s. He was a leading player, with the late Bernie Grant MP in the organisation. BTUSM became a forum for Black workers to mobilise with a common agenda that spanned both the industrial and political wings of the labour movement. More importantly, it was the foremost organisation to challenge the daily and ugly spectre of racism in the workplace, politics and in the wider society.

His first book on 'Race and Trade Unions' published in 1984 was a seminal and defining account of that period in giving voice to the lived experiences of Black people and Black workers' experience of racism in Britain.

This book broke new ground in making a significant contribution to the development of a Black agenda in trade union and labour movement politics of the 1970s and 1980s. It became an agenda that has seen huge transformational changes in trade unions and politics in the last few decades.

Moreover, he articulated a common language in the fight against all forms of oppression in general and racial oppression in particular. The term Black took on a new significance and became to symbolise a radical movement for Black empowerment. Black was now recognised as a political term of unity in the struggle against racism that united people from all background who experienced the daily grind of racism. It was a radical term of ownership that enabled the mobilisation of a generation of people to assert their rights to political engagement, organisation and representation.

There were notable successes in developing a new generation of black activists and leaders in influencing change and taking positions of power in the labour movement. Indeed, it was a period of dynamic progress in putting the politics of race equality centre stage on the trade union and political agenda but also in increasing Black peoples' representation in many areas of local politics as councillors, leaders of councils, mayors and Members of Parliament.

Jim's passionate style in making his point would light up a grey room with the bright sparks of critique he would engender in the debate. His robust style attracted many distractions and detractors who would deride him for his criticisms of persons rather than politics.

Jim can be proud of his contribution as a leader in the struggle for equality and social justice; in seeing transformational change in his lifetime – challenging discrimination, challenging racism and challenging those in positions of power to deliver on their espoused commitment to equality, economic and social progress.

Jim's legacy is based on breaking down barriers and building structures that create sustainable change. Those in positions of power should remember that complacency is the enemy of progress. They stand on the shoulders of giants – and people like Jim whose pioneering work provides a bridge from one generation to the next but moreover, keep the ladder upright to let others rise.

Gloria Mills
First Black President of the Trades Union Council

Paul Mackney

Jim's is an extraordinary story. He began his life as a child labourer on a sugar plantation in Demerara, Guyana, being elected shop steward at 14.

The village may have had no electricity but Jim's parents passed on something as dynamic - their values which have guided him all his life. Whilst, as people have commented, Jim has sometimes seemed impatient or even truculent, he has always been on the side of the underdog.

Jim arrived in Britain in 1961 and did a number of jobs, meeting his wife Doreen when she got on the 187 bus he was conducting in Harlesden. With her support, Jim educated himself. He won a TUC scholarship to Ruskin College and attended a number of higher education establishments after that. But, wherever he studied, Jim was essentially an autodidact.

As a trade unionist and Labour Party activist, Jim was an enthusiastic pioneer organiser and encourager of Black self-organisation. He was one of the first Black paid union officials, very nearly became an MP, and represented a number of unions up to national level.

Jim has served as a councillor and on many committees, public and governing bodies – so many it is difficult to see how he fitted them all in. His principal role seems to have been as critical friend, supporting the organisation, whilst on occasion finding it necessary to remind them of their purpose and how they could alleviate any kind of injustice.

Despite some dramatic health problems in recent years, Jim has continued to campaign through his writing, in his union, at the Black Workers TUC – in recognition of which he was awarded a TUC Silver Badge for his years of commitment.

If things rarely seem calm when Jim is around, we need to remember the words of early Black American freedom fighter Frederick Douglas: "Without struggle, there is no progress. Those who profess freedom, yet deprecate agitation, want crops without digging up the ground; want the ocean without the awful roar of its waters."

Paul Mackney - General Secretary of the National Association of Teachers in Further and Higher Education (NATFHE). NATFHE merged with the Association of University Teachers in 2006 and became the University and College Union (UCU)

Indira Pradhan

It was quite a challenge to write this article for such an incredible personality such as Jim Thakoordin, who has had such a long life of struggle and sacrifice. It is truly an honour for me to be asked to write something about Jim who deserves a place in the annals of the British labour movement! What a struggle he has been through, beginning as a child labourer on a plantation.

I am honoured and proud to be Jim Thakoordin's friend. His resume speaks volumes about his passion for supporting and defending human rights, freedom and democracy wherever it has been violated. A look at his illustrious curriculum vital, tells one of the life-long struggles he has been involved in and has fought on behalf of the working class in Britain and elsewhere. I lived in the UK in the 1970's and am aware of the political climate of those times. I was also a student activist in those days and supported various human rights causes. I say this because I can empathize with Jim's struggles, which began in 1961, when he left Guyana at the tender age of 17 for London. It was a very difficult time for immigrant communities, who were discriminated against and who had to fight very hard for their rights to survive in Britain.

Born and raised in a poor family, Jim who worked in a sugar plantation as a child labourer in Guyana has pulled himself up by his bootstraps to arrive at where he is now. He knows what suffering is and his empathy clearly touches the most downtrodden and marginalized sections of his society in Britain. Having distinguished himself academically in Britain, he pursued his passions to help the working class by immersing himself with their causes. His active involvement in trade union work, the TUC, community relations and race relations to name just a few, reflect his courage of conviction to better society beginning with his new life in London, among his fellow workers.

His 50 years of a remarkable career in the various jobs that he has held reflects his efforts and determination to represent those issues that are close to his heart like mental health, women's rights, housing equality and race equality. They have put him in some very important and much needed critical leadership roles in the various arenas of the labour movement, trade union work and community relations. His entire life has been one of commitment and self-sacrifice and fighting for justice, freedom and democracy. His work among the poor and downtrodden must find an honoured place in the British working class history, over the past 50 years.

Indira Pradhan - Presently live in Columbus, Ohio. I have lived in India, Thailand, Switzerland and the UK. I spent the best years of my life as a student in England. I am involved in various voluntary organisations which provide free education to the poor and marginalized children in the village of Nangli, Punjab in India.

Melanie Sibley

I first met Jim, when he helped my parents to get a meeting together with Bedfordshire County and Luton Borough Councillors and Chief Officers, during the 1980s, in an attempt to resolve a long standing schooling matter involving a member of my family. Jim readily stepped in to help my parents to fight the abuse of my brother by the council. We readily struck up a chord with Jim as we shared common interests as educators and people committed to human and civil rights.

Jim's led no ordinary life. He has dedicated his time to serving the ordinary man and woman, the less fortunate and those who have fell prey to the machinery of heavy handed public and corporate bodies. Jim has committed his life to alleviating any kind of injustice. Not least, he has been a critical friend to many, advising them and helping them in whatever difficulty they might find themselves in. Jim is a true man of the people.

What makes a man, who began his life as a child labourer on a sugar plantation in Demerara, Guyana devote so much of his time to the service and support of others? The answer lies in the fact that he has himself experienced at first-hand what it is like to suffer poverty and discrimination not only in his own country but on his arrival in the UK in 1961.

Yet despite all of his own battles, he has spent his life committed to stamping out racism and supporting those who are oppressed because of their gender, disability, social status, religion, age, beliefs or principles.

Jim met his wife, Doreen on a London bus whilst he was working as a London bus conductor in Alperton. They have been married for over 50 years with two grown up children and four beautiful and talented grandchildren from age 18 to 10 years. Doreen is a graduate who worked as a teacher for 38 years before retiring as the Assistant Head Teacher at Challney High School for Boys, in Luton. With her support, Jim educated himself, after he arrived in London with little formal education and no qualifications. After many years of working full-time and studying part-time Jim won a scholarship to Ruskin College, Oxford, age 31. Jim went on from Oxford to the Universities of Essex, London Warwick and gained qualifications in Teaching, Politics, Economic, Industrial Relations and 15 years later an MBA from the University of Hertfordshire.

He became active in the trade union and the Labour Party within weeks of his arrival in Britain and he was later appointed one of the first Black paid union officials in Britain in 1978, covering London and the Eastern Counties. These were exciting times for Jim as it reminded him of the campaigns he took part in on the plantation fighting for workers' rights and freedom from colonialism.

Jim was instrumental with colleagues in setting up the Black Trade Unionist Solidarity Movement and the Labour Party Black Socialist Society to secure equality for Black workers and solidarity between Black people, the unions and the Labour Party.

His political career continued as a County and Borough councillor for over 20 years. He was the Labour Parliamentary candidate in Milton Keynes in 1983, which he sadly lost. Jim has campaigned tirelessly for local people whilst serving as a councillor and a community leader. I understand that he used his small amounts of councillors' expenses to support the organisation he started and Chaired – The Luton Committee for Racial Harmony, started in 1971 after a period of racist attacks on Asian immigrants in the town. He has always been passionate about defending and promoting human rights issues at home and abroad.

Those who know Jim appreciate him for the work he has done in the communities. Since coming to live in Luton in 1963, he has worked to improve local race relations and has contributed enormously over several decades to race and community relations through the local and regional organisations and the media. Among his many civic duties, he was governor of the Universities of Luton and Bedfordshire and Cranfield. He also served on the Board of Governors for Barnfield and Dunstable Colleges; Chair of Governors of Challney High School for Boys and Girls; member of the Eastern Region Further Education Funding Council and a Board members of the local Hospital, Law Centre and several local and national charities.

As a specialist teacher of young people with dyslexia, I am well aware of the derogatory and damaging labelling of distinct groups of children in British society in the 1970s and 80s. Labelling that could break a child's chances of a good future. What happened to my own family is a prime example. It was partly because my family came from a 'so called' working class background that our parents were denied their rights to educate their children according to their wishes.

Never afraid to speak out, Jim says what he feels and feels what he says. He is a passionate and genuine man who never fails to carry out what he tells people he will do. This is despite some dramatic health problems and his strong personal commitments to his loving family.

Indeed it is his wife Doreen, a Londoner from Irish and English parents, who has stood by him for over 50 years. Their son Michael who turned 50 in February 2014 is married to an African woman and their daughter Jane age 47 married to an Irishman from Northern Ireland. Their family are really multi-racial and multi-cultural.

My parents loved Doreen as she would often sit for hours talking and listening to them in the garden of her home whilst drinking tea and soft drinks together. For nearly four decades Doreen worked as a senior Teacher and had to endure much racist backlash for marrying a Black man. Now retired, Doreen still finds time to teach on a one to one basis in between visiting her extended family including her daughter, a strong feminist who helped Jim to champion gender issues as much as race.

Notably, Jim will always find time for his friends no matter how busy his life may be. If Jim is not writing the next chapter of a book or designing a new flower bed for his garden, he is writing a letter to a newspaper or campaign group about an issue of fairness and democracy. This is the true mark of a man who genuinely feels the suffering of others and whose legacy is one of securing respect, justice and equality for people in Britain and around the world.

Melanie Sibley - 'Teacher and advocate of equal opportunities for all - regardless of gender, race, ability, beliefs, status or class'

Jamie Newell

Jim is one of those people who when you think back you feel like you've always known him but in reality it has only been a short while.

I first met Jim at an Islamaphobia event in Luton at a time when the EDL and another misguided group of young Muslims were creating much tension in the town. Jim had taken the microphone during the Q&A session and reminded the packed hall of our timeless duty to stand together as a community with one voice and to oppose fascism in all its forms. He recounted with great gusto, tales of chasing the National Front out of town in the 1970's and how we must never let our guard down as there are no final victories or defeats.

Following this we met again at various rallies, strikes and meetings and struck up an accord. We met for tea and toast and talked about our backgrounds and cultural upbringing. We found common ground in these areas and struck up a friendship I feel is one of family, like grandfather and grandson. It has not always been smooth, it never is with family, but we have forged a close alliance centered around common principles, that the largely ignored and forgotten class war being waged upon the global society disproportionately affects minority groups but is the one issue that truly transcends colour and culture and could be the unifying feature in building a resistance to these economic terrorist policies.

Jim's legacy is one of the people whom he has taught and inspired over the decades from across all cultures, people like myself inspired by the drive and focus that he still extrudes in his later years, an example of all that is good about the human spirit and what it is to be human.

Who is Jim Thakoordin is a question that could fill an entire debate on the BBC, but for me Jim Thakoordin is an inspiration, a person who despite trouble with ill health, the passing of time and the associated ailments, continues to remain unshaken in his philosophical and moral beliefs even in the face of adversity. Jim Thakoordin is a person who inspired me to think: "what would Jim do?" When faced with a dilemma but more than this Jim is a person of the people, for the people and of his family.

I am aware through Facebook that Jim admires Pope Francis and I believe the quote below reflects to a large extent Jims historic struggles for a better and fairer world for all:

- *"The current crisis is not only economic and financial but is rooted in an ethical and anthropological crisis. Concern with the idols of power, profit, and money, rather than with the value of the human person has become a basic norm for functioning and a crucial criterion for organization. We have forgotten and are still forgetting that over and above business, logic and the parameters of the market is the human being; and that something is men and women in as much as they are human beings by virtue of their profound dignity: to offer them the possibility of living a dignified life and of actively participating in the common good. Benedict XVI reminded us that precisely because it is human, all human activity, including economic activity, must be ethically structured and governed (cf. Encyclical Letter Caritas in Veritate, n. 36). We must return to the centrality of the human being, to a more ethical vision of activities and of human relationships without the fear of losing something."*

- *"The human person and human dignity risk being turned into vague abstractions in the face of issues like the use of force, war, malnutrition, marginalization, violence, the violation of basic liberties, and financial speculation, which presently affects the price of food, treating it like any other merchandise and overlooking its primary function. Our duty is to continue to insist, in the present international context, that the human person and human dignity are not simply catchwords, but pillars for creating shared rules and structures capable of passing beyond purely pragmatic or technical approaches in order to eliminate divisions and to bridge existing differences. In this regard, there is a need to oppose the shortsighted economic interests and the mentality of power of a relative few who exclude the majority of the world's peoples, generating poverty and marginalization and causing a breakdown in society. There is likewise a need to combat the corruption which creates privileges for some and injustices for many others."*

Jamie Newell – Trade Union Officer and community activist

Professor Chris Mullard

I have known Jim since the 1960s, when we were both founding members of the community relations movement in the UK; and during the several decades that have passed since, our paths have crossed repeatedly as we have each pursued the on-going struggle against injustice and discrimination and our commitment to the development of a multi-cultural, multi-racial society that offers equality and justice to all, regardless of their race, gender, faith, sexual orientation, age or disability.

For most of his professional life, informed particularly by his early years as a child labourer on a sugar plantation in Demerara, Jim has been involved in community relations and the fight for justice in various arenas.

In the field of politics, at local, regional and national levels, he has been a Parish, Borough and County Councillor, as well as a Labour Party Parliamentary candidate and an advisor to the last Labour government on education and employment. In the trade unions and Labour movements, he was instrumental in the setting up of the Black Trade Unionists Solidarity Movement and the Labour Party Socialist Society, and in 1971 he was awarded a TUC scholarship to Ruskin College, Oxford, in 1971, having already at that time served as Secretary of the Luton TUC, Secretary of the Post Office Union and on several TUC Committees. And in the field of education he has served as a governor of the Universities of Luton and Cranfield, of Barnfield and Dunstable Colleges, and was Chair of Governors of Challney High School for Boys and Girls.

In fact, the importance of education, particularly as a vehicle for promoting the values that are close to his heart, has always been clear to Jim. Amongst his own many academic qualifications, Jim holds a Post-Graduate Certificate in Education, a BA (Hons) in Government & Sociology, an MBA in Business Administration and an Oxford University Diploma in Social & Labour Studies. He is also an inspirational communicator and has worked as a trainer and a management consultant, putting across his message in fields such as employment law, equality & diversity, and change management, as well as contributing to local and regional media.

It is thanks in part to the unswerving dedication of people like Jim that British society has experienced the seismic changes that have transformed it from the dark days of the 1960s, the days when racial discrimination – in fact, discrimination of all sorts – simply went unquestioned. There is, of course, still much to do but, with Jim and his like as role models, the torch of freedom can pass to the next generation – *e a luta continua!*

Professor Chris Mullard, CBE DL MA PhD Hon LLD FRSA
May 2014

Doreen Thakoordin – My Life Partner

When I first met Jim in 1962, I was studying for my A levels and he was a bus conductor. As you will see from his young photos, he was what used to be called a dish, and I admit to butterflies whenever I happened to get on 'his' bus. When Jim asked me to go to the cinema with him, I thought I had died and gone to Heaven.

As our friendship deepened, I realised that this person was something special. Even though our backgrounds were very different, we discovered that we had a surprising amount of things in common, for example, our hatred of injustice, a belief in the potential of the working class and a determination to try to do something about it. And bright? When Jim amassed Diplomas, a B.A degree and a Master's Degree, I was, of course, very proud but not at all surprised.

Important, well-paid jobs followed, and the hardship of our early years together seemed far away. With his qualifications, experience and gift of oratory, he could have had the pick of what the Labour and Trade Union Movement had to offer - a shadow minister, perhaps, or heading up a large Trade Union. But neither of these things happened because of Jim's undying principles of fairness and justice – and when he saw unfairness, racism and injustice in both those organisations, he spoke out against them.

The details of our first, difficult years together will be well-documented elsewhere in this book, but I can say that whatever Jim earned, which was never very much, he kept enough for himself to buy a snack when he was working a 12-hour shift, and I had the rest. This unselfishness and generosity continues today, to which our children, many colleagues and friends will attest.

Others have written about Jim Thakoordin the public figure.

I can say that, as a husband he has always been loving, loyal, generous and dependable.

Jim always knows what to do. When the fuses in the house have blown, he deals with it in his calm, resourceful way. When we were having filthy, racist phone calls in the middle of the night, he dealt with them similarly. When our beloved pet cat died at 24, he knew what to do and did it with the minimum involvement of me, who was a jibbering wreck

In the company of our grandchildren, he transmogrifies into a blubbering jelly and cherishes each one in a unique and adoring way.

He offers unfailing support to Michael and Jane, both of whom have Masters Degrees; they must get most of their brains from their father.

In short, Jim has been my husband and friend for 52 years and is my earnest wish that this situation will continue well into the future.

Doreen Thakoordin - 25.4.14

Leaving a lasting legacy

Leaving a legacy is a phrase that has become increasingly familiar not only amongst politicians, but also amongst business and other people who felt that they have contributed to their communities, or society. Many are concerned about their personal life; the issues and challenges they faced; their age and achievements and consider their future before entering into the retirement phase of their life. Some people ask "What is a legacy?" Is it what you will be known for in the future by family and friends as well as the public at large, given the unimaginable growth of the social media and information gathering on an international scale that can be accessed by future generations, or is it all irrelevant and over indulgence?

I believe that by asking ourselves how we want to be remembered, we consciously plant the seeds for living our lives in a way that we feel it is important to do so. We live each day, each month, each year as if we matter; we present our own unique legacy through our words, deeds, contributions, associations and lifestyle, with the intention of make the world we live in a better place than we found it. I have seen many people who have lived highly immoral, dishonest, miserable and narrow lives suddenly wish to change their attitudes, behaviour and values in order to create a framework through which they would leave a lasting legacy, such as donating large sums of money, often gained in exploitative or unscrupulous manner to charities or good causes. Others have been consistent, hardworking and diligent as well as caring, compassionate and deliberately active in pursuing issues and campaigns that are aimed at making their environment and the world a more loving, free, equal, fair and democratic place, that may not even be achievable within their lifetime, but during future generations. I would like to see myself in this category.

Everyone leaves behind a legacy of some kind after they die, but only a few people leaves behind a legacy that would make at least their family and close friends feel good about and consider worth sharing. I arrived from Guyana with no skills or qualifications. Within five years I was married with two children and owned a home with my wife. I came to London with years of experience in the University of Life, having endured lots of hard knocks; seen my parents suffering; discovering and being taught to differentiate between right and wrong. My first ambition after getting married was to own our own property, then support my wife through college and university education so she could realise her own career and to prove to her family that they were wrong when they told her that she "will have no future marrying a Black man." She wanted to be a teacher and she started and finished her career as a teacher.

Together, we put our children through school, college and university and they both end up in highly skilled professional careers. We have been saving for each of our grandchildren soon after their birth; we opened separate accounts for them in which we deposit part of our pension. I did all this whilst supporting my family in Guyana; contributing to charities and campaigns in Britain and in Africa and the Caribbean; being involved in trade union work at local and national levels, including 14 years on the National Executive Committee of my trade union; being a county, borough and parish councillor for over 30 years; write several books and policies for employers, trade unions, community and voluntary organisations and helping to shape the voluntary sector into a strategic and successful sector with an annual turnover of around £50 billion and campaigning for equality and justice. Of course, I have upset some people during my voluntary work, including many who either saw me as a threat to their cosy existence; jealous of my achievements including my skills, knowledge and abilities, or simply hated me for what I stood for. I had bitter arguments with people who were hopelessly enslaved, but falsely believe that they were free; those who were self-centred, corrupt, overpaid and underworked, and those who were looking for shoulders to stand on so once they step on the ladder they would kick it away to prevent anyone else can climb on it. I have accepted who I am, who I am not and what my values and principles are. I know I am far from perfect, but I would rather stand-alone instead of being in the majority when I know they are wrong. I am loud and sometimes arrogant and even overbearing, but as long as I genuinely believe I am right or the cause I am fighting for is right, I will not be bullied, silenced, compromised, or run away. I have been the unaccountable bureaucrat nightmare and have challenged wrong doing and incompetence, hypocrisy and untruths unrelentingly throughout my working and political life, without any fear to my own career, popularity or safety. I have lived a life on the frontline of life, confronting those who have failed our society; have threatened our rights; destroyed the lives of vulnerable people; promoting racism, sexism, hate and inequality; abusing their positions and those who fail in their public and professional duties.

I can see much of my principles and values being shared by my children, especially my daughter Jane, who is adorable as a person and a campaigner for rights of women and a committed socialist and anti-racist. She is a highly professional person with lots of energy and determination to fight for a better world. My son is also committed to the environment, promoting development in poorer countries and a caring person. Both my children are confident and assertive professionals with strong views on justice and fairness. My four grandchildren are also conscious of suffering and inequality within our world and have been supported by their parents in their tangible contributions to various charities in Britain and Africa.

I believe I have achieved my goals in life and I am satisfied with my achievements. I could have been a member of parliament many years ago or a trade union leader had I sold my principles for private gain, or being a convert to populism. I have often been told that I have achieved a lot more from fighting from the outside instead of being part of a self-serving cosy cabal, which unfortunately too many committees and boards are. Whenever I am involved in voluntary or paid organisations, I always endeavour to provide leadership, being focused and achieve outcomes by committing people to ownership of the issues. Too many people talk for far too long, without saying anything that will lead to resolution. I frequently prise people out of their comfort zone and push them to declare their position and accept responsibilities. I have had failures and regrets; suffered because of my principles and personality; made mistakes and committed the same mistakes again before I realised that there are more than one way of doing something.

It is better at times do things and fail, rather than doing nothing and still fail. People who take risks, challenge, and question, criticise and are prepared to put forward alternatives are invariably disliked within the British social culture that has become increasingly consensus, passive, compromising, sheepish and polite. Sometimes I remind myself how important it has been for me to be exposed to anther cultures other than the mainstream British culture.

Leaving a legacy that reflects a diversity of interests cannot be a bad thing. During my lifetime I have been the villain, the hero, the good, the bad, the beautiful and the ugly. I have fulfilled many roles as an agitator, the devil's advocate, the kind and compassionate as well as the enforcer of rules and the first to sound the retreat to enable our side to regroup and then press forward. The story I am leaving behind is the story of my life, my humble efforts to do what I could for my fellow human beings that is growing rapidly across the whole world which is constantly changing, sometimes not for the best either. The western capitalist nations started off the 21st Century as they did in the 20th Century with internal conflicts, wars across nations such as the First World War in 1914; the war in Iraq and Afghanistan in 2003, wars in Africa and tensions in Eastern Europe, with NATO forces beating the drums of war against the Russians over the Ukraine. Soon there will be another big clash as the American military, political and corporate beast with three heads on the same body begins to square up to China, or possibly a China/Russia threat to deny the USA and its European poodles their control of the world order, which they have wielded for centuries.

As I sometimes sit down and reflect upon my life and my legacy, which one does with more frequency, when one passes three score years and ten, I wonder whether once I have gone I would leave behind a legacy that would remain in the thoughts and hearts of my family and close friends. I hope they would see me in the light of the life I have carefully designed and lived to the full extent guided by my honest and innate convictions. Some members of my distant family will of course have as little, if any, interest in my legacy as they did when I was alive. They turned against me, because I was unable or, unwilling to continue to support them when they showed me no respect or appreciation and especially since they became successful in their own lives. I am sorry to say that there is some hatred and disrespect for me within certain members who I can only describe as being ungrateful and disrespectful. This is a fact and it is their choice. My conscience is clear and I have no regrets, I have given far more than I have received and I never expected anything in return for what I have given, except the normal acknowledgement. We are living in a world of "I and I" and "me, me, me" where materialism, greed, individualism, memories has become shortened and history is denied.

For me history is my barometer, which has shaped my life and helped me to maintain a good measure of consistency over the decades. I have always tried to be truthful, honest, loving, caring and compassionate for mother earth and all the billions of creatures that populate this forgiving planet. I dislike those people and principles that seek to justify inequality, wars, exploitation, intolerance, abuse, hatred and suffering.

Top –Bottom L-R
Jim leading a Teachers Strike 2013
Moss Evans, General Secretary of the TGWU Supporting Jim's election
campaign for Parliament, Milton Keynes 1983
Jim addressing workers with Moss Evans in Milton Keynes 1983
Jim addressing Striking Teachers in Luton 2014

Top – Bottom L-R
Jim addressing a meeting, organised by Luton Committee for Racial
Harmony in 2013. Jim has chaired LCRH since it started in 1971
Jim's granddaughter Aoife on a community demonstration with her
mother against government cuts in public services
Jim's granddaughter Rohanie at a trade union rally
supporting education for all
Jim at TUC Black Workers Conference with Lee Jasper, Zita Holbourne
and Marcia Rigg 2012

Top-Bottom L-R
Jim with Zita Holbourne NEC Public Services Union At TUC Conference
2012, selling his 12th publication Our Lives, Our History, Our Future
Jim with local community activist at a Black History Month Event 2013
Jim with Gloria Mills, member of the TUC General Council
Jim speaking at the TUC Black Workers Conference, 2014

L-R
Elleyse and Amy
Jim with his personal trainers at his local gym in Luton